CW00591965

THE SOCIAL PSYCHOLOGY
OF ORGANIZATIONAL BEHAVIOR

Key Readings in Social Psychology

General Editor: ARIE W. KRUGLANSKI, University of Maryland at College Park

The aim of this series is to make available to senior undergraduate and graduate students key articles in each area of social psychology in an attractive, user-friendly format. Many professors want to encourage their students to engage directly with research in their fields, yet this can often be daunting for students coming to detailed study of a topic for the first time. Moreover, declining library budgets mean that articles are not always readily available, and course packs can be expensive and time-consuming to produce. **Key Readings in Social Psychology** aims to address this need by providing comprehensive volumes, each one of which will be edited by a senior and active researcher in the field. Articles will be carefully chosen to illustrate the way the field has developed historically as well as current issues and research directions. Each volume will have a similar structure, which will include:

- An overview chapter, as well as introductions to sections and articles,
- Questions for class discussion,
- Annotated bibliographies,
- Full author and subject indexes.

Published Titles

The Self in Social Psychology	Roy F. Baumeister
Stereotypes and Prejudice	Charles Stangor
Motivational Science	E. Tory Higgins and Arie W. Kruglanski
Emotions in Social Psychology	W. Gerrod Parrott
Intergroup Relations	Michael Hogg and Dominic Abrams
Social Psychology: A General Reader	Arie W. Kruglanski and E. Tory Higgins

Titles in Preparation

Social Cognition	David Hamilton
Close Relationships	Harry Reis and Caryl Rusbult
Group Processes	John Levine and Richard Moreland
Language and Communication	Gün R. Semin
Attitudes and Persuasion	Richard E. Petty, Shelly Chaiken, and Russell Fazio
The Social Psychology of Culture	Hazel Markus and Shinobu Kitayama
The Social Psychology of Health	Peter Salovey and Alexander J. Rothman

For continually updated information on published and forthcoming titles in the Key Readings in Social Psychology series, please visit www.keyreadings.com

THE SOCIAL PSYCHOLOGY OF ORGANIZATIONAL BEHAVIOR

Key Readings

Edited by

Leigh L. Thompson

Kellogg School of Management,
Northwestern University

Psychology Press
New York and Hove

Psychology Press
29 West 35th Street
New York, NY 10001
www.psypress.com

Published in Great Britain by
Psychology Press, LTD.
27 Church Road
Hove, East Sussex
BN3 2FA
www.psypress.co.uk

Psychology Press is an imprint of the Taylor & Francis Group.
Printed in the United States of America on acid-free paper.

10 9 8 7 6 5 4 3 2 1

Library of Congress Cataloging-in-Publication Data
The social psychology of organizational behavior : key readings / edited by Leigh L. Thompson.
    p. cm. — (Key readings in social psychology)
   Includes bibliographical references and index.
    ISBN 1-84169-083-X (hc.) — ISBN 1-84169-084-8 (pbk.)
    1. Organizational behavior. 2. Social psychology. I. Thompson, Leigh L. II. Series.

  HD58.7 .S644 2002
  302.3'5—dc21

                            2002032658

Contents

About the Editor   xi
Acknowledgments   xiii
Preface: Doctoral Education and Teaching in OB   xv
    L. Thompson

Organizational Behavior: A Micro Perspective   1
    L. Thompson

PART 1
The Science and Metaphor of Micro OB   7

READING 1
Dressing Up Like an Organization: When Psychological Theories Can
Explain Organizational Action   11
    B. M. Staw

READING 2
What Theory Is *Not*   22
    R. I. Sutton and B. M. Staw

READING 3
Barriers to the Advance of Organizational Science: Paradigm
Development as a Dependent Variable   33
    J. Pfeffer

PART 2
Decision Making   47

READING 4
Knee-Deep in the Big Muddy: A Study of Escalating Commitment to a Chosen Course of Action   51
B. M. Staw

READING 5
Timid Choices and Bold Forecasts: A Cognitive Perspective on Risk Taking   63
D. Kahneman and D. Lovallo

READING 6
The Robust Beauty of Improper Linear Models in Decision Making   79
R. M. Dawes

READING 7
Experimental Tests of the Endowment Effect and the Coase Theorem   91
D. Kahneman, J. L. Knetsch, and R. H. Thaler

READING 8
Social Utility and Decision Making in Interpersonal Contexts   105
G. F. Loewenstein, L. Thompson, and M. H. Bazerman

PART 3
Negotiation and Social Dilemmas   125

READING 9
Integrative Bargaining in a Competitive Market   129
M. H. Bazerman, T. Magliozzi, and M. A. Neale

READING 10
Misperceiving Negotiation Counterparts: When Situationally Determined Bargaining Behaviors Are Attributed to Personality Traits   141
M. W. Morris, R. P. Larrick, and S. K. Su

READING 11
Avoiding Missed Opportunities in Managerial Life: Analogical Training More Powerful Than Individual Case Training   163
L. Thompson, D. Gentner, and J. Loewenstein

READING 12

Choice Behavior in Social Dilemmas: Effects of Social Identity, Group Size, and Decision Framing   174

M. B. Brewer and R. M. Kramer

P A R T   4

Groups and Teams   185

READING 13

Social Influence Processes in Group Brainstorming   188

P. B. Paulus and M. T. Dzindolet

READING 14

Group Versus Individual Training and Group Performance: The Mediating Role of Transactive Memory   204

D. W. Liang, R. L. Moreland, and L. Argote

READING 15

The Common Knowledge Effect: Information Sharing and Group Judgment   216

D. Gigone and R. Hastie

READING 16

Interpersonal Relationships and Task Performance: An Examination of Mediating Processes in Friendship and Acquaintance Groups   238

K. A. Jehn and P. P. Shah

P A R T   5

Procedural Justice   261

READING 17

Voice, Control, and Procedural Justice: Instrumental and Noninstrumental Concerns in Fairness Judgments   265

E. A. Lind, R. Kanfer, and P. C. Earley

READING 18

The Psychology of Procedural Justice: A Test of the Group-Value Model   276

T. R. Tyler

READING 19

Stealing in the Name of Justice: Informational and Interpersonal Moderators of Theft Reactions to Underpayment Inequity   289

J. Greenberg

P A R T 6

Relationships and Trust   305

READING 20

Some Affective Consequences of Social Comparison and Reflection Processes: The Pain and Pleasure of Being Close   308

A. Tesser, M. Millar, and J. Moore

READING 21

Affect- and Cognition-Based Trust as Foundations for Interpersonal Cooperation in Organizations   327

D. J. McAllister

READING 22

Assessing the Political Landscape: Structure, Cognition, and Power in Organizations   350

D. Krackhardt

P A R T 7

Values, Norms, and Politics   373

READING 23

On the Folly of Rewarding A, While Hoping for B   375

S. Kerr

READING 24

Cognitive Biases and Organizational Correctives: Do Both Disease and Cure Depend on the Politics of the Beholder?   384

P. E. Tetlock

READING 25

The Norm of Self-Interest   407

D. T. Miller

Appendix: How to Read a Journal Article in Social Psychology   419
C. H. Jordan and M. P. Zanna

Author Index   429

Subject Index   439

About the Editor

Leigh L. Thompson is the J. Jay Gerber Distinguished Professor of Dispute Resolution and Organizations in the Kellogg School at Northwestern University. An internationally-recognized scholar, Thompson has published three books and over 60 articles in leading management journals and books. Her research and writing include negotiation, learning, decision making, emotions and priming processes, electronic interaction, and team and group behavior. Thompson has received numerous awards and honors for her research, including the National Science Foundation Presidential Young Investigator Award, a fellowship at the Center for Advanced Study in the Behavioral Sciences at Stanford, California, and a grant from the Citigroup Behavioral Science Research Council of Citibank.

Acknowledgments

The authors and publishers are grateful to the following for permission to reproduce the articles in this book:

Reading 1: B. M. Staw, Dressing Up Like an Organization: When Psychological Theories Can Explain Organizational Action. *Journal of Management, 17* (4), 805–819. Copyright © 1991 by *Journal of Management*. Reprinted with permission.

Reading 2: R. I. Sutton and B. M. Staw, What Theory Is *Not. Administrative Science Quarterly, 40,* 371–384. Copyright © 1995 by Johnson Graduate School of Management, Cornell University. Reprinted with permission.

Reading 3: J. Pfeffer, Barriers to the Advance of Organizational Science: Paradigm Development as a Dependent Variable. *Academy of Management Review, 18*(4), 599–620. Copyright © 1993 by the Academy of Management. Reproduced with permission of the Academy of Management in the format Textbook via Copyright Clearance Center.

Reading 4: B. M. Staw, Knee Deep in the Big Muddy: A Study of Escalating Commitment to a Chosen Course of Action. *Organizational Behavior and Human Decisions Processes, 16,* 27–44. Copyright © 1976 by Elsevier Science. Reprinted by permission of the publisher.

Reading 5: D. Kahneman, and D. Lovallo, Timid Choices and Bold Forecasts: A Cognitive Perspective on Risk Taking. *Management Science, 39*(1), 17–3 1. Copyright © 1993 by the Institute for Operations Research and the Management Sciences (INFORMS), 901 Elkridge Landing Road, Suite 400, Linthicum, Maryland 21090-2909 USA. Reprinted by permission.

Reading 6: R. M. Dawes, The Robust Beauty of Improper Linear Models in Decision Making. *American Psychologist, 34,* 571–582. Copyright © 1979 by the American Psychological Association. Reprinted/adapted with permission.

Reading 7: D. Kahneman, J. L. Knetsch, and R. H. Thaler, Experimental Tests of the Endowment Effect and the Coase Theorem. *Journal of Political Economy, 98*(6), 1325–1348. Copyright © 1990 by the University of Chicago Press. Reprinted with permission.

Reading 8: G. F. Loewenstein, L. Thompson, and M. H. Bazerman, Social Utility and Decision Making in Interpersonal Contexts. *Journal of Personality and Social Psychology, 57*(3), 426–441. Copyright © 1989 by the American Psychological Association. Reprinted/adapted with permission.

Reading 9: M. H. Bazerman, T. Magliozzi, and M. A. Neale, Integrative Bargaining in a Competitive Market. *Organizational Behavior and Human Decisions Processes, 36,* 288, 294–313. Copyright © 1985 by Elsevier Science. Reprinted by permission of the publisher.

Reading 10: M. W. Morris, R. P. Larrick, and S. K. Su, Misperceiving Negotiation Counterparts: When Situationally Determined Bargaining Behaviors Are Attributed to Personality Traits. *Journal of Personality and Social Psychology, 77*(1), 52–67. Copyright © 1999 by the American Psychological Association. Reprinted/adapted with permission.

Reading 11: L. Thompson, D. Gentner, and J. Loewenstein, Avoiding Missed Opportunities in Managerial Life: Analogical Training More Powerful Than Individual Case Training. *Organizational Behavior and Human Decision Processes, 82*(1), 60–75. Copyright © 2000 by Elsevier Science. Reprinted by permission of the publisher.

Reading 12: M. B. Brewer and R. M. Kramer, Choice Behaviors in Social Dilemmas: Effects of Social Identity, Group Size, and Decision Framing. *Journal of Personality and Social Psychology, 50*(3), 543–549. Copyright © 1986 by the American Psychological Association. Reprinted/adapted with permission.

Reading 13: P. B. Paulus, and M. T. Dzindolet, Social Influence Processes in Group Brainstorming. *Journal of Personality and Social Psychology, 64*(4), 575–586. Copyright © 1993 by the American Psychological Association. Reprinted/adapted with permission.

Reading 14: D. W. Liang, R. Moreland, and L. Argote, Group Versus Individual Training and Group Performance: The Mediating Role of Transactive Memory. *PSPB, 21*(4), 384–393. Copyright © 1995 by Sage Publications. Reprinted by permission of Sage Publications, Inc.

Reading 15: D. Gigone, and R. Hastie, The Common Knowledge Effect: Information Sharing and Group Judgment. *Journal of Personality and Social Psychology, 65*(5), 959–974. Copyright © 1993 by the American Psychological Association. Reprinted/adapted with permission.

Reading 16: K. A. Jehn and P. P. Shah, Interpersonal Relationships and Task Performance: An Examination of Mediating Processes in Friendship and Acquaintance Groups. *Journal of Personality and Social Psychology, 72*(4), 775–790. Copyright © 1997 by the American Psychological Association. Reprinted/adapted with permission.

Reading 17: E. A. Lind, R. Kanfer, and P. C. Earley, Voice, Control, and Procedural Justice: Instrumental and Noninstrumental Concerns in Fairness Judgments. *Journal of Personality and Social Psychology, 59*(5), 952–959. Copyright @ 1990 by the American Psychological Association. Reprinted/adapted with permission.

Reading 18: T. R. Tyler, The Psychology of Procedural Justice: A Test of the Group-Value Model. *Journal of Personality and Social Psychology, 57*(5), 830–838. Copyright © 1989 by the American Psychological Association. Reprinted/adapted with permission.

Reading 19: J. Greenberg, Stealing in the Name of Justice: Informational and Interpersonal Moderators of Theft Reactions to Underpayment Inequity. *Organizational Behavior and Human Decision Processes, 54,* 81–103. Copyright © 1993 by Elsevier Science. Reprinted by permission of the publisher.

Reading 20: T. R. Tesser, M. Millar, and J. Moore, Some Affective Consequences of Social Comparison and Reflection Processes: The Pain and Pleasure of Being Close. *Journal of Personality and Social Psychology, 54*(1), 49–61. Copyright © 1988 by the American Psychological Association. Reprinted/adapted with permission.

Reading 21: D. J. McAllister, Affect- and Cognition-Based Trust as Foundations for Interpersonal Cooperation in Organizations. *Academy of Management Journal, 38*(1), 24–59. Copyright © 1995 by the Academy of Management. Reproduced with permission of the Academy of Management in the format Textbook via Copyright Clearance Center.

Reading 22: D. Krackhardt, Assessing the Political Landscape: Structure, Cognition, and Power in Organizations. *Administrative Science Quarterly, 35,* 342–369. Copyright © 1990 by Johnson Graduate School of Management, Cornell University. Reprinted with permission.

Reading 23: S. Kerr, On the Folly of Rewarding A, While Hoping for B. *Academy of Management Journal, 18*(4), 769–783. Copyright © 1975 by the Academy of Management. Reproduced with permission of the Academy of Management in the format Textbook via Copyright Clearance Center.

Reading 24: P. E. Tetlock, Cognitive Biases and Organizational Correctives: Do Both Disease and Cure Depend on the Politics of the Beholder? *Administrative Science Quarterly, 45,* 293–326. Copyright © 2000 by Johnson Graduate School of Management, Cornell University. Reprinted with permission.

Reading 25: D. T. Miller, The Norm of Self-Interest. *American Psychologist, 54*(12), 1053–1060. Copyright © 1999 by the American Psychological Association. Reprinted/adapted with permission.

Preface: Doctoral Education and Teaching in OB

Leigh L. Thompson

This book brings together articles that have exerted a tremendous impact on the field of organizational behavior. Many of the articles are also classics in other fields, in particular social psychology, as many of the leading micro OB researchers are social psychologists by training. The articles in this book form the core of the Ph.D.-level micro organization behavior course in the Management and Organizations Department at the Kellogg School of Management. This book is dedicated to the students, past, present, and future, in that course.

Three prominent scholars in organization behavior played an enormous role in shaping the final selection of articles and the sections themselves and offered advice on how to improve the book as a valuable tool for young Ph.D. students: Max Bazerman (Harvard University), Michael Morris (Columbia University), and Philip Tetlock (University of California, Berkeley).

Course Goals

The course is developed around three key themes that serve as goals for the course:

1. *The creation of schemas for scholarly thinking*: The articles in this book and course may be the heaviest dose of reading that students will encounter in their graduate education. These research articles will serve as the foundation for students' own thinking and ideas for several years, perhaps even decades, to come. For this reason, I encourage students to do all of the reading.

2. *Formulating new ideas*: The point of reading articles is not to perfectly memorize the names of the researchers and the exact findings of each research study, but rather to learn how to develop original ideas and use the research studies as supporting arguments for your own ideas. Thus, each week in my course, a student or group is challenged with the task of developing a new framework (or *gestalt*, as I call it) for the papers for that section. The gestalt is limited to one page, and original graphs, charts, and frameworks are encouraged; lists of articles or annotated bibliographies are not allowed. The framework, or gestalt, is one that is novel and, most important, of personal interest to the student. As it turns out, this is a particularly challenging exercise, as most students are inclined to treat each paper on its own merit rather than integrate it into a larger framework.

3. *Writing and publishing*: The grading criteria of the course involve three major components designed to simulate the activities of research and scholarship. With myself acting as "action editor," students submit research papers (introduction and methods section only) by midterm. Next, each student critically reviews two classmates' papers (the reviews are graded). The following week, each student receives a cover letter from the action editor, along with the comments of the two reviewers. All students are invited to "revise and resubmit" their manuscripts. Students then have two to three weeks to revise their paper for resubmission. I choose two to four papers to appear in an online journal supported by our department (visit: http://www.kellogg.nwu.edu/research/ktag/kjob.htm).

Advice for a Successful Graduate School Experience

Along with the course goals comes some advice. (Like most professors of a course populated by first-year Ph.D. students, I am routinely asked for advice.) Much of the essential behavior required for successful completion of a Ph.D. is tacit knowledge, not generally available in writing. In an effort to make this knowledge less tacit and more accessible, I suggest the following as guiding principles for the doctoral years.

Work with More than One Person

It is important that the research community encourage students to work with several people during their doctoral training so as to help them best develop their own skills. Greater exposure to different styles helps students better cultivate their own research strengths. Moreover, students can serve as boundary spanners between individual researchers in profitable ways. (I have personally benefited on several occasions when a doctoral student introduced me to a professor in another discipline.)

Work in More than One Discipline

For similar reasons I encourage students to cross disciplinary boundaries so that they can profitably apply and use theories from different disciplines in their thinking and research.

Put the "Impostor Syndrome" to Rest

Many students suffer from the unfounded belief that they are unworthy and have been admitted to the doctoral program by mistake and that everyone else is much smarter than they are. This feeling is compounded by a sense of pluralistic ignorance—the belief that nobody else feels this way. Most doctoral programs in organization behavior do not attempt to weed out students; quite the contrary, they want every doctoral student to succeed. Moreover, most professors don't have time to sit around and think about how poorly students are doing. Even if they did have the time, they would be motivated for egocentric reasons to look upon students favorably. If you feel compelled to succumb to the "impostor syndrome," I suggest setting up a time (say five minutes per day) to think about yourself as an impostor; the rest of the day, assume you are worthwhile and important, and focus on getting your work done.

Take Every Opportunity to Talk about Your Research

Most doctoral students are extremely reluctant to engage in public speaking, much less present their own research. This makes perfect sense, since they routinely witness faculty members criticizing research presentations (even those of famous scholars). However, there are several important reasons why it is a good idea to present research as often as people are willing to listen to you: (1) At no other time in your professional career will people be as devoted to your growth and development as in your doctoral years. Take advantage of this strange form of tender loving care! (2) Presenting research, like any other skill, can be perfected with practice; the more opportunities you have to practice your presentation skills, the more quickly you can develop expertise. (3) The mere-exposure effect suggests that the more often people are exposed to an idea, the more they grow to like it, even if they did not like it to begin with (Zajonc, 1968); thus, even if people criticize you, they will grow to like you and your ideas the more often you present them!

Write Down All of Your Ideas

Ideas are valuable and they are your key resource as a scholar. During your doctoral career, you are going to be exposed to lots of scholars and ideas and research; consequently, interesting thoughts are going to occur to you. I encourage my students to keep a notebook or a small tape recorder so that they can write down or record all of their ideas.

Embrace Criticism

Tom Cook of Northwestern University has a wonderful saying: "Your enemy is your best friend." Cook is referring to the fact that science advances through the process of peer review. An excellent scholar is responsive to the criticism of peers; consequently, the research improves, which has a positive effect on the field. This means developing a healthy appreciation of criticism. I advise students to take notes when making a research presentation so that they can go back and think about the issues. Alternatively, appoint a friend to take notes for you during your own presentations.

Avoid Competition

It is nice to have friends who are going through the same classes and requirements as you so that you can collaborate with and support one another, but at the same time there is an irrepressible urge to compare yourself with others, to ask, "Do I stack up?" A more enlightened and realistic view is to realize that the other people in your graduate program are not competitors, but rather collaborators. If there is competition, it is from students at other doctoral programs who will compete for the same jobs as you. Even most of these people can ultimately be collaborators rather than competitors.

Learn How to Multitask

The most important skill to learn as a doctoral student is multitasking. Most people are accustomed to working on one task at a time before getting involved in another project. I don't think this is a successful model for graduate education and a research career. I have a Darwinian view of scholarship: I advise students to become involved in as many research projects as interest them; the stronger projects will survive and the weaker will

wither and die. I believe that most doctoral students can get very comfortable having as many as five to 10 ongoing research projects.

Act Like an Assistant Professor

If I have a mental model for graduate school success, it may be summarized by the phrase "Act like an assistant professor." Behaviorally, this means that you are: (1) writing all the time (my own view is that doctoral students should not write anything that they don't plan to submit for publication somewhere), (2) managing multiple research projects, and (3) collaborating with other students (in addition to professors).

Materials and Resources

I believe that information technology can greatly enhance the quality of research and teaching and that information should be widely shared and used and be accessible to all who would like it or benefit from it. To this end I have created materials and have posted them so that students, professors, researchers, teachers, and scholars can use them to enhance the education and development of the next generation of research: our Ph.D. students. I have posted several documents that are designed for graduate students on writing papers, (visit: http://www.leighthompson.com/tips/write_a_paper.htm), reviewing papers (visit: http://www.leighthompson.com/tips/review_a_paper.htm) and making research presentations (visit: http://www.leighthompson.com/tips/present_a_paper.htm). And, I have a special section designed for women and careers (visit: http://www.leighthompson.com/empowering_info.htm).

REFERENCES

Zajonc, R. B. (1968). Attitudinal effects of mere exposure. *Journal of Personality and Social Psychology*, *9* (monograph supplement 2, part 2).

 Suggested Readings

Bem, D. J. (1987). Writing the empirical journal article. In M. P. Zanna & J. M. Darley (Eds.), *The compleat academic: A practical guide for the beginning social scientist* (pp. 171–201). New York: Random House.

Murnighan, K. (1981). Training independent social scientists. *The Organization Behavior Teaching Journal*, *6*(3), 9–11.

Organizational Behavior: A Micro Perspective

Leigh L. Thompson

For better or worse a natural division within the large discipline of organization behavior is that between "micro" and "macro." Very generally stated, micro-organizational behavior focuses on the attitudes, judgments, emotions, and behaviors of individuals and small groups of people within or between organizations. The unit of analysis is the individual, dyad, or small group. Macro-organizational behavior focuses on larger systems, such as the firm, departmental unit, and larger networks connecting these units. This book focuses on micro-organizational behavior. This introductory note is designed to provide an overview of the micro OB field and of this book.

Micro-Organizational Behavior

Micro-organizational behavior, hereafter "micro OB," is a relatively young science. Micro OB has been strongly, nearly uniquely, influenced by social psychology. I define micro OB as "the study of how the thoughts, feelings, and behaviors of individuals and groups in organizations are influenced by the actual, implied, or imagined presence of others." I adapted this definition of micro OB after Allport's (1924) classic definition of social psychology. As such, the major content areas of micro OB, which typically function as the focus of study in research investigations, are:

1. **thought or cognition**, such as decision making, judgment biases, and stereotyping
2. **feelings or emotion**, such as regret or mood in individuals or workgroups
3. **behaviors or action**, such as negotiation or team performance

Thus, micro OB researchers are interested in the classic tripartite of cognition, affect, and behavior. As we shall see, some researchers are interested in all three, and some focus only on one of these content areas in their investigations. Further, these can either serve as independent or dependent variables.

Defining Characteristics of Micro OB

Micro OB as a discipline of study may be characterized by four defining, or hallmark, characteristics: interpersonal level of analysis, experimentation as a research methodology, analytic focus, and application.

Interpersonal Level of Analysis

It is helpful to think of two extremes when describing the interpersonal level of analysis. On one end is the *individual* level of analysis, which is largely the domain of clinical psychologists. On the other end is the *societal* level of analysis, which is largely the domain of sociologists, political scientists, and economists. The focus of micro OB is somewhere in between. This makes the level of analysis interpersonal, rather than at the intrapersonal level. The goal of micro OB is the examination of behavior within organizational settings.

Experimentation as a Research Methodology

The field of micro OB advances nearly uniquely through experimentation via the hypothetical deductive method. That is, researchers develop a hypothesis derived from theory and then design an experiment that will allow cause-and-effect conclusions from the results. This is in contrast to folk wisdom or qualitative ethnographic research. Thus, experimentation is controlled and objective and seeks to establish causality. There are some harsh critiques of experimental research, the chief concern being lack of external validity. However, such claims are usually flawed in two major respects: (1) Experimentation does not exclusively occur in the lab (we will read about investigations that have occurred in field sites and rich settings). (2) External validity is not achievable via case study, as some might argue. Case studies not only do not allow cause-and-effect conclusions; in fact, they represent an even more narrow set of conditions from which to generalize. The first and primary goal of micro OB is internal validity, and replication can best achieve the goal of external validity.

Analytic versus Synthetic Approach

An analytic approach means to become more and more specific and reduce a process down to its key components. In contrast, a synthetic approach is to become more and more general and inclusive. Micro OB research investigations often contain multiple experiments that serve to identify a key process or effect. Thus, a researcher might conduct an initial investigation and find a significant difference between two conditions, experimental and control. The next study might then focus on particular aspects of the experimental condition to determine which factor led to the observed effect. Thus, the analytic method enhances causality.

Application

A key goal of micro OB is not only to investigate the behavior of people in organizational settings, but ultimately to suggest ways to improve the quality of interaction, behavior, judgment, and performance. Many of the research investigations in micro OB are inspired by a problem or concern in an actual company or organization, and the results of micro OB research ideally should apply to real organizational issues.

Theories in Micro OB

A theory is a set of interrelated hypotheses or propositions concerning a phenomenon or a set of phenomena. It is useful to have some understanding and appreciation of key theories that have influenced research in micro OB. I distinguish between normative and descriptive theories (Bell, Tversky, & Raiffa, 1988). Normative theories are theories about human behavior that prescribe what people should do or what they ought to do. Microeconomics is a classic example of a normative theory. In contrast, descriptive theories describe what people actually do, even if the behavior appears to be irrational or suboptimal, by the standards of a normative theory. Most of micro OB focuses on descriptive theory. In fact, there is a premium paid to scholars who specify how organizational actors depart from the predictions of normative theories.

Within descriptive theories, six have played a significant, developmental role on current micro OB: learning theories, cognitive theories, motivational theories, decision-making theories, social exchange, and role theories. Below, we summarize these six classes of theories, without attempting to articulate a particular theory in detail.

Learning Theories

The fundamental idea of most learning theories is that behavior is determined by prior learning and past experience. The 1920s were the heyday of most learning theories; many spanned several decades. Classical conditioning theory (Pavlov, 1927; Watson, 1913), reinforcement theory (Hull, 1943; Skinner, 1953), and social learning theory (Bandura, 1972) are the most common learning theories. Classical conditioning theory focuses on the principle of association; reinforcement theory focuses on rewards and punishment; and social learning theory focuses on observational learning. The distinctive features of most learning theories are that the cause of human behavior lies in the past learning history of the individual, the locus or cause of behavior is in the environment (and therefore not subject to interpretation or perception), and the goal of such theories is to explain observable behavior (as opposed to internal states).

Cognitive Theories

The key idea behind most cognitive theories is the existence of an information-processing system that serves the encoding, representation, and retrieval of information. Perhaps the most widely accepted information-processing theory is the associative network model. The information processing system may use existing concepts and information to interpret and encode new information. The conditions of retrieval may affect recall as well. Information processing and, in particular, the associative network model, argues that a person's memories and ideas are stored in an interconnected network of cognitive nodes, or a semantic network. The strength of the individual connections within the network represents the degree of association between the concepts. Consequently, concepts or ideas that are similar to one another (e.g., *milk* and *cheese*) have much stronger connections than concepts or ideas that are very different from one another (e.g., *milk* and *firefighter*). When a particular node is activated, other nodes with strong connections to that node are also activated. This process is termed *spreading activation* (Andersen & Bower, 1973).

Motivational Theories

In contrast to cognitive theories and learning theories, motivational theories focus on how behavior is motivated from within an individual by internal drives, impulses, and needs. Perhaps the most famous of motivational theories is Freud's (1933) psychoanalytic theory. Motivational theories in micro OB are far from passé. Cognitive dissonance theory, need for cognition, need for closure, and self-regulation theories all have their origins in motivational theories.

Decision-Making Theories

Decision-making theories have their roots in economic analysis and game theory and are largely normative in nature. The basic idea is that individuals must choose among "prospects," with the ultimate goal being to maximize one's utility, which, incidentally, does not necessarily mean monetary wealth.

Social Exchange Theories

Social exchange theories represent a unique blend of group dynamics and micro economic theory. The basic idea is that individuals are attracted to groups and dyads because of the possible rewards that they offer. Strictly speaking, individuals perform a "cost-benefit" analysis of sorts to determine how they will behave in any particular interpersonal encounter, with their ultimate goal being to maximize their rewards.

Role Theories

Role theories have their roots in sociological theory and regard the individual as a "social actor." Accordingly, social actors in organizations serve "roles" and are guided by "norms" and "scripts." Commitment and socialization of actors within organizations focuses on how organizations select members (and vice versa), training, communication of core values, and rewards and promotions.

Organization of the Book

This book is organized into seven major sections: (1) the science of organization behavior; (2) decision making; (3) negotiation and social dilemmas; (4) groups and teams; (5) procedural justice; (6) relationships and trust; and (7) values, norms and politics. The organization of the book reflects a progression through widening levels of analysis. The section on judgment and decision making focuses on the cognition and behavior of the individual actor; the sections on negotiation and groups focus on dyads and groups; and the procedural justice, relationships, and values sections focus on how the organizational actor is embedded in networks, organizational norms, and institutional practices. For each of the major sections, I provide a short overview.

The task of selecting articles for each section was difficult. I used two key criteria: The article should (1) make a substantial impact on the field of OB (as judged by citation rates and inclusion in several doctoral courses offered by leading universities); and (2) contain original data (as opposed to pure theory or overview—however, this is not the case for the first section on the science of micro OB and for a few other articles). I initially targeted over 60 articles for 10 sections, and reduced this to 40 articles. This was reduced to 25 articles spanning seven major areas. I have included a list of suggested supplemental reading in each section; in my own course we read at least two of these articles in addition to what is in this book.

REFERENCES

Allport, F. H. (1924). *Social psychology*. Boston, MA: Houghton Mifflin.

Anderson, J. R., & Bower, G. H. (1973). *Human associative memory*. Washington, DC: V. H. Winston & Sons.

Bandura, A. (1972). Modeling theory: Some traditions, trends, and disputes. In R. D. Parke (Ed.), *Recent trends in social learning theory*. New York: Academic Press.

Bell, D. E., Raiffa, H., & Tversky, A. (Eds.) (1988). Decision making: Descriptive, normative, and prescriptive interactions. New York: Cambridge University Press.

Freud, S. (1933). *New introductory lectures on psychoanalysis*. New York: Harton.

Hull, C. L. (1943). *Principles of behavior*. New York: Appleton-Century-Crofts.

Pavlov, I. P. (1927). *Conditioned reflexes*. London: Oxford University Press.

Skinner, B. F. (1953). *Science and human behavior*. New York: MacMillan.

Watson, J. P. (1913). Psychology as the behaviorist views it. *Psychological Review*, 20, 158–177.

SUGGESTED READINGS

Platt, J. R. (1964). Strong inference. *Science*, *146*, 347–352.

Taylor, S. E. (1998). The social being in social psychology. In D. T. Gilbert, S. T. Fiske, and G. Lindzey (Eds.), *The handbook of social psychology* (4th ed., Vol. 1, pp. 58–95). New York: McGraw-Hill.

The Science and Metaphor of Micro OB

This section contains three articles that focus on the advancement of research and theory in organization behavior.

Macro versus Micro

In the first article, Staw (1991) directly takes up the micro-macro debate and cogently argues that the schism between the two fields may be more apparent than real. He argues that the fundamental processes that are of concern to micro OB researchers are also important for macro organizational researchers. As a direct demonstration of this, he suggests that readers substitute the word *individual* for *organization* when reading a macro OB article (and vice versa).

What Theory Is (Not)

In the second article, Sutton and Staw (1995) vehemently argue that most OB scholars lack theory in their research. They chastise research papers that substitute five things for theory: references (long strings of research citations), data, lists of variables, diagrams (and flowcharts with arrows and boxes), and hypotheses and predictions. They argue that none of these are actually theory and cite some of their own research articles as showing these failings.

Building a Science of OB

The third article, by Pfeffer, "Barriers to the Advance of Organizational Science: Paradigm Development as a Dependent Variable" (1993), argues that micro OB suffers from a lack of paradigm development, or technical certainty (about how to measure concepts) and consensus (agreement among researchers in the field). He then outlines a number of dire consequences that result from a lack of paradigm development, such as the reduced ability of researchers to obtain resources, less collaborative research, lower placement of doctoral students in jobs, higher journal rejection rates, longer time until publication, and increased revise-and-resubmit rates. Pfeffer points to a number of disciplines that have struggled with paradigm development and cites political science as an example of a field that moved from a distinct lack of development to being more highly developed.

Metaphors in Scholarly Research

Most scientists prefer to believe that they are unbiased in terms of how they ask questions about a social phenomenon and the method they use to study its occurrence and cause-effect relationships. However, strong assumptions exist that guide how research questions are formulated and phenomena are investigated. These assumptions may be viewed as metaphors. In the next two sections, I review the key metaphors that guide the conduct of research in micro-organizational behavior, social psychology, and economics.

Metaphors provide insight into the assumptions

that different disciplines make. They also shape the process of research. For example, metaphors affect the nature and choice of dissertation topics. The use of metaphors in research implies that we look at the organizational actor through different lenses, depending upon the particular historical time period. The metaphor that is used to guide research is often driven by the researcher's background (e.g., economics, sociology), and metaphors have different levels of analysis.

Metaphors of OB

Pfeffer (1998) identified four metaphors that characterize the organizational actor: the economic actor, the social model, the retrospective rational model, and the moral model. According to Pfeffer, the economic actor metaphor characterizes a rational person who might sometimes exhibit "bounded rationality" (Simon, 1955) because he or she is in a hurry, but who, for the most part, is strictly self-interested. The social model of organizational behavior stresses the embedded nature of behavior (Granovetter, 1985). Social models of behavior emphasize the context of behavior and networks and the social actor's position in them.

Pfeffer distinguished the "retrospective rational model," which states that people are not really rational but do feel a *need* to be rational. Therefore, they act without thinking or processing and, when they are forced to explain themselves, claim that they acted in a sensible manner and provide an explanation that may have nothing to do with their actions. Because social norms value consistency, people frequently behave in a fashion consistent with their previous attitudes and behaviors. For example, O'Reilly and Caldwell (1981) demonstrated the consistency effect when they found that MBA graduates who had several job offers but accepted a job paying less than the maximum offer were more satisfied and stayed at the job longer.

A fourth metaphor is the "moral model." The moral model postulates that people pursue morality as well as pleasure. Thus, organizational actors are under the influence of pleasure and morality at any given time. For example, symbolic factors are better predictors of political opinions than is self-interest (Sears & Funk, 1990).

Metaphors in Social Psychological Research

It is a useful exercise to contrast Pfeffer's metaphors for the organizational actor with Fiske and Taylor's (1991) metaphors for the social actor. According to Fiske and Taylor, one of the first metaphors that characterized the social actor was that of a "consistency seeker." This research metaphor had its roots in motivational theories and, in particular, cognitive dissonance theory. During the 1960s the focus was on how social actors have needs—and in particular, a strong desire to be consistent. If the social actor believes he or she is inconsistent either in word or in deed, this belief leads to a negative drive state, wherein the social actor attempts to reduce the inconsistency. For instance, if I acknowledge that smoking is bad for my health, but I'm standing outside my office puffing away, I've got a serious problem; this will put me into a state of activation (a drive state), and I'm going to do whatever I can to reduce it.

The cognitive revolution occurred during the end of this period, and with the advent of the computer and cognitive information processing theory, the next major metaphor was that of the naïve scientist. Thus, the social actor was transformed into a rational scientist who willingly and adeptly processed information. It is worth noting that this research metaphor was decidedly "cooler" in terms of affect and motivation than its predecessor. According to social information processing theory, the social actor assesses all of the available information, aggregates it, weights the data appropriately, and produces a judgment, all in a very rational manner. Key examples of this research metaphor include Kelley's (1972) covariance model of attribution and social perception theory.

However, research investigations following the naïve scientist metaphor began surfacing investigations suggesting that people were really not as deliberate, systematic, and rational as these computer metaphors suggested. As a matter of fact, people make a lot of mistakes. Even more interesting, mistakes are not random and haphazard, but are very systematic. One of the biggest mistakes made when people attempt to infer causality is a tendency to attribute the behavior of others to dispositions rather than the situation— also known as the "fundamental attribution error" (Ross, 1977). Thus, the next metaphor was that of the "cognitive miser." According to this research metaphor, the social actor is too busy or too lazy to make systematic judgments, but instead, relies on simple rules of thumb, or heuristics. (We will discuss these terms again in the next section, on decision making.)

The key theoretical assumptions of this research era were largely cognitive in nature. However, research investigations heated up once again, with motivation vying for front-and-center status, as the era of the "motivated tactician" commenced. According to this research metaphor, individuals have several different goals in any given situation. These goals, in turn, influence information processing and guide social behavior. For example, if I am a manager who is accountable for my behavior, I may attend to information more carefully than if I am not accountable (Tetlock, 1983). Similarly, if I desire a job in a particular company, I may engage in more systematic search and appraisal of information. A key distinction emanating from this era of research is the acknowledgment of two types of information processing: deliberate and effortful versus superficial and automatic (Chaiken, 1980).

One of the most recent metaphors in social psychology is the "preconscious actor," the idea that individuals are guided by cognitions and attitudes they are not consciously aware of but that nevertheless may be activated. Studies of cognitive priming and unconscious activation of attitudes suggest that there is a powerful association between cognition and behavior.

REFERENCES

Chaiken, S. (1980). Heuristic versus systematic information processing and the use of source versus message cues in persuasion. *Journal of Personality and Social Psychology, 39*, 752–766.

Fiske, S. T., & Taylor, S. E. (1991). *Social cognition* (2nd ed.). New York: McGraw-Hill.

Granovetter, M. (1985). Economic action and social structure: The problem of embeddedness. *American Journal of Sociology, 91*(3), 481–510.

Kelley, H. H. (1972). Attribution in social interaction. In E. E. Jones, D. E. Kanouse, H. H. Kelley, R. E. Nisbett, S. Valens, & B. Weiner (Eds.), *Attribution: Perceiving the causes of behavior* (pp. 1–26). Morristown, NJ: General Learning Press.

O'Reilly, C. A., & Caldwell, D. F. (1981). The commitment and job tenure of new employees: Some evidence of postdecisional justification. *Administrative Science Quarterly, 26*(4), 597–616.

Pfeffer, J. (1988). Understanding organizations: Concepts and controversies. In D. T. Gilbert, S. T. Fiske, & G. Lindzey (Eds.), *The handbook of social psychology, Vol. 2* (4th ed., pp. 733–777). New York: McGraw-Hill.

Pfeffer, J. (1993). Barriers to the advance of organizational science: Paradigm development as a dependent variable. *Academy of Management Review, 18*(4), 599–620.

Pfeffer, J. (1998). Understanding organizations: Concepts and controversies. In D. T. Gilbert, S. T. Fiske, & G. Lindzey (Eds.), *The handbook of social psychology, Vol. 2* (4th ed., pp. 733–777). New York: McGraw-Hill.

Ross, L. (1977). The intuitive psychologist and his shortcomings: Distortions in the attribution process. In L. Berkowitz (Ed.), *Advances in experimental social psychology* (Vol. 10, pp. 173–220). Orlando, FL: Academic Press.

Sears, D. O., & Funk, C. L. (1990). The limited effect of economic self-interest on the political attitudes of the mass public. *Journal of Behavioral Economics, 19*(3), 247–271.

Simon, H. (1955). A behavioral model of rational choice. *Quarterly Journal of Economics, 69*, 99–118.

Staw, B. M. (1991). Dressing up like an organization: When psychological theories can explain organizational action. *Journal of Management, 17*(4), 805–819.

Sutton, R. I., & Staw, B. M. (1995). What theory is *not*. *Administrative Science Quarterly, 40*, 371–384.

Tetlock, P. E. (1983). Accountability and complexity of thought. *Journal of Personality and Social Psychology, 45*, 74–83.

Suggested Readings

Sternberg, R. J. (1999). In praise of dilettantism. *APS Observer* (May/June).

Dressing Up Like an Organization: When Psychological Theories Can Explain Organizational Action

Barry M. Staw • University of California at Berkeley

This article explores how psychological theories can be used to explain organizational action. It starts by noting that many macro actions may in fact be micro behavior in disguise. It is argued that psychological models are relevant when individuals are able to influence organizational action, when individual-level processes mediate organizational actions, and when theories of human behavior serve as a metaphor for the action of organizations. Once these arguments are posed, how micro research might actually be applied to macro problems is then discussed and specific examples of such "macro-psychological research" are provided.

Shortly after I started my first academic job, a graduate student named Eugene Swajkowski came to me with the idea of doing some research on organizational crime. I knew absolutely nothing about the topic, so I asked some naive questions such as "Do you want to study shoplifting or embezzlement?" He said he wanted to study corporate crimes such as when the entire organization violates the law. The subject sounded interesting to me. So we did the usual things, like conduct a literature search (of which there was not much), construct measures (we used anti-trust and Federal Trade Commission violations), code and analyze data. Everything came out as predicted. Therefore, as a confident young faculty member, I told Gene that this was a "sure publication." The problem was that I did not even know where we should send the paper.

My colleagues assured me that the *American Sociological Review* would be the best outlet for this kind of work. So, being trained primarily by psychologists, I conscientiously reread books by James D. Thompson, Peter Blau, and Richard Scott. I had it all down pat—all the vocabulary, the style of data presentation, the throw-away references to famous sociologists. I sent the paper off and waited 4 months. When the letter from the journal arrived, I anxiously pulled the reviews from the envelope. The opening line from the first reviewer read, "This paper has a curiously non-sociological flavor."

In a sense, this paper is my chance to get even.

It is an effort to demonstrate why psychologists *can* make a contribution to what has traditionally been the sociological study of organizations.

A Land Divided

In the 1960's and 1970's organizational research was considered to be an interdisciplinary field with theoretical inputs from anthropology, psychology, sociology, political science and economics. Since then, as the field has grown and prospered, it has increasingly become a set of specialty topics. Psychologists and those trained in micro organizational behavior have taken issues such as job attitudes, work motivation, absenteeism, turnover, and stress as their purview. Sociologists and those trained in macro organizational behavior have, in turn, laid claim to issues such as organizational structure, power, strategy, and environment. This micro-macro split has also become institutionalized. There are now separate divisions of the American Psychological Association and the American Sociological Association that deal with organizations, and within the Academy of Management, a more applied interdisciplinary organization, separate divisions have become host to micro and macro researchers. At present, not only do experienced academics readily identify themselves as micro versus macro researchers, but graduate students take on this delineation from the outset of their academic careers, choosing up sides in the hunt for data and interpretation of theory. Unfortunately, this division has taken its toll on research. Organizational behavior has moved from a vibrant interdisciplinary field to at least two highly bounded areas of study.

One goal of this article is to try to slow down or reverse what has been an almost centrifugal march in both the micro and macro directions. To do this, I will show how a number of organizational actions can be explained by psychological processes. In an accompanying piece, Pfeffer has noted how sociological processes can explain several aspects of micro organizational behavior. Perhaps these two articles will be seen as raids upon each other's camp to enlarge the territory of one's own subdiscipline. Alternatively, I would like to think of this endeavor as an expansion of common ground— the broadening of a neutral zone where multiple perspectives can be brought to bear on similar issues, with the ultimate goal of returning organiza-

tional behavior to the interdisciplinary field it once was.

Using Micro Models to Explain Macro Actions

To demonstrate how psychological models can be used to explain organizational action I will outline three alternative explanations of macro organizational behavior. I will start with the most radical: that macro actions may in fact be micro behavior. Then, I will move to two weaker forms of the argument: that micro theories may either explain the processes now implicit in macro models or serve as useful metaphors for organization-level theory. Once these arguments have been posed, I will provide some examples of how we might profitably conduct psychological research on the actions of organizations.

When Individuals Are Disguised as Organizations

We have all received letters from companies relating the following sorts of bad news: "It is not company policy to give refunds," or "Your qualifications do not meet the firm's current needs," or "The organization's current priorities unfortunately prevent it from participating in your worthy research project." In each of these instances it is likely that, if we probe the organizational action, we will find an individual decision maker behind the scene. The person in charge (often a lower level person acting autonomously) does not like complainers who want refunds, does not want to hire us, or does not want to be bothered by our valuable research project. In each of these instances, individual and organizational behavior are not just parallel; they are the same thing. Organizational actions can therefore be individual behavior under the cloak of a larger, more impersonal entity.

If organizational actions are actually individual behavior, then psychological theories are obviously useful as explanatory concepts. They are-especially relevant when individuals are given a great deal of discretion in their dealings with outside constituencies. For example, a commodities trader for General Mills, a buyer for Macy's, or an admissions officer at Stanford may each represent the organization and function without close supervision by others. One may of course argue that when an external crisis hits, perhaps in the forms of financial cutbacks or scandal, the representative's autonomy will be restricted (Staw, Sandelands, & Dutton, 1981). However, by nothing this exception one is also implicitly recognizing that the general rule is that they are given relative autonomy.

Another ready argument against using psychological theory to explain the behavior of organizational actors is that their behavior is not really autonomous. Individuals may be socialized to the point that they are acting as full agents of the corporation (Kanter, 1977). They may have absorbed the organization's goals as their own and are simply seeking benefits for the larger system. I do not disagree with this position. Instead, I would argue that even when this is true, psychological theories still apply. Just as in the case of altruistic behavior, where one seeks benefits for another with whom one identifies closely (Batson et al., 1983) or when one acts against an outgroup to demonstrate loyalty to one's own ingroup (Campbell, 1975), psychological theories are useful. In performing their organizational roles, individuals may sometimes behave altruistically so that the institution's interests are furthered, even at the expense of the individual's own interests (Staw, 1983). More often, however, behavior may be determined by a confluence of loyalties, where individual and organizational interests sometimes coincide, sometimes conflict, and at other times are irrelevant to each other. In such a complex world variations of motivation theory, role theory, agency theory, and identity theory would likely provide as many research leads as conventional sociological theories of organizational action.

When Individuals Sway Organizations

Sometimes individuals are not the mere agents of organizations, but instead exert control over them. At the extreme would be a very small, one-person business where organizational action is a direct extension of individual behavior. Consider also a newly founded organization. Here, an individual has expressed his or her ingenuity in the form of entrepreneurial activity, and the way the new business is organized and managed can be expected to be a product of the founder's ideas and predilections. Certainly the type of market one is in, the availability of external role models, and prevailing social norms can all influence how the business is initially organized (Aldrich & Mueller,

1982). However, there is usually enough ambiguity in the environment and equifinality in the structuring of organizations for the individual to come shining through. Thus, it should come as no surprise that Schein (1983) argues that the founder of a firm is the major instigator of its culture. At first, personal preferences are translated into the management of a few employees in ways that are comfortable to the founder. Then, as a firm grows the management style of the founder is likely to become embodied into the culture of the firm, as reflected in its symbols, procedures, and formal structure. Even after the departure of the founder, the legacy of the culture he or she began may endure. Just as the vestiges of an arbitrary norm can persist in small groups over time and changes in membership (Jacobs & Campbell, 1961; Zucker, 1977), one would expect that the modes of internal operation and strategies of dealing with the environment would likely persist in organizations.

Besides founding an enterprise, individuals may also influence organizations through leadership (Kets de Vries & Miller, 1986). The greatest effects would be expected in small firms, because here a CEO's preferences are more directly translatable into organizational action, without the dilution and buffering created by middle management. One might also expect that CEO's would have a greater effect on younger firms (even if the executive is not the founder) than on firms with older and more established cultures. This, in fact, is exactly what Miller and Dröge (1986) found in their research on personality and organizational structure. They showed that the need for achievement of CEO's was a significant predictor of organizational formalization, integration, and centralization, and that these relationships were strongest in smaller and younger firms.

One need not be a CEO to influence organizational action, however, Middle level executives also influence the extent and manner by which organizational policies are enacted. For example, it has long been known that political appointees heading U.S. governmental agencies have a difficult time implementing policies that either threaten the security of middle level bureaucrats or violate long-held goals of the agency. The civil service employees can simply stall in order to "outlive" the political appointee, who is likely to leave after the next national election. In private industry, the same logic can prevail. CEO's proposing radical organizational changes will often meet resistance from those who are asked to do the changing. And as Mechanic (1962) noted long ago, even those lower in the hierarchy have more power than we usually realize. Because it is the employees who complete the product or execute the service, the organization is highly dependent on their efforts to perform in the marketplace (Bower & Schneider, 1988).

Obviously, as one descends the organizational ladder the influence of any single individual decreases. Yet most jobs do entail a degree of discretion, when rules and procedures do not adequately specify behavior; and they also involve some autonomy, where one needs to act without another's supervision. Thus, much of organizational behavior can be viewed as the collection of efforts by a set of quasi-independent actors. At one extreme, when the organization employs a set of professionals, the product of the organization consists of an amalgam of individual behaviors. In universities, for example, each professor conducts courses in a nearly independent manner, and the educational process is an additive product of these individualized efforts. At the other extreme lie machine-like bureaucracies and factories where individuals function as an extension of collective rules and programmed behavior. Fortunately, the success of the Japanese in introducing discretion into the factory floor has had a dramatic impact on our view of doing business in even these highly constrained settings. Being able to stop the assembly line, conduct one's own quality control studies, and redesign various factory operations mean that individuals, even at the lowest level in the organization, can have a direct influence on the product of the organization.

Micro Mediators of Macro Behavior

So far I have argued that at least a portion of what we normally think of as macro-organizational behavior is really individual behavior in disguise. There are, of course, degrees of truth to this assertion, depending on whether individuals act as founders, autonomous agents, or functionaries who are constrained by the structure and rules of the firm. Given the extent of possible individual influence, does this mean that we should trace all organizational actions to their individual originators? Is there not some rationale to macro-level explanations of organizational life?

As things now stand, each branch of the social sciences has its own view of reality and its own corner on the truth. For example, an economic theory of organizations may explain the actions of the firm with only a small set of market variables. Knowing the general economic cycle can help predict the profitability of the firm, its capital expenditures, and changes in employment levels. Likewise, sociological theories of the structure and design of the firm may help predict the actions of the organization in its environment and perhaps even the success of the firm. But such macro models do not necessarily constitute an end in themselves. Just because a significant amount of variance is explained is not reason enough to stop the process of inquiry.

As an example of the merits of reductionism, consider the study of organizational demography (Pfeffer, 1983). The chief premise of this literature is that it is possible to predict organizational outcomes (e.g., the turnover of the employees or work group performance) by knowing the distribution of employees on certain demographic variables (e.g., age, sex, educational background, tenure in the organization). Moreover, in this sociological formulation it is not the demographic characteristic, per se, that is driving the predictions, but the "relational" aspect of the demographic characteristics of the social group. Thus, organizational demography speaks to the consequences of having certain tenure distributions in the firm or skewness in the distribution of women and minorities in the organization.

A common finding in the organizational demography literature is that homogeneous units outperform or are somehow superior to those that are more heterogeneous (O'Reilly & Flatt, 1989; Wagner, Pfeffer, & O'Reilly, 1984). Yet, without knowing the mediating processes involved, we can only guess as to why such effects may occur. Demographic researchers have argued that conflict increases as diversity increases, but seldom is conflict directly measured (see O'Reilly, Caldwell, & Barnett, 1989, for an exception). As a result, we do not know what forms of diversity can create conflict, nor whether this conflict is task or interpersonally based. We also do not know exactly what triggers such difficulties. Is it the lack of commonly held work values, or simply the fact that dissimilar people generally are less likely to be friends than those who are similar? Such questions require the probing of psychological mechanisms underlying macroscopic effects.

By understanding the psychology of demographic variables, one can gain some theoretical power over the problem of interpersonal relations. By knowing why demographic effects have occurred, one is better able to construct a more general theory of social relations at work and perhaps even know when diversity can and cannot help performance. That is not to deny that it is possible to have a sociological model that examines relational variables and their consequences on collective outcomes (i.e., a macro-level theory). However, when one puts psychological flesh on this kind of structural model, the persuasiveness of the basic theory can be increased. With reductionism, each empirical study can become a double test of theory (at both the sociological and psychological levels), requiring data to be consistent across two levels of analysis.

Understanding the psychological dynamics of a macro theory can also make that theory more useful. Lewin's dictum that "there is nothing more practical than a good theory" has by now become a cliché. Yet, anything that increases our understanding of a theoretical process means that we can better know when and where a theory is applicable, how to revise it, and when to ignore it. For example, if we accept the research finding that heterogeneity of work units leads to increases turnover, should we then endeavor to reduce the heterogeneity of the workforce? One reasonable response is that we should do nothing until we know more about the meaning of such heterogeneity. In terms of tenure heterogeneity, for example, do people not get along with people who are of different ages, or does a bimodal or skewed distribution of tenure simply index some other characteristic of organizations? Organizations that have experienced punctuations in employment and hiring levels may have also experienced radical (and conflict-producing) changes in policy, growth, and culture. Thus, the demography of the organization may be a result rather than a cause of conflict.

By understanding more about when or why heterogeneity can cause interpersonal difficulties, we can better design ameliorative programs. With proper intervention we might be able to cope more effectively with the costs of heterogeneity (e.g., learning how to improve communication or reduce hostility) and tap its potential benefits (e.g., a broadening of information and perspective). In this way, we can better adapt to the increase in workforce heterogeneity that will occur in that decade ahead.

In summary, reductionism is not just a way to pick up additional variance missed by macroscopic models. Psychological theories can strengthen and add theoretical substance to macro models by providing the underlying rationale or missing process mechanism. This conclusion does not deny the utility of macro models, but simply recognizes them as an interim solution.

There is no logical limit to the process of reductionism. One could, for example, try to explain the strategic actions of a firm by the psychophysiology of its employees. Though at first blush this may sound like an almost absurd assertion, it could actually be an interesting lead. Connections could be made between chemical bases of aggression in CEO's and the merger/acquisition behavior of their firms, or perhaps between the physiology of workers and their efforts. The question is one of cost and feasibility for such reductionistic research, rather than whether it is a legitimate enterprise to undertake.

I would argue strongly against caveats that sociological explanations *should not* be reduced to the psychological level or that psychological processes cannot be moderating processes in macro-level theory. No doubt, one can construct a highly useful and cost-effective theory at the macro or economic level, just as reinforcement theory has prospered without delving into the psycho-dynamics of the individual. But, as we have seen with the recent merger of goal-setting with reinforcement approaches (e.g., Bandura, 1977, 1986), major advances can also be made by a willingness to move down a level in theoretical explanation—to embrace the call of reductionism.

Micro as a Metaphor for Macro

To this point I have made two arguments for the micro explanation of macro behavior. The strongest or most radical idea is that many macro actions are in fact individual behaviors in disguise. A somewhat weaker position is that it is important to understand the micro mediators of organizational action. A third, even more compromising position, is that micro theory can serve as a useful metaphor for organization-level theory. In making this latter argument, one can admit that real relationships and processes occur at the macro level, but their explanation may still be improved by resorting to psychological theory.

To see how micro metaphors can aid macro theory, one need only scan the horizon of current organizational sociology. There are glaring parallels between macro and micro models. For example, most versions of structural contingency theory (e.g., Lawrence & Lorsh, 1967; Thompson, 1967; Woodward, 1965) imply that there is some impetus toward efficiency of organization or energy minimization. Resource dependence theory (Pfeffer & Salancik, 1978) likewise posits that organizations strive to minimize sources of external control and uncertainty. These models are quite parallel to those of goal-setting, control theory, and expectancy theory—formulations that note how people locomote toward valued end-states—as well as models of personal control and reactance that emphasize motives toward freedom and choice. Consider also institutional theory's central hypotheses that organizations attempt to manage their public image in order to secure external support and legitimacy, and that they readily model their operations after those of other institutions rather than seek the most efficient response (Meyer & Rowan, 1977; Meyer & Scott, 1983). Such reasoning is not too distant from psychological theories of impression management (Schlenker, 1980), social identification (Markus & Wurf, 1987), and modeling (Bandura, 1977).

I have tried reading several of the classics of organization theory (e.g., Pfeffer & Salancik, 1978; Thompson, 1967) and have simply inserted the word *individual* whenever *organization* appears. Not much of the meaning is lost. Why is this so? Why are there such close parallels between micro and macro theories?

Some system theorists (e.g., Miller, 1978) have noted that all social entities have similar properties and predilections. Others, such as economists, might argue that because organizations are basically utility maximizing entities, they will share many behavioral tendencies with self-interested individuals. Finally, it is simply possible that, because organizations are largely populated by individuals, personal predilections are likely to aggregate in determining organizational actions.

My own position is that it is immaterial *why* organizations tend to look or behave like individuals. Because they do, we should therefore use in-dividual psychology as a helpful analogy in organizational theorizing. Many sociologists, I would argue, are already implicitly using psychological concepts in their macro models—almost in a sense asking, "what would I do if I were an organization?" So why not use psychological concepts to their fullest extent? Dress up like an organization and capitalize on the perspective it brings.

Developing a Macro Organizational Psychology[1]

If one were conscientiously to pursue individual explanations of organizational action, where would the most advantageous openings lie? Although it might be theoretically appealing to understand all the dynamics of individual and interpersonal behavior in an organization, this would not likely yield cost-effective insights to organizational actions. A more lucrative source of research would be the study of key organizational decision makers, such as the CEO and the set of top executives in a firm. Current macro theory commonly dubs this collection of policy makers as the "dominant coalition," depersonalizing them into a sociological entity. However, because it is possible to identify key actors in important organizational decisions, psychological research can be applied to these individuals in order to explain organizational actions.

Miller and Dröge (1986) have already shown how personality theory can be applied to the CEO in predicting the structure of organizations. They found that the chief executive's need for achievement could explain how centralized and formalized was the structure of the organization. This research could, of course, be extended to include other personality dimensions as predictors of structure as well as the internal management of the firm. It would not be surprising, for example, to find that executives who are low in interpersonal trust and have difficulty in dealing with others may also tend to use a system of supervision that emphasizes quantitative reports rather than "hands-on" interaction. Likewise, the more suspicious (perhaps even paranoid) is the CEO, the greater the emphasis will be on centralized control rather than employee empowerment (Kets de Vries, 1980).

---

[1]Robert Sutton should be credited with the origination of this term.

Most broadly, one could hypothesize a direct linkage between the personality profile of the CEO (or set of top managers) and the cultural profile of the organization (O'Reilly, Caldwell, & Chatman, 1991). With such research we could find that firms that have aggressive, competitive, or power-oriented CEO's have instituted these same values in the culture of the organization.

In terms of external organizational actions, we may also find that it is possible to use the personality of leaders to predict the behavioral tendencies of the firm. Take for instance the categorization scheme developed by Miles and Snow (1978) in which firms are depicted as "prospectors," "analyzers," "reactors," or "defenders." Some obvious predictions are that firms that work to develop new products and stay ahead of the market ("prospectors") have CEO's that are creative and risk-taking, whereas companies that try to defend their market niche ("defenders") have CEO's that are more passive or cautious. Some tentative support for this notion can be gleaned from the work of Miller, Kets de Vries, and Toulouse (1982). They found that CEO's who scored higher on Rotter's (1966) locus of control measure were likely to lead organizations that innovated in terms of product technology and new product introduction. That is, those CEO's who believed they could exert control over events in their lives ("internals" on the I/E scale) headed the most risk-taking and dynamic organizations. These results were correlational and not causal. But, as one might predict, the smaller the firm and the longer the CEO's tenure, the stronger were the relationships between locus of control and innovation.

In relating dispositional characteristics of managers to organizational characteristics and actions, several often implicit issues must be confronted. The first is how to choose the proper personality dimensions for research. Should we concentrate on the major or most commonly studied aspects of personality and examine their consequences at the macro level? Despite the promising results of Miller, Kets de Vries, and Toulouse (1982) and Miller and Dröge (1986), I think this is a dangerous route to take. My fear is that many low correlations will be found, without enough impact to warrant a shift in resources to this kind of macro-psychological research. Even if we follow the precepts of modern personality research in gathering multiple measures of personality as well as the behavior to be explained (Weiss & Adler, 1984), I

would not be surprised if robust and consistent results are not found. The problem is that most personality measures have been designed to predict individual behavior over an array of family and school situations rather than framed in terms of organizational life. Thus, stronger predictions are likely to be obtained by tailoring dispositional measures to the organizational setting (e.g., instead of using a general scale of competitiveness, one could assess the importance of career advancement and of being the highest paid in one's industry). In addition to grounding measures to the situation, we may also benefit by making our scales more behaviorally based. For example, instead of using an abstract moral reasoning scale (Kohlberg, 1976) to predict legal violations, one might simply use an index of prior infractions (the number of prior speeding and parking tickets) as a proxy for the disposition to break the law. One might note that leaders (such as sports coaches) who have previously been suspected or charged with violations are more likely to head organizations that will be charged with violations in the future, even if they change jobs or organizations.

Besides assessing the disposition of key individuals in the firm and calculating their effects on organizational action, we might also generalize the entire notion of behavioral disposition to the organization level. Here we would treat organizations *as if* they were living, breathing entities with predictable behavioral tendencies. In essence, this is already being done in various categorical schemes, such as Miles and Snow's depiction of the firm's market orientation (i.e., prospector vs. defender). It is also an implicit assumption in the population ecology literature, where it is hypothesized that organizations pursue a given market strategy at birth and that this tendency persists over time (Hannan & Freeman, 1977). Though rarely measured, what apparently underlies the death of firms is their assumed inflexibility to meet changing market conditions—in other words, their strong dispositions to behave consistently over time.

Openly positing that organizations have dispositions makes salient several research routes. The classification of organizations (McKelvey, 1983) looks more interesting as a way of sorting various behavioral tendencies of firms. The study of how particular types of organizations do under differing environmental conditions takes on added urgency (Pennings, in press). And questions such as the mutability of organizations over various stages in their lifespan (cf., Tushman & Romanelli, 1985) become more important with a dispositional approach to organizations.

Using Psychological Processes

Another high yield approach to understanding organizational action may be to examine the psychological processes of managers. If top managers are responsible for organizational decisions, then any universalistic tendency or psychological bias is likely to affect the decisions that are produced by organizations. As an example, consider the well known fact that most people suffer from an overconfidence bias (Einhorn & Hogarth, 1981), believing that they will not be involved in an accident, illness, or some sort of loss. Except for depressives, most people are also perennial optimists, seeing the world in fairly rosy terms (Taylor & Brown, 1988), believing that they have control over the events and vicissitudes of their lives (Langer, 1975). There is, of course, little reason to believe that managers are immune to these tendencies. Thus, we might expect excess risk-taking on the part of organizations, unless specific structures or procedures are present to brake these tendencies.

The list of psychological biases that can potentially affect organizational decision making is large. Bazerman (1990) has described some of the likely effects of decision heuristics, such as representativeness, framing, availability, anchoring, hindsight bias and overconfidence. In addition, one area of psychological research that has already made explicit claims to explaining organization-level action is the escalation of commitment (Brockner & Rubin, 1985; Staw & Ross, 1987). Here the tendency of individuals to become overcommitted to losing courses of action (to throw good money after bad) has been applied to organizations, tendency to persist in losing projects and products.

The list of psychological processes affecting top management behavior need not be limited to decision biases. Any human process such as stereotyping, modeling, or cognitive consistency can be used to understand a general behavioral tendency on the part of managers. Parallel processes at the macro level might include the tendency to view competition in zero-sum terms, the blind adoption of other firms' practices, and the tendency to base strategy on the organization's past actions rather than on future opportunities. The critical question for organizations is not whether psychological tendencies exist, but whether we can expect them to affect additively the resultant actions, policies, or decisions of the organization.

Moving From Micro to Macro

It is reasonable, I believe, to posit that many rather universalistic tendencies on the part of individuals will aggregate into organization-level behavior. As research on group polarization has shown (Lamm & Myers, 1978), if most individuals share a particular bias or opinion, then decisions coming from the larger entity may be even more extreme. In task groups, for example, deviants from a skewed distribution of opinion are likely to censor themselves (or be censored by others), and the bulk of group discussion will probably be supportive of the majority position. Within organizations, there are additional forces for homogeneity. As Schneider (1987) has so adeptly noted, the attraction of individuals to the organization, the socializing of people in the organizations, and the attrition of individuals over time can all contribute to the homogeneity of firms. Thus, if most managers suffer from a particular bias or psychological tendency, it will likely be incorporated into the behavioral profile reinforced within the firm. The organization may, for example, select for those who are optimistic or high in the illusion of control, allow such individuals to assume power, and then weigh these individuals' opinions more heavily than those with minority viewpoints or perspectives (Nemeth & Staw, 1989).

The fact that there are shared psychological biases does not mean that the organization is inevitably locked-in to the foibles of the human mind. As shown in the behavioral decision-making literature (Fischhoff, 1982), people can be trained to counteract some of their inherent biases or cognitive shortcomings. In addition, organizations can be structured to prevent people from acting fully on their own tendencies or to stop these tendencies from aggregating into organizational actions. As an example of the latter procedure, some banks have tried to counteract the common problem of overcommitment to losing courses of action. By setting up work-out groups, these banks have effectively taken troubled loans away from the original lending officers so that a fresh perspective can be provided on the situation. The effort has been one of converting the individual tendency to "save" a project or recoup past losses (a retrospective form of rationality) to an organization-level emphasis on maximizing potential future returns (a more prospective form of rationality).

Multi-Level Processes

Although I have described how psychological tendencies can be responsible for organizational action, the relationship between micro and macro processes may be both complicated and self-sustaining. Again I will use escalation research as an example.

Early studies in the escalation area (e.g., Staw, 1976; Tegar, 1981) examined the effect of self-justification motives on the commitment of resources to a losing course of action. Analogous research has applied decision biases such as the tendency to be influenced by sunk cost (Arkes & Blumer, 1985) and negative framing (Tversky & Kahneman, 1981) to decision situations involving losses. Although nearly all of the escalation literature has been at the individual level, attempting to sort out various theoretical explanations of resource allocation behavior, there has also been a more recent inquiry into the organizational dynamics of escalation.

Staw and Ross (1987) traced escalation across different levels of analysis. They noted that projects are generally initiated by individual administrators who see bright promise in a new product or venture. However, when negative or mixed results start to appear, these same administrators may try to defend the endeavor to both themselves and others. Downplaying adversity and believing that "success is around the corner" are common reactions of those who are responsible for a losing course of action. Yet, an escalation episode rarely ends with this kind of individual rationalization. After a project has been implemented by the organization, it often takes on political overtones, with defenders mobilizing to defend their interests in the venture. In the end, a project or product can become so absorbed into the goals, purposes, and politics of an organization that it is an institutionalized part of the firm.

Discontinuing an institutionalized venture is extremely difficult. Witness Pan American Airlines' actions as they have undergone a slow, steady decline over the past two decades. As revenues fell and losses mounted, Pan Am first sold its profitable Intercontinental Hotel chain. As losses continued, the valuable Pan Am building in New York was put up for sale. Then, when business again soured, the profitable Asian routes were sold to United Airlines. Now Pan Am is in bankruptcy proceedings with competitors bidding for the remainder of its routes. Though it would have seemed heretical at the time, a more sensible leadership might have decided to sell the *airline* and keep the money-making hotel and realestate subsidiaries. This kind of prospective rationality is unlikely, however, when there is an institutionalized form of escalation—when the political core of the firm is dependent on the continuation of a given course of action and it is almost unthinkable to imagine the organization in another line of business.

Longitudinal case studies of escalation (e.g., Ross & Staw, 1986) have delineated some important linkages between psychological processes and organizational actions over time. But, escalation is not the only arena where such cross-level effects are likely to operate. Take, for example, the hypotheses that people are subject to optimistic biases and illusions of control. A direct translation of these psychological tendencies to the organizational level would mean that companies generally overestimate their performance and their prowess in the market place. Yet, one must also realize that a high degree of confidence might also positively contribute to an action orientation on the part of organizations. Thus, some psychological tendencies can have dual or complex effects on organization-level behavior.

To illustrate such dual consequences, consider the area of new product innovation. Here a certain amount of bravado is necessary to push a risky product through to the marketplace. Without some (perhaps illusory) beliefs of control and a set of very positive (perhaps unrealistic) expectations, little energy may be expended on new ventures. However, as has been pointed out in the innovation literature (Amabile, 1988; Kanter, 1988), some filtering of projects is necessary to sort the good ideas from the absurd, as well as difficult goals from the impossible. Thus, innovative firms have found that it is important both to stimulate a diversity of ideas and to filter these varied ideas into a few viable projects (Staw, 1990). To do this, some organizations foster a dialectic in which opposing views are aired fully before irrevocable commitments are made. In addition, organizations may supply seed money for many speculative ventures, but require that an increasingly difficult set of hurdles be surmounted as greater levels of resources are expended. Such structural devices avoid squashing the energy to push new ideas, but instead harness this energy in productive directions. Hence, illusions of control and overoptimism may not always lead to organizational folly, as one might expect from a direct translation of these psychological effects to the organizational level. On the contrary, innovative firms may be exactly those entitites that have best learned to channel these psychological tendencies into appropriate organization-level actions.

Conclusion

This article started with the observation that organizational research has evolved over the past two decades into two separate and identifiable fields—those of micro and macro organizational behavior. In order to slow this movement and help restore some of the interdisiplinary vigor lost by the field, I have outlined ways in which psychological theories can enrich our understanding of organizational action. I have argued that psychological models can be relevant when individual behaviors influence organizational action, when individual-level processes mediate organizational actions, and when theories of human behavior serve as a metaphor for the action of organizations. Following these arguments, I have shown how micro research might actually be applied to macro problems. Examples of this kind of "macro-psychological research" included the effects of leadership characteristics on organizational culture, the consequences of individual decision biases for organizational decision making, how individual tendencies to become overcommitted aggregate into organizational escalation, and how overconfidence and illusory control tendencies can be harnessed by innovative organizations. Of course, these examples are only the tip of a largely unexplored terrain. Dressing up as an organization, I would argue, can be a highly productive enterprise. Its pursuit may not only shed new light on macro research topics, but also help the field of organizational behavior move back to the interdisciplinary field it once was.

ACKNOWLEDGMENTS

This article was made possible by research support from the Institute of Industrial Relations at the University of California at Berkeley, and by staff support from Josef Chytry at Berkeley's Center for Research in Management.

REFERENCES

Aldrich, H., & Mueller, S. 1982. The evolution of organizational forms: Technology, coordination, and control. In B. M. Staw & L. L. Cummings (Eds.), *Research in Organizational Behavior*, 4:33–87. Greenwich, CT: JAI Press.

Amabile, T.M. 1988. A model of creativity and innovation in organizations. In B. M. Staw & L. L. Cummings (Eds.), *Research in Organizational Behavior*, 10:123–167. Greenwich, CT: JAI Press.

Arkes, H. R., & Blumes, C. 1985. The psychology of sunk cost. *Organizational Behavior and Human Decision Processes*, 35:124–140.

Bandura, A. 1977. *Social learning theory*. Englewood Cliffs, NJ: Prentice-Hall.

Bandura, A. 1986. *Social foundations of thought and action: A social cognitive theory*. Englewood Cliffs, NJ: Prentice-Hall.

Batson, C. D., O'Quin, K., Fultz, J., Vanderplas, M., & Isen, A. M. 1983. Influence of self-reported distress and empathy on egoistic vesus altruistic motivation to help. *Journal of Personality and Social Pscychology*, 45:706–718.

Bazerman, M. H. 1990. *Judgment in managerial decision making* (2nd ed.), New York: John Wiley.

Bower, D. E., & Schneider, B. 1988. Services marketing and management: The implications for organizational behavior. In B. M. Staw & L. L. Cummings (Eds.), *Research in Organizational Behavior*, 10:43–80. Greenwich, CT: JAI Press.

Brockner, J., & Rubin, J. Z. 1985. *Entrapment in escalating conflicts*. New York: Springer-Verlag.

Campbell, D. T. 1975. On the conflicts between biological and social evolution and between psychology and moral tradition. *American Psychologist*, 30:1103–1126.

Einhorn, H., & Hogarth, R. 1981. Behavioral decision theory: Processes of judgments and choice. *Annual Review of Psychology*, 32:53–88.

Fischhoff, B. 1982. Debiasing. In D. Kahneman, P. Slovic, & A. Tversky (Eds.), *Judgment under uncertainty: Heuristics and biases*: 422–444. Cambridge: Cambridge University Press.

Hannan, M. T., & Freeman, J. H. 1977. The population ecology of organizations. *American Journal of Sociology*, 32:929–964.

Jacobs, R. C., & Campbell, D. T. 1961. The perpetuation of an arbitrary tradition through several generations of a laboratory microculture. *Journal of Abnormal and Social Psychology*, 62:649–658.

Kanter, R. M. 1977. *Men and women of the corporation*. New York: Basic Books.

Kanter, R. M. 1988. When a thousand flowers bloom: Structural, collective, and social conditions for innovation in organization. In B. M. Staw & L. L. Cummings (Eds.),

Research in Organizational Behavior, 10:169–211. Greenwich, CT: JAI Press.

Kets de Vries, M. F. R. 1980. *Organizational paradoxes: Clinical approaches to management*. London: Tavistock Publications.

Kets de Vries, M. F. R., & Miller, D. 1986. Personality, culture, and organization. *Academy of Management Review*, 11:266–279.

Kohlberg, L. 1976. Moral stages and moralization: The cognitive-deveiopmental approach. In T. Lichona (Ed.), *Moral development and behavior*: 31–53. New York: Holt.

Lamm, H., & Myers, D. G. 1978. Group induced polarization of attitudes and behavior. In L. Berkowitz (Ed.), *Advances in experimental social psychology*, 11:145–195. New York: Academic Press.

Langer, E. J. 1975. The illusion of control. *Journal of Personality and Social Psychology*, 32:311–328.

Markus, H., & Wurf, E. 1987. The dynamic self-concept: A social psychological perspective. *Annual Review of Psychology*, 38:299–337.

McKelvey, B. 1983. *Organizational systematics*. Berkeley: University of California Press.

Mechanic, D. 1962. Sources of power of lower participants in complex organizations. *Administrative Science Quarterly*, 7:349–362.

Meyer, J. W., & Rowan, B. 1977. Institutionalized organizations: Formal structure as myth and ceremony. *American Journal of Sociology*, 83:340–363.

Meyer, J. W., & Scott, W. R. 1983. *Organizational environments: Ritual and rationality*. Beverly Hills, CA: Sage Publications.

Miles, R. E., & Snow, C. C. 1978. *Organizational strategy, structure, and process*. New York: McGraw-Hill.

Miller, D., & Dröge, C. 1986. Psychological and traditional determinants of structure. *Administrative Science Quarterly*, 31:539–560.

Miller, D., Kets de Vries, M. F. R., & Toulouse, J. M. 1982. Top executive locus of control and its relationship to straetgy-making, structure, and environment. *Academy of Management Journal*, 25:237–253.

Miller, J. G. 1978. *Living systems*, New York: Free Press.

Nemeth, C. J., & Staw, B. M. 1989. The tradeoffs of social control and innovation in groups and organizations. In L. Berkowitz (Ed.), *Advances in experimental social psychology*, 22:175–210. New York: Academic Press.

O'Reilly, C. A., Caldwell, D. F., & Barmett, W. P. 1989. Work group demography social integration, and turnover. *Administrative Science Quarterly*, 34:21–37.

O'Reilly, C., Caldwell, D. F., & Chatman, J. 1991. People and organizational culture: A profile comparison approach to assessing person-organization fit. *Academy of Management Journal*, 34:487–516.

O'Reilly, C. A., & Flatt, S. 1989. *Executive team demography, organizational innovation, and firm performance*, Working paper, University of California at Berkeley.

Pennings, J. M. in press. Structural contingency theory: A reappraisal. In B. M. Staw & L. L. Cummings (Eds.), *Research in Organizational Behavior*, 14. Greenwich, CT: JAI Press.

Pfeffer, J. 1983. Organizational demography. In L. L.

Cummings & B. M. Staw (Eds.), *Research in organizational behavior*, 5:299–357. Greenwich, CT: JAI Press.

Pfeffer, J., & Salancik, G. R. 1978. *The external control of organizations*. New York: Harper & Row.

Ross, J., & Staw, B. M. 1986. Expo 86: An escalation prototype. *Administrative Science Quarterly*, 31:274–297.

Schein, E. H. 1983. The role of the founder in creating organizational culture. *Organizational Dynamics*, Summer: 13–28.

Schlenker, B. R. 1980. *Impression management*. Monterey, CA: Brooks/Cole.

Schneider, B. 1987. The people make the place. *Personnel Psychology*, 40:437–453.

Staw, B. M. 1976. Knee-deep in the big muddy: A study of escalating commitment to a chosen course of action. *Organizational Behavior and Human Performnance*, 16:27–44.

Staw, B. M. 1983. Motivation research versus the art of faculty management. *The Review of Higher Education*, 6:301–321.

Staw, B. M. 1990. An evolutionary approach to creativity and innovation. In M. A. West & J. L. Farr (Eds.), *Innovation and Creativity at Work*: 287–308. London: John Wiley & Sons.

Staw, B. M., & Ross, J. 1987. Behavior in escalation situations: Antecedents, prototypes, and solutions. In B. M. Staw & L. L. Cummings (Eds.), *Research in Organizational Behavior*, 9:39–78. Greenwich, CT: JAI Press.

Staw, B. M., Sandelands, L. E., & Dutton, J. E. 1981. Threat-rigidity effects in organizational behavior: A multilevel analysis. *Administrative Science Quarterly*, 26:501–524.

Taylor, S. E., & Brown, J. D. 1988. Illusion and well-being: A social psychological perspective on mental health. *Psychological Bulletin*, 103:193–210.

Tegar, A. 1980. *Too much invested to quit*. New York: Pergamon Press.

Thompson, J. D. 1967. *Organizations in action*. New York: McGraw-Hill.

Tushman, M. L., & Romanelli, E. 1985. Organizational evolution: A metamorphosis model of convergence and reorientation. In L. L. Cummings & B. M. Staw (Eds.), *Research in Organizational Behavior*, 7:171–222. Greenwich, CT: JAI Press.

Tversky, A., & Kahneman, D. 1981. The framing of decisions and the psychology of choice. *Science*, 211:453–458.

Wagner, W. G., Pfeffer, J., & O'Reilly, C. A. 1984. Organizational demography and turnover in top-management groups. *Administrative Science Quarterly*, 29:74–92.

Weiss, H. M., & Adler, S. (1984). Personality and organizational behavior. In B. M. Staw & L. L. Cummings (Eds.), *Research in Organizational Behavior*, 6:1–50. Greenwich CT: JAI Press.

Woodward, J. 1965. *Industrial organization: Theory and practice*. London: Oxford University Press.

Zajac, E. J., & Bazerman, M. H. 1991. Blind spots in industry and competitor analysis: Implications of interfirm (mis)perceptions for strategic decisions. *Academy of Management Review*, 16:37–56.

Zucker, L. G. 1977. The rule of institutionalization in cultural persistence. *American Sociological Review*, 42:726–743.

What Theory Is *Not*

Robert I. Sutton • Stanford University

Barry M. Staw • University of California at Berkeley

This essay describes differences between papers that contain some theory rather than no theory. There is little agreement about what constitutes strong versus weak theory in the social sciences, but there is more consensus that references, data, variables, diagrams, and hypotheses are not theory. Despite this consensus, however, authors routinely use these five elements in lieu of theory. We explain how each of these five elements can be confused with theory and how to avoid such confusion. By making this consensus explicit, we hope to help authors avoid some of the most common and easily averted problems that lead readers to view papers as having inadequate theory. We then discuss how journals might facilitate the publication of stronger theory. We suggest that if the field is serious about producing stronger theory, journals need to reconsider their empirical requirements. We argue that journals ought to be more receptive to papers that test part rather than all of a theory and use illustrative rather than definitive data.

The authors, reviewers, readers, and editors who shape what is published in *ASQ* insist, perhaps above all else, that articles contain strong organizational theory. *ASQ*'s Notice to Contributors states, "If manuscripts contain no theory, their value is suspect." A primary reason, sometimes the primary reason, that reviewers and editors decide not to publish a submitted paper is that it contains inadequate theory. This paper draws on our editorial experiences at *ASQ* and *Research in Organizational Behavior (ROB)* to identify some common reasons why papers are viewed as having weak theory.

Authors who wish to write strong theory might start by reading the diverse literature that seeks to define theory and distinguish weak from strong theory. The *Academy of Management Review* published a forum on theory building in October 1989. Detailed descriptions of what theory is and the distinctions between strong and weak theory in the social sciences can be found, for example, in Dubin's (1976) analysis of theory building in applied areas, Freese's (1980) review of formal theorizing, Kaplan's (1964) philosophical inquiry into the behavioral sciences, Merton's (1967) writings on theoretical sociology, and Weick's (1989) ideas about theory construction as disciplined imagination.

Unfortunately, the literature on theory building can leave a reader more rather than less confused about how to write a paper that contains strong theory (Freese, 1980). There is lack of agreement about whether a model and a theory can be distinguished, whether a typology is properly labeled a theory or not, whether the strength of a theory depends on how interesting it is, and whether falsifiability is a prerequisite for the very existence of a theory. As Merton (1967: 39) put it:

Like so many words that are bandied about, the word theory threatens to become meaningless. Because its referents are so diverse—including everything from minor working hypotheses, through comprehensive but vague and unordered speculations, to axiomatic systems of thought—use of the word often obscures rather than creates understanding.

Lack of consensus on exactly what theory is may explain why it is so difficult to develop strong theory in the behavioral sciences. Reviewers, editors, and other audiences may hold inconsistent beliefs about what constitutes theory and what constitutes strong versus weak theory. Aspiring organizational theorists face further obstacles because there is little consensus about which theoretical perspectives (and associated jargon) are best suited for describing organizations and their members (Pfeffer, 1993). Even when a paper contains a well-articulated theory that fits the data, editors or reviewers may reject it or insist the theory be replaced simply because it clashes with their particular conceptual tastes. Finally, the process of building theory is itself full of internal conflicts and contradictions.

Organizational scholars, like those in other social science fields, are forced to make tradeoffs between generality, simplicity, and accuracy (Weick, 1979) and are challenged by having to write logically consistent and integrated arguments. These difficulties may help explain why organizational research journals have such high rejection rates. Writing strong theory is time consuming and fraught with trial and error for even the most skilled organizational scholars. This is also why there is such great appreciation for those few people, like James March, Jeffrey Pfeffer, and Karl Weick, who are able to do it consistently.

We don't have any magic ideas about how to construct important organizational theory. We will not present a set of algorithms or logical steps for building strong theory. The aim of this essay is more modest. We explain why some papers, or parts of papers, are viewed as containing no theory at all rather than containing some theory. Though there is conflict about what theory is and should be, there is more consensus about what theory is *not*. We consider five features of a scholarly article that, while important in their own right, do not constitute theory. Reviewers and editors seem

to agree, albeit implicitly, that these five features should not be construed as part of the theoretical argument. By making this consensus explicit we hope to help authors avoid some of the most frequent reasons that their manuscripts are viewed as having inadequate theory.

Parts of an Article That Are Not Theory

1. References Are Not Theory

References to theory developed in prior work help set the stage for new conceptual arguments. Authors need to acknowledge the stream of logic on which they are drawing and to which they are contributing. But listing references to existing theories and mentioning the names of such theories is not the same as explicating the causal logic they contain. To illustrate, this sentence from Sutton's (1991: 262) article on bill collectors contains three references but no theory: "This pattern is consistent with findings that aggression provokes the 'fight' response (Frijda, 1986) and that anger is a contagious emotion (Schacter & Singer, 1962; Baron, 1977)." This sentence lists publications that contain conceptual arguments (and some findings). But there is no theory because no logic is presented to explain why aggression provokes "fight" or why anger is contagious.

Calls for "more theory" by reviewers and editors are often met with a flurry of citations. Rather than presenting more detailed and compelling arguments, authors may list the names of prevailing theories or schools of thought, without even providing an explanation of why the theory or approach leads to a new or unanswered theoretical question. A manuscript that Robert Sutton edited had strong data, but all three reviewers emphasized that it had "weak theory" and "poorly motivated hypotheses." The author responded to these concerns by writing a new introduction that added citations to many papers containing theory and many terms like "psycho-social theory," "identity theory," and "social comparison theory." But it still contained no discussion of what these theories were about and no discussion of the logical arguments why these theories led to the author's predictions. The result was that this paper contained almost no theory. despite the author's assertion that much had been added.

References are sometimes used like a smoke screen to hide the absence of theory. Both of us can think of instances in which we have used a string of references to hide the fact that we really didn't understand the phenomenon in question. This obfuscation can unfortunately be successful when references are made to widely known and cited works like Kanter (1977), Katz and Kahn (1978), March and Simon (1958), Thompson (1967), and Williamson (1975). Mark Twain defined a classic as "A book which people praise but don't read." Papers for organizational research journals typically include a set of such throw-away references. These citations may show that the author is a qualified member of the profession, but they don't demonstrate that a theoretical case has been built.

Authors need to explicate which concepts and causal arguments are adopted from cited sources and how they are linked to the theory being developed or tested. This suggestion does not mean that a paper needs to review every nuance of every theory cited. Rather, it means that enough of the pertinent logic from past theoretical work should be included so that the reader can grasp the author's logical arguments. For example, Weick (1993: 644) acknowledged his conceptual debt to Perrow's work and presented the aspects he needed to maintain logical flow in this sentence from his article on the collapse of sensemaking: "Because there is so little communication within the crew and because it operates largely through obtrusive controls like rules and supervision (Perrow, 1986), it acts more like a large formal group with mediated communication than a small informal group with direct communication." Note how there is no need for the reader to know about or read Perrow's work in order to follow the logic in this sentence.

2. Data Are Not Theory

Much of organizational theory is based on data. Empirical evidence plays an important role in confirming. revising, or discrediting existing theory and in guiding the development of new theory. But observed patterns like beta weights, factor loadings, or consistent statements by informants rarely constitute causal explanations. Kaplan (1964) asserted that theory and data each play a distinct role in behavioral science research: Data describe *which* empirical patterns were observed and theory explains *why* empirical patterns were observed or are expected to be observed.

The distinction between the amount and kind of evidence supporting a theory and the theory itself may seem obvious to most readers. Yet in the papers we have reviewed and edited over the years, this is a common source of confusion. We see it in papers by both experienced and inexperienced authors. We also see it our own papers. Authors try to develop a theoretical foundation by describing empirical findings from past research and then quickly move from this basis to a discussion of the current results. Using a series of findings, instead of a blend of findings and logical reasoning, to justify hypotheses is especially common. Empirical results can certainly provide useful support for a theory. But they should not be construed as theory themselves. Prior findings cannot by themselves motivate hypotheses, and the reporting of results cannot substitute for causal reasoning.

One of Sutton's early papers tried to motivate five hypotheses about the relationship between union effectiveness and union members' well-being with the following paragraph:

Recent empirical evidence suggests that the collective bargaining process (Kochan, Lipsky, and Deyer, 1974; Peterson, 1972), the union-management contract (Davis and Sullivan, 1980), and union-management relations in general (Koch and Fox, 1978) all have important consequences for the quality of worklife of unionized workers. Moreover, Hammer (1978) has investigated the relationship between union strength and construction workers' reactions to their work. She found that union strength (operationalized in terms of workers' relative wages) was positively related to both pay satisfaction and perceived job security. Finally, the union's ability to formally increase members' participation in job-related decisions has been frequently cited as contributing to the unionization of teachers and other professionals (e.g., Bass and Mitchell, 1976; Belasco and Alutto, 1969; Chamot, 1976). (Carillon and Sutton, 1982: 172–173).

There is no attempt in this paragraph to explain the logical reasons *why* particular findings occurred in the past or *why* certain empirical relationships are anticipated in the future. We only learn from the paragraph that others had reported certain findings. and so similar patterns would be expected from the data. This is an example of brute empiricism. where hypotheses are motivated by prior data rather than theory.

Although our examples focus on using past quantitative data to motivate theory and hypotheses, qualitative papers are not immune to such problems. Quotes from informants or detailed observations may get a bit closer to the underlying causal forces than, say, mean job satisfaction scores or organizational size, but qualitative evidence, by itself, cannot convey causal arguments that are abstract and simple enough to be applied to other settings. Just like theorists who use quantitative data, those who use qualitative data must develop causal arguments to explain *why* persistent findings have been observed if they wish to write papers that contain theory (Glaser and Strauss, 1967).

In comparing self-managing teams to traditional teams with supervisors, Barker (1993: 408) quoted an informant, "'Now the whole team is around me and the whole team is observing what I'm doing'." This quote doesn't contain causal logic and isn't abstract enough to be generalized to other settings. But these data helped guide and support Barker's inference that because every team member has legitimate authority over every other, and because the surveillance of multiple coworkers is harder to avoid than that of a single boss, self-managing teams constrain members quite powerfully. So, although qualitative data inspired Barker's inferences, they are distinct from his theoretical analysis. Mintzberg (1979: 584) summarized this distinction succinctly: "The data do not generate theory—only researchers do that."

3. Lists of Variables or Constructs Are Not Theory

Pages 249 to 253 of March and Simon's (1958) *Organizations* present a "numerical index" to 206 variables discussed in the classic book. This list of variables and the definitions that March and Simon present of these variables are important parts of their theory but do not, alone, constitute theory. A theory must also explain why variables or constructs come about or why they are connected. Weick (1989: 517) quoted Homans to make this point:

Of particular interest is Homan's irritation with theorists who equate theory with conceptual definitions; he stated that "much official sociological theory consists in fact of concepts and their

difinitions; it provides a dictionary of a language that possesses no sentences."

Papers submitted to organizational journals often are written as if well-defined variables or constructs, by themselves, are enough to make theory. Sometimes the list of variables represents a logical attempt to cover all or most of the determinants of a given outcome or process. Such lists may be useful catalogs of variables that can be entered as predictors or controls in multiple regression equations or LISREL models, but they do not constitute theory. Listing the demographic characteristics of people associated with a given behavior is not theory. Dividing the world into personality versus situational determinants does not, by itself, constitute a theory of behavior. Nor does developing a categorical scheme to cover the determinants of a dependent variable such as escalation (Staw and Ross, 1987) constitute an explanation of that variable.

As an empirically based field, organizational research is often enticed by tests showing the relative strength of one set of variables versus others on particular outcomes. We are attracted to procedures that show the most important influence on dependent variables, as though the contest will show *who the winner is*. Comparative tests of variables should not be confused with comparative tests of theory, however, because a predicted relationship must be explained to provide theory; simply listing a set of antecedents (or even a causal ordering of variables as in LISREL models) does not make a theoretical argument. The key issue is *why* a particular set of variables are expected to be strong predictors.

4. Diagrams Are Not Theory

Diagrams or figures can be a valuable part of a research paper but also, by themselves, rarely constitute theory. Probably the least theoretical representations are ones that simply list categories of variables such as "personality," "environmental determinants," or "demographics." More helpful are figures that show causal relationships in a logical ordering, so that readers can see a chain of causation or how a third variable intervenes in or moderates a relationship. Also useful are temporal diagrams showing how a particular process unfolds over time. On occasion, diagrams can be a useful aid in building theory. For researchers who are not good writers, a set of diagrams can provide structure to otherwise rambling or amorphous arguments. For those researchers who are talented writers, having a concrete model may prevent obfuscation of specious or inconsistent arguments.

Regardless of their merits, diagrams and figures should be considered as stage props rather than the performance itself. As Whetten (1989) suggested, while boxes and arrows can add order to a conception by explicitly delineating patterns and causal connections, they rarely explain *why* the proposed connections will be observed. Some verbal explication is almost always necessary. The logic underlying the portrayed relationships needs to be spelled out. Text about the reasons why a phenomenon occurs, or why it unfolds in a particular manner, is difficult to replace by references to a diagram. A clearly written argument should also preclude the need for the most complicated figures we see in articles—those more closely resembling a complex wiring diagram than a comprehensible theory.

Good theory is often representational *and* verbal. The arguments are clear enough that they can be represented in graphical form. But the arguments are also rich enough that processes have to be described with sentences and paragraphs so as to convey the logical nuances behind the causal arrow. One indication that a strong theory has been proposed is that it is possible to discern conditions in which the major proposition or hypothesis is most and least likely to hold. Pfeffer and Salancik (1978), for example, argued that power is a stronger predictor of resource allocations under conditions of uncertainty. House (1988), likewise, made the case that individuals high in power needs are likely to gain control when organizations are in a state of flux. The reasoning underlying these predictions (even their direction) is not apparent by just showing the existence of moderating variables in a causal diagram. Logical explanations are required.

5. Hypotheses (or Predictions) Are Not Theory

Hypotheses can be an important part of a well-crafted conceptual argument. They serve as crucial bridges between theory and data, making explicit how the variables and relationships that follow from a logical argument will be operationalized. But, as Dubin (1976: 26) noted, "A theoretical model is not simply a statement of hypothesis." Hypotheses do not (and should not) contain logical arguments about why empirical relationships are expected to occur. Hypotheses are concise statements about *what* is expected to occur, not *why* it is expected to occur.

We cannot find a single source that asserts that hypotheses, or other specific predictions, alone constitute theory. As Kaplan (1964: 350) put it, "An explanation rests on a nomological or theoretical generalization, or an intelligible pattern, but a prediction need not have such a basis. ... We can give a reason for making some specific prediction rather than another, but we may be able to give no reason other than past successes for expecting the reason to come true." Homans (1964), Merton (1967), and Weick (1989) are just a few of the authors who made clear that predictions presented without underlying causal logic do not constitute theory.

Although it may seem obvious that a listing of hypotheses cannot substitute for a set of logical explanations, this is exactly what is done in many papers. We have noticed two telltale signs that a paper has presented hypotheses in lieu of theory. First, there may be so many hypotheses that none can be adequately explained or motivated. A second tip-off is when the introduction of a paper ends with a long list of hypotheses, a table of predictions, or a summarizing figure. Often, such lists, tables, or figures are only tenuously linked to causal explanations scattered throughout the introduction, or there may be no linkage at all. In one extreme but by no means uncommon example, Tetrick and LaRocco (1987) tested 21 hypotheses about job stress without presenting the causal logic for any of these predictions. The 21 hypotheses were portrayed in a figure and not otherwise discussed or even listed in the five paragraphs constituting the introduction. Readers were referred to another source for the conceptual logic.

Sometimes authors use a long list of hypotheses to "spread the risk" of empirical research. So much time and effort is invested in research projects that authors naturally want to show something for their labor. They may use a buckshot approach to theory testing, posing a wide range of hypotheses and empirical tests. While this may increase one's publication record, it does not make good theory. Strong theory usually stems from a single or small set of research ideas. Some famous examples have been statements that people are motivated to resolve inconsistencies (Festinger, 1957), that social systems are subject to evolutionary forces (Campbell, 1969; Hannan and Freeman, 1989), and that there can be "normal accidents" (Perrow, 1984). These assertions were simple, though their implications have been widespread. From such simple theoretical arguments have come a set of interrelated propositions and hypotheses that explicated the logical and empirical implications of each theory. Papers with strong theory thus often start with one or two conceptual statements and build a logically detailed case; they have both simplicity and interconnectedness.

Identifying Strong Theory

Though we have noted that it is easier to identify features of manuscripts that are not theory than it is to specify exactly what good theory is, our own prejudices about the matter are already evident. We agree with scholars like Kaplan (1964) and Merton (1967) who assert that theory is the answer to queries of *why*. Theory is about the connections among phenomena, a story about why acts, events, structure, and thoughts occur. Theory emphasizes the nature of causal relationships, identifying what comes first as well as the timing of such events. Strong theory, in our view, delves into underlying processes so as to understand the systematic reasons for a particular occurrence or nonoccurrence. It often burrows deeply into microprocesses, laterally into neighboring concepts, or in an upward direction, tying itself to broader social phenomena. It usually is laced with a set of convincing and logically interconnected arguments. It can have implications that we have not seen with our naked (or theoretically unassisted) eye. It may have implications that run counter to our common sense. As Weick (1995) put it succinctly, a good theory explains, predicts, and delights.

Like other descriptions of strong theory, the prior paragraph reads more like a wish list than a set of realistic expectations. This may be why pleas for better theory fall on receptive ears but recalcitrant hands. Everyone agrees that our theories should be stronger, so long as it does not require us to do anything differently. This is the main reason we decided to write something on what theory is not. Perhaps erecting our five "Wrong Way"

signs will help change behavior in ways that more eloquent road maps have not.

The Case Against Theory

So far, we have made the assumption that theory is good. We have assumed that a stronger theoretical section will help a paper have more impact on the literature and more fully inform the reader. We have also assumed that most researchers would strive to write better theory if they had more knowledge about how to do so or more time and energy to put into their manuscripts. But these assumptions may not be universally shared.

Some prominent researchers have argued the case against theory. John Van Maanen (1989), for example, has stressed that the field first needs more descriptive narratives about organizational life, presumably based on intensive ethnographic work. He called for a ten-year moratorium on theoretical (and methodological) papers. The happy result of such a moratorium, Van Maanen suggested, would be a temporary halt to the proliferation of mediocre writing and theory, a broader audience (attracted by better writing), and better theory—after the moratorium had passed, both old and new models would be grounded in a well-crafted set of organizational narratives. Van Maanen's argument is reminiscent of logic contained in *Zen in the Art of Archery* (Herrigel, 1989). If we avoid aiming at the target for a long while and first develop more fundamental knowledge, we will do a better job of hitting the bull's-eye when we finally do take aim.

More direct arguments against theory can also be mustered from those who rely on quantitative methods. Some evaluation researchers, such as Thomas Cook, have noted that it is more important to isolate a few successful change efforts (those that show consistent positive results) than it is to understand the causal nuances underlying any particular outcome. Likewise, many advocates of meta-analysis view the mission of social science to be an accumulation of empirical findings rather than an ebb and flow of theoretical paradigms (Kuhn, 1970). They tend to see research publications as having value simply because they serve as storage devices for obtained correlations, not because they elaborate a set of theoretical ideas.

An array of organizational research publications have evolved to serve these disparate views of the merits of theory. At the most empirical end of the spectrum are journals such as the *Journal of Applied Psychology* and *Personnel Psychology*. These outlets typically present brief reviews of the literature along with a simple listing of hypotheses. The front end of these journal articles is typically short; the hypotheses are often replications or offshoots of previous work. More attention is paid to describing the methods, variables, data analysis techniques, and findings. Accordingly, the usual reason for rejecting a manuscript at these outlets is that the data do not adequately fit the hypotheses or there is a fatal flaw in the study design. The originality of the hypotheses and the strength of the theoretical arguments are less likely to constitute the major reason for acceptance or rejection.

An outlet such as *Research in Organizational Behavior* resides at the other extreme. The editors of *ROB* view theory development as its primary contribution. If data are presented, they are used for illustrating rather than testing a theory (e.g., Meyer and Gupta, 1994). The philosophy of *ROB* is not antagonistic to data collection and analysis; it simply relegates the role of empirical research to more traditional journal outlets.

Attempting to span the space between theory testing and theory building are journals like *ASQ, Academy of Management Journal*, and *Organization Science*. In the organizational research community, *ASQ* stands as perhaps the most concerned about theoretical issues, with the goal that empirical papers should also make a conceptual contribution. This bridging role is difficult to fulfill, since there are inevitable tradeoffs between theory and empirical research. On the one hand, *ASQ* asks authors to engage in creative, imaginative acts. On the other hand, *ASQ* wants these same authors to be precise, systematic, and follow accepted procedures for quantitative or qualitative analysis. These contradictory requirements can only be captured by phrases such as "disciplined imagination" (Weick, 1989), "wild thoroughness," or "accepted deviance."

Unfortunately, contributors to our field's research journals are rarely skilled at both theory building and theory testing. Most contributors seem to be adept at one or another parts of the trade; either being a good theorist with incomplete empirical skills or a good empiricist with halting theoretical abilities. Northcraft and Neale (1993) have noted that such shortcomings can sometimes

be resolved by building research teams with complementary skills. But we suspect that there may not be enough strong theorists to go around. Organizational researchers are primarily trained in data collection techniques and the latest analytical tools, not the nuances of theory building. Our doctoral programs tend to skip over theory building. Our doctoral programs tend to skip over theory building, perhaps because it is not a step-by-step process that can be taught like LISREL or event-history analysis. Reading major theorists and writing literature review papers is often passed off as training in theory building, even though such assignments really don't teach one how to craft conceptual arguments.

Given our field's likely imbalance of theoretical and empirical skills, is the goal of providing strong theory *and* research a quixotic venture? Should journals make a decision—either to become a home for data or theory, but not both? So far, *ASQ*'s answer to the above quandary is "compensatory education." *ASQ* has tried to fill this breach through the review process, in which authors' attempts to write theory are scrutinized in detail by reviewers and editors. Pages of pointed criticism are conveyed to authors in hopes of "educating them." The product is usually an author who either dutifully complies with whatever theoretical ideas are suggested or who becomes so angered that he or she simply sends the paper elsewhere. By going through rounds of revision, a manuscript may end up with stronger theory, but this is not the same as saying that the authors have actually learned to write better theory. Learning to write theory may or may not occur, and when it does occur, it is almost an accidental by product of the system.

Are We Expecting Too Much?

At this point in the essay we are forced to ask whether we have been naive. Perhaps there are enduring individual differences and preferences that explain why good theory is so hard to find in organizational research papers. Perhaps people who are driven more by data than ideas are enticed to join an empirically based field such as organizational behavior. Perhaps the applied nature of the field attracts practical, no-nonsense types rather than the more dreamy misfits who might naturally be good at theoretical pursuits. If this is so, then the importance of training should become an even larger issue. Without constant pressure for theory building, the field would surely slide to its natural resting place in dust-bowl empiricism.

The problem with theory building may also be structural. Journals could be placing authors in a double bind. On the one hand, editors and reviewers plead for creative and interesting ideas, for there to be an important contribution to organizational theory. On the other hand, authors are skewered for apparent mismatches between their theory and data. Providing a broad theory, in which a given phenomenon is located in a network of interorganizational or cultural influences, will usually lead to complaints that the author did not measure all the variables in his or her model.

Providing a deep theory, in which intervening mechanisms or processes are spelled out in graphic detail, may likewise lead to objections that only the antecedents and consequences of the model are measured. Reviewers will typically say, "If a contextual variable or intervening process is so important, why wasn't it operationalized?"

Contradictory demands for both strong theory and precise measurement are often satisfied only by hypocritical writing. Theory is crafted around the data. The author is careful to avoid mentioning any variables or processes that might tip off the reviewers and editors that something is missing in the article. Peripheral and intervening processes are left out of the theory so as not to expose a gap in the empirical design. We are guilty of these crimes of omission. We have even counseled our graduate students to leave out portions of their theory that are not measured well and to delete otherwise interesting data that did not directly relate to their theoretical argument. The result of these omissions is that the craft of manuscript writing becomes an art of fitting concepts and arguments around what has been measured and discovered. If widely shared, as we suspect they are, these practices mean that our publications have little resemblance to what methodology texts preach as the proper sequence of theory building, design, measurement, and analysis.

So what should journals do to address the inherent difficulties of having strong theory and method in a single research paper? Should these outlets guard even more zealously the scientific sequencing of hypothesis-testing research, for example, by requiring that a list of all variables measured in the study (and their intercorrelations) be included with each submitted manuscript? Should journals spend even more time and energy on the review process, hoping to educate rather than just select manuscripts from the field's constituents? Or might our journals be best served by letting down their guard just a bit?

Some Recommendations

When research manuscripts are divided on the dimensions of theory and method, it is easy to see where the bulk of our contributions lie. Papers with weak theory and method are routinely rejected. Their authors are sent back to the drawing board or on to another journal. At the other end of the spectrum are those few papers with both strong theory and method. These are the exceptional pieces that can become "instant classics," as they are hurriedly passed among scholars and discussed with twinges of jealousy. There are few controversies in the high-high and low-low cells of this matrix.

It is when we turn to the "mixed" cells of the theory-method matrix that we see conflicts of taste and value. Because so few papers are considered strong in both theory and method, journals are forced to make implicit tradeoffs on these dimensions to fill their pages. Even though journals may boldly espouse the goal of theory building, the review process usually works the other way. In practice, it is much easier for a set of reviewers and editors to agree on a carefully crafted empirical piece that has little or no theory than it is for them to go along with a weak test of a new theoretical idea. The author of this second type of manuscript can expect to receive a set of reviews stating, "although some interesting and well-motivated hypotheses were proposed, the author failed to . . ."

Journals specializing in theory testing can live comfortably with the manuscript selection process as it now stands. They can reach consensus on publishing a set of papers that follow strict methodological guidelines to test existing theories. The problem is much greater with journals like *ASQ*. In trying to build theory as well as a database for organizational research, these journals push authors to their limits and beyond. A key difficulty is that papers chosen for revision tend to be those with acceptable methods and undeveloped theory.

Extracting theory from those who could not (or would not) initially provide it can be a grueling and unpleasant process.

Our recommendation is to rebalance the selection process between theory and method. People's natural inclination is to require greater proof of a new or provocative idea than one they already believe to be true (Nisbett and Ross, 1980). Therefore, if a theory is particularly interesting, the standards used to evaluate how well it is tested or grounded need to be relaxed, not strengthened. We need to recognize that major contributions can be made when data are more illustrative than definitive.

We also think journals like *ASQ* need to revise their norms about the linkage between theory and data. Not everything discussed in the introduction of a manuscript need be operationalized in the method section nor show up in a set of regression equations. If theory building is a valid goal, then journals should be willing to publish papers that *really are* stronger in theory than method. Authors should be rewarded rather than punished for developing strong conceptual arguments that dig deeper and extend more broadly than the data will justify. We are not advocating long, rambling introductions that are entirely divorced from empirical analyses. Rather, we believe there is room for sharper discussion of processes underlying a phenomenon as well as grounding of causal forces in the broader social system.

In many ways, our journals have already been imposing these proposed standards on qualitative as opposed to quantitative research. The prevailing wisdom has been that qualitative research is more useful for theory building than theory testing. Rarely are qualitative studies accepted for publication when they simply provide data that validate an existing theory. Seldom are ethnographic descriptions published when they are not also a source of new concepts or ideas. It is even difficult to publish qualitative studies that provide in-depth analysis of a localized phenomenon if reviewers cannot be convinced that such knowledge is applicable to more general social processes.

Perhaps the standards used to judge qualitative papers have the opposite drawback of those used for quantitative papers, with theory emphasized too much and data not emphasized enough. Authors of qualitative studies are often asked to drop much of the description of characters and events, so as to make room for greater theoretical development. The resulting description may end up as little more than a small sequence of vignettes or a summary table of quotations, illustrating those comcepts or hypotheses formulated in a paper. Such paring can deplete a manuscript of much of its value. Lost may be the rich description that Van Maanen (1989) said is necessary for researchers to build strong theory over time. Lost also may be the chance to build cumulative theory from small but comprehensible events. Weick (1992: 177) noted that much of his own work constitutes "knowledge growth by extension," which "occurs when a relatively full explanation of a small region is carried over to an explanation of an adjoining region." We may need to be as careful in not overweighting the theoretical criteria for qualitative papers as in underweighting the theoretical contributions of quantitative research.

Conclusion

We began this essay with the general complaint that many manuscripts we see as reviewers and editors are devoid of theory. In our experience, authors seem to fool themselves into thinking that at least five otherwise worthy features of a research paper can be theory when they are not. So we put up and explained five "Wrong Way" signs for authors. We hope these guidelines will help authors avoid writing manuscripts that contain little or no theory. But we are not so naive as to think that these few signposts will create a rush of new theory in organizational research. The problem is more complex and the solutions more complicated. We explored several structural reasons for the current imbalance between theory and method in organizational research, noting how the problem may stem from both the way we run journals as well as the nature and training of researchers who make up our field. Our conclusions, though sometimes oblique and contradictory, can be read as pleas for more balance in weighing the theoretical versus empirical sides of research. We argue for greater theoretical emphasis in quantitative research, along with more appreciation of the empiricism of qualitative endeavors.

In closing, we ask the reader to consider whether the evidence provided by people such as Freud, Marx, or Darwin would meet the empirical standards of the top journals in organizational research. Would their work be rejected outright, or would they be given the opportunity to go through several rounds of revision? Just thinking about such a question brings forth the essential role of balance (or tolerance) in evaluating research. When theories are particularly interesting or important, there should be greater leeway in terms of empirical support. A small set of interviews, a demonstration experiment, a pilot survey, a bit of archival data may be all that is needed to show why a particular process *might* be true. Subsequent research will of course be necessary to sort out whether the theoretical statements hold up under scrutiny, or whether they will join the long list of theories that only deserve to be true.

ACKNOWLEDGMENTS

We are grateful to Steve Barley, Max Bazerman, Daniel Brass, Gary Alan Fine, Linda Pike, Robert Kahn, James March, Marshall Meyer, Keith Murnighan, Christine Oliver, and David Owens for their contributions to this essay. This essay was prepared while the first author was a Fellow at the Center for Advanced Study in the Behavioral Sciences. We appreciate the financial assistance provided by the Hewlett-Packard Corporation and the National Science Foundation (SBR-9022192).

REFERENCES

Barker, James R. 1993 "Tightening the iron cage: Concertive control in self-managing terms." *Administrative Science Quarterly, 38,* 408–437.

Campbell, Donald T. 1969 "Variation and selective retention in socio-cultural evolution." *General Systems, 16,* 69–85.

Carillon, James W., and Robert I. Sutton 1982 "The relationship between union effectiveness and the quality of teachers' worklife." *Journal of Occupational Behavior, 3,* 171–179.

Dubin, Robert 1976 "Theory building in applied areas." In marvin D. Dunnette (Ed.), *Handbook of Industrial and Organizational Psychology* (pp. 17–40). Chicago: Rand McNally.

Festinger, Leon 1957 *A Theory of Cognitive Dissonance.* Evanston, IL: Row, Peterson.

Freese, Lee 1980 "Formal theorizing." *Annual Review of Sociology, 6,* 187–212. Palo Alto, CA: Annual Reviews.

Glaser, Barney G., and Anselm Strauss 1967 *The Discovery of Grounded Theory: Strategies for Qualitative Research.* London: Wiedenfeld and Nicholson.

Hannan, Michael T., and John Freeman 1989 *Organizational Ecology.* Cambridge, MA: Harvard University Press.

Herrigel, Eugen 1989 *Zen in the Art of Archery.* New York: Vintage Books.

Homans, George C. 1964 "Contemporary theory in sociology." In R. E. L. Farris (Ed.), *Handbook of Modern Sociology* (pp. 951–977). Chicago: Rand-McNally.

House, Robert J. 1988 "Power and personality in complex organizations." In Barry M. Staw and L. L. Cummings (Eds.), *Research in Organizational Behavior, 10,* 305–358. Greenwich, CT: JAI Press.

Kanter, Rosabeth Moss 1977 *Men and Women of the Corporation.* New York: Basic Books.

Kaplan, Abraham 1964 *The Conduct of Inquiry.* New York: Harper & Row.

Katz, Daniel, and Robert L. Kahn 1978 *The Social Psychology of Organizations, 2nd ed.* New York: Wiley.

Kuhn, Thomas 1970 *The Structure of Scientific Revolutions, 2nd ed.* Chicago: University of Chicago Press.

March, James G., and Herbert A. Simon 1958 *Organizations.* New York: Wiley.

Merton, Robert K. 1967 *On Theoretical Sociology.* New York: Free Press.

Meyer, Marshall W., and Vipin Gupta 1994 "The performance paradox." In Barry M. Staw and L. L. Cummings (eds.), *Research in Organizational Behavior, 16,* 309–336. Greenwich, CT: JAI Press.

Mintzberg, Henry 1979 "An emerging strategy of 'direct' research." *Administrative Science Quarterly, 24,* 580–589.

Northcraft, Gregory B., and Margaret A. Neale 1993 "Negotiating successful research collaboration." In J. Keith Murnighan (ed.), *Social Psychology in Organizations: Advances in Theory and Research* (pp. 204–224). Englewood Cliffs, NJ: Prentice Hall.

Nisbett, Richard, and Lee Ross 1980 *Human Inference: Strategies and Shortcomings of Social Judgment.* Englewood Cliffs, NJ: Prentice-Hall.

Perrow, Charles 1984 *Normal Accidents: Living with High-Risk Technologies.* New York: Basic Books.

Pfeffer, Jeffrey 1993 "Barriers to the advance of organizational science: Paradigm development as a dependent variable." *Academy of Management Review, 18,* 599–620.

Pfeffer, Jeffrey, and Gerald R. Salancik 1978 *The External Control of Organizations: A Resource Dependence Perspective.* New York: Harper & Row.

Staw, Barry M., and Jerry Ross 1987 "Behavior in escalation situations: Antecedents, prototypes and solutions." In L. L. Cummings and Barry M. Staw (eds.), *Research in Organizational Behavior, 9,* 39–78. Greenwich, CT: JAI Press.

Sutton, Robert I. 1991 "Maintaining norms about expressed emotions: The case of bill collectors." *Administrative Science Quarterly, 36,* 245–268.

Tetrick, Lois E., and James M. LaRocco 1987 "Understanding, prediction, and control as moderators of the relationships between perceived stress, satisfaction, and psychological well-being." *Journal of Applied Psychology, 72,* 538–543.

Thompson, James D. 1967 *Organizations in Action.* New York: McGraw-Hill.

Van Maanen, John 1989 "Some notes on the importance of writing in organization studies." *Harvard Business School Research Colloquium:* 27–33. Boston: Harvard Business School.

Weick, Karl E. 1979 *The Social Psychology of Organizing. 2nd ed.* Reading, MA: Addison-Wesley.

Weick, Karl E. 1989 "Theory construction as disciplined imagination." *Academy of Management Review, 14,* 516–531.

Weick, Karl E. 1992 "Agenda setting in organizational behavior: A theory-focused approach." *Journal of Management Inquiry, 1,* 171–182.

Weick, Karl E. 1993 "The collapse of sensemaking in organizations: The Mann Gulch disaster." *Administrative Science Quarterly, 38,* 628–652.

Weick, Karl E. 1995 "Definition of 'theory.' " In Nigel Nicholson (ed.), *Blackwell Dictionary of Organizational Behavior.* Oxford: Blackwell (forthcoming).

Whetten, David A. 1989 "What constitutes a theoretical con-tribution?" *Academy of Management Review, 14,* 490–495.

Williamson, Oliver E. 1975 *Markets and Hierarchies.* New York: Free Press.

Barriers to the Advance of Organizational Science: Paradigm Development as a Dependent Variable

Jeffrey Pfeffer • Stanford University

The level of paradigm development—technical certainty and consensus—characterizing a field of study has numerous consequences for the social organization and operation of that field. These consequences, ranging from the ability to obtain resources to the ease of working collaboratively on research, have an impact on the subsequent development of the field (i.e., through a positive feedback loop). Although the degree of technical certainty or consensus is clearly affected by the fundamental nature of the subject of study, consensus is also produced by social practices that differentiate fields that are more or less paradigmatically developed. The study of organizations is arguably paradigmatically not well developed, in part because of values that emphasize representativeness, inclusiveness, and theoretical and methodological diversity. Although these values are attractive ideals, there are consequences for the field's ability to make scientific progress, which almost requires some level of consensus, as well as for its likely ability to compete successfully with adjacent social sciences such as economics in the contest for resources. Recognizing the trade-offs and processes involved in scientific progress seems to be a necessary first step for thinking about the dilemmas that are implicit in the sociology of science literature.

In the sociology of science literature, few concepts have enjoyed as wide acceptance or provided as much conceptual leverage as that of the level of paradigm development. "Thomas Kuhn (1970) differentiates among the sciences by the extent to which they have a developed paradigm or shared theoretical structures and methodological approaches about which there is a high level of consensus" (Cole, 1983: 112). To this point, most, if not all, of the existing research has been devoted to operationalizing the concept of paradigm development, seeing if there really are differences in the sciences in terms of the amount of consensus, and examining the effects of paradigm development on a range of outcomes. In this article, the first part of my argument entails reviewing the evidence that (a) there are differences in the level of paradigm development across scientific fields and that (b) these differences have significant consequences for a number of important outcomes.

Given the importance and predictive power of the concept of the level of paradigm development, it is unfortunate that little attention has been given to asking why it is that some fields have more consensus than others. This is an important issue because the second part of my argument is that consensus is a necessary, although clearly not sufficient, condition for the systematic advancement of knowledge. Thus, because researchers are concerned with the development and growth of organizational science, they can benefit from understanding something about the factors associated with more or less paradigmatically developed fields. This article is far from the first to make this point. Zammuto and Connolly (1984: 30), for instance, argued that "the organizational sciences are severely fragmented and . . . this fragmentation presents a serious obstacle to scientific growth of the field."

After I have shown that paradigm development is theoretically important and that consensus is a critical precondition to scientific advancement, in the third part of my argument I address the factors that seem to affect the development of scientific paradigms in general and organizational science more specifically. In particular, I explore the dual effects of the value placed on theoretical and methodological diversity and participation. As in other contexts, there are trade-offs involved; this is not to say that the trade-offs should be made in one way rather than another, but that researchers should be conscious of them and their long-run implications for the field.

The Measurement and Effects of the Level of Paradigm Development

As originally operationalized by Lodahl and Gordon (1972), paradigm development refers to the technological uncertainty associated with the production of knowledge in a given scientific field or subspecialty. Technological certainty means that there is a wide agreement on the connections between actions and their consequences (Thompson & Tuden, 1959), or in this case, agreement that certain methods, certain sequences and programs of study, and certain research questions will advance training and knowledge in the given field. Whitley (1982: 335) noted that "the meaning, relevance, and significance of research results for theoretical goals vary in clarity and straightforwardness in different fields. Even where techniques are standardized, the overall significance and importance of results may remain vague and subject to disputes."

Measures and Indicators of the Construct

Lodahl and Gordon (1972) surveyed faculty and department chairs in 20 departments in the fields of physics, sociology, chemistry, and political science, and they asked respondents to rank seven fields (the four surveyed plus biology, economics, and psychology) on the "amount of consensus over paradigms (law, theory, and methodology)" (Lodahl & Gordon, 1973a: 192). These authors found good agreement on the rankings of the fields in terms of their paradigm development. They further found that the social scientists reported less agreement over course content, graduate degree requirements, and the content of survey courses than did those in the physical sciences (Lodahl & Gordon, 1973a: 193).

Surveying to obtain measures of consensus is time consuming; this technique also potentially measures perceived rather than actual level of consensus. Therefore, researchers have developed a number of archival or unobtrusive measures of the level of paradigm development of a field. Price (1970) suggested two measures. One is the proportion of Ph.D. graduates employed in college or university teaching. He argued that this number reflected the place of each branch of learning in society:

> In some fields, such as history and philosophy, most of the embryonic researchers get their Ph.D.'s and then proceed toward some sort of career as a teacher. In that case society is paying for students to become teachers to beget students; research becomes an epiphenomenon. In the most "scientific" departments at our universities only about 20 percent of the Ph.D. output is fed back into education, and society gets for its investment ... also the training of Ph.D.'s who become employed in the nonuniversity world. (Price, 1970: 5)

The second measure is the percent of references in published works that were themselves published in the preceding five years, an index that corresponds well with intuitive ideas of hard science, soft science, and nonscience.

Salancik, Staw, and Pondy (1980) reasoned that fields with highly developed paradigms, in which there was more consensus, should be characterized by more efficient communication—less time needed to be spent defining terms or explaining concepts. Lodahl and Gordon (1972: 61) had noted that "the high consensus found in high paradigm fields . . . provides an accepted and shared vocabulary for discussing the content of the field." This idea led to the use of the length of dissertation abstracts (in words), the length of dissertations (in pages), and the proportion of publications in a field that are in the form of articles rather than books (Konrad & Pfeffer, 1990) as indicators of the level of paradigm development (see also Pfeffer & Moore, 1980a).

A high degree of consensus also makes interdependent activity more possible. Thus, another indicator used by Salancik and his colleagues was the length of the longest chain of courses in a department, where a chain is defined as a course being a prerequisite to another course, and that course being a prerequisite to another course, and so on. The length of a course chain was highly correlated with communication efficiency, and for the seven fields measured by Lodahl and Gordon, a scale developed from these indicators correlated above .8 with the survey results (Pfeffer & Moore, 1980a: 397). The possibility of coordinating interdependent activity also means that it is easier to organize and manage the work of others on research. Lodahl and Gordon (1972) found that scientists in fields with highly developed paradigms wanted and used more graduate assistants than those in fields with lower levels of paradigm development. Thus, the preference for and use of graduate students and assistants in the research process is another indicator of the level of paradigm development.

The Effects of the Level of Paradigm Development

The level of a scientific field's paradigm development has a number of substantively important effects. Table 1 presents a listing of many (although certainly not all) of the consequences of the level of paradigm development. There is evidence that more highly developed fields fare better in the contest for resource allocations, both as distributed by external funding agencies and by the administration within a given college or university. For instance, Lodahl and Gordon (1973a, 1973b) found that the physical sciences were much better funded than the social sciences regarding either university funding or funding from outside sources; this finding held true when department size and quality were taken into account. Such a finding is not surprising because "policy makers and the public can be more certain of results from the more developed sciences" (Lodahl & Gordon, 1973a: 196). Pfeffer and Moore (1980b) found that the level of paradigm development affected both the amount of grants received by departments and

the budget allocations to academic departments on two campuses of a large state university. Of course, because research has shown that grants and contracts are an important source of subunit power in universities (Pfeffer & Moore, 1980b; Salancik & Pfeffer, 1974), the fact that external funding advantages translate into internal funding advantages is to be expected. But Pfeffer and Moore's results indicate that paradigm development has an effect on resource allocations, even when departmental power is taken into account. Moreover, because the analysis examined changes over time, it accounted for the possibility of differences in initial funding levels due to inherent differences in the fields.

The level of paradigm development affects not only differences in the level of resource allocations but also the dispersion of such allocations. Lodahl and Gordon (1973a: 197) reported the average level of funding per faculty member in physics, chemistry, sociology, and political science for departments rated as distinguished, strong, good, or adequate plus. They found that "funding is more highly concentrated by quality levels in the physical than in the social sciences. The more distinguished physical science departments enjoy three times the overall funding of lower-quality physical science departments, while the more distinguished social science departments have only one and one-half times the overall funding of their less-

TABLE 1. Outcomes Affected by the Level of Paradigm Development

Resource allocations including funding levels of departments

Dispersion in funding across departments; dispersion in talent

Connection between productivity and pay

Connection between wage dispersion and job satisfaction

Connection between social ties and the National Science Foundation's grant allocations

Connection between social ties and journal publications

Connection between social ties and editorial board appointments

Governance of academic departments

Department head turnover or average tenure

Journal rejection rates

Time to publication for research

Power of fields and departments and salary paid to faculty

Working collaboratively rather than alone on research

Cross-citation practices among fields

distinguished counterparts" (1973a: 196). A study of individual reputation in these four fields revealed that "ability, like funding, is more dispersed in the social sciences" (Lodahl & Gordon, 1973a: 198). Thus, there is less concentration of both talent and resources in less paradigmatically developed fields.

Because paradigm development affects the ease and certainty of evaluating scientific research, Konrad and Pfeffer (1990) observed that in fields with more highly developed scientific paradigms, there was a greater effect of academic research productivity on pay. Pfeffer, Leong, and Strehl (1976) earlier had observed that publication was a more important predictor of both departmental prestige and prestige mobility in more parcdigmatically developed fields. Beyer and Snipper (1974) reported that the quality of faculty degrees and mean research funds per faculty member were more strongly related to the quality ratings of physical science departments as contrasted with social science departments. Thus, it seems that objective measures of performance translate into status or financial rewards with more certainty in more highly developed fields. This consensus over the evaluation of scientific contributions also affects individual reactions to wage inequality. Pfeffer and Langton (In press) used the 1969 Carnegie survey of university faculty to study the effect that wage dispersion within departments had on members' job satisfaction. They found that a given level of wage inequality had less effect on members' dissatisfaction in departments in high-paradigm fields, in which there was more consensus on standards for evaluation.

If consensually shared beliefs about the nature of knowledge and methods in a field are present, such beliefs will guide decisions on grant allocations and publication. If such technological certainty is absent, decisions are more likely to be made on other, more particularistic bases. One such particularistic basis of allocating resources is sharing an affiliation with the recipient of the allocation. Pfeffer, Salancik, and Leblebici (1976) found that the National Science Foundation's grant allocations were more strongly related to institutional presence on the advisory board in fields that were less paradigmatically developed, controlling for departmental size and quality. Pfeffer, Leong, and Strehl (1977) found that institutional membership on editorial boards had a greater effect on institutional representation in journal publications the

less paradigmatically developed the field, even after measures of institutional quality and size were statistically controlled. Beyer (1978) surveyed journal editors in four fields and found some evidence that particularistic criteria (e.g., personal knowledge of the author, institutional affiliation of the author, and position within a professional association) were somewhat more likely to be used in less paradigmatically developed fields.

Yoels (1974), in a study of seven scientific fields, examined the effect of paradigm development on the tendency of editors-in-chief to appoint people from the same institution to their editorial boards. He found that "the selection of editors for social science journals is more subject to the influence of 'particularistic' criteria than for physical and natural science journals" (1974: 271). Yoels's results for editorial board appointments are consistent with the study of grant allocations and journal publications: In each instance, there was evidence that similarity in institutional affiliation affected outcomes more strongly in less paradigmatically developed fields. Another study (Lindsey, 1976) examined the scholarly productivity of members of editorial boards in various journals in psychology, sociology, and social work. Editorial boards were more consistently staffed with more productive scientists in personality and social psychology than in counseling psychology, and psychology, overall, had higher quality (in terms of article publication and citations to their work) editorial board members than did sociology, which, in turn, ranked well ahead of social work. Appointments to prestigious gatekeeping positions were more highly related to scholarly contributions in subspecialties that were more paradigmatically developed. In more developed fields, more universalistic, quality-based measures were employed in allocation decisions.

The level of paradigm development is also related to governance of academic departments. For instance, Lodahl and Gordon (1973a) reported that departments in high-paradigm fields enjoyed more autonomy from the central university administration, in part because of the greater visibility and predictability of consequences of their actions (see also Beyer & Lodahl, 1976). In a study of English universities, Beyer and Lodahl (1976: 120) reported that the authority of the department chair was higher in the more highly developed physical sciences.

The turnover (or average tenure) of academic

department heads is related to the department's level of paradigm development. Not surprisingly, there is more turnover, controlling for other factors, in departments with lower levels of paradigm development (Pfeffer & Moore, 1980a; Salancik et al., 1980). Paradigm development is, after all, an indicator of consensus. The greater the consensus and the greater the certainty on the connections between actions and their consequences, the less the conflict, and the less the conflict, the less either voluntary or involuntary turnover in leadership positions there will be.

Paradigm development is related to journal rejection rates. Hargens (1988) analyzed journal rejection rates for 30 scholarly journals over time, to control for the effects of space shortages as contrasted with paradigm development. He gathered data on both submissions and the number of papers published. He argued that if journal rejection rates were a function of space shortages, changes in submission rates should account for changes in journal rejection rates over time. The fact that journal submission rates had a trivially small effect on rejection rates, even though submission rates varied substantially over the period, whereas the independent effect of earlier rejection rates was strong, Hargens interpreted as impugning the claim that variations in rejection rates were caused by differences in space shortages (Hargens, 1988: 140). He concluded that "space shortages affect journals' backlogs rather than their rejection rates" (Hargens, 1988: 141). Journal acceptance rates in the physical and biological sciences were typically in the .6 and higher range, whereas in anthropology, sociology, psychology, and political science journal acceptance rates were typically .2 or lower (Hargens, 1988: 150).

Hargens also found that review times were substantially shorter in the more paradigmatically developed fields. This finding is consistent with Beyer's (1978) findings that time to publication is shorter in journals in the more paradigmatically developed scientific fields. Garvey, Lin, and Nelson (1970) studied lags in the information flow process and the transfer of information from the informal to the formal (journal publication) domain. They found that the elapsed time from the earliest report of research to publication in a journal was much shorter in the physical sciences compared to the social sciences. However, "these longer lags should not be attributed to lethargy or inefficiency on the part of individual social scien-

tists; rather, they are lags which stem from the characteristics of the dissemination system currently functioning in the social sciences" (Garvey et al., 1970: 68). The biggest factor associated with the lag from research results to dissemination was the higher rejection rate in the social science journals. Even for articles that were eventually published in a so-called core journal, in the social sciences some 25 percent had been previously rejected by one or more journals.

Because of the greater consensus in more paradigmatically developed fields and the greater certainty of technology, collaborative research is easier to organize and accomplish in these areas. Just as communication is more efficient and course sequences can be longer in high-paradigm fields, so too is it easier to organize the activities of larger groups of people in a collaborative research venture. In exploring what affects patterns of research collaboration, Pfeffer and Langton (In press) found that the level of paradigm development was the single most important factor affecting whether or not people worked alone on research, with one or two others, or in a larger group. Work can be better and more efficiently organized in the presence of greater task certainty. Whitley (1982: 337) noted that "the more predictable are task outcomes, the more work can be systematically planned outside the work process, work roles allocated on a full time basis, tasks highly differentiated and results coordinated and controlled through a formal hierarchy, with an elaborate communication system .... Scientific fields where task uncertainty is higher are less likely to formulate and carry out research programmes in a systematic way which directs work across employment organizations."

The level of paradigm development affects researchers' ability to take coordinated action. Beyer and Lodahl (1976: 114) argued that "faculty members who have more consensus can form stronger and more effective coalitions than those in fields rife with internal conflicts." This unity and consensus gives those departments and fields that are more paradigmatically developed more power (Pfeffer, 1992). This power, in turn, can produce higher levels of resource allocations in the form of budgets and higher faculty salaries. Although there is some evidence that within business schools, salaries are higher in fields in which there is more consensus such as finance, accounting, and production and operations management compared to fields such as management and marketing

(AACSB, 1992), Moore and Pfeffer (1980) found that the level of a department's scientific paradigm development had no significant effect on faculty acceleration or deceleration in pay advancement at the University of California.

Finally, because paradigm development is associated with power, it affects patterns of citations. In a social network, one would expect to observe more communication from people in positions of lower power directed to people in positions of more power, and people who have more powerful positions should be more central in the structure. In exactly the same way, there is more tendency, when cross-citations are observed, for citations in low-paradigm fields to come from fields that are more paradigmatically developed. For instance, there are many more citations to economics in both the sociology and organizations literature than there are citations in economics to either organizations or sociology. In a 1992 computer-based search of three bibliographic files covering economics, sociology, and psychology, regarding articles addressing topics in any of these fields or organizational behavior, I found the following: in economics there are 105 articles on organizational behavior, 580 on sociology, and 315 on psychology. By contrast, both sociology and psychology files produced more than 1,000 articles referencing economics. If one examines recent issues of any of the leading organizations journals, one would find substantial citations to economic concepts such as transaction costs, efficiency wages, and agency theory, but one would be hard pressed to find a single citation to organizational articles treating these or related topics in any of the major economics journals. Baron and Hannan (In press) reported a 650 percent increase in citations to economists in the *American Sociological Review* and an 1,100 percent increase in the *American Journal of Sociology* between 1970 and 1980, but no further increase since that time. Although their major point is that there is very little impact of either economics on sociology or the reverse, they noted that "data on cross-journal citation patterns . . . show essentially no influence of the sociology journals . . . either in the late 1970s or at present" (Baron & Hannan, In press: 3).

It is evident that the level of a scientific field or academic departments' paradigm development has a number of effects that follow logically from the impact that consensus and technological certainty have on behavior. It is also clear that a number of these effects are substantively important. But perhaps the most important effect of paradigm development and the consensus implied by that construct is on the subsequent development of knowledge in a field.

Where Does Organization Studies Stand?

The study of organizations has numerous subspecialties, and these certainly vary in terms of the level of paradigm development. Nevertheless, it appears that, in general, the field of organizational studies is characterized by a fairly low level of paradigm development, particularly as compared to some adjacent social sciences such as psychology, economics, and even political science. In addition to the factors already noted (a high rate of citing other social sciences; low salaries compared to other business school disciplines; high rates of manuscript rejection in the major journals), many previous commentators on the field have noted its pre-paradigmatic state. Zammuto and Connolly (1984: 30) noted the low level of interconnection of materials in textbooks, an indicator of a low level of conceptual connection and interdependence. Webster and Starbuck (1988), who examined only industrial and organizational psychology rather than the field as a whole, argued that the development of knowledge was progressing slowly. They called attention to the fact that the strength of relationships reported in research on a set of topics was getting weaker over time. They also cited a study by Campbell, Daft, and Hulin (1982) that asked respondents to suggest the major research needs during the next 10 to 15 years. The 105 respondents produced some 146 suggestions, of which 106 were unique: they were contributed by only one person. Webster and Starbuck believed that this study indicated there was little consensus in the field about what were the most significant research issues.

Miner's (1984) examination of the relationship between usefulness, scientific validity, and frequency of mention by scholars for 24 theories—he found little connection among these three indicators—was prompted by his concern for the absence of a systematically developing scientific paradigm in the field. Burrell and Morgan's (1979) review of only sociological paradigms documented the theoretical diversity in the field. One might have thought, now more than 10 years after the publication of this influential work, that progress would have been made in evaluating the relative usefulness of these different theoretical foci and winnowing down the avenues to be explored. However, if anything, the field is more fragmented and diverse than it has been. Donaldson (1985) asked whether or not there can be a science of organizations. The debate over theory and method that raged in the early 1980s (e.g., Burrell & Morgan, 1979; Clegg, 1977; Donaldson, 1985) is no closer to resolution today (see, e.g., Marsden, 1993). Indeed, whether or not one wants to achieve a high level of paradigm development, to the extent that implies consensus, is itself open to dispute in the field:

> Their [Burrell and Morgan's] prescription is, in fact, a strategy for achieving plurality and diversity in organizational analysis, a guard against "dominant orthodoxies swamping promising heterodoxies and stunting the growth of innovative theoretical development (Reed, 1985: 184)". (Marsden, 1993: 99)

Proponents of functionalism, postmodernism, critical theory, realism, and many other theoretical approaches today contend vigorously in the study of organizations. Whatever else one might think of this state of affairs, it is, by definition, a state that signifies a field that is fragmented and that does not share the consensus characterizing more paradigmatically developed disciplines.

Paradigm Development and the Advance of Knowledge: Positive Feedback Loops

A given level of paradigm development is itself associated with processes that maintain the level of development that exists. In other words, developed fields will tend to advance more consistently and more rapidly, and less developed fields are quite likely to remain comparatively un- or underdeveloped. Fields are unlikely to change their relative positions, but how they do so is an important topic taken up later in this article. At one level, this stability is almost patently obvious. Consider how outcomes affected by paradigm development, listed in Table 1, are themselves likely to affect the subsequent development of knowledge in a field.

Fields that are more paradigmatically developed

fare better in the contest for resources. Although at one point the National Science Board argued for compensating funding to ensure the development of disciplines in a pre-paradigmatic stage, there is little evidence that this advice has been heeded and lots of evidence that in this domain, as in others, the rich get richer. As noted previously, university funding patterns magnify the external inequalities in funding in favor of more paradigmatically developed fields. These resources are not likely to be wasted. Because more developed fields receive a disproportionate share of both external and internal funding, such fields are able to mount more extensive research efforts. These more extensive and better funded research efforts are themselves, other things equal, likely to lead to a greater rate of knowledge accumulation in those fields that are already more paradigmatically developed.

Moreover, the fact that research resources and academic talent are more dispersed in less paradigmatically developed fields also has implications for the rate of development of the field. Lodahl and Gordon (1973b: 82) reported that "quality was not associated as strongly with levels of funding in the social as in the physical sciences. The result was less reinforcement of existing quality patterns." They go on to trace the implications of this resource dispersion for the development of knowledge in these already less paradigmatically developed fields:

> The present diffusion of research support may not be advantageous to the development of the social sciences in universities. It is possible that the best talents are scattered and the funds are following them, but it is also possible that social science funding is being diluted because of . . . the low visibility of consequences in the less developed sciences. (Lodahl & Gordon, 1973b: 82)

Funding may be diffused because particularistic factors operate with more effect and because there is in fact less consensus on quality evaluations in the less paradigmatically developed fields. But whatever the factors producing the results, the diffusion of both talent and research support makes the development of knowledge more difficult. Research support is diffused over a larger number of people of varying skills, so that funds are not allocated to what would necessarily be their highest and best use. And the diffusion of talent makes the benefits of interaction and collaboration more difficult to achieve.

In less paradigmatically developed fields in

which there is less collaboration and in which taking coordinated action is more difficult, it is less likely that dense networks of researchers crossing university boundaries can or will emerge. There will be fewer, smaller, and less well-organized "invisible colleges." But the very absence of these more tightly integrated, cross-organizational networks makes it more difficult to resolve technical uncertainty and to develop consensus that extends across organizational boundaries. As a consequence, the very absence of consensus and the social organization it promotes makes developing more consensus and technical certainty difficult and highly problematic.

The fact that productivity is less closely tied to pay in less paradigmatically developed fields means that there is less reinforcement for producing research in these fields. Although pay is not the only, or even perhaps the most important, incentive for academics, the diminished connection between pay and productivity cannot provide less paradigmatically developed fields with an advantage in terms of incentive or motivation. Furthermore, the lower rates of manuscript acceptance and greater delays in publication also reduce the positive reinforcement of research for those in fields with less developed paradigms.

There are other effects of the higher journal rejection rates. On the one hand, an 80 or a 90 percent rejection rate means that those who are able to publish should (and do) feel comparatively advantaged, part of an elite and very select group. On the other hand, these high rejection rates mean that by far the vast majority of research effort in the field is wasted. Even if some of the rejected articles are subsequently published elsewhere, there is often more effort put forth as authors revise and rewrite the papers. For papers that are ultimately accepted by the first journal to which they are submitted, it is almost certain that the authors will experience the revise-and-resubmit process, a consequence of the lack of agreement among referees. "At most major journals in the social sciences, the overall recommendations given by reviewers of the same paper correlate only about .25" (Marwell, 1992: iii). Revising and resubmitting papers is a process that is unknown in many of the physical sciences, and it requires additional expenditure of time and effort not on advancing knowledge but on getting one's scientific results placed in the public domain. The lack of certainty in the technology that links activity to consequences means, inevitably, that much more activity will be wasted in less paradigmatically developed fields. Although there may be less wasted activity on the part of the more talented or experienced members of any academic discipline, it is nevertheless the case that a high rate of rejection speaks to a substantial waste of effort and resources—a waste much less likely to occur in fields in which there is more certainty about what to do and how to do it.

The fact that social ties and other particularistic criteria loom larger in decisions about funding, journal publication, and editorial board appointments in less paradigmatically developed fields means that there is less reinforcement provided for quality work and, instead, there is more reinforcement for engaging in political strategies of career advancement. This differential reinforcement must inevitably lead to wasted effort (from the point of view of the development of knowledge and advancement of the field) in influence activities, a point made with respect to organizational resource allocation more generally by Milgrom and Roberts (1988). Thus, the very reward system in less paradigmatically developed fields tends to divert efforts to social influence and political strategies and does not send a consistent message that productive scholarly effort is the surest way to achieve status and recognition.

The fact that coordination is more difficult in less paradigmatically developed fields and collaborative research is less likely as a consequence means that such fields will tend to lose out on the advantages of social facilitation effects, peer influence, and support in the research and teaching process. Although academic teaching and research are not identical to production work, it is likely to be the case that many of the advantages of teamwork now being discovered in other work settings also operate, at least to some degree, in academic environments. If researchers work in isolation, it is harder for them to achieve the benefits of social support and intellectual cross-stimulation.

The fact that fields with less developed paradigms are more likely to import ideas from fields with highly developed paradigms (witness the importation of economic concepts and theories into sociology, political science, and organizational behavior) means that the boundaries and domain of the less paradigmatically developed fields are more often in contest and being negotiated. A lot of boundary maintenance and definition activity occurs that would otherwise not be required. Moreover, this process, if carried to the extreme, means that the less developed field simply disappears, as it is taken over by its more developed rival. Although this is one way to develop a field of knowledge (to have its questions subsumed by another, more paradigmatically developed specialty), it is a course of development that leaves the research questions of the absorbed field not necessarily answered in the way they would have been had the field retained its boundaries and its academic integrity.

The Importance of Consensus for Knowledge Development

The preceding ideas make the point that the very effects of paradigm development work in a self-reinforcing way to maintain fields at their given comparative level of development. But a more fundamental point should be made; namely, that consensus itself, however achieved, is a vital component for the advancement of knowledge in a field. Without some minimal level of consensus about research questions and methods, fields can scarcely expect to produce knowledge in a cumulative, developmental process.

This argument is neither new nor novel. "Kuhn (1970), Polanyi (1958), Lakatos (1970), and Ziman (1968) have argued convincingly that some degree of consensus is a necessary though not a sufficient condition for the accumulation of knowledge in science or in any other type of intellectual activity" (Cole, 1983: 134). As Stephen Cole (1983: 134–135) argued:

> Accumulation of knowledge can occur only during periods of normal science which are characterized by the adherence of the scientific community to a paradigm. It is only when scientists are committed to a paradigm and take it as the starting point for additional research that progress can be made. Without agreement on fundamentals, scientists will not be able to build on the work of others and will spend oil their time debating assumptions and first principles. . . . Most new and contradictory ideas prove to be of little value. If scientists were too willing to accept every unorthodox theory, method, or technique, the established consensus would be destroyed, and the intellectual structure of science would become chaotic. Scientists would be faced with a multi-

tude of conflicting and unorganized theories and would lack research guidelines and standards.

Webster and Starbuck (1988: 95) noted that an absence of consensus about theories fostered "divergent findings and incomparable studies that claim to be comparable." They argued that theories should play a stabilizing role in the social sciences, as they do in the physical sciences, organizing the collection of data and interpretations of the world, and they should not be discarded too readily or replaced for reasons of fad or fashion. They noted:

> As much as correctness, theories need the backing of consensus and consistency. When scientists agree among themselves to explain phenomena in terms of base-line theories, they project their findings into shared perceptual frameworks that reinforce the collective nature of research by facilitating communication and comparison and by defining what is important or irrelevant. (Webster and Starbuck, 1988: 127)

Whitley (1982: 338) noted that in fields with greater task uncertainty, "local considerations and exigencies will have more impact on the nature of the work carried out and how it is done." Although local adaptation may be useful in some circumstances, it is likely to lead to proliferation of concepts and methods that make the development of knowledge difficult. As Zammuto and Connolly (1984: 32) noted, doctoral students "are confronted with a morass of bubbling and sometimes noxious literature. Theories presented are incompatible, research findings inconsistent." This lack of agreement leads to difficulties in doctoral training, including high rates of attrition, a long period of time needed to complete the degree, and problems in training doctoral students in distinguishing good from bad theory and methods.

In the study of organizations, it is almost as if consensus is systematically avoided. Journal editors and reviewers seem to seek novelty, and there are great rewards for coining a new term. The various divisions of the Academy of Management often give awards for formulating "new concepts" but not for studying or rejecting concepts that are already invented.

Where Does Consensus Come From?

Why is it that some fields are more paradigmatically developed and have more consensus than others? One answer to this question, which un-doubtedly has some empirical validity, is that there are simply inevitable, irreducible differences across scientific areas of inquiry that are inherent in the very nature of the phenomena being studied and the knowledge of these different subjects. For instance, it may be that people, the subject of or-ganizational science, sociology, and psychology, are simply more unpredictable and difficult to ex-plain than the behavior of either light waves or physical particles or the course of chemical reac-tions. This answer, however, does not explain the difference in paradigm development between, for instance, economics and either sociology or orga-nizational studies. Economic activity is activity undertaken by individuals, and there is little evi-dence that such activity is either more predictable or easier to comprehend than the subject matter of organizational science. Moreover, there are differ-ences even across subspecialties of organizational studies. For example, it is my impression that population ecology is characterized by much more consensus either than the field as a whole or than most other topic domains within it. There is enor-mous consistency in terms of the methods used (event-history analysis, most often using the com-puter program RATE), the dependent variables studied, the literature that is cited, and most im-portant, on what are judged to be the next impor-tant problems to work on (e.g., Carroll, 1988). This is the one branch of organization studies in which one can frequently hear (as I have) that it is im-portant to get research done and published quickly, because, otherwise, in a year or so, it will be made obsolete by what other researchers are doing. This time urgency, because of the predictable advance of the domain of inquiry is one sign of a highly developed paradigm.

As one who has been a participant-observer of business schools specifically and universities more generally for some time, it seems clear to me that consensus it, at least to some degree, created and imposed in those fields or subspecialties where it exists. It is imposed in several ways.

Cole (1983: 137–138), describing how science works generally, noted:

> One of the primary mechanisms through which consensus is maintained is the practice of vesting authority in elites. . . . Generally, the stars of a discipline occupy the main gatekeeping roles. . . . For the gatekeepers to establish consen-sus, they must have legitimated authority. . . . Le-

gitimacy is granted by virtue of one's being a star. If the gatekeeper positions are filled by "average" scientists, it will be difficult for the authority ex-ercised to be granted legitimacy.

The Academy of Management has, for good reasons, intentionally constituted itself as a repre-sentative body, and representativeness is a trea-sured value of the organization. Elitism is shunned. Compare the editorial boards of any of the Acad-emy journals to the editorial board of *Econometrica*, for instance, in terms of the num-ber of different institutions and the institutional prestige represented. Similar comparisons in the officers of professional associations will reveal the same, simple fact: that the Academy and other or-ganizations and journals involved in the discipline of organization studies are substantially less elit-ist and more egalitarian, and they have spread the distribution of power much more widely than one will observe in more paradigmatically developed physical science fields or even economics. The explicit incorporation of representativeness when slates of officers or editorial board members are selected—where representativeness is defined in terms of geography, public/private college or uni-versity, field of specialization, gender, career stage and academic rank, theoretical perspective, and academic achievement—as is often done in this field, may have a number of desirable effects, but building consensus on a paradigm is not likely to be one of them.

Consensus is enforced when members of a field develop a set of methodological standards and ensure that these are consistently maintained. In the study of organizations at present, a good idea can obviate obvious empirical shortcomings. For instance, although some researchers of the effects of personality on organizational behavior adhere to methodological rigor, many authors do not (see, e.g., Davis-Blake & Pfeffer, 1989). In fields with highly developed paradigms, researchers also pre-fer some issues and points of view rather than oth-ers. The difference in this case is their commit-ment to enforce a set of research standards that are more central to the definition of science in those fields, more agreed upon, and zealously main-tained.

Members of high-paradigm fields enforce both theoretical and methodological conformity. They do this by reserving the most desirable places only for those who conform to the disciplinary ortho-doxy and criticizing, regardless of their power or the validity of their ideas, those who depart from the established paths. For instance, shortly after the election of Bill Clinton to the presidency in 1992, Robert Reich was appointed to the team advising the president-elect on economic policies. This appointment enraged conventional economists, and an article in the *New York Times* provides a good illustration of how a discipline maintains consensus and enforces its standards:

> Although the general approach of Mr. Reich is increasingly shared by others, his specific work has nevertheless been criticized by trained economists, mostly on the ground that he is a lawyer, not a Ph.D. in economics, and his insights lack the rigor and precision that economists provide through their training in mathematics and economic theory.
>
> That criticism has been one reason that Mr. Reich . . . has failed to get a tenured professorship at the Kennedy School, where he has been a lecturer . . . for more than a decade, under a contract renewed every few years . . . the criticism of Mr. Reich's credentials . . . has intensified with his appointment last week as chief of the economics transition team. (Uchitell, 1992: 17)

Michael Piore (Doeringer & Piore, 1971; Piore & Sabel, 1984) holds a somewhat similar position in the discipline because of his different use of methodology and different theoretical approach. Although he is a tenured member of the economics department at MIT, many economists in private conversations maintain that he isn't really an economist—regardless of their opinion of his work—because he doesn't think like one.

Contrast these examples with organization studies. The contents of the July 1992 special issue of the *Academy of Management Review*, although perhaps an extreme example of the proliferation of theoretical perspectives ranging from feminism to conversation analysis and radical humanism, make the point that the field not only has, to use the current political parlance, a very large "tent," but a tent in which fundamentally any theoretical perspective or methodological approach is as valid as any other. Those who study organizations energetically seek out ideas, perspectives, and techniques from numerous allied social sciences, the humanities, economics, anthropology, political science, psychology, and with the current play given to deconstruction and conversation analysis, from linguistics and English.

My argument is, at its heart, a very simple one:

A substantial amount of the variation in the level of paradigm development is a consequence of the social structure, culture, and power relations that characterize the discipline (i.e., how it is organized and the factors that create and perpetuate that organization). Here, again, there are forces at work that tend toward stability of whatever system is in place. A field in which control is concentrated in the hands of a comparatively small elite is one in which power is much more institutionalized and control by the dominant paradigm is quite likely to be perpetuated. By contrast, an area of inquiry characterized by diffuse perspectives, none of which has the power to institutionalize its dominance, is one in which consensus is likely to remain elusive and the dispersion in resources, rewards, and activity will be great.

Conclusion

There is evidence that disciplines can change in their level of paradigm development, in spite of the many self-reinforcing feedback loops described in this paper. When Lodahl and Gordon (1972) conducted their survey, political science was the least paradigmatically developed field. But over time, actually beginning in the 1960s, political science evolved. Adopting many of the methods and theoretical assumptions of economics, political science became noninstitutional, as researchers emphasized theories that are (a) reductionist (behavior is seen as the aggregate consequence of individual action); (b) utilitarian (behavior is presumed to result from calculated self-interest); (c) functionalist (history and the passage of time tend to produce appropriate and efficient outcomes); and (d) instrumentalist (the allocation of resources and decision making are seen as the central foci of interest) (March & Olsen, 1989: 3). Those in political science have developed a much more coherent, consensually shared paradigm, and it is now probably one of the more paradigmatically developed social sciences.

This evolution may have come at a cost, at least according to some theorists. As the evolution was unfolding and the rational choice paradigm was gaining increasing preeminence, Ball (1976: 172) argued for "being tenacious in defending and tolerant in criticizing research programs." He noted that in response to Kuhn, critics "emphasized the narrowing of focus and the 'dogmatism' of 'normal science.' If that is what a normal or mature science looks like, then political scientists should want no part of it. Paradigms . . . tyrannize; and so political scientists committed to free inquiry should resist all blandishments to make theirs a 'normal' science" (Ball, 1976: 153). Ball's pleas fell largely on deaf ears as the discipline evolved in the directions already mentioned.

The question for organizational science is whether the field can strike an appropriate balance between theoretical tyranny and an anything-goes attitude, which seems to be more characteristic of the present state. Those who bemoan the present condition of presumed positivist hegemony (e.g., Marsden, 1993) need only to consider economics or political science, adjacent social sciences whose members are interested in many of the same things, to see how truly open and unstructured organizational theory really is.

It is crucial to distinguish among disagreement over (a) the substantive research questions that are considered to be important, or the goals of knowledge development in the field; (b) the ways in which relevant variables should be measured and modeled; (c) the methods used to collect and analyze relevant data; (d) the theoretical models of behavior used to guide the measurement process, to analyze the data, and to comprehend the phenomena of interest; and (e) the rules for determining which approach to each of these four domains is more or less fruitful. A field characterized by disagreements over all five areas will almost certainly be unable to make progress of any consequence. Theoretical and methodological diversity may be adaptive as long as there is some agreement over fundamental goals and on a set of rules to winnow the measures, methods, and theories on the basis of accumulated evidence. In the study of organizations, there appears to have been more agreement on these issues in the past than there is at present, when almost every aspect of the research process is contested.

A diversity in ideas and in methodology can be useful to the field as long as the diversity can be resolved at some point. The question is whether the social structure and organization of the field encourage resolution of diverse ideas or the continued particularistic advancement of separate agendas, often with explicitly political undertones. At present, I believe that the field encourages the development and advancement of differences and separate agendas rather than attempts at integra-

tion or resolution. More than 10 years ago, I (Pfeffer, 1982: 1) argued that "the domain of organization theory is coming to resemble more of a weed patch than a well-tended garden. Theories . . . proliferate along with measures, terms, concepts, and research paradigms. It is often difficult to discern in what direction knowledge of organizations is progressing." The situation has not changed, and, if anything, there are now more diversity of ideas and measures and more contention over the rules for organizational science than there were a decade ago.

Richard Marsden (1993: 101) noted:

> Paradigmatic change is not a purely cerebral affair, but depends on the outcome of political conflicts between custodians and opponents of a paradigm. Resistance to change is the norm; breakthroughs typically occur when the hegemony of the "invisible college" is broken.

But Marsden's unit of analysis needs to be extended outside the boundaries of the discipline to adjacent fields of inquiry. In this context, the contest is not just within the various branches of organizational science; it is between organizational science and related disciplines. The hegemony of the invisible college that may be broken is the hegemony of those who have fostered theoretical dissensus.

It already seems clear that the 1990s are not going to be a great decade for higher education in general or for business schools in particular. In state after state, budgets for colleges and universities are being severely constrained, and tuition, in both public and private schools, is rising rapidly. Business school applications are down some 20 percent this academic year and have fallen in the past several years, although not as dramatically. After all the articles in the popular press criticizing business schools and business education, and after the decades of truly phenomenal growth, it is scarcely surprising that the halcyon days are over.

I think we know two things about political processes: (a) power is more likely to be exercised when resources are scarce (e.g., Salancik & Pfeffer, 1974) and (b) unity of perspective and the ability to take collective action with ease provide an important source of power (Pfeffer, 1992). It seems fair to forecast that contests for resources are likely to increase in universities and in schools of administration in the coming years. It also seems reasonable to suggest that the theoretical and methodological diversity and disagreements that characterize the study of organizations are disadvantages rather than advantages in this coming struggle.

Do researchers in the organizational sciences have to become like their competitors to survive and prosper? Must they, to use a phrase of one commentator on this argument, follow the lead of economics and mutilate the phenomena they are studying in order to compete and survive?

Disagreement in theoretical approaches and even in methodology will not prove detrimental as long as there is some agreement about what the fundamental questions or issues are and as long as there are some agreed upon ways of resolving theoretical and methodological disputes. At the moment neither condition holds. There is no commitment to a unifying set of research goals or questions being pursued by varied means. There is no agreement as to whether the field should serve the powerful, presumably business and government interests, or the powerless. There is little apparent agreement about how to resolve the controversies among competing paradigms—not only disagreement about which one is correct or useful, but disagreement about how to even go about figuring this out. Because of these fundamental disagreements, debates about basic epistemological issues, even though useful at one level, never seem to produce much resolution. Rather, they are repeated periodically, often covering the same ground.

It would be interesting and useful to study the history of related fields such as political science and economics to understand exactly how paradigm consensus was achieved. My sense is that such consensus was developed by a group of individuals forming a dense network of connections and unified view, who then intentionally and systematically took over positions of power and imposed their views, at times gradually and at times surreptitiously, on the field. There seems to be nothing in the natural order of things that suggests that mathematical rigor should be valued over empirical richness or realism. Rather, the criteria, the status hierarchy, and the enforcement of rules were and are very much political processes.

Many researchers entered the field of organizations because of its theoretical and methodological openness and pluralism. But anything carried to an extreme can be harmful, and given the current climate, downright dangerous. Without a recommitment to a set of fundamental questions—

perhaps pursued in a multitude of ways—and without working through a set of processes or rules to resolve theoretical disputes and debates, the field of organizational studies will remain ripe for either a hostile takeover from within or from outside. In either case, much of what is distinctive, and much of the pluralism that is so valued, will be irretrievably lost.

ACKNOWLEDGMENTS

This article is a revised version of a paper presented at the 1992 annual meeting of the Academy of Management in Las Vegas, Nevada, as the distinguished scholar address to the Organization and Management Theory division. I appreciate the comments of Joanne Martin, the suggestions of Charles O'Reilly, and the benefit of discussions about these issues with Jim Baron.

REFERENCES

American Assembly of Collegiate Schools of Business (AACSB). 1992. Annual salary survey: The recession hits home. *Newsline, 22* (Winter): 1–3.

Ball, T. 1976. From paradigms to research programs: Toward a post-Kuhnian political science. *American Journal of Political Science, 20,* 151–177.

Baron, J. N., & Hannan, M. T. In press. The impact of economics on contemporary sociology. *Journal of Economic Literature.*

Beyer, J. M. 1978. Editorial policies and practices among leading journals in four scientific fields. *Sociological Quarterly, 19,* 68–88.

Beyer, J. M., & Lodahl, T. M. 1976. A comparative study of patterns of influence in United States and English universities. *Administrative Science Quarterly,* **21,** 104–129.

Beyer, J. M., & Snipper, R. 1974. Objective versus subjective indicators of quality in graduate education. *Sociology of Education, 47,* 541–557.

Burrell, G., & Morgan, G. 1979. *Sociological paradigms and organizational analysis.* London: Heinemann.

Campbell, J. P., Daft, R. L., & Hulin, C. L. 1982. *What to study: Generating and developing research questions.* Beverly Hills, CA: Sage.

Carroll, G. R. 1988. Organizational ecology in theoretical perspective. In G. R. Carroll (Ed.), *Ecological models of organizations:* 1–6. Cambridge, MA: Ballinger.

Clegg, S. R. 1977. Power, organization theory, Marx and critique. In S. R. Clegg & D. Dunkerly (Eds.), *Critical issues in organizations:* 21–40. London: Routledge & Kegan Paul.

Cole, S. 1993. The hierarchy of the sciences? *American Journal of Sociology, 89,* 111–139.

Davis-Blake, A., & Pfeffer, J. 1989. Just a mirage: The search for dispositional effects in organizational research. *Academy of Management Journal, 14,* 385–400.

Doeringer, P., & Piore, M. 1971. *Internal labor markets and manpower analysis.* Lexington, MA: Heath.

Donaldson, L. 1985. *In defence of organization theory: A reply to the critics.* Cambridge, England: Cambridge University Press.

Garvey, W. D., Lin, N., & Nelson, C. E. 1970. Some comparisons of communication activities in the physical and social sciences. In C. E. Nelson & D. K. Pollock (Eds.), *Communication among scientists and engineers*: 61–84. Lexington, MA: Heath.

Hargens, L. L. 1988. Scholarly consensus and journal rejection rates. *American Sociological Review, 53,* 139–151.

Konrad, A. M., & Pfeffer, J. 1990. Do you get what you deserve? Factors affecting the relationship between productivity and pay. *Administrative Science Quarterly, 35,* 258–285.

Kuhn, T. S. 1970. *The structure of scientific revolutions* (2nd ed.). Chicago: University of Chicago Press.

Lakatos, L. 1970. Falsification and the methodology of research programmes. In L. Lakctos & A. Musgrave (Eds.), *Criticism and the growth of knowledge*: 91–96. Cambridge. England: Cambridge University Press.

Lindsey, D. 1976. Distinction, achievement, and editorial board membership. *American Psychologist, 31,* 799–804.

Lodahl, J. B., & Gordon, G. 1972. The structure of scientific fields and the functioning of university graduate departments. *American Sociological Review, 37,* 57–72.

Lodahl, J. B., & Gordon, G. 1973a. Differences between physical and social sciences in university graduate departments. *Research in Higher Education, 1,* 191–213.

Lodahl, J. B., & Gordon, G. 1973b. Funding the sciences in university departments. *Educational Record, 54,* 74–82.

March, J. G., & Olsen, J. P. 1989. *Rediscovering institutions: The organizational basis of politics*, New York: Free Press.

Marsden, R. 1993. The politics of organizational analysis. *Organization Studies, 14,* 93–124.

Marwell, G. 1992. Let's train reviewers: Editors comment. *American Sociological Review, 57,* iii–iv.

Milgrom. P., & Roberts, J. 1988. An economic approach to influence activities in organizations. *American Journal of Sociology, 94* (Supplement): S154–S179.

Miner, J. B. 1984. The validity and usefulness of theories in an emerging organizational science. *Academy of Management Review, 9,* 296–306.

Moore, W. L., & Pfeffer, J. 1980. The relationship between departmental power and faculty careers on two campuses: The case for structural effects on faculty salaries. *Research in Higher Education, 13,* 291–306.

Pfeffer, J. 1982. *Organizations and organization theory*. Marshfield, MA: Pitman.

Pfeffer, J. 1992. *Managing with power: Politics and influence in organizations*. Boston: Harvard Business School Press.

Pfeffer, J., & Langton, L. In press. The effect of wage dispersion on satisfaction, productivity, and working collaboratively: Evidence from college and university faculty. *Administrative Science Quarterly.*

Pfeffer, J., Leong, A., & Strehl, K. 1976. Publication and prestige mobility of university departments in three scientific disciplines. *Sociology of Education, 49,* 212–218.

Pfeffer, J., Leong, A., & Strehl, K. 1977. Paradigm development and particularism: Journal publication in three scientific disciplines. *Social Forces, 55,* 938–951.

Pfeffer, J., & Moore, W. L. 1980a. Average tenure of academic department heads: The effects of paradigm, size, and departmental demography. *Administrative Science Quarterly, 25,* 387–406.

Pfeffer, J., & Moore, W. L. 1980b. Power in university budgeting: A replication and extension. *Administrative Science Quarterly, 25,* 637–653.

Pfeffer, J., Salancik, G. R., & Leblebici, H. 1976. The effect of uncertainty on the use of social influence in organizational decision making. *Administrative Science Quarterly, 21,* 227–245.

Piore, M., & Sabel, C. 1984. *The second industrial divide*. New York: Basic Books.

Polanyi, M. 1958. *Personal knowledge*. London: Routledge & Kegan Paul.

Price, D. J. de Solla. 1970. Citation measures of hard science, soft science, technology, and nonscience. In C. E. Nelson & D. K. Pollock (Eds.), *Communication among scientists and engineers*: 3–22. Lexington, MA: Heath.

Reed, M. I. 1985. *Redirections in organizational analysis*. London: Tavistock.

Salancik, G. R., & Pfeffer, J. 1974. The bases and use of power in organizational decision making: The case of a university. *Administrative Science Quarterly, 19,* 453–473.

Salancik, G. R., Staw, B. M., & Pondy, L. R. 1980. Administrative turnover as a response to unmanaged organizational interdependence. *Academy of Management Journal, 23,* 422–437.

Thompson, J. D., & Tuden, A. 1959. Strategies, structures and processes of organizational decision. In J. D. Thompson, P. B. Hammond, R. W. Hawkes, B. H. Junker, & A. Tuden (Eds.), *Comparative studies in administration*: 195–216. Pittsburgh: University of Pittsburgh Press.

Uchitelle, L. 1992. Clinton's economics point man. *New York Times*, November 21: 17.

Webster, J., & Starbuck, W. H. 1988. Theory building in industrial and organizational psychology. In C. L. Cooper & I. Robertson (Eds.), *International review of industrial and organizational psychology 1988*: 93–138. London: Wiley.

Whitley, R. 1982. The establishment and structure of the sciences as reputational organizations. In N. Elias, H. Martins, & R. Whitley (Eds.), *Scientific establishments and hierarchies*: 313–357. Dordrecht, Holland: D. Reidel.

Yoels, W. C. 1974. The structure of scientific fields and the allocation of editorships on scientific journals: Some observations on the politics of knowledge. *Sociological Quarterly, 15,* 264–276.

Zammuto, R. F., & Connolly, T. 1984. Coping with disciplinary fragmentation. *Organizational Behavior Teaching Review, 9,* 30–37.

Ziman, J. 1968. *Public knowledge*. Cambridge, England: Cambridge University Press.

Decision Making

Judgment and decision making constitute a key area within micro OB. Within the area of judgment and decision making, there are several distinctions that guide research endeavors, some of which are outlined below. A major distinction concerns individual judgment and interpersonal decision making.

Decision Making Metaphors

With the economic model serving as the perfect whipping boy, the judgment and decision making research domain characterizes the organizational actor as generally deficient when it comes to making decisions. Because descriptive research defies normative economic theory, this raises interesting questions about human cognition and motivation. Within the judgment and decision-making domain there are different views about judgment. Following our analysis of metaphors in OB and social psychology, we outline metaphors of the decision maker following Abelson and Levi (1985). One of these metaphors is known as the "corrigible rationalist" model (cf., Edwards, 1968). This model is highly similar to Pfeffer's (1998) "economic actor" metaphor. According to this research metaphor, people are fundamentally rational, but through no fault of their own they make mistakes, for completely idiosyncratic reasons. However, there is no particular pattern or direction to their mistakes.

Simon's (1955) principle of "bounded rationality" largely displaced the corrigible rationalist model. According to Simon, people "satisfice," or take shortcuts, rationalize, or otherwise don't try as hard as they might if they were perfectly rational. The key reasons that lead people to satisfice are lack of time and lack of resources.

The "error-prone intuitive scientist" metaphor differs from the "bounded rationalist" model in that people apparently lack a fundamental appreciation of key normative assumptions. Simply stated, even if they had more time and greater cognitive resources, organizational actors might very well continue to make critical mistakes in their judgments.

There are two other metaphors in the area of decision-making research and theory that are worth mentioning: the "slave to motivational forces" and the "butt of faulty normative models." According to the "slave" metaphor, people make faulty decisions on gambles not because they have cognitive shortcomings (as Tversky and Kahneman (1974) argued), but because they become emotional and they are stressed. The "butt" metaphor suggests that the experiments are designed by researchers to make organizational actors look stupid. This research metaphor essentially asks the question, "If people are so stupid, how did they put a person on the moon?" The idea behind this model is that normative models are wrong; people are correct, and we should look at things in a different way (cf., Lopes, 1994; Beach, 1990).

Domains of Decision Making

In connection with judgment and decision making, there are three main areas of research: riskless choice, uncertainty, and risky choice. *Riskless choice* (also known as *decision making under certainty*) focuses on how organizational actors choose from among sure courses of action. For example: You are shopping for an apartment and have located three having slightly different prices and amenities. You must decide which one to rent. There is essentially no risk involved, because all the choices are essentially the same. The main model of riskless choice is the multi-attribute utility theory (or MAUT); if you are choosing between apartments, you put each apartment choice in a different column; along the rows, you list each relevant attribute, such as price, size, distance from work, and so on. Within this grid, or matrix, you can assign a value for each apartment on each attribute. Then it is possible to sum up the value of each apartment and determine which one is the best choice.

The next decision type is *decision making under uncertainty*, in which you don't know what the future will bring, nor can you assign meaningful probabilities to it. For example, you live in the American Northwest and are planning a wedding. Should you have it outdoors? You cannot predict whether it will rain because you are planning six months in advance. How do you make a choice?

The third type is *decision making under risk* (or *risky choice*), in which the decision maker knows the exact probabilities. In experiments, researchers can assign probabilities from which participants can choose.

The first article in this section is an example of risky decision making that illustrates the powerful principle of risk seeking in the face of unfavorable information. Staw (1976) provides several examples of how managers continue to allocate resources to a course of action even in the face of information that suggests the course of action is unwise.

The second article, by Kahneman and Lovallo (1993), argues that decision makers—managers in organizations—often treat problems as unique, neglecting both the statistics of the past and the multiple opportunities of the future. This makes managers likely to succumb to two biases (or "isolation errors"), such that managers' forecasts of the future are often anchored on plans and scenarios of success rather than on past results, and their evaluations of single, risky prospects neglect the possibilities of pooling risks, and are therefore overly timid. Kahneman and Lovallo identify several organizational implications of this human bias, including the tendency of managers to adopt an "inside view" of the problem, when in fact, an "outside view" may lead to better judgment. They also suggest that reducing the frequency of managers' evaluations may mitigate the inhibiting effects of some of these biases.

The third article, by Dawes (1979), on linear decision making, attests to the power of inappropriate naïve theories when it comes to making decisions. Dawes's article is an example of decision making under certainty in which the decision makers' own judgments are more errorful than a model of their judgment process.

The fourth article, by Kahneman, Knetsch, and Thaler (1990), introduced an important inconsistency in individual decision making known as the *endowment effect*. According to the endowment effect, the value of goods increases when they become part of a person's endowment. Kahneman, Knetsch, and Thaler experimentally demonstrate that when people are asked to name a selling price for something that they own (e.g., chocolate bar, pen, or coffee mug), they often require much more money than they themselves would pay to own the very same item. According to Kahneman and his colleagues, the reason for this effect is that losses (of the good in question) are felt more strongly than equivalent gains. This asymmetry is routinely exploited by companies that offer products on a trial basis (Plous, 1993). Specifically, trial ownership often increases the value of a product and makes customers more reluctant to return it.

Interpersonal Decision Making

In contrast to individual decision making, which focuses on the biases that organizational actors hold and how it can lead to less-than-optimal personal outcomes for the actor, interpersonal decision making focuses on how decision making is affected by interpersonal relationships with others.

Loewenstein, Thompson, and Bazerman (1989) used Messick and Sentis's (1985) concept of social utility functions to specify the relationship conditions that affect actors' preferences for different allocations of payments to self and others. They explored two key factors: the nature of the relationship (positive, neutral, or negative) and the type of relationship (business or social). Several competing models were tested prior to specifying the social utility function. Under nearly all circumstances, the social utility function was tent-shaped, such that people preferred equal outcomes even more than they desired to earn more than the other party (except in the case of negative and business relationships). However, the tent was lopsided, such that if inequality must occur, people overwhelmingly preferred to be better off than the other party. The article includes a direct test of Kahneman & Tversky's (1979) framing effect in an individual versus interpersonal context, and the results suggest that concerns for the other party can push around the value function curve.

REFERENCES

Abelson, R., & Levi, A. (1985). Decision making and decision theory. In G. Lindzey & E. Aronson (Eds.), *The handbook of social psychology, Vol. 1* (3rd ed., pp. 231–310). New York: Random House.

Beach, L. R. (1990). *Image theory: Decision making in personal and organizational contexts.* Chichester, England: Wiley.

Dawes, R. (1979). The robust beauty of improper linear models in decision making. *American Psychologist, 34,* 571–582.

Edwards, W. (1968). Conservatism in human information processing. In B. Kleinmuntz (Ed.), *Formal representation of human judgment* (pp. 17–52). New York: Wiley.

Kahneman, D., & Lovallo, D. (1993). Timid choices and bold forecasts: A cognitive perspective on risk taking. *Management Science, 39*(1), 17–31.

Kahneman, D., Knetsch, J. L., & Thaler, R. H. (1990). Experimental tests of the endowment effect and the Coase theorem. *Journal of Political Economy, 98*(6), 1325–1348.

Loewenstein, G. F., Thompson, L., & Bazerman, M. H. (1989). Social utility and decision making in interpersonal contexts. *Journal of Personality and Social Psychology, 57*(3), 426–441.

Lopes, L. L. (1994). Psychology and economics: Perspectives on risk, cooperation, and the marketplace. *Annual Review of Psychology, 45,* 197–227.

Messick, D. M., & Sentis, K. P. (1985). Estimating social and nonsocial utility functions from ordinal data. *European Journal of Social Psychology, 15,* 389–399.

Pfeffer, J. (1998). Understanding organizations: Concepts and controversies. In D. T. Gilbert, S. T. Fiske, & G. Lindzey (Eds.), *The handbook of social psychology, Vol. 2* (4th ed., pp. 733–777). New York: McGraw-Hill.

Plous, S. (1993). *The psychology of judgment and decision making.* New York: McGraw Hill.

Simon, H. (1955). A behavioral model of rational choice. *Quarterly Journal of Economics, 69,* 99–118.

Staw, B. M. (1976). Knee deep in the Big Muddy: A study of escalating commitment to a chosen course of action. *Organizational Behavior and Human Decision Processes, 16,* 27–44.

Suggested Readings

Bazerman, M. H. (1998). *Judgment in managerial decision making* (4th ed.) New York: John Wiley & Sons.

Dawes, R. M. (1998). Behavioral decision making and judgment. In D. T. Gilbert & S. T. Fiske (Eds.), *The handbook of social psychology, Vol. 1* (4th ed., pp. 497–548). Boston: McGraw-Hill.

Knetsch, J., & Sinden, J. A. (1984). Willingness to pay and compensation demanded: Experimental evidence of an unexpected disparity in measures of value. *Quarterly Journal of Economics, 99*(3), 507–521.

Kray, L., & Gonzalez, R. (1999). Differential weighting in choice versus advice: I'll do this, you do that. *Journal of Behavioral Decision Making, 12*(3), 207–217.

MacCrimmon, K. R., & Messick, D. M. (1976). A framework for social motives. *Behavioral Science, 21,* 86–100.

Messick, D. M., Bloom, S., Boldizar, J. P., & Samuelson, C. D. (1985). Why we are fairer than others. *Journal of Experimental Social Psychology, 21,* 480–500.

Knee-Deep in the Big Muddy: A Study of Escalating Commitment to a Chosen Course of Action

Barry M. Staw • Northwestern University

It is commonly expected that individuals will reverse decisions or change behaviors which result in negative consequences. Yet, within investment decision contexts, negative consequences may actually cause decision makers to increase the commitment of resources and undergo the risk of further negative consequences. The research presented here examined this process of escalating commitment through the simulation of a business investment decision. Specifically, 240 business school students participated in a role- playing exercise in which personal responsibility and decision consequences were the manipulated independent variables. Results showed that persons committed the greatest amount of resources to a previously chosen course of action when they were personally responsible for negative consequences.

Intuitively, one would expect individuals to reverse decisions or to change behaviors which result in negative consequences. Yet, there seem to be many important instances in which persons do not respond as expected to the reward/cost contingencies of their environments. Specifically, when a person's behavior leads to negative consequences we may find that the individual will, instead of changing his behavior, cognitively distort the negative consequences to more positively valenced outcomes (see, e.g., Abelson et al. 1968; Aronson, 1966; Staw, 1976; Weick, 1966). The phenomenon underlying this biasing of behavioral outcomes is often said to be a self-justification process in which individuals seek to rationalize their previous behavior or psychologically defend themselves against adverse consequences (Aronson, 1968, 1972; Festinger, 1957).

No doubt, the largest and most systematic source of data on the justification of behavior following adverse consequences is provided by the literature of forced compliance. Typically, in forced compliance studies an individual is induced to perform an unpleasant or dissatisfying act such as lying to fellow subject about the nature of a task (e.g., Festinger & Carlsmith. 1959; Collins & Hoyt, 1972; Calder, Ross, & Insko, 1973), writing an essay against one's own position (e.g., Cohen, 1962; Linder, Cooper, & Jones, 1967; Sherman, 1970), eating a disliked food (Brehm. 1959), or performing a dull task (e.g., Freedman, 1963; Weick, 1964; Pallak, Sogin, & Van Zante, 1974). Negative consequences result from carrying out each of these counter attitudinal acts when no external rewards are present to compensate for the dissatisfying nature of the experimental task (Collins & Hoyt, 1972). However, since it is difficult for the subject in forced compliance experiments to undo the consequences of his acts, it is predicted that the individual will bias his attitude on the experimental task (or change his opinion on an attitudinal issue) so as to cognitively reduce any negative outcomes resulting from his behavior. In short, the individual is predicted to justify his previous behavior or defend himself from negative consequences through the perceptual biasing of behavioral outcomes.[1]

Recent empirical research has shown that there are two basic preconditions for the biasing of outcomes within forced compliance situations. First, the individual must have committed himself to behavioral consequences which are irrevocable or at least not easily changed (Brehm & Cohen, 1962). If it is readily possible to reverse one's own behavior, then this course of action may often be taken to reduce negative consequences rather than any biasing of behavioral outcomes (Staw, 1974). Secondly, the individual must feel personally responsible for the negative consequences of his behavior (Carlsmith & Freedman, 1968; Copper, 1971). That is, a person must perceive at least a moderate degree of choice in his behavior (Linder, Cooper, & Jones, 1967), and the possibility of negative consequences should have been anticipated at an earlier decision point (Brehm & Jones, 1970; Cooper, 1972).

Self-Justification in Investment Decision Contexts

Though forced compliance studies have provided a great deal of data on the biasing of behavioral outcomes, there remain a large number of situations in which individuals may be able to go beyond the distortion of negative consequences to rationalize a behavioral error. For example, one societally important context in which individuals may take new and concrete actions to justify their behavior following negative consequences is that of investment decision making. Investment decision contexts are considered broadly here as situations in which resources are allocated to one decisional alternative over others, and in which the level of resources can be increased or decreased at the discretion of the decision maker.

When negative consequences are incurred within an investment context, it is often possible for a decision maker to greatly enlarge the commitment of resources and undergo the risk of additional negative outcomes in order to justify prior behavior or demonstrate the ultimate rationality of an original course of action. It follows, however, that committing additional resources to a losing decisional alternative can also turn into a negative cyclical process. That is, due to a need to justify prior behavior, a decision maker may increase his commitment in the face of negative consequences, and this higher level of commitment may, in turn, lead to further negative consequences. Within the sphere of governmental policy making, just such an example of committing resources to a costly decisional alternative was described by George Ball, the former Under Secretary of State, in some early observations on U.S. involvement in Indochina.

> Once large numbers of U.S. troops are committed to direct combat. they will begin to take heavy casualties in a war they are ill-equipped to fight in a non-cooperative if not downright hostile countryside. Once we suffer large casualties we will have started a well-high irreversible process. Our involvement will be so great that we cannot—without national humiliation—stop short of achieving our complete objectives. Of the two possibilities, I think humilitation would be more likely than the achievement of our objectives—even after we have paid terrible costs. (Memo from George Ball to President Lyndon Johnson, July, 1965; source: *The Pentagon Papers*, 1971)

Obviously, many factors may have influenced governmental decision making in the commitment of men and material to the war in Indochina. But, the comments of this high level official do underscore the need for research on the possibility that important resource investment decisions may be influenced by the reluctance of individuals to admit past mistakes or a need to justify prior behavior.

Assessing Self-Justification in Investment Decisions

An empirical test of self-justification in an investment decision context would seem to involve an assessment of whether or not negative consequences serve to increase individual's commitment to a decisional alternative. However, an unambiguous test of self-justification would necessitate more than the simple manipulation of consequences and

---

[1]An active controversy exists over the theoretical interpretation of the data from forced compliance studies (see Bem, 1967, 1972; Jones et al. 1968; Ross & Shulman, 1973). However, the issue of self-justification versus self-perception will be addressed in a later section of the paper.

the measurement of subsequent commitment. This is because other theoretical mechanisms might also account for the same empirical relationship between commitment and consequences. One such mechanism might be the desire of decision makers to maximize their own outcomes, since sometimes it is precisely when negative consequences have been incurred that a new and larger commitment to a decisional alternative will pay off in the future. A separate but related mechanism which may also account for the effect of negative consequences on the commitment of resources may be a "gambler's fallacy" that resources should always be placed in a losing decisional alternative since "things are bound to get better" Implicit in the notion of a gambler's fallacy is the perception of long-run equality of investment alternatives and the nonindependence of outcomes over time (see Lee, 1971).

The separation of self-justification from alternative theoretical mechanisms within an investment decision context may depend upon manipulations conceptually similar to those used in previous forced compliance studies. As noted in several earlier studies (e.g., Collins & Hoyt, 1972; Calder, Ross, & Insko, 1973), the rationalization of one's behavior has been shown to be significantly affected by the manipulation of prior choice and negative consequences. Within an investment decision context, self-justification may similarly depend upon the level of personal responsibility one has had in determining a particular course of action and the outcomes resulting from those actions. The experiment described below was therefore designed to test self-justification within an investment decision context by manipulating these two independent variables and measuring their effects upon the commitment of resources to a previously chosen course of action. Through the maximization of gain or a gambler's fallacy, one might expect negative consequences to cause an increase in the commitment of resources to a decisional alternative. In addition, due to the simple consistency of actions over time, one might also expect individuals to increase their commitment to a decisional alternative for which they have had some prior choice. However, only self-justification would predict an interaction of personal responsibility and decision consequences such that increases in commitment would be even greater than the additive effects of these two separate factors.

Method

Subjects

The subjects of this experiment were 240 undergraduate students enrolled in the College of Commerce and Business Administration at the University of Illinois, Urbana-Champaign. Subjects had volunteered to participate in a study on financial problem-solving as one means of fulfilling a course research requirement. Upon arrival, the subjects were asked to work on the "A & S Financial Decision Case" in which it was necessary to play the role of a corporate executive in making some decisions about the allocation of research and development funds.

As students in a business school, subjects generally were experienced in working on written cases in which an organizational or financial scenario is presented and some action or set of actions are called for by the student. However, in order to maximize the involvement of subjects and to provide a rationale for the study, the experimenter told each subject that the purpose of the case was to examine the effectiveness of business decision-making under various amounts of information. Each subject was told that the particular case on which he would be working contained only a limited amount of information, but that the information provided should still be sufficient for a business school student to make "a good financial decision." Subjects were asked to do the best job they could on the cases and to place their names on each page of the case material.

The A & S Financial Decision Case

The financial decision case used in this study describes a hypothetical corporation in the year 1967. The case depicts the financial history (including ten prior years of sales and earnings data) of the "Adams & Smith Company," and a scenario is presented in which the subject is asked to play a major role in financial decision-making. As stated in the case, the profitability of the A & S Company, a large technologically-oriented firm, has started to decline over several preceding years, and the directors of the company have agreed that one of the major reasons for the decline in corporate earnings (and a deterioration in competitive position) lay in some aspect of the firm's program of research and development. The case further states that the company's directors have concluded that 10 million dollars of additional R & D funds should be made available to its major operating divisions, but, that for the time being, the extra funding should be invested in only *one* of the corporation's *two* largest divisions. The subject is then asked to act in the role of the Financial Vice President in determining which of the two corporate divisions, Consumer Products or Industrial Products, should receive the additional R & D funding. A brief description of each corporate division is included in the case material, and the subject is asked to make the financial investment decision on the basis of the potential benefit that R & D funding will have on the future earnings of the divisions. In addition to circling the chosen division, subjects were also asked to write a brief paragraph defending their allocation decisions.

After completing the above section of the case and turning it in to the experimenter, subjects were administered a second section of the case which necessitated another financial investment decision. Part 11 of the Financial Decision Case presents the subject with the condition of Adams & Smith Company in 1972, five years after the initial allocation of research and development funds. As stated in Part 11, the R & D program of Adams & Smith is again up for re-evaluation, and the management of the company is convinced that there is an even greater need for expenditure on research and development. In fact. 20 million dollars has been made available from a capital reserve for R & D funding, and the subject, as the Financial Vice President, is again asked to decide upon its proper allocation. This time, however, the subject is allowed to divide the R & D money in any way he wishes among the two major corporate divisions. Financial data (e.g., sales and earnings) is provided for each of the five years since the initial allocation decision and, as earlier, the investment decision is to be made on the basis of future contribution to earnings. Subjects made this second investment decision by specifying the amount of money that should be allocated to either the Consumer Products or Industrial Products division (out of a total of 20 million) and again wrote a paragraph defending the decision.

Manipulation of Consequences

Decision consequences were experimentally manipulated in this study through the random assign-

ment of financial information. One half of the subjects were provided information that the division initially chosen for R & D funds subsequently performed better than the unchosen division, while one half were given information showing the reverse. For example, in the positive consequences condition, subjects received financial data which showed that the chosen division had returned to profitable levels while the unchosen division continued to decline. In a parallel manner, subjects in the negative consequences condition received financial data which showed a deepening decline in the profitability of the chosen division but an improvement in the unchosen division. The exact nature of the financial data provided to subjects is shown in Tables 1 and 2.

Manipulation of Personal Responsibility

One half of the subjects were randomly assigned to the high personal responsibility condition in which two investment decisions were sequentially made by the subject. This condition conformed to the two-part financial decision case described above in which subjects made an initial decision to allocate R & D funds, discovered its consequences, and then made a second investment decision. However, one half of the subjects were also randomly assigned to a low personal responsibility condition in which the entire financial decision case was presented in one section. In the low personal responsibility condition, subjects were asked to make the second allocation decision without having made a prior choice as to which corporate division was most deserving of R & D funds. Subjects in this condition received one set of case materials which described the financial condition of the Adams & Smith Company *as of 1972,* the time of the second R & D funding decision. They were told in the case that an earlier R & D funding decision had been made in 1967 *by another financial officer of the company* and that the preceding officer had decided to invest all the R & D funds in the Consumer (or Industrial) Products division. The financial results of each corporate division (e.g., sales and earnings data) were presented from 1957 to 1972, and, like other subjects, persons in the low responsibility condition were asked to make the (second) R & D funding decision based upon the potential for future earnings. In sum, the information presented to low personal responsibility subjects was identical to that given to other

TABLE 1. Consumer Products Contribution to Sales and Earnings of Adams & Smith Company[a]

Fiscal year	Sales [b]	Earnings [b]
1957	624	14.42
1958	626	10.27
1959	649	8.65
1960	681	8.46
1961	674	4.19
1962	702	5.35
1963	717	3.92
1964	741	4.66
1965	765	2.48
1966	770	(.12)
1967	769	(.63)

	First R & D funding decision as of 1967			
	Manipulated improvement		Manipulated decline	
Fiscal year	Sales [b]	Earnings [b]	Sales [b]	Earnings [b]
1968	818	.02	771	(1.12)
1969	829	(.09)	774	(1.96)
1970	827	(.23)	762	(3.87)
1971	846	.06	778	(3.83)
1972 (est)	910	1.28	783	(4.16)

Second R & D funding decision as of 1972

[a] Parentheses denote net losses in earnings.
[b] In millions of dollars.

subjects except for the fact that the case's scenario began at a later point in time (1972 rather than 1967) and necessitated making the second investment decision without having participated in an earlier choice.

Dependent Variable

The dependent variable utilized in this study was the individuals' commitment to a previously chosen investment alternative. This variable was operationalized by the amount of money subjects allocated on the second R & D funding decision to the corporate division chosen earlier (either chosen earlier by the subject or the other financial officer mentioned in the case). The amount allocated to the previously chosen alternative could range between zero and 20 million dollars.

Summary of Treatment Groups

Of the 120 subjects in the high personal responsibility condition, 64 initially chose the Consumer Products Division as the best investment for R & D funds, while 55 initially chose the Industrial Prod-

ucts Division. (One subject was unable to make a choice between Consumer and Industrial Products and therefore had to be excluded from further analyses). Since subjects self-selected themselves to prior choices and then financial information was randomly assigned, four cells were created by initial choice and financial information. However, as shown in Table 3, these four cells can be collapsed into two primary treatment groups of positive decision consequences and negative decision consequences.

Of the 120 subjects assigned to the low personal responsibility condition, thirty were also assigned to each of the four cells described above. For example, thirty were given cases in which another financial officer had chosen the Consumer Products Division and it continued to decline; thirty were given cases in which another financial officer had chosen the Consumer Products Division and it started to improve; thirty were given cases in which another financial officer had chosen the Industrial Products Division and it continued to decline; and, thirty worked on cases in which Industrial Products was chosen and it started to improve. Again, the four cells can be collapsed into

TABLE 2. Industrial Products Contribution to Sales and Earnings of Adams & Smith Company[a]

Fiscal year	Sales [b]	Earnings [b]
1957	670	15.31
1958	663	10.92
1959	689	11.06
1960	711	10.44
1961	724	9.04
1962	735	6.38
1963	748	5.42
1964	756	3.09
1965	784	3.26
1966	788	(.81)
1967	791	(.80)

	First R & D funding decision as of 1967			
	Manipulated improvement		Manipulated decline	
Fiscal year	Sales [b]	Earnings [b]	Sales [b]	Earnings [b]
1968	818	.02	771	(1.12)
1969	829	(.09)	774	(1.96)
1970	827	(.23)	762	(3.87)
1971	846	.06	778	(3.83)
1972 (est)	910	1.28	783	(4.16)

Second R & D funding decision as of 1972

[a] Parentheses denote net losses in earnings.
[b] In millions of dollars.

two treatment groups of positive and negative decision consequences comprising 60 subjects in each.

The final form of the design of this experiment was a 2 × 2 factorial in which personal responsibility and decision consequences were the manipulated independent variables. As stated earlier, the amount of money invested in the previously chosen corporate division (previously chosen either by the subject or the other financial officer mentioned in the case) was the dependent measure utilized in the study.

Results

Preliminary Analysis

A preliminary analysis was conducted to determine whether the object of a subject's prior choice (Consumer Products-Industrial Products) or the exact form of financial information (C↑|↓ or C↑|↓) affected the amount of money allocated to the previously chosen alternative. If there were main effects of either of these two variables, then it would not be possible to collapse the eight cells shown

in Table 3 into a 2 × 2 analysis of variance. As can be seen from the data of Table 4, there were no main effects of either the object of prior choice ($F < 1.00$, $df = 1/231$, n.s.) or the exact form of financial information ($F < 1.00$, $df = 1/231$, n.s.).

Effects of Personal Responsibility and Decision Consequences

Since there were no main effects of the object of prior choice and financial information, a 2 × 2 analysis of variance was conducted in which personal responsibility and decision consequences were the independent variables. Table 5 shows that there were significant main effects of both personal responsibility and decision consequences, and a significant interaction of the two independent variables.[2]

---

[2] In a 2 ×2 § 2 analysis of variance there was a corresponding main effect of personal responsibility, an interaction of prior choice and financial information (same as main effect of decision consequences). and a triple interaction of personal responsibility, prior choice, and financial information (same as interaction of responsibility and decision consequences.

TABLE 3. Schematic Analysis of the Cells to Which Subjects Were Assigned Under Both High and Low Responsibility Conditions

HIGH PERSONAL RESPONSIBILITY

Financial Information

		C ↑|↓	C ↑|↓
		Positive	Negative
	Consumer Products	consequences	consequences
		($n = 32$)	($n = 32$)
Initial Choice		Negative	Positive
	Industrial Products	consequences	consequences
		($n = 27$)	($n = 28$)

LOW PERSONAL RESPONSIBILITY

Financial Information

		C ↑|↓	C ↑|↓
		Positive	Negative
	Consumer Products	consequences	consequences
		($n = 30$)	($n = 30$)
Initial Choice		Negative	Positive
	Industrial Products	consequences	consequences
		($n = 30$)	($n = 30$)

Under high personal responsibility conditions, subjects allocated an average of 11.08 million dollars to the corporate divisions they had earlier chosen for extra R & D funding. Under low personal responsibility conditions, subjects allocated an additional 8.89 million dollars to the corporate divisions previously chosen by another financial officer. Under positive decision consequences, subjects allocated an average of 8.77 million to the previously chosen alternative, while 11.20 million was allocated under negative consequences.

Interaction of Personal Responsibility and Decision Consequences

When subjects (personally) made an initial investment decision which declined, they subsequently allocated an average of 13.07 million dollars to this same alternative in the second funding decision. As shown in Fig. 1. the amount invested in the previously chosen alternative was greater in the high personal responsibility-negative consequences condition than in any of the other three experimental conditions. Although this result could

TABLE 4. Amount of Money (in Millions) Allocated to Previously Chosen Alternative by Level of Personal, Responsibility, Object of Prior Choice, and Financial Information

Personal responsibility	Prior choice	Financial Information	
		c↑|↓	c↑|↓
High	Consumer Products	9.36 positive consequences	12.56 negative consequences
	Industrial Products	13.46 negative consequences	9.00 positive consequences
Low	Consumer Products	8.22 positive consequences	9.22 negative consequences
	Industrial Products	9.65 negative consequences	8.48 positive consequences

have been expected from two significant main effects of personal responsibility and consequences, the difference between the high personal responsibility-negative consequence condition and the other cells was of such magnitude as to produce a significant interaction. Further more, a close analysis of Fig. 1 shows that the *only* significant differences among any of the four experimental conditions were between the high responsibility-negative consequences cell and the other three experimental conditions. For example, consequences did not have a significant effect under low personal responsibility conditions ($t = 1.20$, $df = 118$; $n.s.$), and responsibility did not significantly affect results under positive consequences conditions ($f = 1.13$, $df = 118$, $n.s.$).

Discussion

Interpretation of Effects

The main effect of decision consequences upon commitment to a previously chosen alternative

could be explained by a maximization of gain hypothesis. Either through the objective reappraisal of action-outcome contingencies following negative consequences or through a "gambler's fallacy" that the probability of gain is increased by prior failure, individuals could have decided to increase their investment of resources. However, it is interesting to note that, although a maximization of gain hypothesis provides an adequate explanation of the main effect in analysis of variance terms, its explanatory power is somewhat weakened when individual cell means are considered. Specifically, while maximization can account for the effect of decision consequences under the high responsibility condition, it is less clear why there was no significant effect of consequences under the low responsibility condition.[3]

---

[3]It is possible, of course, to postulate (post-hoc) that the valence of future outcomes was less for subjects under low rather than high responsibility conditions, and, thus, the motive to maximize gain was correspondingly weaker in low rather than high responsibility conditions.

TABLE 5. Analysis of Variance of Effects of Personal Responsibility and Decision Consequences upon Allocation of Resources to a Previously Chosen Alternative

Source	df	MS	F	P
Personal Responsibility (P)	1	282.36	14.40	<.001
Decision Consequences (D)	1	351.57	17.93	<.001
Interaction (P × D)	1	109.12	5.56	<.019
Error	235	19.61	—	

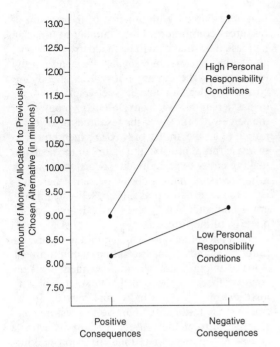

FIGURE 1 ■ Amount of money allocated to previously chosen alternative by personal responsibility and decision consequences.

A related interpretive problem also weakens the consistency of choice explanation of the main effect of personal responsibility. For example, it may well be true that, due to consistency in choice decisions, individuals will allocate more money to an investment alternative that was personally chosen at an earlier point in time (e.g., under high responsibility) than one chosen previously by someone else (e.g., under low responsibility). However, when the individual cells of the analysis of variance are examined (see Fig. 1), it appears that the main effect of personal responsibility is not fully explained by consistency. Only under negative consequences was there a significant difference between the high and low responsibility conditions, although there was a nonsignificant trend under positive consequences.

Thus, from the data of this study, it is not unreasonable to conclude that the primary effect of responsibility and consequences was that individuals invested a substantially greater amount of resources when they were *personally responsible for negative consequences*. The significantly greater commitment of resources under this one experimental condition clearly accounted for the inter-

action of personal responsibility and decision consequences. However, a close examination of Fig. 1 also shows that the substantial difference between the condition of high personal responsibility–negative consequences and the other cells could also underlie the statistical significance of the two main effects. As a result, the data from this study provide even somewhat stronger support than expected for the hypothesis that individuals who are personnally responsible for negative consequences will increase the investment of resources in a previously chosen course of action.

Self-Justification versus Self-Perception

Frequently, when a self-justification process is experimentally tested, its outcroppings are difficult to separate from those derived from self-perception theory (Bem, 1967, 1972). The distinction between self-justification and self-perception is also important to the interpretation of the present study and should be considered in some depth.

In essence, the question of self-justification versus self-perception revolves around dual formulations of the process of rationalization. On the one hand, self-justification (Aronson, 1968, 1972) or dissonance theory (Festinger, 1957) posits that individuals possess a potent need to restore the "appearance" of rationality to their own behavior. As a result, the theory predicts that individuals will cognitively re-evaluate decisional alternatives after an important choice (e.g., Walster, 1964; Knox & Inkster, 1968; Vroom, 1966) or actively distort the characteristics of a behavioral task (e.g., Festinger & Carlsmith, 1959; Weick, 1966) On the other hand, self-perception theory posits that individuals retrospectively restore rationality to their behavior by simply inferring the causes of their own actions within a social context. Self-perception theory predicts that individuals will re-evaluate their behavior so that it conforms to their own notions of how one might feel or behave *if he were acting rationally.* Thus, like self-justification, the retrospective analysis of behavior which comprises self-perception theory can also account for the re-evaluation of alternatives following a decisional choice (see Kelley, 1967, 1971) or changes in the perception of the characteristics of a behavioral task (see Calder & Staw, 1975; Deci, 1971, 1972; Salancik, 1975; Staw, 1976).

It is possible that a self-perception analysis can also be usefully applied to the effects of personal responsibility and decision consequences within an investment decision context. For example, when individuals personally select a course of action which results in negative consequences, they may retrospectively infer that their prior choices were especially meritorious in that they required some suffering and, as a result, they may subsequently choose to invest even greater amounts of resources in the losing alternative. This cause–effect sequence, however, does not appear as plausible an explanation of the present data as an individual need or predisposition to justify behavior. The primary interpretive problem facing a self-perception analysis is the fact that there is a substantial body of evidence which shows that individuals attempt to avoid the self-attribution of causality when behavior leads to negative consequences or results in personal failure (see Weiner, Frieze, Kukla, Reed, Rest, & Rosenbaum, 1971). Thus, it would seem very unlikely for individuals to attribute greater internal causality (and therefore invest more) in a previously chosen alternative which has led to negative consequences. In contrast, it would seem more likely for individuals to take concrete actions to reduce negative consequences for which they are responsible or at least to attempt to reduce those negative outcomes which cannot be attributed to an external source. This latter interpretation is consistent with a self-justification notion that individuals actively seek to maintain or restore the appearance of rationality to a previously chosen course of action.[4]

Self-Justification and the Escalation of Commitment

As we have seen, when individuals are personally responsible for negative consequences, they may decide to increase the investment of resources to a prior course of action. It follows that this same process of escalation may also occur in many decision contexts in which additional time, effort, and resources are committed to an unsatisfactory policy alternative. Thus, further research should focus on the critical factors underlying the escala-

tion of resources, both in terms of the amount of resources committed and the number of times an increase in resources will be made to a decisional alternative. Specific independent variables worthy of study may be the amount of loss already incurred by a decision maker (see Weick, 1974, for discussion of the "Vietnam Dollar" phenomenon), the perceived efficacy of the resources being committed (e.g., the ability of R & D expenditures to increase future profits), the nature of the decision making entity (e.g., individual decision maker vs group decision making body), personal characteristics of the decision maker (e.g., self-esteem, tolerance for ambiguity), and the evaluative consequences of the situation.

One conceptual note which could prove useful in future studies of the escalation of commitment is the distinction that, within investment decision contexts, there may be two separate sources of self-justification. First, an individual may desire to demonstrate rationality to himself or restore consistency between the consequences of his actions and a self-concept of rational decision making (Aronson, 1968). This may be a rather ubiquitous phenomena as has been demonstrated by research on cognitive dissonance and other consistency theories (see Abelson, Aronson, McGuire, Newcomb, Rosenberg, & Tannenbaum, 1968). Secondly, the individual may attempt to demonstrate rationality to others or to prove to others that a costly error was really the correct decision over a longer term perspective. This second form of self-justification would seem to be most important in organizational contexts where a decision maker may be uncertain of his own status within a social hierarchy or in governmental policy situations in which a decision maker may be anxious about his political standing among constituents. No doubt, these two forms of self-justification could both be viewed as face-saving activities (Goffman, 1959), with the distinction of an internal versus external orientation on the part of the decision maker. However, while the first form of self-justification may be based on a general human need to be consistent and correct (Festinger, 1957; White, 1959), the second form may relate to individual desires for social approval (Crowne & Marlow, 1964). Future research should be directed toward the specification of each of these forms of self-justification and the determination of their relative influence within investment decision contexts.

---

[4] Other studies which (indirectly) demonstrate the escalation of commitment using a "foot in the door" technique (e.g., Freedman & Fraser, 1966) can be interpreted by *either* an increase in the perception of internal causality following increases in commitment or by an individual need to justify prior behavior.

ACKNOWLEDGMENTS

The author wishes to express his gratitude to William Brighton for his help in the preparation of experimental materials, to Greg R. Oldham, Louis R. Pondy, and Gerald R. Salancik for their comments on an earlier version of this manuscript, and to The Center for Advanced Study at the University of Illinois, Urbana-Champaign for the facilities necessary to complete this study.

REFERENCES

Abelson, R. P., Aronson, E., McGuire, W. J., Newcombe, T. M., Rosenberg, M. J., & Tannenbaum, P. H. (Eds.). *Theories of cognitive consistency*. Chicago: Rand McNally, 1968.

Aronson, E. The psychology of insufficient justification: An analysis of some conflicting data. In S. Feldman (Ed.), *Cognitive consistency*. New York: Academic Press. 1966.

Aronson, E. Dissonance theory: Progress and problems. In R. Abelson, E. Aronson W. McGuire, T. Newcomb, M. Rosenberg, & P. Tannenbaum (Eds.), *Theories of cognitive consistency*. Chicago: Rand McNally, 1968.

Aronson, E. *The social animal*. San Francisco: Freeman, 1972.

Bem, D. J. Self-perception: An alternative interpretation of cognitive dissonance phenomena, *Psychological Review*, 1967, 74, 183–200.

Bem, D. J. Self-perception theory. In L. Berkowitz (Ed.), *Advances in experimental social psychology*. New York: Academic Press, 1972. Vol. 6.

Brehm, J. W. Increasing cognitive dissonance by a fait-accompli. *Journal of Abnormal and Social Psychology*, 1959, 58, 379–382.

Brehm, J. W., & Cohen, A. E. *Explorations in cognitive dissonance*. New York: Wiley, 1962.

Brehm, J. W., & Jones, R. A., The effect on dissonance of surprise consequences. *Journal of Personality and Social Psychology*, 1970.

Calder, B. J., Ross, M., & Insko, C. A. Attitude change and attitude attribution: Effects of incentive, choice, and consequences, *Journal of Personality and Social Psychology*, 1973, 25, 84–100.

Calder, B. J. & Staw, B. M. The self-perception of intrinsic and extrinsic motivation. *Journal of Personality and Social Psychology*, 1975, 31, 599–605.

Carlsmith, J. M., & Freedman, J. L. Bad decisions and dissonance: Nobody's perfect. In R. Abelson, E. Aronson, W. McGuire, T. Newcomb, M. Rosenberg, & P. Tannenbaum (Eds.), *Theories of cognitive consistence*. Chicago: Rand McNally, 1968.

Cohen, A. R. An experiment on small rewards for discrepant compliances and attitude change. In J. W. Brehm & A. R. Cohen (Eds.), *Exploration in cognitive dissonance*. New York: Wiley, 1962.

Collins, B. E., & Hoyt, M. F. Personal responsibility-for-consequences: An integration and extension of the "forced compliance" literature. *Journal of Experimental Social Psychology*, 1972. 8, 558–593.

Cooper, J. Personal responsibility and dissonance: The role of foreseen consequences: An integration and extension of the "forced compliance" literature. *Journal of Experimental Social Psychology*, 1971, 8, 558–594.

Crowne, D. P. & Marlowe, D. *The approval motive: studies in evaluative dependence*. New York: Wiley, 1964.

Deci, E. L. The effects of externally mediated rewards on intrinxic motivation. *Journal of Personality and Social Psychology*, 1971, 18, 105–115.

Deci, E. L. The effects of contingent and noncontingent rewards and controls on intrinsic motivation. *Organizational Behavior and Human Performance*. 1972, 8, 217–229.

Festinger, L. *A Theory of Cognitive Dissonance*, Stanford: Stanford Univ. Press. 1957.

Festinger, L., & Carlsmith, J. M. Cognitive consequences of forced compliance. *Journal of Abnormal and Social Psychology*, 1959, 58, 203–210.

Freedman, J. L. Attitudinal effects on inadequate justification. *Journal of Personality*, 1963, 31, 371–385.

Freedman, J. L., & Fraser, S. C. Compliance without pressure: The foot-in-the-door technique, *Journal of Personality and Social Psychology*, 1966, 4, 195–202.

Goffman, E. *The presentation of self in everyday life*. Garden City, N. Y.: Doubleday 1959.

Jones, R. A., Linder, D. E., Kiesler, C. A., Zanna, M., & Brehm, J. W. Internal states or external stimulus: Observer's attitude judgments and the dissonance-self-persuasion controversy. *Journal of Experimental Social Psychology*, 1968, 4, 247–269.

Kelley, H. H. Attribution theory in social psychology. In D. Levine (Ed.), *Nebraska Symposium on Motivation*. Lincoln: Univ. of Nebraska Press. 1967.

Kelley, H. H. *Attribution in social interaction*. New York: General Learning Press, 1971.

Knox, R., & Inkster, J. Postdecision dissonance at post time. *Journal of Personality and Social Psychology*, 1968, 8, 319–323.

Lee, W. *Decision theory and human behavior*. New York: Wiley, 1971.

Linder, E. D., Cooper, J., & Jones, E. E. Decision freedom as a determinant of the role of incentive magnitude in attitude change. *Journal of Personality and Social Psychology*, 1967, 6, 245–254.

Pallak, M. S., Sogin, S. R., & Van Zante, A. Bad decisions: Effects of volition, locus of cauality, and negative consequences on attitude change. *Journal of Personality and Social Psychology*, 1974, 30, 217–227.

Pentagon papers. The New York. Times (based on investigation reporting of Neil Sheehan). New York: Bantam Books, 1971.

Ross, M., & Shulman, R. F. Increasing the salicnce of initial attitudes: Dissonance versus self-perception theory. *Journal of Personality and Social Psychology*, 1973, 28, 138–144.

Salancik, J. R. Interaction effects of performance and money on self-perception of intrinsic motivation. *Organizational Behavior and Human Performance*, 1975, 13, 339–351.

Sherntan, S. J. Effects of choice and incentive on attitude change in a discrepant behavior situation. *Journal of Personality and Social Psychology*, 1970, 15, 245–252.

Staw, B. M. Attitudinal and behavioral consequences of changing a major organizational reward: A natural field experiment. *Journal of Personality and Social Psychology*, 1974, 6, 742–751.

Staw, B. M. Attribution of the "causes" of performance: A general alternative interpretution of cross-sectional research on organization. *Organizational Behavior and Human Performance*, 1975, 13, 414–432.

Staw, B. M. *Intrinsic and Extrinsic Motivation*. New York:

General Learning Press, 1976

Vroom, V. H. Organizational choice: A study of pre- and post-decision processes. *Organizational Behavior and Human Performance*, 1966, 1, 212–225.

Walster, E. The temporal sequence of post-decision processes. In L. Festinger (Ed.), *Conflict, decision, and dissonance.* Stanford: Stanford Univ. Press, 1964.

Weick, K. E. Reduction of cognitive dissonance through task enhancement and effort expenditure. *Journal of Abnormal and Social Psychology*, 1964, 68, 533–539.

Weick, K. E. Task acceptance dilemmas: A site for research on cognition. In S. Feldman (Ed.), *Cognitive consistency.* New York: Academic Press, 1966.

Weick, K. E. Amendments to organizational theorizing. *Academy of Management Journal*, 1974, 17, 487–502.

Weiner, B., Frieze, I., Kukla, A., Reed, L., Rest, S., & Rosenbaum, R. M. *Perceiving the causes of success and failure.* New York: General Learning Press, 1971.

White, R. W. Motivation reconsidered: The concept of competence. *Psychological Review*, 1959, 66, 297–334.

Timid Choices and Bold Forecasts: A Cognitive Perspective on Risk Taking

Daniel Kahneman and Dan Lovallo • University of California, Berkeley

Decision makers have a strong tendency to consider problems as unique. They isolate the current choice from future opportunities and neglect the statistics of the past in evaluating current plans. Overly cautious attitudes to risk result from a failure to appreciate the effects of statistical aggregation in mitigating relative risk. Overly optimistic forecasts result from the adoption of an inside view of the problem, which anchors predictions on plans and scenarios. The conflicting biases are documented in psychological research. Possible implications for decision making in organizations are examined.

The thesis of this essay is that decision makers are excessively prone to treat problems as unique, neglecting both the statistics of the past and the multiple opportunities of the future. In part as a result, they are susceptible to two biases, which we label isolation errors: their forecasts of future outcomes are often anchored on plans and scenarios of success rather than on past results, and are therefore overly optimistic; their evaluations of single risky prospects neglect the possibilities of pooling risks and are therefore overly timid. We argue that the balance of the two isolation errors affects the risk-taking propensities of individuals and organizations.

The cognitive analysis of risk taking that we sketch differs from the standard rational model of economics and also from managers' view of their own activities. The rational model describes business decisions as choices among gambles with financial outcomes, and assumes that managers' judgments of the odds are Bayesian, and that their choices maximize expected utility. In this model, uncontrollable risks are acknowledged and accepted because they are compensated by chances of gain. As March and Shapira (1987) reported in a well-known essay, managers reject this interpretation of their role, preferring to view risk as a challenge to be overcome by the exercise of skill and choice as a commitment to a goal. Although managers do not deny the possibility of failure, their idealized self-image is not a gambler but a prudent and determined agent, who is in control of both people and events.

The cognitive analysis accepts choice between gambles as a model of decision making, but does not adopt rationality as a maintained hypothesis.

The gambling metaphor is apt because the consequences of most decisions are uncertain, and because each option could in principle be described as a probability distribution over outcomes. However, rather than suppose that decision makers are Bayesian forecasters and optimal gamblers, we shall describe them as subject to the conflicting biases of unjustified optimism and unreasonable risk aversion. It is the optimistic denial of uncontrollable uncertainty that accounts for managers' views of themselves as prudent risk takers, and for their rejection of gambling as a model of what they do.

Our essay develops this analysis of forecasting and choice and explores its implications for organizational decisions. The target domain for applications includes choices about potentially attractive options that decision makers consider significant and to which they are willing to devote forecasting and planning resources. Examples may be capital investment projects, new products, or acquisitions. For reasons that will become obvious, our critique of excessive risk aversion is most likely to apply to decisions of intermediate size: large enough to matter for the organization, but not so large as to be truly unique, or potentially fatal. Of course, such decisions could be perceived as both unique and potentially fatal by the executive who makes them. Two other restrictions on the present treatment should be mentioned at the outset. First, we do not deal with decisions that the organization explicitly treats as routinely repeated. Opportunities for learning and for statistical aggregation exist when closely similar problems are frequently encountered, especially if the outcomes of decisions are quickly known and provide unequivocal feedback; competent management will ensure that these opportunities are exploited. Second, we do not deal with decisions made under severely adverse conditions, when all optins are undesirable. These are situations in which high-risk gambles are often preferred to the acceptance of sure losses (Kahneman and Tversky 1979a), and in which commitments often escalate and sunk costs dominate decisions (Staw and Ross 1989). We restrict the treatment to choices among options that can be considered attractive, although risky. For this class of projects we predict that there will be a general tendency to underestimate actual risks, and a general reluctance to accept significant risks once they are acknowledged.

Timid Choices

We begin by reviewing three hypotheses about individual preferences for risky prospects.

RISK AVERSION

The first hypothesis is a commonplace: most people are generally risk averse, normally preferring a sure thing to a gamble of equal expected value, and a gamble of low variance over a riskier prospect. There are two important exceptions to risk aversion. First, many people are willing to pay more for lottery tickets than their expected value. Second, studies of individual choice have shown that managers, like other people, are risk-seeking in the domain of losses (Bateman and Zeithaml 1989, Fishburn and Kochenberger 1979, Laughhunn et al. 1980).[1] Except for these cases, and for the behavior of addictive gamblers, risk aversion is prevalent in choices between favorable prospects with known probabilities. This result has been confirmed in numerous studies, including some in which the subjects were executives (MacCrimmon and Wehrung 1986, Swalm 1966).[2]

The standard interpretation of risk aversion is decreasing marginal utility of gains. Prospect theory (Kahneman and Tversky 1979a; Tversky and Kahneman 1986, 1992) introduced two other causes: the certainty effect and loss aversion. The certainty effect is a sharp discrepancy between the weights that are attached to sure gains and to highly probable gains in the evaluation of prospects. In a recent study of preferences for gambles the decision weight for a probability of 0.95 was approximately 0.80 (Tversky and Kahneman 1992). Loss aversion refers to the observation that losses and disadvantages are weighted more than gains and advantages. Loss aversion affects decision making in numerous ways, in riskless as well as in risky contexts. It favors inaction over action and the status quo over any alternatives, because the disadvantages of these alternatives are evaluated

---

[1] Observed correlations between accounting variability and mean return have also been interpreted as evidence of risk-seeking by unsuccessful firms (Bowman 1982, Fiegenbaum 1990, Fiegenbaum and Thomas 1988), but this interpretation is controversial (Ruefli 1990).

[2] A possible exception is a study by Wehrung (1989), which reported risk-neutral preferences for favorable prospects in a sample of executives in oil companies.

as losses and are therefore weighted more than their advantages (Kahneman et al. 1991, Samuelson and Zeckhauser 1988, Tversky and Kahneman 1991). Loss aversion strongly favors the avoidance of risks. The coefficient of loss aversion was estimated as about 2 in the Tversky-Kahneman experiment, and coefficients in the range of 2 to 2.5 have been observed in several studies, with both risky and riskless prospects (for reviews, see Kahneman, Knetsch and Thaler 1991; Tversky and Kahneman 1991).

NEAR-PROPORTIONALITY

A second important generalization about risk attitudes is that, to a good first approximation, people are proportionately risk averse: cash equivalents for gambles of increasing size are (not quite) proportional to the stakes. Readers may find it instructive to work out their cash equivalent for a 0.50 chance to win $100, then $1,000 and up to $100,000. Most readers will find that their cash equivalent increases by a factor of less than 1,000 over that range, but most will also find that the factor is more than 700. Exact proportionality for wholly positive prospects would imply that value is a power function, $u(x) = x^a$, where x is the amount of gain (Keeney and Raiffa 1976). In a recent study of preferences for gambles (Tversky and Kahneman 1992), a power function provided a good approximation to the data over almost two orders of magnitude, and the deviations were systematic: cash equivalents increased slightly more slowly than prizes.

Much earlier, Swalm (1966) had compared executives whose planning horizons, defined as twice the maximum amount they might recommend be spent in one year, ranged from $50,000 to $24,000,000. He measured their utility functions by testing the acceptability of mixed gambles, and observed that the functions of managers at different levels were quite similar when expressed relative to their planning horizons. The point on which we focus in this article is that there is almost as much risk aversion when stakes are small as when they are large. This is unreasonable on two grounds: (i) small gambles do not raise issues of survival or ruin, which provide a rationale for aversion to large risks; (ii) small gambles are usually more common, offering more opportunities for the risk-reducing effects of statistical aggregation.

NARROW DECISION FRAMES

The third generalization is that people tend to consider decision problems one at a time, often isolating the current problem from other choices that may be pending, as well as from future opportunities to make similar decisions. The following example (from Tversky and Kahneman 1986) illustrates an extreme form of narrow framing:

Imagine that you face the following pair of concurrent decisions. First examine both decisions, then indicate the options you prefer.

Decision (i) Choose between:
(A) a sure gain of $240 (84%)
(B) 25% chance to gain $1000 and 75% chance to gain nothing (16%)

Decision (ii) Choose between:
(C) a sure loss of $750 (13%)
(D) 75% chance to lose $1000 and 25% chance to lose nothing (87%)

The percentage of respondents choosing each option is shown in parentheses. As many readers may have discovered for themselves, the suggestion that the two problems should be considered concurrently has no effect on preferences, which exhibit the common pattern of risk aversion when options are favorable, and risk seeking when options are aversive. Most respondents prefer the conjunction of options A & D over other combinations of options. These preferences are intuitively compelling, and there is no obvious reason to suspect that they could lead to trouble. However, simple arithmetic shows that the conjunction of preferred options A & D is dominated by the conjunction of rejected options B & C. The combined options are as follows:

A & D: 25% chance to win $240 and 75% chance to lose $760,
B & C: 25% chance to win $250 and 75% chance to lose $750.

A decision maker who is risk averse in some situations and risk seeking in others ends up paying a premium to avoid some risks and a premium to obtain others. Because the outcomes are ultimately combined, these payments may be unsound. For a more realistic example, consider two divisions of a company that face separate decision problems.[3] One is in bad posture and faces a choice

---

[3] We are endebted to Amos Tversky for this example.

between a sure loss and a high probability of a larger loss; the other division faces a favorable choice. The natural bent of intuition will favor a risk-seeking solution for one and a risk-averse choice for the other, but the conjunction could be poor policy. The overall interests of the company are better served by aggregating the problems than by segregating them, and by a policy that is generally more risk-neutral than intuitive preferences.

People often express different preferences when considering a single play or multiple plays of the same gamble. In a well-known problem devised by Samuelson (1963), many respondents state that they would reject a single play of a gamble in which they have equal chances to win $200 or to lose $100, but would accept multiple plays of that gamble, especially when the compound distribution of outcomes is made explicit (Redelmeier and Tversky 1992). The question of whether this pattern of preferences is consistent with utility theory, and with particular utility functions for wealth has been discussed on several occasions (e.g., Lopes 1981, Tversky and Bar-Hillel 1983). the argument that emerges from these discussions can be summarized as "If you wish to obey the axioms of utility theory and would accept multiple plays, then it is logically inconsistent for you to turn down a single play". We focus on another observation: the near-certainty that the individual who is now offered a single play of the Samuelson gamble is not really facing her last opportunity to accept or reject a gamble of positive expected value. This suggests a slightly different argument: "If you would accept multiple plays, then you should accept the single one that is offered now, because it is very probable that other bets of the same kind will be offered to you later". A frame that includes future opportunities reduces the difference between the two versions of Samuelson's problem, because a rational individual who is offered a single gamble will adopt a policy for $m + 1$ such gambles, where m is the number of similar opportunities expected within the planning horizon. Will people spontaneously adopt such a broad frame? A plausible hypothesis, supported by the evidence for narrow framing in concurrent decisions and by the pattern of answers to Samuelson's problems, is that expectations about risky opportunities of the future are simply ignored when decisions are made.'

It is generally recognized that a broad view of decision problems is an essential requirement of rational decision making. There are several ways of broaderning the decision frame. Thus, decision analysts commonly prescribe that concurrent choices should be aggregated before a decision is made, and that outcomes should be evaluated in terms of final assets (wealth), rather than in terms of the gains and losses associated with each move. The recommended practice is to include estimates of future earnings in the assessment of wealth. Although this point has attracted little attention in the decision literature, the wealth of an agent or organization therefore includes future risky choices, and depends on the decisions that the decision maker anticipates making when these choices arise.[4] The decision frame should be broadened to include these uncertainties: neglect of future risky opportunities will lead to decisions that are not optimal, as evaluated by the agent's own utility function. As we show next, the costs of neglecting future opportunities are especially severe when options are evaluated in terms of gains and losses, which is what people usually do.

The Costs of Isolation

The present section explores some consequences of incorporating future choice opportunities into current decisions. We start from an idealized utility function which explains people's proportional risk preferences for single gambles. We then compute the preferences that this function implies when the horizon expands to include a portfolio of gambles.

Consider an individual who evaluates outcomes as gains and losses, and who maximizes expected utility in these terms. This decision maker is risk-averse in the domain of gains, risk-seeking in the domain of losses, loss-averse, and her risky choices exhibit perfect proportionality. She is indifferent between a 0.50 chance to win $1,000 and a sure gain of $300 (also between 0.50 chance to win $10,000 and $3,000 for sure) and she is also indif-

---

[4]Two agents that have the same current holdings and face the same series of risky choices do not have the same wealth if they have different attitudes to risk and expect to make different decisions. For formal discussions of choice in the presence of unresolved uncertainty, see Kreps (1988) and Spence and Zeckhauser (1972).

ferent between the status quo and a gamble that offers equal chances to win $250 or to lose $100. The aversion to risk exhibited by this individual is above the median of respondents in laboratory studies, but well within the range of observed values. For the sake of simple exposition we ignore all probability distortions and attribute the risk preferences of the individual entirely to the shape of her utility function for gains and losses. The preferences we have assumed imply that the individual's utility for gains is described by a power function with an exponent of 0.575 and that the function in the domain of losses is the mirror image of the function for gains, after expansion of the X-axis by a factor of 2.5 (Tversky and Kahneman 1991). The illustrative function was chosen to highlight our main conclusion: with proportional risk attitudes, even the most extreme risk aversion on individual problems quickly vanishes when gambles are considered part of a portfolio.

The power utility function is decreasingly risk averse, and the decrease is quite rapid. Thus, a proportionately risk averse individual who values a 0.50 chance to win $100 at $30 will value a gamble that offers equal chances to win either $1,000 or $1,100 at $1,049. This preference is intuitively acceptable, indicating again that the power function is a good description of the utility of outcomes for single gambles considered in isolation. The power function fits the psychophysical relation of subjective magnitude to physical magnitude in many other contexts (Stevens 1975).

To appreciate the effects of even modest aggregation with this utility function, assume that the individual owns three independent gambles:

one gamble with a 0.50 chance to win $500,
two gambles, each with a 0.50 chance to win $250.

Simple arithmetic yields the compound gamble:

0.125 chance to win $1,000, and 0.25 to win $750, $500, and $250.

If this individual applies the correct probabilities to her utility function, this portfolio will be worth $433 to her. This should be her minimum selling price if she owns the gamble, her cash equivalent if she has to choose between the portfolio of gambles and cash. In contrast, the sum of the cash equivalents of the gambles considered one at a time is only $300. The certainly premium the individual would pay has dropped from 40% to 13% of expected value. By the individual's own utility function, the cost of considering these gambles in isolation is 27% of their expected value, surely more than any rational decision maker should be willing to pay for whatever mental economy this isolation achieves.

The power of aggregation to overcome loss aversion is equally impressive. As already noted, our decision maker is indifferent between accepting or rejecting a gamble that offers a 0.50 chance to win $250 and a 0.50 chance to lose $100. However, she would value the opportunity to play two of these gambles at $45, and six gambles at $304. Note that the average incremental value of adding the third to the sixth gamble is $65, quite close to the EV of $75, although each gamble is worth nothing on its own.

Finally, we note that decisions about single gambles will no longer appear risk-proportional when gambles are evaluated in the context of a portfolio, even if the utility function has that property. Suppose the individual now owns a set of eleven gambles:

one gamble with a 0.50 chance to win $1,000,

ten gambles, each with a 0.50 chances to win $100.

The expected value of the set is $1,000. If the gambles were considered one at a time, the sum of their cash equivalents would be only $600. With proper aggregation, however, the selling price for the package should be $934. Now suppose the decision maker considers trading only one of the gambles. After selling a gamble for an amount X, she retains a reduced compound gamble in which the constant X is added to each outcome. The decision maker, of course, will only sell if the value of the new gamble is at least equal to the value of the original portfolio. The computed selling price for the larger gamble is $440, and the selling price for one of the smaller gambles is $49. Note that the premium given up to avoid the risk is 12% of expected value of the large gamble, but only 2% for the small one. A rational decision maker who applies a proportionately risk averse utility function to aggregate outcomes will set cash equivalents closer to risk neutrality for small gambles than for large ones.

As these elementary examples illustrate, the common attitude of strong (and proportional) aversion to risk and to losses entails a risk policy that quickly approaches neutrality as the portfolio is extended.[5] Because possibilities of aggregation over future decisions always exist for an ongoing concern, and because the chances for aggregation are likely to be inversely correlated with the size of the problem, the near-proportionality of risk attitudes for gambles of varying sizes is logically incoherent, and the extreme risk aversion observed for prospects that are small relative to assets is unreasonable. To rationalize observed preferences one must assume that the decision maker approaches each choice problem as if it were her last—there seems to be no relevant tomorrow. It is somewhat surprising that the debate on the rationality of risky decisions has focused almost exclusively on the curiosities of the Allais and Ellsberg paradoxes, instead of on simpler observations, such as the extraordinary myopia implied by extreme and nearly proportional risk aversion.

Risk Taking in Organizations: Implications and Speculations

The preceding sections discussed evidence that people, when faced with explicitly probabilistic prospects in experimental situations, tend to frame their decision problem narrowly, have near-proportional risk attitudes, and are as a consequence excessively risk averse in small decisions, where they ignore the effects of aggregation. Extending these ideas to business decisions is necessarily speculative, because the attitudes to risk that are implicit in such decisions are not easily measured. One way to approach this problem is by asking whether the organizational context in which many business decisions are made is more likely to enhance or to inhibit risk aversion, narrow framing and near-proportionality. We examine this question in the present section.

RISK AVERSION

There is little reason to believe that the factors that produce risk aversion in the personal evaluation of explicit gambles are neutralized in the context of managerial decisions. For example, attempts to measure the utility that executives attach to gains and losses of their firm suggest that the principle of decreasing marginal values applies to these outcomes (MacCrimmon and Wehrung 1986, Swalm 1966). The underweighting of probable gains in

comparisons with sure ones, known as the certainty effect, is also unlikely to vanish in managerial decisions. The experimental evidence indicates that the certainty effect is not eliminated when probabilities are vague or ambiguous, as they are in most real-life situations, and the effect may even be enhanced (Curley et al. 1986, Hogarth and Einhorn 1990). We suspect that the effect may become even stronger when a choice becomes a subject of debate, as is commonly the case in managerial decisions: the rhetoric of prudent decision making favors the certainty effect, because an argument that rests on mere probability is always open to doubt.

Perhaps the most important cause of risk aversion is loss aversion, the discrepancy between the weights that are attached to losses and to gains in evaluating prospects. Loss aversion is not mitigated when decisions are made in an organizational context. On the contrary, the asymmetry between credit and blame may enhance the asymmetry between gains and losses in the decision maker's utilities. The evidence indicates that the pressures of accountability and personal responsibility increase the status quo bias and other manifestations of loss aversion. Decision makers become more risk averse when they expect their choices to be reviewed by others (Tetlock and Boettger 1991) and they are extremely reluctant to accept responsibility for even a small increase in the probability of a disaster (Viscusi et al. 1987). Swalm (1966) noted that managers appear to have an excessive aversion to any outcome that could yield a net loss, citing the example of a manager in a firm described as "an industrial giant," who would decline to pursue a project that has a 50–50 chance of either making for his company a gain of $300,000 or losing $60,000. Swalm hypothesized that the steep slopes of utility functions in the domain of losses may be due to control procedures that bias man-

[5] The conclusions of the present section do not critically depend on the assumption of expected utility theory, that the decision maker weights outcomes by their probabilities. All the calculations reported above were repeated using cumulative prospect theory (Tversky and Kahneman 1992) with plausible parameters ($a = 0.73$; $b = c = 0.6$ and a loss aversion coefficient of 2.5). Because extreme outcomes are assigned greater weight in prospect theory than in the expected utility model, the mitigation of risk aversion as the portfolio expands is somewhat slower. Additionally, the risk seeking that prospect theory predicts for single low-probability positive gambles is replaced by risk aversion for repeated gambles.

agers against choices that might lead to losses. This interpretation seems appropriate since "several respondents stated quite clearly that they were aware that their choices were not in the best interests of the company, but that they felt them to be in their own best interests as aspring executives."

We conclude that the forces that produce risk aversion in experimental studies of individual choice may be even stronger in the managerial context. Note, however, that we do not claim that an objective observer would describe managerial decisions as generally risk averse. The second part of this essay will argue that decisions are often based on optimistic assessments of the chances of success, and are therefore objectively riskier than the decision makers perceive them to be. Our hypothesis about risk in managerial decisions are: (i) in a generally favorable context, the threshold for accepting risk will be high, and acceptable options will be *subjectively* perceived as carrying low risk, (ii) for problems viewed in isolation the willingness to take risks is likely to be approximately constant for decisions that vary greatly in size, and (iii) decisions will be narrowly framed even when they could be viewed as instances of a category of similar decisions. As a consequence, we predict (iv) an imbalance in the risks that the organization accepts in large and in small problems, such that relative risk aversion is lower for the aggregate of small decisions than for the aggregate of large decisions. These hypotheses are restricted to essentially favorable situations, which often yield risk aversion in laboratory studies. We specifically exclude situations in which risk seeking is common, such as choices between essentially negative options, or choices that involve small chances of large gain.

NARROW FRAMING

We have suggested that people tend to make decisions one at a time, and in particular that they are prone to neglect the relevance of future decision opportunities. For both individuals and organizations, the adoption of a broader frame and of a consistent risk policy depends on two conditions: (i) an ability to group together problems that are superficially different; (ii) an appropriate procedure for evaluating outcomes and the quality of performance.

A consistent risk policy can only be maintained if the recurrent problems to which the policy applies are recognized as such. This is sometimes easy: competent organizations will identify obvious recurring, questions—for example, whether or not to purchase insurance for a company vehicle—and will adopt policies for such questions. The task is more complex when each decision problem has many unique features, as might be the case for acquisitions or new product development. The explicit adoption of a broad frame will then require the use of an abstract language that highlights the important common dimensions of diverse decision problems. Formal decision analysis provides such a language, in which outcomes are expressed in money and uncertainty is quantified as probability. Other abstract languages could be used for the same purpose. As practitioners of decision analysis well know, however, the use of an abstract language conflicts with a natural tendency to describe each problem in its own terms. Abstraction necessarily involves a loss of subtlety and specificity, and the summary descriptions that permit projects to be compared almost always appear superficial and inadequate.

From the point of the individual executive who faces a succession of decisions, the maintenance of a broad decision frame also depends on how her performance will be evaluated, and on the frequency of performance reviews. For a schematic illustration, assume that reviews occur at predictable points in the sequence of decisions and outcomes, and that the executive's outcomes are determined by the *value* of the firm's outcomes since the last review. Suppose the evaluation function is identical to the utility function introduced in the preceding numerical examples: the credit for gaining 2.5 units and the blame for losing 1 unit just cancel out. With this utility function, a single gamble that offers equal probabilities to win 2 units or to lose 1 unit will not be acceptable if performance is evaluated on that gamble by itself. The decision will not change even if the manager knows that there will be a second opportunity to play the same gamble. However, if the evaluation of outcomes and the assignment of credit and blame can be deferred until the gamble has been played twice, the probability that the review will be negative drops from 0.50 to 0.25 and the compound gamble will be accepted. As this example illustrates, reducing the frequency of evaluations can mitigate the inhibiting effects of loss aversion on risk taking, as well as other manifestations of myopic discounting.

The attitude that "you win a few and you lose a few" could be recommended as an antidote to narrow framing, because it suggests that the outcomes of a set of separable decisions should be aggregated before evaluation. However, the implied tolerance for "losing a few" may conflict with other managerial imperatives, including the setting of high standards and the maintenance of tight supervision. By the same token, of course, narrow framing and excessive risk aversion may be unintended consequences of excessive insistence on measurable short-term successes. A plausible hypothesis is that the adoption of a broad frame of evaluation is most natural when the expected rate of success is low for each attempt, as in drilling for oil or in pharmaceutical development.[6] The procedures of performance evaluation that have evolved in these industries could provide a useful model for other attempts to maintain consistent risk policies.

NEAR PROPORTIONALITY OF RISK ATTITUDES

Many executives in a hierarchical organization have two distinct decision tasks: they make risky choices on behalf of the organization, and they supervise several subordinates who also make decisions. For analytical purposes, the options chosen by subordinates can be treated as independent (or imperfectly correlated) gambles, which usually involve smaller stakes than the decisions made personally be the superior. A problem of risk aggregation inevitably arises, and we conjecture that solving it efficiently may be quite difficult.

To begin, ignore the supervisory function and assume that all decisions are made independently, with narrow framing. If all decision makers apply the same nearly-proportional risk attitudes (as suggested by Swalm 1966), an unbalanced set of choices will be made: The aggregate of the subordinates' decisions will be more risk averse than the supervisor's own decisions on larger problems—which in turn are more risk averse than her global utility for the portfolio, rationally evaluated. As we saw in an earlier section, the costs of such inconsistencies in risk attitudes can be quite high.

Clearly, one of the goals of the executive should be to avoid the potential inefficiency, by applying a consistent policy to risky choices and to those she supervises—and the consistent policy is *not* one of proportional risk aversion. As was seen earlier, a rational executive who considers, a portfolio consisting of one large gamble (which she chose herself) and ten smaller gambles (presumably chosen by subordinates) should be considerably more risk averse in valuing the large gamble than in valuing any one of the smaller gambles. The counterintuitive implication of this analysis, is that, in a generally favorable context, an executive should encourage subordinates to adopt a higher level of risk-acceptance than the level with which she feels comfortable. This is necessary to overcome the costly effects of the (probable) insensitivity of her intuitive preferences to recurrence and aggregation. We suspect that many executives will resist this recommendation, which contradicts the common belief that accepting risks is both the duty and the prerogative of higher management.

For several reasons, narrow framing and near-proportionality could be difficult to avoid in a hierarchical organization. First, many decisions are both unique and large at the level at which they are initially made. The usual aversion to risk is likely to prevail in such decisions, even if from the point of view of the firm they could be categorized as recurrent and moderately small. Second, it appears unfair for a supervisor to urge acceptance of a risk that a subordinate is inclined to reject—especially because the consequences of failure are likely to be more severe for the subordinate.

In summary, we have drawn on three psychological principles to derive the prediction that the risk attitudes that govern decisions of different sizes may not be conherent. The analysis suggests that there may be too much aversion to risk in problems of small or moderate size. However, the conclusion that greater risk taking should be encouraged could be premature at this point, because of the suspicion that agents' view of prospects may be systematically biased in an optimistic direction. The combination of a risk-netural attitude and an optimistic bias could be worse than the combination of unreasonable risk aversion and unjustified optimism. As the next sections show, there is good reason to believe that such a dilemma indeed exists.

Bold Forecasts

Our review of research on individual risk attitudes suggests that the substantial degree of risk to which

---

[6] We owe this hypothesis to Richard Thaler.

individuals and organizations willingly expose themselves is unlikely to reflect true acceptance of these risks. The alternative is that people and organizations often expose themselves to risk because they misjudge the odds. We next consider some of the mechanisms that produce the 'bold forecasts' that enable cautious decision makers to take large risks.

Inside and Outside Views

We introduce this discussion by a true story, which illustrates an important cognitive quirk that tends to produce extreme optimism in planning.

In 1976 one of us (Daniel Kahneman) was involved in a project designed to develop a curriculum for the study of judgment and decision making under uncertainty for high schools in Israel. The project was conducted by a small team of academics and teachers. When the team had been in operation for about a year, with some significant achievements already to its credit, the discussion at one of the team meetings turned to the question of how long the project would take. To make the debate more useful, I asked everyone to indicate on a slip of paper their best estimate of the number of months that would be needed to bring the project to a well-defined stage of completion: a complete draft ready for submission to the Ministry of Education. The estimates, including my own, ranged from 18 to 30 months. At this point I had the idea of turning to one of our members, a distinguished expert in curriculum development, asking him a question phrased about as follows:

"We are surely not the only team to have tried to develop a curriculum where none existed before. Please try to recall as many such cases as you can. Think of them as they were in a stage comparable to ours at present. How long did it take them, from that point, to complete their projects?" After a long silence, something much like the following answer was given, with obvious signs of discomfort: "First, I should say that not all teams that I can think of in a comparable stage ever did complete their task. About 40% of them eventually gave up. Of the remaining, I cannot think of any that was completed in less than seven years, nor of any that took more than ten". In response to a further question, he answered: "No, I cannot think of any relevant factor that distinguishes us favorably from the teams I have been thinking about. Indeed, my impression is that we are slightly below average in terms of our resources and potential".

This story illustrates several of the themes that will be developed in this section.

Two distinct modes of forecasting were applied to the same problem in this incident. The *inside view* of the problem is the one that all participants in the meeting spontaneously adopted. An inside view forecast is generated by focusing on the case at hand, by considering the plan and the obstacles to its completion, by constructing scenarios of future progress, and by extrapolating current trends. The *outside view* is the one that the curriculum expert was encouraged to adopt. It essentially ignores the details of the case at hand, and involves no attempt at detailed forecasting of the future history of the project. Instead, it focuses on the statistics of a class of cases chosen to be similar in relevant respects to the present one. The case at hand is also compared to other members of the class, in an attempt to assess its position in the distribution of outcomes for the class (Kahneman and Tversky 1979b). The distinction between inside and outside views in forecasting is closely related to the distinction drawn earlier between narrow and broad framing of decision problems. The critical question in both contexts is whether a particular problem of forecast or decision is treated as unique, or as an instance of an ensemble of similar problems.

The application of the outside view was particularly simple in this example, because the relevant class for the problem was easy to find and to define. Other cases are more ambiguous. What class should be considered, for example, when a firm considers the probable costs of an investment in a new technology in an unfamiliar domain? Is it the class of ventures in new technologies in the recent history of this firm, or the class of developments most similar to the proposed one, carried out in other firms? Neither is perfect, and the recommendation would be to try both (Kahneman and Tversky 1979b). It may also be necessary to choose units of measurement that permit comparisons. The ratio of actual spending to planned expenditure is an example of a convenient unit that permits meaningful comparisons across diverse projects.

The inside and outside views draw on different sources of information, and apply different rules to its use. An inside view forecast draws on knowledge of the specifics of the case, the details of the plan that exists, some ideas about likely obstacles and how they might be overcome. In an extreme form, the inside view involves an attempt to sketch a representative scenario that captures the essential elements of the history of the future. In contrast, the outside view is essentially statistical and comparative, and involves no attempt to divine future history at any level of detail.

It should be obvious that when both methods are applied with equal intelligence and skill, the outside view is much more likely to yield a realistic estimate. In general, the future of a long and complex undertaking is simply not foreseeable in detail. The ensemble of possible future histories cannot be defined. Even if this could be done, the ensemble would in most cases be huge, and the probability of any particular scenario negligible.[7] Although some scenarios are more likely or plausible than others, it is a serious error to assume that the outcomes of the most likely scenarios are also the most likely, and that outcomes for which no plausible scenarios come to mind are impossible. In particular, the scenario of flawless execution of the current plan may be much more probable a priori than any scenario for a specific sequence of events that would cause the project to take four times longer than planned. Nevertheless, the less favorable outcome could be more likely overall, because there are so many different ways for things to go wrong. The main advantage of the outside approach to forecasting is that it avoids the snares of scenario thinking (Dawes 1988). The outside view provides some protection against forecasts that are not even in the ballpark of reasonable possibilities. It is a conservative approach, which will fail to predict extreme and exceptional events, but will do well with common ones. Furthermore, giving up the attempt to predict extraordinary events is not a great sacrifice when uncertainty is high, because the only way to score 'hits' on such events is to predict large numbers of other extraordinary events that do not materialize.

This discussion of the statistical merits of the outside view sets the stage for our main observation, which is psychological: the inside view is overwhelmingly preferred in intuitive forecasting. The natural way to think about a problem is to bring to bear all one knows about it, with special attention to its unique features. The intellectual detour into the statistics of related cases is seldom chosen spontaneously. Indeed, the relevance of the outside view is sometimes explicitly denied: physicians and lawyers often argue against the application of statistical reasoning to particular cases. In these instances, the preference for the inside view almost bears a moral character. The inside view is valued as a serious attempt to come to grips with the complexities of the unique case at hand, and the outside view is rejected for relying on crude analogy from superficially similar instances. This attitude can be costly in the coin of predictive accuracy.

Three other features of the curriculum story should be mentioned. First, the example illustrates the general rule that consensus on a forecast is not necessarily an indication of its validity: a shared deficiency of reasoning will also yield consensus. Second, we note that the initial intuitive assessment of our curriculum expert was similar to that of other members of the team. This illustrates a more general observation: statistical knowledge that is known to the forecaster will not necessarily be used, or indeed retrieved, when a forecast is made by the inside approach. The literature on the impact of the base rates of outcomes on intuitive predictions supports this conclusion. Many studies have dealt with the task of predicting the profession or the training of an individual on the basis of some personal information and relevant statistical knowledge. For example, most people have some knowledge of the relative sizes of different departments, and could use that knowledge in guessing the field of a student seen at a graduating ceremony. The experimental evidence indicates that base-rate information that is explicitly mentioned in the problem has some effect on predictions, though usually not as much as it should have (Griffin and Tversky 1992, Lynch and Ofir 1989: for an alternative view see Gigerenzer et al. 1988). When only personal information is explicitly offered, relevant statistical information that is known to the respondent is largely ignored (Kahneman and Tversky 1973, Tversky and Kahneman 1983).

The sequel to the story illustrates a third general observation: facing the facts can be intolerably demoralizing. The participants in the meeting had professional expertise in the logic of forecasting, and none even ventured to question the relevance of the forecast implied by our expert's statistics: an even chance of failure, and a completion time of seven to ten years in case of

---

[7] For the purposes of this exposition we assume that probabilities exist as a fact about the world. Readers who find this position shocking should transpose the formulation to a more complex one, according to their philosophical taste.

success. Neither of these outcomes was an acceptable basis for continuing the project, but no one was willing to draw the embarrassing conclusion that it should be scrapped. So, the forecast was quietly dropped from active debate, along with any pretense of long-term planning, and the project went on along its predictably unforeseeable path to eventual completion some eight years later.

The contrast between the inside and outside views has been confirmed in systematic research. One relevant set of studies was concerned with the phenomenon of overconfidence. There is massive evidence for the conclusion that people are generally overconfident in their assignments of probability to their beliefs. Overconfidence is measured by recording the proportion of cases in which statements to which an individual assigned a probability p were actually true. In many studies this proportion has been found to be far lower than p (see Lichtenstein et al. 1982; for a more recent discussion and some instructive exceptions see Griffin and Tversky 1992). Overconfidence is often assessed by presenting general information questions in a multiple-choice format, where the participant chooses the most likely answer and assigns a probability to it. A typical result is that respondents are only correct on about 80% of cases when they describe themselves as "99% sure." People are overconfident in evaluating the accuracy of their beliefs one at a time. It is interesting, however, that there is no evidence of overconfidence bias when respondents are asked after the session to estimate the number of questions for which they picked the correct answer. These global estimates are accurate, or somewhat pessimistic (Gigerenzer et al. 1991, Griffin and Tversky 1992). It is evident that people's assessments of their overall accuracy does not control their confidence in particular beliefs. Academics are familiar with a related example: finishing our papers almost always takes us longer than we expected. We all know this and often say so. Why then do we continue to make the same error? Here again, the outside view does not inform judgments of particular cases.

In a compelling example of the contrast between inside and outside views, Cooper et al. (1988) interviewed new entrepreneurs about their chances of success, and also elicited from them estimates of the base rate of success for enterprises of the same kind. Self-assessed chances of success were uncorrelated to objective predictors of success such as college education, prior supervisory experience and initial capital. They were also wildly off the mark on average. Over 80% of entrepreneurs perceived their chances of success as 70% or better. Fully one-third of them described their success as certain. On the other hand, the mean chance of success that these entrepreneurs attributed to a business like theirs was 59%. Even this estimate is optimistic, though it is closer to the truth: the five-year survival rate for new firms is around 33% (Dun and Bradstreet 1967).

The inside view does not invariably yield optimistic forecasts. Many parents of rebellious teenagers cannot imagine how their offspring would ever become a reasonable adult, and are consequently more worried than they should be, since they also know that almost all teenagers do eventually grow up. The general point is that the inside view is susceptible to the fallacies of scenario thinking and to anchoring of estimates on present values or on extrapolations of current trends. The inside view burdens the worried parents with statistically unjustified premonitions of doom. To decision makers with a goal and a plan, the same way of thinking offers absurdly optimistic forecasts.

The cognitive mechanism we have discussed is not the only source of optimistic errors. Unrealistic optimism also has deep motivational roots (Tiger 1979). A recent literature review (Taylor and Brown 1988) listed three main forms of a pervasive optimistic bias: (i) unrealistically positive self-evaluations, (ii) unrealistic optimism about future events and plans, and (iii) an illusion of control. Thus, for almost every positive trait—including safe driving, a sense of humor, and managerial risk taking (MacCrimmon and Wehrung 1986)—there is a large majority of individuals who believe themselves to be above the median. People also exaggerate their control over events, and the importance of the skills and resources they possess in ensuring desirable outcomes. Most of us underestimate the likelihood of hazards affecting us personally, and entertain the unlikely belief that Taylor and Brown summarize as "The future will be great, especially for me."

Organizational Optimism

There is no reason to believe that entrepreneurs and executives are immune to optimistic bias. The prevalence of delusions of control among managers has been recognized by many authors (among others, Duhaime and Schwenk 1985, March and Shapira 1987, Salancik and Meindl 1984). As we noted earlier, managers commonly view risk as a challenge to be overcome, and believe that risk can be modified by "managerial wisdom and skill" (Donaldson and Lorsch 1983). The common refusal of managers to refuse risk estimates provided to them as "given" (Shapira 1986) is a clear illustration of illusion of control.

Do organizations provide effective controls against the optimistic bias of individual executives? Are organizational decisions founded on impartial and unbiased forecasts of consequences? In answering these questions, we must again distinguish problems that are treated as recurrent, such as forecasts of the sales of existing product lines, from others that are considered unique. We have no reason to doubt the ability of organizations to impose forecasting discipline and to reduce or eliminate obvious biases in recurrent problems. As in the case of risk, however, all significant forecasting problems have features that make them appear unique. It is in these unique problems that biases of judgment and choice are most likely to have their effects, for organizations as well as for individuals. We next discuss some likely causes of optimistic bias in organizational judgments, some observations of this bias, and the costs and benefits of unrealistic optimism.

CAUSES

Forecasts often develop as part of a case that is made by an individual or group that already has, or is developing a vested interest in the plan, in a context of competition for the control of organizational resources. The debate is often adversarial. The only projects that have a good chance of surviving in this competition are those for which highly favorable outcomes are forecast, and this produces a powerful incentive for would-be promoters to present optimistic numbers. The statistical logic that produces the winner's curse in other contexts (Capen, Clapp and Campbell 1971; Bazerman and Samuelson 1983; Kagel and Levin 1986) applies here as well: the winning project is more likely than others to be associated with optimistic errors (Harrison and March 1984). This is an effect of regression to the mean. Thus, the student who did best in an initial test is also the one for whom the most regression is expected on a

subsequent test. Similarly, the projects that are forecast to have the highest returns are the ones most likely to fall short of expectations.

Officially adopted forecasts are also likely to be biased by their secondary functions as demands, commands and commitments (Lowe and Shaw 1968, Lawler and Rhode 1976, Lawler 1986, Larkey and Smith 1984). A forecast readily becomes a target, which induces loss aversion for performance that does not match expectations, and can also induce satisficing indolence when the target is exceeded. The obvious advantages of setting high goals is an incentive for higher management to adopt and disseminate optimistic assessments of future accomplishments—and possibly to deceive themselves in the process.

In his analysis of "groupthink," Janis (1982) identified other factors that favor organizational optimism. Pessimism about what the organization can do is readily interpreted as disloyalty, and consistent bearers of bad news tend to be shunned. Bad news can be demoralizing. When pessimistic opinions are suppressed in this manner, exchanges of views will fail to perform a critical function. The optimistic biases of individual group members can become mutually reinforcing, as unrealistic views are validated by group approval.

The conclusion of this sketchy analysis is that there is little reason to believe organizations will avoid the optimistic bias—except perhaps when the problems are considered recurrent and subjected to statistical quality control. On the contrary, there are reasons to suspect that many significant decisions made in organizations are guided by unrealistic forecasts of their consequences.

OBSERVATIONS

The optimistic bias of capital investment projects is a familiar fact of life: the typical project finishes late, comes in over budget when it is finally completed, and fails to achieve its initial goals. Grossly optimistic errors appear to be especially likely if the project involves new technology or otherwise places the firm in unfamiliar territory. A Rand Corporation study on pioneer process plants in the energy field demonstrates the magnitude of the problem (Merrow et al. 1981). Almost all project construction costs exceeded initial estimates by over 20%. The norm was for actual construction costs to more than double first estimates. These conclusions are corroborated by

PIMS data on start-up ventures in a wide range of industries (cited by Davis 1985). More than 80% of the projects studied fell short of planned market share.

In an interesting discussion of the causes of failure in capital investment projects, Arnold (1986) states:

> Most companies support large capital expenditure programs with a worst case analysis that examines the projects' loss potential. But the worst case forecast is almost always too optimistic. . . . When managers look at the downside they generally describe a mildly pessimistic future rather than the worst possible future.

As an antidote against rosy predictions Arnold recommends staying power analysis, a method used by lenders to determine if organizations under severe strain can make payments. In effect, the advice is for managers to adopt an outside view of their own problem.

Mergers and acquisitions provide another illustration of optimism and of illusions of control. On average, bidding firms do not make a significantly positive return. This striking observation raises the question of why so many takeovers and mergers are initiated. Roll (1986) offers a "hubris hypothesis" to explain why decision makers acquiring firms tend to pay too much for their targets. Roll cites optimistic estimates of "economies due to synergy and (any) assessments of weak management" as the primary causes of managerial hubris. The bidding firms are prone to overestimate the control they will have over the merged organization, and to underestimate the "weak" managers who are currently in charge.

COSTS AND BENEFITS

Optimism and the illusion of control increase risk taking in several ways. In a discussion of the Challenger disaster, Landau and Chisholm (1990) introduced a "law of increasing optimism" as a form of Russian roulette. Drawing on the same case, Starbuck and Milliken (1988) noted how quickly vigilance dissipates with repeated successes. Optimism in a competitive context may take the form of contempt for the capabilities of opponents (Roll 1986). In a bargaining situation, it will support a hard line that raises the risk of conflict. Neale and Bazerman (1983) observed a related effect in a final-offer arbitration setup, where the arbiter is constrained to choose between the final offers made by the contestants. The participants were asked to state their subjective probability that the final offer they presented would be preferred by the arbiter. The average of these probabilities was approximately 0.70; with a less sanguine view of the strength of their case the contestants would surely have made more concessions. In the context of capital investment decisions, optimism and the illusion of control manifest themselves in unrealistic forecasts and unrealizable plans (Arnold 1986).

Given the high cost of mistakes, it might appear obvious that a rational organization should want to base its decisions on unbiased odds, rather than on predictions painted in shades of rose. However, realism has its costs. In their review of the consequences of optimism and pessimism, Taylor and Brown (1988) reached the deeply disturbing conclusion that optimistic self-delusion is both a diagnostic indication of mental health and well-being, and a positive causal factor that contributes to successful coping with the challenges of life. The benefits of unrealistic optimism in increasing persistence in the face of difficulty have been documented by other investigators (Seligman 1991).

The observation that realism can be pathological and self-defeating raises troubling questions for the management of information and risk in organizations. Surely, no one would want to be governed entirely by wishful fantasies, but is there a point at which truth becomes destructive and doubt self-fulfilling? Should executives allow or even encourage unrealistic optimism among their subordinates? Should they willingly allow themselves to be caught up in productive enthusiasm, and to ignore discouraging portents? Should there be someone in the organization whose function it is to achieve forecasts free of optimistic bias, although such forecasts, if disseminated, would be demoralizing?

Should the organization maintain two sets of forecasting books (as some do, see Bromiley 1986)? Some authors in the field of strategy have questioned the value of realism, at least implicitly. Weick's famous story of the lost platoon that finds its way in the Alps by consulting a map of the Pyrenees indicates more respect for confidence and morale than for realistic appraisal. On the other hand, Landau and Chisholm (1990) pour withering scorn on the "arrogance of optimism" in organizations, and recommend a pessimistic failure-avoiding management strategy to control risk. Before further progress can be made on this difficult issue, it is important to recognize the existence of a genuine dilemma that will not yield to any simple rule

Concluding Remarks

Our analysis has suggested that many failures originate in the highly optimistic judgments of risks and opportunities that we label bold forecasts. In the words of March and Shapira (1987), "managers accept risks, in part, because they do not expect that they will have to bear them." March and Shapira emphasized the role of illusions of control in this bias. We have focused on another mechanism—the adoption of an inside view of problems, which leads to anchoring on plans and on the most available scenarios. We suggest that errors of intuitive predication can sometimes be reduced by adopting an outside view, which forecasts the outcome without attempting to forecast its history (Kahneman and Tversky 1979b). This analysis identifies the strong intuitive preference for the inside view as a source of difficulties that are both grave and avoidable.

On the issue of risk we presented evidence that decision makers tend to deal with choices one at a time, and that their attitudes to risk exhibit risk-aversion and near-proportionality. The reluctance to take explicit responsibility for possible losses is powerful, and can be very costly in the aggregate (for a discussion of its social costs see Wildavsky 1988). We claimed further that when the stakes are small or moderate relative to assets the aversion to risk is incoherent and substantively unjustified. Here again, the preference for treating decision problems as unique causes errors that could be avoided by a broader view.

Our analysis implies that the adoption of an outside view, in which the problem at hand is treated as an instance of a broader category, will generally reduce the optimistic bias and may facilitate the application of a consistent risk policy. This happens as a matter of course in problems of forecasting or decision that the organization recognizes as obviously recurrent or repetitive. However, we have suggested that people are strongly biased in favor of the inside view, and that they will normally treat significant decision problems as unique even when information that could support an outside view is available. The adoption of an outside view in such cases violates strong intuitions about the relevance of information. Indeed, the deliberate neglect of the features that make the current problem unique can appear irresponsible. A deliberate effort will therefore be required to foster the optimal use of outside and inside views in forecasting, and the maintenance of globally consistent risk attitudes in distributed decision systems.

Bold forecasts and timid attitudes to risk tend to have opposite effects. It would be fortunate if they canceled out precisely to yield optimal behavior in every situation, but there is little reason to expect such a perfect outcome. The conjunction of biases is less disastrous than either one would have been on its own, but there ought to be a better way to control choice under risk than pitting two mistakes against each other. The prescriptive implications of the relation between the biases in forecast and in risk taking is that corrective attempts should deal with these biases simultaneously. Increasing risk taking could easily go too far in the presence of optimistic forecasts, and a successful effort to improve the realism of assessments could do more harm than good in an organization that relies on unfounded optimism to ward off paralysis.[8]

REFERENCES

Arnold, J. III, "Assessing Capital Risk: You Can't Be Too Conservative," *Harvard Bus. Rev.,* 64 (1986), 113–121.

Bateman, T. S. and C. T. Zeithaml, "The Psychological Context of Strategic Decisions: A Model and Convergent Experimental Findings," *Strategic Management J.,* 10 (1989), 59–74.

Bazerman, M. H. and W. F. Samuelson, "I Won the Auction but Don't Want the Price," *J. Financial Econ.,* 27 (1983), 618–634.

Bowman, E., "Risk Seeking by Troubled Firms," *Sloan Management Rev.,* 23 (1982), 33–42.

Bromiley, P., *Corporate Capital Investment: A Behavioral*

---

[8] An earlier version of this paper was presented at a conference on Fundamental Issues in Strategy, held at Silverado, CA, in November 1990. The preparation of this article was supported by the Center for Management Research at the University of California, Berkeley, by the Russell Sage Foundation, and by grants from the Sloan Foundation and from AFOSR, under grant number 88–0206. The ideas presented here developed over years of collaboration with Amos Tversky, but he should not be held responsible for our errors. We thank Philip Bromiley, Colin Camerer, George Loewenstein, Richard Thaler, and Amos Tversky for their many helpful comments.

Approach, Cambridge University Press, New York, 1986.

Capen, E. C., R. V. Clapp and W. M. Campbell, "Competitive Bidding in High-Risk Situations," *J. Petroleum Technology*, 23 (1971), 641–653.

Cooper, A., C. Woo and W. Dunkelberg, "Entrepreneurs' Perceived Chances for Success," *J. Business Venturing*, 3 (1988), 97–108.

Curley, S. P., F. J. Yates and R. A. Abrams, "Psychological Sources of Ambiguity Avoidance," *Org. Behavior and Human Decision Processes*, 38 (1986), 230–256.

Davis, D., "New Projects: Beware of False Economies," *Harvard Bus. Rev.*, 63 (1985), 95–101.

Dawes, R. M., *Rational Choice in an Uncertain World*, Harcourt Brace Jovanovich, Orlando, FL, 1988.

Donaldson, G. and J. Lorsch, *Decision Making at the Top*, Basic Books, New York, 1983.

Duhaime, I. and C. Schwenk, "Conjectures on Cognitive Simplification in Acquisition and Divestment Decision Making," *Academy of Management Rev.*, 10 (1985), 287–295.

Dun and Bradstreet, *Patterns of Success in Managing a Business*, Dun and Bradstreet, New York, 1967.

Fiegenbaum, A., "Prospect Theory and the Risk-Return Association," *J. Econ. Behavior and Organization*, 14 (1990), 187–203.

——— and H. Thomas, "Attitudes Toward Risk and the Risk Return Paradox: Prospect Theory Explanations," *Academy of Management J.*, 31 (1988), 85–106.

Fishburn, P. C. and G. A. Kochenberger, "Two-Piece von Neumann-Morgenstern Utility Functions, *Decision Sci.*, 10 (1979), 503–518.

Gigerenzer, G., U. Hoffrage and H. Kleinbölting, "Probabilistic Mental Models" A Brunswikian Theory of Confidence," *Psychological Rev.*, 98 (1991), 506–528.

———, W. Hell and H. Blank, "Presentation and Content," *J. Experimental Psychology: Human Perception and Performance*, 14 (1988), 513–525.

Griffin, D. and H. Tversky, "The Weighting of Evidence and the Determinants of Confidence," *Cognitive Psychology*, 24 (1992), 411–435.

Harrison, J. R. and J. G. March, "Decision Making and Post-Decision Surprises," *Admin. Sci. Quarterly*, 29 (1984), 26–42.

Hogarth, R. M. and H. J. Einhorn, "Venture Theory: A Model of Decision Weights," *Management Sci.*, 36 (1990), 780–803.

Janis, I. L., *Groupthink* (2nd Ed.), Houghton-Mifflin, Boston, MA, 1982.

Kagel, J. H. and D. Levin, "The Winner's Curse and Public Information in Common Value Auctions," *American Econ, Rev.*, 76 (1986), 894–920.

Kahneman, D., J. L. Knetsch and R. H. Thaler, "The Endowment Effect, Loss Aversion, and Status Quo Bias," *J. Econ. Perspectives*, 5 (1991), 193–206.

——— and A. Tversky, "On the Psychology of Prediction," *Psychological Rev.*, 80 (1973), 237–251.

——— and ———, "Prospect Theory: An Analysis of Decision Under Risk," *Econometrica*, 47 (1979a), 263–290.

——— and ———, "Intuitive Prediction: Biases and Corrective Procedures," *Management Sci.*, 12 (1979b), 313–327.

Keeney, R. and A. Raiffa, *Decisions with Multiple Objectives: Preference and Value Tradeoffs*, Wiley, New York, 1976.

Kreps, D. M., "Static Choice in the Presence of Unforseen Contingencies," Working Paper: Stanford Graduate School of Business, Stanford, CA. 1988.

Landau, M. and D. Chisholm, "Fault Analysis, Professional Football, and the Arrogance of Optimism: An Essay on the Methodology of Administration," Working Paper: Univ. of California, 1990.

Larkey, P. and R. Smith, Eds., "Misrepresentation in Government Budgeting," *Advances in Information Processing in Organizations*, JAI Press, Greenwich, CT, 1984, 68–92.

Laughhunn, D., J. Payne and R. Crum, "Managerial Risk Preferences for Below-Target Returns," *Management Sci.*, 26 (1980), 1238–1249.

Lawler, E., "Control Systems in Organizations," *Handbook of Industrial and Organizational Psychology*, Rand-McNally, Chicago, IL, 1986, 1247–1291.

——— and J. Rhode, *Information and Control in Organizations*, Goodyear, Pacific Palisades, CA, 1976.

Lichtenstein, S., B. Fischhoff and L. D. Phillips, "Calibration of Probabilities: The State of the Art to 1980," in D. Kahneman, T. Slovic and A. Tversky (Eds.), *Judgement under Uncertainty: Heuristics and Biases*, Cambridge Univ. Press, New York, 1982, 306–334.

Lopes, L., "Decision Making in the Short Run," *J. Experimental Psychology: Human Learning and Memory*, 7 (1981), 377–385.

Lowe, E. and R. Shaw, "An Analysis of Managerial Biasing: Evidence From a Company's Budgeting Process," *J. Management Studies*, 5 (1968), 304–315.

Lynch, J. G. and C. Ofir, "Effects of Cue Consistency and Value on Base-Rate Utilization," *J. Personality and Social Psychology*, 56 (1989), 170–181.

MacCrimmon, K. and D. Wehrung, *Taking Risks*, Free Press, New York, 1986.

March, J. and Z. Shapira, "Managerial Perspectives on Risk and Risk Taking," *Management Sci.*, 33 (1987), 1404–1418.

Merrow, E., K. Phillips and C. Myers, *Understanding Cost Growth and Performance Shortfalls in Pioneer Process Plants*, Rand Corporation, Santa Barbara, CA, 1981.

Neale, M. and M. Bazerman, "The Effects of Perspective-taking Ability under Alternate Forms of Arbitration on the Negotiation Process," *Industrial and Labor Relations Review*, 36 (1983), 378–388.

Redelmeier, D. A. and A. Tversky, "On the Framing of Multiple Prospects," *Psychological Sci.*, 3 (1992), 191–193.

Roll, L., "The Hubris Hypothesis of Corporate Takeovers," *J. Business*, 59 (1986), 197–218.

Ruefli, T. W., "Mean-Variance Approaches to Risk-Return Relationships in Strategy: Paradox Lost," *Management Sci.*, 36 (1990), 368–380.

Salancik, G. R. and J. R. Meindl, "Corporate Attributions as Strategic Illusions of Management Control," *Admin. Sci. Quarterly*, 29 (1984), 238–254.

Samuelson, P. A., "Risk and Uncertainty: A Fallacy of Large Numbers," *Scientia*, 98 (1963), 108–113.

Samuelson, W. and R. Zeckhauser, "Status Quo Bias in Decision Making," *J. Risk and Uncertainty*, 1 (1988), 7–59.

Seligman, M. E. P., *Learned Optimism*, Alfred A. Knopf, New York, 1991.

Shapira, Z., "Risk in Managerial Decision Making," Working Paper: Hebrew Univ. School of Business Administration, 1986.

Spence, M. and R. Zeckhauser, "The Effect of the Timing of Consumption Decisions and the Resolution of Lotteries on the Choice of Lotteries," *Econometrica*, 40 (1972), 401–403.

Starbuck, W. and F. Milliken, "Challenger: Fine-Tuning the Odds Until Something Breaks," *J. Management Studies*, 25 (1988), 319–340.

Staw, B. and J. Ross, "Understanding Behavior in Escalation Situations," *Science*, 246 (1989), 216–220.

Stevens, S. S., *Psychophysics*, John Wiley and Sons, New York, 1975.

Swalm, R. O., "Utility Theory: Insights into Risk Taking," *Harvard Bus. Rev.*, 44 (1966), 123–136.

Taylor, S. E. and J. D. Brown, "Illusion and Well-Being: A Social Psychological Perspective on Mental Health," *Psychological Bull.*, 103 (1988), 193–210.

Tetlock, P. E. and R. Boettger, "Accountability Amplifies the Status Quo Effect When Change Creates Victims," Working Paper: University of California at Berkeley, Berkeley, CA, 1992.

Tiger, L., *Optimism: The Biology of Hope*, Simon and Schuster, New York, 1979.

Tversky, A. and M. Bar-Hillel, "Risk: The Long and the Short," *J. Experimental Psychology: Learning, Memory, and Cognition*, 9 (1983), 713–717.

—— and D. Kahneman, "Extensional Verses Intuitive Reasoning: The Conjunction Fallacy in Probability Judgment, *Psychological Review*, 90 (1983), 293–315.

—— and ——, "Rational Choice and the Framing of Decisions," *J. Business*, 59 (1986), S251–S278.

—— and ——, "Reference Theory of Choice and Exchange," *Quart. J. Economics*, (1991), 1039–1061.

—— and ——, "Advances in Prospect Theory: Cumulative Representation of Uncertainty," *J. Risk and Uncertainty*, 5 (1992), 297–323.

Viscusi, K., W. Magat and J. Huber, "An Investigation of the Rationality of Consumer Valuations of Multiple Health Risks," *Rand J. Economics*, 18 (1987), 465–479.

Wehrung, D. A., "Risk Taking Over Gains and Losses: A Study of Oil Executives," *Ann. Oper. Res.*, 19 (1989), 115–139.

Wildavsky, A., *Searching for Safety*, Transaction Books, New Brunswick, 1988.

The Robust Beauty of Improper Linear Models in Decision Making

Robyn M. Dawes

Paul Meehl's (1954) book *Clinical Versus Statistical Prediction: A Theoretical Analysis and a Review of the Evidence* appeared 25 years ago. It reviewed studies indicating that the prediction of numerical criterion variables of psychological interest (e.g., faculty ratings of graduate students who had just obtained a Ph.D.) from numerical predictor variables (e.g., scores on the Graduate Record Examination, grade point averages, ratings of letters of recommendation) is better done by a proper linear model than by the clinical intuition of people presumably skilled in such prediction. The point of this article is to review evidence that even improper linear models may be superior to clinical predictions.

A *proper linear model* is one in which the weights given to the predictor variables are chosen in such a way as to optimize the relationship between the prediction and the criterion. "Simple regression analysis is the most common example of a proper linear model; the predictor variables are weighted in such a way as to maximize the correlation between the subsequent weighted composite and the actual criterion. Discriminant function analysis is another example of a proper linear model; weights are given to the predictor variables in such a way that the resulting linear composites maximize the discrepancy between two or more groups. Ridge regression analysis, another example (Darlington, 1978; Marquardt & Snee, 1975), attempts to assign weights in such a way that the linear composites correlate maximally with the criterion of interest in a new set of data.

Thus, there are many types of proper linear models and they have been used in a variety of contexts. One example (Dawes, 1971) involved the prediction of faculty ratings of graduate students. All graduate students at the University of Oregon's Psychology Department who had been admitted between the fall of 1964 and the fall of 1967— and who had not dropped out of the program for nonacademic reasons (e.g., psychosis or marriage) —were rated by the faculty in the spring of 1969; faculty members rated only students whom they felt comfortable rating. The following rating scale was used: 5, outstanding; 4, above average; 3, average; 2, below average; 1, dropped out of the program in academic difficulty. Such overall ratings constitute a psychologically interesting criterion because the subjective impressions of faculty members are the main determinants of the job (if any) a student obtains after leaving graduate school. A total of 111 students were in the sample; the number of faculty members rating each of these students ranged from 1 to 20, with the mean number being 5.67 and the median being 5. The ratings were reliable. (To determine the reliability, the ratings were subjected to a one-way analysis of variance in which each student being rated was regarded as a treatment. The resulting between-treatments variance ratio (n^2) was .67, and it was significant beyond the .001 level.) These faculty ratings were predicted from a proper linear model based on the student's Graduate Record Examination (GRE) score, the student's undergraduate grade point average (GPA), and a measure of the selectivity of the student's undergraduate institution.[1] The cross-validated multiple correlation between the faculty ratings and predictor variables was .38. Congruent with Meehl's results, the correlation of these latter faculty ratings with the average rating of the people on the admissions committee who selected the students was .19,[2] that is, it accounted for one fourth as much variance. This example is typical of those found in psychological research in this area in that (a) the correlation with the model's predictions is higher than the correlation with clinical prediction, but (b) both correlations are low. These characteristics often lead psychologists to interpret the findings as meaning that while the low correlation of the model indicates that linear modeling is deficient as a method, the even lower correlation of the judges indicates only that the wrong judges were used.

An *improper linear model* is one in which the weights are chosen by some nonoptimal method. They may be chosen to be equal, they may be chosen on the basis of the intuition of the person making the prediction, or they may be chosen at random. Nevertheless, improper models may have great utility. When, for example, the standardized GREs, GPAs, and selectivity indices in the previous example were weighted equally, the resulting linear composite correlated .48 with later faculty rating. Not only is the correlation of this linear composite higher than that with the clinical judgment of the admissions committee (.19), it is also higher than that obtained upon cross-validating the weights obtained from half the sample.

An example of an improper model that might be of somewhat more interest—at least to the general public—was motivated by a physician who was on a panel with me concerning predictive systems. Afterward, at the bar with his wife and me, he said that my paper might be of some interest to my colleagues, but success in graduate school in psychology was not of much general interest: "Could you, for example, use one of your improper linear models to predict how well my wife and I get along together?" he asked. I realized that I could—or might. At that time, the Psychology Department at the University of Oregon was engaged in sex research, most of which was

behavioristically oriented. So the subjects of this research monitored when they made love, when they had fights, when they had social engagements (e.g., with in-laws), and so on. These subjects also made subjective ratings about how happy they were in their marital or coupled situation. I immediately thought of an improper linear model to predict self-ratings of marital happiness: rate of lovemaking minus rate of fighting. My colleague John Howard had collected just such data on couples when he was an undergraduate at the University of Missouri–Kansas City, where he worked with Alexander (1971). After establishing the intercouple reliability of judgments of lovemaking and fighting, Alexander had one partner from each of 42 couples monitor these events. She allowed us to analyze her data, with the following results: "In the thirty happily married couples (as reported by the monitoring partner) only two argued more often than they had intercourse. All twelve of the unhappily married couples argued more often" (Howard & Dawes, 1976, p. 478). We then replicated this finding at the University of Oregon, where 27 monitors rated happiness on a 7-point scale, from "very unhappy" to "very happy," with a neutral midpoint. The correlation of rate of lovemaking minus rate of arguments with these ratings of marital happiness was .40 ($p < .05$); neither variable alone was significant. The findings were replicated in Missouri by Edwards and Edwards (1977) and in Texas by Thornton (1977a), who found a correlation of .81 ($p < .01$) between the sex-argument difference and self-rating of marital happiness among 28 new couples. (The reason for this much higher correlation might be that Thornton obtained the ratings of marital happiness after, rather than before, the subjects monitored their lovemaking and fighting; in fact, one subject decided to get a divorce after realizing that she was fighting more than loving; Thornton 1977b.) The conclusion is that if we love more than we hate, we are happy; if we hate more than we love, we are miserable. This conclusion is not

---

[1] This index was based on Cass and Birnbaum's (1968) rating of selectivity given at the end of their book *Comparative Guide to American Colleges.* The verbal categories of selectivity were given numerical values according to the following rule: most selective, 6; highly selective, 5; very selective (+), 4; very selective, 3; selective, 2; not mentioned, 1.

[2] Unfortunately, only 23 of the 111 students could be used in this comparison because the rating scale the admissions committee used changed slightly from year to year.

very profound, psychologically or statistically. The point is that this very curde improper linear model predicts a very important variable: judgments about marital happiness.

The bulk (in fact, all) of the literature since the publication of Meehl's (1954) book supports his generalization about proper models versus intuitive clinical judgment. Sawyer (1966) reviewed a plethora of these studies, and some of these studies were quite extensive (cf. L.R. Goldberg, 1965). Some 10 years after his book was published, Meehl (1965) was able to conclude, however, that there was only a single example showing clinical judgment to be superior, and this conclusion was immediately disputed by L.R. Goldberg (1968a) on the grounds that even the one example did not show such superiority. Holt (1970) criticized details of several studies, and he even suggested that prediction as opposed to understanding may not be a very important part of clinical judgment. But a search of the literature fails to reveal any studies in which clinical judgment has been shown to be superior to statistical prediction when both are based on the same codable input variables. And though most nonpositivists would agree that understanding is not synonymous with prediction, few would agree that it doesn't entail some ability to predict.

Why? Because people—especially the experts in a field—are much better at selecting and coding information than they are at integrating it.

But people *are* important. The statistical model may integrate the information in an optimal manner, but it is always the individual (judge, clinician, subject) who chooses variables. Moreover, it is the human judge who knows the directional relationship between the predictor variables and the criterion of interest or who can code the variables in such a way that they have clear directional relationships. And it is in precisely the situation where the predictor variables are good and where they have a conditionally monotone relationship with the criterion that proper linear models work well.[3]

The linear model cannot replace the expert in deciding such things as "what to look for," but it is precisely this knowledge of what to look for in reaching the decision that is the special expertise people have. Even in as complicated a judgment as making a chess move. It is the ability to code the board in an appropriate way to "see" the proper moves that distinguishes the grand master from the expert from the novice (deGroot, 1965; Simon

& Chase, 1973). It is not in the ability to integrate information that people excell (Slovic, 1972b). Again, the chess grand master considers no more moves than does the expert; he just knows which ones to look at. The distinction between knowing what to look for and the ability to integrate information is perhaps best illustrated in a study by Einhorn (1972). Expert doctors coded biopsies of patients with Hodgkin's disease and then made an overall rating of the severity of the process. The overall rating did not predict survival time of the 193 patients, all of whom died. (The correlations of rating with survival time were all virtually 0, some in the wrong direction.) The variables that the doctors coded did, however, predict survival time when they were used in a multiple regression model.

In summary, proper linear models work for a very simple reason. People are good at picking out the right predictor variables and at coding them in such a way that they have a conditionally monotone relationship with the criterion. People are bad at integrating information from diverse and incomparable sources. Proper linear models are good at such integration when the predictions have a conditionally monotone relationship to the criterion.

Consider, for example, the problem of comparing one graduate applicant with GRE scores of 750 and an undergraduate GPA of 3.3 with another with GRE scores of 680 and an undergraduate GPA of 3.7. Most judges would agree that these indicators of aptitude and previous accomplishment should be combined in some compensatory fashion, but the question is how to compensate. Many judges attempting this feat have little knowledge of the distributional characteristics of GREs and GPAs, and most have no knowledge of studies indicating their validity as predictors of graduate

---

[3] Relationships are conditionally monotone when variables can be scaled in such a way that higher values on each predict higher values on the criterion. This condition is the combination of two more fundamental measurement conditions: (a) independence (the relationship between each variable and the criterion is independent of the values on the remaining variables) and (b) monotonicity (the ordinal relationship is one that is monotone). (See Krantz, 1972; Krantz. et al., 1971.) The true relationships need not be linear for linear models to work; they must merely be approximated by linear models. It is not true that "In order to compute a correlation coefficient between two variables the relationship between them must be linear" (advice found in one introductory statistics text). In the first place, it is always possible to compute something.

success. Moreover, these numbers are inherently incomparable without such knowledge, GREs running from 500 to 800 for viable applicants, and GPAs from 3.0 to 4.0. Is it any wonder that a statistical weighting scheme does better than a human judge in these circumstances?

Suppose now that it is not possible to construct a proper linear model in some situation. One reason we may not be able to do so is that our sample size is inadequate. In multiple regression, for example, b weights are notoriously unstable; the ratio of observations to predictors should be as high as 15 or 20 to 1 before *b* weights, which are the optimal weights, do better on cross-validation than do simple unit weights. Schmidt (1971), L.R. Goldberg (1972), and Claudy (1972) have demonstrated this need empirically through computer simulation, and Einhorn and Hogarth (1975) and Srinivisan (1977) have attacked the problem analytically. The general solution depends on a number of parameters such as the multiple correlation in the population and the covariance pattern between predictor variables. But the applied implication is clear. Standard regression analysis cannot be used in situations where there is not a "decent" ratio of observations to predictors.

Another situation in which proper linear models cannot be used is that in which there are no measurable criterion variables. We might, nevertheless, have some idea about what the important predictor variables would be and the direction they would bear to the criterion *if* we were able to measure the criterion. For example, when deciding which students to admit to graduate school, we would like to predict some future long-term variable that might be termed "professional self-actualization." We have some idea what we mean by this concept, but no good, precise definition as yet. (Even if we had one, it would be impossible to conduct the study using records from current students, because that variable could not be assessed until at least 20 years after the students had completed their doctoral work.) We do, however, know that in all probability this criterion is positively related to intelligence, to past accomplishments, and to ability to snow one's colleagues. In our applicant's files, GRE scores assess the first variable; undergraduate GPA, the second; and letters of recommendation, the third. Might we not, then, wish to form some sort of linear combination of these variables in order to assess our applicants' potentials? Given that we cannot perform a standard regression analysis, is there nothing to do other than fall back on unaided intuitive integration of these variables when we assess our applicants?

One possible way of building an improper linear model is through the use of *bootstrapping* (Dawes & Corrigan, 1974; L.R. Goldberg, 1970). The process is to build a proper linear model of an expert's judgments about an outcome criterion and then to use that linear model in place of the judge. That such linear models can be accurate in predicting experts' judgments has been pointed out in the psychological literature by Hammond (1955) and Hoffman (1960). (This work was anticipated by 32 years by the late Henry Wallace, Vice-President under Roosevelt, in a 1923 agricultural article suggesting the use of linear models to analyze "what is on the corn judge's mind.") In his influential article, Hoffman termed the use of linear models a *paramorphic* representation of judges, by which he meant that the judges' psychological processes did not involve computing an implicit or explicit weighted average of input variables, but that it could be simulated by such a weighting. Paramorphic representations have been extremely successful (for reviews see Dawes & Corrigan, 1974; Slovic & Lichtenstein, 1971) in contexts in which predictor variables have conditionally monotone relationships to criterion variables.

The bootstrapping models make use of the weights derived from the judges; because these weights are not derived from the relationship between the predictor and criterion variables themselves, the resulting linear models are improper. Yet these paramorphic representations consistently do better than the judges from which they are derived (at least when the evaluation of goodness is in terms of the correlation between predicted and actual values).

Bootstrapping has turned out to be pervasive. For example, in a study conducted by Wiggins and Kohen (1971), psychology graduate students at the University of Illinois were presented with 10 background, aptitude, and personality measures describing other (real) Illinois graduate students in psychology and were asked to predict these students' first-year graduate GPAs. Linear models of every one of the University of Illinois judges did a better job than did the judges themselves in predicting actual grade point averages. This result was replicated in a study conducted in conjunction with Wiggins, Gregory, and Diller (cited in Dawes &

Corrigan, 1974). L.R. Goldberg (1970) demonstrated it for 26 of 29 clinical psychology judges predicting psychiatric diagnosis of neurosis or psychosis from Minnesola Multiphasic Personality Inventory (MMPI) profiles, and Dawes (1971) found it in the evaluation of graduate applicants at the University of Oregon. The one published exception to the success of bootstrapping of which I am aware was a study conducted by Libby (1976). He asked 16 loan officers from relatively small banks (located in Champaign–Urbana, Illinois, with assets between $3 million and $56 million) and 27 loan officers from large banks (located in Philadelphia, with assets between $.6 billion and $4.4 billion) to judge which 30 of 60 firms would go bankrupt within three years after their financial statements. The loan officers requested five financial ratios on which to base their judgments (e.g., the ratio of present assets to total assets). On the average, the loan officers correctly categorized 44.4 businesses (74%) as either solvent or future bankruptcies, but on the average, the paramorphic representations of the loan officers could correctly classify only 43.3 (72%). This difference turned out to be statistically significant, and Libby concluded that he had an example of a situation where bootstrapping did not work – perhaps because his judges were highly skilled experts attempting to predict a highly reliable criterion. L.R. Goldberg (1976), however, noted that many of the ratios had highly skewed distributions, and he reanalyzed Libby's data, normalizing the ratios before building models of the loan officers. Libby found 77% of his officers to be superior to their paramorphic representations, but Goldberg, using his rescaled predictor variables, found the opposite; 72% of the models were superior to the judges from whom they were derived.[4]

Why does bootstrapping work? Bowman (1963), L.R. Goldberg (1970), and Dawes (1971) all maintained that its success arises from the fact that a linear model distills underlying policy (in the implicit weights) from otherwise variable behavior (e.g., judgments affected by context effects or extraneous variables).

Belief in the efficacy of bootstrapping was based on the composition of the validity of the linear model of the judge with the validity of his or her judgments themselves. This is only one of two logically possible comparisons. The other is the validity of the linear model of the judge versus the validity of linear models in general; that is, to demonstrate that bootstrapping works because the linear model catches the essence of the judge's valid expertise while eliminating unreliability, it is necessary to demonstrate that the weights obtained from an analysis of the judge's behavior are superior to those that might be obtained in other ways, for example, randomly. Because both the model of the judge and the model obtained randomly are perfectly reliable, a comparison of the random model with the judge's model permits an evaluation of the judge's underlying linear representation, or *policy*. If the random model does equally well, the judge would not be "following valid principles but following them poorly" (Dawes, 1971, p. 182), at least not principles any more valid than any others that weight variables in the appropriate direction.

Table 1 presents five studies summarized by Dawes and Corrigan (1974) in which validities (i.e., correlations) obtained by various methods were compared. In the first study, a pool of 861 psychiatric patients took the MMPI in various hospitals; they were later categorized as neurotic or psychotic on the basis of more extensive information. The MMPI profiles consist of 11 scores, each of which represents the degree to which the respondent answers questions in a manner similar to patients suffering from a well-defined form of psychopathology. A set of 11 scores is thus associated with each patient, and the problem is to predict whether a later diagnosis will be psychosis (coded 1) or neurosis (coded 0). Twenty-nine clinical psychologists "of varying experience and training" (L.R. Goldberg, 1970, p. 425) were asked to make this prediction on an 11-step forced-normal distribution. The second two studies concerned 90 first-year graduate students in the Psychology Department of the University of Illinois who were elevated on 10 variables that are predictive of academic success. These variables included aptitude test scores, college GPA, various peer ratings (e.g., extraversion), and various self-ratings (e.g., conscientiousness). A first-year GPA was computed

---

[4] It should be pointed out that a proper linear model does better than either loan officers or their paramorphic representations. Using the same task, Beaver (1966) and Deacon (1972) found that linear models predicted with about 78% accuracy on cross-validation. But I can't resist pointing out that the simplest possible improper model of them all does best. The ratio of assets to liabilities (!) correctly categorizes 48 (80%) of the cases studied by Libby.

TABLE 1. Correlations between predictions and criterion values

Example	Average validity of judge	Average validity of judge model	Average validity of random model	Validity of equal weighting model	Cross-validity of regression analysis	Validity of optimal linear model
Prediction of neurosis vs. psychosis	.28	.31	.30	.34	.46	.46
Illinois students' predictions of GPA	.33	.50	.51	.60	.57	.69
Oregon students' predictions of GPA	.37	.43	.51	.60	.57	.69
Prediction of later faculty ratings at Oregon	.19	.25	.39	.48	.38	.54
Yntema & Torgerson's (1961) experiment	.84	.89	.84	.97	—	.97

Note: GPA = grade point average.

for all these students. The problem was to predict the GPA from the 10 variables. In the second study this prediction was made by 80 (other) graduate students at the University of Illinois (Wiggins & Kohen, 1971), and in the third study this prediction was made by 41 graduate students at the University of Oregon. The details of the fourth study have already been covered; it is the one concerned with the prediction of later faculty ratings at Oregon. The final study (Yntema & Torgerson, 1961) was one in which experimenters assigned values to ellipses presented to the subjects, on the basis of figures' size, eccentricity, and grayness. The formula used was $ij + kj + ik$, where $i, j,$ and k refer to values on the three dimensions just mentioned. Subjects in this experiment were asked to estimate the value of each ellipse and were presented with outcome feedback at the end of each trial. The problem was to predict the true (i.e., experimenter-assigned) value of each ellipse on the basis of its size, eccentricity, and grayness.

The first column of Table 1 presents the average validity of the judges in these studies, and the second presents the average validity of the paramorphic model of these judges. In all cases, bootstrapping worked. But then what Corrigan and I constructed were *random linear models,* that is, models in which weights were randomly chosen except for sign and were then applied to standardized variables.[5]

The sign of each variable was determined on an a priori basis so that it would have a positive relationship to the criterion. Then a normal deviate was selected at random from a normal distribution with unit variance, and the absolute value of this deviate was used as a weight for the variable. Ten thousand such models were constructed for each example. (Dawes & Corrigan, 1974, p. 102)

On the average, these random linear models perform about as well as the paramorphic models of the judges; these averages are predicted in the third column of the table. Equal-weighting models, presented in the fourth column, do even better. (There is a mathematical reason why equal-weighting models must outperform the average random model.[6]) Finally, the last two columns present the cross-validated validity of the standard regression model and the validity of the optimal linear model.

Essentially the same results were obtained when the weights were selected from a rectangular distribution. Why? Because linear models are robust over deviations from optimal weighting. In other words, the bootstrapping finding, at least in these studies, has simply been a reaffirmation of the ear-

[5] Unfortunately, Dawes and Corrigan did not spell out in detail that these variables must first be standardized and that the result is a standardized dependent variable. Equal or random weighting of incomparable variables – for example, GRE score and GPA – without prior standardization would be nonsensical.

[6] Consider a set of standardized variables S_1, X_2, X_m, each of which is positively correlated with a standardized variable Y. The correlation of the average of the Xs with the Y is equal to the correlation of the sum of the Xs with Y. The covariance of this sum with Y is equal to

$$\left(\tfrac{1}{n}\right) \sum_i y_i (x_{i1} + x_{i2} \ldots x_{im})$$

$$= \left(\tfrac{1}{n}\right) \sum_i y_i x_{i1} + \left(\tfrac{1}{n}\right) \sum_i y_i x_{i2} \ldots + \left(\tfrac{1}{n}\right) \sum_i y_i x_{im}$$

$$= r_1 + r_2 \ldots + r_m \; (\textit{the sum of the correlations})$$

The variance of y is 1, and the variance of the sum of the Xs is $M + M(M - 1) r$, where r is the average inter-correlation between the Xs. Hence, the correlation of the average of the Xs with Y is $(\Sigma r_i)/(M + M(M - 1)r)^{1/2}$; this is greater than $(\Sigma r_i)/(M + M^2 - M)^{1/2}$ – average r_i. Because each of the random models is positively correlated with the criterion, the correlation of the average, which is the unit-weighted model, is higher than the average of the correlations.

lier finding that proper linear models are superior to human judgments the weights derived from the judges' behavior being sufficiently close to the optimal weights that the outputs of the models are highly similar. The solution to the problem of obtaining optimal weights is one that – in terms of von Winterfeldt and Edwards (1973) – has a "flat maximum." Weights that are near to optimal level produce almost the same output as do optimal beta weights. Because the expert judge knows at least something about the direction of the variables, his or her judgments yield weights that are nearly optimal (but note that in all cases equal weighting is superior to models based on judges' behavior).

The fact that different linear composites correlate highly with each other was first pointed out 40 years ago by Wilks (1938). He considered only situations in which there was positive correlation between predictors. This result seems to hold generally as long as these intercorrelation: are not negative; for example, the correlation between $X + 2Y$ and $2X + Y$ is .80 when X and Y are uncorrelated. The ways in which outputs are relatively insensitive to changes in coefficients (provided changes in sig. are not involved) have been investigated most recently by Green (1977) Wainer (1976), Wainer and Thissen (1976), W. Edwards (1978), and Gardiner and Edwards (1975).

Dawes and Corrigan (1974, p. 105) concluded that "the whole trick is to know what variables to look at and then know how to add." That principle is well illustrated in the following study, conducted since the Dawes and Corrigan article was published. In it, Hammond and Adelman (1976) both investigated and influenced the decision about what type of bullet should be used by the Denver City Police, a decision having much more obvious social impact than most of those discussed above. To quote Hammond and Adelman (1976):

> In 1974, the Denver Police Department (DPD), as well as other police departments throughout the country, decided to change its handgun ammunition. The principle reason offered by the police was that the conventional round-nosed bullet provided insufficient "stopping effectiveness" (that is, the ability to incapacitate and thus to prevent the person shot from firing back at a police officer or others). The DPD chief recommended (as did other police chiefs) the conventional bullet be replaced by a hollow-point bullet. Such bullets, it was contended, flattened on impact, thus decreasing penetration, increasing stopping effectiveness,

and decreasing ricochet potential. The suggested change was challenged by the American Civil Liberties Union, minority groups, and others. Opponents of the change claimed that the new bullets were nothing more than outlawed "dum-dum" bullets, that they created far more injury than the round-nosed bullet, and should, therefore, be barred from use. As is customary, judgments on this matter were formed privately and then defended publicly with enthusiasm and tenacity and the usual public hearings were held. Both sides turned to ballistics experts for scientific information and support. (p. 392)

The disputants focused on evaluating the merits of specific bullets—confounding the physical effect of the bullets with the implications for social policy; that is, rather than separating questions of what it is the bullet should accomplish (the social policy question) from questions concerning ballistic characteristics of specific bullets, advocates merely argued for one bullet or another. Thus, as Hammond and Adelman pointed out, social policymakers inadvertently adopted the role of (poor) ballistics experts, and vice versa. What Hammond and Adelman did was to discover the important policy dimensions from the policymakers, and then they had the ballistics experts rate the bullets with respect to these dimensions. These dimensions turned out to be stopping effectiveness (the probability that someone hit in the torso could not return fire), probability of serious injury, and probability of harm to bystanders. When the ballistics experts rated the bullets with respect to these dimensions, it turned out that the last two were almost perfectly confounded, but they were not perfectly confounded with the first. Bullets do not vary along a single dimension that confounds effectiveness with lethainess. The probability of serious injury of harm to bystanders is highly related to the penetration of the bullet, whereas the probability of the bullet's effectively stopping someone from returning fire is highly related to the width of the entry wound. Since policymakers could not agree about the weights given to the three dimensions, Hammond and Adelman suggested that they be weighted equally. Combining the equal weights with the (independent) judgments of the ballistics experts, Hammond and Adelman discovered a bullet that "has greater stopping effectiveness and is less apt to cause injury (and is less apt to threaten bystanders) than the standard bullet then in use by the

DPD" (Hammond & Adelman, 1976, p. 395). The bullet was also less apt to cause injury than was the bullet previously recommended by the DPD. That bullet was "accepted by the City Council and all other parties concerned, and is now being used by the DPD" (Hammond & Adelman, 1976, p. 395).[7] Once again, "the whole trick is to decide what variables to look at and then know how to add" (Dawes & Corrigan, 1974, p. 105).

So why don't people do it more often? I know of four universities (University of Illinois; New York University; University of Oregon; University of California, Santa Barbara – there may be more) that use a linear model for applicant selection, but even these use it as an initial screening device and substitute clinical judgment for the final selection of those above a cut score. L.R. Goldberg's (1965), actuarial formula for diagnosing neurosis or psychosis from MMPI profiles has proven superior to clinical judges attempting the same task (no one to my or Goldberg's knowledge has ever produced a judge who does better), yet my one experience with its use (at the Ann Arbor Veterans Administration Hospital) was that it was discontinued on the grounds that it made obvious errors (an interesting reason, discussed at length). In 1970, I suggested that our fellowship committee at the University of Oregon apportion cutbacks of National Science Foundation and National Defense Education Act fellowships to departments on the basis of a quasi-linear point system based on explicitly defined indices, departmental merit, and need; I was told "you can't systemize human judgment." It was only six months later, after our committee realized the political and ethical impossibility of cutting back fellowships on the basis of intuitive judgment, that such a system was adopted. And so on.

In the past three years, I have written and talked about the utility (and in my view, ethical superiority) of using linear model's in socially important decisions. Many of the same objections have been raised repeatedly by different readers and audiences. I would like to conclude this article by cataloging these objections and answering them.

Objections to Using Linear Models

These objections may be placed in three broad categories: technical, psychological, and ethical. Each category is discussed in turn.

Technical

The most common technical objection is to the use of the correlation coefficient; for example, Remus and Jenicke (1978) wrote:

It is clear that Dawes and Corrigan's choice of the correlation coefficient to establish the utility of random and unit rules is inappropriate [sic, inappropriate for what?]. A criterion function is also needed in the experiments cited by Dawes and Corrigan. Surely there is a cost function for misclassifying neurotics and psychotics or refusing qualified students admissions to graduate school while admitting marginal students. (p. 221)

Consider the graduate admission problem first. Most schools have k slots and N applicants. The problem is to get the best k (who are in turn willing to accept the school) out of N. What better way is there than to have an appropriate rank? None. Remus and Jenicke write as if the problem were not one of comparative choice but of absolute choice. Most social choices, however, involve selecting the better or best from a set of alternatives: the students that will be better, the bullet that will be best, a possible airport site that will be superior, and so on. The correlation coefficient, because it reflects ranks so well, is clearly appropriate for evaluating such choices.

The neurosis–psychosis problem is more subtle and even less supportive of their argument. "Surely," they state, "there is a cost function," but they don't specify any candidates. The implication is clear: If they could find it, clinical judgment would be found to be superior to linear models. Why? In the absence of such a discovery on their part, the argument amounts to nothing at all. But this argument from a vacuum can be very compelling to people (for example, to losing generals and losing football coaches, who know that "surely" their plans would work "if" – when the plans are in fact doomed to failure no matter what).

A second related technical objection is to the comparison of average correlation coefficients of judges with those of linear models. Perhaps by averaging, the performance of some really out-

---

[7] It should be pointed out that there were only eight bullets on the Pareto frontier; that is, there were only eight that were not inferior to some particular other bullet in both stopping effectiveness and probability of harm (or inferior on one of the variables and equal on the other). Consequently, any weighting rule whatsoever would have chosen one of these eight.

standing judges is obscured. The data indicate otherwise. In the L.R. Goldberg (1970) study, for example, only 5 of 29 trained clinicians were better than the unit-weighted model, and none did better than the proper one. In the Wiggins and Kohen (1971) study, no judges were better than the unit-weighted model, and we replicated that effect at Oregon. In the Libby (1976) study, only 9 of 43 judges did better than the ratio of assets to liabilities at predicting bankruptcies (3 did equally well). While it is then conceded that clinicians should be able to predict diagnosis of neurosis or psychosis, that graduate students should be able to predict graduate success, and that bank loan officers should be able to predict bankruptcies, the possibility is raised that perhaps the experts used in the studies weren't the right ones. This again is arguing from a vacuum: If other experts were used, then the results would be different. And once again no such experts are produced, and once again the appropriate response is to ask for a reason why these hypothetical other people should be any different. (As one university vice-president told me, "Your research only proves that you used poor judges; we could surely do better by getting better judges"—apparently not from the psychology department.)

A final technical objection concerns the nature of the criterion variables. They are admittedly short-term and unprofound (e.g., GPAs, diagnoses); otherwise, most studies would be infeasible. The question is then raised of whether the findings would be different if a truly long-range important criterion were to be predicted. The answer is that of course the findings *could* be different, but we have no reason to suppose that they *would* be different. First, the distant future is in general less predictable than the immediate future, for the simple reason that more unforeseen, extraneous, or self-augmenting factors influence individual outcomes. (Note that we are not discussing aggregate outcomes, such as an unusually cold winter in the Midwest in general spread out over three months.) Since, then, clinical prediction is poorer than linear to begin with, the hypothesis would hold only if linear prediction got much worse over time than did clinical prediction. There is no a priori reason to believe that this differential deterioration in prediction would occur, and none has ever been suggested to me. There is certainly no evidence. Once again, the objection consists of an argument from a vacuum.

Particularly compelling is the fact that people who argue that different criteria or judges or variables or time frames would produce different results have had 25 years in which to produce examples, and they have failed to do so.

Psychological

One psychological resistance to using linear models lies in our selective memory about clinical prediction. Our belief in such prediction is reinforced by the availability (Tversky & Kahneman, 1974) of instances of successful clinical prediction—expecially those that are exceptions to some formula: "I knew someone once with . . . who . . ." (E.g., "I knew of someone with a tested IQ of only 130 who got an advanced degree in psychology.") As Nisbett, Borgida, Crandall, and Reed (1976, 7) showed, such single instances often have greater impact on judgment than do much more valid statistical compilations based on many instances. (A good prophylactic for clinical psychologists basing resistance to actuarial prediction on such instances would be to keep careful records of their own predictions about their own patients—prospective records not subject to hindsight. Such records could make all instances of successful and unsuccessful prediction equally available for impact; in addition, they could serve for another clinical versus statistical study using the best possible judge—the clinician himself or herself.)

Moreover, an illusion of good judgment may be reinforced due to selection (Einhorn & Hogarth, 1978) in those situations in which the prediction of a positive or negative outcome has a self-fulfilling effect. For example, admissions officers who judge that a candidate is particularly qualified for a graduate program may feel that their judgment is exonerated when that candidate does well, even though the candidate's success is in large part due to the positive effects of the program. (In contrast, a linear model of selection is evaluated by seeing how well it predicts performance *within* the set of applicants selected.) Or a waiter who believes that particular people at the table are poor tippers may be less attentive than usual and receive a smaller tip, thereby having his clinical judgment exonerated.[8]

A second psychological resistance to the use of linear models stems from their "proven" low va-

---

[8] This example was provided by Einhorn (1979).

lidity. Here, there is an implicit (as opposed to explicit) argument from a vacuum because neither changes in evaluation procedures, nor in judges, nor in criteria, are proposed. Rather, the unstated assumption is that these criteria of psychological interest are in fact highly predictable, so it follows that if one method of prediction (a linear model) doesn't work too well, another might do better (reasonable), which is then translated into the belief that another *will* do better (which is not a reasonable inference)—once it is found. This resistance is best expressed by a dean considering the graduate admissions, who wrote, "The correlation of the linear composite with future faculty ratings is only 4, whereas that of the admissions committee's judgment correlates .2. Twice nothing is nothing." In 1976, I answered as follows (Dawes, 1976, pp. 6–7):

> In response, I can only point out that 16% of the variance is better than 4% of the variance. To me, however, the fascinating part of this argument is the implicit assumption that that other 84% of the variance is predictable and that we can somehow predict it.
>
> Now what are we dealing with? We are dealing with personality and intellectual characteristics of [uniformly bright] people who are about 20 years old. . . . Why are we so convinced that this prediction can be made at all? Surely, it is not necessary to read *Ecclesiastes* every night to understand the role of chance. . . . Moreover, there are clearly positive feedback effects in professional development that exaggerate threshold phenomena. For example, once people are considered sufficiently "outstanding" that they are invited to outstanding institutions, they have outstanding colleagues with whom to interact—and excellence is exacerbated. This same problem occurs for those who do not quite reach such a threshold level. Not only do all these factors mitigate against successful long-range prediction, but studies of the success of such prediction are necessarily limited to those accepted, with the incumbent problems of restriction of range and a negative covariance structure between predictors. (Dawes, 1975)

Finally, there are all sorts of nonintellectual factors in professional success that could not possibly be evaluated before admission to graduate school, for example, success at forming a satisfying or inspiring libidinal relationship, not yet evident genetic tendencies to drug or alcohol addiction, the misfortune to join a research group that "blows up," and so on, and so forth.

Intellectually, I find it somewhat remarkable that we are able to predict even 16% of the variance. But I believe that my own emotional response is indicative of those of my colleagues who simply assume that the future is more predictable. *I want it to be predictable, especially when the aspect of it that I want to predict is important to me.* This desire, I suggest, translates itself into an implicit assumption that the future is in fact highly predictable, and it would then logically follow that if something is not a very good predictor, something else might do better (although it is never correct to argue that it necessarily will).

Statistical prediction, because it includes the specification (usually a low correlation coefficient) of exactly how poorly we can predict, bluntly strikes us with the fact that life is not all that predictable. Unsystematic clinical prediction (or "postdiction"), in contrast, allows us the comforting illusion that life is in fact predictable and that we can predict it.

Ethical

When I was at the Los Angeles Renaissance Fair last summer, I overheard a young woman complain that it was "horribly unfair" that she had been rejected by the Psychology Department at the University of California, Santa Barbara, on the basis of mere numbers, without even an interview. "How can they possibly tell what I'm like?" The answer is that they can't. Nor could they with an interview (Kelly, 1954). Nevertheless, many people maintain that making a crucial social choice without an interview is dehumanizing. I think that the question of whether people are treated in a fair manner has more to do with the question of whether or not they have been dehumanized than does the question of whether the treatment is face to face. (Some of the worst doctors spend a great deal of time conversing with their patients, read no medical journals, order few or no tests, and grieve at the funerals.) A GPA represents 3½ years of behavior on the part of the applicant. (Surely, not all the professors are biased against his or her particular form of creativity.) The GRE is a more carefully devised test. Do we really believe that we can do a better or a fairer job by a 10-minute folder evaluation or a half-hour interview than is done by these two mere numbers? Such cognitive conceit (Dawes, 1976, p. 7) is unethical, especially given the fact of no evidence whatsoever indicating that we do a better job than does the linear equation. (And even making exceptions must be done with extreme care if it is to be ethical, for if we admit someone with a low linear score on the basis that he or she has some special talent, we are automatically rejecting someone with a higher score, who might well have had an equally impressive talent had we taken the trouble to evaluate it.)

No matter how much we would like to see this or that aspect of one or another of the studies reviewed in this article changed, no matter how psychologically uncompelling or distasteful we may find their results to be, no matter how ethically uncomfortable we may feel at "reducing people to mere numbers," the fact remains that our clients are people who deserve to be treated in the best manner possible. If that means—as it appears at present—that selection, diagnosis, and prognosis should be based on nothing more than the addition of a few numbers representing values on important attributes, so be it. To do otherwise is to cheat the people we serve.

REFERENCE NOTES

1. Thornton, B. Personal communication, 1977.
2. Slovic, P. Limitations of the mind of man: Implications for decision making in the nuclear age. In H. J. Otway (Ed.), *Risk vs. benefit: Solution or dream?* (Report LA 4860-MS). Los Alamos, N.M.: Los Alamos Scientific Laboratory, 1972. [Also available as Oregon Research Institute Bulletin 1971, *11*(17).]
3. Srinivisan, V. *A theoretical comparison of the predictive power of the multiple regression and equal weighting procedures* (Research Paper No. 347). Stanford, Calif.: Stanford University, Graduate School of Business, February 1977.
4. von Winterfeldt, D., & Edwards, W. Costs and payoffs in perceptual research. Unpublished manuscript, University of Michigan, Engineering Psychology Laboratory, 1973.
5. Einhorn, H. J. Personal communication, January 1979.

REFERENCES

Alexander, S. A. H. *Sex, arguments, and social engagements in marital and premarital relations.* Unpublished master's thesis, University of Missouri—Kansas City, 1971.
Beaver, W. H. Financial ratios as predictors of failure. In *Empirical research in accounting: Selected studies.* Chicago: University of Chicago, Graduate School of Business, Institute of Professional Accounting, 1966.
Bowman, E. H. Consistency and optimality in managerial decision making. *Management Science,* 1963, *9,* 310–321.
Cass, J., & Birnbaum, M. *Comparative guide to American colleges.* New York: Harper & Row, 1968.
Claudy, J. G. A comparison of five variable weighting procedures. *Educational and Psychological Measurement,* 1972, *32,* 311–322.
Darlington, R. B. Reduced-variance regression. *Psychological Bulletin,* 1978, *85,* 1238–1255.
Dawes, R. M. A case study of graduate admissions: Application of three principles of human decision making. *American Psychologist,* 1971, *24,* 180–188.
Dawes, R. M. Graduate admissions criteria and future success. *Science,* 1975, *187,* 721–723.
Dawes, R. M. Shallow psychology. In J. Carroll & J. Payne (Eds.), *Cognition and social behavior.* Hillsdale, N.J.: Erlbaum, 1976.
Dawes, R. M., & Corrigan, B. Linear models in decision making. *Psychological Bulletin,* 1974, *81,* 95–106.
Deacon, E. B. A discriminant analysis of predictors of business failure. *Journal of Accounting Research,* 1972, *10,* 167–179.
deGroot, A. D. *Het denken van den schaker [Thought and choice in chess].* The Hague, The Netherlands: Mouton, 1965.
Edwards, D. D., & Edwards, J. S. Marriage: Direct and continuous measurement. *Bulletin of the Psychonomic Society,* 1977, *10,* 187–188.
Edwards, W. M. Technology for director dubious: Evaluation and decision in public contents. In K. R. Hammond (Ed.), *Judgement and decision in public policy formation.* Boulder, Colo.: Westview Press, 1978.
Einhorn, H. J. Expert measurement and mechanical combination. *Organizational Behavior and Human Performance,* 1972, *7,* 86–106.
Einhorn, H. J., & Hogarth, R. M. Unit weighting schemas for decision making. *Organizational Behavior and Human Performance,* 1975, *13,* 171–192.
Einhorn, H. J., & Hogarth, R. M. Confidence in judgment: Persistence of the illusion of validity. *Psychological Review,* 1978, *85,* 395–416.
Gardiner, P. C., & Edwards, W. Public values: Multi-attribute-utility measurement for social decision making. In M. F. Kaplan & S. Schwartz (Eds.), *Human judgment and decision processes.* New York: Academic Press, 1975.
Goldberg, L. R. Diagnosticians vs. diagnostic signs: The diagnosis of psychosis vs. neurosis from the MMPI. *Psychological Monographs,* 1965, *79*(9, Whole No. 602).
Goldberg, L. R. Seer over sign: The first "good" example? *Journal of Experimental Research in Personality,* 1968, *3,* 168–171.
Goldberg, L. R. Man versus model of man: A rationale, plus some evidence for a method of improving on clinical inferences. *Psychological Bulletin,* 1970, 73, 422–432.
Goldberg, L. R. Parameters of personality inventory construction and utilization: A comparison of prediction strategies and tactics. *Multivariate Behavioral Research Monographs,* 1972, No. 72-2.
Goldberg, L. R. Man versus model of man: Just how conflicting is that evidence? *Organizational Behavior and Human Performance,* 1976, *14,* 13–22.
Green, B. F., Jr. Parameter sensitivity in multivariate methods. *Multivariate Behavioral Research,* 1977, *3,* 263.
Hammond, K. R. Probabilistic functioning and the clinical method. *Psychological Review,* 1955, *42,* 255–262.
Hammond, K. R., & Adelman, L. Science, values, and human judgment. *Science,* 1976, *194,* 389–396.

Hoffman, P. J. The paramorphic representation of clinical judgment. *Psychological Bulletin*, 1960, *57*, 116–131.

Holt, R. R. Yet another look at clinical and statistical prediction. *American Psychologist*, 1970, *25*, 337–339.

Howard, J. W., & Dawes, R. M. Linear prediction of marital happiness. *Personality and Social Psychology Bulletin*, 1976, *2*, 478–480.

Kelly, L. Evaluation of the interview as a selection technique. In *Proceedings of the 1953 Invitational Conference on Testing Problems*. Princeton, N.J.: Educational Testing Service, 1954.

Krantz, D. H. Measurement structures and psychological laws. *Science*, 1972, *175*, 1427–1435.

Krantz, D. H., Luce, R. D., Suppes, P., & Tversky, A. *Foundations of measurement* (Vol. 1). New York: Academic Press, 1971.

Libby, R. Man versus model of man: Some conflicting evidence. *Organizational Behavior and Human Performance*, 1976, *14*, 1–12.

Marquardt, D. W., & Snee, R. D. Ridge regression in practice. *American Statistician*, 1975, *29*, 3–19.

Meehl, P. E. *Clinical versus statistical prediction: A theoretical analysis and a review of the evidence*. Minneapolis: University of Minnesota Press, 1954.

Meehl, P. E. Seer over sign: The first good example. *Journal of Experimental Research in Personality*, 1965, *1*, 27–32.

Nisbett, R. F., Borgida, E., Crandall, R., & Reed, H. Popular induction: Information is not necessarily normative. In J. Carrol & J. Payne (Eds.), *Cognition and social behavior*. Hillsdale, N.J.: Erlbaum, 1976.

Remus, W. E., & Jenicke, L. O. Unit and random linear models in decision making. *Multivariate Behavioral Research*, 1978, *13*, 215–221.

Sawyer, J. Measurement and prediction, clinical and statistical. *Psychological Bulletin*, 1966, *64*, 178–200.

Schmidt, F. L. The relative efficiency of regression and simple unit predictor weights in applied differential psychology. *Educational and Psychological Measurement*, 1971, *31*, 699–714.

Simon, H. A., & Chase, W. G. Skill in chess. *American Scientist*, 1973, 61, 394–403.

Slovic, P., & Lichtenstein, S. Comparison of Bayesian and regression approaches to the study of information processing in judgment. *Organizational Behavior and Human Performance*, 1971, *6*, 649–744.

Thornton, B. Linear prediction of marital happiness: A replication. *Personality and Social Psychology Bulletin*, 1977, *3*, 674–676.

Tversky, A., & Kahneman, D. Judgment under uncertainty: Heuristics and biases. *Science*, 1974, *184*, 1124–1131.

Wainer, H. Estimating coefficients in linear models: It don't make no nevermind. *Psychological Bulletin*, 1976, *83*, 312–317.

Wainer, H., & Thissen, D. Three steps toward robust regression. *Psychometrika*, 1976, *41*, 9–34.

Wallace, H. A. What is in the corn judge's mind? *Journal of the American Society of Agronomy*, 1923, *15*, 300–304.

Wiggins, N., & Kohen, E. S. Man vs. model of man revisited: The forecasting of graduate school success. *Journal of Personality and Social Psychology*, 1971, *19*, 100–106.

Wilks, S. S. Weighting systems for linear functions of correlated variables when there is no dependent variable. *Psychometrika*, 1938, *8*, 23–40.

Yntema, D. B., & Torgerson, W. S. Man–computer cooperation in decisions requiring common sense. *IRE Transactions of the Professional Group on Human Factors in Electronics*, 1961, *2*(1), 20–26.

Experimental Tests of the Endowment Effect and the Coase Theorem

Daniel Kahneman • University of California, Berkeley

Jack L. Knetsch • Simon Fraser University

Richard H. Thaler • Cornell University

Contrary to theoretical expectations, measures of willingness to accept greatly exceed measures of willingness to pay. This paper reports several experiments that demonstrate that this "endowment effect" persists even in market settings with opportunities to learn. Consumption objects (e.g., coffee mugs) are randomly given to half the subjects in an experiment. Markets for the mugs are then conducted. The Coase theorem predicts that about half the mugs will trade, but observed volume is always significantly less. When markets for "induced-value" tokens are conducted, the predicted volume is observed, suggesting that transactions costs cannot explain the undertrading for consumption goods.

I. Introduction

The standard assumptions of economic theory imply that when income effects are small, differences between an individual's maximum willingness to pay (WTP) for a good and minimum compensation demanded for the same entitlement (willingness to accept [WTA]) should be negligible (Willig 1976). Thus indifference curves are drawn without reference to current endowments; any difference between equivalent and compensating variation assessments of welfare changes is in practice ignored;[1] and there is wide acceptance of the Coase theorem assertion that, subject to income effects, the allocation of resources will be independent of the assignment of property rights when costless trades are possible.

The assumption that entitlements do not affect value contrasts sharply with empirical observations of significantly higher selling than buying prices. For example, Thaler (1980) found that the minimal compensation demanded for accepting a .001 risk of sudden death was higher by one or two orders of magnitude than the amount people were willing to pay to eliminate an identical existing risk. Other examples of similar reported findings are summarized in table 1. The disparities observed in these examples are clearly too large to be explained plausibly by income effects.

Several factors probably contribute to the discrepancies between the evaluations of buyers and sellers that are documented in table 1. The perceived illegitimacy of the transaction may, for example, contribute to the extraordinarily high de-

---

[1] For example, the conventional prescription for assessing environmental and other losses is that, "practically speaking, it does not appear to make much difference which definition is accepted" (Freeman 1979, p. 3).

TABLE 1. Summary of Past Tests of Evaluation Disparity

Study and Entitlement	Means			Medians		
	WTP	WTA	Ratio	WTP	WTA	Ratio
Hypothetical surveys:						
Hammack and Brown (1974): marshes	$247	$1,044	4.2			
Sinclair (1978): fishing				35	100	2.9
Banford et al. (1979):						
Fishing pier	43	120	2.8	47	129	2.7
Postal service	22	93	4.2	22	106	4.8
Bishop and Heberlein (1979): goose hunting permits	21	101	4.8			
Rowe et al. (1980): visibility	1.33	3.49	2.6			
Brookshire et al. (1980): elk hunting*	54	143	2.6			
Heberlein and Bishop (1985): deer hunting	31	513	16.5			
Real exchange experiments:						
Knetsch and Sinden (1984): lottery tickets	1.28	5.18	4.0			
Heberlein and Bishop (1985): deer hunting	25	172	6.9			
Coursey et al. (1987): taste of sucrose octa-acetate[†]	3.45	4.71	1.4	1.33	3.49	2.6
Brookshire and Coursey (1987): park trees[‡]	10.12	56.60	5.6	6.30	12.96	2.1

* Middle-level change of several used in study.
† Final values after multiple iterations.
‡ Average of two levels of tree plantings.

mand for personal compensation for agreeing to the loss of a public good (e.g., Rowe, d'Arge, and Brookshire 1980). Standard bargaining habits may also contribute to a discrepancy between the stated reservation prices of buyers and sellers. Sellers are often rewarded for overstating their true value, and buyers for understating theirs (Knez, Smith, and Williams 1985). By force of habit they may misrepresent their true valuations even when such misrepresentation confers no advantage, as in answering hypothetical questions or one-shot or single transactions. In such situations the buying-selling discrepancy is simply a strategic mistake, which experienced traders will learn to avoid (Coursey, Hovis, and Schulze 1987; Brookshire and Coursey 1987).

The hypothesis of interest here is that many discrepancies between WTA and WTP, far from being a mistake, reflect a genuine effect of reference positions on preferences. Thaler (1980) labeled the increased value of a good to an individual when the good becomes part of the individual's endowment the "endowment effect." This effect is a manifestation of "loss aversion," the generalization that losses are weighted substantially more than objectively commensurate gains in the evaluation of prospects and trades (Kahneman and Tversky 1979; Tversky and Kahneman, in press). An implication of this asymmetry is that if a good is evaluated as a loss when it is given up and as a

gain when it is acquired, loss aversion will, on average, induce a higher dollar value for owners than for potential buyers, reducing the set of mutually acceptable trades.

There are some cases in which no endowment effect would be expected, such as when goods are purchased for resale rather than for utilization. A particularly clear case of a good held exclusively for resale is the notional token typically traded in experimental markets commonly used to test the efficiency of market institutions (Plott 1982; Smith 1982). Such experiments employ the induced-value technique in which the objects of trade are tokens to which private redemption values that vary among individual participants have been assigned by the experimenter (Smith 1976). Subjects can obtain the prescribed value assigned for the tokens when redeeming them at the end of the trading period; the tokens are otherwise worthless.

No endowment effect would be expected for such tokens, which are valued only because they can be redeemed for cash. Thus both buyers and sellers should value tokens at the induced value they have been assigned. Markets for induced-value tokens can therefore be used as a control condition to determine whether differences between the values of buyers and sellers in other markets could be attributable to transaction costs, misunderstandings, or habitual strategies of bargaining. Any discrepancy between the buying and selling values can be isolated in an experiment by comparing the outcomes of markets for real goods with those of otherwise identical markets for induced-value tokens. If no differences in values are observed for the induced-value tokens, then economic theory predicts that no differences between buying and selling values will be observed for consumption goods evaluated and traded under the same conditions.

The results from a series of experiments involving real exchanges of tokens and of various consumption goods are reported in this paper. In each case, a random allocation design was used to test for the presence of an endowment effect. Half of the subjects were endowed with a good and became potential sellers in each market; the other half of the subjects were potential buyers. Conventional economic analysis yields the simple prediction that one-half of the goods should be traded in voluntary exchanges. If value is unaffected by ownership, then the distribution of values in the two groups should be the same except for sampling variation. The supply and demand curves should therefore be mirror images of each other, intersecting at their common median. The null hypothesis is, therefore, that half of the goods provided should change hands. Label this predicted volume V^*. If there is an endowment effect, the value of the good will be higher for sellers than for buyers, and observed volume V will be less than V^*. The ratio V/V^* provides a unit-free measure of the undertrading that is produced by the effect of ownership on value. To test the hypothesis that market experience eliminates undertrading, the markets were repeated several times.

A test for the possibility that observed undertrading was due to transaction costs was provided by a comparison of the results from a series of induced-value markets with those from the subsequent goods markets carried out with identical trading rules. Notice that this comparison can also be used to eliminate numerous other possible explanations of the observed undertrading. For example, if the instructions to the subjects are confusing or misleading, the effects should show up in both the induced-value markets and the experimental markets for real goods. Section II describes studies of trading volume in induced-value markets and in consumption goods markets. Section III provides a further test for strategic behavior and demonstrates that the disparity findings are not likely caused by this. Section IV investigates

the extent to which the undertrading of goods is produced by reluctance to buy and reluctance to sell. Section V examines undertrading in bilateral negotiations and provides a test of the Coase theorem. Section VI describes an experiment that rules out income effects and a trophy effect as explanations of the observed valuation disparity. Implications of the observed effects are discussed in Section VII.

II. Repeated Market Experiments

In experiment 1, 44 students in an advanced undergraduate law and economics class at Cornell University received a packet of general instructions plus 11 forms, one for each of the markets that were conducted in the experiment. (The instructions for all experiments are available from the authors.) The first three markets were conducted for induced-value tokens. Sellers received the following instructions (with differences for buyers in brackets):

> In this market the objects being traded are tokens. You are an owner, so you now a token [You are a buyer, so you have an opportunity to buy a token] which has a value to you of $x. It has this value to you because the experimenter will give you this much money for it. The value of the token is different for different individuals. A price for the tokens will be determined later. For each of the prices listed below, please indicate whether you prefer to: (1) Sell your token at this price and receive the market price. [Buy a token at this price and cash it in for the sum of money indicated above.] (2) Keep your token and cash it in for the sum of money indicated above. [Not buy a token at this price.] For each price indicate your decision by marking an X in the appropriate column.
>
> Part of the response form for sellers follows:
>
> At a price of $8.75 I will sell _____
>   I will not sell_____
> At a price of $8.25 I will sell _____
>   I will not sell_____

The same rectangular distribution of values—ranging from $0.25 to $8.75 in steps of $0.50—was prepared for both buyers and sellers. Because not all the forms were actually distributed, however, the induced supply and demand curves were not always precisely symmetrical. Subjects alternated between the buyer and seller role in the three successive markets and were assigned a different individual redemption value in each trial.

Experimenters collected the forms from all participants after each market period and immediately calculated and announced the market-clearing price,[2] the number of trades, and the presence or absence of excess demand or supply at the market-clearing price.[3] Three buyers and three sellers were selected at random after each of the induced markets and were paid off according to the preferences stated on their forms and the market-clearing price for that period.

Immediately after the three induced-value markets, subjects on alternating seats were given Cornell coffee mugs, which sell for $6.00 each at the bookstore. The experimenter asked all participants to examine a mug, either their own or their neighbor's. The experimenter then informed the subjects that four markets for mugs would be conducted using the same procedures as the prior induced markets with two exceptions: (1) One of the four market trials would subsequently be selected at random, and only the trades made on this trial would be executed. (2) In the binding market trial, *all* trades would be implemented, unlike the subset implemented in the induced-value markets.[4] The initial assignment of buyer and seller roles was maintained for all four trading periods. The clearing price and the number of trades were announced after each period. The market that "counted" was indicated after the fourth period, and transactions were executed immediately. All sellers who had indicated that they would give up their mugs for a sum at the market-clearing price exchanged their mugs for cash, and successful buyers paid this same price and received their mugs. This design was used to permit learning to take place over successive trials and yet make each trial potentially binding. The same procedure was then followed for four more successive markets using boxed ballpoint pens with a visible bookstore price tag of $3.98, which were distributed to the subjects who had been buyers in the mug markets.

For each goods market, subjects completed a form similar to that used for the induced-value tokens, with the following instructions:

You now own the object in your possession. [You do not own the object that you see in the possession of some of your neighbors.] You have the option of selling it [buying one] if a price, which will be determined later, is acceptable to you. For each of the possible prices below indicate whether you wish to: (1) Sell your object and receive this price [Pay this price and receive an object to take

home with you] or (2) Keep your object and take it home with you. [Not buy an object at this price.] For each price indicate your decision by marking an X in the appropriate column.

The buyers and sellers in the consumption goods markets faced the same incentives that they had experienced in the induced-value markets. Buyers maximized their potential gain by agreeing to buy at all prices below the value they ascribed to the good, and sellers maximized their welfare by agreeing to sell at all prices above the good's worth to them. As in the induced-value markets, it was in the best interest of the participants to act as price takers.

As shown in table 2, the markets for induced-value tokens and consumption goods yielded sharply different results. In the induced-value markets, as expected, the median buying and selling prices were identical. The ratio of actual to predicted volume (V/V^*) was 1.0, aggregating over the three periods. In contrast, the median selling prices in the mug and pen markets were more than twice the median buying prices, and the V/V^* ratio was only .20 for mugs and .41 for pens. Observed volume did not increase over successive periods in either the mug or the pen markets, providing no indication that subjects learned to adopt equal buying and selling prices.

The results of the first and last markets for coffee mugs are also displayed in figure 1. There are five features to notice in this figure: (1) Both buy-

---

[2] The instructions stated that "*it is in your best interest to answer these questions truthfully.* For any question, treat the price as fixed. (In economics jargon, you should act as 'price takers'.)" All the subjects were junior and senior economics majors, so they were familiar with the terms used. If subjects asked how the market prices were determined, they were told, truthfully, that the market price was the point at which the elicited supply and demand curves intersected. The uniformity of the results across many different experiments suggests that this information had no discernible effect on behavior. Furthermore, the responses of the subjects in the induced-value portion of the experiments indicate that nearly all understood and accepted their role as price takers. See also experiment 5, in which a random price procedure was used.

[3] When this occurred, a random draw determined which buyers and sellers were accommodated.

[4] The experimental design was intended to give the markets for consumption goods every possible chance to be efficient. While in the induced-value markets not everyone was paid, in the consumption goods markets everyone was paid. Also, the consumption goods markets were conducted after the induced-value markets and were repeated four times each, to allow the subjects the maximum opportunity for learning.

TABLE 2. Results of Experiment 1 Induced-Value Markets

Trial	Actual Trades	Expected Trades	Price	Expected Price
1	12	11	3.75	3.75
2	11	11	4.75	4.75
3	10	11	4.25	4.25

		Consumption Goods Markets		
Trial	Trades	Price	Median Buyer Reservation Price	Median Seller Reservation Price
		Mugs (Expected Trades = 11)		
4	4	4.25	2.75	5.25
5	1	4.75	2.25	5.25
6	2	4.50	2.25	5.25
7	2	4.25	2.25	5.25
		Pens (Expected Trades = 11)		
8	4	1.25	.75	2.50
9	5	1.25	.75	1.75
10	4	1.25	.75	2.25
11	5	1.25	.75	1.75

ers and sellers display a wide range of values, indicating that in the absence of an endowment effect there would be enough rents to produce gains from trade. Indeed, the range of values is similar to that used in the induced-value markets, which had near-perfect market efficiency. (2) The distribution of selling prices has a single mode, unlike some recent results in which an evaluation discrepancy could be explained by a bimodal distribution of compensation demanded (Boyce et al. 1990). (3) The payment of a small commission for trading, such as $0.25 per trade, would not significantly alter the results. (4) The mugs were desirable. Every subject assigned a positive value to the mug, and the lowest value assigned by a seller was $2.25. (5) Neither demand nor supply changed much between the first and last markets.

Quantity

Experiment 2 was conducted in an undergraduate microeconomics class at Cornell ($N = 38$). The procedure was identical to that of experiment 1, except that the second consumption good was a pair of folding binoculars in a cardboard frame, available at the bookstore for $4.00. The results are reported in table 3.

In experiments 3 and 4, conducted in Simon Fraser University undergraduate economics classes, the subjects were asked to provide minimum selling prices or maximum buying prices rather than to answer the series of yes or no questions used in experiments 1 and 2. The induced-value markets were conducted with no monetary pay-offs and were followed by four markets for pens in experiment 3 and five markets for mugs in experiment 4. In experiment 3, subjects were told that the first three markets for pens would be used for practice, so only the fourth and final market would be binding. In experiment 4, one of the five markets was selected at random to count, as in experiments 1 and 2. Other procedures were unchanged. The results are shown in table 4.

Experiments 2–4 all yielded results similar to those obtained in experiment 1. Summing over the induced-value markets in all four experiments produced a V/V^* index of .91. This excellent performance was achieved even though the participants did not have the benefit of experience with the trading rules, there were limited monetary incentives in experiments 1 and 2, and there were no monetary incentives in experiments 3 and 4. In the markets for consumption goods, in which all participants faced monetary incentives and experience

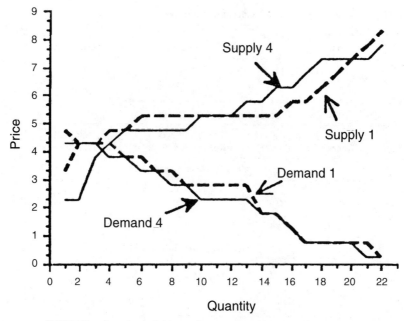

FIGURE 1 ■ Supply and demand curves, markets 1 and 4.

with the market rules gained from the induced-value markets, V/V^* averaged .31, and median selling prices were more than double the corresponding buying prices. Trading procedures were precisely identical in markets for goods and for induced-value tokens. The high volume of trade in money tokens therefore eliminates transaction costs (or any other feature that was present in both types of markets) as an explanation of the observed undertrading of consumption goods.

TABLE 3. Results of Experiment 2 Induced-Value Markets

Trial	Actual Trades	Expected Trades	Price	Expected Price
1	10	10	3.75	4.25
2	9	10	4.75	4.25
3	7	8	4.25	4.75

	Consumption Goods Markets			
Trial	Trades	Price	Median Buyer Reservation Price	Median Seller Reservation Price
		Mugs (Expected Trades = 9.5)		
4	3	3.75	1.75	4.75
5	3	3.25	2.25	4.75
6	2	3.25	2.25	4.75
7	2	3.25	2.25	4.25
		Binoculars (Expected Trades = 9.5)		
8	4	1.25	.75	1.25
9	4	.75	.75	1.25
10	3	.75	.75	1.75
11	3	.75	.75	1.75

TABLE 4. Results of Experiments 3 and 4

Trial	N	Object	Actual Trades	Expected Traders	Ratio of Seller Median Value to Buyer Median Value
			Experiment 3		
1	26	Induced	5	6.5	
2	26	Pen	2	6.5	6.0
3	26	Pen	2	6.5	6.0
4	26	Pen	2	6.5	5.0
5	26	Pen	1	6.5	5.0
			Experiment 4		
1	74	Induced	15	18.5	
2	74	Induced	16	18.5	
3	74	Mug	6	18.5	3.8
4	74	Mug	4	18.5	2.8
5	72	Mug	4	18	2.2
6	73	Mug	8	18	1.8
7	74	Mug	8	18.5	1.8

It should be noted that subjects in the position of buyers were not given money to use for purchases, but rather had to make transactions using their own money. (Subjects were told to bring money to class and that credit and change would be available if necessary. Some subjects borrowed from friends to make payments.) The aim was to study transactions in a realistic setting. While the present design makes potential sellers slightly wealthier, at least in the first market, the magnitude of the possible income effect is trivial. In one of the markets the equilibrium price was only $0.75, and the prices in other markets were never above a few dollars. Also, as shown in experiments 7 and 8 below, equal undertrading was found in designs that eliminated the possibility of an income effect or cash constraint.

As shown in tables 2–4, subjects showed almost no undertrading even in their first trial in an induced-value market. Evidently neither bargaining habits nor any transaction costs impede trading in money tokens. On the other hand, there is no indication that participants in the markets for goods learned to make valuations independent of their entitlements. The discrepant evaluations of buyers and sellers remained stable over four, and in one case five, successive markets for the same good and did not change systematically over repeated markets for successive goods.

A difference in procedure probably explains the apparent conflict between these results and the conclusion reached in some other studies, that the WTA-WTP discrepancy is greatly reduced by market experience. The studies that reported a disciplinary effect of market experience assessed this effect by comparing the responses of buyers and sellers in preliminary hypothetical questions or nonbinding market trials to their behavior in a subsequent binding trial with real monetary payoffs (Knez et al. 1985; Brookshire and Coursey 1987; Coursey et al. 1987). In the present experiments, the markets for consumption goods were real and potentially binding from the first trial, and the WTA-WTP discrepancy was found to be stable over a series of such binding trials.

It should be stressed that previous research did not actually demonstrate that the discrepancy between buyers and sellers is eliminated in markets. Although the discrepancy between the final selling and buying prices in the sucrose octa-acetate experiment of Coursey et al. (1987) was not statistically significant, the ratio of median prices of sellers and buyers was still 2.6.[5] If the buyers and sellers had been allowed to trade according to their final bids, a total of nine advantageous exchanges would have occurred between the two groups, compared to the theoretical expectation of 16 trades (for details, see Knetsch and Sinden [1987]). This V/V* ratio of .56 is quite similar to the ratios ob-

---

[5] The ratio of the mean selling and buying prices is 1.4 if all subjects are included. However, if one buyer and one seller with extreme valuations are excluded, the ratio is 1.9. These numbers were reported in an earlier version of Coursey et al. (1987).

served in experiments 1–4. In the study by Brookshire and Coursey (1987), the ratio of mean prices was indeed reduced by experience, from a high of 77 for initial hypothetical survey responses to 6.1 in the first potentially binding auction conducted in a laboratory. However, the ratio remained at 5.6 in the final auction.

III. Testing for Misrepresentation

As previously stated, subjects faced identical incentives in the induced-value and consumption goods phases of experiments 1–4. Therefore, it seems safe to attribute the difference in observed trading to the endowment effect. However, some readers of early drafts of this paper have suggested that because of the way market prices were determined, subjects might have felt that they had an incentive to misstate their true values in order to influence the price, and perhaps this incentive was perceived to be greater in the consumption goods markets. To eliminate this possible interpretation of the previous results, experiment 5 was carried out in a manner similar to the first four experiments, except that subjects were told that the price would be selected at random. As is well known, this is an incentive-compatible procedure for eliciting values (see Becker, DeGroot, and Marschak 1964).

Each participant received the following instructions (with appropriate alternative wording in the buyers' forms):

> After you have finished, one of the prices listed below will be selected at random and any exchanges will take place at that price. If you have indicated you will sell at this price you will receive this amount of money and will give up the mug; if you have indicated that you will keep the mug at this price then no exchange will be made and you can take the mug home with you.
>   . . . Your decision can have no effect on the price actually used because the price will be selected at random.

The experiment was conducted in a series of six tutorial groups of a business statistics class at Simon Fraser University. The use of small groups helped assure complete understanding of the instructions, and the exercises were conducted over the course of a single day to minimize opportunities for communication between participants. Each group was divided equally: half of the subjects were designated as sellers by random selection,

and the other half became buyers. A total of 59 people took part.

Two induced-value markets for hypothetical payoffs and a subsequent third real exchange market for money and mugs were conducted with identical trading rules used in all three. All participants maintained the same role as either buyers or sellers for the three markets. As in experiments 1 and 2, the prices that individuals chose to buy or to sell were selected from possible prices ranging from $0.00 to $9.50 listed by increments of $0.50.

The results of this experiment were nearly identical to the earlier ones in which the actual exchanges were based on the market-clearing price. Even though possibly less motivating hypothetical values were used in the two induced-value markets, nearly all participants pursued a profit-maximizing selection of prices to buy or sell the assets. Fourteen exchanges at a price of $4.75 were expected in the first induced-value market on the basis of the randomly distributed values written on the forms. Thirteen trades at this price were indicated by the prices actually selected by the participants. The results of the second hypothetical induced-value market were equally convincing, with 16 of the 17 expected exchanges made at the expected price of $5.75. The procedures and incentives were apparently well understood by the participants.

Mugs, comparable to those used in other experiments, were distributed to the potential sellers after the induced-value markets were completed. A mug was also shown to all the potential buyers. The following form with instructions, nearly identical to the ones used in the induced-value markets, was then distributed (with the alternative wording for buyers in brackets):

> You now [do not] have, and own a mug which you can keep and take home. You also have the option of selling it and receiving [buying one to take home by paying] money for it.
>   For each of the possible prices listed below, please indicate whether you wish to: (1) Receive [pay] that amount of money and sell your [buy a] mug, or (2) Not sell your [buy a] mug at this price.
>   After you have finished, one of the prices listed below will be selected at random and any exchanges will take place at that price. If you have indicated you will sell [buy] at this price you will receive this amount of money [a mug] and will give up the mug [pay this amount of money]; if you have indicated that you will keep the [not buy a] mug at this price then no exchange will be made

and you can take the mug home with you [do not pay anything].

Notice the following two things: (1) Your decision can have no effect on the price actually used because the price will be selected at random. (2) It is in your interest to indicate your true preferences at each of the possible prices listed below.

For each price indicate your decision by marking an X in the appropriate column.

	I Will Sell [Buy]	I Will Keep [Not Buy] the Mug
If the price is $0	_____	_____
If the price is $0.50	_____	_____
.		
.		
.		
If the price is $9.50	_____	_____

After the instructions were read and reviewed by the experimenter and questions were answered, participants completed the forms indicating either their lowest selling price or their highest buying price. A random price, from among the list from $0.00 to $9.50, was then drawn, and exchanges based on this price were completed.

The results again showed a large and significant endowment effect. Given the 29 potential buyers, 30 potential sellers, and the random distribution of the mugs, 14.5 exchanges would be expected if entitlements did not influence valuations. Instead, only six were indicated on the basis of the values actually selected by the potential buyers and sellers ($V/V^* = .41$). The median selling price of $5.75 was over twice the median buying price of $2.25, and the means were $5.78 and $2.21, respectively.

IV. Reluctance to Buy versus Reluctance to Sell

Exchanges of money and a good (or between two goods) offer the possibilities of four comparisons: a choice of gaining either the good or money, a choice of losing one or the other, buying (giving up money for the good), and selling (giving up the good for money) (Tversky and Kahneman, in press). The endowment effect results from a difference between the relative preferences for the good and money. The comparison of buying and selling to simple choices between gains permits an analysis of the discrepancy between WTA and WTP into two components: reluctance to sell (ex-

changing the good for money) and reluctance to buy (exchanging money for the good).

Experiments 6 and 7 were carried out to assess the weight of reluctance to buy and reluctance to sell in undertrading of a good similar to the goods used in the earlier experiments. The subjects in experiment 6 were 77 Simon Fraser students, randomly assigned to three groups. Members of one group, designated sellers, were given a coffee mug and were asked to indicate whether or not they would sell the mug at a series of prices ranging from $0.00 to $9.25. A group of buyers indicated whether they were willing to buy a mug at each of these prices. Finally, choosers were asked to choose, for each of the possible prices, between a mug and cash.

The results again reveal substantial undertrading: While 12.5 trades were expected between buyers and sellers, only three trades took place ($V/V^* = .24$). The median valuations were $7.12 for sellers, $3.12 for choosers, and $2.87 for buyers. The close similarity of results for buyers and choosers indicates that there was relatively little reluctance to pay for the mug.

Experiment 7 was carried out with 117 students at the University of British Columbia. It used an identical design except that price tags were left on the mugs. The results were consistent with those in experiment 6. Nineteen trades were expected on the basis of valuation equivalence, but only one was concluded on the basis of actual valuations ($V/V^* = .05$). The median valuations were $7.00 for sellers, $3.50 for choosers, and $2.00 for buyers.

It is worth noting that these results eliminate any form of income effect as an explanation of the discrepant valuations since the positions of sellers and choosers were strictly identical. The allocation of a particular mug to each seller evidently induced a sense of endowment that the choosers did not share: the median value of the mug to the sellers was more than double the value indicated by the choosers even though their choices were objectively the same. The results imply that the observed undertrading of consumption goods may be largely due to a reluctance to part with entitlements.

V. Bilateral Bargaining and the Coase Theorem

According to the Coase theorem, the allocation of resources to individuals who can bargain and trans-act at no cost should be independent of initial property rights. However, if the marginal rate of substitution between one good and another is affected by endowment, then the individual who is assigned the property right to a good will be more likely to retain it. A bilateral bargaining experiment (experiment 8) was carried out to test this implication of the endowment effect.

The subjects were 35 pairs of students in seven small tutorials at Simon Fraser University. The students were enrolled in either a beginning economics course or an English class. Each student was randomly paired with another student in the same tutorial group, with care taken to assure that students entering the tutorial together were not assigned as a pair. A game of Nim, a simple game easily explained, was played by each pair of participants. The winners of the game were each given a 400-gram Swiss chocolate bar and told it was theirs to keep.

An induced-value bargaining session was then conducted. The member of each pair who did not win the Nim game, and therefore did not receive the chocolate bar, was given a ticket and an instruction sheet that indicated that the ticket was worth $3.00 because it could be redeemed for that sum. The ticket owners were also told that they could sell the ticket to their partner if mutually agreeable terms could be reached. The partners (the chocolate bar owners) received instructions indicating that they could receive $5.00 for the ticket if they could successfully buy it from the owner. Thus there was a $2.00 surplus available to any pair completing a trade.

The pairs were then given an unlimited amount of time to bargain. Subjects were told that both credit and change were available from the experimenter. Results of the bargaining sessions were recorded on their instruction sheets.

Of the 35 pairs of participants, 29 agreed to an exchange ($V/V^* = .83$). The average price paid for the 29 tickets was $4.09, with 12 of the exchange prices being exactly $4.00. Payments of the redemption values of the tickets were made as soon as the exchanges were completed. These payments were made in single dollar bills to facilitate trading in the subsequent bargaining session. After the ticket exchanges were completed, owners of the chocolate bars were told that they could sell them to their partners if a mutually agreeable price could be determined. The procedures used for the tick-

ets were once again applied to these bargaining sessions.

An important effect of the preliminary induced-value ticket bargains was to provide the ticket owners with some cash. The average gain to the ticket owners (including the six who did not sell their tickets) was $3.90. The average gain to their partners (the chocolate bar owners) was only $0.76. Thus the potential chocolate bar buyers were endowed with an average of $3.14 more than the owners, creating a small income effect toward the buyers. Also, to the extent that a windfall gain such as this is spent more casually by subjects than other money (for evidence on such a "house money effect," see Thaler and Johnson [1990]), trading of chocolate bars should be facilitated.

Results of the chocolate bar bargains once again suggest reluctance to trade. Rather than the 17.5 trades expected from the random allocations, only seven were observed ($V/V^* = .4$). The average price paid in those exchanges that did occur was $2.69 (the actual prices were $6.00, $3.10, $3.00, $2.75, $2.00, $1.00, and $1.00). If the six pairs of subjects who did not successfully complete bargains in the first stage are omitted from the sample on the grounds that they did not understand the task or procedures, then six trades are observed where 14.5 would be expected ($V/V^* = .414$). Similarly, if two more pairs are dropped because the prices at which they exchanged tickets were outside the range $3.00–$5.00, then the number of trades falls to four, and V/V^* falls to .296. (No significant differences between the students in the English and economics classes were observed.)[6]

To be sure that the chocolate bars were valued by the subjects and that these valuations would vary enough to yield mutually beneficial trades, the same chocolate bars were distributed to half the members of another class at Simon Fraser. Those who received chocolate bars were asked the minimum price they would accept to sell their bar, while those without the bars were asked the maxi-

---

[6] We conducted two similar bargaining experiments that yielded comparable results. Twenty-six pairs of subjects negotiated the sale of mugs and then envelopes containing an uncertain amount of money. Buyers had not been given any cash endowment. These sessions yielded six and five trades, respectively, where 13 would be expected. Also, some induced-value bilateral negotiation sessions were conducted in which only $0.50 of surplus was available (the seller's valuation was $1.50 and the buyer's was $2.00). Nevertheless, 21 of a possible 26 trades were completed.

mum price they would pay to acquire a bar. The valuations of the bars varied from $0.50 to $8.00. The average value ascribed by sellers was $3.98, while the buyers' average valuation was $1.25. (The median values were $3.50 and $1.25.)

VI. The Endowment Effect in Choices between Goods

The previous experiments documented undertrading in exchanges of money and consumption goods. A separate experiment (Knetsch 1989) establishes the same effect in exchanges between two goods. Participants in three classes were offered a choice between the same two goods. All students in one class were given a coffee mug at the beginning of the session as compensation for completing a short questionnaire. At the completion of the task, the experimenters showed the students a bar of Swiss chocolate that they could immediately receive in exchange for the mug. The students in another class were offered an opportunity to make the opposite exchange after first being given the chocolate bar. The students in a third class were simply offered a choice, at the beginning of the session, between a chocolate bar and a mug. The proportion of students selecting the mug was 89 percent in the class originally endowed with mugs ($N = 76$), 56 percent in the class offered a choice ($N = 55$), and only 10 percent in the class originally endowed with chocolate bars ($N = 87$). For most participants a mug was more valuable than the chocolate when the mug had to be given up but less valuable when the chocolate had to be given up. This experiment confirms that undertrading can occur even when income effects are ruled out. It also demonstrates an endowment effect for a good that was distributed to everyone in the class and therefore did not have the appeal of a prize or trophy.

VII. Discussion

The evidence presented in this paper supports what may be called an instant endowment effect: the value that an individual assigns to such objects as mugs, pens, binoculars, and chocolate bars appears to increase substantially as soon as that individual is given the object.[7] The apparently instantaneous nature of the reference point shift and consequent value change induced by giving a person possession of a good goes beyond previous discussions of the endowment effect, which focused on goods that have been in the individual's possession for some time. While long-term endowment effects could be explained by sentimental attachment or by an improved technology of consumption in the Stigler-Becker (1977) sense, the differences in preference or taste demonstrated by more than 700 participants in the experiments reported in this paper cannot be explained in this fashion.

The endowment effect is one explanation for the systematic differences between buying and selling prices that have been observed so often in past work. One of the objectives of this study was to examine an alternative explanation for this buying-selling discrepancy, namely that it reflects a general bargaining strategy (Knez and Smith 1987) that would be eliminated by experience in the market (Brookshire and Coursey 1987; Coursey et al. 1987). Our results do not support this alternative view. The trading institution used in experiments 1–7 encouraged participants to be price takers (especially in experiment 5), and the rules provided no incentive to conceal true preferences. Furthermore, the results of the induced-value markets indicate that the subjects understood the demand-revealing nature of the questions they were asked and acted accordingly. Substantial undertrading was nevertheless observed in markets for consumption goods. As for learning and market discipline, there was no indication that buying and selling prices converged over repeated market trials, though full feedback was provided at the end of each trial. The undertrading observed in these experiments appears to reflect a true difference in preferences between the potential buyers and sellers. The robustness of this result reduces the risk that the outcome is produced by an experimental artifact. In short, the present findings indicate that the endowment effect can persist in genuine market settings.

The contrast between the induced-value markets and the consumption goods markets lends

---

[7] The impression gained from informal pilot experiments is that the act of giving the participant physical possession of the good results in a more consistent endowment effect. Assigning subjects a chance to receive a good, or a property right to a good to be received at a later time, seemed to produce weaker effects.

support to Heiner's (1985) conjecture that the results of induced-value experiments may not generalize to all market settings. The defining characteristic of the induced-value markets is that the values of the tokens are unequivocally defined by the amount the experimenter will pay for them. Loss aversion is irrelevant with such objects because transactions are evaluated simply on the basis of net gain or loss. (If someone is offered $6.00 for a $5.00 bill, there is no sense of loss associated with the trade.) Some markets may share this feature of induced-value markets, especially when the conditions of pure arbitrage are approached. However, the computation of net gain and loss is not possible in other situations, for example, in markets in which risky prospects are traded for cash or in markets in which people sell goods that they also value for their use. In these conditions, the cancellation of the loss of the object against the dollars received is not possible because the good and money are not strictly commensurate. The valuation ambiguity produced by this lack of commensurability is necessary, although not sufficient, for both loss aversion and a buying-selling discrepancy.

The results of the experimental demonstrations of the endowment effect have direct implications for economic theory and economic predictions. Contrary to the assumptions of standard economic theory that preferences are independent of entitlements,[8] the evidence presented here indicates that people's preferences depend on their reference positions. Consequently, preference orderings are not defined independently of endowments: good A may be preferred to B when A is part of an original endowment, but the reverse may be true when initial reference positions are changed. Indifference curves will have a kink at the endowment or reference point (see Tversky and Kahneman, in press), and an indifference curve tracing acceptable trades in one direction may even cross another indifference curve that plots the acceptable exchanges in the opposite direction (Knetsch 1989).

The existence of endowment effects reduces the gains from trade. In comparison with a world in which preferences are independent of endowment, the existence of loss aversion produces an inertia in the economy because potential traders are more reluctant to trade than is conventionally assumed. This is not to say that Pareto-optimal trades will not take place. Rather, there are simply fewer mutually advantageous exchanges possible, and so the volume of trade is lower than it otherwise would be.

To assess the practical significance of the endowment effect, it is important to consider first some necessary conditions for the effect to be observed. Experiments 6 and 7 suggest that the endowment effect is primarily a problem for sellers; we observed little reluctance to buy but much reluctance to sell. Furthermore, not all sellers are afflicted by an endowment effect. The effect did not appear in the markets for money tokens, and there is no reason in general to expect reluctance to resell goods that are held especially for that purpose. An owner will not be reluctant to sell an item at a given price if a perfect substitute is readily available at a lower price. This reasoning suggests that endowment effects will almost certainly occur when owners are faced with an opportunity to sell an item purchased for use that is not easily replaceable. Examples might include tickets to a sold-out event, hunting licenses in limited supply (Bishop and Heberlein 1979), works of art, or a pleasant view.

While the conditions necessary for an endowment effect to be observed may appear to limit its applicability in economic settings, in fact these conditions are very often satisfied, and especially so in the bargaining contexts to which the Coase theorem is applied. For example, tickets to Wimbledon are allocated by means of a lottery. A standard Coasean analysis would imply that in the presence of an efficient ticket brokerage market, winners of the lottery would be no more likely to attend the matches than other tennis fans who had won a similar cash prize in an unrelated lottery. In contrast, the experimental results presented in this paper predict that many winners of Wimbledon tickets will attend the event, turning down opportunities to sell their tickets that exceed their reservation price for buying them.

Endowment effects can also be observed for firms and other organizations. Endowment effects are predicted for property rights acquired by historic accident or fortuitous circumstances, such as government licenses, landing rights, or transferable pollution permits. Owing to endowment ef-

---

[8] Although ownership can affect taste in the manner suggested by Stigler and Becker (1977), in the absence of income effects, it is traditional to assume that the indifference curves in an Edgeworth box diagram do not depend on the location of the endowment point.

fects, firms will be reluctant to divest themselves of divisions, plants, and product lines even though they would never consider buying the same assets; indeed, stock prices often rise when firms do given them up. Again, the prediction is not an absence of trade, just a reduction in the volume of trade.

Isolating the influence of endowment effects from those of transaction costs as causes of low trading volumes is, of course, difficult in actual market settings. Demonstrations of endowment effects are most persuasive where transaction costs are very small. By design, this was the case in the experimental markets, where the efficiency of the induced-value markets demonstrated the minimal effect of transaction costs, or other impediments, on exchange decisions, leaving the great reluctance to trade mugs and other goods to be attributable to endowment effects.

Endowment effects are not limited to cases involving physical goods or to legal entitlements. The reference position of individuals and firms often includes terms of previous transactions or expectations of continuation of present, often informal, arrangements. There is clear evidence of dramatically asymmetric reactions to improvements and deteriorations of these terms and a willingness to make sacrifices to avoid unfair treatment (Kahneman, Knetsch, and Thaler 1986). The reluctance to sell at a loss, owing to a perceived entitlement to a formerly prevailing price, can explain two observations of apparent undertrading. The first pertains to housing markets. It is often observed that when housing prices fall, volume also falls. When house prices are falling, houses remain on the market longer than when prices are rising. Similarly, the volume for stocks that have declined in price is lower than the volume for stocks that have increased in value (Shefrin and Statman 1985; Ferris, Haugen, and Makhija 1988), although tax considerations would lead to the opposite prediction.

Another manifestation of loss aversion in the context of multiattribute negotiations is what might be termed "concession aversion": a reluctance to accept a loss on any dimension of an agreement. A straightforward and common instance of this is the downward stickiness of wages. A somewhat more subtle implication of concession aversion is that it can produce inefficient contract terms owing to historic precedents. Old firms may have more inefficient arrangements than new ones because new companies can negotiate without the

reference positions created by prior agreements. Some airlines, for example, are required to carry three pilots on some planes while others—newer ones—operate with two.

Loss aversion implies a marked asymmetry in the treatment of losses and forgone gains, which plays an essential role in judgments of fairness (Kahneman et al. 1986). Accordingly, disputes in which concessions are viewed as losses are often much less tractable than disputes in which concessions involve forgone gains. Court decisions recognize the asymmetry of losses and forgone gains by favoring possessors of goods over other claimants, by limiting recovery of lost profits relative to compensation for actual expenditures, and by failing to enforce gratuitous promises that are coded as forgone gains to the injured party (Cohen and Knetsch 1989).

To conclude, the evidence reported here offers no support for the contention that observations of loss aversion and the consequential evaluation disparities are artifacts; nor should they be interpreted as mistakes likely to be eliminated by experience, training, or "market discipline." Instead, the findings support an alternative view of endowment effects and loss aversion as fundamental characteristics of preferences.

ACKNOWLEDGMENTS

Financial support was provided by Fisheries and Oceans Canada, the Ontario Ministry of the Environment, and the behavioral economics program of the Alfred P. Sloan Foundation. We wish to thank Vernon Smith for encouraging us to conduct these experiments and for providing extensive comments on earlier drafts. Of course, the usual disclaimer applies.

REFERENCES

Banford, Nancy D.; Knetsch, Jack L.; and Mauser, Gary A. "Feasibility Judgements and Alternative Measures of Benefits and Costs." *J. Bus. Admin.* 11, nos. 1, 2 (1979): 25–35.

Becker, Gordon M.; DeGroot, Morris H.; and Marschak, Jacob. "Measuring Utility by a Single-Response Sequential Method." *Behavioral Sci.* 9 (July 1964): 226–32.

Bishop, Richard C., and Heberlein, Thomas A. "Measuring Values of Extramarket Goods: Are Indirect Measures Biased?" *American J. Agricultural Econ.* 61 (December 1979): 926–30.

Boyce, Rebecca R.; Brown, Thomas C.; McClelland, Gary D.; Peterson, George L.; and Schulze, William D. "An Experimental Examination of Intrinsic Environmental Values." Working paper. Boulder: Univ. Colorado, 1990.

Brookshire, David S., and Coursey, Don L. "Measuring the Value of a Public Good: An Empirical Comparison of Elicitation Procedures." *A.E.R.* 77 (September 1987): 554–66.

Brookshire, David S.; Randall, Alan; and Stoll, John R. "Valuing Increments and Decrements in Natural Resource Service Flows." *American J. Agricultural Econ.* 62 (August 1980): 478–88.

Cohen, David, and Knetsch, Jack L. "Judicial Choice and Disparities between Measures of Economic Values." Working paper. Burnaby, B.C.: Simon Fraser Univ., 1989.

Coursey, Don L.; Hovis, John L.; and Schulze, William D. "The Disparity between Willingness to Accept and Willingness to Pay Measures of Value." *Q.J.E.* 102 (August 1987): 679–90.

Ferris, Stephen P.; Haugen, Robert A.; and Makhija, Anil K. "Predicting Contemporary Volume with Historic Volume at Differential Price Levels: Evidence Supporting the Disposition Effect." *J. Finance* 43 (July 1988): 677–97.

Freeman, A. Myrick. *The Benefits of Environmental Improvement.* Washington: Resources for the Future, 1979.

Hammack, Judd, and Brown, Gardner Mallard, Jr. *Waterfowl and Wetlands: Toward Bio-economic Analysis.* Baltimore: Johns Hopkins Press (for Resources for the Future), 1974.

Heberlein, Thomas A., and Bishop, Richard C. "Assessing the Validity of Contingent Valuation: Three Field Experiments." Paper presented at the International Conference on Man's Role in Changing the Global Environment, Italy, 1985.

Heiner, Ronald A. "Experimental Economics: Comment." *A.E.R.* 75 (March 1985): 260–63.

Kahneman, Daniel; Knetsch, Jack L.; and Thaler, Richard. "Fairness as a Constraint on Profit Seeking: Entitlements in the Market." *A.E.R.* 76 (September 1986): 728–41.

Kahneman, Daniel, and Tversky, Amos. "Prospect Theory: An Analysis of Decision under Risk." *Econometrica* 47 (March 1979): 263–91.

Knetsch, Jack L. "The Endowment Effect and Evidence of Nonreversible Indifference Curves." *A.E.R.* 79 (December 1989): 1277–84.

Knetsch, Jack L., and Sinden, J. A. "Willingness to Pay and Compensation Demanded: Experimental Evidence of an Unexpected Disparity in Measures of Value." *Q.J.E.* 99 (August 1984): 507–21.

—. "The Persistence of Evaluation Disparities." *Q.J.E.* 102 (August 1987): 691–95.

Knez, Marc, and Smith, Vernon L. "Hypothetical Valuations and Preference Reversals in the Context of Asset Trading." In *Laboratory Experiments in Economics: Six Points of View*, edited by Alvin E. Roth. Cambridge: Cambridge Univ. Press, 1987.

Knez, Peter; Smith, Vernon L.; and Williams, Arlington W. "Individual Rationality, Market Rationality, and Value Estimation." *A.E.R. Papers and Proc.* 75 (May 1985): 397–402.

Plott, Charles R. "Industrial Organization Theory and Experimental Economics." *J. Econ. Literature* 20 (December 1982): 1485–1527.

Rowe, Robert D.; d'Arge, Ralph C.; and Brookshire, David S. "An Experiment on the Economic Value of Visibility." *J. Environmental Econ. and Management* 7 (March 1980): 1–19.

Shefrin, Hersh, and Statman, Meir. "The Disposition to Sell Winners Too Early and Ride Losers Too Long: Theory and Evidence." *J. Finance* 40 (July 1985): 777–90.

Sinclair, William F. *The Economic and Social Impact of Kemano II Hydroelectric Project on British Columbia's Fisheries Resources.* Vancouver: Dept. Fisheries and Oceans, 1978.

Smith, Vernon L. "Experimental Economics: Induced Value Theory." *A.E.R. Papers and Proc.* 66 (May 1976): 274–79.

—. "Macroeconomic Systems as an Experimental Science." *A.E.R.* 72 (December 1982): 923–55.

Stigler, George J., and Becker, Gary S. "De Gustibus Non Est Disputandum." *A.E.R.* 67 (March 1977): 76–90.

Thaler, Richard. "Toward a Positive Theory of Consumer Choice." *J. Econ. Behavior and Organization* 1 (March 1980): 39–60.

Thaler, Richard, and Johnson, Eric J. "Gambling with the House Money and Trying to Break Even: The Effects of Prior Outcomes on Risky Choice." *Management Sci.* 36 (June 1990).

Tversky, Amos, and Kahneman, Daniel. "Reference Theory of Choice and Exchange." *Q.J.E.* (in press).

Willig, Robert D. "Consumer's Surplus without Apology." *A.E.R.* 66 (September 1976): 589–97.

Social Utility and Decision Making in Interpersonal Contexts

George F. Loewenstein • University of Chicago
Leigh Thompson • University of Washington
Max H. Bazerman • Northwestern University

Three studies examined preferences for outcomes to self and a codisputant. Studies 1 and 2 estimated social utility functions from judgments of satisfaction with alternative outcomes. Comparing functional forms, we found that a utility function, including terms for own payoff and for positive and negative discrepancies between the parties' payoffs (advantageous and disadvantageous inequality), provides a close fit to the data. The typical utility function is steeply increasing and convex for disadvantageous inequality and weakly declining and convex for advantageous inequality. We manipulated dispute type (personal, business) and disputant relationship (positive, neutral, or negative) and found that both strongly influence preferences for advantageous but not disadvantageous inequality. A third study contrasted implications of the social utility functions with predictions of individual utility theories.

People care about the outcomes of others. We sacrifice our own interests to help loved ones or harm adversaries. Participants withdraw from profitable participation in a laboratory experiment if they perceive inequity in remuneration (Schmitt & Marwell, 1972). Players in two-person ultimatum games (in which one player proposes a distribution of a fixed amount of money that the other has the option of either accepting or rejecting) frequently reject a positive but inequitable offer even though the alternative is no gain at all (Guth, Schmittberger, & Schwarze, 1982). Negotiations between parties often collapse when one party becomes incensed with the other and attempts to "maximize his opponent's displeasure rather than his own satisfaction" (Seigel & Fouraker, 1960, p. 100). In general, disputants are concerned not only with the outcomes they receive, but also with the outcomes of their opponents (Pruitt & Rubin, 1986).

The importance of interpersonal comparisons has long been recognized by social psychologists. Equity theorists (Adams, 1963, 1965; Homans, 1961; Walster, Walster, & Berscheid, 1978) have argued that people attempt to maintain proportionality between inputs and outcomes to themselves and comparison others. Research on relative deprivation has enumerated preconditions for experiencing deprivation as a result of adverse social comparison (Crosby, 1976). Social comparison theory (Festinger, 1954) has focused mainly on the question of with whom people choose to compare themselves.

Recently, a number of researchers have experimented with different ways of graphically or mathematically encoding individuals' concern for others' outcomes. The main focus of this work has been on decomposing individuals' concern for the outcomes of others into underlying primary motives and graphically depicting these motives using indifference curves, a tool widely used by economists. One of the earliest of these analyses (Scott, 1972) distinguished between three motives underlying concern for other people's outcomes: avarice, altruism, and egalitarianism, each with its own characteristically shaped pattern of indifference curves. Later, MacCrimmon and Messick (1976) proposed that concern for others' payoff could be decomposed into six basic motives, consisting of self-interest (choosing so as to increase own payoffs), self-sacrifice (choosing so as to decrease your own payoffs), altruism (choosing so as to increase the payoffs to the other party), aggression (choosing so as to decrease the payoffs to the other party), cooperation (choosing so as to increase the sum of your payoff and the other's payoff), and competition (choosing so as to increase the difference between your payoffs; see also Griesinger & Livingston, 1973). MacCrimmon and Messick also identified a series of supplementary motives that reflected the assumption of equity theory that concern about the other party depends on the ratio of, rather than the difference between, the parties' attainments. Most recently, Lurie (1987) has developed an indifference curve analysis based on the idea that people are concerned with both the difference and the ratio between their own and another party's outcomes.

The indifference curve approach is basically a theory-free tool that permits free expression of preferences. It is useful as a tool for studying preferences, but it has two major limitations. First, it is difficult to make specific behavioral predictions using indifference curves, especially in situations different from those in which the indifference curves were estimated. Second, it is difficult to compare indifference curves to the utility models that have formed the main thrust of work on decision making under uncertainty. An alternative approach that avoids these problems encodes interpersonal preferences using *social utility functions*. Social utility functions specify level of satisfaction as a function of outcome to self and other. Although more restrictive than indifference curves

because they impose a specific functional form on preferences, social utility functions permit easier comparison with other decision models such as prospect theory (Kahneman & Tversky, 1979) and make specific behavioral predictions in a wide range of situations.

Although less developed than the work on indifference curves, there has been limited research on social utility. Conrath and Deci (1969) conjectured about different shapes that social utility functions could assume and explored how different basic social motives would manifest themselves in utility function curvature. Other research has empirically estimated social utility functions in different contexts (e.g., Messick & Sentis, 1985). Our research extends the work on social utility in a number of directions.

First, we estimate a separate utility function for each subject. Earlier estimates of social utility functions have fitted a single, aggregate, utility function to all subjects (e.g., Messick & Sentis, 1985). Individual-level estimates permit an examination of the consistency of preferences across decision makers as well as the identification of individual differences in social utility functions.

Second, we examine social and contextual factors that may affect decision making in interpersonal contexts. Although the importance of these factors has been demonstrated in research on social dilemmas (e.g., Orbell & Dawes, 1981), their impact on social utility functions has not been examined systematically.[1] Two important factors that may influence decision making in interpersonal contexts are the nature of the relationship between the individual and the comparison other and the nature of the dispute (dispute type), for example, a business or personal matter. At a simple level, relationships may be dichotomously characterized as positive and harmonious or as negative and disruptive (Heider, 1958; Kelley, 1979). On the basis of prior research (e.g., Walster et al., 1978), one might expect individuals in positive or neutral relationships to value equity. In negative relationships, people may prefer to receive more than the other party (advantageous inequality) and be particularly averse to situations in which the

---

[1] A recent exception is Lurie (1987). Lurie included a relationship condition comparable to ours in his empirical indifference curve analysis. However, his study used too few subjects to systematically compare the different conditions.

other party receives more than the self (disadvantageous inequality).

The dispute type refers to the issue being negotiated (e.g., a business or personal matter). Lewicki and Litterer (1985) suggested that the norms' of a situation affect decision making. For example, with friends and neighbors, the equality norm is expected to prevail (Austin, 1980). However, business transactions often dictate a greater concern for self, with the implicit value being that individuals should maximize their own outcomes. Business disputes generally occur in the context of exchange relationships, whereas personal disputes occur in communal relationships (Clark & Mills, 1979). Exchange relationships are characterized by strict norms of reciprocity, which is expected to be overt, immediate, and typically in kind. Although reciprocity is also important in communal relationships (Thibaut & Kelley, 1959), it is generally less overt and occurs over longer time intervals.

Third, we compare the goodness of fit of a variety of functional forms reflecting different social motives. Earlier research on social utility functions assumed a particular functional form, without testing alternatives.

The functional form that we ultimately estimated has properties that permit a direct comparison to Kahneman and Tversky's prospect theory (1979). A central idea of prospect theory is that people evaluate the utility of alternative courses of action relative to a reference point. Outcomes below the reference point are viewed as losses; outcomes above the reference point are perceived as gains. The reference point represents a state to which individuals have adapted and is usually assumed to correspond to the status quo. However, in an interpersonal context the outcomes of another person may emerge as an alternative (or additional), potentially salient reference point. The prospect theory value function is concave in the region of gains, indicating risk aversion, and convex in the region of losses, indicating risk seeking. A major interest of ours is whether the typical social utility function has a similar shape.

Our studies examined social utility in a dispute context. We were interested in estimating social utility functions that could be used to predict individual behavior in situations, such as negotiations, in which decisions have consequences not only for the self, but also for another party. In Study 1, we performed multiple regressions to estimate a separate utility function for each subject. We examined the impact of the relationship between the disputants and the environmental context on the shape of the utility function. Study 2 extended and replicated the findings from the first study using a separate data set. In Study 3, we used the model specifications from the first two studies to contrast decision making in individual and interpersonal contexts. The primary question addressed in Study 3 is whether the introduction of interpersonal concerns leads to consistent departures from the predictions of prospect theory in competitive decision-making tasks.

Study 1

Method

Subjects and procedure. A total of 148 subjects participated in the study; 98 were undergraduate students and participated in partial fulfillment of an introductory psychology course requirement; 50 were students in a graduate management program in a business school.[2]

Materials and procedure. The experimenter told participants that the purpose of the study was to examine individuals' reactions to situations involving disputes between two people. Participants were each given a booklet consisting of 10 pages. The 1st page instructed participants to assume the role of the disputant described in each situation. The 2nd page described a dispute between two people. On the 3rd and 4th pages, participants indicated their satisfaction with each of 42 possible outcomes of the dispute by making a slash mark on a scale with endpoints labeled *very unsatisfied* (−5) and *very satisfied* (5). The outcomes described exact dollar payoffs to the self and the other party. The 5th page described a different dispute, and participants rated their satisfaction with outcomes on Pages 6 and 7. The 8th page described a third dispute, and participants rated their satisfaction with outcomes on Pages 9 and 10.

Design. Our design included two within-subjects variables: relationship between disputants

---

[2] There were no significant differences between the two groups on any of the analyses. Therefore, the analyses reported in this study are based on the total sample.

(positive, negative, or neutral) and dispute type. Dispute type included three conditions, two occurring between people of the same status in a nonbusiness setting and one occurring between a customer and salesperson in a business setting. In one nonbusiness dispute ("invention") two students were faced with the task of splitting the proceeds or costs resulting from a joint invention:

One day while eating lunch, a student who lives in your dorm, Pat, mentioned to you an idea for a new product: cross-country water skis. They are similar to conventional cross-country skis except that they are floatable pontoons that permit you to "ski" over water. Pat thought of the idea several years ago, but had not done anything with it and had not been able to interest anyone in it.

You find the idea of whisking over the water in a standing position exciting. You suggest to Pat that the two of you work together on the project.

Over the next month you spend long hours together constructing a prototype of the water skis in the basement of your dorm. Since it was Pat's idea, you agree to pay for the materials you use to construct the prototype. After extensively testing and refining the skis at the university pool, you decide that you are ready to patent the invention. You hire a patent lawyer to determine whether there is an existing patent on the invention. At your first meeting with the lawyer, he draws up a patent application document for the two of you to examine.

[relationship manipulation goes here]

Loss: Several weeks after your meeting with the patent lawyer, he returns with the news that cross-country water skis have already been patented. Nevertheless, you are responsible for paying him for his services. Both you and Pat receive copies of his bill and negotiate how to split the cost.

Gain: Several weeks after your meeting with the patent lawyer, he returns with the news that cross-country water skis have already been patented. However, he has contacted the current holder of the patent, who is interested in buying one of the innovative features incorporated in your design. You and Pat agree that the amount offered seems reasonable. The two of you negotiate how to split the profit.

In the other nonbusiness scenario ("lot"), two neighbors split revenue or tax payments from a vacant lot located between their houses. The business dispute scenario ("business") described a conflict between a customer and a sales manager at a computer retail outlet in which the disputants split either the revenue from a retroactive rebate or the cost of repairs. The stimuli for the lot and business disputes are presented in the appendix.

We manipulated the relationship between the two disputants by including details about prior encounters with the other disputant. In the positive relationship condition, participants read a description of a positive, harmonious relationship between the parties. In the invention dispute, this description read as follows: "In perusing the patent application at home later that day, you find that Pat has listed your name as the primary inventor of the skis. You are pleased, but believe that he really deserves this designation." In the negative relationship condition, participants read a description of a negative, acrimonious relationship between the parties. The text for the invention condition read as follows: "In perusing the patent application at home later that day, you find that Pat has not listed your name on the patent. You feel snubbed since, although it was his initial idea, he had taken it nowhere without your assistance." In the neutral relationship condition, the participants were not provided with any information about the disputants' prior relationship.

We combined the three dispute situations (two personal and one business) with the three relationship conditions using a Latin square design. If we label the dispute situations as A, B, and C and the relationship conditions as 1, 2, and 3, then the three sets of stimuli were composed as follows: (A1, B2, C3), (A2, B3, C1), and (A3, B1, C2). These were randomly assigned to participants.

We constructed 21 positive outcomes by combining 3 outcomes to self ($300, $500, and $600) with 7 outcomes to the other party determined by adding one of seven dollar amounts (–$300, –$200, –$100, 0, $100, $200, and $300) to the amount received by self. As a result, the outcomes to the other party ranged from $0 to $900. We constructed 21 negative outcome combinations by expressing the same dollar values as amounts to be paid rather than received. Participants rated their satisfaction with the 21 outcomes involving gains to the self and the other party and then with the 21 outcomes involving losses to the self and the other party for each of the disputes. Because subjects completed these 42 judgments in three different relationship–dispute-type conditions, each subject made a total of 126 judgments. To avoid response set and automatic responding, outcome pairs were randomly ordered on the page; however, all subjects received the same order.

TABLE 1. Adjusted R^2 by Relationship and Dispute Type: Study 1

Condition		Equation									
		1		2		3		4		5	
Relationship	Dispute type	R^2	SD	R^2	SD	R^2	SD	R^2	SD	R^2	SD
Positive	Invention	.41	.33	.52	.24	.35	.32	.25	.27	.66	.26
Neutral	Invention	.46	.33	.55	.25	.30	.32	.31	.25	.65	.25
Negative	Invention	.59	.31	.63	.23	.41	.30	.47	.31	.70	.20
Positive	Lot	.43	.34	.55	.27	.33	.33	.17	.18	.74	.23
Neutral	Lot	.33	.31	.51	.21	.40	.32	.15	.23	.72	.22
Negative	Lot	.60	.30	.65	.25	.18	.30	.25	.22	.79	.21
Positive	Business	.70	.25	.70	.24	.18	.30	.39	.27	.73	.22
Neutral	Business	.75	.16	.71	.15	.27	.30	.55	.25	.72	.16
Negative	Business	.75	.17	.72	.17	.31	.33	.53	.28	.73	.17
All conditions		.56	.32	.62	.24	.30	.32	.34	.29	.72	.32

Results

Specification of the model. The first stage of our analysis involved selecting a functional form for the social utility function. We considered three criteria in evaluating different functional specifications: (a) goodness of fit across subjects—the selected functional form should explain a large amount of the variation in an individual subject's ratings; (b) simplicity—it should incorporate a minimum number of explanatory variables; and (c) flexibility—it should be capable of depicting qualitative differences between subjects' patterns of responses. We experimented with several functional forms, each of which included terms for the individual's own payoff and own payoff squared, permitting estimation of both slope and curvature.[3] The first functional form we examined assumes that people are concerned with absolute level of payments both to self and other. Defining U as utility, SELF as payoff to self, and OTHER as the opponent's payoff, the regression equation is as follows:

$$U = c + B_1 \text{SELF} + B_2 \text{SELF}^2 + B_3 \text{OTHER} + B_4 \text{OTHER}^2 \quad (1)$$

Equation 1 is appropriate if the utility one obtains from the other person's payoff does not depend on the payoff to oneself.

An alternative formulation includes the difference between the payment to the other party and one's own payment rather than the absolute payment to the other party. Defining DIFF as the difference between own and other's payoff,

$$U = c + B_1 \text{SELF} + B_2 \text{SELF}^2 + B_3 \text{DIFF} + B_4 \text{DIFF}^2 \quad (2)$$

Equation 2 is the bivariate utility function proposed by Conrath and Deci (1969). Note that by suitable manipulation, Equation 2 can be rewritten as Equation 1 plus an interaction term. Thus, we would expect Equation 2 to outperform Equation 1 if preferences for own payoff are not independent of the payoff to the other party.

A third form, suggested by equity theory, incorporates the absolute difference between self and other and the absolute difference squared. This formulation is applicable if people dislike disparity in either direction between own and other payoff. Let |DIFF| represent the absolute difference between own and other payoff. Then,

$$U = c + B_1 \text{SELF} + B_2 \text{SELF}^2 + B_3 |\text{DIFF}| + B_4 |\text{DIFF}|^2 \quad (3)$$

Finally, we tested a formulation based on the social motive that MacCrimmon and Messick (1976) defined as *proportionate competition*. This involves "choosing so as to increase the ratio of your payoff to the other's payoff" (MacCrimmon & Messick, 1976, p. 90). Defining PROP as payments to self divided by total payoffs,

$$U = c + B_1 \text{SELF} + B_2 \text{SELF}^2 + B_3 \text{PROP}^+ + B_4 \text{PROP}^- \quad (4)$$

---

[3] Although there is no reason to assume that a power function expresses the curvature of the utility function better than any other functional form, the amount of data collected and the limited number of values of own payoff that were collected made it impractical to compare the relative fit of alternative second-order terms.

Because a higher proportion of payments may be desirable when payoffs are gains, but undesirable when payments are losses, we included separate PROP terms for losses and gains.

To compare the goodness of fit of the four specifications, we performed separate regressions for each subject, and within subjects, for each disputant relationship condition (positive, neutral, or negative) and dispute-type (personal or business) combination. Goodness of fit across the four equations was compared on the basis of adjusted R^2s. The Equation 1–4 columns of Table 1 present the means of the adjusted R^2s for each of the four specifications in each of the relationship and dispute-type conditions.[4] Equations 1 and 2 provided systematically higher R^2s than did Equations 3 and 4, all $ts(725) > 141$, $p < .0001$, and Equation 2 also significantly outperformed Equation 1 in terms of R^2, $t(725) = 13.8$, $p < .0002$.[5] Looking across the nine relationship-dispute–type combinations in Table 1, it can be seen that Equation 2 is superior to Equation 1 in six combinations, equal in one, and inferior in two.

In a second round of estimation, we compared Equation 2 with a modified function that permitted a different slope and curvature for positive and negative values of DIFF. We also dropped the self-squared term because it failed to achieve significance in a majority of the regression equations.

$$U = c + B_1\text{SELF} + B_2\text{NEGDIFF} + B_3\text{NEGDIFF}^2 + B_4\text{POSDIFF} + B_5\text{POSDIFF}^2. \quad (5)$$

The prefixes NEG and POS act as binary switches that activate the terms for negative and positive values of DIFF respectively.

The mean adjusted R^2 for Equation 5 under each relationship and dispute type is presented in the last column of Table 1.

Difference Between Own and Other Payoff

Across the nine relationship–dispute-type conditions, the mean adjusted R^2 for Equation 5 was .72, a significant improvement over the average adjusted R^2 of .62 for Equation 2, $t(725) = 58.6$, $p < .0001$. The fact that the inclusion of separate terms for positive and negative differences leads to such a great improvement in R^2 suggests that in interpersonal, as in individual, decision making, there is a discontinuity in the treatment of positive

and negative departures from one's reference level (Kahneman & Tversky, 1979; Walster et al., 1978).

The functional form represented by Equation 5 has several desirable qualities. First, it allows one to assess the relative importance of intrapersonal and interpersonal concerns by comparing the parameter values applied to SELF and to the various DIFF terms. Second, and as noted previously, it makes it possible to separate subjects' attitudes toward advantageous and disadvantageous inequality. Finally, the functional form is sufficiently flexible to permit comparison with individual-level models of decision making such as prospect theory.

The estimated utility function is illustrated in Figure 1, averaging across the three relationship conditions and three dispute types. Three different curves correspond to different levels of SELF (payoff to self). The predominant shape is upward sloping and convex for negative values of DIFF. For positive values of DIFF, the curve slopes downward and is also convex.

Relationship and dispute type. Table 2 summarizes the results of the regression analysis in tabular form, disaggregating the data by disputant relationship and dispute type. Each estimate is the mean of individual subjects' parameter estimates. To facilitate comparisons of parameter estimates across different relationship–dispute-type conditions, we performed separate analyses of variance (ANOVAS) with the regression parameters SELF, NEGDIFF, and POSDIFF serving as dependent variables and the relationship and dispute-type conditions as independent variables.

Concern for own payoff (as indicated by the

---

[4] The interpretations of the differences between adjusted R^2s is questionable, due both to the problematic nature of the adjusted R^2 statistic and to the fact that the different adjusted R^2s were estimated from the same population. Nevertheless, we believe the differences between the adjusted R^2s, and the significance of these differences looking across subjects, permits a reasonable qualitative comparison of goodness of fit across equations.

[5] We estimated all t statistics from an analysis of variance (ANOVA) in which the adjusted R^2 of the regression equations served as the dependent variable and the equation type (1–5) served as the independent variable. All comparisons that were significant on the basis of the conventional t test were also significant at the .05 level, using Scheffé's test, which controls for experimentwise error. Each pairwise comparison is based on 888 regressions (148 subjects × 3 conditions × 2 equations): however, this number was reduced to 871 because of missing data. Correcting for the repeated measures nature of the design absorbed 145 degrees of freedom, leaving 725 degrees of freedom.

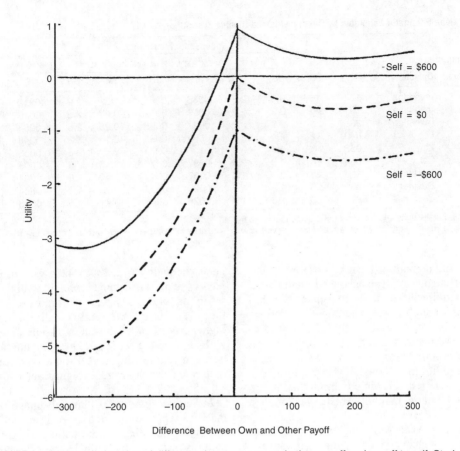

FIGURE 1 ■ Utility as a function of difference between own and other payoff and payoff to self: Study 1.

parameter value for SELF) differed across the three types of disputes, $F(2,284) = 36.9, p < .0001$. Subjects displayed greatest concern for their own payoff in the invention and business disputes, whereas concern for own payoff in the lot scenario was significantly lower, all $ts(284) > 40.7, p < .0001.$[6] The disputant relationship also had a significant effect on concern for self. $F(2, 284) = 19.4, p < .0001.$ Concern for own payment was highest in the negative relationship condition, followed by the neutral condition, and lowest in the positive relationship condition, with all three conditions significantly different from one another, all $ts(284) > 9.1, p < .003$. The interaction between relationship and dispute type was also significant, $F(2, 284) = 3.18, p < .02$; in the invention and business dispute settings, the value of SELF was substantially greater in the negative than in the positive relationship condition, but the effect was less pronounced in the lot condition.

Figure 2 compares the shape of the social utility function on the basis of mean parameter values for the positive, neutral, and negative relationship conditions. [7] The utility functions for all three conditions are positively sloped and convex for negative differences between own and other payoff (disadvantageous inequality); people do not like to do worse than the other party regardless of the relationship between the parties. However, the relationship between disputants did affect preference for disadvantageous inequality (NEGDIFF), $F(2, 284) = 6.5, p < .001$, although the magnitude of the effect was small.

---

[6] The between-conditions comparisons reported were based on conventional t tests. All pairwise comparisons reported in Studies 1 and 2 were also evaluated using the more conservative Schefé multiple-comparison procedure; the results were qualitatively indistinguishable.

[7] Figures 2, 3, and 5 are all based on a value of own outcome equal to 0.

TABLE 2. Mean Parameter Estimates by Relationship and Dispute Type: Study 1

Condition		Independent variables									
		SELF		NEGDIFF		NEGDIFF^2		POSDIFF		POSDIFF^2	
Relationship	Dispute type	M	SD	M	SD	M	SD	M	SD	M	SD
Positive	Invention	.12	.16	3.5	2.8	.0065	.0065	−1.2	2.9	.0012	.0073
Neutral	Invention	.13	.20	3.3	2.2	.0059	.0052	−0.87	2.6	.0013	.0048
Negative	Invention	.30	.25	2.2	2.2	.0037	.0055	−0.28	2.5	−.0004	.0065
Positive	Lot	.043	.12	4.4	3.0	.0082	.0081	−2.1	3.2	.0048	.0072
Neutral	Lot	.068	.15	5.1	3.0	.0100	.0075	−2.5	2.6	.0053	.0055
Negative	Lot	.064	.16	4.3	2.9	.0087	.0070	−0.17	2.8	.0006	.0065
Positive	Business	.11	.23	2.3	1.8	.0037	.0046	0.41	1.6	−.0001	.0051
Neutral	Business	.26	.20	1.6	1.4	.0029	.0037	0.73	1.2	−.0004	.0037
Negative	Business	.29	.25	1.6	1.7	.0026	.0043	0.71	1.5	.0003	.0035

Note. All parameter values and standard devisations multiplied by 100.
NEGDIFF − negative difference between own and other payoff, POSDIFF − positive difference between own and other payoff.

It is in the domain of positive differences between self and other (advantageous inequality) that the most striking differences between relationship conditions were observed. The effect of relationship on POSDIFF was significant, $F(2, 284) = 11.6$, $p < .0001$. Averaging across the three dispute types, the slope of POSDIFF was positive under all relationship conditions, although it was much smaller in the negative relationship condition than in the positive and neutral conditions, $ts(284) > 16$, $p < .0001$.

In general, subjects were much more concerned with disadvantageous ineqality than with advantageous inequality. The mean parameter estimate for POSDIFF given a positive or neutral relationship was approximately one-third the magnitude of that for NEGDIFF; subjects did not like to obtain a higher payoff than their opponent, but they much preferred a positive discrepancy between their own and the other party's payoff to a negative discrepancy of equal magnitude.

Figure 3 depicts the shape of the social utility function for each of the three dispute-type conditions. Again, the utility functions are all positively sloped and convex for negative differences between own and other payoff, although the slope of the utility function in the region of disadvantageous inequality was affected by dispute type, $F(2, 284) = 76.3$, $p < .0001$. Subjects were most concerned about falling below the other party in the lot dispute, were less concerned in the invention dispute, and were least concerned in the business conditions, all $ts(284) > 26.8$, $p < .0001$. The effect of dispute type on utility for advantageous inequality is again more striking than that for disadvanta-

geous inequality, $F(2, 284) = 42.2$, $p < .0001$. Subjects were most resistant to receiving a higher payoff in the lot dispute, were next most resistant in the invention dispute, and actually preferred a higher payoff in the business dispute condition, with all $ts(284) > 11.4$, $p < .001$. The interactions between relationship and dispute type for both POSDIFF and NEGDIFF were not significant, $Fs(4, 284) < 1.45$, $p > .2$.

Individual differences. One advantage to estimating a separate equation for each subject is that it permits classification of qualitatively different patterns of behavior. Table 3 shows the percentage of subjects in each of the relationship–dispute-type conditions who had positive parameter estimates for NEGDIFF and negative parameter estimates for POSDIFF, the modal response pattern. As noted earlier, a negative parameter value for NEGDIFF would mean that the subject preferred to obtain a lower payoff than his opponent. A positive value for POSDIFF would indicate that the subject receives satisfaction from obtaining a superior outcome than his opponent.

Looking down the Dislike disadvantageous inequality column, it is evident that very few subjects in any condition obtained positive satisfaction from receiving an inferior payoff. On the other hand, there is considerable diversity among subjects and across conditions in preferences for obtaining a higher payoff than the other player. For the invention and lot disputes, a majority of subjects in the positive and neutral relationship conditions (66%) disliked getting a higher payoff than the other player. On the other hand, in the negative relationship condition a majority (59%) pre-

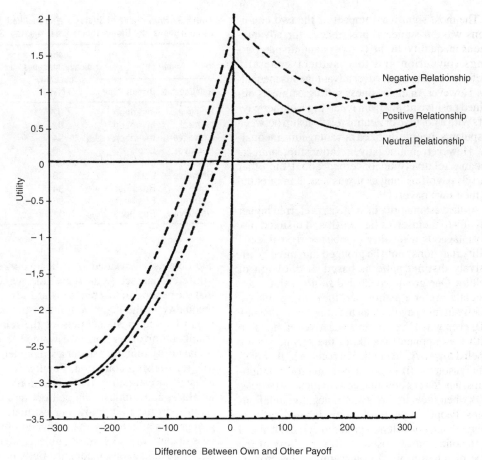

FIGURE 2 ■ The effect of disputant relationship on the social utility function: Study 1.

ferred to come out ahead. In the business dispute, the relationship between disputants had little impact on preferences; in all conditions, approximately 73% of subjects increased their level of satisfaction by increasing advantageous inequality.

Discussion

In general, subjects were very concerned with the comparison of their own payoffs to those of the other party. This was true in all of the dispute settings and in each relationship condition. In fact, subjects were more concerned with the comparison of their own outcomes with those of the other party than they were with the value of their own outcomes. Most subjects preferred that rewards or costs be equitably shared, although they were more averse to disadvantageous inequality than to advantageous inequality. Similar results were ob-

tained by Messick and Sentis (1985) in examining individuals' preferences for payoffs to the self and to the other party in an employment situation. Messick and Sentis found that when inputs were equal (students worked the same amount of hours), individuals preferred equal payments. When equality was not possible, however, subjects preferred that the other party be at a disadvantage relative to the self. We had expected the effect to be stronger when there was a negative relationship between disputants, but this was not observed. Instead, the relationship between the disputants had a significant effect on concern with own payoff in two of the three negotiating settings. In both the lot and business disputes, we observed what could be called a "selfish shift"—a move toward greater concern for own payoff as the relationship shifted from positive to negative—that was mediated by dispute type.

The most significant impact of the two conditions was on subjects' preferences for advantageous inequality. In the two personal dispute settings (invention and lot), subject generally preferred equal payoffs over advantageous inequality. However, in the business setting, subjects obtained positive utility from receiving a higher payoff. With a positive or neutral relationship between disputants, people disliked advantageous inequality. However, in a negative relationship, subjects became relatively unconcerned about the other party's payoff as long as it was less than or equal to their own payoff.

As the vast majority of subjects preferred higher payoffs to themselves (SELF > 0) and disliked disadvantageous inequality (NEGDIFF < 0), subjects' utility functions could be grouped into three qualitatively distinct patterns based on the sign of POSDIFF. One group we labeled *saints:* saints consistently prefer equality, and they do not like to receive higher payoffs than the other party (POSDIFF < 0) even when they are in a negative relationship with the opponent. People in the second group, labeled *loyalists*, do not like to receive higher payoffs (POSDIFF < 0) in positive or neutral relationships, but do seek advantageous inequality (POSDIFF > 0) when they are involved in negative relationships. People in the third group, labeled *ruthless competitors*, consistently prefer to come out ahead of the other party (POSDIFF > 0) regardless of the type of relationship. In our sample, the proportions of saints, loyalists, and ruthless competitors were 24%, 27%, and 36%, respectively. The remaining 18% of subjects could not be neatly classified into any of the three categories. We suspect that the proportions of loyalists and ruthless competitors were elevated by the inclusion of the business condition, in which most subjects derived positive satisfaction from advantageous inequality, regardless of the nature of the relationship.

Study 2

Some of the results of the first study surprised us. We had expected that people would prefer to receive superior outcomes to the other except, perhaps, in the positive relationship condition. Instead, even in the negative relationship condition subjects were relatively indifferent to advantageous inequality. Given the unexpectedness of this result, and the notorious instability of regression

TABLE 3. Proportions of Subjects Who Disliked Advantageous and Disadvantageous Inequality: Study 1

Condition		Dislike disadvantageous inequality (%)	Dislike advantageous inequality (%)
Relationship	Dispute Type		
Positive	Invention	92	61
Neutral	Invention	92	55
Negative	Invention	94	42
Positive	Lot	98	68
Neutral	Lot	100	80
Negative	Lot	98	40
Positive	Business	94	26
Neutral	Business	96	27
Negative	Business	91	27

coefficients, we wanted to replicate our results on a different data set. At the same time, we suspected that the general indifference toward advantageous inequality in the negative relationship condition might be due to the subtiety of the relationship manipulation. Therefore, we wanted to estimate social utility functions under a strengthened negative relationship condition. Finally, we were interested in estimating the proportions of saints, loyalists, and ruthless competitors in a different sample. In the first study, our estimate of these groups was affected by the inclusion of the business dispute in which most subjects weakly preferred advantageous inequality but were mainly concerned with their own payoff, regardless of the relationship condition. We conducted the second study, which included a strengthened relationship manipulation and which dropped the business dispute-type condition, to accomplish these goals. The two personal (i.e., nonbusiness) disputes provided a more uniform backdrop against which to observe the effect of the relationship between disputants on preferences for outcomes.

Method

Forty-four graduate students of management participated in the study. The materials and procedures were the same as those used in Study 1. Our design included two within-subjects variables, relationship between disputants and dispute type. Subjects responded to two dispute situations, the lot and invention scenarios from Study 1. Half the subjects received the lot scenario first: the other half completed the invention scenario first. The

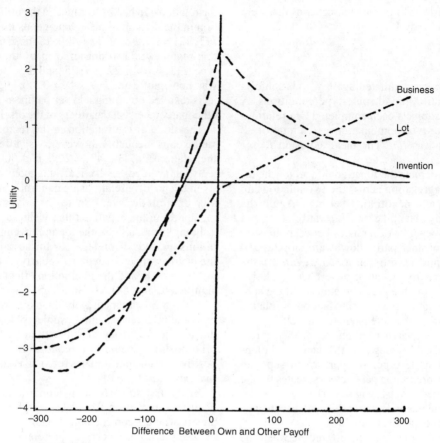

FIGURE 3 ■ The effect of dispute type on the social utility function: Study 1.

relationship manipulations were similar to those in the Study 1, but were more detailed and explicit. For example, in the lot scenario, the positive relationship manipulation read as follows:

> The Smiths are your neighbors. You like the Smiths a lot, and other neighbors consider the Smiths to be very nice as well. The Smiths always help out others. The Smiths are more than happy to take care of pets, water plants, and collect mail. Last week; the Smiths baby-sat for your children on very short notice, loaned you some very expensive tools for a repair project, and offered their guest bedroom for one of your out-of-town guests. In short, the Smiths are kind, friendly, sincere, responsible, and dependable.

The negative relationship manipulation was as follows:

> The Smiths are your neighbors. You have had many unpleasant personal experiences with the Smiths. Your other neighbors also consider the Smiths to be obnoxious. The Smiths complain about others' lawn and house maintenance, yet they do not do any work on their own home. The Smiths borrow tools, but they do not say *thank you* and often fail to return items. Last week, the Smiths threatened to call the police on a small party you were having, damaged your lawn furniture after borrowing it for a larger party, and failed to pick up after their dog had been in your yard. In short, the Smiths are selfish, irresponsible, argumentative, demanding, and insincere.

The relationship manipulations for the invention dispute are included in the appendix. Following each dispute description, participants indicated their satisfaction with the same 42 outcomes for each of the two scenarios that were evaluated in Study 1.

Results

Equation 5 was estimated again for all subjects and all relationship–dispute-type conditions. A total of 44 subjects each completed two relationship–dispute-type combinations, so a total of 88 regressions was run. The mean adjusted R^2 for these regressions was .66.

Figure 4 depicts the functional form for the regression, aggregating across the two relationship conditions and negotiating settings. Again the curve displays a tentlike form, upward sloping and convex for negative differences between the subject and the other party, downward sloping and convex for positive differences. Also evident is the steeper slope for negative differences (relative losses hurt more than relative gains) and the substantially greater effect on satisfaction of relative payoffs than of absolute payments to self.

Table 4 summarizes the results of the regression analysis, disaggregating the data by relationship and dispute type. We performed separate ANOVAS with regression parameter estimates for the variables SELF, NEGDIFF, and POSDIFF serving as dependent variables and relationship and dispute type serving as independent variables.

Concern for own payoff differed between the two negotiating settings, $F(1, 42) = 8.6, p < .005$, and across the two relationship conditions, $F(1, 42) = 12.3, p < .001$, but these effects were qualified by a significant interaction, $F(1, 84) = 8.9, p < .004$.[8] In the invention scenario, subjects again displayed a selfish shift; they were almost three times as concerned with their own payoff in the negative relationship condition as they were in the positive relationship condition. However, no such effect was observed in the lot dispute type.

Figure 5 depicts the shape of the social utility functions based on mean parameter values given a positive and negative disputant relationship. Again,

the relationship had little effect on the utility function in the domain of disadvantageous inequality, $F(1, 42) = 1.7, p > .2$. The slope of the function in this region was also not affected by the dispute type, $F(1, 42) = 1.27, p > .25$, and the interaction was nonsignificant, $F(1, 84) = 0.3, p > .5$. Subjects disliked obtaining a lower payment than the other party received, regardless of the dispute type.

The slope of the function in the region of advantageous inequality, however, was affected by the relationship, $F(1, 42) = 26.6, p < .0001$. Subjects, on average, disliked advantageous inequality in the positive relationship condition and actually exhibited a weak taste for advantageous inequality in the negative relationship condition. Echoing the results for the lot and invention conditions in Study 1, preferences for advantageous inequality were unrelated to dispute type, $F(1, 42) = 0.04, p > .8$, and the interaction effect was not significant, $F(1, 84) = 0.36, p > .5$.

We again examined individual differences in outcome preferences among subjects. Table 5 indicates the frequency of subjects in each of the relationship–dispute-type conditions who had positive parameter estimates for NEGDIFF and negative estimates for POSDIFF.

Again, few subjects in any condition obtained positive satisfaction from obtaining an inferior payoff, whereas considerable diversity was evident between subjects concerning preferences for a superior payoff. Averaging across the two disputes, a majority of subjects (77%) in the positive relationship condition disliked getting a higher payoff than the other party. In the negative relationship condition, a majority (68%) preferred obtaining a higher payoff. The proportions of saints, loyalists, and ruthless competitors were 20%, 52%, and 22%, respectively. The remaining 6% of subjects could not be classified into any of these three groups.

Discussion

The purpose of Study 2 was to replicate the results of Study 1 and to explore the effects of relationships characterized by strong negative and positive affect on interpersonal decision making. Overall, the results of Study 2 closely parallel those of Study 1. Although the strengthened relationship condition did cause subjects, on average, to seek out advantageous inequality in the negative relationship condition, the social utility functions

---

[8] Because subjects were always run in diagonal within-subjects cells, it was impossible to simultaneously examine interactions and take account of the repeated measures nature of the design. Therefore, the reported interaction effects are based on a simple ANOVA that treats the same subject in different conditions as two independent observations. It seems unlikely to us that this had much of an impact on the results. When we examined the main effects, both taking and not taking account of the repeated measures nature of the design, the results from the two analyses were virtually indistinguishable.

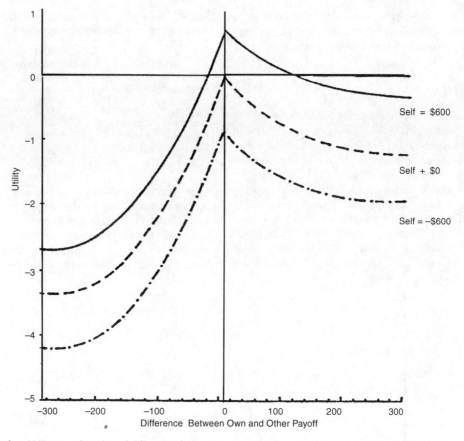

Figure 4 ■ Utility as a function of difference between own and other payoff and payoff to self: Study 2.

estimated in Study 2 were similar to those derived in Study 1, and the impact of the manipulations was comparable. Again, relationship conditions (i.e., positive, negative) strongly influenced preferences for advantageous inequality, but did not affect concern for disadvantageous inequality. Also, individuals showed a selfish shift (e.g., greater concern for own payoff) in the invention

dispute as interpersonal relationships became more negative.

As in Study 1, most individuals could be classified into one of three groups, reflecting desires for advantageous equality in interpersonal contexts. There was a larger fraction of loyalists in the present study, which may reflect the more explicit relationship manipulations. Subjects were gener-

TABLE 4. Mean Parameter Estimates by Disputant Relationship and Dispute Type: Study 2

Condition		Independent variables									
		SELF		MEGDIFF		NEGDIFF^2		POSDIFF		POSDIFF^2	
Relationship	Dispute type	M	SD	M	SD	M	SD	M	SD	M	SD
Positive	Invention	.060	0.12	2.7	3.0	.0044	.0075	−2.0	3.1	.0034	.0072
Negative	Invention	0.31	0.32	1.8	1.6	.0034	.0040	0.44	1.3	−.0011	.0034
Positive	Lot	0.081	0.15	2.8	2.7	.0052	.0063	−1.7	2.6	.0034	.0060
Negative	Lot	0.081	0.12	2.6	2.5	.0052	.0060	0.067	1.9	.0004	.0038

Note. All parameter values and standard deviations multiplied by 100.
NEGDIFF = negative difference between own and other payoff, POSDIFF - positive difference between own and other payoff.

ally more favorably disposed to the opponent in the positive relationship condition and more hostile in the negative relationship condition.

Study 3

The striking correspondence between the results from Studies 1 and 2 increases our confidence in the reliability of the findings. However, the validity of the estimated social utility functions—whether they accurately predict choice behavior in dispute settings—is uncertain. To assess the predictive accuracy of the estimated social utility functions, we conducted a third study that compared choice behavior in individual and interpersonal decision tasks. Subjects in this study made three hypothetical choices in an individual choice

TABLE 5. Proportions of Subjects Who Disliked Advantageous and Disadvantageous Inequality: Study 2

Condition		Dislike disadvantageous inequality (%)	Dislike advantageous inequality (%)
Relationship	Dispute type		
Positive	Invention	86	78
Negative	Invention	96	27
Positive	Lot	82	77
Negative	Lot	82	42

setting and three choices—between arbitrating or accepting a certain offer—in an interpersonal setting. The two sets of choices were matched in terms of payoffs to self, but the interpersonal choice task introduced consequences for another decision maker. The three choices in the individual choice

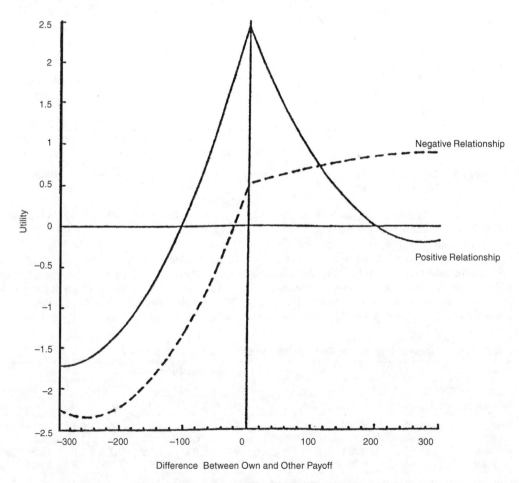

FIGURE 5 ■ The effect of disputant relationship on the social utility function: Study 2.

condition are summarized on the lefthand side of Table 6; the three interpersonal choices are summarized on the right-hand side. Disputant relationship (positive or negative) was manipulated between subjects.

The three choices were designed to test implications of the specific features of the social utility functions estimated in the first two studies. The first presented a choice between a sure $5,000 and a risky alternative offering a .7 chance of $6,000 and a .3 chance of $4,000. In the interpersonal choice condition, the payoffs to self were identical, but the other party received the balance of $10,000, that is, $5,000 if the sure settlement was chosen and $4,000 or $6,000 under arbitration. On the basis of its relatively low level of risk and significantly higher expected value ($5,400 vs. $5,000), we expected subjects to prefer the risky option in the individual choice setting. In the interpersonal choice condition, however, we predicted that preferences would depend on the relationship between the disputants. In the positive relationship condition, most subjects dislike either form of inequality, making the arbitration option, which results in either advantageous or disadvantageous inequality, especially unattractive. In the negative relationship condition, people dislike disadvantageous inequality but are relatively indifferent to advantageous inequality. Hence, we expected a larger proportion of subjects in the negative relationship condition to opt for arbitration. Furthermore, we anticipated a greater preference for the sure thing in both interpersonal settings than in the individual decision setting, as aversion to either type of inequality tends to favor the $5,000–$5,000 split.

The second choice offered subjects in both settings (individual or interpersonal) a choice between a sure $4,000 and a .5 chance at $3,000 and at $5,000. In the interpersonal setting, the other party received the balance of $10,000. We expected subjects to prefer the sure thing in the individual choice condition, given the general tendency toward risk aversion for gains. However, we anticipated that subjects would opt for arbitration in the interpersonal condition. First, one of the outcomes involved a $5,000–$5,000 split, which is especially attractive, particularly given a positive relationship between disputants. Second, the slope of the utility function in the region of disadvantageous inequality is convex, so the potential negative discrepancy of $4,000 under the arbitration option is not twice as bad as the negative discrepancy of $2,000 under the sure-thing option. We did not anticipate that preferences would be significantly affected by disputant relationship, which has little impact on preferences for disadvantageous inequality.

The third item involved losses rather than gains. In the individual choice condition, subjects were offered a choice between losing $5,000 for sure or a .5 chance of losing $10,000. On the basis of the tendency toward risk seeking in the domain of losses (Kahneman & Tversky, 1979), we expected subjects to prefer the risky outcome in the individual choice condition. However, in the interpersonal choice condition, because of the attractiveness of the equal-split option, we hypothesized that subjects would prefer the equal split of –$5,000: – $5,000 over equal chances of –$10,000–$0 and $0–$10,000. Furthermore, we predicted that subjects in the positive relationship condition would exhibit a greater preference for the equal split owing to their aversion to both types of inequality.

Method

A total of 111 graduate students of management participated in the study. The experimenter ex-

TABLE 6. Payoffs to Self and Other: Study 3

	Individual choice condition			Interpersonal choice condition				
		Risky choice		Sure thing		Risky choice		
Choice	Sure thing, Payoff to self	Probability	Payoff to self	Payoff to self	Payoff to opponent	Probability	Payoff to self	Payoff to opponent
1	$5,000	.3	$4,000	$5,000	$5,000	.3	$4,000	$6,000
		.7	$6,000			.7	$6,000	$4,000
2	$4,000	.5	$3,000	$4,000	$6,000	.5	$3,000	$7,000
		.5	$5,000			.5	$5,000	$5,000
3	–$5,000	.5	–$10,000	–$5,000	–$5,000	.5	–$10,000	$0
			$0			.5	$0	–$10,000

plained that the purpose of the study was to examine decision making under different conditions. There were two phases, each conducted on different days separated by a 1-week interval. In Phase 1, half the participants completed individual choice questionnaires and half completed interpersonal choice questionnaires. In Phase 2, each group completed the questionnaire that they had not previously encountered. The individual choice questionnaire contained three hypothetical choices on a single page, with the instructions: "Below you are given choices between a SURE THING and a GAMBLE. Decide which option you prefer and indicate your choice to each question by circling either A or B." The interpersonal choice questionnaire was based on the lot condition from Studies 1 and 2. The questionaire began with these instructions: "Below you are given a description of an incident involving you and a neighbor. Please read the description and then answer each question." It then introduced the lot scenario and the disputant relationship manipulation (positive or negative), which was adopted verbatim from Study 2 (see Appendix). The questionnaire described three situations in which the subject and neighbor either jointly owed or were to be paid $10,000. Subjects were then given a choice between accepting a settlement proposed by the neighbor or taking the risky option of arbitrating.

Results and Discussion

Table 7 summarizes the results from Study 3. In general, they conformed to predictions. On the first item, the disputant relationship had a significant impact on preferences. In the positive relationship condition. 15% opted for arbitration, whereas in the negative relationship condition 73% of subjects preferred the risky alternative, $\chi^2(1, N = 67) = 32.7, p < .0001$. Generally, in the interpersonal relationship condition subjects were likely to select the risky alternative. Averaging across the two relationship conditions, 38% of subjects chose the risky alternative in the interpersonal choice condition, and 81% did so in the individual choice condition—a significant difference, Cochran $Q(1) = 27, p < .0001$.

On the second item there was, as predicted, a greater tendency to select the sure thing in the individual choice than in the interpersonal choice condition. In the individual choice condition, a majority of subjects (73%) preferred the sure

TABLE 8.7. Response Proportions: Individual Versus Interpersonal Choice: Study 3

	Individual choice ($n = 67$)	Interpersonal choice	
		Positive relationship ($n = 35$)	Negative relationship ($n = 32$)
Question			
Question 1			
Sure thing	19%	85%	27%
Gamble-arbitrate	81%	15%	73%
	100%	100%	100%
Question 2			
Sure thing	73%	56%	33%
Gamble-arbitrate	27%	44%	67%
	100%	100%	100%
Question 3			
Sure thing	25%	85%	82%
Gamble-arbitrate	75%	15%	18%
	100%	100%	100%

$4,000 over the 50–50 chance at $3,000 and $5,000. In the interpersonal condition, 55% preferred the risky option of arbitration, $Q(1) = 10.8$, $p < .001$. However, contrary to our prediction, we observed a significant effect of disputant relationship on preference for arbitration. Subjects in the negative relationship condition were more likely to opt for arbitration (67%) than were subjects in the positive relationship condition (44%), $\chi^2(1, N = 67) = 4.9, p < .05$. The effect of disputant relationship may reflect a generally negative attitude toward arbitrating a dispute against a friend.

Finally, the results for the third item were largely as predicted. In the individual decision condition, a majority (75%) of subjects selected the risky option, whereas in the interpersonal choice condition 85% preferred the sure $5,000–$5,000 split, $Q(1) = 38.1, p < .0001$. The difference between the positive and negative relationship conditions was not significant, $\chi^2(1, N = 67) = 0.67, p > .15$, although, as predicted, a higher proportion in the positive relationship condition opted for the equal split. It is possible that the nonsignificance of the relationship manipulation was due to ceiling effects; even in the negative relationship condition a full 82% chose the equal split.

General Discussion

Our goal was to estimate social utility functions in a dispute context. We were especially interested in the effect of the relationship between disputants on preferences for own and other outcomes. The following conclusions summarize our main findings.

First, individuals' utilities for disputed outcomes depended on the magnitude of their own outcomes and on the difference between their own and the other party's outcomes. This finding is consistent with earlier research (e.g., Messick & Sentis, 1985), indicating that individuals' concern with own and others' payoffs is well captured by an additive function of nonsocial utility (own payment) and social utility (difference between own and other's payment). Second, most disputants preferred equal payoffs over either advantageous or disadvantageous inequality. The modal utility function was tent shaped: increasing and convex for disadvantageous inequality, decreasing and convex for advantageous inequality. Third, if inequality was unavoidable, people preferred advantageous over disadvantageous inequality. Fourth, the disputant relationship and negotiation context exerted their main impact on concern with own payoff and attitude toward advantageous inequality, but had little impact on attitudes toward disadvantageous inequality. Fifth, as the disputant relationship shifted from positive to negative, subjects displayed a selfish shift: They became more concerned with their own payoff, independent of the other party's, and more tolerant of advantageous inequality. Sixth, we found that subjects could be neatly categorized according to their preferences toward advantageous inequality. We labeled as saints those subjects who preferred equality over inequality, regardless of the relationship between disputants. Loyalists preferred equality when involved in a positive relationship, but preferred advantageous inequality under conditions of a negative relationship. Ruthless competitors sought advantageous inequality under all conditions, even in the positive relationship condition. Averaged across the first two studies, the proportions of saints, loyalists, and ruthless competitors in our samples were, respectively, 22%, 39%, and 29%.

In general, interpersonal concerns overshadowed concern for own outcome independent of the other's outcome, thus providing further evidence for the importance of relative comparisons in decision making, a prominence that has already been recognized in research on decision making under uncertainty (see, e.g., Bell, 1982; Fishburn, 1977; Loomes & Sugden, 1982). Most prominent among theories of decision making under uncertainty that incorporate relative concerns is prospect theory (Kahneman & Tversky, 1979). Prospect theory examines decision making in individual contexts in which decision outcomes affect only the decision maker, the reference point is most frequently modeled as the current state of the decision maker, although it can also assume other psychologically relevant values. One such value, particularly relevant in interpersonal negotiations, is the payoff to another party. If this payoff is adopted as a reference point, then the x-axis will correspond to the difference between the two parties' payoffs as in the social utility functions illustrated in Figures 1–5.

Although further underscoring the importance of relative comparisons, the current findings challenge the generalizability of prospect theory's specific qualitative features to an interpersonal setting. The predominant shape of the social utility function we estimated resembles the prospect theory value function in the domain of losses; it is upward sloping and convex. However, for positive differences in payoffs, the curve slopes downward and is also convex. Prospect theory's value function is upward sloped and concave for gains. We found that prospect theory makes accurate predictions of decision behavior in the individual decision contexts we examined, but that decision making departs systematically from these predictions in an interpersonal context—in ways predicted by a tent-shaped social utility function.

An important question concerns the generalizability of the present results to decision making in real-world disputes. Although having subjects rate their satisfaction with, or choose between, hypothetical outcomes is a common practice in psychological research, the problem of generalizability may be especially significant in interpersonal contexts for several reasons. First, emotions are likely to play a more important role in interpersonal decision making than in other situations, and hypothetical questions are unlikely to evoke the same intensity of emotions as real-world situations. We cannot predict whether or how the emotions that often arise during negotiations would influence social utility functions. Our analysis, however, provides a framework within which to examine such effects. Would concern for own payoff be greater or smaller in a real dispute than in our study? Would the slope of the utility function in the domain of advantageous inequality slope more steeply downward? These questions could be addressed by interrupting an actual dispute, asking disputants to confidentially rate their satisfaction with different outcomes, and using these ratings to estimate individual-level social utility functions. We suspect that emotions would intensify the effects we observed, but not change them qualitatively. Answers to these questions await further research.

A second concern in this, and in most experimental and observational research, is that subjects' responses may be influenced by considerations of social desirability. Norms of behavior for social situations are better established than are those applying to, for example, decision making under uncertainty. However, it is difficult to assess, a priori, the direction of the bias that social desirability considerations introduce. Behavior in real-world settings is also influenced by norms of behavior, and it is unclear whether norms exert a greater impact in real or experimental settings.

A final concern is that the outcomes in our studies were presented to the subjects without any account of how they were arrived at. In real negotiations, any settlement has a history that may influence participants' satisfaction. For example, disputants are generally more satisfied with outcomes when they feel personally responsible in the sense of having obtained concessions from the other party. Earlier research has examined the effects of concession rates and other variables relating to settlement history on negotiator attitudes and behavior (e.g., Pruitt & Drews, 1969). We chose to abstract away from historical variables and to focus instead on the effect of the relationship between negotiators and the nature of the dispute on social utility. Again, our estimation methodology would provide an excellent structure for assessing the impact of settlement history on negotiator preferences.

The social utility functions we estimated paint a rather benevolent picture of disputant preferences in a wide range of situations. Most of our subjects either disliked or exhibited only a weak preference for advantageous inequality. Even for ruthless competitors, parameter estimates for advantageous inequality were, if positive, close to zero. In contrast, the negotiation literature (e.g., Raiffa, 1982; Seigel & Fouraker, 1960) highlights the fact that negotiators often fail to reach agreements because of invidious social comparisons. What fac-

tors might explain why individuals in our experiments focused on clearly equitable agreements, but individuals in real-world contexts have difficulty reaching mutually acceptable decisions and often appear to be trying to beat the other party?

One possible explanation stems from the great complexity of most interpersonal decision tasks. Most disputes involve a number of issues and often call into play competing norms of distributive justice. Furthermore, disputants are often ignorant of the other party's interests. Complexity and imperfect information permit subjective interpretations of equity. Faced with ambiguous information, egocentric biases (Ross & Sicoly, 1979) may pervade individuals' judgments regarding the fairness of different potential settlements (see, e.g., Raiffa, 1982, p. 75, p. 94). When faced with the task of dividing scarce resources, disputants may invoke norms and reasoning that favor the self, causing both parties to simultaneously perceive themselves as being in the domain of disadvantageous inequality. In this region, most subjects can enhance their utility by decreasing the payoff to the other party, even at the expense of some decrement to their own payoff. Each party is likely to see its own attempts to decrease the other party's relative payoff as an attempt to restore equity, whereas the other party's efforts are seen as efforts to gain an unfair advantage. The likely outcome of these combined efforts to restore equity will be a destructive downward spiral of recriminations and joint losses.

The preceding discussion suggests that one interesting direction for future research would be to examine interpersonal decision making under different levels of complexity and uncertainty regarding the parties' inputs and interests and in situations in which multiple norms of distributive justice are operative. In our study, the neutral dispute situation was relatively unambiguous, and individuals probably focused on a single criterion of equity: equal payoffs or payments by both parties. Thus, we were unable to observe self-serving interpretations of equity and their effect on social utility and decision making. It would be informative to explore whether breakdowns in negotiations are typically due to individual factors, such as the presence of ruthless competitors on one or more sides, or to environmental factors, such as complexity and imperfect information, that permit egocentric interpretations of equity.

Appendix

Stimuli: Experiment 1, Lot Scenario

You live adjacent to an empty lot separating you from your next-door neighbor to your left. No one knows who owns the lot, despite the fact that you and your next-door neighbor have lived there for more than 2 years. However, the city recently informed you that the lot actually belongs to both you and your neighbor, but the percentage owned by each of you has to be negotiated.

POSITIVE RELATIONSHIP

You have always been found of your neighbors: They take care of your pets when you are out of town, and they always invite you to their parties.

NEGATIVE RELATIONSHIP

You have never been found of your neighbors: they let their dogs roam in your yard and you frequently have to pick up after the dogs. Adding insult to injury, last New Year's Eve they called the police a few minutes after midnight to disrupt your party.

LOSS

The lot is too small a sell. However, the city has assessed taxes on the property that you and your neighbor must pay. You and your neighbor need to decide how to split the costs of the taxes.

GAIN

A third neighbor who lacks a backyard has agreed to buy the property for gardening purpose. You and your neighbor would both be happy to have a garden between your houses. You and your neighbor need to decide how to split the profit.

Stimuli: Experiment 1, Business Scenario

You bought a new computer system for word processing. Having a computer system has been a major advantage in your life. With each new year of college, you have found that the amount of writing required has increased. You do not know how you would get the work done without the computer.

POSITIVE RELATIONSHIP

During your visit to the computer store, the salesperson gave you excellent information and personal attention. When it appeared that delivery of your computer would be delayed, he personally drove to the warehouse to get the computer in time for your final exams.

NEGATIVE RELATIONSHIP

During your visit to the computer store, the salesperson treated you in a rude manner. Moreover, he tried to sell you an inferior brand. Clearly, he was trying to take advantage of your lack of knowledgs.

LOSS

Your computer had a warranty of only 30 days. On the 29th day, a Saturday, the computer broke down. You called the store, but they could not be reached until Monday—2 days after the warranty ended. The manufacturer would not give the extension. The dealer arranged for the computer to be repaired. However, the bill has to be divided between you and the dealer. You and the dealer need to decide how to split the cost.

GAIN

After buying the computer, you and the dealer found out that the manufacturer was offering a rebate. The rebate was a negotiated rebate, meaning that it can be divided between the dealer and customer as the two parties choose. You and the dealer must decide how to split the rebate.

Study 2: Strengthened Relationship Manipulations (Invention Dispute Type)

NEGATIVE RELATIONSHIP

Pat is a student who lives in your dorm. You have had many unpleasant personal experiences with Pat, and other people in the dorm also consider Pat to be obnoxious. Pat complains about others' living habit, yet does not do any work. Pat borrows notes and copies assignments, but does not say *thank you* and often fails to return items. Last week. Pat failed to pick up some party supplies after promising to do so, did not show up for an important intramurals playoff game, and insulted one of your friends. In short, Pat is selfish, irresponsible, argumentative, demanding, and insincere.

POSITIVE RELATIONSHIP

Pat is a student in your dorm. You like Pat a lot, and other people in the dorm also consider Pat to be very nice. Pat always helps out when others need help in everyday dorm activities. Pat takes notes and picks up assignments for people who miss classes. Last week, Pat made all the arrangements for a small dorm party, gathered everyone together to visit a sick friend in the health center, and offered his room to you for your out-of-town guest. In short, Pat is kind, friendly, sincere, responsible, and dependable.

ACKNOWLEDGMENTS

The research reported in this article was supported by grants from the Dispute Resolution Research Center in Northwestern University's Kellogg School of Management, the Russell Sage Foundation, the Alfred P. Sloan Foundation, and the IBM Faculty Research Fund at the University of Chicago.

We gratefully acknowledge comments and suggestions from Colin Camerer, Steve Hoch, Norbert Kerr, and Dave Messick and statistical advice from Dawn Iacobucci.

REFERENCES

Adams, J. S. (1963). Toward an understanding of inequity. *Journal of Abnormal and Social Psychology: 67*, 422–436.

Adams, J. S. (1965). Inequity in social exchange. In L. Berkowitz (Ed.), *Advances in experimental social psychology* (Vol. 2, pp. 267–299). New York: Academic Press.

Austin, W. (1980). Friendship and fairness: Effects of type of relationship and task performance on choice of distribution rules. *Personality and Social Psychology Bulletin, 6,* 402–408.

Bell, D. E. (1982). Regret in decision making under uncertainty. *Operations Research, 30,* 961–981.

Clark, M. S., & Mills, J. (1979). Interpersonal attraction in exchange and communal relationships. *Journal of Personality and Social Psychology, 37,* 12–24.

Conrath, D. W., & Deci, E. L. (1969). The determination and scaling of a bivariate utility function. *Behavioral Science, 14,* 316–327.

Crosby, F. (1976). A model of egoistical relative deprivation. *Psychological Review, 83,* 85–113.

Festinger, L. (1954). A theory of social comparison processes. *Human Relations, 7,* 117–40.

Fishburn, P. C. (1977). Mean-risk analysis with risk associated with below-target returns. *American Economic Review, 67,* 116–126.

Griesinger, D. W., & Livingston, J. W., Jr. (1973). Toward a model of interpersonal motivation in experimental games. *Behavioral Science, 18,* 173–188.

Guth, W., Schmittberger, R. & Schwarze, B. (1982). An experimental analysis of ultimatum bargaining. *Journal of Economic Behavior and Organization, 3,* 367–388.

Heider, F. (1958). *The psychology of interpersonal relations.* New York: Wiley.

Homans, G. C. (1961). *Social behavior: Its elementary forms.* New York: Harcourt, Brace & World.

Kahneman, D., & Tversky, A. (1979). Prospect theory: An analysis of decision under risk. *Econometrica, 47,* 263–291.

Kelley, H. (1979). *Personal relationships: Their structures and processes.* Hillsdale, NJ: Erlbaum.

Lewicki, R. J., & Litterer, J. A. (1985). *Negotiation.* Homewood, IL. Irwin.

Loomes, G., & Sugden, R. (1982). Regret theory: An alternative theory of rational choice under uncertainty. *Economic Journal, 92,* 805–824.

Lurie, S. (1987). A parametric model of utility for two-person distributions. *Psychological Review. 94,* 42–60.

MacCrimmon, K. R., & Messick, D. M. (1976). A framework for social motives. *Behavioral Science, 21,* 86–100.

Messick, D. M., & Sentis, K. P. (1985). Estimating social and nonsocial utility functions from ordinal data. *European Journal of Social Psychology, 15,* 389–399.

Orbell, J. M., & Dawes, R. M. (1981) Social dilemmas. In G. M. Stephenson & J. H. Davis (Eds.), *Progress in applied social psychology* (Vol. 1, pp. 37–65). Chichester, England: Wiley.

Pruitt, D. G., & Drews, J. L. (1969). The effect of time pressure, time elapsed, and the opponent's concession rate on behavior in negotiation. *Journal of Experimental and Social Psychology, 31,* 553–60.

Pruitt, D. G., & Rubin, J. Z. (1986). *Social conflict.* New York: Random House.

Raiffa, H. (1982). *The art and science of negotiation.* Cambridge, MA: Harvard University Press.

Ross, M., & Sicoly, F. (1979). Egocentric biases in availability and attribution. *Journal of Personality and Social Psychology, 37,* 322–336.

Schmitt, D. R. & Marwell, G. (1972). Withdrawal and reward reallocation in response to inequity. *Journal of Experimental Social Psychology, 8,* 207–221.

Scott, R. H. (1972). Avarice, altruism, and second party preferences. *Quarterly Journal of Economics, 86,* 1–18.

Seigel, S., & Fouraker, L. E. (1960). *Bargaining and group decision making: Experiments in bilateral monopoly.* New York McGraw-Hill.

Thibaut, J. W., & Kelley, H. H. (1959). *The social psychology of groups.* New York: Wiley.

Walster, E., Walster, G. W., & Berscheid, E. (1978). *Equity: Theory and research.* Boston: Allyn and Bacon.

Negotiation and Social Dilemmas

Negotiation theory and research has a strong descriptive, as well as prescriptive, tradition. Prescriptively, it is important to note that there are two major components involved in nearly any negotiation. They are known as the distributive and integrative aspects. The distributive element of negotiation involves a mutual decision by negotiators on how to allocate resources. For example, two people negotiating over salary might settle upon a point midway between their stated demands. The scholarly study of distributive negotiation is concerned with topics of fairness and power. Integrative bargaining, by contrast, is the study of how people reach mutually beneficial agreements. A common research finding is that people often "leave money on the table" because they fail to discover mutually beneficial agreements.

The negotiation literature, because of its rich multidisciplinary tradition, has been analyzed from a number of theoretical vantage points. For example, Thompson and Loewenstein (in press) analyzed the negotiation literature and found that there were five key metaphors for describing the nature of theory and research on negotiation, which they called: (1) power and persuasion, (2) game playing, (3) decision making, (4) relationship building, and (5) problem solving. Thompson and Loewenstein argued that these metaphors serve descriptive, prescriptive, and paradigmatic functions for theory and research. The present set of papers represents three popular metaphors in the study of negotiation behavior: negotiation as decision making, negotiation as social perception, and negotiation as problem solving.

Negotiation as Decision Making

Negotiation as decision making has its roots in behavioral decision theory. The negotiator is viewed as a person who is confronted with several alternatives among which to decide. Most often, the decision maker is viewed as using cognitive shortcuts that result in errors. The first article, by Bazerman, Magliozzi, and Neale (1985), represents the essence of the decision-making-meets-organizational-behavior era. Using principles and theories derived from Kahneman and Tversky's decision-making theory, Bazerman et al. demonstrated that individual biases operate in a negotiation context. The research was especially exciting and important because the biases, which heretofore had simply existed on paper and pencil measures of uncertain consequence, were actually associated with performance in a quantifiable and managerially relevant negotiation task. Furthermore, Bazerman et al. ushered in an era of examining the social context of negotiation; in this case, the dyad was embedded in a larger social network or market.

Negotiation as Social Perception

Negotiation as social perception has its roots in social psychology and, in particular, focuses on the negotiator as an observer of social processes, using intuition to answer many questions about a given negotiation situation, such as "Is my partner trustworthy?"

The second article, by Morris, Larrick, and Su (1999), focuses on attribution theory and social perception. Specifically, Morris et al. demonstrate that negotiators who have attractive alternatives (also known as BATNAs, standing for "best alternative to a negotiated agreement") are more likely to be regarded by their opponents as disagreeable. Thus, negotiators fall prey to a classic attributional error: the tendency to make dispositional attributions when a situational attribution would be more accurate.

Negotiation as Problem Solving

In the third article, Thompson, Gentner, and Loewenstein (2000) use theories of learning in cognitive psychology to examine how and when negotiators are able to apply a solution from one situation to another. People often fail to apply knowledge learned from one situation to another because it does not occur to them to do so. This is known as the "inert knowledge" problem. Thompson et al. reasoned that one cause for failure to transfer is that negotiators do not have a "portable" problem-solving schema. Most people use superficial, surface-level details as encoding and retrieval devices. For example, if a person learns a useful negotiation technique in the context of buying a new car, he or she may apply that technique to a negotiation situation involving, say, the purchase of a new truck, but not a negotiation involving salary. Thompson et al. compared two conditions designed to help make problem-solving strategies more portable (and hence more usable): an analogy-training condition and a separate-cases condition (built around principles of MBA-style teaching). The analogy-training condition led to nearly twice the knowledge transfer rate.

Social Dilemmas

Social dilemmas are situations in which the individual pursuit of self-interest leads to collective disaster. Several organizational systems, ranging from small groups and teams within organizations to organizations themselves, may be modeled as social dilemmas. Different disciplines have different frames of reference for studying social dilemmas. According to economic theory, it is not rational for individuals to cooperate in social dilemmas, as defection is always better for self-interest. Defection (not cooperating) is a dominant strategy, meaning that it results in greater payoffs under any condition. Thus, economists are perplexed at why anyone would cooperate in a social dilemma. In contrast, social psychologists and organization theorists have the goal of increasing cooperation in social dilemmas and thus view defection as a negative outcome.

Brewer and Kramer (1986) argue that a key factor that leads people to behave cooperatively is the extent to which they identify themselves with the group. Building upon social identity theory, they argue that people derive a certain amount of their identity from their association with particular groups and collectives (Tajfel, 1978). Identification with groups motivates individuals to maintain or enhance the welfare of the group. This can lead to positive behaviors such as contributing to the group and behaving cooperatively; however, it can also lead to negative and destructive behaviors, such as downward social comparison and in-group favoritism (Wills, 1981). Most notably, Brewer and Kramer (1986) as well as Mannix (1993) note that the locus of social identity is highly malleable, meaning that subtle factors can exert a powerful influence on an individual's locus of identity and the resulting behavior.

REFERENCES

Bazerman, M. H., Magliozzi, T., & Neale, M. A. (1985). Integrative bargaining in a competitive market. *Organizational Behavior and Human Decision Processes*, *35*(3), 294–313.

Brewer, M. B., & Kramer, R. M. (1986). Choice behavior in social dilemmas: Effects of social identity, group size, and decision framing. *Journal of Personality and Social Psychology*, *50*(3), 543–549.

Mannix, E. A. (1993). Organizations as resource dilemmas: The effects of power balance on coalition formation in small groups. *Organizational Behavior and Human Decision Processes*, *55*, 1–22.

Morris, M. W., Larrick, R. P., & Su, S. K. (1999). Misperceiving negotiation counterparts: When situationally determined bargaining behaviors are attributed to personality traits. *Journal of Personality and Social Psychology*, *77*(1), 52–67.

Tajfel, H. (Ed.) (1978). *Differentiation between social groups: Studies in the social psychology of intergroup relations*. London: Academic Press.

Thompson, L., & Loewenstein, J. (in press). Mental models of negotiation: Descriptive, prescriptive, and paradigmatic implications. To appear in M. A. Hogg & J. Cooper, *Sage Handbook of Social Psychology*. London: Sage Publications, Ltd.

Thompson, L., Gentner, D., & Loewenstein, J. (2000). Avoiding missed opportunities in managerial life: Analogical training more powerful than individual case training. *Organizational Behavior and Human Decision Processes*, *82*(1), 60–75.

Wills, T. A. (1981). Downward comparison principles in social psychology. *Psychological Bulletin*, *90*, 245–271.

Suggested Readings

Dawes, R., van de Kragt, A., & Orbell, J. (1990). Cooperation for the benefit of us—not me or my conscience. In J. Mansbridge (Ed.), *Beyond self-interest* (pp. 97–110). Chicago: University of Chicago Press.

Deutsch, M., & Krauss, R. M. (1960). The effect of threat upon interpersonal bargaining. *Journal of Abnormal Social Psychology, 61*(2), 181-189.

Hogg, M. A., & Cooper, J. (Eds.) (19xx). *Sage Handbook of Social Psychology*. London: Sage.

Kelley, H. H. (1966). A classroom study of dilemmas in interpersonal negotiations. In K. Archibald (Ed.), *Strategic intervention and conflict* (pp. 49–73). Berkeley, CA: University of California, Institute of International Studies.

Kray, L., Thompson, L., & Galinsky, A. (in press). Battle of the sexes: Gender stereotype confirmation and reactance in negotiations. *Journal of Personality and Social Psychology*.

Larrick, R. P., & Blount, S. (1997). The claiming effect: Why players are more generous in social dilemmas than in ultimatum games. *Journal of Personality and Social Psychology, 72*(4), 810–825.

Messick, D. M., & Brewer, M. (1983). Solving social dilemmas: A review. In L. Wheeler & P. Shaver (Eds.), *Review of personality and social psychology, Vol. 4* (pp. 11–44). Beverly Hills, CA: Sage.

Moore, D., Kurtzberg, T., Thompson, L., & Morris, M. W. (1999). Long and short routes to success in electronically mediated negotiations: Group affiliations and good vibrations. *Organizational Behavior and Human Decision Processes, 77*(1), 22–43.

Roth, A. E. (1993). Bargaining experiments. In J. Kagel & A. E. Roth (Eds.), *Handbook of experimental economics*. Princeton, NJ: Princeton University Press.

Sally, D. F. (1995). Conversation and cooperation in social dilemmas: Experimental evidence from 1958 to 1992. *Rationality and Society, 7*(1), 58–92.

Thompson, L. (2001). *The mind and heart of the negotiator* (2nd ed.). Upper Saddle River, NJ: Prentice Hall.

Thompson, L., & Loewenstein, J. (in press). Mental models in negotiations. In M. A. Thompson, L., & Nadler, J. (in preparation). Email negotiations. *Journal of Social Issues*.

Integrative Bargaining in a Competitive Market

Max H. Bazerman • Massachusetts Institute of Technology
Thomas Magliozzi • Boston University
Margaret A. Neale • University of Arizona

The behavioral decision theory literature was used to identify the determinants of negotiation success in an integrative bargaining, free-market exercise. This study provides a novel methodology for studying negotiation. Specifically, buyers and sellers were allowed to engage in negotiations with as many competitors as possible in a fixed time period. The results suggest that integrative bargaining behavior increases and the market converges toward a Nash equilibrium as negotiators gain experience. In addition, the results suggest that (1) positively framed negotiators ("What will be my net profit from the transaction?") complete more transactions than negatively framed negotiators ("What will be my expenses on this transaction?"). (2) negotiators who are given moderately difficult profit constraints in order to be allowed to complete a transaction achieve more profitable transactions than negotiators without such constraints, and (3) both framing and the existence of constraints affect the total profitability of the negotiator.

The investigation of negotiation has occupied a central position in labor relations (Kochan, 1980; Walton and McKersie, 1965) and social psychology (Pruitt. 1981; Rubin. 1980; Rubin and Brown, 1975). More recently, the study of negotiation has emerged as a concern of organizational scholars as they try to understand such phenomena as budgeting, transfer pricing, and market transactions (Bazerman and Lewicki, 1983).

One of the primary topics of negotiation research concerns the processes that lead to the development of integrative agreements. An agreement is said to be integrative when the negotiators locate and adopt options that reconcile the needs of both parties and produce solutions of high joint benefit. This study is based on the behavioral decision theory literature and investigates the deter-minants of integrative behavior in a free-market simulation.

Integrative agreements are illustrated by the story of the two sisters who fought over an orange (Follett, 1940). The two sisters agreed to split the orange in half—a compromise—allowing one sister to use her portion for juice and the other sister to use the peel of her half for a cake. The two parties in this conflict overlooked the *integrative* agreement of giving one sister all the juice and the other sister all the peel.

Walton and McKersie (1965) proposed two contrasting models of the bargaining process. The distributive model views negotiation as a procedure for dividing a fixed pie of resources—"How much of the orange does each sister receive?" According to this model, what one side gains, the other side loses. In contrast, Walton and McKersie's integrative bargaining model views negotiation as a means by which parties can make trade-offs or jointly solve problems to the mutual benefit of both parties—"How can the orange be divided to maximize the joint benefit of the two sisters?" According to this model, the success of the two sisters at joint problem solving will determine the size of the pie of resources to be distributed.

Pruitt (cf. 1983) has conducted extensive experimental work on the determinants of integrative bargaining behavior. In his studies, subjects engaged in a single negotiation with a single opponent. He found that negotiators who had an incentive to cooperate and moderately high aspiration levels were far more likely to behave integratively than were negotiators without an incentive to cooperate or with low aspiration levels. Consistent with this result is the further finding that integrative behavior was especially likely to occur when negotiators had a positive relationship with the other party and were highly accountable to a constituency (Ben Yoav and Pruitt, 1984).

In contrast to Pruitt's work on a single-transaction, single-opponent task, the research presented here examines negotiator behavior in a freemarket context in which negotiators can make transactions with multiple opponents in a fixed amount of time. Thus, the same high aspiration level that creates a higher likelihood of an integrative agreement in Pruitt's single transaction (without a specified time limit) may prove to be a costly time drain in the simulated market. In addition, Pruitt's research suggests that, under many conditions, negotiators deviate significantly from achieving the fully integrative (and pareto optimal) agreements that exist.

The current research explores whether this is a permanent effect or whether this effect is limited to Pruitt's one-trial, one-opponent methodology. Plott and Agha (1983) propose the alternative hypothesis that markets converge to an equilibrium, implying that negotiators will learn to become integrative over time.

This research explores the determinants of integrative behavior and success for the negotiator. While integrative behavior and success are conceptually related, success is determined by both the quality of transactions (which are affected by the integrative nature of the agreement) and the quantity of transactions. The variables that are examined as determinants of integrative behavior and success in a free market are (1) the frame (positive versus negative) of the negotiators and (2) the existence of limit setting (constraints) on negotiators. Each of these is explored in the sections that follow.

The Frame of Negotiation

Consider the following two scenarios:

> The average employee is currently earning $10/h. The inflation rate is 10%. The union is demanding a $1/h increase to keep up with inflation, Your side, management, maintains that no increase is possible in the current economic environment. Would a $0.40/h increase represent a nominal loss to management of $0.40/h or a real dollar gain of $0.60/h?

> You are a wholesaler of refrigerators. Corporate policy does not allow any flexibility in pricing. However, flexibility does exist in terms of expenses that you can incur (shipping, financing terms, etc.), which have a direct effect on the profitability of the transaction. These expenses can all be costed out in dollar value terms. When you negotiate the terms of a transaction, are you trying to minimize the losses resulting from the expenses incurred or maximize the overall net gain of that sale?

In each situation, the answer to the question posed is "both." Each question is similar to the famous question, "Is the cup half full or half empty?" From a normative perspective, and based on our intuition, the difference in the two points of view is irrelevant. Recently, however, Kahneman and Tversky (1979, 1982; Tversky and Kahneman, 1981) have suggested that important differences exist between how individuals respond to questions framed as losses versus those framed as gains. This section explores the impact of this framing effect on negotiators in a free market.

Tversky and Kahneman (1981) presented the following problem to a group of subject:

The U.S. is preparing for the outbreak of an unusual Asian disease which is expected to kill 600 people. Two alternative programs are being considered. Which would you favor?

1. If Program A is adopted, 200 will be saved.
2. If Program B is adopted, there is a one-third probability that all will be saved and a two-thirds probability that none will be saved.

Of 158 respondents, 76% chose Program A, while only 24% chose Program B. The prospect of being able to save 200 lives for certain was more valued by most of the subjects than a risky prospect of equal expected value. Thus, most subjects were risk averse.

A second group of subjects received the same cover story and the following two choices:

1. If Program A is adopted, 400 people will die.
2. If Program B is adopted, there is a one-third probability that no one will die and a two-thirds probability that 600 people will die.

Out of the 169 respondents in the second group, only 13% chose Program A, while 87% chose Program B. The prospect of 400 people dying was less acceptable to most of the subjects than a two-thirds probability that 600 will die. Thus, most subjects were risk seeking to the second set of choices.

Careful examination of two problems finds them to be *objectively* identical. However, changing the description of outcomes from lives saved (gains) to lives lost (losses) was sufficient to shift the majority of subjects from a risk-averse to a risk-seeking orientation. This result is inconsistent with utility theory, which predicts the same response when objectively identical problems are presented. These findings, however, are consistent with Kahneman and Tversky's (1979) prospect theory, which predicts risk-averse behavior when individuals are evaluating gains and riskseeking behavior when individuals are evaluating losses.

To exemplify the importance of "framing" to negotiation, consider the following labor–management situation: The union claims that they need a raise to $12/h, and that anything less would represent a *loss* given the current inflationary environment. Management argues that they cannot pay more than $10/h, and that anything more would impose an unacceptable *loss*. What if each side had the choice of settling for $11/h (a certain settlement) or going to binding arbitration (a risky settlement)? Since each side is viewing the conflict in terms of what they have to lose, following Tversky and Kahneman's (1981) findings, each side is predicted to be risk seeking to losses and unwilling to take the certain settlement. Changing the frame of the situation, however, results in a very different predicted outcome: If the union views anything above $10/h as a *gain* and management views anything under $12/h as a *gain*, then positive frames

will exist, risk aversion will dominate, and a negotiated settlement is predicted (Neale and Bazerman, in press).

This study explores the impact of the frame of buyers and sellers in an open-market simulation. The open-market simulation allowed buyers and sellers to complete transactions on a three-issue integrative bargaining problem with as many opponents as possible in a fixed amount of time—with total profit the goal. Negotiators were led to view a transaction in terms of either (1) net profit (gains) or (2) expenses (losses) away from the gross profit of the transaction. While net profit is equal to gross profit less expenses, the logic above suggests that positively (gain) framed negotiators will be more risk averse and have a stronger desire to achieve resolutions than negatively (loss) framed negotiators. In our market context, this leads to the prediction that positively framed negotiators will complete more transaction than negatively framed negotiators.

Limit Setting (Constraints) in Negotiation

Pruitt (cf. 1983) has demonstrated repeatedly that paired negotiators who both have moderately difficult goals reach more integrative agreements (when they agree) than paired negotiators with no externally set goals. Simple compromises cannot satisfy the externally set goals in Pruitt's simulation. Essentially, his results demonstrate that when both negotiators have limitation on the transaction that they can accept due to organizationally set profit constraints, an environment is produced which necessitates the search for integrative solution if agreement is to be reached. Without any time limitations, the result is clear—greater integrative behavior results.

Pruitt's results are consistent with goal-setting research in the motivation literature (cf. Latham and Locke, 1979). The goal-setting literature shows that employees exposed to moderately difficult goals outperform employees with either no externally set goals or very difficult goals. Pruitt's goal-setting condition implies the existence of moderately difficult goals.

In contrast, a basic axiom of economics states that additional choices can only make a decision maker better off and that additional constraints can only make a decision maker worse off (Thaler, 1980). This position would argue that the existence of a constraint on the offers that a negotiator is allowed to accept can only hinder his/her effectiveness. That is, the economically rational negotiator without a constraint should achieve the same high-quality agreements that the negotiator with a constraint achieves when such high-quality agreements are possible. In addition, the absence of constraints should produce greater flexibility to the negotiator, allowing additional opportunities for profit.

In summary, Pruitt argues that imposing constraints which limit the negotiator to only accepting agreements above a moderately challenging profit standard positively affects integrative behavior and the negotiator's success. The economic position argues that these constraints will have a negative effect on negotiator effectiveness. This study will treat these as opposing hypotheses to be tested in a market simulation.

Based on the argument developed above, the following hypotheses are proposed:

Hypothesis 1. As negotiators gain experience in a market, their behavior will become more integrative and converge to the economically proposed equilibrium.

Hypothesis 2. In a market context, positively framed negotiators will complete more transactions than negatively framed negotiators.

Hypothesis 3. In a market context, the increase in the number of transactions completed (as specified in Hypothesis 2) will lead positively framed negotiators to be more profitable than negatively framed negotiators.

Hypothesis 4. Negotiators with moderately difficult externally set profit constraints will achieve more profitable individual agreements than negotiators without externally set constraints.

Hypothesis 5a. The increase in the quality of agreements (as specified in Hypothesis 4) will result in negotiators with moderately difficult externally set constraints achieving greater overall profitability than negotiators without externally set constraints (Pruitt's prediction).

Hypothesis 5b. (competing hypothesis). Negotiators with moderately difficult externally set constraints will achieve less overall profitability that negotiators without externally set constraints (the economist's position).

Methods

Subjects

One hundred seventy-eight graduate and undergraduate students from Boston University and the University of Arizona participated in one of six runs of a free-market simulation. Each run was part of a class.

Design

Subjects were randomly assigned to be (1) either a buyer or seller, (2) either positively or negatively framed, and (3) either in a constraint condition or in a no-constraint condition—resulting in a $2 \times 2 \times 2$ design. All six runs of the simulation had exactly equal number of buyers and sellers. However, slight variation in cell sizes across the other two factors was necessary due to the number of subjects in the run.

Procedure

Instructions that described the exercise as a simulation of a free market between buyers (retail stores) and sellers (manufacturers of refrigerators) were provided to all subjects. Participants were told that product quality among all manufacturers was undifferentiable and that profits (or expenses) were affected by only three factors: delivery terms, discount level, and financial terms. The information packet included a profit schedule showing nine levels labeled "A" through "I" for each of the factors (see Tables 1a and b for seller and buyer profit schedules). Subjects saw only the profit schedule for their role.

Buyers achieve their highest profits and sellers their lowest profits at the "A" levels of delivery, discount, and financing, whereas sellers achieve their highest profits and buyers their lowest profits at the "I" levels. In addition, delivery time holds the highest profit potential and financing terms holds the lowest profit potential for buyers. In contrast, delivery time holds the lowest profit potential and financing terms holds the highest profit potential for sellers. Although an extremely unlikely possibility, if either party were able to convince the other party to accept his/her optimal terms (A–A–A for buyers, I–I–I for sellers), then

TABLE 1. Buyer and Seller Schedules for Positively and Negatively Framed Negotiations

	Delivery time	Discount terms	Financing terms		Delivery time	Discount terms	Financing terms
	\(a)Seller net profit schedule				(c) Seller expense schedule (Gross Profit = $8000)		
A	$000	$000	$000	A	$–1600	$–2400	$–4000
B	200	300	500	B	–1400	–2100	–3500
C	400	600	1000	C	–1200	1800	–3000
D	600	900	1500	D	–1000	–1500	–2500
E	800	1200	2000	E	–800	–1200	–2000
F	1000	1500	2500	F	–600	–900	–1500
G	1200	1800	3000	G	–400	–600	–1000
H	1400	2100	3500	H	–200	–300	–500
I	1600	2400	4000	I	000	000	000
	(b)Buyer net profit schedule				(d) Buyer expense schedule (gross profit = $8000)		
A	$4000	$2400	$1600	A	$000	$000	$000
B	3500	2100	1400	B	–500	–300	–200
C	3000	1800	1200	C	–1000	–600	–400
D	2500	1500	1000	D	–1500	–900	–600
E	2000	1200	800	E	–2000	–1200	–800
F	1500	900	600	F	–2500	–1500	–1000
G	1000	600	400	G	–3000	–1800	–1200
H	500	300	200	H	–3500	–2100	–1400
I	000	000	00	I	–4000	–2400	–1600

his/her profit for the transaction would be equal to $8000. The opponent would receive $0. The simple compromise solution of E–E–E yields $4000. to each party. However. If the parties are able to reach the fully integrative agreement of A–E–I, then each would receive a profit of $5200.

The market methodology used in this study responds to the limitations of field research on negotiation (e.g., inaccessibility of private negotiations, the difficulties of obtaining causal data, and the difficulty in obtaining data on the same variables across transactions). The market methodology also overcomes many of the limitations accepted by most social psychological laboratory studies of negotiation (e.g., one-shot negotiations, external validity, and ignoring the existence of economic markets that surround the transaction). This experiment uses a rich-context simulation (Greenhalgh and Neslin, 1983) that purists of both the laboratory and field research traditions may find to be less than fully satisfactory. However, the market experiments may provide the best joint optimization of (1) the control necessary to understand the decision processes of negotiators and (2) the reduction of the inherent limitaions of laboratory studies.

Each subject was told that he/she was either a buyer or seller in a market in which they could complete as many transactions as possible in a fixed (30 min) amount of time. For example, a buyer could potentially complete as many transactions as the number of sellers in the room. Since an equal number of buyers and sellers existed in each market and the simulation was perfectly symmetrical, all negotiators in a particular market had indentical profit potential. A buyer (seller) could complete only one transaction with any one seller (buyer). The logistics of the market required buyers and sellers to make contact at the front of the classroom and then proceed to a "bargaining area" to engage in the actual negotiation. Once an agreement was reached, a "transaction form" was completed, which identified the buyer and seller and the delivery, discount, and financing terms agreed upon. In addition, the time of the transaction (0 to 30 min) was recorded by the experimenters for each transaction. After jointly turning in the form, the buyer and seller were free to return to the front of the classroom in order to make contact for another transaction. This cyclical procedure continued until the end the 30-min market session.

The framing manipulation. Positively framed

subjects were given the role-specific profit tables (1a and b) previously discussed. For the negatively framed condition, these tables were converted into "expenses" that the subject would incur—that would be taken away from the $8000 gross profit that would be received for each completed transaction. This transformation can be seen for buyers and sellers in Tables 1c and d. Since net profit is defined to be equal to gross profit minus expenses, Tables 1a and b are identical objectively to Tables 1c and d. For example, the seller's profit for A–E–I is $5200, the sum of $0 + $1200 + $4000 (Table 1b). In Table 1d, this same transaction would result in expenses of $2800, the sum of $1600 + $1200 + $0. When $2800 is subtracted from the $8000 gross profit, the same $5200 net profit is received. Thus both forms of the schedules yield the same profit results, with the only difference being that the positively framed negotiators see the terms as net profits, whereas the negatively framed negotiators see the same terms as expenses. In addition, all further instructions were given in terms of profits for positively framed negotiators and in terms of expenses for negatively framed negotiators. However, all subjects were told to maximize their total profit during the 30-min market.

Limit setting (constraints). Limit setting was manipulated by including a "confidential memo." in the information packet of subjects in the "constrained" condition. The memo was not included in the packets of those in the "unconstrained" condition.[1] The memo was signed by the negotiator's supervisor. This memo stated that it was against company policy to accept any transaction that did not meet minimum requirements. For example, subjects in the positive frame/constrained condition read:

> do not under any circumstances make any deals which result in total profit of less than $4,600. At this limit, the transaction is detrimental to the overall financial welfare of the company. If you cannot reach this goal with a particular seller, you should break off negotiations since there are other firms we can deal with.

In the negative frame/constrained level condition, subjects read the following:

> do not under any circumstances make any deals which result in expenses of more than $3,400. At this limit . . .

After they had taken a short quiz to ensure that the profit and expense schedules were understood,

subjects were given final instructions prior to negotiations. For example, positively framed sellers were told:

> Talk to buyers and make deals which specify all three factors. That is you should propose three-letter deals in your negotiations . . . overall net profit will be determined by summing the net profits of all the transactions that you complete . . . assume that market conditions are such that your firm can produce all the refrigerators that you can sell.

After these final instructions, the market began. Upon completion of the market, all participants completed a postsimulation questionnaire that further verified their understanding of the exercise and assessed a number of common attitudes about negotiation. Finally, subjects were given detailed personal and general feedback in the following class session.

Results

Preliminary Analyses

Two items were included in the postsimulation questionnaire as manipulation checks on the constraint and frame manipulations. The constraint manipulation was assessed by asking all subjects the open ended question: "Was there an explicitly stated rule concerning minimum requirements for you to be allowed to accept a transaction? If yes, explain." Eighty-two of the 89 subjects in the constrained condition responded "yes" and identified the existence of the minimum profitability rule that was included in their packet. None of the 89 subjects in the unconstrained condition mentioned any minimum requirements. Thus, it is assumed that the manipulation was effective.

To assess the framing manipulation, all subjects were asked to respond to the following question on a 7-point scale: "When negotiating a transaction, how did you think about your goal (1 = "minimize expenses," 7 = "maximize net profits")? Positively framed negotiators responded significantly higher than negatively framed negotiators (5.88 vs. 3.40, $p < .01$), confirming the framing manipulation.

---

[1] While subjects in the unconstrained condition may determine their own constraints, the theoretical development of this paper is concerned with the impact of *externally* set constraints.

Finally, to verify that subjects understood the differential payoffs across issues (that created the integrative problem), all subjects were asked which of the three factors was most important to them and which one was least important to them. When responding to these questions, subjects no longer had their payoff tables in front of them. Overall, 86% of the responses to these questions were consistent with the payoff tables provided to the subjects.

Hypothesis 1

It was predicted that negotiators would become more integrative over time. We examined this pattern for each of the six markets separately, as well as in the aggregate. Figure 1 shows the average profit for buyers and sellers for each 5-min time interval (0–5 min, 5–10 min . . . , 25–30 min). The diagonal line running from the top left to the bottom right represents the nonintegrative agreements available to negotiators. Notice that all points on this line result in a joint profit of $8000. The outermost boundary represents the pareto frontier available to negotiators, with the point $5200, $5200 representing the Nash equilibrium solution that is the economic prediction of the solution that two negotiators will achieve. The Nash equilibrium is defined to be equal to the point that maximizes the product of the utilities of the two parties (Nash, 1950).

Figure 1 plots the averages of buyer and seller profit of all agreements reached in each 5-min segment of the market (aggregated across all six markets. This figure shows that negotiators tend to start the exercise by achieving distributive agreements—the result of compromises rather than the integration of their interests. As the market continues, negotiators become increasingly integrative. By the end of the market, many transactions are fulfilling the Nash prediction. The general pattern depicted in Fig. 1 was consistently obtained for each of the six markets (separate figures and data on each market are available from the first author). The impact of time on joint profit is shown formally for the six markets combined by the regression (N = 942)

$$\text{JPROFIT} = \$8551 + \$55.4T + \varepsilon, \; R^2 := .25,$$
$$F = 312.1. \qquad (1)$$
$$(p < .001)$$

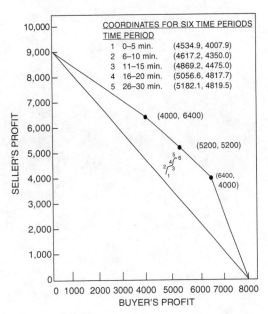

FIGURE 1 ▪ Average profit for buyers and sellers of transactions completed in each 5-min segment of the market (aggregated across markets).

where, JPROFIT is equal to the joint profit of the two negotiators and T is equal to the minute (from 0 to 30) of the market in which the transaction was completed. The results suggest clearly that integrative behavior increases as the market develops and that the market moves toward the Nash equilibrium.

An important question to answer about the increased integration over time concerns "Who gets the added profit?" Figure 2 plots the profit of the more profitable negotiator in a transaction, the less profitable negotiator in a transaction, and their joint profit in 5-min intervals of the market. The general pattern shows that the joint profit increases primarily due to the increased profit of the *less* profitable negotiator. The profit of the more profitable negotiator remains relatively constant across the market. This suggests (1) that one negotiator can often help the other negotiator without incurring costs and (2) that integrative bargaining increases the equity between two negotiators. The general pattern depicted in Fig. 2 was also consistently obtained for each of the six markets (again, separate figures and data on each market are available from the first author).

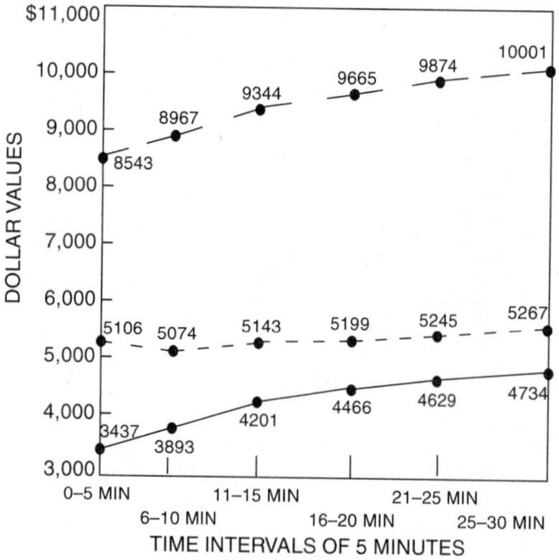

FIGURE 2 ■ Means of more and less successful negotiators in each 5-min segment of the market (aggregated across markets).

Hypotheses 2 through 5

These hypotheses dealt with the impact of constraints and frame on the success of negotiators, Specifically, the hypotheses made predictions about (1) the number of transactions that a negotiator completed. (2) the profitability of the transactions that a negotiator completed, and (3) the total profitability of negotiators. Table 2 provides the means of the three dependent variables for each cell in the design, collapsing across the buyer/seller factor. The means are provided for each (as well as the total) of the six markets. In addition, the number of subjects in each cell of each market is specified in Table 2. The pattern of results suggests that (1) positively framed negotiators complete more transactions than negatively framed negotiators, (2) constrained negotiators complete more profitable transactions than unconstrained negotiators, (3) both independent variables affect the total profitability of the negotiator, and (4) wide variation exists in the average profitability of negotiators across markets.

Before creating regressions which will test the predicted relationships for statistical significance, it is appropriate to identify other factors in the experiment that are likely to affect the three dependent variables. First, Table 2 suggested that significant differences exist in these variables between the six markets that were run. That is, holding constant the impact of the hypothesized independent variables, the negotiator's market significantly affected his/her performance. Consequently, in the interest of obtaining the best assessment of the impact of the hypothesized independent variables, dummy variables were included to control for the variation in the dependent variables due to market differences. Second, the

TABLE 9.2. Cell Means for Transactions, Average Profit per Transaction, and Total Profit

	Frame									
	Negative					Positive				
CONSTRAINT	MARKET	TRANS	AVPRF	TOTAL	*n*	MARKET	TRANS	AVPRF	TOTAL	*n*
4600 Limit	1	4.20	4955	20,820	5	1	6.40	4884	31,280	5
	2	9.38	4849	45,025	8	2	8.75	4708	41,063	8
	3	8.14	5103	41,200	7	3	9.50	5101	48,388	8
	4	11.43	5047	57,343	7	4	11.00	4988	54,938	8
	5	12.33	4957	61,167	6	5	12.63	4872	61,338	8
	6	13.40	5287	70,520	10	6	16.00	5066	80,822	9
	Total	10.26	5052	51,774	43	Total	11.11	4943	54,991	46
None	1	4.83	4285	20,866	6	1	5.33	4852	26,033	6
	2	7.88	4280	33,125	8	2	8.63	4293	36,838	8
	3	7.63	4856	37,050	8	3	8.14	5025	39,957	7
	4	9.88	4872	47,417	6	4	11.00	4795	52,586	7
	5	12.75	4383	55,013	8	5	14.38	4418	63,400	8
	6	15.44	4581	70,622	9	6	15.88	4572	72,125	8
	Total	10.07	4540	45,484	45	Total	10.84	4639	49,611	44

Note. Overall means: TRANS = 10.57 (*SD* = 3.88). AVPRF = 4792 (*SD* = 502). TOTAL = 50,481 (*SD* = 18,761)

exercise was set up symmetrically, leading to the expectation that, on average, buyers and sellers would do equally well. Surprisingly, this was not the case. Thus, a dummy variable is entered for whether the negotiator was a buyer or seller. These additions resulted in the following three regressions ($N = 178$)[2]:

$$\text{TRANS} = 3.83 + 0.85 \text{ FRAME} + 0.05 \text{ LIMIT} + \underset{0.00 \text{ BUYSEL}}{\text{LIMIT}} + 3328 \text{ BUYSEL} + 3.47 \text{ D2}$$

$$(p < .001) \quad (ns) \quad (ns) \quad (p < .001)$$

$$+ 3.18 \text{ D3} + 5.64 \text{ D4} + 7.86 \text{ D5} + 9.95 \text{ D6} + \varepsilon.$$

$$R^2 = .70, F = 49.8 \quad (2)$$

$$(p < .001) \qquad (p < .001) \qquad (p < .001)$$
$$(p < .001)$$

$$\text{AVPRF} = 4011 - 2.6 \text{ FRAME} + 394 \text{ LIMIT} + 296 \text{ BUYSEL} - 213 \text{ D2}$$

$$(ns) \ (p < .001) \qquad (p < .001) \qquad (p < .001)$$

$$+ 273 \text{ D3} + 170 \text{ D4} - 95 \text{ D5} + 139 \text{ D6} + \varepsilon. R^2 = .37. F = 12.2. \quad (3)$$

$$(p < .001) \quad (p < .05) \quad (ns) \quad (ns)$$

$$\text{TOTAL} = 10004 + 3934 \text{ FRAME} + 4856 \text{ LIMIT} + 3327 \text{ BUYSEL}$$

$$(p < .001) \qquad (p < .001) \qquad (p < .001)$$

$$+ 14160 \text{ D2} + 16867 \text{ D3} + 28173 \text{ D4} + 35345 \text{ D5} + 48600 \text{ D6} + \varepsilon. \quad R^2 = .73, F = 57.6. \quad (4)$$

$$(p < .001) \qquad (p < .001) \quad (p < .001)$$
$$(p < .001) \qquad (p < .001)$$

In these regressions, TRANS was equal to the number of transactions a negotiator completed, AVPRF was equal to the negotiator's average profit per transaction, and TOTAL was equal to the negotiator's total profit. All indepedent variables were dummy variables, where FRAME was equal to 0 for negatively framed negotiators and 1 for positively framed negotiators; LIMIT was equal to 0 for the unconstrained condition and 1 for the constraint; BUYSEL was equal to 0 for sellers and 1 for buyers; and Di was equal to 1 if the negotiator was in the ith market and 0 otherwise.

Overall, the betas from these regressions demonstrate the earlier observed effects described by the mean differences in Table 2. Specifically, positively framed negotiators, on the average, completed .85 more transactions than negatively framed negotiators [Eq. (2), $p < .001$].[3] This effect confirms Hypothesis 2. The average profit from transactions completed by constrained negotiators was, on average, worth $394 more than the average profit from transactions completed by unconstrained negotiators [Eq. (3), $p < .001$]. This effect confirms Hypothesis 4. The total profit of positively framed negotiators was, on the average, $3934 higher than the total profit of negatively framed negotiators [Eq. (4), $p < .001 =$]. This effect confirms Hypothesis 3. And finally, the total profit of constrained negotiators was, on average, $4856 higher than the total profit of unconstrained negotiators [Eq. (4), $p < .001$]. This effect confirms Hypothesis 5a, and rejects Hypothesis 5b.

These regressions also show that buyers are significantly more successful than sellers [Eq. (3) and (4)]. In addition, Eqs. (2)–(4) show dramatic differences in the quantity and quality of transactions across markets.

Discussion

The results demonstrate that experience has a very powerful influence on the degree to which nego-

---

[2]
$$\text{TRANS} = -5.60 + 0.85 \text{ FRAME} + 0.02 \text{ LIMIT} + 0.00 \text{ BUYSEL}$$

$$(p < .001) \qquad (ns) \qquad (ns)$$

$$+ 4.27 \text{ MBA} + 0.42 \text{ NMARKET} + e,$$

$$R^2 = .68, F = 76.0. \quad (2^1)$$

$$(p < .001) \qquad (p < .001)$$

$$\text{AVPRF} = 4056 - 6.2 \text{ FRAME} + 402 \text{ LIMIT} + 296 \text{ BUYSEL}$$

$$(ns) \ (p < .001) \ (p < .001)$$

$$+ 61 \text{ MBA} - 1.3 \text{ NMARKET} + e.$$

$$R^2 = .26, F = 11.8. \quad (3^1)$$

$$(ns) \qquad\qquad (ns)$$

$$\text{TOTAL} = - 34924 + 3841 \text{ FRAME} + 4787 + 20877 \text{ MBA} + 1974 \text{ NMARKET} + \varepsilon,$$

$$R^2 = .71, F = 85.7. \quad (4^1)$$

$$(p < .001) \qquad (p < .001)$$

In these alternative regressions, MBA was equal to 1 for MBA classes and 0 for undergraduate classes and NMARKET was equal to the number of individuals in the market. These regressions show that the experience (MBA) and size of the market affected significantly the number of transactions completed and the total profitability of negotiators. This change in the model, however, has virtually no impact on any of the other effects that were examined in the text of the paper.

[3] An alternative interpretation of the framing manipulation (offered independently by David Schkade and Dean Pruitt) is that the negative frame simple requires more time from the negotiator to evaluate the quality of an offer. This could slow down negatively framed negotiators, reducing the number of transactions that they could complete. While this is a viable alternative interpretation, the explanations in the text is consistent with the framing effect observed by Neale and Bazerman (1983) on negotiators in a labor-management simulation. In the Neale and Bazerman (1983) study, the negatively framed task was no harder to evaluate than the positively framed task.

tiators exhibit integrative behavior. Early in the markets, negotiators generally arrived at distributive agreements. This suggests that negotiators start the simulation with a fixed-pie assumption, consistent with Bazerman and Neale's (1983; Bazerman, 1983) argument that negotiators have a fundamental bias that leads them to enter bargaining situations with a win–lose, fixed-pie perspective. As the market develops, however, negotiators acquire the information to break this fundamental bias, which allows them to engage in integrative behavior. This research raises questions about the extent of generalizability of one-shot studies of negotiator behavior. While one-shot investigations may capture accurately the context of some negotiations, they do not capture the dynamic nature of many competitive interactions. Further, the differential effects of integrative behavior over time suggest that negotiation researchers should understand the learning process as they explain the degree to which negotiators develop integrative agreements.

The analyses demonstrate that limit setting, or constraints, on negotiators can be very effective in improving their performance. Specifically, negotiators with moderately difficult goals achieved more profitable agreements than negotiators without specified goals. This result is consistent with Pruitt's (1983; Ben Yoav and Pruitt, 1982) research. Further, this constraint had no effect on the number of transactions that a negotiator completed. This latter result refutes the economist's prediction that imposing a constraint on a decision maker can only hinder his/her overall performance. This result, which is paradoxical given the rationality of the economist's prediction, can be explained in terms of the learning process created by the constraint. Constrained negotiators need to learn quickly how to develop integrative solutions, since simple compromises will not allow them to achieve their goals. Once they arrived at integrative agreements early in the market, their new integrative behaviors were useful in arriving at future agreements in a very efficient manner. Once a subject learned of the A–E–I solution, arriving at mutually acceptable agreements was a very easy task.

The results found that positively framed negotiators completed significantly more transactions than negatively framed negotiators. This results consistent with Kahneman and Tversky's prospect theory and contradicts the form of rationality suggested by the utility theory. That is, negotiators with the same objective information may compromise to very different degrees depending on the frame (gains vs. losses) in which they view the transaction. Future research should address (1) how an understanding of framing affects negotiator performance. (2) how negotiators can frame the behaviors of their opponent, and (3) how mediators can frame the behaviors of negotiators to be more effective at dispute resolution.

A few unexpected results also occurred. First, despite the existence of a completely symmetrical simulation, buyers outperformed sellers. This effect was consistent across markets. We do not have a clear explanation of this result. However, it may reflect the perceived bargaining power that many buyers feel—"If you don't lower the price, I will buy elsewhere." Obviously, in the simulation, the reverse argument should have been, but was not, just as persuasive. The second result that was not part of the theoretical development concerns the extreme differences in negotiator performance between markets. While some differences were expected. the six markets performed at fundamentally different levels. Part of this may have been due to differences in the intelligence, maturity, etc., of the participants in the various markets. In addition, as the number of participants in a market increases, the nature of the competitive situation increases the potential of all subjects, since there are more potential opponents. Unfortunately, identifying the accurate causation of the market effect is not possible with only six observations.

This study identifies some important determinants of integrative behavior in a market simulation. To place the importance of these results in perspective, it is useful to identify the benefits of integrative agreements:

(1) Integrative agreements maximize the joint benefit of the two parties.
(2) If high aspirations exist on both sides, it may not be possible to resolve a conflict unless a way can be found to integrate the two parties' interests (Pruitt, 1983).
(3) Because integrative agreements are mutually rewarding, they tend to strengthen the relationship between the parties. This facilitates future interaction between the parties (Pruitt, 1983).
(4) Integrative agreements often contribute to the

welfare of a broader community of which the two parties are members (Pruitt, 1983). For example, if firms in the United States behave more integratively, increasing their profitability, they can be more competitive with foreign competitors.

Thus while the study only demonstrates the impact of constraints and framing on increasing the joint profit of the two parties, the increase in integrative agreements that these variables create is likely to have more extensive benefits.

Finally, this paper introduces the study of decision biases as a new approach for understanding negotiator behavior. However, the fixed-pie assumptions and the impact of framing are a small sampling of the systematic deviations from rationality that affect negotiator judgment (Bazerman and Neale, 1982, 1983; Neale and Bazerman, 1983). Future empirical research should further identify how the behavioral decision theory literature can be used to understand and improve negotiator behavior. While the description of systematic biases that affect negotiators is a critical step in the development of negotiation literature, research needs to advance to the point of providing prescriptive recommendations for eliminating these judgmental deficiencies. With these advances, the study of negotiator cognition has the potential both to improve negotiator outcomes and to enhance the probability of negotiators reaching settlements that are in society's interest.

In conclusion, this paper has identified a new conceptual direction for improving negotiation effectiveness and has specified a new methodology for studying negotiation that integrates the benefits of traditional methodologies. This research on negotiator cognition complements the existing negotiation literature that (1) provides normative prescriptions (e.g., Raiffa, 1982), (2) identifies structural interventions (Pruitt, 1981), and (3) specifies the role of personality characteristics (Rubin and Brown, 1975).

ACKNOWLEDGMENTS

This research was funded by National Science Foundation Grant BNS-8107331. The author thanks Elizabeth Lepkowski for data analysis assistance. In addition, the insightful comments of John Carroll, Len Greenhalgh, Leigh McAlister, Dean Pruitt, David Schkade, Richard Thaler, Bart Weitz, the participants in the MIT Marketing Seminar, the participants in the MIT Summer Research Seminar, and an anonymous reviewer on previous drafts of this paper significantly improved the quality of this manuscript.

REFERENCES

Bazerman, M. H. (1983). A critical look at the rationality of negotiator judgment. *American Behavioral Scientist, 27*, 211–228.

Bazerman. M. H., & Lewicki, R. J. (Eds.) (1983), *Negotiation in organizations.* Beverly Hills, CA: Sage.

Bazerman, M. H., & Neale, M. A. (1982). Improving negotiation effectiveness under final offer arbitration: The role of selection and training. *Journal of Applied Psychology.* 67, 543–548.

Bazerman, M. H., & Neale, M. A. (1983). Heuristics in negotiation: Limitations to dispute resolution effectiveness. In M.H. Bazerman & R.J. Lewicki (Eds), *Negotiation in organizations.* Beverly Hills, CA: Sage.

Ben Yoav, O., & Pruitt, D.G. (1982, August). *Level of aspiration and expectation of future interaction in negotiation.* Paper presented at the annual convention of the American Psychological Association. Washington D.C.

Ben Yoav, O., & Pruitt, D.G. (1984). Accountability to constituents: A two-edged sword. *Organizational Behavior and Human Performance*, 34, 283–295.

Follett, M. P. (1940) Constructive conflict. In H.C. Metcalf & L. Urwick (Eds.), *Dynamic administration: The collected papers of Mary Parker Follett.* New York: Harper.

Greenhalgh, L., & Neslin, S. A. (1983). Empirical assessment of the determinants of outcomes of negotiations in organizational settings. In M.H. Bazerman & R.J. Lewicki (Eds.), *Negotiation in organizations.* Beverly Hills, CA: Sage.

Kahneman, D., & Tversky, A. (1979). Prospect theory: An analysis of decision under risk. *Econometrica, 47,* 263–291.

Kahneman, D., & Tversky, A. (1982). Psychology of preferences. *Scientific American*, 161–173.

Natham, G. P., & Locke, E. A. (1979) Goal-setting: A motivational techinique that works. *Organizational Dynamics, 8,* 68–80.

Neale, M., & Bazerman, M. H. (1983). The role of perspective-taking ability in negotiating under different forms of arbitration. *Industrial and Labor Relations Review.*

Neale, M., & Bazerman, M. H. (in press). Systematic deviations from rationality in negotiator behavior: The framing of conflict and negotiator overconfidence. *Academy of Management Journal.*

Plott, C. R., & Agha, G. (1983). Intertemporal speculation with a random demand in an experimental market. In R. Tietz (Ed.), *Aspiration oriented decision making.* New York/ Berlin: Springer-Verlag.

Pruitt, D. G. (1981). *Negotiation behavior.* New York: Academic Press.

Pruitt, D. G. (1983). Integrative agreements: Nature and antecedents. In M. H. Bazerman & R. J. Lewicki (Eds.), *Negotiation in organization.* Beverly Hills, CA: Sage.

Raiffa, H. (1982). *The art and science of negotiation.* Boston: Harvard Univ. Press.

Rubin, J. (1980). Experimental research on third party intervention in conflict: Toward some generalizations. *Psychological Bulletin, 87,* 379–391.

Rubin, J., & Brown, B. (1975). *The social psychology of bargaining and negotiation*. New York: Academic Press.

Thaler, R. (1980). Toward a positive theory of consumer choice. *Journal of Economic Behavior and Organization, 1,* 39–80.

Tversky, A., & Kahneman, D. (1981). The framing of decisions and the psychology of choice. *Science (Washington, D.C.), 40,* 453–463.

Walton, R., & McKersie, R. (1965). *A behavioral theory of negotiation*. New York: McGraw–Hill.

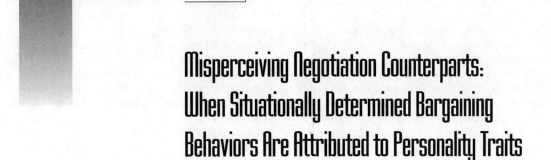

Misperceiving Negotiation Counterparts: When Situationally Determined Bargaining Behaviors Are Attributed to Personality Traits

Michael W. Morris • Stanford University and University of California, Berkeley
Richard P. Larrick • University of Chicago
Steven K. Su • The European Institute of Business Administration (INSEAD)

Several experiments provided evidence that negotiators make systematic errors in personality-trait attributions for the bargaining behaviors of their counterparts. Although basic negotiation behavior is highly determined by bargaining positions negotiators primarily interpret their counterpart's behavior in terms of the counterpart's personality. such as his or her level of cooperativeness or agreeableness. Data support a model of 4 processes that contribute to misperceptions: (a) the primacy of situations in determining bargaining behavior, (b) the primacy of personality traits in attributions, (c) the lack of sufficient information about the other's situation to discount personality attributions, and (d) the potentially self-confirming consequences of personality attributions for subsequent interactions. The authors discuss implications for research areas such as social cognition in negotiation, accuracy in social perception, and the dynamics of belief confirmation.

The psychology of resolving mixed-motive conflicts has long been of interest to social psychologists, sociologists, and political scientists, not only because explicit negotiations are ubiquitous and consequential phenomena in work and political life, but also because many other interpersonal relations can be modeled as negotiations of mixed-motive conflicts (Axelrod, 1984: Kelley & Thibaut, 1954; Strauss, 1964). In the psychology of conflict resolution, an important role is played by negotiators' perceptions of their counterparts. Social psychologists have argued that interpersonal conflicts are particularly likely to give rise to attributions of personality traits to one's counterpart

(Orvis, Kelley, & Butler, 1976). Conflict theorists have suggested that a negotiator's attributions for a counterpart's behavior exert a pivotal influence on the negotiator's strategic decisions (Schelling, 1960). A first purpose of the current research is to investigate regularities in the personal dispositions perceived in negotiation counterparts as a function of structural features of the conflict. A second purpose is to investigate the consequences of these attributions on decisions in subsequent interactions with the counterpart.

If attributions in conflict have far-reaching consequences, it is important to know whether attributions are accurate—whether the perceived causes of negotiation behavior correspond to the actual causes. To address this, we reviewed the literature on the actual and perceived causes of negotiation behavior and then we developed hypotheses about systematic attributional biases in which effects of specific negotiation situations are misinterpreted in terms of specific personality traits. Our methods are influenced by recent social perception researchers (e.g., McArthur & Baron, 1983; Swann, 1984) who have mounted challenges to traditional evidence that attributions are biased and have defended more stringent criteria for identifying attribution errors. In a first experiment we tested hypotheses about two general patterns of misperception. In a second experiment we tested hypotheses about four component social psychological processes that contribute to misperceptions in negotiations.

Background

Actual Causes of Negotiation Behavior

A point where the findings of social psychology diverge from the core beliefs of conventional Western social thought is the degree to which an individual's behavior is shaped by stable personal characteristics as opposed to temporary social situations. Milgram's (1963) famous obedience experiment, in which pressure from an authority figure led participants to deliver painful electric shocks, illustrates the extent to which people's behavior is determined by the pressures and incentives of a situation. Sometimes even minor factors in a person's situation shape behavior to a greater extent than the most central factors in the person's character. A classic illustration is Darley and Batson's (1973) study of the determinants of altruistic behavior. They observed whether seminary students heading across campus to deliver a sermonette on the Good Samaritan stopped to assist a stranger in medical need. The probability of stopping was not at all influenced by whether the student had indicated "helping others" was a central religious value. However, stopping was influenced by whether the student had been made to feel that he or she was running late to deliver the sermon. In sum, acting as a Good Samaritan was determined more by the superficial constraints of a person's situation than by the person's deepest values.

Empirical research on the determinants of negotiation behavior has yielded similar conclusions. Many researchers have modeled negotiations by running experiments in which participants play bargaining games. Recent reviews of this work have concluded that important components of bargaining behavior, such as the extent to which a negotiator haggles with his or her counterpart instead of making concessions, are greatly determined by a player's economic bargaining situation and little determined by personality traits (Thompson, 1990). A second research paradigm has been direct observation of naturally occurring negotiations. Although researchers in this tradition have generally not been able to take the measurements required for testing causal hypotheses, their interpretive conclusions about the causes of negotiators' behavior have paralleled those from bargaining game experiments in their emphasis on the importance of situations and unimportance of personality. From one of the more comprehensive studies of industrial negotiators inside and outside the bargaining room, Douglas (1962) concluded that a negotiator "more nearly resembles his opposite number in the conference room than himself outside the conference room" (p. 159).

Perceived Causes of Negotiation Behavior

The fascination of social psychologists with attributions for behavior is owed in part to discoveries of systematic biases, which seem to play a pivotal role in many social interactions. Ichheiser noted that we have "in everyday life the tendency to interpret and evaluate the behavior of other people in terms of *specific personality characteristics* rather than in terms of *specific social situations* in which these people are placed" (Ichheiser, 1943, p. 151; emphasis added). This bias was explained by Heider (1958) in terms of a gestalt perceptual process and more recently by Nisbett and Ross (1980) in terms of judgmental heuristics; it is referred to as the *fundamental attribution error* (Ross, 1977) or the tendency to make correspondent inferences from behaviors to traits (Jones, 1990). It is most clearly documented in contexts where the actual causes of behavior are known. For example. Safer (1980) found that observers of a film of Milgram's (1963) experiment attributed the actions of obedient participants to sadistic personalities rather than to the situational pressure to comply with authority. Likewise, Pietromonaco and Nisbett (1982) found that participants who read about Darley and Batson's (1973) seminarians attributed the behavior of the hurried seminarians to their personalities rather than their situation.

The attribution of negotiation behavior to personality traits rather than situational constraints (although familiar to those who have been privy to the thoughts of disputants in a contentious strike or divorce) has been the subject of relatively few experimental studies. Although researchers have run many experiments using detailed simulations of negotiation procedures to search for actual effects of personality in negotiations, research on perceptions of opponents has primarily involved abstract conflict games and perceptions of strategy or intent. Nonetheless, studies have found that an opponent's situational constraints are often misunderstood. Dorris, Gentry, and Kelley (1966) created a bidding game in which a buyer and a seller were each given a limit on the price on which they could settle and still make a profit. When sellers had a high limit, deals were less likely. Interestingly, although participants knew their counterparts were constrained by an externally imposed limit, they nonetheless attributed their counterparts' behavior to personal intent: sellers in the high-limit condition were perceived by counterparts to have a competitive intent. In similar studies of buyer-seller games. participants have systematically underestimated their counterpart's limit (Kelley et al., 1970; Pruitt & Drews, 1969). When participants had the option of attributing a behavior to both personal and situational factors, they primarily attributed it to personal factors (Kelley et al., 1967). These early studies of perceptions of conflict counterparts did not specify what sort of inferences are drawn. Evidence from other domains suggested that perceivers draw mistaken inferences about enduring personality traits (Nisbett & Ross, 1980).

Although systematic errors in social perception were widely accepted a decade ago, recently critics have challenged the evidence. Some challenges focus on the contexts in which errors have been demonstrated. McArthur and Baron (1983) argued that attributions drawn about a target person on the basis of a vignette description or on abstract information about moves in a game are responses to impoverished social stimuli; hence, errors may occur that would not occur in the ecology of real-world social interactions, where responses are based on a richer flow of information (for a review of related issues. see Funder, 1995). Another point is that social perception accuracy increases in contexts where perceivers are motivated to perceive another person accurately, such as when the perceiver's and the target person's outcomes are interdependent (Neuberg & Fiske, 1987; Ruscher & Fiske, 1990). Other challenges focus on how researchers model lay conceptions of personality. Swann (1984) pointed out that instructions in some studies may tap perceptions of a target's disposition within a bounded social situation, and these perceptions may indeed have circumscribed accuracy. Other researchers have objected to the contrived trait lists on which perceivers' impressions have been measured. Studies with more comprehensive measures have identified distinctive types of bias on particular personality dimensions (Robins, Spranca, & Mendelsohn, 1996).

In part because of concerns about the methods used to establish attribution errors, another tradition of research on social perception in conflicts has eschewed experiments in favor of retrospective surveys of naturally occurring conflicts. Surveys have revealed general biases in attribution, such as the difference between the attributions made for behavior by oneself and for behavior by the other person (i.e., the actor–observer difference, Jones & Nisbett, 1971). For example, members of romantic couples in conflict ascribed negative traits (e.g., *selfishness*) more often for behaviors of their partner than for their own behaviors (Orvis, Kelley, & Butler, 1976). Likewise, college students ascribed *uncooperativeness* more to their roommates (Sillars, 1980) and executives ascribed *competitiveness* more to their rivals (Thomas & Pondy, 1977) than they did to themselves. It is tempting to integrate these actor–observer differences in natural conflicts with the findings of Kelley et al. (1967) that competitive intent is overattributed to opponents in bargaining games. However, actor–observer differences can reflect either error in the perceiver's self-attribution or error in his or her attributions about the counterpart, and it is not clear which of these underlines the findings. A second complication in integrating actor–observer findings from field studies of conflict is that some of the identified personality traits are semantically unrelated to uncooperativeness. For instance, negotiators have been observed to overattribute to opponents characteristics such as *anxiety* (Douglas, 1962) and *insincerity* (Baron, 1984, 1988). This suggests that there may be more than one dimension on which negotiators misperceive their counterparts' personalities.

Hypothesis Development

Our general hypothesis is that certain bargaining behaviors are primarily determined by the negotiator's situational constraints but are attributed by their opponents to personality traits. Through a review of literature on the dimensions of bargaining situations, we will work toward more specific hypotheses about the content of particular misperceptions. A negotiator's bargaining situation can be described in terms his or her alternative option, the option he or she will take if no agreement is reached in the negotiation (Raiffa, 1982; White & Neale, 1991). A negotiator's alternative is like the ground from which he or she negotiates, it is the basic situational factor that determines his or her bargaining style and behav-

ior. Negotiation alternatives vary on two basic dimensions: value and risk.

Value is the amount of a negotiator's alternative. For instance, a job recruit's bargaining position depends greatly on whether his or her offer from an alternative employer is relatively low or high in value. Figure 1 illustrates the bargaining position of a recruit occupying four different bargaining position varying in value and risk. The top row of the matrix shows that a recruit with an alternative offer that is relatively high in value is like a seller with a high minimum price: In the negotiation with the recruiter, this recruit has a relatively small zone of possible agreements (i.e., where the recruiter pays no more and the recruit earns no less than with their respective alternatives). To achieve an agreement appreciably better than his or her alternative, the recruit will likely have to engage in hard bargaining, or *haggling*, with the recruiter—it will not be easy to find a mutually pleasing outcome. By contrast, when the recruit's alternative is relatively low and the zone is relatively large (as shown in the bottom row of Figure 1), then the recruit will not have to haggle much to reach an acceptable agreement (Thomp-

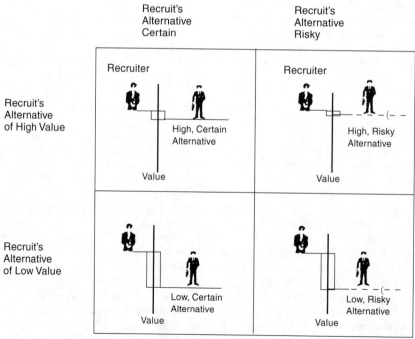

Figure 1 ■ An illustration of four different bargaining situations created by crossing the value (high vs. low) and risk (certain vs. risky) of the recruit's alternative. In the right column, the dashed line indicates that the recruit's alternative is an expected value corresponding to the mean of the market distribution.

son, 1997). Although negotiators know that their own haggling depends on the situation, we suspect that they nonetheless misattribute their counterpart's level of haggling to his or her personality. Hence, the first error pattern we predict is that negotiators misattribute the trait of uncooperativeness to counterparts who have a relatively high-value alternative in the negotiation where they meet.

A second aspect of a negotiator's alternative option is its level of risk. In some cases, a recruit may have a definite offer of a specific salary from another employer as his or her alternative. In other cases, a recruit's alternative may be uncertain or risky—a risky alternative is an expected value based on knowing that one will draw an offer from a distribution, such as a market (for further definition see Larrick & Boles, 1995). In Figure 1, the recruits in the left column are standing on the secure ground of a definite offer from another company; recruits in the right column are in the more precarious position of not being certain about the value of their alternative, having only an expectation based on the distribution from which the offer will be drawn. Having a risky, as opposed to a certain, alternative affects one's bargaining in several ways. A recruit without a definite, concrete alternative will have more difficulty setting a consistent lower limit (or *reservation price*) in the negotiation, because this limit must take into account not only the expected value of the alternative but also the value that he or she places on certainty. A recruit without a firm alternative offer is also more likely to be vague about his or her alternatives during the negotiation. In sum, a certain alternative option makes it more likely that negotiators will be consistent and steady, whereas a risky alternative makes it more likely that negotiators will *waffle* in the limits they set and in the justifications they offer for these limits. Although we expect that waffling is induced by the situation of uncertainty, we expect that it will be primarily interpreted by perceivers in terms of personality traits such as inconsistency or insincerity. Hence, our second prediction is that negotiators will misattribute dishonesty or insincerity to counterparts who have relatively risky alternatives.

In a pilot experiment, a test of these predictions was conducted by having master of business administration (MBA) students participate in a negotiation exercise that closely simulated a job compensation negotiation typical of the ones they were currently involved in at the time. One hundred twenty students were randomly assigned to roles of recruiter and recruit for a scenario in which they were negotiating the compensation of a possible position for the recruit. The recruit role varied in the value and certainty of the alternative, resulting in the four conditions illustrated by Figure 1. After negotiating, participants rated themselves and their opponent on an ad hoc list of traits relevant to negotiation. Recruits in different experimental conditions did not differ in self-ratings, yet they differed in how they were rated by their opponents. The pattern of differences fit our predictions. Compared with recruits with a low-value alternative, those with a high-value alternative were perceived as more stubborn (4.60 vs. 3.73 on a 7-point scale ranging from 1 = *disagree* to 7 = *agree*), $F(1, 57) = 3.29, p < .10$, and more competitive (5.30 vs. 4.40), $F(1, 57) = 6.21, p < .05$. Recruits with a risky, as opposed to a certain, alternative were rated less sincere (4.85 vs. 5.38), $F(1, 57) = 3.0, p < .10$. However, differences on other trait dimensions, such as that recruits were rated lower on the *friendly* dimension when they had a high-value alternative (4.89 vs. 5.54), $F(1, 57) = 3.69, p < .10$, and when they had a risky alternative (4.81 vs. 5.58), $F(1, 57) = 4.82, p < .05$, suggested that misperceptions involve more general personality constructs than specific trait terms.

Experiment 1: Patterns of Personality Misperception in Negotiations

To frame hypotheses at the most general level that conveys the content of misperceptions, we drew on models of the major dimensions of personality differences and personality perceptions (Goldberg, 1990). Four major factors that reemerge in analyses of trait terms in different languages (Yik & Bond, 1993) are usually labeled as follows: (a) Extraversion, (b) Agreeableness, (c) Conscientiousness, and (d) Emotional Instability or Neuroticism. In numerous studies, researchers using reliable indexes of these general dimensions rather than ratings of isolated trait terms have found a considerable degree of consensus in perceivers' impressions of a target person's personality (John & Robins, 1994). Scales measuring these dimensions seem to capture content-general constructs in lay perceptions of personality (McCrae & John,

1992). For instance, a target person rated high in Agreeableness is expected to be more cooperative than the average person in the wide range of domains for which this trait is relevant. If biases in negotiators' personality perceptions affect their core impressions of others, then it should be possible to specify their biases in terms of basic personality dimensions. We propose that the traits to which people should attribute haggling and waffling behavior (if they are making correspondent inferences) map closely onto two of these factors (to the extent that uncooperativeness is an element of low Agreeableness and to the extent that insincerity and inconsistency are related to Emotional Instability). Hence, we can frame our predictions in terms of these more general constructs as follows: (a) Negotiators with high-value alternatives will haggle more and hence evoke perceptions of low Agreeableness, and (b) negotiators with risky alternatives will waffle more and hence evoke perceptions of Emotional Instability.

Our goal was to test these predictions with methods that meet the criteria for error in social perception emphasized in recent scholarship. That is, in our research personality perception is measured in an ecologically valid context, in which errors have personal consequences for participants and competition motivates accurate perception. Also, our instructions emphasized to participants that they were to indicate their inferences about enduring characteristics of the other person, not merely describe the other's behavioral patterns. Specifically, we asked them to indicate characteristics that they would expect to see again in a future interaction with the other person. Also, they rated this person on a comprehensive set of trait descriptors.

Method

Participants. Participants were 376 MBA students from four sections of a course on negotiation at Stanford University (1 year after the pilot study) and from three sections of a course on negotiation at the University of Chicago. To make the motivation to succeed in one's outcome more salient, one randomly selected participant in each role was publicly awarded a cash payment in direct proportion to the value of their settlement (the payment ranged from $0 to $24) in class after the negotiation simulation.

Procedure. The data were collected during negotiations in a simulation exercise conducted during the 2nd week of a course on negotiation. The negotiation exercise was condutced between two students acting as, respectively, a recruiter from Alpha Inc., a consulting firm, and an MBA recruit. It concerned only one issue: the salary the firm would offer the recruit (all other terms, such as the signing bonus, had been settled). It was clearly stated that the two individuals would never be working together in the future, so the relationship between the two players was not an issue in the negotiation.

Negotiators in both roles were given private information about their alternatives. On the one side, recruiters were told that if they did not reach a satisfactory agreement with this recruit then they would definitely sign an alternative candidate. The alternative candidate had asked only that Alpha Inc. match the salary offer being sent in the mail by another firm; because this figure was as yet unknown, the recruiter's alternative was risky. Recruiters were told that their expectation of what they would have to pay the alternative candidate came from an office survey that found salaries of recruits from the top five schools in this industry fell on a normal distribution with a mean of $90,000 and with most offers falling in a range from $75,000 to $105,000.

On the other side, recruits were told that in addition to their offer from Alpha Inc., they had an offer from another consulting firm, Lambda. If the negotiation with Alpha Inc. led to a satisfactory salary offer, they would sign immediately and not pursue the offer from Lambda. However, if the negotiation did not lead to a satisfactory offer, they would accept the offer from Lambda, which would be a first and final offer (this firm does not negotiate salary). The recruits' expectation about their salary with Lambda varied across four conditions, which corresponded to the conditions in Figure 1:

1. In the *risky, high-value* condition, recruits were uncertain of the amount Lambda would offer but expected a value around $85,000, an estimate based on a market survey in *Fortune* of the offers to graduates of the top five business schools that showed essentially a normal distribution with a mean of $85,000 and with most offers falling in the range from $75,000 to $95,000.

2. In the *certain, high-value* condition, the role differed only in that recurits knew for certain

that the Lambda salary offer would be $85,000.

3. In the *risky, low-value* condition, recruits were uncertain of the amount Lambda would offer but expected a value around $70,000 on the basis of a market survey that showed essentially a normal distribution with a mean of $70,000 and with most offers falling in the range from $60,000 to $80,000.

4. In the *certain, low-value* condition, the role differed form Condition 3 only in that recruits knew for certain that the Lambda salary offer would be $70,000.

Negotiation measures. Participants were given 20 min to study their role. They then answered several prenegotiation questions about their strategy and plans for the negotiation. One of these asked participants to state their reservation price—the lowest salary amount that they would accept in the negotiation instead of resorting to their alternative option. After completing the prenegotiation questions, each participant was randomly assigned to a couterpart. The pairs of participants were directed to a private area for a 0.5-hr-long negotiation session. They were then separated to answer postnegotiation questions about whether they reached an agreement and if so, the amount of the salary contract.

Situation perception measures. Next, we asked recruiters for their perceptions of the recruit's bargaining situation. Participants were familiar from negotiation class with the concepts of the value and risk of an alternative option and had been taught guidelines for estimating these from an opponent's negotiation behavior (see Lewicki & Litterer, 1985). Perceptions of value were measured with the following question: "What do you think is the amount of the recruit's best alternative to a negotiated agreement? The amount the recruit expected to receive from an alternative firm if the negotiation with you ended in an impasse is $___." Perceptions of risk were measured with the following question: "How certain was the recruit's alternative offer?" Responses were taken on a 5-point scale with one end (1) labeled *known with certainty,* the midpoint labeled *estimated precisely,* and the other end (5) labeled *estimated loosely.*

Personality perception measures. Finally, we asked recruiters about their perceptions of the recruit's personality traits. We requested that recruiters share their perceptions of stable, global characteristics by asking participants to indicate "personality characteristics that you would expect to see again in future interactions with this person" on a 5-point scale (1 = *disagree strongly,* 5 = *agree strongly*). We emphasized that the question applied to cross-temporal, cross-situational traits so that participants would not merely select characteristics that described the other's behavior in this one bounded situation. We then presented 28 randomly ordered trait descriptors that marked the first four factors of personality perception (O.P. John, personal communication, January 30, 1995). These items and the scale reliability statistics may be seen in Table 1.

TABLE 1. Trait Descriptors for Four Factors of Personality Perception

		$\propto$	
Factor	Trait descriptors	study 1	study 2
Agreeableness		.83.	.85
	Cooperative, trustful, helpful, considerate (+)		
	Demanding, cold, selfish (−)		
Emotional Instability		.78	.78
	Insecure, nervous, touchy, highstrung (+)		
	Relaxed, not stressed; emotionally steady and stable; calm, not tense (−)		
Extraversion		.75	.68
	Talkative, assertive, energetic, candid (+)		
	Reserved, quiet, shy (−)		
Conscientiousness		.72	.67
	Efficient, thorough, systematic (+)		
	Inconsistent, careless, undependable (−)		

Note. The plus sign denotes trait descriptors that load positively on the factor; the minus sign denotes trait descriptors that load negatively on the factor.

Results and Discussion

Negotiation measures. Recruiters set reservation prices (M = \$94.95K) above the level of their alternative option.[1] Recruits in the low-value conditions set reservation prices (M = \$73.55K) slightly above their alternative option, which created the intended large settlement zones in this condition. Recruits in the high-value conditions set their reservation prices much higher (M = \$85.83K), $F(1, 175) = 169.65, p < .001$, which created the intended smaller settlement zones. There was a slight tendency for the recruit's reservation prices to be higher in the risky (M = \$80.83K) than in the certain conditions (M = \$77.95K), $F(1, 175) = 5.24, p <. 05$. There was no interaction of risk and value manipulations in determining reservation prices.

Not surprisingly, the outcome of negotiations was highly affected by the manipulation of the value of a recruit's alternative. As may be seen in Table 2, when the value of the recruit's alternative was high rather than low, the settlement rate was lower (86% vs.97%), $\chi^2(1, N = 188) = 25.36, p < .001$, and the average settlement amount was higher (\$89.21K vs. \$84.67K), $F(1, 170) = 20.50, p < .001$. Negotiation outcomes were not significantly affected by the recruit's level of risk nor by the interaction of the risk and value manipulations.

Situation perception measures. The result suggest that participants were partially successful in estimating their counterparts' bargaining position. Recruiters ascribed an alternative to the recruit that was higher in the high-value conditions (M = \$89.10K) than in the low-value conditions (M = \$84.04K), $F(1, 185) = 13.01, p < .001$. Not surprisingly, perceptions of the value of the recruit's alternative did not vary as a function of the risk manipulation. There was an unanticipated interaction effect, $F(1, 185) = 6.57, p < .05$, which reflected a greater difference between perceptions of recruit's alternatives in the low-value versus high-value conditions when the alternative was risky (Ms = \$82.33K vs. \$91.43K) than when it was certain (\$85.46K vs. \$87.19K). However, participants were not successful in perceiving the recruit's level of risk. Perceptions of the recruit's level of risk did not differ at all between recruits who had a certain versus a risky alternative (Ms = 3.66 vs. 3.57).[2] Not surprisingly, perceptions of the recruit's risk did not differ as a function of the value manipulation or as a function of the interaction.

TABLE 2. Negotiation Outcomes and Perceptions of the Recruit's Personality as a Function of the Recruit's Situation (Experiment 1)

| Measure | Recruit's alternative offer | | | |
| | Low value | | High value | |
	Risky	Certain	Risky	Certain
Negotiation outcomes				
Proportion reaching agreement (%)	93	100	84	88
Settlement amount (in dollars)	82.93K	85.97K	89.63K	88.74K
Personality perceptions				
Agreeableness	3.69	3.61	3.42	3.35
Emotional Instability	2.24	2.10	2.26	1.99
Extraversion	3.33	3.24	3.31	3.35
Conscientiousness	3.71	3.73	3.77	3.78

Note. Relative to the recruiter's alternative, the recruit's alternative was of either low or high value.

Personality perception measures. Summary scores for perceived personality factors were created by reverse coding the negative items and then averaging the seven ratings for each factor. Perceptions of Agreeableness and Emotional Instability were predicted to vary as a function of the manipulated factors, whereas perceptions of Extraversion and Conscientiousness were not. As may be seen in Table 2, the predicted difference but no other differences were obtained. Recruiters ascribed a more agreeable character to recruits who had a low-value (M = 3.65) rather than a high-value (M =3.38) alternative offer, $F(1, 179) = 7.75, p < .01$. Recruiters ascribed a more emotionally unstable character to recruits who had a risky (M = 2.25) rather than a certain (M = 2.04) alternative offer, $F(1, 178) = 5.31, p < .05$. In sum, recruits placed in a situation that induced or required haggling were taken to be disagreeable persons, and recruits placed in a situation that induced waffling were taken to be emotionally unstable persons.

[1] This is consistent with results of previous studies (Larrick & Boles, 1995) and probably indicates either risk aversion or aversion to the transaction costs of hiring the alternative recruit.

[2] A troubling aspect of the data for this variable is that almost all responses were above the scale midpoint of *estimated precisely*. Because the region of the scale between *known with certainty* and *estimated precisely* was hardly used by participants, we thought it possible that these labels struck participants as being synoymous. To avoid this possible problem, we dropped the midpoint scale label in the subsequent study.

A question that the reader may ask is, Why did participants in the recruiter role ascribe traits even though their ascriptions of the counterpart's situational constraints did in fact correspond to the counterpart's actual situation? Classical models portray personality and situational attributions as hydraulically related (Heider, 1958), yet our results indicate that situational and personality ascriptions were both elevated. Our interpretation is based on a model of attributional judgment (Morris & Larrick, 1995), which holds that after observing a behavioral effect, a perceiver raises his or her confidence in each of its multiple possible causes to a degree depending on the pereceived extremity of effect. If the behavior is perceived as extreme (i.e., a high degree of haggling or waffling in the role-play procedure), then a strong situational attribution does not discount a strong personality attribution (Morris, Smith, & Turner, 1988). In our next study, we measured the perceiver's impression of the extremity of the bargaining behavior to test this interpretation and more incisive hypotheses about the roots of social misperceptions.

Experiment 2: Processes Contributing to Misperceptions

Heretofore we have tested predictions at the level of overall pattern of misperception. At this point. we refine our analysis to four specific hypotheses about processes that contribute to misperceptions of personality. Misperceptions originate from the combination of the primacy of situations in the actual causes of negotiation behavior (Hypothesis 1) and the primacy of personality in the perceived causes of negotiation behavior (Hypothesis 2). These two hypotheses are expressed in Figure 2 as the first two links in a sequential process that leads negotiators to misperceive their counterparts. In Experiment 2 we tested each of these links separately by measuring the recruits' actual personalities in addition to manipulating recruits' situation and by measuring recruiters' perceptions of bargaining behavior, situation, and personality.

Misperceptions of personality persist in negotiations because the information a perceiver receives about the counterpart's situation is too uncertain to discount his or her personality attributions (Hypothesis 3). Although one can estimate a counterpart's degree of situational constraint from his or her words and actions in the negotiation, the information is rarely clear and trustworthy enough for one to be certain of the presence of the situational factor. Both in normative analyses and in empirical studies, little discounting of personality attributions follows from information about the mere possibility that a situational factor is present (see Morris & Larrick, 1995).

A final process that perpetuates personality misperceptions is the effect of personality ascriptions on subsequent interactions with the perceived. Personality ascriptions shape decisions that affect the other person and can induce behavior consistent with the ascribed personality. There is

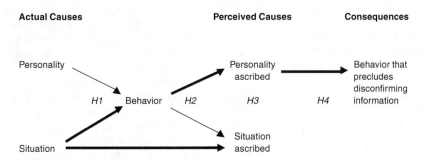

Figure 2 ■ Illustration of four hypothesized processes that contribute to misperceptions of negotiation counterparts: Primacy of situational rather than personality causes of bargaining behavior (Hypothesis 1, or H1); primacy of personality rather than situation in ascriptions for bargaining behavior (Hypothesis 2, or H2); personality ascriptions that persist rather than being discounted by the uncertain situational information a negotiator receives (Hypothesis 3, or H3); and self-confirming consequences of personality ascriptions (Hypothesis 4, or H4). As the bold arrows indicate, we expect that perceivers misjudge their counterpart's personality, even though they pick up some cues to the counterpart's bargaining situation.

considerable evidence that an impression of an opponent as uncooperative leads one to choose uncooperative strategies in future rounds of conflicts. This has been observed in studies of conflict games, such as the multiple-round prisoner's dilemma (Radlow & Weidner, 1966), and in studies of naturally occurring multiple-round confilcts, such as those between roommates (Sillars, 1980) and nations (Jervis, 1976; Bar-Tal & Geva, 1986). Because uncooperative strategies beget uncooperative responses from one's counterpart (Kelley & Stahelski, 1970), they prevent the disconfirmation of one's original impression and even create spurious confirmatory evidence for one's initial impression. In organizational settings, there are several ways in which a perceiver, such as a recruiter, makes decisions that place others in situations that lead them to act consistently with the perceiver's impression of their personality (Hypothesis 4).

A first organizational mechanism for belief confirmation is the choice of how to resolve a future conflict. One can either proceed through direct negotiation or through the arbitration of a third party, such as an ombudsperson or mutual supervisor (Ury, Brett, & Goldberg, 1989). We predict that employees who perceive their counterpart to be low in Agreeableness will avoid negotiation because they expect that the other person will not exhibit the cooperativeness and flexibility needed for negotiation to proceed effectively. Instead they will choose arbitration, which does not require active cooperation from the parties. Yet, the structure of arbitration limits flexibility and evokes competitive behaviors (Lewicki & Litterer, 1985). In sum, having the impression that the other's personality is low in Agreeableness begets conflict resolution through arbitration, which, in turn, induces uncooperative inflexible behavior consistent with one's initial impression.

A second organizational mechanism for belief confirmation is the process of recommending others for role assignments. For example, a new employee who comes across as having a low-Agreeableness personality would be recommended for roles that require inflexible behavior (e.g., the role of handling external bargaining over one-time purchases, such as real estate, which requires a demanding, intransigent stance). This new employee would not likely be recommended for roles that require high-Agreeableness behaviors (e.g.,

the role of managing relationships with important long-term clients. which requires cooperativeness and flexibility). As with conflict resolution decisions, role assignment decisions that are influenced by perceptions of Agreeableness will work to confirm that personality perception.

Method

Participants. Participants were 210 MBA students from two sections of a course on negotiation at Stanford University and from two sections of a course on negotiation at the University of Chicago (1 year after Experiment 1). A week before the negotiation exercise. participants were asked to fill out the Big Five Index (BFI), a reliable and valid self-report inventory for the basic factors of personality (see John & Donahue, 1994). Respondents were presented with 44 short phrases that completed the sentence "I see myself as someone who . . . " and rated each on a 5-point scale (1 = *disagree strongly,* 5 = *agree strongly*). Examples of phrases that load on the five factors are as follows: for Agreeableness, "Is considerate and kind to almost anyone"; for Emotional Instability, "Gets nervous easily"; for Extraversion, "Is outgoing, social"; for Conscientiousness, "Does a thorough job"; and for Openness to Experience, "Is curious about many different things." Students were given this instrument along with several other questionnaires in a packet. This provided our measure of actual personality.

Procedure. The procedure was almost identical to that followed in Experiment 1 except for the addition of several measures of the recruiter's perceptions of the recruit's bargaining behaviors and of his or her organizational decisions affecting the recruit. The only change to the basic manipulation was that the value of the recruit's alternative in the high-value conditions was increased by $10,000. This was because recruiters in Experiment 1 had been willing to pay more than their alternative was worth, and the average salary on the job market had increased. Immediately after negotiating, participants indicated the extent to which their counterpart had engaged in a number of specific tactical behaviors on a 5-point agreement scale (1 = *disagree,* 5 = *agree*). Some items on the list were designed as measures of haggling, some as measures of waffling, and some as filler. Some items designed to capture perceived haggling were the following: "haggled' (argued over the number) a lot before settling," "made extreme requests," "moved quickly to a reasonable position" (reverse scored), and "responded to my requests for concessions" (reverse scored), Some items designed to capture perceived waffling were the following: "waffled" (changed his or her mind) about his or her limit, "was unsure or uncertain at moments," "stated a limit and stuck to it consistently"(reverse scored), "remained confident in his or her bargaining stance" (reverse scored).

After completing the situation perception and personality perception questions, recruiters were asked to make two decisions involving the recruit. First, recruiters were asked to imagine that in the future they found themselves working in the same business organization with the person who was their counterpart in this negotiation. Recruiters were asked to decide how to respond if a conflict arose between themselves and the recruit. They were then to describe their intentions and expectancies by rating on a 5-point scale (1 = *disagree*, 5 = *agree*) the following four statements: "I would be willing to negotiate the issue with the recruit," "I would be willing to let a third party settle the issue," "Negotiating the issue would prevent tension or animosity," and "Letting a third party settle the issue would prevent tension or animosity."

In the final measure, recruiters were asked to make recommendations about which role in the organization the recruit should be assigned to. The following four roles were described: "*relationship manager* role, which involves contact with important, long-term clients and requires positive interpersonal skills"; "*external bargaining* role, which involves handling one-time transactions such as real estate purchases and which requires assertiveness and competitiveness"; "*scheduling and crisis management* role, which requires precision in planning and firmness in decisions"; and "*innovation and research* role, which requires the ability to perform unstructured tasks." The descriptions of these roles made it clear that an employee would be required to display particular sorts of behavior in the performance of each role. The first two were designed to be roles that require and thereby induce high-agreeableness and low-agreeableness behaviors, respectively. The second two were an attempt to create roles that induce high-stability and low-stability behaviors.

Results and Discussion

Negotiation measures. Recruiters set reservation prices (M = \$96.24K) above the value of their alternative, as in Experiment 1. Recruits with a low-value alternative set relatively low reservation prices (M = \$73.65K), which allowed a broad settlement zone, whereas those recruits with a high-value alternative set substantially higher reservation prices (M = \$98.02K), $F(1, 97)$ = 261.02, $p < .001$. Reservation prices in the risky conditions (M= \$85.80K) were not significantly different than those in the certain conditions (M = \$85.11K), $F(1, 97)$ = 0.49, *ns*.

As in the previous study, the value of a recruit's alternative greatly affected the outcomes that were obtained. As may be seen in Table 3, moving from the low to the high condition, the settlement rate decreases (98% vs. 54%), $\chi^2 (1, N = 94)$ = 35.43, $p < .001$, but the average settlement amount increases (\$84.93K vs. \$94.24K), $F(1, 70)$ = 19.26, $p < .001$. The rate and amount of the settlement were not affected by the certainty of the recruit's alternative or by the interaction of the manipulated factors.

Measures of recruits' tactical bargaining behaviors were important for testing hypotheses about the determinants of personality perceptions. To derive measures of haggling and waffling behaviors by recruits, we performed a principal components factor analysis across ratings of behaviors

TABLE 3. Negotiation Outcomes and Perceptions of the Recruit's Personality as a Function of the Recruit's Situation (Experiment 2)

| | Recruit's alternative offer | | | |
| | Low value | | High value | |
Measure	Risky	Certain	Risky	Certain
Negotiation outcomes				
Proportion reaching agreement (%)	96	100	62	41
Settlement amount (in dollars)	85.56K	84.32K	93.28K	96.71K
Perceived personality factors				
Agreeableness	3.70	3.91	3.17	3.15
Emotional Instability	1.97	2.04	1.98	2.01
Extraversion	3.27	3.14	3.61	3.25
Conscientiousness	3.81	3.84	3.92	3.79

Note. Relative to the recruiter's alternative, the recruit's alternative was of either low or high value.

on a list of 16 specific tactics. Two factors emerged that accounted for 26% and 16% of the total variance, respectively. The pattern of items loading on these corresponded to the priori haggling and waffling categories.[3] Scales for haggling ($\alpha = .85$) and for waffling ($\alpha = .71$) were constructed, using the items that loaded onto each of the two factors, by reverse coding the negatively loading items and then averaging. Haggling behavior was much more marked among recruits who had a high-value alternative ($M = 3.36$) than among those who had a low-value alternative ($M = 2.35$), $F(1, 94) = 53.10$, $p < .001$. By regressing a recruit's haggling score on the relevant personality factor (the recruit's actual score on the Agreeableness dimension of the BFI) and the relevant situational factor (the value of the recruit's alternative), we can test the hypothesis that situations are primary in the actual causes of bargaining behavior (Hypothesis 1). As may be seen in Table 4, results support the hypothesis that bargaining behavior is primarily driven by situational rather than personality factors.[4]

Whereas results suggest that the haggling scale captured the dimension of behavior perception that mediates the pattern of misperceived disagreeableness that we have observed (in Experiment 1 and the pilot experiment), the results do not suggest that the waffling scale captures the bargaining behavior dimension underlying the pattern of misperceived emotional instability that we have observed. Contrary to predictions, recruits' waffling behavior was not significantly higher among recruits who had a risky ($M = 2.73$) as opposed to a certain alternative ($M = 2.62$), $F < 1$. Although, as expected, perceived waffling was not correlated

with the relevant personality factor (Emotional Instability), the lack of an effect of the situational factor means a failure to support the first hypothesis. This failure may reflect that the waffling scale missed the target—the bargaining behavior affected by risk.

Situation perception measures. As in Study 1, participants were somewhat successful at perceiving their counterpart's bargaining situation. Recruiters' perceptions of the value of the recruits' alternative varied as a function of its actual value ($\$83.51K$ vs. $\$95.89K$), $F(1, 92) = 33.72$, $p < .001$. Yet, as in Experiment 1, recruiters' perceptions of risk were not responsive to the actual level of risk. Oddly, perceptions of risk were responsive to the value of the recruits' alternative: Recruits who actually had a higher value alternative were perceived to have a more certain offer. Perhaps participants in the recruiter role assumed their opponents were averse to risk, so an opponent with a higher apparent reservation price was inferred to have a more certain alternative. However, given the inconsistent results with the certainty-perception variable, conclusions cannot be drawn until further studies using more fine-grained measures are conducted.

Perceptions of the counterpart's personality. Measures of the four trait factors reached acceptable levels of reliability (see Table 1). Personality

TABLE 4. Recruit's Haggling Behavior Regressed on the Actual Value of the Recruit's Alternative and the Recruit's Actual Agreeableness Score

Predictor	Regression equation		
	1	2	3
Actual value of alternative	.60***		.53$***
Actual Agreeableness score		−.08	−.09
Adjusted R^2	.36	−.01	.27
df	96	70	69

Note. Coefficients are standardized weights. Actual value of alternative is a dummy variable with, the high value condition coded as 1 and the low-value condition coded as 0. Actual Agreeableness score is the recruit's self-rated Agreeableness score on the Big Five Index (John & Donahue, 1994).
***$p < .001$.

[3]There was an exception: Some of the intended waffling items failed to load on the waffling factor.

[4]How would a more context-specific dispositional measure fare? In line with the general notion of a fidelity–bandwidth tradeoff, we expected that a scale specifically tuned to competitiveness in workplace conflicts (Rahim, 1983) would have higher fidelity in predicting haggling in our exercise. This scale (composed of items such as "In conflicts at work, I am usually firm in pursuing my goals") provided a better prediction of bargaining behavior (work conflict competitiveness. $\beta = .24$, $p < .05$. vs. Agreeableness, $\beta = -.09$, $-$ ns). Yet, the personality effect was still quite small in comparison with the effect of the situation manipulation ($\beta = .46$, $p < .001$). Hence, substituting a context-specific measure does not alter the qualitative pattern of findings. We also investigated our expectation that a fine-tuned, context-specific measure would have a more limited bandwidth in predicting conflict behavior. Participants played an ultimatum game that was not framed in a workplace context (Larrick, 1998) in which the measure of conflict behavior was the amount of resources that a player claimed from a fixed pool. Consistent with the expectation of reduced bandwidth, the measure of competitive style in workplace conflicts was worse in predicting this non workplace conflict ($r = .15$, ns) than was the context-general measure of agreeableness ($r = -.28$, $p < .05$).

Table 5. Recruiter's Perception of the Recruit's Disagreeableness Regressed on Predictor Variables

Predictor	Regression equation						
	1	2	3	4	5	6	7
Actual value of alternative	.47***				.40***	.10	.09
Actual Agreeableness score		−.29***			−.29**	−.25**	−.23*
Haggling behavior				.72***		.55***	.55***
Ascribed value of alternative				.41***			.02
Adjusted R^2	.22	.07	.51	.16	.22	.44	.43
df	96	70	98	95	69	67	64

Note. Coefficients are standardized weights. Value of alternative is a dummy variable with the high-value condition coded 1 and the low-value condition coded 0. Actual Agreeableness score is the recruit's self-rated Agreeableness. score on the Big Five Index (John & Donahue, 1994).
* $p < .05$. ** $p < .01$. *** $p < .001$.

perceptions across conditions of the experiment may be seen in Table 3. As in Study 1, the value of the alternative offer had a strong effect on the recruit's perceived agreeableness. Perceptions of agreeableness were greater for recruits with low-value versus high-value alternative offers (3.81 vs. 3.16), $F(1, 94) = 26.63$, $p < .001$. To test that this effect of the situational factor was mediated by the recruiter's perception of the recruit's haggling behavior, we regressed perceptions of disagreeableness on all of the variables that are prior to it in the proposed path model (Figure 2). We obtained evidence for a mediation relationship, according to the criteria of Baron and Kenny (1986): The two independent variables (actual situation and actual personality) individually predicted perceived disagreeableness, as did the proposed mediator, haggling (Equations 1, 2, and 3 in Table 5). When haggling was included with the independent variables, haggling still significantly predicted the dependent variable, whereas the recruit's actual situation did not (Equation 6), which indicates

that the effect of the recruit's situation on the attribution of a disagreeable disposition to the recruit is indeed mediated by the recruit's level of haggling.[5] As can be seen in Figure 3, there was

[5]It might be argued that perceptions of disagreeableness were picking up the recruiter's dissatisfaction with the recruit rather than an assessment of the recruit's personality. However, Agreeableness is only one of four dimensions by which the recruiters could portray the recruit unfavorably, and effects of the manipulation were limited to Agreeableness. We also measured recruiters' satisfaction with the outcome on a rating scale, and although it was affected by the size of alternative offer, it did not mediate any of the relationships between the manipulation, haggling behavior, and attributions of disagreeableness. Moreover, in recent studies featuring a *negative* bargaining zone where it quickly becomes apparent that no deal is possible (Larrick, Morris, & Su, 1999), we have found that disagreeableness perception does not increase steadily as the bargaining zone becomes more negative and the settlement rate declines. Rather, perception of disagreeableness is highest in a narrow but positive bargaining zone. In sum, disagreeableness seems to be a correspondent inference drawn directly from perceived bargaining behavior not from postnegotiation feelings about impasse versus settlement.

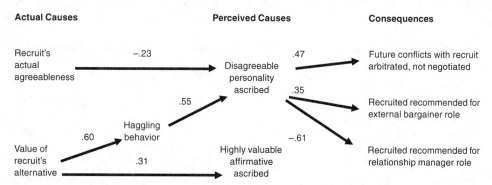

FIGURE 3 ■ Observed relationships in Experiment 2 between actual causes of haggling behavior, perceived causes, and decisions about future interactions. Only the significant paths from the full regression models in Table 4 (Equation 3), Table 5 (Equation 7), Table 6 (Equation 7), and Table 9 (Equation 7) are shown.

an effect of the recruit's actual personality on perceived agreeableness that was not mediated by the recruit's level of haggling. An interpretation (for which we thank a reviewer) is that agreeableness affects other behaviors besides haggling, and the recruiters had some ability to read these behaviors.

An isomorphic regression model of antecedents of recruiters' ascription of situational factors was also run. Haggling, although primarily caused by the recruit's situation, was not primarily attributed to the situation. As Equation 7 reveals, haggling predicted ascription of a high-value alternative to the recruit only marginally ($\beta = .23, p < .10$, Table 6), not nearly as well as it predicted ascription of a disagreeable personality ($\beta = .55, p < .001$, Table 5). As illustrated in Figure 3, the one significant predictor of perceptions of the value of the recruit's situation was its actual value. This influence, which was not mediated by haggling, reflects that some other cues to the value of the recruit's alternative were available.

Counter to our prediction and to the pattern observed in Experiment 1, perceptions of emotional instability were not affected by the manipulation of the risk in the recruit's alternative, as may be seen in Table 3. One possible explanation for the failure to replicate the pattern of misperception is that the introduction of the waffling perception questions inhibited the trait attribution on this dimension. That is, the pejorative connotations of waffling may have led participants to be reticent in their trait ratings. Consistent with this interpretation, ratings of emotional instability in Experiment 2 were generally lower than those in in Experiment 1, and this depression of ratings was specific to emotional instability rather than being a general pattern. Furthermore, in subsequent stud-

ies that have omitted the behavior perception measures, the effect of the recruit's level of risk on the recruit's perceived personality was observed once again. Although in Experiment 2 we have no evidence for a misperception of personality and hence obviously cannot test mediating variables, there was support for the notion that a negotiator's attribution on this personality dimension was predicted more by his or her counterpart's waffling behavior than by the counterpart's actual level of emotional instability, as the regression model in Table 7 reveals. Finally, perceptions of the Extraversion and Conscientiousness dimensions were not affected by the manipulations.

Persistence of personality trait ascriptions. Regression analyses also allowed us to test our third hypothesis that ascription of personality traits persists in the face of information about possible situational causes for behavior. We predicted that people's confidence in ascribing a personality factor would not be appreciably discounted by cues to a situational factor that fall short of definite information about a sufficient alternative (Morris & Larrick, 1995). The observed haggling behavior should lend credence to both unobserved possible causes: a disagreeable personality and an attractive alternative. Because more extreme levels of perceived haggling should lend relatively more credence to both attributions, we have interpreted the positive association between personality and situational attributions observed in Experiment 1 as arising from variation in the extremity of perceived haggling behavior across dyads. Accordingly, we expected to once again observe a positive bivariate relationship between personality and situational ascriptions, but we predicted that this association would disappear once variation in per-

TABLE 6. Recruiter's Perception of the Value of the Recruit's Alternative Regressed on Predictor Variables

Predictor	Regression equation						
	1	2	3	4	5	6	7
Actual value of alternative	.51***				.46***	.31*	.31*
Actual Agreeableness score		−.16			−.16	−.13	−.12
Haggling behavior			.52***			.25†	.23†
Ascribed disagreeableness				.41***			.03
Adjusted R^2	.25	.01	.26	.16	.22	.23	.22
df	94	70	95	95	69	66	64

Note. Coefficients are standardized weights. Value of alternative is a dummy variable with the high-value condition coded 1 and low-value condition coded 0. Actual Agreeableness score is the recruit's self-rated Agreeableness score on the Big Five Index (John & Donahue, 1994).
† $p < .10$ (marginally significant). * $p < .05$. *** $p < .001$.

TABLE 7. Recruiter's Perception of Recruit's Emotional Instability Score and the Recruit's Waffling Behavior

	Regression equation		
Predictor	1	2	3
Actual Emotional Instability score	−.12		−.04
Waffling behavior		.45***	.40***
Adjusted R^2	.00	.20	.14
df	70	96	68

Note. Coefficients are standardized weights. Actual Emotional Instability score is the recruit's self-rated Neuroticism score on the Big Five Index (John & Donahue, 1994). Waffling behavior is an index of six negotiation behaviors.
*** $p < .001$.

ceived haggling was controlled (in Figure 2 we predict no direct association between the ascription of situational and personality factors). In Tables 5 and 6 we can see that that the bivariate relationship is strongly positive (Equation 4), but this relationship disappears when haggling is controlled (Equation 7).

Future behavior toward the perceived. The fourth hypothesis is that erroneous perceptions of disagreeableness lead to decisions regarding one's counterpart that induce behavior confirming one's misperceptions. A first test of this hypothesis drew on questions about how the recruiter would choose to resolve a dispute with the recruit if they ended up working in the same organization in the future: Would he or she resolve the conflictual issues through direct discussion and negotiation or let a third party arbitrate the matter? As may be seen in the means presented in Table 8, the experimental

TABLE 8. Recruiter's Decisions About Future Interaction as a Function of the Recruit's Situation

	Recruit's alternative offer			
	Low		High	
Measure	Risky	Certain	Risky	Certain
Dispute resolution preference				
Willingness to negotiate	4.52	4.64	3.92	4.21
Confidence in negotiation	4.12	4.08	3.79	3.37
Willingness to seek arbitration	2.20	2.20	2.50	3.11
Confidence in arbitration	1.88	1.92	2.29	2.63
Role assignment preference				
Relationship manager	3.80	3.83	3.50	3.52
External bargaining	2.68	2.50	3.75	3.57

Note. Relative to the recruiter's alternative, the recruit's alternative was of either low or high value.

manipulation of the value of the recruit's alternative produced differences in recruiters' expectancies and preference for arbitration versus negotiation. To test that the difference across conditions of the experiment was mediated by personality perceptions (as illustrated in Figure 2), we performed a set of linear regressions using a summary variable that summarized preference for arbitration. The composite variable was created from the four future conflict variables through a principal component factor analysis, which indicated that the four variables loaded onto a single dimension that explained 52% of the variance in the variables. Factor scores for the four variables were approximately equal, and a composite variable was created by summing the two variables that tapped preference for arbitration and subtracting the sum of the two variables that tapped preference for negotiation. The regression results presented in Table 9 reveal that willingness to use arbitration is strongly predicted by ascription to the recruit of a disagreeable personality. Importantly, as hypothesized, effects of more remote variables, such as the recruit's alternative (see Equation 1) and the recruit's level of haggling (see Equation 3), are mediated by the ascription variable (see Equation 7). Moreover, a parallel analysis revealed that the effect of a high ascribed alternative was also mediated by ascribed disagreeableness.

A second belief-confirmatory dynamic was tested by asking recruiters to recommend the recruit for organizational roles. They considered roles that demand different kinds of behavior from the people that fill them. Of interest are the two roles that require, respectively, high-and low-agreeableness behavior.[6] As predicted, the manipulation of the recruit's alternative value led to differences in the extent to which the recruit was later recommended for the relationship manager and external bargaining roles—the relevant means may be seen in Table 8. Recruits in the high-value alternative condition were recommended more for the external bargaining role (3.67 vs. 2.58), $F(1, 89) = 22.54$, $p < .001$, and were deemed less appropriate for the relationship manager role (3.51 vs. 3.82), although this latter difference was nonsignificant, $F(1, 89) = 1.69$, *ns*. Recommendation decisions were submitted to regression analyses,

---

[6]The two job roles that were designed to require high or low degrees of stability are not discussed because the certainty manipulation did not have an effect on either perceived emotional stability or assignment to these roles.

TABLE 9. Recruiter's Preference for Arbitration (vs. Negotiation) Regressed on Predictor Variables

Predictor	Regression equation						
	1	2	3	4	5	6	7
Actual value of alternative	.38***				.34**	.22†	.18
Actual Agreeableness score		−.02			.02	−.01	.10
Haggling behavior			.44***			.25*	.01
Ascribed disagreeableness				.47***			.47***
Adjusted R^2	.13	.00	.18	.21	.09	.13	.25
df	95	69	97	98	68	66	65

Note. Coefficients are standardized weights. Preference for arbitration is a unit-weighted index created by summing willingness to arbitrate, confidence in arbitration, willingness to negotiate (reverse coded), and confidence in negotiation (reverse coded). Value of alternative is a dummy variable with the high-value condition coded as 1 and the low-value condition coded as 0.
† $p < .10$ (marginally significant). * $p < .05$. ** $p < .01$. *** $p < .001$.

isomorphic to those described for the conflict resolution decision. As summarized in Figure 3, we again observed that ascribed disagreeableness mediated the effect of more remote variables. In sum, results of Experiment 2 supported the hypothesis that the personality misperceptions that arise in negotiations have consequences for decision making in organizations. False attributions of a disagreeable personality led to organizational decisions regarding the new recruit that make him or her unlikely to disconfirm the false impression and likely to reinforce it.

General Discussion

The current research greatly clarifies the dynamics of attribution errors and their consequences in conflicts. In a pilot experiment we found support for two predicted patterns in which bargaining behaviors arising from basic aspects of a counterpart's situation are erroneously attributed to corresponding traits in the counterpart's personality. In Experiment 1 we found that these misperceptions affect major dimensions of personality perception. Counterparts who had a highly attractive alternative offer and hence required a higher salary to accept the job were perceived to be lower on the Agreeableness dimension of personality. Also, counterparts who had a less certain alternative offer and hence were less able to refer openly and consistently to their alternative were perceived to be higher on the Emotional Instability dimension of personality.

In Experiment 2 we tested hypotheses about specific processes that contribute to and sustain misperceptions of the personalities of conflict counterparts. Misperceptions originate from the combination of the primacy of situations in the actual causes of bargaining behavior (Hypothesis 1) and the primacy of personality in attributions (Hypothesis 2), Misperceptions are sustained by the lack of discounting of personality ascriptions based on uncertain information about situational causes (Hypothesis 3) and by the self-confirming effects of personality impressions on subsequent interactions with the other person (Hypothesis 4). All four hypotheses were clearly supported with regard to the pattern of perceived disagreeableness. Perceptions of disagreeableness arose from the fact that a recruit's level of haggling depended primarily on the situational factor (the value of his or her alternative), not on the corresponding personality factor (level of Agreeableness), yet haggling was attributed by the recruiter almost exclusively to the personality factor rather than to the situational factor. As expected, although recruiters' estimates of the recruits' alternative did respond to the clues they received about its actual level, recruiters did not significantly discount their personality ascriptions on the basis of their (uncertain) estimates of the situational factor. And, finally, impressions of the recruit as being a disagreeable type influenced future decisions to place the recruit in situations that induce further low-agreeableness behavior: (a) the decision to resolve a future conflict with the recruit through the adversarial procedure of arbitration rather than the collaborative procedure of negotiation and (b) the decision to assign the recruit to an organizational role that requires demandingness and intransigence rather than to a role that requires cooperativeness and flexibility. In sum, results of Experiment 2 unequivocally reveal a systematic misperception in which negotiators in a commanding economic position are attributed demanding, uncooperative personalities.

Our data are not inconsistent with recent findings that Agreeableness has a weak impact on competitive bargaining in some situations (Barry & Friedman, 1998), but our emphasis is that the impact of personality is small in comparison with the impact of the economic bargaining situation and in comparison with the role that lay perceivers accord personality.

With regard to perceptions of Emotional Instability, it was not possible to test hypotheses about component processes because the basic effect of the certainty condition on emotional instability perceptions (seen in the pilot experiment and Experiment 1) failed to replicate in Experiment 2. Various features of the current findings and subsequent findings in our research suggest that this misattribution vanished because the derogatory connotation of the waffling items reduced their endorsement. Which carried over to the emotional instability items. In ongoing work, we have found that the misperception of emotional instability reappears when the waffling measure is removed. Also, the effect occurs more strongly when the recruit's alternative is high in value, probably because the alternative is more salient when it is attractive. Hence, although our findings in general point to a pattern of misperception in which negotiators in an uncertain, insecure economic position are attributed unstable, insecure personalities, we are less confident (than with regard to the first pattern) that our measures fully capture this pattern or that the pattern is very robust. The behavioral effects of a risky alternative may not be captured by the construct of waffling, and they may be attributed to a personality disposition that does not fall squarely on the Emotional Instability dimension. For example, the trait of insincerity (which we used successfully in the pilot experiment) may be a correspondent inference evoked by the behavior of inconsistent statements in bargaining, but not a trait that loads on the dimension of Emotional Instability. Although the findings about Emotional Instability did not allow a test of specific hypotheses, results were consistent with the general claim that major dimensions of personality perceived in negotiation counterparts are mirages. Perceptions of a counterpart's personality on the Agreeableness and Emotional Instability dimensions had little to do with the counterpart's actual personality.

The Issue of Context Specificity in Personality Dispositions

We have conceived of personality in terms of the five-factor model of context-general traits, such as Agreeableness. Although this is currently the leading approach to the study of dispositions in psychology generally (McCrae & John, 1992) and in negotiation research specifically (Barry & Friedman, 1998), it is not the only fruitful approach. An increasingly influential alternative is defended by Mischel and Shoda (1995), who have argued that personality can be conceptualized in terms of behavioral dispositions specific to particular situational contexts. In extensive studies of domains involving sustained social interaction, such as a summer camp, they have found that tailor-made, context-specific measures do better than context-general measures in predicting behavior. This can be understood in terms of the general notion that increased specificity in constructs brings gains in fidelity (predictive validity) albeit losses in bandwidth (generality and parsimony). The magnitude of these gains and losses will, of course. very from domain to domain. Proponents of context-general constructs such as Agreeableness argue that in many domains, the gains in fidelity from narrowing one's constructs are small. To assess this we compared the performance of the Agreeableness scale with a similar instrument that taps the disposition to be competitive specifically in workplace conflicts (Rahim, 1983). We found (see Footnote 4) that the context-specific measure does allow slightly better prediction of haggling behavior, but the effect remains small relative to that of the situational variable and relative to the role accorded personality by perceivers.

A second, and independent, claim about context specificity is that lay perceivers form impressions of others in terms of context-specific traits (Mischel & Shoda, 1995; Shoda & Mischel, 1993). Undoubtedly person perception is this nuanced in some social settings, for instance, the impressions formed by perceptive camp counselors. Yet, there are features of the domain we studied—one-round negotiations between strangers—that impede such impressions. First, the perceiver has information about the target person in only one situation (negotiating in the context of one specific bargaining position) and hence cannot observe situation–behavior covariation. Second, the perceiver cannot easily detect the target person's situation; negotiations create strong situational pressure for actors to hide their true situation (strategically, negotiators strive to create the impression that they have a favorable alternative). Hence, our expectation is that perceivers interpret bargaining behavior in terms of context-general dispositions. We investigated this in an exploratory study using a distributive negotiation similar to the narrow-bargaining-zone conditions of Experiments 1 and 2. Two weeks prior to the study, all participants were asked to rate themselves on a series of eight descriptors of negotiation behavior in one of two contexts: Four synonymous questions asked about their behavior in an advantageous bargaining situation (having a favorable alternative), and four asked about their behavior in a disadvantageous bargaining situation (having an unfavourable alternative). For example, they were asked to rate their agreement with the statement "If I am in a *strong* bargaining position, I negotiate aggressively" and were also asked to rate their behavior in the converse situation: "If I am in a *weak* bargaining position, I negotiate aggressively." Following the negotiation excercise, negotiation opponents were asked to rate their counterpart on six similar if . . . then items. For instance, they were asked to rate their opponent on descriptors such as "would negotiate aggressively if in a *strong* bargaining position" and "would negotiate aggressively if in a *weak* bargaining position."

Relations between these actor ratings and observer ratings on the situation-contingent dispositions are shown in Table 10. As may be seen in Table 10, actors believed that their own behavior is only weakly related across strong and weak ne-

gotiation situations, $r(1, 2) = .19$, whereas perceivers expected actors to show a great deal of consistency. $r(5, 6) = .50$. This fits the expectation that perceivers, having only one observation of the other person, do not have information about situational variability, unlike actors who can recall their own behavior across different kinds of conflict situations. It may also be seen in Table 10 that actor self-ratings in particular contexts did not correlate highly with the corresponding perceiver ratings, as would be expected if actual personality and perceived personality existed at this context-specific level (these correlations were no higher than for context-general agreeableness perceptions in Study 2). Indeed, the correlation is highest between actors' self-ratings in strong situations and perceivers' ratings of the actor in weak situations, $r(1, 6) = .29$, suggesting that perceivers encoded behavior not as context-specific but in terms of a context-general impression of the actor's competitiveness. In support of this, a regression of perceived behavior in strong situations (Variable 5) on actor's self-rating in strong situations (Variable 1) and on perceived behavior in weak situations (Variable 6) showed that the relationship to actor's self-rating disappeared ($\beta = -.09$), $p > .30$, whereas the relationship to the perceiver rating remained high ($\beta = .46$), $p < .001$. Finally, Table 10 also shows that self-rated context-specific measures predicted perceived haggling poorly, $r(1, 4) = .15$ and $r(2, 4) = .07$, *ns*, but perceived haggling predicted context-specific perceptions very well, $r(4, 5) = .41$ and $r(4, 6) = .45$, $p < .001$. It seems that perceivers were using negotiation behavior to form impressions of the target in strong and weak situations, and they were doing so equally. Once again, this result suggests that perceivers, in this domain, worked with a context-general impression of cooperativeness. To test this, we conducted a partial

Table 10. Correlations Between Context-Specific Measures of Personality and Personality Perceptions

Variable	1	2	3	4	5	6
1. Self (if strong)	—					
2. Self (if weak)	.19*	—				
3. Perc (agreeable)	−.06	.16	—			
4. Perc (haggle)	.15	.07	−.66***	—		
5. Perc (if strong)	.22*	.01	−.50***	.41***	—	
6. Perc (if weak)	.29**	.07	−.49***	.45***	.50***	—

Note $N = 107$, self-reported ratings; Perc = perceiver's ratings of target.
*$p < .05$. **$p < .01$. ***$p < .001$.

correlation between perceived haggling and each of the context-specific if . . . then measures controlling for perceptions of global Agreeableness (Variable 3). The previous correlations of .41 and .45 decreased to .13 (*ns*) and .19 (*p* < .05), indicating that the global impression largely mediated the relationship between perceived behavior and context-specific perceptions. In sum, the empirical findings converge with our conceptual arguments to support the assumption that first impressions of negotiation counterparts are formed in terms of context-general constructs, such as Agreeableness.

Implications for Theory

Social psychological processes in negotiation. Early social psychological research on negotiation focused on personality dispositions that affect negotiation outcomes (e.g., Rubin & Brown, 1975) and was not, on the whole, successful in identifying strong, reliable effects (Thompson, 1990). The social psychological study of negotiation dwindled in the 1980s, at the same time that the study of cognitive biases in negotiation, led by Neale and Bazerman (1991), flourished and redefined the field. Of late, researchers of social cognition and perception in negotiation (Thompson, 1997) have carved out a new territory for social psychological studies of negotiation. Most of the studies in this stream of research have explored social psychological factors that distort a negotiator's perceptions of an opponent's preferences (Thompson & Hastie, 1990) or of a third party's preferences (Thompson & Loewenstein, 1992). The current research extends this approach to perceptions of an opponent's personality. More generally, we draw on the traditional social psychological themes that situations primarily determine the behaviors one sees, and yet one's subjective attributions for such behaviors, which guide one's response, often miss the role of situational factors (Ross & Nisbett, 1991). We apply this situationist, subjectivist analysis to elucidate how negotiation counterparts are misperceived.

Accuracy in social perception. As we have reviewed, the portrait of the error-prone social perceiver painted during the 1970s and early 1980s (e.g., Nisbett & Ross, 1980; Ross, 1977) has been questioned by recent theorists who have put forth more stringent criteria for errors. These criteria are met by the current studies in the negotiation context. The ecological validity (McArthur & Baron, 1983) is high because the interaction was natural and in a context that is familiar and motivating to participants. Although the ecological validity of a role-play method might be questionable in a study of interactions that are spontaneous or involve deep personal feelings, it is less problematic in a study of negotiation, which, as a task, requires conscious stage-management of impressions (Goffman, 1969). Furthermore, in the current studies we have examined biases with summary measures of the major dimensions of personality perception rather than mere ad hoc lists of specific traits. We have hypothesized and found that patterns of error are specific to major content dimensions such as Agreeableness, as in other work that has comprehensively measured trait perception (Robins et al., 1996). Finally, we have established that the misattributions are made to stable dispositions and hence affect decisions about future interactions; they are not just descriptions of the other person's behavior within the bounds of one interaction (Swann, 1984). In sum, evidence that meets the recently proffered criteria suggests that the fundamental attribution error (Ross, 1977) or correspondence bias (Jones, 1990) is alive and well and living at the bargaining table.

Dynamics of self-confirming beliefs. The notion that prophecies are self-fulfilling—that beliefs result in actions that evoke confirmatory responses from others—was first developed by the sociologist Merton (1940) to account for phenomena he observed in organizations. However, the concept has been refined primarily by social psychologists, particularly those interested in stereotypes (e.g., Rosenthal & Rubin, 1978). Psychologists have provided detailed evidence for several distinct ways that beliefs work toward their own confirmation. The simplest process, which almost certainly occurs in interpersonal conflicts, is that beliefs guide a perceiver's attention to details of the environment that are confirmatory (Jones, 1990). In face-to-face conversation, this process could occur through a negotiator selectively seeking, attending to, and remembering those actions of the counterpart that confirm prior impressions (Snyder & Swann, 1978). A more complex process, which has been studied in interpersonal conflicts, is that beliefs support actions that constrain the opponent's behavior and evoke behavior by the other person that is confirmatory of the beliefs. A classic demonstration is Kelley and Stahelski's

(1970) experiment with the repeated-trial prisoner's dilemma game in which a competitive player's attribution of competitiveness to a counterpart supported the competitive player's behavior of defecting, the expectation of competitiveness was then confirmed when this defection induced defection from the counterpart. Also, within the context of a more informationally rich negotiation conversation, there is a resonance whereby a recruiter's negative expectancies about a recruit manifest themselves in negative nonverbal behaviors that evoke confirming responses (Word, Zanna, & Cooper, 1974).

The contribution of the current research, however, lies in identifying longer-term organizational processes through which specific misperceptions born in negotiation work toward their own confirmation. In the spirit of Merton's examples, we examined two kinds of organizational decisions that routinely occur following a negotiation and that clearly influence what will be observed in the counterpart's subsequent behavior. We found that erroneous personality perceptions affected (a) decisions about the procedure in which one will meet the other person to resolve a future conflict and (b) decisions about work roles to which the other person will be assigned. These decisions place the other person in situations that constrain behavior; hence, they shape the other person's behavior and, as a result, the behavior the decision maker will observe in the future. Notice also that these organizationally mediated self-confirming dynamics not only perpetuate the decision maker's mistaken personality impression but also potentially spread this false personality impression to many other observers because they shape a person's long-term public behavior.

Implications for Practice

The current findings about systematic negotiator misperceptions suggest a few speculative recommendations for people negotiating everyday conflicts. Our findings highlight that negotiations have not only an economic outcome but also a *social outcome*. Acting to maximize one's economic outcome by obtaining a valuable alternative can involve the cost of appearing to be a person low in Agreeableness. However, the trade-off is not inevitable—the misperception can be avoided. Research in progress (Larrick, Morris, & Su, 1999) suggests that if, after the settlement, negotiators

are provided with trustworthy, certain information about their counterpart's alternative, then negotiators can discount their ascription of disagreeableness. A recommendation about avoiding misperceived Emotional Instability is easier to make because there does not seem to be a trade-off between the economic and the social outcomes. Both outcomes were better if negotiators had a certain rather than risky alternative option. Even when the certain alternative was of only average value, negotiators with certain alternatives achieved economic outcomes just as high as those with risky alternatives and came across as having more stable personalities. Hence, certain alternatives should be obtained in preparing for negotiations in which social outcomes matter.

ACKNOWLEDGMENTS

We acknowledge helpful comments at various stages of this research from Max Bazerman, Jonathon Bendor, Oliver John, Roderick Kramer, Keith Murnighan, Margaret Neale, Richard Nisbett, Richard Robins, Lee Ross, and Amos Tversky. We gratefully acknowledge research funding from the Stanford University Graduate School of Business, the University of Chicago Graduate School of Business, and the William S. Fishman fellowship.

REFERENCES

Axelrod, R. (1984). *The evolution of cooperation*. New York: Basic Books.

Baron, R. A. (1984). Reducing organizational conflict: An incompatible response approach. *Journal of Applied Psychology, 69,* 272–279.

Baron, R. A. (1988). Attributions and organizational conflict: The mediating role of apparent sincerity. *Organizational Behavior and Human Decision Processes, 41,* 111–127.

Baron, R., & Kenny, D. A. (1986). The moderator-mediator variable distinction in social psychological research: Conceptual, strategic, and statistical considerations. *Journal of Personality and Social Psychology, 51,* 1173–1182.

Barry, B., & Friedman, R. A. (1998). Bargainer characteristics in distributive and integrative negotiation. *Journal of Personality and Social Psychology, 74,* 345–359.

Bar-Tal, D., & Geva, N. (1986). A cognitive basis of international conflicts. In S. Worchel & W. G. Austin (Eds.), *Psychology of intergroup relations* (pp. 118–133). Chicago: Nelson-Hall.

Darley, J. M., & Batson, C. D. (1973). From Jerusalem to Jericho: A study of situational and dispositional variables in helping behavior. *Journal of Personality and Social Psychology, 27,* 100–108.

Dorris, W., Gentry. G., & Kelley. H. H. (1966). Unpublished raw data. University of California, Los Angeles.

Douglas, A. (1962). *Industrial peacemaking*. New York: Columbia University Press.

Funder, D. C. (1995). On the accuracy of personality judgement: A realistic approach. *Psychological Review, 102,* 652–666.

Goffman, E. (1969). *Strategic interaction*. Philadelphia: University of Pennsylvania Press.

Goldberg, L. R. (1990). An alternative "description of personality": The Big-Five Factor structure. *Journal of Personality and Social Psychology, 52*, 409–418.

Heider, F. (1958). *The psychology of interpersonal relations*. New York: Wiley.

Ichheiser, G. (1943). Misinterpretations of personality in everyday life and the psychologists's frame of reference. *Character and Personality, 12*, 145–160.

Jervis, R. (1976). *Perception and misperception in international policies*. Princeton. NJ: Princeton University Press.

John, O. P., & Donahue, E. M. (1994). *The Big Five inventory: Technical report of the 44- item version*. Berkeley, CA: Institute of Personality and Social Research.

John, O. P., & Robins, R. W. (1994). Determinants of interjudge agreement on personality traits: The Big Five domains, observability. evaluativeness, and the unique perspective of the self. *Journal of Personality, 61*, 521–551.

Jones, E. E. (1990). *Interpersonal perception*. New York: Freeman.

Jones, E. E., & Nisbett, R. E. (1971). The actor and the observer: Divergent perceptions of the causes of behavior. In E. E. Jones, D. E. Kanouse, H. H. Kelley, R. E. Nisbett, S. Valins, & B. Weiner (Eds.), *Attribution: Perceiving the causes of behavior* (pp. 79–94). Morristown, NJ: General Learning Press.

Kelley, H. H., Helus. Z., Lamm, H., Servais, M., Veen, P., Zaleska, M., & Wouters, K. (1967). *Direction of change in problem difficulty and perceived source of change as independent variables in a negotiation game*. Unpublished manuscript. Training Center, Catholic University of Louvain.

Kelley, H. H., Shure, G. H., Deutsch, M., Faucheux, C., Lanzena, J. L., Moscovici, S., Nuttin, J. M., Rabbie, J. M., & Thibaut, J. W. (1970). A comparative experimental study of negotiation behavior. *Journal of Personality and Social Psychology, 16*, 411–438.

Kelley, H. H., & Stahelski, A. J. (1970). Social interaction basis of cooperators' and competitors' beliefs about others. *Journal of Personality and Social Psychology, 16*, 66–91.

Kelley, H. H., & Thibaut, J. W. (1954). Experimental studies of group problem-solving and process. In G. Lindzey (Ed.). *Handbook of social psychology* (Vol. 2., pp. 1–101). Cambridge, MA: Addison-Wesley.

Larrick, R. P. (1998). [Predictors of ultimatum game play]. Unpublished raw data, Graduate School of Business. University of Chicago.

Larrick, R. P., & Boles, T. L. (1995). Avoiding regret in decisions with feedback: A negotiation example. *Organizational Behavior and Human Decision Processes, 63*, 87–97.

Larrick, R. P., Morris, M. W., & Su, S, K. (1999). *Agreeing to disagree: From limiting conditions on negotiator misperceptions to an intervention strategy*. Unpublished manuscript. Graduate School of Business, University of Chicago.

Lewicki, R. J., & Litterer, J. A. (1985). *Negotiation*. Homewood, IL: Irwin.

Loewenstein, G., Thompson, L., & Bazerman. M. H. (1989). Social utility and decision making in interpersonal contexts. *Journal of Personality and Social Psychology, 57*, 426–441.

McArthur, L., & Baron, R. M. (1983). Toward an ecological theory of social perception. *Psychological Review, 90*, 215–238.

McCrae, R. R., & John, O. P. (1992). An introduction to the five-factor model and its applications. *Journal of Personality, 60*, 175–219.

Merton, R. K. (1940). Bureaucratic structure and personality. *Social Forces, 17*, 560–568.

Milgram, S. (1963). Behavioral study of obedience. *Journal of Abnormal and Social Psychology, 46*, 961–978.

Mischel, W., & Shoda, Y. (1995). A cognitive-affective system theory of personality: Reconceptualizing situations, dispositions, dynamics, and invariance in personality structure. *Psychological Review, 102*, 246–268.

Morris, M. W., & Larrick, R. P. (1995). When one cause casts doubt on another: A normative analysis of discounting in causal attribution. *Psychological Review, 102*, 331–355.

Morris, M. W., Smith, E. E., & Turner, K. (1998). Parsimony in intuitive explanations for behavior: Reconciling the discounting principle and preference for conjunctive explanations. *Basic and Applied Social Psychology, 20*, 71–85.

Neale, M. A., & Bazerman, M. H. (1991). *Cognition and rationality in negotiation*. New York: Macmillan.

Neuberg, S. L., & Fiske, S. T. (1987). Motivational influences on impression formation: Outcome dependency, accuracy-driven attention, and individuating processes. *Journal of Personality and Social Psychology, 53*, 431–444.

Nisbett, R. E., & Ross, L. (1980). *Human inference strategies and shortcomings of social judgment*. Englewood Cliffs, NJ: Prentice Hall.

Orvis, B. R., Kelley, H. H., & Butler, D. (1976). Attributional conflict in young couples. In H. H. Harvey, W. J. Ickes, & R. F. Kidd (Eds.). *New directions in attribution research* (Vol. 1., pp. 353–386). Hillsdale, NJ: Erlbaum.

Pietromonaco, P., & Nisbett, R. E. (1982). Swimming upstream against the fundamental attribution error: Subjects' weak generalizations from the Darley and Batson study. *Social Behavior and Personality, 10*, 1–4.

Pruitt, D. G., & Drews, J. L. (1969). The effect of time pressure, time elapsed, and the opponent's concession rate on behavior in negotiation. *Journal of Experimental Social Psychology, 5*, 43–60.

Radlow, R., & Weidner, M. F. (1966). Unenforced commitments in "co-operative" and "noncooperative" non-constant-sum games. *Journal of Conflict Resolution, 10*, 497–505.

Rahim, M. A. (1983). A measure of styles of handling interpersonal conflict. *Academy of Management Journal, 26*, 368–376.

Raiffa, H. (1982). *The art and science of negotiation*. Cambridge. MA: Belknap Press.

Robins, R. W., Spranca, M. D., & Mendelsohn, G. A. (1996). The actor-observer effect revisited: Effects of individual difference and repeated social interactions on actor and observer attributions. *Journal of Personality and Social Psychology, 71*, 375–389.

Rosenthal, R., & Rubin, D. B. (1978). Interpersonal expectancy effects: The first 345 studies. *Behavioral and Brain Sciences, 3*, 377–415.

Ross, L. D. (1977). The intuitive psychologist and his shortcomings: Distortions in the attribution process. In I. Berkowitz (Ed.). *Advances in experimental social psychology* (Vol. 10., pp. 173–220). New York: Random House.

Ross, L. D., & Nisbett, R. E. (1991). *The person and the situation: Perspectives of social psychology*. New York: McGraw-Hill.

Rubin, J. Z., & Brown, B. (1975). *The social psychology of bargaining and negotiation*. New York: Academic Press.

Ruscher, J. B., & Fiske, S. T. (1990). Interpersonal competition can cause individuating processes. *Journal of Personality and Social Psychology. 58,* 832–843.

Safer, M. A. (1980). Attributing evil to the subject, not the situation: Student reactions to Milgram's film on obedience. *Personality and Social Psychological Bulletin, 11,* 315–325.

Schelling, T. C. (1960). *The strategy of conflict*. New York: Oxford University Press.

Shoda, Y., & Mischel, W. (1993). Cognitive social approach to dispositional inferences: What if the perceiver is a cognitive social theorist? *Personality and Social Psychology Bulletin, 19,* 574–585.

Sillars, A. L. (1980). The sequential and distributional structure of conflict interactions as a function of attributions concerning the locus of responsibility and stability of conflicts. In. D. Nimmo (Ed.), *Communication yearbook* (Vol. 4., pp. 218–235). Edison. NJ: Transaction Books.

Snyder, M., & Swann, W. B., Jr. (1978). Hypothesis-testing processes in social interaction. *Journal of Personality and Social Psychology, 36,* 1202–1212.

Strauss, A. L. (1964). *Psychiatric ideologies and institutions*. New York: Free Press.

Swann, W. B., Jr. (1984). Quest for accuracy in person perception: A matter of pragmatics. *Psychological Review, 91,* 457–477.

Thomas, K. W., & Pondy, L. R. (1977). Toward an "intent" model of conflict management among principal parties. *Human Relations, 30,* 1089–1102.

Thompson, L. L. (1990). Negotiation: Empirical evidence and theoretical issues. *Psychological Bulletin, 108,* 515–532.

Thompson, L. L. (1997). *The heart and mind of the negotiator*. Englewood Cliffs, NJ: Prentice Hall.

Thompson, L. L., & Hastie, R. M. (1990). Social perception in negotiation. *Organizational Behavior and Human Decision Processes, 47,* 98–123.

Thompson, L., & Loewenstein. G. (1992). Egocentric interpretations of fairness and interpersonal conflict. *Organizational Behavior and Human Decision Processes, 51,* 176–197.

Ury, W., Brett, J., & Goldberg, S. (1989). *Designing dispute systems*. San Francisco: Jossey-Bass.

White, S. B., & Neale, M. A. (1991). Reservation prices, resistance points, and BATNAs: Determining the parameters of acceptable negotiation outcomes. *Negotiation Journal, 7,* 378–388.

Word, C. O., Zanna, M. P., & Cooper, J. (1974). The nonverbal mediation of self-fulfilling prophecies in interracial interaction. *Journal of Experimental Social Psychology, 10,* 109–120.

Yik, M. S. M., & Bond, M. H. (1993). Exploring the dimensions of Chinese person perception with indigenous and imported constructs: Creating a culturally balanced scale. *International Journal of Psychology, 28,* 75–95.

Avoiding Missed Opportunities in Managerial Life: Analogical Training More Powerful Than Individual Case Training

Leigh Thompson, Dedre Gentner, and Jeffrey Loewenstein
• Northwestern University

We examined the ability of Masters of Management students to transfer knowledge gained from case studies to face-to-face negotiation tasks. During a study phase, students either read two cases and gave advice to the protagonist in each case ("Advice" condition) or derived an overall principle by comparing two cases ("Comparison" condition). Management students in the Comparison condition were nearly three times more likely to transfer the principle in an actual, face-to-face bargaining situation than those in the Advice condition. Further, content analysis of students' open-ended responses revealed that the quality of the advice given in the Advice condition did not predict subsequent behavior, whereas the quality of the principles given in the Comparison condition did predict successful transfer to the negotiation situation. Perhaps most striking is the fact that not a single person in the Advice condition drew a parallel between the two cases, even though they were presented on the same page. We conclude that the value of examples is far greater if analogical comparisons among examples are encouraged. We propose that this simple and cost-effective method can substantially improve the benefits of professional training and education.

One of the more lamentable experiences in life is feeling that you knew something after the fact, but not when the opportunity presented itself. The assumption that we can use what we know underlies much of our intuition about how managers solve problems and make decisions. However, studies of problem solving reveal that people often do not retrieve their relevant knowledge at appropriate times (Bassok, 1990; Bassok & Holyoak, 1989; Gentner & Landers, 1985; Gentner, Rattermann, & Forbus, 1993; Gick & Holyoak, 1980; Ross, 1984, 1987; see Reeves & Weisberg, 1994, for a recent review). Thus knowledge transfer hinges on memory access. Our ability to access knowledge from memory depends crucially upon how we learned it.

Transfer of knowledge is of critical importance to managers who typically spend tens of thousands of dollars for an MBA degree and to companies who invest hundreds of thousands of dollars on the continuing management education of their employees. Typically, investigations of knowledge transfer have focused on dissemination and adoption of practices and knowledge between individuals or firms (e.g., Argote, 1993; Argote & Epple, 1990). A large body of research has examined the generalization of learned material to job behavior and the maintenance of trained skills over time (see Baldwin & Ford, 1988, for a review). The research reported here focused on cognitive processes involved in transfer. Virtually no research has dealt with the question of whether managers can transfer *their own* knowledge to novel-appearing organizational problems and challenges. In fact, the implicit assumption that underlies management training is that once presented and understood, managerial knowledge can be applied to future problems that managers may confront. There may be obstacles to implementing the knowledge, but not to retrieving it from memory. Our research investigation provides evidence that challenges this assumption. We argue that optimal learning processes leading to accessible knowledge available for transfer are not intuitively obvious. This may help explain why knowledge transfer is often so difficult.

Although retrieving previous experiences can help to solve novel-appearing problems, people appear to have limited ability to retrieve appropriate information. For example, Perfetto, Bransford, and Franks (1983) had people judge sentences for their validity (e.g., "A minister marries several people each week") and then had them solve riddles (e.g., "A man . . . married 20 different women of the same town. All are still living and he has never divorced one of them. Yet, he has broken no law. Can you explain?"). Participants who were not told that the initial sentences could help them solve the riddles not only solved fewer riddles but were no more likely to solve the riddles than participants who never read the initial sentences.

Furthermore, actively learning the initial information may not provide much advantage in knowledge transfer. Having solved one problem does not offer much help in solving an analogous problem when the two problems come from different contexts (e.g., Catrambone & Holyoak, 1989; Gick & Holyoak, 1980, 1983; Keane, 1988; Novick, 1988; Reed, Ernst, & Banerji, 1974; Ross, 1987, 1989; Schumacher & Gentner, 1988; Simon & Hayes, 1976; see Bransford, Franks, Vye, & Sherwood, 1989; and Reeves & Weisberg, 1994, for reviews). For example, Ross taught students mathematical principles by having them solve problems embodying those principles. Students were then given a new set of problems from different contexts that

required them to use the same principles they had just learned. Students solved less than 30% of the new problems correctly.

One key problem in knowledge transfer is that people tend to access previous knowledge that bears *surface*, rather than *structural*, similarity to the problem at hand. Consider the following example from Gentner and Schumacher (reported in Gentner & Medina, 1998). Gentner and Schumacher gave participants 100 proverbs, asking after each one if it reminded them of any of the previous proverbs. Very commonly, participants were reminded of proverbs with surface similarities. For example, the proverb "A hair from here, a hair from there will make a beard" reminded participants of "It is not the beard that makes the philosopher." However, participants were far less often reminded of proverbs with matching relational structure. For example, "Remove the dirt from your own eye before you wipe the speck from mine" is structurally similar to "He who laughs at the crooked man should walk very straight," but few people recalled these kinds of matches. Subsequently, participants judged the structurally similar pairs as both more sound and more similar than the surface similarity matches—even when they had failed to recall proverbs that were structurally similar to one another. Thus, the very matches judged by participants to be most useful in reasoning were the ones that came to mind least readily.

In another investigation involving more elaborate materials, Gentner, Rattermann, and Forbus (1993) gave students several stories prior to reading a target story. Some of the prior "source" stories bore a surface similarity to the critical target story (e.g., they shared similar characters or objects). In contrast, other stories did not bear much surface similarity, but were structurally equivalent. Stories containing surface feature matches were recalled 55% of the time, as compared with 12% of the time for recall based on purely analogical matches. Yet, when the same participants were presented with the original source stories, they clearly regarded those with structural similarity to be more useful for reasoning about the target story than those bearing only surface similarity. These results point to a striking dissociation between what is most accessible in memory and what is most useful in reasoning: We often fail to recall what is ultimately most valuable for solving new problems (Forbus, Gentner, & Law, 1995; Gentner

& Landers, 1985; Gentner, Rattermann, & Forbus, 1993; Gick & Holyoak, 1980, 1983; Holyoak & Koh, 1987; Reeves & Weisberg, 1994; Ross, 1987, 1989).

Are there ways to foster analogical transfer, that is, to encourage knowledge transfer based on retrieving structurally similar, rather than superficially similar, instances? We think so. Successful analogical transfer relies on relational similarity between the current problem and stored experiences. If people abstract general schemas or principles during learning, perhaps these principles can form the basis for experiencing similarities with new cases involving the same principles (Forbus, Gentner, & Law, 1995). If so, it would allow people to better capitalize on their experiences. One method for promoting schema-abstraction is to draw a comparison between two or more instances (Gick & Holyoak, 1983). People seem to draw such abstractions readily when explicitly asked to compare (e.g., Brown, Kane, & Echols, 1986; Catrambone & Holyoak, 1989; Gick & Holyoak, 1983, Kotovsky & Gentner, 1996; Loewenstein & Gentner, 1997, submitted; Ross & Kennedy, 1990).

According to structure-mapping theory, comparison entails a structural alignment and mapping process that highlights the similar aspects of the two examples (Falkenhainer, Forbus, & Gentner, 1989; Gentner & Markman, 1997; Medin, Goldstone, & Gentner, 1993). Focusing on shared aspects between examples with different surface features promotes the abstraction of a common relational structure that can then be stored as a schema. Such a schema is useful for the learner because it is uncluttered with irrelevant surface information. In this way, judicious comparison can inform the learner as to which aspects of experience are relevant, and which are causally irrelevant. Thus, our hypothesis is that comparing two or more instances during learning leads managers to derive a problem-solving schema that can be retrieved and applied to future instances. Analogical encoding fosters subsequent knowledge transfer.

To date, most studies of analogical reasoning of the kind we have described have used mathematical and logic puzzles. Because we were particularly interested in the role of analogical encoding in managerial life, we focused on negotiation, an important and complex managerial skill (Thompson, 1998). Negotiation is not only considered to be an essential skill in the managerial repertoire (Bazerman & Neale, 1992), but one that

needs to be accessible in high-stress, cognitively demanding situations. Successful transfer in management situations requires that the principles and strategies underlying successful negotiation be accessed and adapted to vastly different contexts. Therefore, negotiation poses a serious challenge for cross-domain analogizing.

The cost of ineffective negotiation is dramatic. People often settle for suboptimal negotiation agreements, leaving large portions of money on the bargaining table. For example, in incidence of lose–lose outcomes is strikingly high: 50% of negotiators fail to realize that they have perfectly compatible interests with the other party and 20% of the pairs fail to settle on the value that both parties prefer (Thompson & Hrebec, 1996). These findings are particularly disturbing when viewed in light of research that suggests that people—even including managers—do not seem to know when they have negotiated well (Thompson, Valley, & Kramer, 1995). Further, when their mistakes are explained, people often feel that they understand fully, yet go on to repeat their errors in subsequent negotiations that have different surface (but similar deep) structures (Thompson & DeHarpport, 1994).

Overview of Research

We conducted a research investigation to address whether and how analogical encoding during negotiation training promotes subsequent transfer. This experiment was a test of transfer from written case analysis to actual face-to-face negotiation. We compared the transfer ability of people who received analogical comparisons during learning with that of people who did not. In the learning phase, students read two cases. In the test phase, students had an opportunity to use what they had learned from the cases in a face-to-face negotiation.

We focused on an especially difficult, yet important, negotiation principle—the formation of contingency contracts (Lax & Sebenius, 1986; Bazerman & Gillespie, 1999). Most people tend to resolve negotiations through the use of compromise. However, compromise (or splitting-the-difference strategies) are suboptimal when negotiators have differing beliefs concerning relevant events. For example, suppose that an author is optimistic about book sales and wants a prospective publisher to agree to a high royalty rate. However, the prospective publisher is much less optimistic about book sales and consequently only wants to offer a standard minimal royalty rate. The two parties could compromise on the royalty rate. However, a more elegant solution would involve a contingency agreement, wherein the royalty rate is contingent upon book sales. Such an agreement has the beneficial effects of meeting both parties' interests, maximizing negotiators' profits, and allowing agreements to be reached in situations that might otherwise end in stalemate. As in betting, contingency contracts capitalize on parties' differing expectations regarding the outcome of a future event. Contingency contracts are effective in increasing negotiators' profits (and, hence, increasing joint profits) because they often allow negotiators to avoid impasse. Further, even though one person will eventually be right (and the other wrong) about the future, *at the time negotiators make the agreement*, they each believe in their own predictions.

In some areas of business—compensation, for example—contingent contracts are common, as with the case of book publishing. For example, when a CEO agrees to a salary tied to the company's stock price, that CEO is entering into a contingent contact. Similarly, an actor who takes points in a movie in return for a lower up-front payment is agreeing to a contingent contract. But in many business negotiations, contingent contracts are either ignored entirely or rejected outright for three reasons (Bazerman & Gillespie, 1999). First, many negotiators are simply unaware of the possibility of using contingent contracts. Second, contingent contracts are often seen a form of gambling and are therefore antithetical to good business judgment. Finally, most companies lack a systematic way of thinking about the formulation of such contracts.

In an initial investigation, we tested the power of comparison in promoting subsequent knowledge transfer for contingent contracts (Loewenstein, Thompson, & Gentner, 1999). In a management class, half of the participants were instructed to compare training cases and draw out their common solution; the other half were asked to draw out the solution in each training case separately. In addition, we orthogonally examined whether providing participants with an explicit reference to a particular principle in the training phase would affect knowledge transfer. The result were dramatic

and straightforward: managers who explicitly compared the cases were three times as likely to use contingency contracts in the subsequent negotiation case as those who did not compare the cases. Mentioning the principle during training had no effect.

The goal of the present experiment was to examine the efficacy of case comparison in a more realistic managerial context. Specifically, we contrasted the effectiveness of *comparing cases* versus *providing advice on a case-by-case basis*. Managers and executives, particularly those enrolled in MBA programs and consulting firms, are regularly in the position of giving advice. One view of advice is that it requires deep thinking about a specific case, particularly through an analysis of costs and benefits, and therefore should induce subsequent knowledge transfer. Another view is that giving advice may prevent comparison and abstraction, if the advice-giver becomes too focused on particulars present in a single instance, thereby inhibiting subsequent knowledge transfer.

All participants read two brief cases embodying the principle of contingency contracts prior to engaging in an actual face-to-face negotiation which contained the opportunity to apply this principle. Further, all participants received the two written cases presented on a single page. In the Advice condition, participants were asked to give advice to the protagonist for each of the two cases. In the Comparison condition, participants were asked to compare the two cases and draw out their similarities. We hypothesized that Management students in the Comparison condition would show superior transfer of the contingency contract principle to their face-to-face negotiation in the test phase because comparison entails a structural alignment process that promotes abstraction of a common schema (Gentner, 1983; Gentner & Medina, 1998; Markman & Gentner, 1997). In addition to measuring participant negotiation performance, we content-coded negotiators' responses so we could trace their paths of learning and reasoning.

Method

Participants

Participants were 88 Masters of Management students enrolled in a 10-week course in negotiation at Northwestern University's Kellogg Graduate School of Management. For their training in negotiation, the students were given a week to prepare for the face-to-face negotiation before spending up to an hour and a half at the bargaining table working out an agreement. Half of the students were randomly assigned to the Comparison condition ($n = 22$ dyads), and half were assigned to the Advice condition ($n = 22$ dyads). Students in the same condition were paired together to form dyads who negotiated with one another.[1]

Materials and Procedure

In the test phase, each student randomly received one of two roles to play in a face-to-face negotiation (buyer or seller) and was matched with a partner who was to play the opposing role. The task concerned a negotiation between a general manager of a theater (buyer) and a producer of a Broadway show (seller).[2] The issues to be negotiated concerned the profit-sharing among parties, number of shows, salaries for cast and crew, and so on. Each party had different expectations about the profitability of the show—the seller anticipated sell-out performances; the buyer was much less optimistic. A contingency contract could be developed between parties concerning profit-sharing based on the number of ticket sales. For example, negotiators could agree to split profits 60/40 (buyer/seller) if ticket sales were in line with the buyer's conservative estimation; and 40/60 if the seller's optimistic prediction was borne out. This is an example of a contingency contract that is ultimately more beneficial for both parties than is a simple compromise agreement, such as splitting ticket revenues 50/50. For example, say that the producer of the show believes that ticket sales will gross $1M; however, the theater owner believes that ticket sales will barely gross $750K. One way to share profits would involve a compromise, wherein the parties agree to split ticket sales 50/50; this would mean an expected value of $500K for the producer and an expected value of $375K for the theater owner. However, a more elegant and mutually profitable solution would be for the parties to agree to a 60/40 split in the case of ticket sales over $1M and a 40/60 split in the case of ticket sales under $750K. Because the parties have different beliefs, the expected value of their profits is higher—in this case, $600K for the producer and $450K for the theater owner. Of course, both parties cannot be right about the future; however, because they each believe that they will be right at the time they form the contingency contract, their subjective value of the deal is greater. In hindsight, contingency contracts seem not only sensible but obvious; however, they rarely occur to the negotiator embroiled in the heat of conflict.

In the study phase, one week prior to the test phase, the students received a packet of materials to prepare for the negotiation. There were two pages of questions (all open-ended), the first of which asked students four questions concerning their expectations about the outcome of the negotiation and what strategies they planned to employ to reconcile differences of opinion, preference, and beliefs. The second page contained the training materials: two 225-word summaries of cases involving contingency contracts (see Appendix 1). We deliberately chose the two training cases with little or no surface similarity to the face-to-face negotiation case. Thus, to profit from their training experience, students would need to rely on relational, rather than surface-level, similarities.

In the Comparison condition, the cases were read one after another, and then the participants were asked to respond to the following questions: "Think about the similarities between these two cases. What are the key parallels in the two negotiations? In the space below, identify an overall principle that captures the essence of the strategy of betting on differences." In the Advice condition, the cases were read one at a time, after which the participants were asked to respond to the following question: "Suppose you are advising [the main character]. What should she do? Why?" Participants' responses to the Comparison/Advice questions were collected prior to the negotiation and coded for quality of response. Our key hypothesis was that negotiators who engaged in active comparison before the negotiation would be more likely to employ a contingency contract during the actual, face-to-face negotiation.

---

[1] All data are analyzed at the level of the dyad.
[2] The negotiation case *Oceania!* is available upon request through the Dispute Resolution Research Center, Kellogg School of Management, Northwestern University, 2001 Sheridan Road, Evanston. IL 60208-2011. E-mail: drrc@kellogg.northwestern.edu.

Results

Negotiated Outcomes

The final contracts negotiated by participants were scored in terms of the inclusion of a contingency contract and also their overall monetary value to each negotiator. The results supported our prediction that making a comparison is crucial for encoding the relational commonalities necessary for analogical transfer. Specifically, only 5 (23%) of the 22 dyads in the Advice condition made contingency contracts; in contrast, 14 (64%) of the 22 dyads in the Comparison condition made contingency contracts. Thus, participants who explicitly compared the cases were nearly three times as likely to use contingency contracts as those who responded to separate cases: $\chi^2 (1, N = 44) = 7.503$, $p < .01$. This held true despite the fact that all participants read the same two cases and both cases were presented on a single page.

A second indication of the influence of comparison is the monetary outcomes of the negotiations. As expected, using a contingency contract resulted in a higher gain than using a compromise solution. Negotiating dyads who compromised on ticket sales grossed, on average, $987,500 from the negotiation, whereas dyads using a contingency contract grossed, on average, $1,049,500, a $52,000 (6%) gain, $t(42) = 2.484$, $p < .05$. Greater use of the contingency contract by participants in the Comparison condition meant an average gain of $21,000 (2%) over the dyads in the Advice condition, a nonsignificant trend.

Content Coding

We examined participants' answers in the Advice and Comparison conditions. Although all participants in both conditions read the same two cases, the questions asked of them afterwards differed. Thus, we cannot compare the two conditions directly. Therefore, we performed a content analysis within each condition. We had complete data for 19 dyads in each condition. Two trained raters read all of the responses and rated the responses on several dimensions explained below. Although the coders were not blind to conditions (e.g., it was obvious whether a participant was in the Advice or Comparison condition), they had no knowledge of the hypotheses. For those cases in which there was a discrepancy, coders jointly resolved their differences. We report individual reliability statistics for each dimension below.

Advice Condition

Our first analysis concerned whether the quality of advice that participants gave in the Advice condition led to better negotiated agreements. If many people thought it unwise to accept the contingency proposed in the case, for example, then it would not be surprising that these participants did not develop contingency contracts in their actual negotiations. To examine this, we looked at only those participants in our Advice condition and coded their responses to the two cases in terms of whether they advised the protagonist to accept the contingency contract (or, in the language of the mini-case, "to take the bet") or not. Specifically, two raters coded the advice given on each particular case (0 = not to take the bet; 1 = indeterminate; 2 = to take the bet). The reliability measure was 87%. The results showed that the nature of the advice was unrelated to actual negotiation performance. Those dyads in which both people had advised taking the bet in 75% of the training cases (operationalized as at least one dyad member recommending the bet in both cases and the other member recommending the bet in at least one case) made contingency contracts in the actual face-to-face negotiation 25% of the time (2 of 8 dyads). Those dyads whose members had advised not taking the bet made contingency contracts 18% of the time (2 of 11 dyads). Thus, recognizing that the contingency contract was advisable was not related to transferring the betting principle to the face-to-face negotiation situation subsequently encountered by participants.

A second question is whether people in the Advice condition spontaneously noticed the parallels between the two cases. Not a single person in the Advice condition referenced the first case when talking about the second case in any meaningful way. Had participants noticed this common structure, it is reasonable to assume that they would have responded to the second case by referring to their advice for the first case. However, no suggestion of linking the cases was found among these participants' responses.

If participants offered what they regarded to be a better solution to the case, this was noted. A total of 85% of the dyads in the Advice condition made at least one suggestion that they considered to be a better solution to the case than the bet. These suggestions were often based on the particular idiosyncrasies of each case. In contrast, only three people in the Comparison condition suggested something they thought would be better than the bet.

Comparison Condition

We examined the quality of the principles articulated by participants in the Comparison condition. Each participant's response to the directive to "derive a principle that captures the essence of these two cases . . . " was rated on a 3-point scale in terms of depth of understanding, with 0 for little understanding (e.g., "Each party will pay what they think is fair after the event" $N = 2$), 1 for some understanding (e.g., "Both are negotiating with regard to their risks and are willing to pay a price if they are wrong" $N = 10$); and 2 for sophisticated understanding (e.g., "They are similar in that there are uncertain future events and different beliefs about the outcome of those events. The strategy is to create a bet that hinges on the outcome of uncertain future events" $N = 7$). The reliability measure was 82%. Developing contingency contracts in the negotiation was highly related to the quality of the principles derived by the participants. When only one member of the dyad abstracted a good principle, development of a contingency contract was only moderately likely (45%, or 5 of 11 dyads). However, if one person stated the principle and the other person stated at least elements of it, then making bets was extremely likely—88%, or 7 of 8 of these dyads made bets. As in Gick and Holyoak's (1983) study, better extraction of principles lead to greater tendency to apply the principles, marginal by a Fisher's exact test, $p = .08$.

Despite the fact that the two cases were printed on the same page in both conditions, we found widely different responses between groups. In the Advice condition, there was no evidence that participants spontaneously compared cases. Not one participant mentioned the first case when giving advice about the second. In contrast, only 1 person (of 38) in the Comparison condition failed to discuss the two cases together. What did participants in the Advice condition do? Nearly everyone in the Advice condition attempted to come up with new solutions to the cases, typically appealing to expected values when they were trying to make the case for or against what to do. In contrast, virtually no one in the Comparison condi-

tion mentioned expected values. Only 2 people in the Comparison condition talked about the cases separately, and 1 of them first stated an overall principle and then wrote how it played out in each case. Comparing the cases led people to derive and understand the common betting principle; in contrast, for people studying the cases separately, the common principle did not emerge.

Discussion

Management students who compared two cases were more likely to transfer their knowledge to a face-to-face negotiation than students who read the same two training cases but gave advice. In both the Advice and Comparison conditions, participants read the same two cases that were presented on a single page. The cases were presented merely as an addendum to the role participants were learning and in a written format quite unlike the actual face-to-face negotiation scenario. Yet, the simple presence of explicit instructions to compare the two cases and derive a principle led to a large advantage in negotiation performance. Making a comparison enabled students to recognize the principle in common to the cases and carry it forward to the negotiation nearly three times as often as those students giving sequential advice. Moreover, in a related study we found that simply giving instructions to compare two cases without mentioning an abstract principle likewise led to superior performance in the comparison group (54% of dyads transferred the principle to their negotiations) over the advice group (13%) (Loewenstein, Thompson, & Gentner, 1999). Thus the advantage of the comparison group in the current study does not appear to stem from the directive to "derive a principle that captures the essence of the two cases." These results support our hypothesis that comparison of instances can promote knowledge transfer.

Professional education in management, law, and medicine is often based on the case method. The traditional case method relies upon the belief that people can and will abstract higher order relations from the analysis of individual examples. The current findings cast doubt on this assumption. The present investigation corroborates and extends the findings of Loewenstein, Thompson, and Gentner (1999). Students showed little transfer of knowledge learned from individual examples. On the basis of the results of our experiments, we conclude that comparing cases does not automatically occur—even when cases are physically juxtaposed. It is not enough simply to be presented with multiple cases; rather, it is *comparing* multiple cases that leads to abstracting their common principles thereby facilitating later memory access and knowledge transfer. Given elaborate proposals for educational innovation and on-the-job training, our technique of simply encouraging people to compare available cases seems refreshingly cost-effective.

We might conjecture that the truly seasoned manager or executive would be able to retrieve appropriate experiences when confronted with a novel-appearing situation. However, an investigation of expertise in mathematics (Novick, 1988) suggests that although experts show somewhat more appropriate retrieval than novices, they too retrieve many surface-similar cases. The experts did show an advantage over novices in their ability to dismiss inappropriate cases quickly. However, although experts performed better than novices, they still failed to retrieve appropriate cases in many instances (Novick, 1988).

The available evidence suggests that although seasoned professionals will show a higher hit rate of accessing genuinely relevant prior experiences, they too are vulnerable to the problem of retrieval by surface similarities. The Management students in our experiment were not experts in negotiation—few people are—but they were not naive and they were highly motivated, intelligent, and competitive. Such people would seem to be an ideal group for recognizing parallels and connections. Yet, even when presented with relevant cases prior to a face-to-face negotiation, few of them drew upon principles embedded in the cases. Their difficulty (in the Advice condition) in transferring principles from a learning situation to a test situation shows that transfer difficulty holds even for highly motivated participants working on problems they find relevant.

Our own qualitative observations of our participants yield further insights about comparison and transfer. In a debriefing of the negotiation case after the fact, we asked participants whether they had thought about the two preceding mini-cases. Many of those in the Comparison condition said they had; fewer in the Advice condition reported doing so. Yet when we revealed the contingency solution to the negotiation case and pointed out the relational parallels to the test cases, participants often expressed regret. The conceptual parallels seemed completely obvious when pointed out to them, yet did not provoke spontaneous recall before the fact, a pattern reminiscent of Gentner, Rattermann, and Forbus' (1993) findings.

Mundane and Creative Analogy

Throughout this article, we have been arguing that managers need to access their relevant knowledge to apply to current problems they face. Many case-based retrievals are highly mundane (Gentner, Rattermann, & Forbus, 1993) and rightly so: If one is preparing an account statement, it is typical (and optimal) to be reminded of last quarter's account statement. Cases that share surface properties often share structural properties as well. But analogical retrieval processes can also yield distant analogies, as happens in scientific discovery. For example, Kepler's proposal that the sun causes planetary motion depended on positing an attractive force analogous to light: Like light, the attractive force diminishes with distance; and most importantly, like light, it shows "action at a distance": it travels unseen between the source and the distant object, yet has clear effects on the distant object (Gentner, Brem, Ferguson, Wolff, Markman, & Forbus, 1997). Reasoning by analogical comparison is most often ordinary, but can be extraordinary.

Analogical Reasoning in Individuals and Groups

There is a great deal of interest in team-based learning and transfer (Moreland, Argote, & Krishnan, 1996). Yet, little is known about analogical training in dyads and groups. Virtually all prior studies have involved individuals. To our knowledge, we are the first to examine the effect of analogical training on dyadic interaction. However, the analogical training in our study did in fact occur at an individual (nondyadic) level. It is interesting to speculate on the efficacy of dyadic versus individual analogical training effects. On the one hand, substantial evidence suggests that groups are poor at discussing noncommon information (Stasser & Stewart, 1992), which might result in poorer transfer of principles if comparison necessitates the discussion of unique examples. On the other hand, groups have access to a potentially richer source of experiences from which to compare. For example, Dunbar's (1994) direct observations of molecular biologists at work demonstrate that comparison is frequently used in the everyday practice of science. Dunbar's observations of the research process suggest three factors that make a lab creative: frequent use of comparison, attention to inconsistency, and heterogeneity of the research group (which contributes to the group's ability to think of many different analogs). Similarly, Hargadon and Sutton (1997) report qualitative evidence that teams of design engineers use analogies quite frequently in brainstorming sessions for new product design. Obviously, there is no connection necessarily between what makes for a creative organization and what makes for a creative manager. Nonetheless, there are some striking commonalities. The microbiology laboratories that showed the most progress were those that used analogies in quantity and took them seriously. Dunbar's analyses of transcripts show that in the successful lab groups, analogies are extended and "pushed" in group discussion.

Summary

We believe that ordinary case-based training may often leave learning on the table. We have introduced a method of training whereby students explicitly compare examples in order to derive common schemas or principles. Principles learned in this fashion have a greater likelihood of later being accessed and used than principles learned through the common practice of giving advice about individual examples. We suggest that this simple change in training procedures—to promote the opportunity to make fruitful comparisons—can dramatically improve people's ability to put their learning into practice.

APPENDIX 1

Cases Used in Advice and Comparison Conditions

Case 1: Syd, a recently-promoted head buyer of a major retail store, has bought some wholesale goods from an Asian merchant. All aspects of the deal have been successfully negotiated except the transfer of the goods. The merchant tells Syd that he will pay to ship the goods by boat. Syd is concerned because the U.S. has announced that a trade embargo is likely to be placed on all goods from that country in the near future. The Asian merchant tells Syd not to worry because the boat will arrive at the U.S. dock before the embargo occurs. Syd, however, thinks the boat will be late. Syd wants the merchant to pay to ship the goods by air freight (which is substantially more expensive). The merchant refuses because of the higher cost. They argue about when the boat will arrive.

The Asian merchant suggests that they "make a bet." The Asian merchant will ship the goods air freight but they will both watch when the boat actually docks in the U.S. If the boat arrives on time (as the Asian merchant believes it will), Syd will pay for all of the air freight. However, if the boat arrives late (as Syd believes it will), the Asian merchant will pay the entire air freight bill.

Advice Condition: Suppose that you are advising Syd. What should she/he do? Why?

Case 2: Two fairly poor brothers, Ben and Jerry, have just inherited a working farm whose main crop has a volatile price. Ben wants to sell rights to the farm's output under a long-term contract for a fixed amount rather than depend upon shares of an uncertain revenue stream. In short, Ben is risk-averse. Jerry, on the other hand is confident that the next season will be spectacular and revenues will be high. In short, Jerry is risk-seeking. The two argue for days and nights about the price of the crop for next season. Ben wants to sell now because he believes the price of the crop will fall; Jerry wants to hang onto the farm because he believes the price of the crop will increase. Jerry cannot afford to buy Ben out at this time.

Then, Jerry proposes a bet to his brother: They keep the farm for another season. If the price of the crop falls below a certain price (as Ben thinks it will), they will sell the farm and Ben will get 50% of today's value of its worth, adjusted for inflation; Jerry will get the rest. However, if the price of the crop rises (as Jerry thinks it will), Jerry will buy Ben out for 50% of today's value of the farm, adjusted for inflation, and keep all of the additional profits for himself.

Advice Condition: Suppose that you are advising Ben. What should he do? Why?

Comparison Condition: Think about the similarities between these two cases. What are the key parallels in the two negotiations? In the space below, identify an overall principle that captures the essence of the strategy of betting on differences.

ACKNOWLEDGMENTS

The research was supported by National Science Foundation Grant 9870892 awarded to the first author and National Science Foundation Grant SBR-9511757 and Office of Naval Research Grant N00014–92-J-1098 awarded to the second author. We thank the Similarity and Analogy group at Northwestern University for helpful discussions.

REFERENCES

Argote, L. (1993). Group and organizational learning curves: Individual, system, and environmental components. *British Journal of Social Psychology, 32,* 31–51.

Argote, L, & Epple, D. (1990). Learning curves in manufacturing. *Science, 247,* 920–924.

Baldwin, T. T., & Ford, J. K. (1988). Transfer of training: A review and directions for future research. *Personnel Psychology, 41,* 63–105.

Bassok, M. (1990). Transfer of domain-specific problem-solving procedures. *Journal of Experimental Psychology, Learning, Memory, & Cognition, 16*(3), 522–533.

Bassok, M., & Holyoak, K. J. (1989). Interdomain transfer between isomorphic topics in algebra and physics. *Journal of Experimental Psychology, Learning, Memory, & Cognition, 15*(1), 153–166.

Bazerman, M. H., & Gillespie, J. J. (1999). Betting on the future: The virtues of contingent contracts. *Harvard Business Review, 77*(5), 155–160.

Bazerman, M. H., & Neale, M. A. (1992). *Negotiating rationally*. New York: Free Press.

Bransford, J. D., Franks, J. J., Vye, N. J., & Sherwood, R. D. (1989). New approaches to instruction: because wisdom can't be told. In S. Vosniadou & A. Ortony (Eds.), *Similarity and analogical reasoning* (pp. 470–497). New York: Cambridge Univ. Press.

Brown, A. L., Kane, M. J., & Echols, C. H. (1986). Young children's mental models determine analogical transfer across problems with a common goal structure. *Cognitive Development, 1,* 103–121.

Catrambone, R., & Holyoak, K. J. (1989). Overcoming contextual limitations on problem-solving transfer. *Journal of Experimental Psychology: Learning, Memory and Cognition, 15*(6), 1147–1156.

Dunbar, K. (1994). Scientific discovery heuristics: How current-day scientists generate new hypotheses and make scientific discoveries. In A. Ram & K. Eislet (Eds.), *Proceedings of the 16th Annual Conference of the Cognitive Science Society* (pp. 985–986). Atlanta, GA: Erlbaum.

Falkenhainer, B., Forbus, K. D., & Gentner, D. (1989). The structure-mapping engine: Algorithm and examples. *Artificial Intelligence, 41,* 1–63.

Forbus, K. D., Gentner, D., & Law, K. (1995). MAC/FAC: A model of similarity-based retrieval. *Cognitive Science, 19,* 141–205.

Gentner, D. (1983). Structure-mapping: A theoretical framework for comparison. *Cognitive Science, 7,* 155–170.

Gentner, D. & Landers, R. (1985). Analogical reminding: A good match is hard to find. In *Proceedings of the International Conference on Cybernetics and Society* (pp. 607–613). New York: Institute of Electrical and Electronics Engineers.

Gentner, D., & Markman, A. B. (1997). Structure-mapping in analogy and similarity. *American Psychologist, 52*(1) 45–56.

Gentner, D., & Medina, J. (1998). Similarity and the development of rules. *Cognition, 65*(2–3), 263–297.

Gentner, D., Rattermann, M. J., & Forbus, K. D. (1993). The roles of similarity in transfer: Separating retrievability and inferential soundness. *Cognitive Psychology, 25,* 524–575.

Gentner, D., Brem, S., Ferguson, R., Wolff, P., Markman, A. B., & Forbus, K. D. (1997). Comparison and creativity in the works of Johannes Kepler. In T. B. Ward, S. M. Smith, & J. Vaid (Eds.), *Creative thought: An investigation of conceptual structures and processes* (pp. 403–459). Washington, DC: American Psychological Association.

Gick, M. L., & Holyoak, K. J. (1980). Analogical problem solving. *Cognitive Psychology, 12,* 306–355.

Gick, M. L., & Holyoak, K. J. (1983). Schema induction and analogical transfer. *Cognitive Psychology, 15,* 1–38.

Hargadon, A., & Sutton, R. I. (1997). Technology brokering and innovation in a product development firm. *Administrative Science Quarterly, 42*(4), 716–749.

Holyoak, K. J., & Koh, K. (1987). Surface and structural similarity in analogical transfer. *Memory & Cognition, 15,* 332–340.

Keane, M. T. (1988). *Analogical problem solving*. Chichester, England: Ellis Horwood.

Kotovsky, L., & Gentner, D. (1996). Comparison and categorization in the development of relational similarity. *Child Development, 67,* 2797–2822.

Lax, D. A., & Sebenius, J. K. (1986). *The manager as negotiator*. New York: Free Press.

Loewenstein, J., & Gentner, D. (1997). *Using comparison to improve preschoolers' spatial mapping ability*. Poster presented at the Biennial meeting of the Socity for Research in Child Development, Washington, DC.

Loewenstein, J., & Gentner, D. (submitted). *Comparison promotes relational mapping in preschoolers*.

Loewenstein, J., Thompson, L., & Gentner, D. (1999). Analogical encoding facilitates knowledge transfer in negotiation. *Psychonomic Bulletin & Review, 6*(4), 586–597.

Markman, A. B., & Gentner, D. (1997). The effects of alignability on memory. *Psychological Science, 8*(5), 363–367.

Medin, D. L., Goldstone, R. L., & Gentner, D. (1993). Respects for similarity. *Psychological Review, 100*(2), 254–278.

Moreland, R. L., Argote, L., & Krishnan, R. (1996). Socially shared cognition at work: Transactive memory and group performance. In J. L. Nye & A. M. Brower, (Eds.), *What's social about social cognition? Research on socially shared cognition in small groups* (pp. 57–84). Thousand Oaks, CA: Sage.

Novick, L. (1988). Analogical transfer, problem similarity, and expertise. *Journal of Experimental Psychology: Learning, Memory and Cognition, 14,* 510–520.

Perfetto, G. A., Bransford, J. D., & Franks, J. J. (1983). Constraints on access in a problem solving context. *Memory & Cognition, 11,* 24–31.

Reed, S. K., Ernst, G. W., & Banerji, R. (1974). The role of comparison in transfer between similar problem states. *Cognitive Psychology, 6,* 436–450.

Reeves, L. M., & Weisberg, R. W. (1994). The role of content and abstract information in analogical transfer. *Psychological Bulletin, 115*(3), 381–400.

Ross, B. H. (1984). Remindings and their effects in learning a cognitive skill. *Cognitive Psychology, 16,* 371–416.

Ross, B. H. (1987). This is like that: The use of earlier problems and the separation of similarity effects. *Journal of Experimental Psychology: Learning, Memory & Cognition, 13*(4), 629–639.

Ross, B. H. (1989). Distinguishing types of superficial similarities: Different effects on the access and use of earlier problems. *Journal of Experimental Psychology: Learning, Memory & Cognition, 15,* 456–468.

Ross, B. H., & Kennedy, P. T. (1990). Generalizing from the use of earlier examples in problem-solving. *Journal of Experimental Psychology: Learning, Memory and Cognition, 16*(1), 42–55.

Schumacher, R. M., & Gentner, D. (1988). Transfer of training as analogical mapping. *IEEE Transactions on Systems, Man, and Cybernetics, 18*(4), 592–600.

Simon, H. A., & Hayes, J. R. (1976). The understanding process: Problem isomorphs. *Cognitive Psychology, 8*(2), 165–190.

Stasser, G., & Stewart, D. (1992). The discovery of hidden profiles by decision making groups: Solving a problem versus making a judgment. *Journal of Personality and Social Psychology, 62,* 426–434.

Thompson, L. (1998). *The mind and heart of the negotiator.* Upper Saddle River, NJ: Prentice Hall.

Thompson, L., & DeHarpport, T. (1994). Social judgment, feedback, and interpersonal learning in negotiation. *Organization Behavior and Human Decision Processes, 58,* 327–345.

Thompson, L., & Hrebec, D. (1996). Lose–lose agreements in interdependent decision making. *Psychological Bulletin, 120*(3), 396–409.

Thompson, L., Valley, K. L., & Kramer, R. (1995). The bittersweet feeling of success: An examination of social perception in negotiation. *Journal of Experimental Social Psychology, 31*(6), 467–492.

Choice Behavior in Social Dilemmas: Effects of Social Identity, Group Size, and Decision Framing

Marilynn B. Brewer • University of California, Los Angeles
Roderick M. Kramer • Stanford University

Social dilemmas appear in two basic forms: the *public goods* problem (in which the individual must decide whether to contribute to a common resource) and the *commons dilemma* (in which the individual must decide whether to take from a common resource). The two forms of choice dilemma are equivalent in terms of outcomes, but because they involve different decision frames, they are not psychologically equivalent. In this research, framing effects on decisions involving use of a common resource pool were explored in a $2 \times 2 \times 2$ (Public Goods vs. Commons Dilemma Task Structure × Small vs. Large Group Size × Individualistic vs. Collective Social Identity) experiment. That the two versions of the decision task were not psychologically equivalent was evidenced both by a main effect of task structure and by interactions involving task structure, group size, and social identity. Overall, subjects kept more of the common resource for themselves under the public goods version of the task than under the commons dilemma frame. Furthermore, under the commons dilemma structure, group size had no effect on choice behavior, but in the public goods version individuals in large groups kept more than did individuals in small groups. Lastly, as the resource pool was depleted, the social identity manipulation had opposite effects for large groups under commons dilemma and public goods frames.

Social dilemmas exist whenever the cumulative result of reasonable individual choices is collective disaster. There are, for example, many situations in which each member of a collective has a greater incentive to act in a self-interested way, in disregard of the social consequences, even though if everyone else does the same, all will be worse off (Messick & Brewer, 1983). Contemporary examples are commonplace. In a heat wave, each individual is most comfortable using his or her air conditioner at full power; yet, if all do so, an electrical overload may result, leaving everyone hotter. If enough people use moderate restraint, on the other hand, all may be reasonably comfortable, and a supply of the common resource remains available for future use. Similarly, many of us might prefer not to contribute any of our own money toward medical research, but if everyone fails to contribute, all will be worst off in the long run.

These two examples illustrate the most extensively studied forms of social dilemma: the commons dilemma, in which individuals must decide how much of a shared resource to take for themselves, and the problem of the provision of public goods, in which individuals must decide whether to contribute in order to establish or sustain a common resource. Both types of dilemma are characterized by free access to the resource and by the fact that cooperative or prosocial outcomes are dependent on voluntary actions by individuals (viz., that individuals exercise appropriate self-restraint on consumption in a commons, and that they be willing to contribute their share towards provision of a public good).

Much of the current theory and research on these problems has treated the commons dilemma and provision of public goods as somewhat distinct or separate issues. Social psychologists and ecologists have given relatively more attention to commons dilemma situations (see, e.g., reviews by Dawes, 1980; Edney, 1980), and sociologists and economists have focused more on factors affecting the provision of public goods (e.g., Chamberlain, 1984; Marwell & Ames, 1979).

Despite differences in the way the two collective problems are studied, however, the basic structures of the decision faced by individuals in both cases are equivalent. In the commons dilemma situation, the individual must decide whether to accept a smaller immediate benefit to the self in order to sustain the collective resource and accumulate more in the long run. In the public goods situation, the individual must decide whether to give up some immediate benefit to the self for the collective good. In either case, the outcome is such that individuals have less for themselves if they choose to act in the collective interest than they would have if they do not.

To the extent that individuals are concerned primarily with the net outcomes of their actions, it should make no difference in structural terms whether their decision entails not taking from a common resource or contributing towards its provision, so long as the end result is the same. From this perspective, the commons dilemma and public goods problem can be viewed as logically (i.e., rationally or economically) equivalent.

Recent work on prospect theory by Kahneman and Tversky (1984) suggests that even though decisions may be equivalent in terms of objective appraisal of gains and losses, they may not be regarded as equivalent psychologically. According to this theory, individuals' preferences among various choices or prospects may be influenced by the way in which a decision is initially formulated or framed. Kahneman and Tversky (1984) reviewed a variety of studies that demonstrated that although, from a normative standpoint, preferences should not be affected by such things as the order or temporal relation between gains and losses, individuals' preferences often reflect greater sensitivity to either gains or losses relative to the status quo rather than to objective or final states. When formulated in terms of gains, individuals' preferences among alternative courses of action may reflect risk aversion (i.e., individuals will prefer a "sure thing" over a gamble, even though the monetary expectation on the gamble may be greater). Conversely, when the same decision is framed in terms of the losses associated with it, individuals' preferences may reflect risk seeking (i.e., they will prefer a gamble that carries the possibility of larger future losses over acceptance of an immediate certain loss).

Differences in the nature of the decisions confronting individuals in a public goods or commons dilemma situation may, in a similar way, tend to make salient different reference points against which prosocial or cooperative choices are evaluated. In the case of providing for a public good, individuals must decide how much to contribute of something of value already in their possession. In relation to what one starts with, such a decision entails giving up something—that is, enduring an immediate and certain loss in order to gain an uncertain future benefit. With this frame of reference, the prediction of prospect theory is that individuals will be risk seeking (i.e., that they will prefer to risk long-term loss in order to keep as much as possible of what they have in the short run).

In the case of the commons dilemma, on the other hand, an individual begins, in a sense, with nothing and must decide how much to take for self. In relation to this "zero" starting point, anything taken constitutes a definite gain. This frame of reference should make individuals comparatively more risk averse, in the sense that they will settle for a smaller immediate gain rather than take a larger gain that carries the risk of long-term loss. Thus, using prospect theory, we predict that a collective choice problem framed as a commons dilemma will be more likely to lead to individual self-restraint or cooperation than will the same problem framed as a public goods dilemma.

We can assess whether decisions that are structurally equivalent are not psychologically equivalent in at least two ways. First, the final outcomes of decisions made under the different framing conditions should be different, as described earlier. Second, the contextual factors that influence individuals' decisions under one task structure may not have the same effects when the decision is framed in a different way. Two conditions that have been found to influence outcomes of social dilemma situations in the past are the size of the collective and the social group identity of the individual decision makers. Whether these two factors have equivalent effects, regardless of whether the decision is framed as a public goods problem or as a commons dilemma, has yet to be examined.

Effects of Group Size

In his influential book, *The Logic of Collective Action,* Olson (1965) argued that "the larger a group is, the farther it will fall short of providing an optimal supply of any collective good . . . in short, the larger the group, the less it will further common interests" (p. 65). This argument has been applied both to situations involving the provision of public goods, such as contributing towards formation of a union (Messick, 1973) or willingness to support public over private resources (Marwell & Ames, 1979), and to commons dilemma situations (Dawes, 1975). Among the reasons offered for the deleterious effects of group size are decreases in the incentives or payoffs associated with cooperating in larger groups (Dawes, 1975; Messick, 1973), deindividuation (Hamburger, Guyer, & Fox, 1975), and social loafing or diffusion of responsibility (Messick & McClelland, 1983; Stroebe & Frey, 1982).

The results of empirical tests of the relation between prosocial behavior and group size in social dilemmas are equivocal. Messick and McClelland (1983), for example, found that individuals (group size = 1) did better than groups of 3 or 6 subjects, and groups of 3 did better than groups of 6, both in maintaining a replenishing resource longer and in showing greater restraint. Liebrand (1984), however, found no differences in levels of cooperation between groups of size 7 and 20 in a commons dilemma-type task. Using *n*-person Prisoner's Dilemma tasks, both Hamburger et al. (1975) (3- versus 7-person groups)

and Komorita and Lapworth (1982) (2-, 3-, and 6-person groups) found declining cooperation as a function of increasing group size. Bonacich, Shure, Kahan, and Meeker (1976), however, reported mixed results after using groups of 3, 6, and 9 persons in a public goods task.

These mixed findings may result from competing effects of group size on perceived risk and concern about the long-term consequences of one's own behavior. On the one hand, when a group is large, the consequences of collective overuse of common resource may be more salient and more impressive than when the group (and the total resource pool) is fairly small. On the other hand, the larger the group is, the less the impact that one's own choice has on the collective outcome and hence the lower is the perceived risk associated with self-interested behavior. Intuitively, we might expect that individuals who are risk averse are more sensitive to the former aspect of group size (enhanced salience of collective risk), whereas the diffusion of risk aspect would have more impact on those who are risk seeking. On this basis, we predict an interaction between group size and task structure, such that the predicted negative effects of group size will be more likely when the problem is framed as a public goods dilemma than when it is framed as a commons dilemma.

Level of Social Group Identity

In theoretical arguments regarding the detrimental effects of group size on collective outcomes, researchers implicitly assume that the individual decision maker is the basic unit of interest. Thus group size is defined in terms of the number of individuals in the collective. Research on social identity theory (e.g., Tajfel & Turner, 1986), however, demonstrates that self-interest may not always be defined at the individual level. As Coleman (1961) noted,

> Classic economic theory always assumes that the individual will act in "his" interest; but it never examined carefully the entity to which "his" refer . . . in many situations men act as if the "his" refers to some entity larger than themselves. That is, they appear to act in terms, not of their own interest, but in the interests of a collectivity. (p. 24)

In an analysis of why individuals might be willing to forfeit individual gain in favor of collective interests, Brewer (1979, 1981) argued that salience of a collective or common social identity may result in greater weight being given to joint (collective) gains over individual gains alone. Inclusion within a common social boundary acts to reduce social distance among group members, making it less likely that they will make sharp distinctions between their own and others' welfare. Thus whether individuals respond prosocially to a social dilemma may depend on whether they think of themselves as single and autonomous individuals or whether, in contrast, they regard themselves as sharing membership in and identification with a larger aggregate or social unit.

Kramer and Brewer (1984) found some evidence to support this theoretical analysis. In a series of laboratory experiments in which they used a replenishing-resource-use dilemma, the level of social group identity made salient to individuals in small heterogeneous groups did affect their decision making. Individuals were more likely to exercise cooperative restraint when a collective-level identity was made salient than when differentiating subgroup identities were made salient.

These findings suggest that the potentially deleterious effects on collective outcomes of increasing group size may be overridden when collective identity is high. If group members think of the collective as a single entity, then the number of individuals within the collective should be irrelevant and the effect of group size should be eliminated or diminished in relation to situations in which individual identity is more salient. Furthermore, the enhanced salience of collective outcomes should have most impact when individuals are risk averse. On this basis, we predict that the positive effects of collective group identity will be greater when the choice problem is framed as a commons dilemma than when it is framed as a public goods dilemma.

Method

Design of the Study

The design of the study was a 2 × 2 × 2 (Task Structure × Level of Social Identity × Size of Group) factorial design. The task was structured as either a public goods problem or commons dilemma; level of social identity was manipulated so as to make salient either an individual or col-

lective-level identification; and feedback was varied in order to suggest that the groups were either small (containing 8 persons) or large (32 persons). Experimental sessions were randomly assigned to group size condition, and the other four treatment conditions were randomly assigned within sessions (i.e., each terminal was programmed to display a different Task Structure × Level of Social Identity condition).

Subjects

Subjects were 88 undergraduate students from the University of California at Los Angeles, who participated in the experiment in partial fulfillment of a course requirement. Eight subjects were recruited for each session and there were 11 subjects in each condition.

Apparatus

The apparatus used in the experiment consisted of a DEC PDP-11 computer connected to eight individual terminals, each located in a private booth. Subjects were led to believe that the terminals were linked together; in actuality, however, all of the feedback, other than that pertaining to subjects' own choices, was predetermined and controlled by the central processing unit.

Procedure

As subjects arrived at the computer facility, they were met by the experimenter, who explained that they would be participating with either 7 or 31 others via a system of connected computer terminals that would allow them to be linked together. As subjects arrived, the experimenter conspicuously checked their names from a prominently displayed list with 8 or 32 names listed for their session. To reinforce the group size manipulation the large laboratory facility had signs indicating that Cubicles 1–4 or 1–16 were on one side of the facility and Cubicles 5–8 or 17–32 were on the other. Each subject was individually led to one of the private cubicles and told the experiment would begin as soon as all of the other 7 or 31 participants arrived.

When all 8 actual subjects were seated, the experimenter went to each cubicle and announced that all of the 8 or 32 subjects were present and told each subject to activate his or her own terminal. In order to protect the confidentiality of their responses and further enhance the credibility of the group size manipulation, subjects were assigned identification numbers ranging from 1–8, whereas those in the large-groups condition received numbers ranging from 1–32. All of the remaining instructions and manipulations were introduced directly via the terminals to each subject individually.

Subjects first received a brief set of instructions regarding operation of their computer terminals and the nature of the interactive computer system. In order to reinforce the group size manipulation and increase the believability of the interdependence of their responses, subjects were told to enter the number assigned to them to activate linkage of their terminals with those of the others. After subjects entered their number, false feedback was used to indicate that either 7 or 31 others were present. The display also indicated that 5 or 20 of the terminals, including the subject's own, had been successfully linked and that the computer was still waiting for 3 or 12 others to finish reading the instructions regarding terminal operation. After a brief pause, the computer then displayed an updated panel indicating that all 8 or 32 terminals were linked and all participants ready to continue with the task.

Subjects in all conditions were told that they would have an opportunity to accumulate points from a resource pool during the experiment, with each point worth a certain amount of money. The procedure for assigning the monetary value of the points provided an opportunity to introduce the social identity manipulation.

Level of social identity. The level of social identity manipulation used in this experiment was similar to that described by Kramer and Brewer (1984, Experiment 3) and other researchers (e.g., Rabbie & Horwitz, 1969). The manipulation varies the "common fate" (Campbell, 1958) or implicit level of interdependence among decision makers so as to make salient either a superordinate or collective-level social identity that encompasses all of the individuals in a group (*collective identity* condition) or an individual-level identity that differentiates among them (*individual identity* condition).

The experimenter explained to subjects that the monetary value of the resource points in the different experimental sessions would be either 1¢

or 2¢ depending on the results of a lottery to be conducted by the computer. In the condition designed to make salient the collective level of identity, subjects were told that a single lottery would be used to determine the value of the points for all the 8 or 32 group members in that session. The computer would generate a number using its random number generator. If the number was odd, the points would be worth 1¢ each; if the number was even, they would be worth 2¢. In the individual level of identity condition, subjects were told that there would be 8 or 32 separate lotteries that would independently determine the pay rate for each of the 8 or 32 individuals in the session.

The computer was programmed so that, regardless of condition, the outcome of the lottery in all sessions was always the same; that is, points were always worth 2¢ each. We further reinforced level of social identity in subsequent instructions by labeling the participants as *group members* in the collective identity condition versus *individuals* in the individual identity condition.

Overview of the task. The task that we used was generally patterned after the replenishing resource dilemma that was described by Messick and Brewer (1983) and used in previous experiments by Messick et al. (1983) and Kramer and Brewer (1984). Subjects were told that they would share access to a resource pool initially containing 1,200 points in the small-groups condition and 4,800 in the large-groups condition.[1]

On each of a series of separate trials, subjects could accumulate from 0 to 25 points for themselves. Subjects were told that after all of the participants had decided how many points they wish to accumulate on a given trial, the computer would subtract that number of points from the common pool. The size of the remaining pool was then increased by a replenishment factor, which varied between 1% and 10% per trial. Thus the number of points in the resource pool for the next trial was affected ostensibly by both total group use and the variable replenishment function.

Subjects were told they should try to accumulate as many points as possible for themselves (because this would determine how much they would

---

[1]In the present experiment, group size and absolute pool size are confounded. However, relative pool size, in terms of the ratio of pool size to group size, is constant. (See Hamburger, Guyer, & Fox, 1975, and Bonacich, Shure, Kahan, & Meeker, 1976, for a discussion of this issue.)

be paid at the end of the session), but that they should also try to maintain the common resource pool for as long as possible because, by doing so, everyone (including themselves) could continue to accumulate points for a longer period, and thus earn more in the long run.

Practice trials were included so that subjects could see the relation among total group use of the resource, the variable replenishment factor, and the state of the common resource pool. Specifically, the practice trials demonstrated that if subjects did not try to accumulate too much for themselves on a given trial, and the replenishment rate selected was high enough, then the common resource pool could be sustained at a high level. If, on the other hand, subjects did accumulate too much for themselves, or the replenishment rate was too low, then the common pool level would decline and eventually be depleted.

Task structure manipulation. We manipulated task structure by varying the nature of the resource use decision that subjects made on each trial. In the *public-goods-contribution* version of the task, subjects were given instructions beginning with the following description:

There exist many public services and resources, such as public television stations, which are available to everyone and whose existence depends upon voluntary contributions. If enough persons contribute enough money, these resources will continue to be available. If voluntary contributions fall below a certain point, however, they will be undersupported and cease to exist. Obviously, the more people who contribute, the less each has to give. But, of course, it is possible to contribute nothing and still enjoy the resource since access is open to all. On the other hand, if everyone fails to contribute, or if the total contributions are insufficient, the resource cannot be sustained and no one will enjoy access to it. Thus, each person must decide whether to contribute to the resource and, if so, how much to contribute.

After this explanation of the problem, the task itself was further described. Each subject was told that at the start of every trial, 25 points (50 cents' worth) would be deposited in a personal resource account assigned to him or her. The number of points in this personal account at the end of the experiment would determine the amount of money that he or she earned. On every trial, therefore, the common pool level temporarily dropped by 200 or 800 points. Subjects had to decide how many,

if any, of the 25 points given to them they wanted to contribute (return to) the common pool. Subjects were informed that the common pool size for the next trial would be determined both by the total contributions made by the group and the replenishment rate randomly selected for that trial.

At this point, the trials began. At the end of each trial, after subjects had entered their contribution decision, feedback was provided regarding the total number of points ostensibly contributed by all of the subjects on that trial, as well as the size of the smallest and largest individual contributions, and the replenishment rate for that trial. Subjects were then told the size of the common pool available for the next trial and were asked how many points they wish to contribute for the next trial.

In the *commons-dilemma-restraint* version of the task, subjects had to decide on each trial how many points (from 0 to 25) to take from the common resource pool. These points were then added to their personal resource pool.

In both conditions, at the end of a trial, feedback was provided about the behavior of the group and the resulting state of the common resource pool. In every respect, therefore, the feedback provided regarding pool size, total group use, variance in others' behavior, and rate of replenishment were equivalent across the two conditions. For example, if on Trial 5, feedback in the public goods version indicated that the highest contribution was 10 points (i.e., someone kept 15 points for himself or herself), then the corresponding feedback in the commons dilemma version would indicate that someone had taken 15 points for himself or herself on that trial. Similarly, if the feedback indicated that the total group contribution was 120 points (meaning that members of the group as a whole had kept 60 points for themselves and that the common pool had dropped by 60 points), then the feedback in the commons version would indicate that the total group take was 60 points (meaning that 120 points remained in the resource pool). Thus, regardless of subjects' own decisions, the aggregate pattern of feedback was controlled across conditions.

Outcomes to subjects as a consequence of their decisions were exactly equivalent in the two versions of the task (i.e., comparable resource-use decisions produced identical net consequences with regard to both individual as well as collective gains and losses). The only aspect that varied across the task structure conditions was the nature of the initial decision that subjects had to make (i.e., with whether the collective choice entailed returning resource points to the common pool versus not taking points from it).

Feedback. The resource use trials were separated into two phases. There were 14 trials in Phase 1, during which the false feedback indicated that the common resource pool had declined from an initial size of 1,200 or 4,800 points to only 291 or 1,164 points. The task was then interrupted briefly and a summary display showing the initial size of the common resource pool, as well as its current size (i.e., number of points remaining for the next set of trials), was presented to all subjects. The experiment then continued for another six trials, during which the common pool level dropped from 291 or 1,164 down to only 5 or 20 points at the start of the 20th trial. At the end of the 20th trial, the computer announced that the resource pool had been depleted.

The false feedback about the behavior of the other individuals indicated that, from trial to trial, others were accumulating for themselves an average number of points ranging from 8 to 18 per trial (i.e., were contributing 17 to 7 points per trial in the public goods version, or taking 8 to 18 points per trial in the commons version).

Subjective measures. In addition to the behavioral data collected during the trials themselves, a number of questions were included in order to assess subjects' perceptions and evaluations of own and others' performance at various stages of the experiment. Before the first trial, for example, subjects responded to a series of questions intended to assess their understanding of the task, their confidence in being able to earn what they hoped, and their expectations about others' behavior. A series of intertrial questions were included at the break between Phase 1 and Phase 2 in order to assess subjects' expectations about and evaluation of their group's performance up to that point, their perception of others' motivations and intentions, and their expectations about their own outcomes in the next set of trials. Lastly, after the last trial, a series of similar posttrial questions was administered.

After subjects had responded to the last question, the computer was programmed to notify the experimenter, who debriefed each subject individually, paid them $3.00, and thanked them for their participation.

Results

The primary dependent variable in this study was the number of points subjects chose to accumulate for themselves rather than leave in or return to the common pool. Because the break between Phase 1 and Phase 2 trials during the experimental task created an opportunity to reinforce feedback regarding depletion of the resource pool and to make salient issues that may have altered subsequent resource use, resource-use decisions during the two phases were analyzed separately.

Phase 1 Decisions

Initial trial. One way to assess the impact of the manipulated conditions is to examine their effects on subjects' initial decisions (i.e., those that they made before receiving any feedback regarding others' behavior). These initial decisions are presumably free from the effects of any social influence or norms regarding appropriate behavior that might be inferred from feedback about others' decisions. Accordingly, we performed a $2 \times 2 \times 2$ (Task Structure × Level of Social Identity × Size of Group) analysis of variance (ANOVA), using individuals' first resource-use decision as the dependent variable. A highly significant main effect was obtained for task structure, $F(1, 80) = 26.19, p < .001$. The direction of this effect is consistent with the argument that individuals in a public goods situation would be less likely to give up resources already in their possession (keeping, on average, 15.45 points initially), in comparison with subjects in a commons dilemma, who took from the shared resource an average of only 12.13 points initially. There was also a group size effect, $F(1, 80) = 3.86$, $p < .05$, such that individuals' initial decisions reflected relatively more self-interest in large groups ($M = 14.42$ points kept) than in smaller groups ($M = 13.15$ points). The social identity effect was not significant at this early stage of decision making, nor were there any significant interaction effects.

Across trials. At the time that these initial decisions were made, of course, the common resource was at maximum size. The feedback that was subsequently provided across trials indicated that its future availability was threatened by collective overuse in relation to the replenishment rate. In order to assess changes in individuals' responsiveness over time, the number of points that subjects kept for themselves (resource-use decisions) were summed across adjacent trials in order to form trial blocks. A $2 \times 2 \times 2 \times 7$ (Task Structure × Level of Social Identity × Size of Group × Trial Blocks) ANOVA with repeated measures was performed on these resource use measures.

A significant Task × Trials interaction effect, $F(6, 480) = 2.60$, $p < .05$, indicated that subjects in the public goods version of the task altered their choices across trial blocks more than did subjects in the commons dilemma structure. Across Phase 1 trials, commons dilemma subjects did not vary significantly from an average of 11.68 points per trial, but subjects in the public goods task averaged 12.76 points per trial, varying from a high of 15.16 points in the first trial block to a mean of 12.11 on the last trial block.

Over all of the Phase 1 trials there was also a significant Task Structure × Group Size interaction effect, $F(1, 80) = 3.75$, $p = .05$. With the commons dilemma task structure, there was virtually no effect of group size on individual resource-use decisions ($M = 11.89$ vs. 11.62 for group sizes 8 and 32, respectively). With the public goods structure, however, individuals kept more for themselves in large groups ($M = 13.90$) than they did in small groups ($M = 11.47$). Results of simple effects analyses indicated that the effect of group size was marginally significant in the public goods condition, $F(1, 80) = 3.05$, $p < .10$, but nonsignificant in the commons dilemma version, $F(1, 80) < 1.00$.

Phase 2 Decisions

We expected, on the basis of the results of prior studies (Kramer & Brewer, 1984; Messick et al., 1983), that the effects of these manipulations—particularly the social identity manipulation—on individuals' resource-use decisions would be most evident under conditions in which the future of the shared resource is increasingly threatened by collective overuse. Depletion of the common resource would be most severe during the Phase 2 trials. Therefore, we performed a separate $2 \times 2 \times 2 \times 2$ (Task Structure × Level of Social Identity × Size of Group × Phase 2 Trial Blocks) ANOVA with repeated measures.[2]

Overall, resource use was reduced in Phase 2, dropping from an average of 12.22 points per trial in Phase 1 to 7.96 for the two trial blocks in Phase

2. This was due in part to the effects of the interpolated feedback and intertribal ratings, which call subjects' attention to the state of the resource pool and heighten awareness of the consequences of one's own and others' decisions. Apart from this general effect, interesting differences in Phase 2 resource use emerged as a function of all three experimental treatments. A significant task main effect, $F(1, 80) = 10.91$, $p < .002$, reflected the fact that individuals in the public goods situation responded to continued and increasingly severe depletion of the resource by keeping more for themselves ($M = 9.32$) than did those in the commons dilemma version of the same situation ($M = 6.60$).

A Task × Social Identity × Group Size interaction, $F(1, 80) = 4.30$, $p < .05$, revealed that under severe resource depletion conditions, individuals' decisions were affected by level of social identity, but this effect varied depending on the task structure and group size (See Table 1). Results of simple effects analyses indicated that within the commons dilemma structure, there was no significant interaction between group size and social identity, $F(1, 80) < 1.00$, but this interaction was marginally significant, $F(1, 80) = 3.88$, $p < .10$, in the public goods version of the task. Regardless of the size of the group they were in, individuals in the commons dilemma task for whom a collective identity had been made salient took less for themselves than did individuals with an individual-level identity, and this was also the case in the small-group–public goods condition. In the large-group–public goods task condition, however, this outcome was reversed, and it deviated from that obtained in any of the other conditions. In this case, individuals who adopted a collective identity kept more for themselves in comparisons with those with an individual-level identity.

Subjective Measures

In order to explore further the psychological meaning of the interaction effects that our manipula-

---

[2] Data from the last two rounds were excluded from the analyses because the size of the resource pool had dropped so low by that time that subjects no longer had any hope of restoring the pool. At this point, choices were artificially constrained and differences in resource choices across conditions were necessarily eliminated.

tions had on resource-use decisions, three measures of subjective expectations regarding the nature of the situation and the behavior of other group members were included in a multivariate analysis of variance (MANOVA).

Before the first trial, subjects were asked to indicate their confidence in being able to accumulate the number of points that they would like during the session (0 = Not at all confident, 100 = Very confident.) At the end of Phase 1, they were asked again to indicate the confidence they had in being able to achieve their goal. At this point they were also asked to indicate, on a scale from 0 (Very unlikely) to 100 (Very likely), their belief that if they were to respond cooperatively, others would do so also. This is the measure that Messick et al. (1983) referred to as "reciprocal trust," the belief that one's own choice decisions could influence the decision of others in the group through reciprocity. If individuals behave in accord with economic rationality, both expectations of reciprocity and confidence in the impact of one's own behavior on long-run outcomes should be positively related to self-restraint, and both should be lower in larger groups than in smaller ones. To test this, we assessed the effects of group size and task structure on the two confidence measures and the measure of reciprocal trust in a MANOVA.

The results of the MANOVA revealed that the experimental groups did differ overall in responses to the psychological measures, $F(3, 78) = 503.53$, $p < .001$. Univariate analyses indicated that the locus of these experimental effects differed for the different measures, which suggested some complex interrelations among our manipulated variables, resource use, and mediating psychological variables.

Neither group size nor task structure had significant main effects on the subjective measures, even though both had direct effects on initial behavioral measures. The social identity manipulation, in contrast, did have a main effect on both

Table 1. Mean Resource-Use Decisions per Trial During Phase 2

| | Task structure | | | |
| | Commons | | Public goods | |
Level of social identity	Small group	Large group	Small group	Large group
Individual	7.04	7.15	9.50	9.06
Collective	6.22	6.00	6.34	12.38

TABLE 2. Mean Perceived Reciprocity

| | Task structure | | | |
| | Commons | | Public goods | |
Level of social identity	Small group	Large group	Small group	Large group
Individual	74.00	56.36	56.18	48.18
Collective	43.64	42.09	54.55	64.00

Note. 0 = Very unlikely; 100 = Very likely.

the confidence measures, $F(1, 80) = 8.45$ and 3.71, respectively, and on expected reciprocity, $F(1, 80) = 2.62$, but no direct effect on resource-use decisions. Lastly, although the interaction between task structure and social identity conditions affected perceived reciprocity, $F(1, 80) = 9.86$ (see Table 2 for means), it did not affect the other measures.

The cumulative effects of these factors are represented in threeway interactions affecting confidence measures at Time 1, $F(1, 80) = 3.29$, and Time 2, $F(1, 80) = 5.27$ (see Table 3). However, the pattern of effects is not related in any simple way to observed differences in resource-use decisions. Results of regression analyses indicated that the three psychological measures did not account for a significant amount of variance in Phase 1 or Phase 2 resource decisions, either between or within experimental conditions. When we controlled for experimental treatment effects, there was a negative relation between confidence at the end of Phase 1 and resource use during Phase 1 trials ($\beta = -.27$, $p < .05$). but this apparently reflected (rather than caused) subjects' willingness to exercise self-restraint in the collective interest. Neither expectations of reciprocity nor initial confidence apparently mediated individual differences in self-restraint, at least not consistently across experimental treatments.[3]

Discussion

In general, the effects of task structure on resource-use decisions in this experiment were consistent with predictions derived from Kahneman and Tversky's (1984) prospect theory. The interactive effect of task structure and group size appeared

[3]The absence of any simple correlation between subjective measures and resource use also indicates that choice behavior during the Phase 2 trials of the experiment was not dictated by the potentially reactive nature of the interpolated ratings.

relatively early in the resource task, but, as in our previous experiments, the influence of the social identity manipulation was apparent only when depletion of the common resource had become severe. This latter result is not altogether surprising, insofar as the conflict between individual self-interest and collective well-being is not very acute or obvious when an ample supply of a common resource exists (Kramer & Brewer, 1984; Messick et al., 1983).

When the group was small or the choice problem was framed as a commons dilemma, or both, the effect of collective identity on individual self-restraint was generally consistent with previous research on social identity effects (Kramer & Brewer, 1984). The anomalous finding from this experiment was obtained only in the large public goods–collective identity condition, and this, too, may be accounted for by differences in orientation toward risk associated with the framing effect.

When the choice problem was framed as a commons dilemma, so that individuals had to decide whether to take resources from a common pool, resource-use decisions were not altered by group size. They were, however, affected by level of social identity when the collective resource was endangered. For subjects in the commons dilemma structure, self-restraint increased under collective identity conditions, in comparison with individual identity conditions, and this effect was strongest when group size was large. This held true even though expectations of reciprocity and overall confidence in one's own ability to influence outcomes

were low in the large-group–collective condition. Thus, in the commons dilemma setting, subjects were apparently responding more to the salience of collective loss than to the diffusion of risk in the large-group situation.

When the choice was framed as a public goods dilemma, in contrast, individuals appeared to be more sensitive to diffusion effects, so that large groups undermined the positive effects of collective identity. When collective identity was not made salient, public goods subjects kept a moderately high amount for themselves on each trial in both large and small groups, although they were less confident that they could affect their own total outcomes in the large group condition. The introduction of a collective identity condition, however, had paradoxical effects on behavior in the public goods dilemma, depending on group size. With a small group, in which one's own contribution to the resource pool could be expected to make a difference, increasing the salience and imminence of collective loss apparently increased willingness to sacrifice personal gain for the collective welfare in a manner that was parallel to that obtained with the commons dilemma structure. With large groups, in which the perceived impact of one's own contribution in determining collective outcomes is greatly reduced, however, enhancing the salience of the group as a whole apparently increased preference for risk in that individuals chose to keep as much as possible for themselves in the short run despite the potential loss of long-term benefits. Thus the public goods problem seems to be particularly vulnerable to the predicted deleterious effects of group size, which are not overridden by group identification.

ACKNOWLEDGMENTS

Preparation of this article was supported by National Science Foundation Grant BNS83–02674 to the first author. We thank Matt Futterman for his assistance with computer programming and operation.

REFERENCES

Bonacich, P., Shure, G. H., Kahan, J. P., & Meeker, R. J. (1976). Cooperation and group size in the *N*-person prisoners' dilemma. *Journal of Conflict Resolution, 20,* 687–706.

Brewer, M. B. (1979). In-group bias in the minimal intergroup situation: A cognitive–motivational analysis. *Psychological Bulletin, 86,* 307–324.

Brewer, M. B. (1981). Ethnocentrism and its role in interpersonal trust. In M. B. Brewer & B. E. Collins (Eds.) *Scien-*

Table 3. Mean Ratings of Own Confidence

Level of social identity	Task structure			
	Commons		Public goods	
	Small group	Large group	Small group	Large group
Individual				
Own confidence (Time 1)	64.09	67.73	74.55	59.55
Own confidence (Time 2)	56.82	60.45	66.82	53.18
Collective				
Own confidence (Time 1)	55.45	50.82	54.18	59.55
Own confidence (Time 2)	54.55	39.55	49.36	58.82

Note. 0 = *Not at all confident;* 100 = *Very confident.*

tific inquiry in the social sciences (pp. 345–360), New York: Jossey-Bass.

Campbell, D. T. (1958). Common fate, similarity, and other indices of the status of aggregates of persons as social entities, *Behavioral Science, 3*, 14–25.

Chamberlain, J. (1984). Provision of collective goods as a function of group size, *American Political Science Review, 68*, 6–74.

Coleman, J. S. (1961). *Papers on non-market decision-making.* New York: Vantage.

Dawes, R. M. (1975). Formal models of dilemmas in social decision making, In M. Kaplan & S. Schwartz (Eds.), *Human judgment and decision processes* (pp. 87–107). New York: Academic Press.

Dawes, R. M. (1980). Social dilemmas. *Annual Review of Psychology, 31*, 169–193.

Edney, J. J. (1980). The commons problem: Alternative perspectives. *American Psychologist, 35*, 131–150.

Hamburger, H., Guyer, M., & Fox, J. (1975). Group size and cooperation. *Journal of Conflict Resolution, 19*, 503–531.

Kahneman, D., & Tversky, A. (1984). Choices, values, and frames. *American Psychologist, 39*, 341–350.

Komorita, S. S., & Lapworth, C. W. (1982). Cooperative choice among individuals versus groups in an *N*-person dilemma situation. *Journal of Personality and Social Psychology, 42*, 487–496.

Kramer, R. M., & Brewer, M. B. (1984). Effects of group identity on resource use in a simulated commons dilemma. *Journal of Personality and Social Psychology, 46*, 1044–1057.

Liebrand, W. G. (1984). The effect of social motives, communication, and group size on behavior in an *N*-person multi-stage mixed-motive game. *European Journal of Social Psychology, 14*, 239–264.

Marwell, G., & Ames, R. E. (1979). Experiments on the provision of public goods, I. Resources, interest, group size, and the free-rider problem. *American Journal of Sociology, 84*, 1335–1360.

Messick, D. M. (1973). To join or not to join: An approach to the unionization decision. *Organizational Behavior and Human Performance, 10*, 145–156.

Messick, D. M., & Brewer, M. B. (1983). Solving social dilemmas: A review. In L. Wheeler & P. Shaver (Eds.), *Review of Personality and Social Psychology* (Vol. 4. pp. 11–44). Beverly Hills, CA: Sage.

Messick, D. M., & McClelland, C. L. (1983). Social traps and temporal traps. *Personality and Social Psychology Bulletin, 9*, 105–110.

Messick, D. M., Wilke, H., Brewer, M. B., Kramer, R. M., Zemke, P., & Lui, L. (1983). Individual adaptation and structural change as solutions to social dilemmas. *Journal of Personality and Social Psychology. 44*, 294–309.

Olson, M. (1965). *The logic of collective action.* Cambridge, MA: Harvard University Press.

Rabbie, J. M., & Horwitz, M. (1969). Arousal of ingroup–outgroup bias by a chance win or loss. *Journal of Personality and Social Psychology, 13*, 269–277.

Stroebe, W., & Frey, B. S. (1982). Self-interest and collective action: The economics and psychology of public goods. *British Journal of Social Psychology, 21*, 121–137.

Tajfel, H., & Turner. J. C. (1986). The social identity theory of intergroup behavior. In S. Worchel & W. Austin (Eds.), *Psychology of intergroup relations* (pp. 7–24). Chicago: Nelson-Hall.

Groups and Teams

The research literature on groups and teams has a rich social psychological tradition. The group and team literature segments itself in many ways, including group conflict, group decision making, group problem solving, group voting, creativity, minority influence, and intergroup behavior. One of the oldest questions guiding group research, especially within the context of organizations, concerns whether individuals or groups are superior at decision making, creativity, problem solving, and so on. In recent years, research has moved beyond comparisons of individuals with groups and examined the conditions under which groups are more or less effective. The study of group- and team-level biases has raised a number of application issues, as well as theoretical questions. The four articles in this section have broken new theoretical ground in terms of identifying new phenomena.

Group Creativity and Brainstorming

A large body of research suggests that, contrary to popular intuition, groups are not more creative than individuals. In fact, several carefully controlled research investigations have revealed the opposite: Namely, individuals working alone generate more and better ideas than do teams. The first article, by Paulus and Dzindolet (1993), raises the question of why teams perform worse than do the same number of people working independently, and outlines the key reasons why groups might underperform when it comes to brainstorming. Using Steiner's (1972) group productivity model, brainstorming groups are thought to suffer from motivational and process loss. Specifically, people in brainstorming sessions may contribute less (social loafing) and may block the ability of others to think and talk (production blocking). Furthermore, Paulus and Dzindolet demonstrate that performance levels in brainstorming groups are strongly affected by the behavior of others through a process of social matching.

Group Decision Making

Group decision making has been the subject of research by both social psychologists and economists and political scientists who want to understand the best means of maximizing social welfare and political representation. Numerous paradoxes in voting that plague group effectiveness have been documented by economists. In terms of social psychology, several group decision-making problems and challenges have been documented, probably the most memorable being the "risky shift" phenomenon, later aptly referred to as "group polarization" (Stoner, 1961).

Within the organizational behavior literature, two group decision-making phenomena have proved particularly important in terms of theoretical advance and prescriptive application: the study of transactive memory systems in groups and the common information effect. The second article, Liang, Moreland, and Argote's (1995) paper on transactive memory, began a new paradigm of research that bridged principles of cognitive psychology, distributed intelligence, and group behavior. Liang et al. take a simple group task—the construction of an AM radio—and examine the impact of four different types of training methods on the performance of the group. Their theory is intriguing: Groups that have had an opportunity to train and work together develop a nuanced, socially shared understanding of who knows what. Thus, the key prediction is that groups who train together should outperform groups who don't train together. Liang et al. develop a number of interesting and new dependent measures for tracking the group's process and performance, such as the number of corrections members make to others' statements, how close members sit to one another, the number of "we"-to-"I" statements, and so on.

The third article, by Gigone and Hastie (1993), on the common information effect, also began a new domain of research in the organizational study of groups. Again, their methods were simple, powerful, and highly realistic. They "distributed" information relevant to an organizational decision among members of a group. Some of the informational clues were shared by everyone in the group (common information); some were partially shared; and some were known only by one member of the group. The task was constructed in such a manner that if team members perfectly shared all information, a superior decision alternative would emerge. However, groups did not share all information; rather, they tended to discuss only the information that they happened to have in common. This failure to share unique information led to an inferior decision.

Group Composition

Group composition is the study of how the selection of particular persons affects group performance. In the fourth article, Jehn and Shah (1997) take an applied approach to how group composition affects performance. They reason that friendship is often a consequence of teamwork; similarly, friendship often can lead to teamwork. They used a simple 2 x 2 experimental design to examine how relationships among team members (friends vs. acquaintances) and type of task (decision making vs. motor) affected performance. They found that friendship groups performed significantly better than acquaintance groups on both decision making and motor tasks because of a greater degree of group commitment and cooperation. Jehn and Shah, then, go beyond a demonstration effect by providing a fascinating look at the actual group processes that produce the effect.

REFERENCES

Gigone, D., & Hastie, R. (1993). The common knowledge effect: Information sharing and group judgment. *Journal of Personality and Social Psychology, 65*(5), 959–974.

Jehn, K. A., & Shah, P. P. (1997). Interpersonal relationships and task performance: An examination of mediating processes in friendship and acquaintance groups. *Journal of Personality and Social Psychology, 72*(4), 775–790.

Liang, D. W., Moreland, R., & Argote, L. (1995). Group versus individual training and group performance: The mediating role of transactive memory. *Personality and Social Psychology Bulletin, 21*(4), 384–393.

Paulus, P. B., & Dzindolet, M. T. (1993). Social influence processes in group brainstorming. *Journal of Personality and Social Psychology, 64*, 575–586.

Steiner, I. (1972). *Group process and productivity.* New York: Academic Press.

Stoner, J. A. F. (1961). *A comparison of individual and group decision involving risk.* Unpublished master's thesis, Massachusetts Institute of Technology.

Suggested Readings

Arrow, H., McGrath, J. E., & Berdahl, J. L. (2000). *Small groups as complex systems: Formation, coordination, development, and adaptation.* Newbury Park, CA: Sage.

Diehl, M., & Stroebe, W. (1987). Productivity loss in brainstorming groups: Toward the solution of a riddle. *Journal of Personality and Social Psychology, 53*(3), 497–509.

Diehl, M., & Stroebe, W. (1991). Productivity loss in idea-generating groups: Tracking down the blocking effect. *Journal of Personality and Social Psychology, 61*(3), 392–403.

Thompson, L. (2000). *Making the team: A guide for managers.* Upper Saddle River, NJ: Prentice Hall.

Wegner, D. M., Erber, R., & Raymond, P. (1991). Transactive memory in close relationships. *Journal of Personality and Social Psychology, 61*(6), 923–929.

Social Influence Processes in Group Brainstorming

Paul B. Paulus • University of Texas
Mary T. Dzindolet • Cameron University

A series of studies examined the role of social influence processes in group brainstorming. Two studies with pairs and 1 with groups of 4 revealed that the performance of participants in interactive groups is more similar than the performance of those in nominal groups. A 4th study demonstrated that performance levels in an initial group session predicted performance on a different problem 2 sessions later. In a 5th study it was found that the productivity gap between an interactive and nominal group could be eliminated by giving interactive group members a performance standard comparable with the typical performance of nominal groups. These studies indicate that performance levels in brainstorming groups are strongly affected by exposure to information about the performance of others. It is proposed that social matching of low performance levels by interactive group members may be an important factor in the productivity loss observed in group brainstorming.

There has been a recent resurgence of interest in group brainstorming (cf. Diehl & Stroebe, 1987; Mullen, Johnson, & Salas, 1991; Paulus, Dzindolet, Poletes, & Camacho, 1993). Brainstorming involves generation of ideas in groups with an emphasis on generating as many ideas as possible (Osborn, 1957). To facilitate this process, four guidelines are provided. The participants are instructed not to be critical of ideas but state any ideas that come to mind no matter how wild. It is emphasized that they should aim for a large quantity of ideas, and they are encouraged to build on the ideas of others. The general philosophy behind these rules is that generating a large number of ideas will stimulate the generation of high quality ideas as well. Although it was initially expected that group interaction would facilitate both the generation of number and quality of ideas (Osborn, 1957), almost all studies have found that brainstorming in groups leads to lower productivity in

comparison with the combined productivity of a similar number of individuals brainstorming in isolation (nominal groups; Diehl & Stroebe, 1987; Mullen et al., 1991). The only exceptions involve comparisons of brainstorming of interactive pairs with that of noninteractive pairs. In this case, productivity is generally similar for both groups. In cases in which the quality of ideas has been rated, no differences have been found in the quality of the ideas (e.g., Bouchard, 1969; Diehl & Stroebe, 1987, 1991).

A major concern of recent analyses has been the search for an adequate explanation of the productivity loss experienced in brainstorming groups. Initial investigations examined the possibility that in interactive groups, individuals feel some degree of evaluation apprehension in spite of the instructions designed to minimize such concerns. This apprehension would result in withholding of ideas because of a concern for what others might think of the ideas. There is some evidence that concern with evaluation does play a role in the productivity of brainstorming groups (Collaros & Anderson, 1969; Diehl & Stroebe, 1987; Harari & Graham, 1975). However, it does not appear to account for the productivity gap, because such a gap is similar in both low and high evaluative conditions (Diehl & Stroebe, 1987).

One other explanation for the productivity loss is that individuals may free ride in interactive groups (Diehl & Stroebe, 1987). Although each person's performance is identifiable to other group members, there may be a tendency to let other generate the bulk of the ideas (Borgatta & Bales, 1953). When group members are made individually accountable, they do tend to increase their production of ideas. However, increased accountability in groups does not eliminate the productivity gap (Diehl & Stroebe, 1987).

Diehl and Stroebe (1987) concluded that something about the interactive procedure itself is responsible for the productivity loss. Obviously, only one person can talk effectively at one time in groups. This procedure may inhibit the generation of ideas in various ways. Individuals may forget ideas while waiting for others to state theirs or decide not to state ideas similar to those of others. Of course, individuals in groups of four have available only one fourth of the person-hours of individuals in nominal groups because group members must share their time. In several explicit tests of the production-blocking interpretation, Diehl and Stroebe (1987, 1991) have varied the type of blocking condition and found that not being able to speak when others are talking inhibits individual productivity. Diehl and Stroebe (1991) also found that time constraints in groups are not a major factor in accounting for the productivity gap.

Diehl and Stroebe's (1987, 1991) findings are consistent with a procedural interpretation of productivity loss in groups. However, they do not clearly demonstrate that this factor actually mediates productivity loss. The causal role of blocking in actual interactive brainstorming groups remains to be demonstrated (Bond & Van Leeuwen, 1991). Diehl and Stroebe's (1987) manipulations of blocking have involved the use of individual subjects under very controlled conditions and not actual interactive groups. Another problem with the procedural blocking interpretation is that it cannot account for the impact of variables that influ-

ence group brainstorming without changing the nature of the interaction. For example, variations in degree of evaluation, accountability, and experimenter presence do not affect the group procedures but do influence performance (Diehl & Stroebe, 1987; Mullen et al., 1991). It is therefore not surprising that different investigators have come to somewhat different conclusions in evaluating the brainstorming literature. Stroebe and Diehl (1991) stated that procedural blocking is the major factor in productivity loss, whereas Mullen et al. (1991) proposed that social psychological mechanisms such as group-induced arousal and self-attention are more important. Bond and Van Leeuwen (1991) concluded that neither of these positions can account adequately for the data.

We agree with Mullen et al. (1991) and Bond and Van Leeuwen (1991) that it is premature to conclude that procedural factors are primarily responsible for the productivity loss in brainstorming groups. Although it seems likely that the procedural constraints of brainstorming in a group do play a significant role, we feel that social factors may also be quite influential. In fact, we propose that procedural and social factors may work in concert to produce the observed productivity loss.

The presence of other group members in a brainstorming exercise can have a variety of nondirective and directive effects (cf. Casey, Gettys, Pliske, & Mehle, 1984). The simple presence of others can be arousing and enhance performance of simple tasks (cf. Geen, 1989; Zajonc, 1980). Assuming that the mere generation of ideas without regard to quality is a fairly simple task, one would predict that the presence of others would enhance one's rate of generating ideas. Some support for this prediction is derived from the finding that while others are present (as independent coactors), one generates more ideas than when one is alone (Harkins, 1987; Mullen et al., 1991). However, to the extent that one feels that the pooling of one's ideas with those of others reduces accountability for one's performance, individuals in groups may exert less effort (social loafing) than those performing alone (Diehl & Stroebe, 1987; Harkins, 1987). While support exists for the role of arousal and accountability in group brainstorming, it seems unlikely that these are major factors. Reviews of the social facilitation literature suggest that the effects of other presence are generally quite weak (Bond & Titus, 1983). Similarly, accountability effects are weak relative to the impact of the type of brainstorming session (interactive vs. nominal; Diehl & Stroebe, 1987). Furthermore, social loafing studies suggest that loafing effects are not likely to occur when individuals can be identified with their ideas (Williams, Harkins, & Latane, 1981), as is the case with the typical interactive brainstorming situation.

We suggest that rather than looking for an important role of these nondirective effects of other presence, investigators should examine the impact of directive effects. There are various types of directive effects. First, when someone generates ideas, these ideas may stimulate others to generate unique ideas of their own. This may be particularly true if others propose ideas that are counter to the majority view (Nemeth, 1985). However, because interactive brainstorming is not associated with increases in number of unique ideas relative to nominal groups (Diehl & Stroebe, 1987), it is likely that any such social stimulation effects (if they exist) are overwhelmed by other factors.

One type of directive effect that has not been considered in the brainstorming literature is the potential influence of group members on each other's rate of performance. Individuals in nominal groups have no information about the rate of other individuals' performance because they work in isolation. Thus, the performance rate of these individuals will depend on their personal characteristics (e.g., intelligence and motivation) and situational factors (e.g., task characteristics and instructions). Whereas these factors also will influence the performance of individuals in interactive groups, these individuals will have the additional impact of information about the rate of performance of other members of their group. Assuming that individuals will tend to compare their performance with that of others (Goethals & Darley, 1987) and will be motivated to match their performance with that of others (Seta, Seta, & Donaldson, 1991), one would expect the similarity in performance to be greater among members of interactive groups than among members of randomly constituted nominal groups. Of course, directive effects may occur in conjunction with nondirective ones. Social comparison processes may motivate matching but also could be a source of frustration if one is not able to match the performance of one's partner (cf. Seta & Seta, 1983). However, in this article we focus primarily on the degree to which matching occurs. We present the results of several studies designed to determine whether there is evidence for a matching process in brainstorming groups. Then we test various predictions implied by a matching analysis of group brainstorming.[1]

Study 1

The dyadic brainstorming paradigm provides an opportunity to assess social influence processes in a fairly straightforward manner. If a matching process occurs in interactive brainstorming, the performance data of the members of the interactive pairs should be more similar than that of the nominal pairs. In addition to assessing the existence of performance matching, we wanted to determine whether the nature of the interaction procedure would have an impact on performance and matching. One group of subjects performed alone and were randomly paired with other subjects to form nominal groups. A second group was asked to perform in pairs with a common microphone and recorder for their responses (interaction-share microphone). In three other pair conditions, participants were provided individual microphones and recorders. In one condition, they were given the same instructions as those with a common microphone (interaction-independent microphone). In a second condition, they were told to take turns in presenting their ideas. They could opt to pass if they did not have an idea at their turn (alternating). In a third condition, individuals were seated at opposite ends of the room and told to individually generate ideas and not communicate with the other person. However, they were encouraged to listen to and build on the ideas of the other person (overhear).

It was expected that the procedures in the alternating and overhear conditions would facilitate performance because they ensured that each person would have a full opportunity to present their ideas. In each of the interactive conditions, it was expected that the performance levels of the members of the pair would be more similar than the

---

[1]Studies 2 and 3 present new data from experiments published previously to demonstrate the illusion of productivity (Paulus, Dzindolet, Poletes, and Camacho, 1993). Because the focus of this article and that of Paulus et al. (1993) are quite different, this overlap was not deemed to be a problem by us or by the Editor.

performance of the members of nominal pairs because in each of the interactive conditions participants were exposed to the performance of another individual. Although the interactive procedure might affect the degree of similarity, we did not anticipate a specific pattern of differences among these groups. The degree of similarity in number of ideas generated was not assessed for the interaction-share microphone group because of the difficulty of identifying the source of the ideas. This group was included only to replicate the type of interactive condition used in past studies.

Method

Subjects. Ninety-eight female students from introductory psychology classes participated to fulfill a course requirement. Twenty students participated in each of the conditions, with the exception of 18 participating in the alternating condition. They were assigned randomly to one of the four experimental conditions. If only one participant arrived, this person was assigned to the nominal condition. At the end of the experiment, students were thoroughly informed about the purposes of the research.

Procedure. When students arrived for the experiment, they were given an informed-consent form that provided general information about the nature of the research. After signing the informed-consent form, the experimenter provided detailed instructions about the brainstorming procedure. This included the presentation of the four rules: Criticism is ruled out, freewheeling is welcome, quantity is desirable, and combination and improvement are sought (see Bouchard & Hare, 1970). Students were asked to brainstorm about what would happen if everyone had an extra thumb on their hand. This problem has been used frequently in past brainstorming research (e.g., Bouchard, 1969, Maginn & Harris, 1980; Taylor, Berry, & Block, 1958). Participants were provided 15 min to work on the problem. They were seated at a table with a microphone in front of them. In the nominal condition and interaction-share condition, only one microphone and tape recorder were provided. In the other three conditions two microphones and recorders were provided. In the interaction-independent microphone and the alternating conditions, subjects were seated at the same table, and in the overhear condition they were seated at separate tables. Participants in the interaction-independent microphone conditions were

given the same task instructions as those in the interaction-share microphone condition, but they were told that their ideas were being recorded separately. The alternating subjects were instructed to alternate turns in providing ideas. They were told not to communicate with each other except for exchanging ideas and saying "pass" if they were temporarily out of ideas. In the overhear condition, subjects were told they would be generating ideas in their own recorder at the same time as the other person. They were instructed not to communicate but were told they could listen to the ideas of the other person and build on them. A written version of the instructions and the problem were provided to each subject throughout the experimental session.

At the end of the experimental session individuals were provided with a questionnaire designed to tap some of the underlying processes. Each of the questions was rated on a 9-point scale. Only a few of these questions are relevant to this article. Participants were asked how much effort they put into generating ideas, how hard it was to generate ideas while the other person was talking, and how hard it was to concentrate while generating new ideas. Nominal participants were asked to rate the extent to which they would have generated more ideas or greater quality ideas if they brainstormed with another person (*many more* or *much greater quality* to *many less* or *much less quality*). The other participants were asked these same questions about brainstorming alone. For purposes of data analyses, these items were recorded so that high scores were favorable to group brainstorming.

Results

The recordings generated by each pair were transcribed and the number of distinct ideas coded by two raters. The interrater agreement for this task was .96. To develop comparable scores for all of the conditions, overlapping ideas were eliminated from the scores of the nominal pairs as well as the interactive pairs. This coding was done by two assistants with a reliability of .94.[2] Although the

---

[2]Interrater agreement in this and the other studies was measured by Person product–moment correlation. This is a more conservative approach than that used by Diehl and Stroebe (1987), which involves the number of pairs of ideas for which raters have discrepant decisions. The Diehl and Stroebe formula yields a reliability of above .99 for each of the studies in this article.

TABLE 1. Results: Study 1

	Nonrepetitive ideas		Mean difference		Intraclass correlation	F	df	p
Condition	M	SD	M	SD				
Nominal	32.7	13.4	9.6	6.2	.11	1.24	9.10	ns
Interaction								
Share[a]	20.8	7.9						
Independent	31.0	15.9	8.1	7.4	.44	2.56	9,10	.08
Alternating	21.8	17.3	5.6	5.1	.82	10.10	8, 9	.001
Overhear	26.3	11.7	3.7	4.3	.88	15.59	9,10	.001

[a]Because the performance of the individual members of the pairs in this condition were not separable, the mean difference and intraclass correlation cannot be computed. Standard deviations are for pair scores.

nominal pairs generated more ideas than the pairs in the other conditions, a comparison of the nominal condition with the other conditions for the number of ideas generated for pairs was not significant, $F(1, 44) = 2.58$, $p > .10$. If some degree of matching was occurring in conditions in which individuals were exposed to another's ideas, the difference between the number of ideas generated by the paired partners should be smaller then that for the nominal pairs. The results are in line with this prediction, but a comparison of the nominal group with the other conditions for the mean difference scores was not significant, $F(1, 38) = 2.94$, $p > .10$ (Table 1).

A more precise analysis of interdependence among pair members is provided by the intraclass correlation statistic. This statistic is a measure of the relative homogeneity of the number of ideas generated by subjects within a pair in relation to the total variation among the number of ideas generated by all subjects (Haggard, 1958). The intraclass correlations and related statistics are shown in Table 1. It should be noted that intraclass correlations also indicate the percentage of variance accounted for by similarity in performance. The pattern of results indicates the existence of intrapair similarity for the interacting pairs but not for the nominal pairs. Intraclass correlations were also computed separately for three 5-min time blocks to determine whether these changed systematically over time. If it takes some time for the group influence processes to develop, intraclass correlations might be stronger in the later time periods. Some suggestion of such a pattern is evident in the interaction-independent condition but not in the alternating and overhear conditions (Table 2).

There were no significant effects of condition for the questionnaire items. However, consistent with prior research (Paulus et al., 1993), most students felt that they would generate more ideas (70% for interactive and 80% for nominal) and better quality ideas (60% for both interactive and nominal) in groups than alone.

Discussion

The results of this study are consistent with the predictions of the matching hypothesis. Compared with individuals in nominal pairs, the performance of partners in interactive pair conditions was more similar, as reflected in the intraclass correlations.

Table 2. Intraclass Correlations Over Blocks of Time: Study 1

	0–5min				6–10min				11–15min			
Condition	R	F	df	p	R	F	df	p	R	F	df	p
Nominal	.28	1.78	9,10	ns	.17	1.41	9,10	ns	.14	1.31	9,10	ns
Interaction												
Independent	−.02	0.96	9,10	ns	.70	5.76	9,10	.01	.42	2.42	9,10	ns
Alternating	.74	6.57	8, 9	.01	.65	4.74	8, 9	.02	.80	9.09	8, 9	.01
Overhear	.52	3.13	9,10	.05	.88	16.24	9,10	.001	.41	2.40	9,10	ns

Note. R is the intraclass correlation.

The relative stability of the intraclass correlations over 5-min blocks suggests that the social influence process develops early in the interaction process and is maintained over time. Inspection of the distributions indicated that 4 of the 5 best performances and 14 of the 15 worst performances were by interactive pairs. Thus, it appears that the matching process may stimulate some pairs of individuals to reach fairly high levels of performance, whereas other pairs may influence each other to perform at a rather low level. This pattern of results may explain in part why interacting pairs do not show strong overall productivity losses relative to nominal pairs in spite of interacting pairs being exposed to procedural blocking. The productive interacting pairs may have felt some sense of competition (cf. Beck & Seta, 1980; Harkins & Jackson, 1985), and the individuals may have been concerned with doing as well or better than their partners. Furthermore, the tendency for upward comparison of abilities (Festinger, 1954) suggests that less productive performers would be motivated to increase their performance to the level of the superior performer unless there is too great a discrepancy in the initial performance levels (Seta, 1982). Indeed, Paulus et al. (1993) found that members of pairs who discovered they had generated fewer ideas than their partner increased their performance level during the subsequent interactive session relative to that of their partner. Therefore, the potentially competitive aspects of dyadic brainstorming may increase the motivation levels of some interactive subjects sufficiently to compensate for the potential inhibitory effects of procedural blocking and the matching of low performance levels in some pairs.

It is apparent that the degree of matching is somewhat greater in the alternating and overhear conditions than in the interaction-independent microphone condition. The alternating and overhear procedures may have fostered a sense of competition.

Study 2

Further evidence of a matching process in dyadic brainstorming can be derived from data obtained in a study in which same-sex pairs of individuals brainstormed in two 15-min sessions on the same problem (Paulus et al., 1993).[3] Instead of talking aloud, participants wrote their ideas on paper. In the first session, all of the participants brainstormed individually while separated by a partition. There were four different pair conditions in the second session, which varied in whether individuals were allowed to share their ideas by exchanging their slips of paper through a common bin and whether the experimenter announced aloud at the beginning of the pair session the number of ideas the two subjects had generated in the solitary phase. The resulting four conditions were share–feedback, share–no feedback, no share–feedback, and no share–no feedback. One hundred students participated in this study and the coding procedures were similar to those in Study 1 (see Paulus et al., 1993, for details).

Only in those conditions in which some feedback or sharing occurred would one expect a tendency for members of the pairs to match performance levels. The intraclass correlations for the various conditions are consistent with this expectation. During the initial solitary phase, there was no correspondence between the performance of the members of the pair ($R = -.15$), $F(73, 26) = 1.35$, $p > .05$. If the pair did not exchange ideas in the second session and was not provided feedback about the first session, the performances of the members of the pair continued to be independent ($R = -.174$), $F(14, 11) = 1.428$, $p > .05$. In the other three conditions, numbers of ideas generated in Session 2 by the members of the pair showed some degree of correspondence: no share–feedback $R = .392$, $F(10, 13) = 2.29$, $p < .10$; share–no feedback $R = .755$, $F(10, 13) = 7.16$, $p < .001$; share–feedback $R = .413$, $F(11, 14) = 2.41$, $p < .10$.

The results for Study 2 are consistent with those of Study 1 in demonstrating that the performance of those who brainstormed as interactive pairs tends to be more similar than the performance of noninteractive individuals. That the strongest intraclass correlation was observed in the share–no feedback condition is intriguing. This result can be seen as consistent with the basic tenet of social comparison theory that individuals tend to compare with others to reduce uncertainty about their abilities or opinions (Festinger, 1954). Because subjects in this condition were not provided performance feedback, they may have been more highly motivated to attend to the performance of

---

[3]This study was part of an undergraduate honors thesis by George Poletes.

their partners than those who were provided such feedback.

Study 3

Although Studies 1 and 2 have demonstrated that social influence processes play a role in dyadic brainstorming, it remains to be demonstrated that a similar process occurs in larger groups. Data of this type are available from a study in which nominal groups of four were compared with interactive groups of four with individual microphones and recorders. These two conditions were part of a larger study designed to assess the illusion of group productivity in brainstorming groups (Paulus et al., 1993). The independent microphone feature in interactive groups allows one to compare the degree of correspondence among group members with that of nominal groups. It was predicted that performance scores of individuals in the same interactive groups would be more similar than those of individuals in the nominal groups.

For our matching perspective to account for productivity loss in interactive groups of four or larger, the matching process must be related to the occurrence of productivity loss. As discussed earlier, as the size of brainstorming groups increases, a number of factors may contribute to a tendency of individuals to inhibit their performance. When individuals in a group are performing the same task, they may feel that their efforts are dispensible and demonstrate lowered task performance (Harkins & Petty, 1982). This may occur even when they are individually identifiable (Kerr & Bruun, 1983). Concerns about evaluation by other group members and procedural blocking should also contribute to inhibition of individual performance (Diehl & Stroebe, 1987). Thus, the various inhibitory aspects of interactive brainstorming ensure that group members will have an initially low level of performance. The matching process helps to make this a "normative" level of performance for the group. Consequently, even though groups often use only a portion of the time available in the later stages of their session, this normative level is then maintained throughout the task session. Thus, whereas blocking, evaluation apprehension, and free riding are factors that may inhibit initial performance in interactive groups, we propose that it is the social-matching process that explains the continued low performance of interactive groups

members even though they may have sufficient opportunity to express their ideas. Moreover, we suggest that various constraints on group brainstorming would lead to a tendency toward downward comparison, with the low producers being more influential in setting the performance standard than the high producers. In laboratory settings, there is little or no external incentive for performing at a high level other than the experimental instructions. Furthermore, because the group has little stake in their product, there should be minimal social pressure on low performers to increase their performance level. Instead, high performers may not want to look foolish or "play the sucker" by taking the experiment more seriously than the other group members (cf. Kerr, 1983). These various predictions were assessed in Study 3.

Method

Eighty male and female volunteers from introductory psychology classes participated in same-sex groups of four. One half of the subjects brainstormed together in the same room; the other half brainstormed alone in separate rooms. All subjects were provided with individual microphones and tape recorders and were given brainstorming instructions similar to those in the interaction-independent microphone and nominal pair conditions in Study 1. Two different brainstorming problems were used. Nine of the groups brainstormed on the thumbs problem, while 11 generated ways to improve their university. The procedure was similar to that of Study 1 except that subjects brainstormed for 25 min. The tapes were transcribed and coded for the number of ideas relevant to the topic. Overlapping ideas were eliminated from the pool of ideas in the nominal groups. Interrater agreement on this task was obtained for nine groups and was .95.

Results and Discussion

The nominal groups performed better than the interactive groups in terms of the number of ideas generated (68.7 vs. 51.4), but this difference was not significant, $t(18) = 1.50$, $p > .05$. As reported by Paulus et al. (1993), nominal groups did perform better than interactive groups with a common microphone. An assessment of intraclass correlations revealed that there was a high degree of interdependence among the members of the interactive groups ($R = .44$), $F(9, 30) = 4.10$, $p < .002$, but not among the members of the nominal groups ($R = -.07$), $F(30, 9) = 1.33$, $p > .05$. As with Study 1, the intraclass correlations were quite consistent over time for both the nominal and interactive groups. For each of five 5-min blocks of the brainstorming session the intraclass correlations for the nominal groups were (in order) $-.06$, $-.12$, $.01$, $-.01$, and $-.21$ (all nonsignificant). For the interactive groups, these intraclass correlations were $.30$, $.41$, $.17$, $.46$, and $.37$. These were significant ($p < .05$) for the first, second, and fourth blocks and marginally significant for the fifth ($p < .06$).

If the performance of individuals in groups is influenced by that of their co-workers, groups may quickly develop a normative level of performance. Therefore, one would expect the performance of groups in the early phases of group performance to be predictive of the performance in the later phases. Furthermore, because we presume that the social comparison process in brainstorming groups (in contrast to interacting pairs) tends to be downward, we predicted that the performance of the least productive members of the group would be most predictive of later performance. For one analysis, we determined the correlation between performance in the first 5 min with that of the last 5 min separately for the two high performers and the two low performers in each group. In the nominal condition, these correlations were low and nonsignificant, $r(19) = .07$ for the high performers and $r(19) = .13$ for the low performers. In the interactive condition, these correlations were strong and significant, $r(19) = .57$, $p < .02$, for the high performers and $r(19) = .74$, $p < .001$, for the low performers, Although the correlation was stronger for the low performers, the difference between the correlation for the low and high performers was not significant. We also examined the degree of correlation between the overall performance of the group and the group's performance in the first 5 min. According to our social influence analysis, there should be a stronger correlation for interactive groups, than for nominal groups. Furthermore, this correlation should be stronger for the low performers than the high ones. On the basis of their performance in the first 5 min, individuals within each group were assigned a rank from 1 (top) to 4 (bottom). For the nominal groups, the correlations for the four ranks from 1 to 4 were $r(10) = .46$, $p > .10$; $r(9) = .57$, $p > .10$;

$r(9) = .67$, $p < .05$; and $r(10) = .60$, $p < .07$. For the interactive groups. each of the four correlations was higher and significant, Rank 1 $r(10) = .80$, $p < .01$; Rank 2 $r(9) = .77$, $p < .02$; Rank 3 $r(9) = .69$, $p < .05$; and Rank 4, $r(10) = .83$, $p < .01$. However, the four correlations were not significantly different from one another.

Items from a questionnaire were correlated with individual performance for group subjects to determine the predictive power of theoretically relevant factors such as effort, concern with evaluation, distraction, pressure to generate many ideas, and the extent to which other group members facilitated performance. None of these correlations were significant.

The results of this study are consistent with our social influence perspective of brainstorming. The performance of members of interactive groups is more similar than that of members of nominal groups, indicating that matching does occur among interactive groups of four. For interactive groups, the performance in the early phase of the brainstorming session strongly predicts the performance at the end of the session as well as the overall performance. This result suggests that the initial phase of group performance establishes a performance norm that influences subsequent performance. Moreover, that this relationship tends to be stronger for the low than the high performers in the group for the last 5-min measure is consistent with the view that downward comparison characterizes brainstorming groups in laboratory settings.

Study 4

We have noted that the inhibitory aspects of interactive brainstorming ensure that group members will have an initially low level of performance. The matching process helps to make this a normative level of performance for the group, and this level is then maintained throughout the task session. Consistent with this analysis, in Study 3 the performance level during the first 5 min of group interaction predicted the performance during the last 5 min. If the level of performance in brainstorming groups achieved some degree of normative character, one would expect that performance level in one session would predict performance level quite well in a later session, even if a different brainstorming problem were used. Although individual performance will probably also show some degree of correspondence across different tasks (because of consistency in motivation, intelligence, etc.), the degree of correspondence for interactive groups should be greater because of the additional stability provided by the group norm.

The potential carryover effect of group performance level was examined in a study in which individuals were asked to perform three different brainstorming problems in three separate sessions. In one condition, individuals performed in interactive groups of four for each session (group-group-group). In a second condition, individuals performed alone in the first two sessions and as part of an interactive group of four in the third session (alone-alone-group). It was expected that the degree of correspondence among the three sessions would be greatest in the condition in which all three sessions involved group interaction.

Method

Seventy-two female psychology students participated to fulfill a course requirement. The procedures and instructions for the individual and group brainstorming sessions were the same as those used in Study 3. Three different problems were used: the thumbs problem, an education problem, and a tourist problem. The education problem was concerned with ways to assure that the effectiveness of instruction in public schools could be maintained in the face of increasing enrollments in the future. The tourist problem was concerned with ways to encourage Europeans to vacation in the United States.

Students were recruited in groups of four and brought to one room for instructions. In the interactive group sessions, participants performed at a table in this room and their responses were re-

corded by a common microphone. In the alone conditions, they were taken to individual rooms adjacent to this room These rooms contained individual microphones and recorders. Each of the three sessions lasted 10 min. At each session, subjects were given instructions appropriate to their condition and problem. The last session was always a group condition in which participants discussed the education problem. One half of the groups in each of the two conditions had the thumbs problem in the first session and the tourist problem in the second session. The order was reversed for the other half. A copy of the instructions and problems remained with the participants during each session.

Results

Each of the tapes was transcribed and the number of ideas was coded. The interrater agreement for this task was checked for eight of the groups and was .99. For the sessions in which individuals performed as a nominal group, repetitive ideas were deleted in deriving a total score. The average agreement for raters on this task was .99. Table 3 summarizes the results for the number of nonrepetitive ideas generated in the various conditions. The results for Session 1 were analyzed in a Problem Order × Brainstorm Condition analysis of variance. There was a significant effect for brainstorm condition due to the superior performance of the nominal groups, $F(1,14) = 5.43$, $p < .04$. More ideas were generated by groups that began with the thumbs problem than by those that began with the tourist problem, although this was not a significant effect, $F(1, 14) = 1.36$, $p > .05$. In Session 2, there was again a condition effect due to the superior performance of the nominal groups relative

TABLE 3. Means and Standard Deviations for Numbers of Nonrepetitive Ideas Generated: Study 4

Condition	Session 1		Session 2		Session 3	
	M	SD	M	SD	M	SD
Alone-alone-group						
Thumbs-tourist	45.0	10.6	54.1	8.6	17.1	3.5
Tourist-thumbs	39.7	13.4	34.0	8.6	9.0	5.4
Group-group-group						
Thumbs-tourist	31.7	9.5	27.4	8.9	17.1	3.6
Tourist-thumbs	21.1	19.9	18.6	14.7	10.0	9.6

Note. In the thumbs-tourist condition, the thumbs task was performed in Session 1 and the tourist task in Session 2. In the tourist-thumbs condition, this order was reversed. In all conditions, the education task was used in Session 3. Standard deviations are for group scores.

to the interactive groups, $F(1, 14) = 17.00, p < .001$. It is interesting that the groups that began with the thumbs problem continued to perform better than those that began with the tourist problem even though they were now working on the other problem, $F(1, 14) = 7.99, p < .02$. This enhanced performance for those who had the thumbs problem first persisted in Session 3, with a significant effect of problem order, $F(1, 14) = 6.53, p < .03$.

The performance scores of groups in the two brainstorming conditions were examined for degree of correlation between sessions. For both the alone-alone-group and the group-group-group conditions, Sessions 1 and 2 were somewhat (although not significantly) correlated, $r(7) = .51$, $p > .05$ and $r(7) = .65. p < .06$, respectively. However, there was a stronger correlation between the performance of groups in Sessions 1 and 3 for groups in the group-group-group condition than for those groups in the alone-alone-group condition, $r(7) = .92, p < .0005$ and $r(7) = .28, p > .05$, respectively. These correlations were significantly different from one another, $Z = 2.25, p < .05$. Correlations between Sessions 2 and 3 were high both for the alone-alone-group and the group-group-group conditions, $r(7) = .88, p < .002$ and $r(7) = .72, p < .03$, but not significantly different from one another, $Z = .81, p > .05$.

Discussion

The pattern of results of Study 4 is generally consistent with our hypotheses. The performance level established in Session 1 and 2 carried over to the subsequent sessions. However, only for the group-group-group condition was there a strong carryover from Session 1 to Session 3. Furthermore, as would be expected on the basis of serial dependency, the predictive power of the performance of nominal groups in Session 1 decreased over sessions. The experience with a second different problem should diminish the impact of the Session 1 experience, and the performance level in the second session should be more predictive of performance in Session 3 than would be the case for Session 1 performance. However, the predictive power of Session 1 performance remains strong and even increases over sessions for the interactive groups. If groups develop a normative rate of performance in the first session, this norm should carry over to a second session and should not be greatly disturbed by the experience of a different task. The pattern of results obtained in the two different conditions therefore is consistent with that of our social influence analysis. Because the alone-alone-group condition involves a change in experimental context and the all-group condition does not, this change itself could be responsible for the lower correlation between Sessions 1 and 3 found in the former condition. However, in Study 3 there was no change in context in either the nominal or interaction conditions, and a significant relationship between early performance and later performance was obtained only for interacting students. Additional studies are required to demonstrate clearly that exposure to different group norms on one brainstorming task will be reflected in differences in performance on a second group-brainstorming task.

The thumbs problem yielded a higher number of ideas in Session 1 than the tourist problem. Those subjects who had the thumbs problem in Session 1 performed at a higher level in Sessions 2 and 3 even though they had different problems during these sessions. This effect occurred both for the alone-alone-group and the group-group-group subjects and is similar to entrainment effects reported by Kelly (1988). These results are of course consistent with the correlational analyses showing that performance levels established by individuals or groups can carry over to subsequent sessions with different problems It should be noted, however, that the performance difference between nominal and interactive groups for Sessions 1 and 2 is not reflected in a "carried over" performance difference in Session 3. Possibly, the change in context from solitary to group performance for the alone-alone participants inhibited the carryover of their higher performance level. Yet the fact that the correlations between Sessions 2 and 3 were similar for the alone-alone-group and the group-group-group conditions suggests that this is not a major factor.

Study 5

The studies reported have provided evidence that members of interactive brainstorming groups match their performance to that of other members of their group. Because of the situational constraints that exist for interactive groups, interactive group members should evidence a rather low level of performance at the beginning of the session. If this performance level takes on normative qualities, it may carry over to later parts of the session when these constraints are no longer a major factor.

As indicated by Diehl and Stroebe (1987), interactive brainstorming groups often run out of ideas before the end of the session. However, because interactive groups typically generate about half of the ideas of nominal groups, it is unlikely that groups actually run out of ideas. Instead, interactive group members may decide that they have generated a sufficient number of ideas because they typically perceive their performance quite favorably (Paulus et al., 1993). This perception may reduce the motivation to generate ideas. The impact of this lowered motivation may be enhanced by the social matching of low levels of performance.

The social-matching perspective suggests that the low level of performance of interactive groups could be counteracted if the groups were provided with high normative standards. Such standards could eliminate the illusion of group productivity in interactive groups and motivate the group members to achieve these higher standards. These predictions were tested in Study 5.[4] Consistent with these predictions, some studies have shown that providing explicit goals can facilitate brainstorming. However, these studies have not involved comparisons of nominal and interactive groups (cf. Hyams & Graham, 1984).

Method

Subjects and design. Ninety-six female students participated in this study to fulfill a course requirement. They were asked to brainstorm in groups of four or as individuals. One half of the subjects in each condition was provided information about the "typical performance" of other subjects, and the other half was not provided with such information.

Procedure. Students were brought to the experimental room in groups of four. The procedures and instructions were similar to those in the previous studies. Participants brainstormed on the thumbs problem for 25 min. Subjects in the nominal brainstorming conditions were assigned to separate rooms for their brainstorming activity. Each room contained a tape recorder to record the ideas generated. The ideas generated by the group were recorded by a common microphone in the middle of

the table at which the four group members were seated. Participants were instructed to keep track of the number of ideas they (or the group) had generated by making slash marks on a slip of paper. This procedure was designed to enhance the social comparison process.

In the information conditions, subjects were told about the typical performance of others just before starting the brainstorming session.

In preliminary research, it was found that nominal subjects could generate about 25 ideas in 25 min. Thus, the group subjects were informed that "the average number of ideas generated by one individual is about 25. So for this group to equal this amount, you would have to generate about 100 ideas." This level of performance was actually about 2½ times greater than that attained by interacting groups in our preliminary studies. This information should inhibit overestimation of the adequacy of group performance and motivate higher levels of performance compared with uninformed groups. Of course, comparative information can also have a motivational impact on nominal subjects. Therefore, the nominal subjects in the information condition were given a standard 2½ times greater than their typical performance. They were informed that "the average number of ideas generated by one individual alone is about 65. So for you to equal this amount you would have to generate about 65 ideas."

When the brainstorming session was finished, participants were provided with a brief questionnaire. A number of the questions focused on evaluations of performance. Participants were asked to rate the number and quality of ideas they generated on 9-point scales (from *very many* or *very high* to *very few* or *very low*). For the interactive group subjects, these questions were asked both for their individual performance and the performance of the group. Interactive group subjects were also asked to predict whether they would have generated more or fewer ideas if they had been asked to brainstorm alone (*many more* to *many less*) and whether these ideas would be of greater or lesser quality (*much greater* to *much less*). Nominal group participants were asked to predict whether they would have generated more or fewer ideas and ideas of greater or lesser quality if they

---

[4]The preliminary results of this study were presented at several conferences (Dzindolet & Paulus, 1990; Paulus, Dzindolet, & Camacho, 1990).

had been asked to brainstorm in a group with three other people. A number of questions were designed to tap some of the underlying processes and emotions, all using 9-point scales. Participants were asked about effort, difficulty of generating ideas while others were talking, and difficulty of concentrating while generating new ideas. Participants in the individual conditions were asked the same questions, modified in some cases to make them appropriate for solitary performers. Of course, questions pertaining solely to rating group performance were not used in these conditions. All participants were asked to rate how they felt during brainstorming on 12 emotion dimensions. These were *tense-calm, nervous-relaxed, stimulated-understimulated, aroused-unaroused, embarrassed-comfortable, very anxious-not at all anxious, very concerned with making a good impression-not at all concerned with making a good impression, very aware of myself-not at all aware of myself, very aware of my own thoughts-not at all aware of my own thoughts, very attentive to my inner feelings-not at all attentive to my inner feelings, very reflective about myself-not at all reflective about myself.*

At the conclusion of the experiment, the subjects were thoroughly debriefed about the experiment. Subjects in the information condition were informed that the standards provided were higher than those achieved by typical subjects or groups.

Results

Questionnaire. The significant results for the questionnaire items and performance are shown in Table 4. Participants in interactive groups thought that they individually had generated more ideas than did subjects in the nominal group conditions, $F(1,93) = 4.63, p < .04$. Interactive group participants also rated the quality of their ideas higher than participants in the nominal conditions, $F(1,93) = 13.64, p < .001$. Interactive group members tended to feel that they would generate fewer ($M = 6.33$) and lower quality ($M = 5.42$) ideas if they brainstormed alone, whereas nominal participants believed they would have generated more ($M = 6.93$) and better quality ($M = 6.48$) ideas in groups of four. Nominal participants were significantly more favorable about quality of ideas in group brainstorming than group participants, $F(1,92) = 11.82, p < .001$. Subjects in interactive groups also indicated they felt they could generate a larger number of additional ideas with more time than did nominal group subjects, $F(1,93) = 28.80, p < .0001$. Nominal group subjects indicated more difficulty concentrating while generating ideas than subjects in interactive groups, $F(1,93) = 18.03, p < .0001$. There were no differences in reported effort between nominal and interactive group subjects, $F(1,93) = .23, p > .05$. It is interesting that the information manipulation did not affect any of the questionnaire items in terms of main effects or interaction with group condition.

The results for the emotion items were subjected to a multivariate analysis of variance that yielded only a significant effect of group condition, Wilks's $\lambda = .75, F(12,75) = 2.06, p < .03$. Univariate analyses yielded significant effects only for arousal and embarrassment. Individuals in interactive groups

TABLE 4. Results: Study 5

Measure	Nominal groups				Interactive groups			
	No information		Information		No information		Information	
	M	SD	M	SD	M	SD	M	SD
Number of ideas[a]	66.6	16.0	96.3	36.6	39.9	14.1	62.4	25.9
Rating of number of ideas	4.2	2.3	4.1	2.3	4.7	2.1	5.7	2.1
Rating of quality of ideas	4.1	2.0	4.0	1.8	5.1	1.8	5.8	1.2
Rating of quality of ideas in groups	6.2	1.5	6.7	1.6	5.4	1.4	5.5	1.1
More ideas with more time	7.7	1.5	7.5	1.7	5.9	2.3	5.1	2.1
Concentration	5.2	2.5	4.6	2.1	7.0	1.8	6.6	1.7
Arousal	6.3	1.8	6.1	1.9	5.5	1.9	5.0	2.0
Embarrassment	5.2	2.2	5.4	2.6	7.5	1.1	6.2	2.2

Note. For the number and quality of ideas items, higher ratings are more favorable. For the other items, the lower the number, the more ideas with more time, the harder to concentrate, the more aroused, and the more embarrassed.
[a]Standard deviations are for group scores.

felt more aroused but less embarrassed than those in nominal groups, $F(1,86) = 6.11, p < .02, F(1,86) = 10.66, p < .01$, respectively.

Task performance. To analyze the number of ideas generated, nominal groups were composed by combining the performance of groups of four individual subjects. In cases in which four subjects were not run at the same time, the nominal groups were composed by randomly assigning subjects to form groups of four. For the nominal and interactive groups, overlapping ideas were eliminated to derive a total score of nonoverlapping ideas. The tapes were transcribed by one assistant. All transcripts were scored for number of relevant ideas by two raters whose overall degree of agreement was .98. The agreement for these raters in determining the number of nonoverlapping ideas was .99.

The number of ideas generated by interactive and nominal groups was subjected to a Group Type × Information Condition analysis of variance. This yielded significant main effects for type of group, $F(1,19) = 7.65, p < .02$, and information condition, $F(1,19) = 5.68, p < .03$. It can be seen in Table 4 that nominal groups generated more ideas than interactive groups and the information manipulation led to the generation of a larger number of ideas.

The ideas were also coded in 5-min blocks, but in this coding process it was not feasible to eliminate overlapping ideas because these often occurred in different time blocks. An analysis of these data in a Group Type × Information Condition × Time Block analysis of variance yielded significant effects of group type, $F(1,13) = 14.11, p < .01$, information condition, $F(1,13) = 5.20, p < .05$, and time blocks, $F(4,52) = 45.27, p < .001$, an Information Condition × Time Block interaction, $F(4,52) = 3.81, p < .01$, and a Group Condition ×

Time Block interaction, $F(4, 52) = 11.27, p < .001$. As can be seen in Table 5, the number of ideas generated decreased over time blocks, and the differences in number of ideas generated between the nominal and interacting conditions and between the no-information and information conditions became smaller over time.

Discussion

The results of this study provide further support for the role of social factors in brainstorming performance. Providing the interactive groups with information about the typical performance level of nominal groups led the interactive groups to attain a level similar to that of the uninformed nominal groups. Thus, this informed interactive group was able to overcome the entire productivity gap in performance that existed for the uninformed group. This is quite remarkable because the various manipulations used by Diehl and Stroebe (1987) diminished the gap only slightly between the regular nominal group and the manipulated interaction group (e.g., personal assessment instructions, Experiment 1). Although we did not supply the uninformed nominal group with a performance standard, it is presumed that providing this group with the same standard, as the informed interactive group would lead to similar results. This presumption seems quite reasonable in light of the fact that when the nominal groups were given a standard of 260 ideas (4 × 65) they generated 96 ideas, 37% of the standard. The informed interactive groups with a standard of 100 generated 62 ideas, 62% of the standard. Providing nominals with a standard more than 2½ times higher than that for the informed interactive groups increased their performance by only 45%, possibly because of a ceiling effect. Thus, it seems un-

Table 5. Number of Ideas (Including Repeats) Generated by the Three Brainstorming Conditions Over Blocks of Time: Study 5

Condition	0–5 min		6–10 min		11–15 min		16–20 min		21–25 min	
	M	SD	M	SD	M	SD	M	SD	M	SD
Nominal										
No information	29.7	5.4	17.7	4.5	13.1	5.6	10.3	4.6	6.2	5.1
Information	45.2	9.0	24.8	7.4	19.2	6.1	14.2	7.1	3.0	2.6
Interactive										
No information	12.9	2.4	9.1	2.8	9.9	4.8	7.6	1.4	5.5	2.5
Information	19.0	13.0	15.2	6.8	16.5	13.1	7.7	3.2	4.2	5.6

Note. Standard deviations are for group scores.

likely that providing nominals with a standard of 100 would lead to performance superior to that of interactive groups with the same standard. In any case, this study has clearly demonstrated that brainstorming groups are strongly affected by performance information about other groups. This does not prove that a matching process occurs naturally within interacting groups, but the results of this study do provide additional evidence for our perspective that social influence processes can affect the performance of brainstorming groups.

Although providing even higher external standards or norms could increase further the performance of the interactive groups, it is likely that having to share one's production time with others will place limits on the ability of interactive groups to attain ever increasing standards. Four-person nominal groups have four times as much total production time as four-person interactive groups. If production time of interactive and nominal groups were equated, the potential facilitative impact of normative information or other procedural or motivational interventions should be fairly similar for both of these groups. Under such conditions, interactive groups might be able to achieve levels similar to that of comparable nominal groups. Some evidence for this possibility already exists. Panman and Rosenbaum (1964, cited in Kanekar & Rosenbaum, 1972) extended the brainstorming session to 50 min (thus reducing time constraints on interactive groups), and the experimenter encouraged subjects to continue generating ideas by restating the problem when no one spoke for 30 s. Under the extended time period and motivating conditions, the performance of individuals in interactive groups reached the same level as that of nominal groups. They found nominal group performance to be superior to interactive group performance for the first 20 min, but during the last 30 min, interactive group performance was superior to nominal group performance. In our own research we have also found that the productivity gap between nominal and interactive groups becomes smaller over the course of the brainstorming session (Paulus et al., 1993; Study 5). Diehl and Stroebe (1991) reported that a significant reduction in the productivity gap over time does not occur when one analyzes the performance in the 20-min session for 10 2-min intervals. However, when one examines the means for nominal and interactive groups, it is clear that most of the productivity gap occurs in the early phases of performance. The gap between groups that brainstorm for 10 min is 19.25 ideas, whereas that for groups that brainstorm for 20 min is 23.5 ideas. Thus, providing an additional 10 min of brainstorming increased the gap by only 22%. Although Diehl and Stroebe (1991) found that providing groups with extra time does not reduce the productivity gap, if groups are stimulated to overcome the "normative brakes" of social interaction, they may be able to use the extra time to overcome much if not all of the productivity gap.

Evidence for the potential facilitative impact of social information has also been obtained in dyadic brainstorming. When members of a dyad are provided information about their relative performance in a prior independent session, the member with the lowest performance demonstrates an increased level of performance in the second session in comparison with a condition in which subjects are not provided with social comparison information (Paulus et al., 1993).

Some of the questionnaire results are inconsistent with some of the interpretations of productivity losses in group brainstorming. Contrary to social loafing or economic interpretations, there was no difference in rated effort for interactive and nominal group subjects. That group members report less difficulty in concentrating than individual participants seems inconsistent with a blocking perspective. Interactive group members indicated a lower level of embarrassment compared with individual subjects, contrary to expectations from an evaluation interpretation.

In accord with our prior research on the illusion of group productivity (Paulus et al., 1993), participants in interactive brainstorming groups rated their performance quite favorably relative to participants in nominal brainstorming conditions. Furthermore, participants in both interactive and nominal group conditions felt that interactive group brainstorming was more productive than individual brainstorming both in terms of number and quality of ideas. However, actual performance data replicated that of past studies in that interactive groups generated fewer distinct ideas than nominal groups. It was somewhat surprising that the information manipulations did not affect the rated perception of performance. It is possible that whereas the information had motivational effects, it also provided a high standard for subjective evaluations of one's performance. Subjects in the no-information conditions did not have such a high

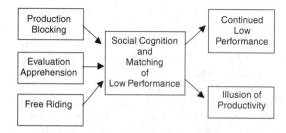

FIGURE 1 ■ Social influence model of productivity losses in group brainstorming.

standard to use as a basis for judging the subjective quality of their performance.

The social comparison-matching process that appears to be important in affecting task performance in group brainstorming may also be responsible for the illusion of group productivity that is found in brainstorming groups. When group members compare their performance with that of others in the group, most should discover that they are either above or fairly close to the performance level of others. Those who perform in isolation do not have the benefit of such a comparison process and may be less confident about the adequacy of their performance. A social influence model that incorporates these ideas and the others proposed in this article is presented in Figure 1.

Conclusion

Our studies have provided evidence for the role of social factors in group brainstorming. Members of interactive groups are influenced by the performance of their fellow group members as well as by information about performance of other groups. Performance levels attained by groups in early phases of their interaction are carried over to later phases, even when different problems are used. The social influence perspective is not necessarily inconsistent with the other explanations of productivity in brainstorming groups. In fact we have proposed that procedural blocking, evaluation apprehension, and free riding may be inhibiting factors in initial performance in group brainstorming. This state of affairs provides the occasion for social matching of low performance levels, which in turn results in maintenance of low levels of productivity in later task phases, when blocking, apprehension, and free riding may no longer be major factors (as suggested by the questionnaire data

obtained at the end of the session). At the same time, because individuals in groups discover that their performance is fairly similar to that of others, they may perceive their performance in a fairly positive way. Although significant progress has been made in solving the riddle of productivity losses in groups, it will take a series of studies with varying approaches to fully illuminate the interrelationship of blocking, evaluation apprehension, free riding, social matching, and perception of productivity.

ACKNOWLEDGMENTS

We thank the following students for their loyal assistance in this research project: Robin Brunner, Ayman Ghousheh, Lisa Kucharski, Ingrid Maghias, Jacqueline Miller, and Christopher Young. The assistance of William Ickes and Vic Bissonette in the data analyses is greatly appreciated.

REFERENCES

Beck, H. P., & Seta, J. J. (1980). The effects of frequency of feedback on a simple coaction task. *Journal of Personality and Social Psychology, 38*, 75–80.

Bond, C. F., & Titus, L. J. (1983). Social facilitation: A meta-analysis of 241 studies. *Psychological Bulletin, 94*, 265–292.

Bond, C. F., & Van Leeuwen, M. D. (1991). Can a part be greater than the whole? On the relationship between primary and meta-analytic evidence. *Basic and Applied Social Psychology, 12*, 33–40.

Borgatta, E. F., & Bales, R. F. (1953). Interaction of individuals in reconstituted groups. *Sociometry, 16*, 302–320.

Bouchard, T. J. (1969). Personality, problem-solving procedure, and performance in small groups. *Journal of Applied Psychology Monograph, 53*, 1–29.

Bouchard, T. J., & Hare, M. (1970). Size, performance, and potential in brainstorming groups. *Journal of Applied Psychology, 54*, 51–59.

Casey, J. T., Gettys, C. F., Pliske, R. M., & Mehle, T. (1984). A partition of small group predecision performance into informational and social components. *Organizational Behavior and Human Performance, 34*, 112–139.

Collaros, P. A., & Anderson, L. R. (1969). Effect of perceived expertness upon creativity of members of brainstorming groups. *Journal of Applied Psychology, 53*, 159–163.

Diehl, M., & Stroebe, W. (1987). Productivity loss in brainstorming groups: Toward the solution of a riddle. *Journal of Personality and Social Psychology, 53*, 497–509.

Diehl, M., & Stroebe, W. (1991). Productivity loss in idea-generating groups: Tracking down the blocking effect. *Journal of Personality and Social Psychology, 61*, 392–403.

Dzindolet, M. T., & Paulus, P. B. (1990, April). *The role of performance perception and standards in brainstorming.* Paper presented at the meetings of the Southwestern Psychological Association, Dallas.

Festinger, L. (1954). A theory of social comparison processes. *Human Relations, 7*, 117–140.

Geen, R. G. (1989). Alternative conceptions of social facilitation. In P. B. Paulus (Ed.), *Psychology of group influence* (2nd ed., pp. 15–52) Hillsdale, NJ: Erlbaum.

Goethals, G. R., & Darley, J. M. (1987). Social comparison theory: Self-evaluation and group life. In B. Mullen & G. R. Goethals (Eds.), *Theories of group behavior* (pp. 21–48), New York: Springer-Verlag.

Haggard, E. A. (1958). *Intraclass correlation and the analysis of variance*. New York: Dryden Press.

Harari, O., & Graham, W. K. (1975). Tasks and task consequences as factors in individual and group brainstorming. *Journal of Social Psychology, 95*, 61–65.

Harkins, S. (1987). Social loafing and social facilitation. *Journal of Experimental Social Psychology, 23*, 1–18.

Harkins, S. G., & Jackson, J. M. (1985). The role of evaluation in the elimination of social loafing. *Personality and Social Psychology Bulletin. 11*, 457–465.

Harkins, S. G., & Petty, R. E. (1982). Effects of task difficulty and task uniqueness on social loafing. *Journal of Personality and Social Psychology, 43*, 1214–1229.

Hyams, N. B., & Graham, W. K. (1984). Effects of goal setting and initiative on individual brainstorming. *Journal of Social Psychology, 123*, 283–284.

Kanekar, S., & Rosenbaum, M. E. (1972). Group performance on a multiple-solution task as a function of available time. *Psychonomic Science, 27*, 331–332.

Kelly, J. R. (1988). Entrainment in individual and group behavior. In J. E. McGrath (Ed.), *The social psychology of time: New perspectives* (pp. 89–110). Newbury Park, CA: Sage.

Kerr, N. L. (1983). Motivation losses in small groups: A social dilemma analysis. *Journal of Personality and Social Psychology, 45*, 819–828.

Kerr, N. L., & Bruun, S. E. (1983). The dispensability of member effort and group motivation losses: Free rider effects. *Journal of Personality and Social Psychology, 44*, 78–94.

Maginn, B. K., & Harris, R. J. (1980). Effects of anticipated evaluation on individual brainstorming performance. *Journal of Applied Psychology, 65*, 219–225.

Mullen, B., Johnson, C., & Salas, E. (1991). Productivity loss in brainstorming groups: A meta-analytic integration. *Basic and Applied Social Psychology, 12*, 3–24.

Nemeth, C. J. (1985). Dissent, group process, and creativity: The contribution of minority influence. *Advances in Group Processes, 2*, 57–75.

Osborn, A. F. (1957). *Applied imagination*. New York: Scribner.

Panman, R. A., & Rosenbaum, M. E. (1964, May). *A comparison of real groups and nominal groups in the solution of open-ended problems*. Paper presented at the meeting of the Midwestern Psychological Association, St. Louis, MO.

Paulus, P. B., Dzindolet, M. T., & Camacho, L. M. (1990, June). *Perceived and actual productivity in brainstorming groups*. Paper presented at the general meeting of the European Association of Experimental Social Psychology, Budapest, Hungary.

Paulus, P. B., Dzindolet, M. T., Poletes, G. W., & Camacho, L. M. (1993). Perception of performance in group brainstorming: The illusion of group productivity. *Personality and Social Psychology Bulletin, 19*, 78–89.

Seta, J. J. (1982). The impact of comparison processes on coactors' task performance. *Journal of Personality and Social Psychology. 42*, 281–291.

Seta, J. J., & Seta, C. E. (1983). The impact of personal equity processes on performance in a group setting. In P. B. Paulus (Ed.), *Basic group processes* (pp. 121–147). New York: Springer-Verlag.

Seta, J. J., Seta, C. E., & Donaldson, S. (1991). The impact of comparison processes on coactors' frustration and willingness to expend effort. *Personality and Social Psychology Bulletin, 17*, 560–568.

Stroebe, W., & Diehl, M. (1991). You can't beat good experiments with correlational evidence: Mullen & Johnson's meta-analytic misinterpretations. *Basic and Applied Social Psychology, 12*, 25–32.

Taylor, D. W., Berry, P. C., & Block, C. H. (1958). Does group participation when using brainstorming facilitate or inhibit creative thinking? *Administrative Science Quarterly, 3*, 23–47.

Williams, K., Harkins, S., & Latane, B. (1981). Identifiability as a deterrent to social loafing: Two cheering experiments. *Journal of Personality and Social Psychology, 40*, 303–311.

Zajonc, R. B. (1980). Compresence. In P. B. Paulus (Ed.), *Psychology of group influence* (pp. 35–60). Hillsdale, NJ: Erlbaum.

Group Versus Individual Training and Group Performance: The Mediating Role of Transactive Memory

Diane Wei Liang • Carlson School of Management, University of Minnesota
Richard L. Moreland • University of Pittsburgh
Linda Argote • Graduate School of Industrial Administration, Carnegie Mellon University

The task performance of laboratory work groups whose members were trained together or alone was investigated. At an initial training session, subjects were taught to assemble transistor radios. Some were trained in groups, others individually. A week later, subjects were asked to recall the assembly procedure and actually assemble a radio. Everyone performed these tasks in small work groups, each containing three persons of the same gender. Subjects in the group training condition worked in the same groups where they were trained, whereas subjects in the individual training condition worked in newly formed groups. Groups whose members were trained together recalled more about the assembly procedure and produced better-quality radios than groups whose members were trained alone. Through an analysis of videotape data, the mediating effects of various cognitive and social factors on the relationship between group training and performance were explored. The results indicated that group training improved group performance primarily by fostering the development of transactive memory systems among group members.

Training is used widely in organizations. Estimates of the amount that American corporations spend annually on training range from $30 billion to $100 billion (Baldwin & Ford, 1988; "Labor Letter," 1991). And this amount is likely to increase as a result of changes in the nature of work and characteristics of the work force (Goldstein, 1989, 1991; "Labor Letter," 1992; Webb & Smith, 1991).

Training programs can be very helpful. In a meta-analysis of the effects of various interventions on worker productivity, Guzzo, Jette, and Katzell (1985) found that interventions designed to enhance productivity through learning, including training programs, had strong positive effects overall. However, there was also considerable variability in the effectiveness of different training programs. Workers cannot always apply the knowledge and skills acquired in training programs to their jobs (Georgenson, 1982), and many examples of training programs that failed to improve worker productivity can be found (e.g., Baldwin & Ford,

1988; Goldstein, 1986; Wexley & Latham, 1981). A few researchers have even reported that investments in training can lead to productivity losses rather than gains (e.g., Galbraith, 1990; Hayes & Clark, 1986).

The real issue, then, is to specify the conditions under which training programs enhance job performance. Researchers are beginning to identify some of these conditions (Burke & Day, 1986; Guzzo et al., 1985). Although many factors may be important, one critical factor is the *fidelity* of training programs. Fidelity refers to the degree of similarity between workers' experiences during training and their experiences on the job. In general, training programs with greater fidelity are more likely to improve job performance, because they facilitate the transfer of knowledge from training to the job site.

One important factor that may weaken the fidelity and thereby limit the effectiveness of training programs is their emphasis on individual learning. Workers are often trained individually or in large cohorts whose members do not work together. Participants in these training programs generally work on their own (guided by an instructor) to learn new procedures. Afterward, they are assigned or return to job sites, where those procedures can be applied. But the work at those job sites is often performed by groups of people (Argote & McGrath, 1993), whose procedures may differ from those taught during training. Such differences can arise from variation over time in the content of training programs or from the emergence among group members of shared views about how their work should be performed (Levine & Moreland, 1991; Salas, 1993). In either case, misunderstandings, coordination problems, and interpersonal conflicts are likely.

Some corporations have begun to acknowledge the limits of individual training. Ray Stata of Analog Devices argues that training employees in their work groups is more effective than training them individually (Stata, 1989). John Seely Brown of Xerox believes that most learning in organizations takes place in groups (Brown & Duguid, 1991). And the military is investing considerable resources in training group members together as well as alone (Andrews, Wang, & Bell, 1992; Morgan, Glickman, Woodard, Blaiwes, & Salas, 1986).

Despite this enthusiasm for group training, only a few empirical studies have actually compared the performance of work groups whose members were trained together or alone (see Dyer, 1985, for a review), and the results of these studies are quite mixed. Some researchers (e.g., George, 1967) have found that group training is superior to individual training, whereas others (e.g., Briggs & Naylor, 1965) have found that group training is inferior. Several researchers (e.g., Laughlin & Sweeney, 1977) have found no difference at all These divergent findings are puzzling, and their interpretation is further clouded by methodological problems and a general lack of theory. Clearly, further research is needed to determine whether group or individual training produces better group performance. Several recent reviews of the training literature have called for such research (e.g., Druckman & Bjork, 1991).

The present research was designed to clarify the effects of group versus individual training on group performance. We propose and test a theoretical account for why group training should be superior to individual training. That account is based on Wegner's (1986) notion of *transactive memory*. According to Wegner, shared experiences often lead groups of people to encode, store, and retrieve relevant information together. As a result, a transactive memory system can develop within the group. This system is a combination of the knowledge possessed by particular group members and an awareness of who knows what. A transactive memory system is useful because it can serve as an external storage device (like a library or computer) for everyone in the group. Individual group members are thus able to locate and retrieve information that might otherwise be unavailable to them.

An example may help to clarify transactive memory systems. Imagine a group of people who work together at assembling radios for a small consumer electronics firm. The knowledge and abilities of these workers probably overlap considerably, which can be valuable in situations where one worker must cover for another. But workers are not clones; there is always some variability in the knowledge and abilities of group members. For example, one worker may know more than the others about electronics, whereas another worker is especially adept at connecting certain radio components. If group members are unaware of such expertise, they cannot easily take advantage of it (see Stasser, 1992). But if a transactive memory system exists, so that each group member knows the strengths and weaknesses of his or her coworkers, then the group can make better use of its human resources.

Only a few researchers have investigated transactive memory systems. Giuliano and Wegner (described in Wegner, 1986) studied the operation of such systems within dating couples. Each couple in their study was presented with many items of information (e.g., "The Kaypro II is a personal computer") representing various domains of expertise (e.g., computers). Each person's beliefs about who was more expert in each domain (self, other, both, neither) were measured, and the amount of time available for studying the items was manipulated to give each partner an advantage over the other on some items. The ability of each person to recall the items was then assessed. The results showed that items were more likely to be recalled when they represented domains of self- rather than other-expertise and when they were studied longer. Perceived expertise and study time also interacted in intriguing ways. For example, when someone had more time than his or her partner to study an item, that item was more likely to be recalled if the partner's expertise in the relevant domain was believed to be low. But when someone had less time than his or her partner to study an item, the partner's perceived expertise in the relevant domain had no effect on recall. These results suggest that partners collaborated at some level to maximize their collective recall, using perceived expertise and available study time as guides for deciding which items of information each person should remember. Such behavior indicated that a transactive memory system was at work.

Wegner, Erber, and Raymond (1991) studied the operation of natural or imposed transactive memory systems within real or artifical couples. As in the previous study, the subjects were all members of dating couples. Some of those couples were left intact, whereas the members of others were randomly assigned to new partners of the other sex. Once again, each couple (real or artificial) was presented with many items of information representing various domains of expertise. Within some of the couples, responsibility for remembering items from each domain was randomly assigned to one partner or the other, as an attempt to impose transactive memory systems on these couples. Within the remaining couples, however, responsibility for remembering items from each domain was left entirely to the subjects themselves. As before, the ability of each person to recall the items was later assessed. The results showed that real couples recalled more items when they used natural rather than imposed transactive memory systems, perhaps because the latter systems were unfamiliar, confusing, or maladaptive. In contrast, artifical couples recalled more items when they used imposed transactive memory systems. Without some help from the researchers, these "couples" probably had troubly deciding who should remember what, because they lacked any natural transactive memory systems.

If the results of these studies can be extrapolated to work groups, then they have important implications for understanding the effects of group versus individual training on group performance. We believe that training the members of a work group together rather than alone may be helpful because it allows them to develop a transactive memory system. When they are trained together, workers can acquire a common language for describing tasks, divide those tasks among themselves in ways that reflect their abilities and interests, and observe one another while they are actually acquiring task expertise. Because they know who is good at what, the members of such a group can seek information from the right person(s) when problems arise and trust that the information they receive will be correct. Knowing who is good at what also improves coordination within the group, because its members can anticipate one another's behavior and therefore react to that behavior more quickly and easily. Group training thus provides workers with a valuable resource—a transactive memory system—that facilitates knowledge distribution and coordination within the group. This resource should improve the group's performance.

The following experiment compared the performance of groups whose members were trained together or alone, with a special focus on the development of transactive memory systems. We hypothesized that:

1. Groups whose members are trained together rather than alone will recall more about how to perform a task.

2. Groups whose members are trained together

will perform that task more quickly and accurately than groups whose members are trained alone.

3. Groups whose members are trained together will develop stronger transactive memory systems than groups whose members are trained alone.

4. The development of transactive memory systems will mediate the effects of group training on task performance.

Group training could have other consequences (aside from the development of transactive memory systems) that affect task performance. For example, the performance of a work group often reflects the motivation of its members. There is clear evidence (e.g., O'Reilly & Caldwell, 1979; White & Mitchell, 1979) that motivation depends not only on the objective characteristics of whatever tasks someone performs but also on that person's subjective evaluations of those tasks. These evaluations are often shaped by social influence processes within a work group (see Salancik & Pfeffer, 1978)—processes that should operate more strongly among workers who are trained together rather than alone. Another factor that might be important is the level of cohesion within a work group. Several studies have shown that more cohesive groups exhibit better task performance (Evans & Dion, 1991; Keller, 1986; Murdock, 1989). Group training may strengthen cohesion, because workers who are trained together rather than alone spend more time with one another, share more common experiences, and so on. Finally, social identity theory (Tajfel & Turner, 1986) suggests another way in which group training might affect task performance. According to that theory, people derive part of their self-esteem from the groups to which they belong. A general desire to maximize self-esteem leads to a preference for membership in more successful groups, especially among individuals whose social identities are stronger (see Wilder, 1986). Workers who are trained together rather than alone probably identify more strongly with their groups. If so, then they may be more concerned about improving the performance of those groups.

All three of these factors—task motivation, group cohesion, social identity—are clearly worth exploring, because they represent alternative ways in which group training might improve task performance. While measuring various cognitive fac-

tors associated with the operation of transactive memory systems, we consequently obtained measures of these social factors as well. Those measures allowed us to investigate alternative explanations of differences in performance between groups whose members were trained together or alone.

Method

Subjects

Ninety students (66 males and 24 females) enrolled in undergraduate business courses at Carnegie Mellon University participated in the experiment to meet course requirements. Half of the sample was randomly assigned to an individual training condition, half to a group training condition.

Task

Subjects were required to assemble the AM portion of an AM/FM radio. This task was chosen to simulate the type of work found in many manufacturing organizations. Radio kits were purchased from the Tandy Corporation (Model 28-175). Each kit included a circuit board and dozens of mechanical and electronic components (e.g., resistors, transistors, capacitors). The circuit board contained prepunched holes with special symbols indicating where different components should be placed. Assembling just the AM portion of the radio required subjects to insert dozens of components into different places on the circuit board and then to connect each component to the others in the proper manner. No special tools for performing this task were provided.

Procedure

The experiment was carried out in two phases. During the first phase, subjects were trained to assemble the radio. This training was conducted either individually or in groups. In the group training condition, subjects were randomly assigned to small groups for training. Each group contained three subjects of the same sex. There were 10 male groups and 5 female groups in the group trainig condition.

When subjects arrived for the first phase of the experiment, they were told that our research examined how training can affect work group performance. Subjects were then given an overview of the experiment so that they knew what to expect during each phase. In particular, all subjects knew that they would later be asked to work in groups, whose performance would be videotaped and evaluated. Subjects in the individual training condition did not know who would belong to their groups, whereas subjects in the group training condition expected to remain in their current groups. Subjects were promised that members of the best work group would receive a prize of $20 per person.

The same basic training was provided to subjects in the two conditions. The experimenter began by demonstrating how the radio's components should be placed on the circuit board and connected to one another. This demonstration lasted about 15 min, and subjects were allowed to ask questions about the radio while the experimenter assembled it. Next, the subjects were given up to 30 min to practice assembling the radio themselves. No individual or group was allowed to assemble more than one radio during this practice period. Finally, the experimenter reviewed with the subjects every component and connection in the radio they had produced, identifying any errors and describing how such errors could be corrected.

The second phase of the experiment, in which subjects' ability to assemble the radios was tested, occurred 1 week later. During this phase, all subjects worked together in groups. Subjects who were trained individually were now assigned randomly to small groups, each containing three persons of the same sex. There were 12 male groups and 3 female groups in this individual training condition. Subjects who were trained as groups remained in those same groups.

Subjects in the two conditions were tested in exactly the same way. First, the members of each group were asked to recall together (as a group) how the radio should be assembled and then record the assembly procedure on a single piece of paper. Up to 7 min was allotted for this free recall task. During that time, subjects talked freely with one another, but they could not consult the experimenter or examine any radios or components. Next, each group was given up to 30 min to actually assemble a radio. The subjects were told to work as quickly as possible but also to make as few errors as possible. While working on the radio, subjects could not consult the experimenter,

nor could they examine their own recall sheet. Every group's performance was recorded on videotape, with the subjects' permission.

After assembling their radio, the subjects in each group were given 10 min to complete (individually and privately) a brief questionnaire. This questionnaire requested several items of biographical information, including the subject's age, sex, college major, and prior familiarity with the other group members. Measures of subjects' beliefs about the task (complexity, difficulty, enjoyment) and their group (cohesion, cooperation, role differentiation, memory differentiation) were also included. Afterward, subjects were debriefed, thanked for their participation, and dismissed.

Results

Three measures of group performance were available from the testing phase of the experiment. First, we measured how well each group remembered the procedure for assembling a radio by reviewing its recall sheet and counting the steps in that procedure that were recorded correctly. Higher scores on this measure indicated better group performance. Second, we measured how well each group actually assembled its radio by examining that radio and counting the misplaced or misconnected components it contained. Higher scores on this measure indicated poor performance by the group. (These scores could have been divided by the number of radio components that each group used, but every group used all the components it was given, and so this alternative measure would have correlated perfectly with the simpler one that we used). Finally, we measured how quickly each group assembled its radio by recording the number of minutes that it took to complete the task. Higher scores on this measure again indicated worse performance by the group.

A summary of the scores earned on all three of these performance measures by groups from the two training conditions can be found in the top portion of Table 1. The results for procedural recall supported our first hypothesis. As we predicted, groups whose members were trained together remembered significantly more about how to assemble a radio than groups whose members were trained alone, $t(28) = 3.08$, $p < .01$. The results for assembly errors supported our second hypothesis. As we predicted, groups whose members were

TABLE 1. Some Effects of Group Versus Individual Training on Group Performance and Process

Effect	Group Training		Individual Training	
	M	SD	M	SD
Performance measures				
Procedural recall (number of steps recalled)	25.53	6.91	16.40	9.16
Assembly errors	1.93	1.98	5.06	3.11
Assembly time (minutes)	16.11	4.13	15.67	3.24
Process measures				
Memory differentiation	0.80	0.61	-0.87	0.43
Task coordination	0.43	0.90	-0.47	0.93
Task credibility	0.73	0.16	-0.80	0.91
Task motivation	0.01	0.95	-0.01	1.11
Group cohesion	0.26	0.96	-0.29	1.01
Social identity	0.62	0.85	-0.68	0.66

NOTE: Scores on performance measures are based on 30 groups; scores on process measures are based on only 21 groups (11 in the group training condition and 10 in the individual training condition). Scores on the process measures were standardized before analysis.

trained together made significantly fewer errors while assembling a radio than groups whose members were trained alone, $t(28) = -3.30$, $p < .01$. Our second hypothesis, however, was not supported by the results for assembly time. Groups whose members were trained together or alone took about the same amount of time to assemble a radio, $t(28) = 0.32$, n.s.

Several regression analyses were performed to determine whether support for our hypotheses varied as a function of the subjects' gender or their prior familiarity with one another. To investigate gender, we regressed each group's performance on dummy variables representing its gender, training condition, and the interaction between gender and training condition. This analysis was performed three times, once for each performance measure. No significant ($p < .05$) interactions between gender and training condition were observed in any of these analyses. This suggests that the support for our hypotheses was equally strong among male and female groups. To investigate prior familiarity, we regressed each group's performance on the mean number of other group members that each subject knew prior to the experiment, a dummy variable representing the group's training condition, and the interaction between prior familiarity and training condition. Once again, this analysis was performed three times, once for each performance measure. No significant ($p < .05$) interactions between prior familiarity and training condition were observed in any of these analyses. This suggests that support for our hypotheses was

equally strong among groups whose members had different levels of prior familiarity with one another.

Earlier we suggested that both cognitive and social factors could mediate the effects of group training on group performance. The videotapes taken of the groups while they assembled their radios allowed us to measure several such factors. Unfortunately, the sound quality was poor in the videotapes for 9 groups, 5 in the individual training condition and 4 in the group training condition. There was no evidence that these groups differed from the others on any of the performance measures, and so we decided to code only the videotapes from the remaining 21 groups. Two judges, one of whom was blind to the research hypotheses and to each group's condition, coded these videotapes for evidence of these factors. A list of specific behaviors exemplifying each factor was provided to the judges to facilitate their coding. The judges were asked to watch each videotape carefully, keeping these behaviors in mind, and then make an overall rating of the group on each factor.

Three cognitive factors, all of which were assumed to reflect the operation of a transactive memory system among group members, were coded from the videotapes. The first factor was *memory differentiation,* or the tendency for group members to specialize in remembering distinct aspects of assembling the radio. One member, for example, might remember where different radio components should be placed on the circuit board, while another one remembered how those components should be connected. Such specialization is, of course, a key feature of transactive memory systems. The judges rated each group on a 7-point differentiation scale, higher ratings indicating a greater degree of memory differentiation among group members. The second factor was *task coordination*, or the ability of group members to work together smoothly while assembling the radio. In groups with stronger transactive memory systems, there should be less need for planning, greater cooperation, less confusion, fewer misunderstandings, and so on. The judges rated each group on a 7-point coordination scale, higher ratings indicating a greater degree of task coordination among group members. Finally, the third factor was *task credibility*, or how much group members trusted one another's knowledge about assembling the radio. This represents another key feature of transactive memory systems—group members already know how much and what kind of information each person possesses. In groups with stronger transactive memory systems, there should be less need to make claims of expertise, better acceptance of any procedural suggestions, less criticism of work by others, and so on. The judges rated each group on a 7-point credibility scale, higher ratings indicating a greater degree of trust among group members while assembling the radio.

Three social factors were also coded from the videotapes, but these factors were not assumed to reflect the operation of any single underlying process. The first factor was *task motivation*, or how eager group members were to win the prize by assembling their radio quickly and correctly. Group members whose motivation is stronger should express more enthusiasm for the task, encourage one another more often, work harder, and so on. The judges rated each group on a 7-point motivation scale, higher ratings indicating stronger motivation among group members. The second factor was *group cohesion*, or the level of interpersonal attraction among group members. Members of more cohesive groups should sit closer together, speak more warmly to one another, and so on. The judges rated each group on a 7-point cohesion scale, higher ratings indicating greater attraction among group members. Finally, the third factor was *social identity*, or subjects' tendency to think about themselves as group members rather than as individuals. This was the only factor for which behavioral counts rather than ratings were

obtained. The two judges counted the times that individual personal pronouns (e.g., *I, me, mine, he, she, him, her, his, hers*) and collective personal pronouns (*e.g., we, us, our, ours*) were used while the members of each group assembled their radio. The ratio of collective pronouns to all personal pronouns (individual and collective) used was then computed to create an index of social identity. Higher scores on that index indicated a stronger sense of social identity among group members.

For each of these factors, an intraclass correlation was computed to evaluate how reliably the two judges coded the videotapes. These correlations ranged from .61 (for memory differentiation) to .96 (for social identity) and were all significant ($p < .05$), indicating adequate coding reliability. Any disagreements between judges were resolved by averaging their ratings together. This procedure took advantage of the fact that both judges coded every videotape (cf. Hill, 1982) but may have allowed ratings by the nonblind judge to bias the results. To explore this issue, we later reran all our data analyses, using only the ratings from the blind judge. The results indicated that averaging the videotape ratings across judges did not affect any of our findings.

A summary of the standardized scores for each of the cognitive and social factors among groups from the two training conditions can be found in Table 1. It should be noted that alternative measures for a few factors (task motivation, group cohesion, and memory differentiation) were available from the questionnaires. Questionnaire and videotape measures of the same factors were significantly correlated ($p < .05$) with each other. We chose to rely on the videotape measures because their validity was probably better and it seemed preferable to measure all six behavioral factors using the same data source.

A series of t tests was performed to determine whether videotape scores on the six factors varied significantly across conditions. Our third hypothesis was clearly supported. Transactive memory systems operated much more strongly among groups whose members were trained together rather than alone. Groups whose members were trained together thus exhibited significantly greater memory differentiation, $t(19) = 7.17, p < .01$, task coordination, $t(19) = 2.24, p < .05$, and task credibility, $t(19) = 5.50, p < .01$. The effects of group or individual training on the social factors were much weaker. There were no significant differences in task motivation, $t(19) = 0.056$, or group cohesion, $t(19) = 1.28$, between groups whose members were trained together or alone. However, when group members were trained together, they did exhibit significantly stronger social identities, $t(19) = 3.87$, $p < .01$.

These results suggest that any of the cognitive factors, and one of the social factors (social identity), could have mediated the observed effects of group training on group performance. To test our fourth hypothesis, we carried out two sets of regression analyses. The only performance measure examined in these analyses was assembly errors. Neither the cognitive nor the social factors we measured could have mediated the effects of group training on procedural recall, because that performance measure was assessed before the videotapes were made. And because group training had no effects on assembly time, any possible mediation of such effects was excluded. Following procedures suggested by Baron and Kenny (1986), each set of analyses tested whether (a) group training significantly affected group performance, (b) group training significantly affected a potential mediator from the videotape data, and (c) the effects of group training were significantly reduced when that mediator was included as an additional predictor of group performance. All three findings were necessary to confirm mediation.

The first mediator we explored was a composite scale representing each group's average score on the memory differentiation, task coordination, and task credibility measures. These three scores were combined because they were all assumed to reflect the operation of transactive memory systems. Some evidence for that assumption was found in the correlations between these measures, which were all significant ($p < .01$) and positive. Coefficient alpha for the composite scale was .96, indicating a high degree of internal consistency. As we expected, scores on this composite scale were significantly higher, $t(19) = 6.96$, $p < .01$, among groups whose members were trained together rather than alone.

We began our mediation analysis by regressing each group's assembly errors (P) on its training condition (T). A dummy variable (0 = individual training, 1 = group training) was used to represent training condition in this and other regression analyses. The first regression equation, $P = 6.10 - 4.28T$, accounted for about 42% of the variance and was significant, $F(1, 19) = 15.66$, $p < .01$. As

we reported earlier, groups whose members were trained together made fewer errors while assembling their radios. We then regressed each group's transactive memory *(TM)* score on its training condition. This regression equation, $TM = -0.87 + 1.66\ T$, accounted for about 70% of the variance in the transactive memory scores and was also significant, $F(1, 19) = 48.46$, $p < .01$. As we reported earlier, transactive memory systems were stronger among groups whose members were trained together. Finally, we regressed each group's assembly errors on both its training condition and its transactive memory score. This regression equation, $P = 3.92 - 0.12T - 2.52TM$, accounted for about 57% of the variance and was significant, $F(2, 18) = 14.65$, $p < .01$. The coefficient for transactive memory was significant, $t(19) = -2.82$, $p < .05$, but the coefficient for training condition was not significant, $t(19) = -0.07$. This suggests that the transactive memory systems mediated the effects of group training on group performance, because when variability on the transactive memory measure was taken into account, groups whose members were trained together no longer performed better than groups whose members were trained alone. Our fourth hypothesis was thus supported.

In a second set of analyses, each group's social identity score was tested as a potential mediator. Once again, we began by regressing each group's assembly errors on its training condition. Then we regressed each group's social identity *(S)* score on its training condition. This regression equation, $S = -0.68 + 1.30T$, accounted for about 41% of the variance in social identity scores and was significant, $F(1, 19) = 15.03$, $p < .01$. As we reported earlier, groups whose members were trained together had stronger social identities. Finally, we regressed each group's assembly errors on both its training condition and its social identity score. This regression equation, $P = 6.80 - 5.61\ T + 1.02S$, accounted for about 45% of the variance and was significant, $F(2, 18) = 9.25$, $p < .01$. But this time, the regression coefficient for training condition remained significant, $t(19) = -3.98$, $p < .01$, whereas the coefficient for social identity was not significant, $t(19) = 1.02$. This suggests that social identity did not mediate the effects of group training on group performance, because when variability among groups on the social identity measure was taken into account, groups whose members were trained together still performed better than groups whose members were trained alone.

Discussion

The results of our experiment suggest that a work group's performance can indeed be improved by training its members together rather than alone. As we predicted, groups whose members were trained together recalled more about how to assemble their radios, and made fewer errors while assembling those radios, than groups whose members were trained alone. However, groups whose members were trained together did not assemble their radios more quickly. Perhaps assembly time was an unsuitable measure of group performance. A review of the videotapes revealed that most of the groups worked at a very rapid pace. This emphasis on speed may have reduced variability on the assembly time measure, thereby obscuring any differences between the training conditions.

We also predicted that stronger transactive memory systems would emerge among groups whose members were trained together rather than alone. Behavioral evidence gathered from the videotapes confirmed this prediction. When the members of a group were trained together, they were more likely to (a) recall different aspects of the task, (b) coordinate their task activities, and (c) trust one another's expertise. These findings represent the first direct evidence that transactive memory systems can operate within work groups, as Wegner (1986) claimed.

Finally, we predicted and found that transactive memory systems would mediate the effects of training on group performance. Training the members of a group together strengthened that group's transactive memory system, which, in turn, improved its task performance. Training had no direct effects on group performance when these indirect effects were taken into account. However, direct effects of transactive memory systems on group performance were observed, even after differences in training were taken into account. That is, groups with stronger transactive memory systems performed the task better, whether their members were trained together or alone. This suggests that other procedures, which may be less difficult or costly than training group members together, might be used to strengthen a group's transactive memory system and thereby improve its performance. For example, the members of a group could be trained individually but then provided with some of the information (e.g., the distribution of abilities among workers) normally found in a transactive memory system. Or a supervisor could impose some structure (e.g., task assignments based on the distribution of abilities among workers) on a group that would produce the kinds of behavior normally associated with a transactive memory system. The latter procedure was used in this way by Wegner et al. (1991) in their study of how natural and imposed transactive memory systems can affect the memories of real and artificial couples.

The fact that transactive memory systems mediated the effects of training on group performance helps to discount two alternative interpretations for our results. One such interpretation involves the role of contextual cues in memory. There is some evidence (Bjork & Richardson-Klavehn, 1989; Davies & Thomson, 1988) that people remember what they have learned better when memory is assessed under the same conditions in which learning occurred. This effect probably occurs because associations arise between various aspects of the context in which material is learned and the material itself. As a result, contextual factors can later serve as cues for retrieving that material from memory.

In our experiment, subjects in both training conditions could have used contextual cues involving the experimenter (e.g., her appearance or demeanor) or the laboratory setting (e.g., its sounds or appearance or temperature) as memory aids. However, another source of contextual cues was also available to subjects who were trained together rather than alone. Perhaps these subjects, whose skills at assembling radios were tested in the same groups where those skills were acquired, used *one another's* appearance or demeanor as memory cues. That might account for the superior performance of their groups. Note that this interpretation is quite different from our own. A contextual cues interpretation requires little interaction among group members, whose mere presence during testing may have been enough to help subjects remember how the radios should be assembled. In contrast, interaction among group members is essential for a transactive memory interpretation, which claims that people consulted one another during testing when they lacked information that others were believed to possess about assembling the radios.

Although a contextual cues interpretation of our results is interesting, the available evidence does not support it. When differences in transactive memory among groups were taken into account, the effect of training on group performance was no longer significant. In other words, *other* possible advantages associated with group training, such as providing group members with additional contextual cues, did not have much impact on group performance. Of course, the effects of contextual cues on group performance could be controlled through procedural rather than statistical means. In future research, we may modify the individual training condition so that group members are trained to assemble radios at the same time but cannot talk to one another, work together, or obtain information about one another's performance. This would allow contextual cues to operate in both the individual and group training conditions but still limit the creation of transactive memory systems to the group training condition.

A second alternative explanation for our results involves the role of group development in group performance. Group members who were trained together rather than alone spent much more time with one another, shared more work experiences, and so on. As a result, their groups probably attained higher levels of development (see LaCoursiere, 1980; Tuckman, 1965), resolving some of the problems (e.g., anxieties about acceptance, interpersonal conflicts) that can plague newer groups. Perhaps the superior performance of groups whose members were trained together reflected their developmental progress rather than their transactive memory systems.

This interpretation of our results is interesting as well, but the available evidence does not support it either. Group development is another potential advantage of group training. Although transactive memory systems may be found more often in older groups, they need not arise there. That is, a group may or may not develop an effective system of transactive memory as time passes. Group development and transactive memory are thus correlated but distinct phenomena. Our finding that training had no significant effects on group performance when differences in transactive memory among groups were taken into account thus becomes relevant once again. As we noted earlier, it means that *other* possible advantages associated with group training; such as fostering group development, did not have much impact on group performance. Two other findings from our research also seem relevant to this issue. First, behavioral evidence gathered from the videotapes allowed us to investigate such social factors as group cohesion and social identity, both of which are associated with group development (Ewert & Heywood, 1991; Kuypers, Davies, & Hazewinkel, 1986; Louche & Magnier, 1978). Yet training had no effects on group cohesion, and although social identity was indeed strengthened by training group members together rather than alone, social identity did not mediate the effects of training on group performance. Second, some of the groups we studied contained members who already knew one another prior to the experiment. Yet these groups, which probably developed more quickly and easily, did not perform any better than groups whose members were complete strangers. All these findings indicate that group development was not responsible for the superior performance of groups whose members were trained together rather than alone.

The results of our experiment suggest many directions for future research, but we are especially interested in several factors that might moderate the effects of group training on performance. We do not believe that groups whose members are trained together will always perform better than groups whose members are trained alone. But when will the advantages of group training be especially strong or weak? Several factors could be important in this regard. These factors include characteristics of the group, the task that the group performs, and the environment in which the group operates.

The composition of a work group (see Moreland & Levine, 1992) may be one important moderating factor. Some groups are relatively homogeneous— their members come from similar backgrounds, have comparable abilities, and share interests. But other groups are more heterogeneous, and the performance of these groups can suffer when differences among group members produce confusion and conflict (Jackson, 1991). Training the members of a heterogeneous group together rather than alone, so that they can learn to work together more smoothly, may therefore be especially advantageous. Another moderating factor that may be important is a group's task (see Steiner, 1972). Some tasks require little coordination among group members, but other tasks require group members to interact quickly and in complex ways (Argote, 1982; Murnighan & Conlon, 1991). Training the members of a group together rather than alone may be especially advantageous for tasks with greater coordination requirements. Finally, the amount of stress that a group experiences may also be an important moderating factor. Stressful working conditions, arising from time pressure, competition with other groups, or even physical danger, affect many groups. Staw, Sandelands, and Dutton (1981) have suggested that groups often respond to such conditions by becoming more "rigid." This rigidity involves a restriction in information processing (e.g., narrower or reduced attention) as well as a constriction in control (e.g., reliance on tradition or centralized power). More rigid groups generally perform less well, unless their members have developed strong and effective work routines. Such routines are more likely to be found in a group whose members were trained together rather than alone (see Goodman & Shah, 1992; Hall & Williams, 1966). This suggests that group training may be especially advantageous when a group must operate under stressful working conditions.

Some theorists (see Druckman & Bjork, 1991) have argued that group training is an interesting notion but is probably impractical because of turnover. Every group eventually loses some of its members, whose departure could damage the group's transactive memory system, especially when they possess unique knowledge or abilities. Indeed, Wegner, Giuliano, and Hertel (1985) have described with great poignancy the distress that people feel when broken relationships leave them unable to recover valuable information that their group once possessed. This suggests that turnover may actually have more harmful effects on groups whose members were trained together rather than alone. Of course, there may be ways to minimize these effects, such as building greater redundancy into the group's transactive memory system or selecting newcomers who match as closely as possible the oldtimers they are replacing. Moreland and Levine (1992) have also described several ways in which the socialization of newcomers might be altered to help them participate in a group's transactive memory system more quickly and easily. These ideas seem worthy of further investigation.

ACKNOWLEDGMENTS

This research was presented at the 1992 meetings of the Operations Research Society of America/The Institute of Management Science in San Francisco and at Carnegie Mellon University. The authors wish to thank participants in these forums for their very helpful comments.

REFERENCES

Andrews, D. H., Wang, W. L., & Bell, H. H. (1992). Training technologies applied to team training: Military examples. In R. W. Swezey & E. Salas (Eds.), *Teams: Their training and performance* (pp. 283–327). Norwood, NJ: Ablex.

Argote, L. (1982). Input uncertainty and organizational coordination in hospital emergency service units. *Administrative Science Quarterly, 27,* 420–434.

Argote, L. & McGrath, J. E. (1993). Group processes in organizations: Continuity and change. *International Review of Industrial and Organizational Psychology, 8,* 333–389.

Baldwin, T. T., & Ford, J. K. (1988). Transfer of training: A review and direction for future research. *Personnel Psychology, 41,* 63–105.

Baron, R. M., & Kenny, D. A. (1986). The moderator-mediator variable distinction in social psychological research: Conceptual, strategic, and statistical considerations. *Journal of Personality and Social Psychology, 51,* 1173–1182.

Bjork, R. A., & Richardson-Klavehn, A. (1989). On the puzzling relationship between environmental context and human memory. In I. Chizuko (Ed.), *Current issues in cognitive processes: The Tulane Flowerree Symposium on Cognition* (pp. 313–344). Hillsdale, NJ: Lawrence Erlbaum.

Briggs, G. E., & Naylor, J. C. (1965). Team versus individual training, training task fidelity, and task organization effects on transfer performance by three-man teams. *Journal of Applied Psychology, 49,* 387–391.

Brown, J. S., & Duguid, P. (1991). Organizational learning and communities of practice: Towards a unified view of working, learning, and innovation. *Organization Science, 2,* 40–57.

Burke, M. J., & Day, R. R. (1986). A cumulative study of the effectiveness of managerial training. *Journal of Applied Psychology, 71,* 232–245.

Davies, G. M., & Thomson, D. M. (1988). *Memory in context: Context in memory.* Chichester, England: Wiley.

Druckman, D., & Bjork, R. A. (Eds.). (1991). *In the mind's eye: Enhancing human performance.* Washington, DC: National Academy Press.

Dyer, J. L. (1985). *Annotated bibliography and state-of-the-art review of the field of team training as it relates to military teams.* Fort Benning, GA: Army Research Institute for the Behavioral and Social Sciences.

Evans, C. R., & Dion, K. (1991). Group cohesion and performance: A meta-analysis. *Small Group Research, 22,* 175–186.

Ewert, A., & Heywood, J. (1991). Group development in the natural environment: Expectations, outcomes, and techniques. *Environment and Behavior, 23,* 592–615.

Galbraith, C. S. (1990). Transferring core manufacturing technologies in high-technology firms. *California Management Review, 32,* 56–69.

George, C. E. (1967). Training for coordination within rifle squads. In T. O. Jacobs, J. S. Ward, T. R. Powers, C. E. George, & H. H. McFann (Eds.), *Individual and small-unit training for combat operations.* Alexandria, VA: George Washington University.

Georgenson, D. L. (1982). The problem of transfer calls for partnership. *Training and Development Journal, 36*(10), 75–78.

Goldstein, I. L. (1986). *Training in organizations: Needs as-*

sessment, development, and evaluation. Pacific Grove, CA: Brooks/Cole.

Goldstein, I. L. (1989). Critical training issues: Past, present, and future. In I. L. Goldstein and Associates, *Training and development in organizations.* San Francisco: Jossey-Bass.

Goldstein, I. L. (1991). Training in work organizations. In M. D. Dunnette & L. M. Hough (Eds.), *Handbook of industrial and organizational psychology* (2nd ed.). Palo Alto, CA: Consulting Psychologists Press.

Goodman, P. S., & Shah, S. (1992). Familiarity and work group outcomes. In S. Worchel. W. Wood, & J. A. Simpson (Eds.), *Group process and productivity* (pp. 276–298). Newbury Park, CA: Sage.

Guzzo, R. A. Jette, R. D., & Katzell, R. A. (1985). The effects of psychologically based intervention programs on worker productivity: A meta-analysis. *Personnel Psychology, 38,* 275–291.

Hall, J., & Williams, M. S. (1966). A comparison of decision-making performances in established and ad hoc groups. *Journal of Personality and Social Psychology, 3,* 214–222.

Hayes, R. H., & Clark, K. B. (1986, September-October). Why some factories are more productive than others. *Harvard Business Review,* pp. 66–73.

Hill, G. W. (1982). Group versus individual performance: Are N+1 heads better than one? *Psychological Bulletin, 91,* 517–539.

Jackson, S. E. (1991). Team composition in organizational settings: Issues in managing an increasingly diverse work force. In S. Worchel, W. Wood, & J. A. Simpson (Eds.), *Group process and productivity* (pp. 138–173). Newbury Park, CA: Sage.

Keller, R. T. (1986). Predictors of the performance of project groups in R & D organizations. *Academy of Management Journal, 29,* 715–726.

Kuypers, B. C., Davies, D., & Hazewinkel, A. (1986). Developmental patterns in self-analytic groups. *Human Relations, 39,* 793–815.

Labor letter: Training the workforce–corporate committment. (1991, October 22). *Wall Street Journal,* p. A-1.

Labor letter: Training holds. (1992, July 14). *Wall Street Journal,* p. A-1.

LaCoursiere, R. (1980). *The life cycle of groups: Group developmental stage theory.* New York: Human Sciences Press.

Laughlin, P. R., & Sweeney, J. D. (1977). Individual-to-group and group-to-individual transfer in problem solving. *Journal of Experimental Psychology: Human Learning and Memory, 3,* 246–254.

Levine, J. M., & Moreland, R. L. (1991). Culture and socialization in work groups. In L. B. Resnick, J. M. Levine, & S. D. Teasley (Eds.), *Perspectives on socially shared cognition* (pp. 257–279). Washington, DC: American Psychological Association.

Louche, C., & Magnier, J. P. (1978). Group development: Effects on intergroup and intragroup relations. *European Journal of Social Psychology, 8,* 387–391.

Moreland, R. L., & Levine, J. M. (1992). The composition of small groups. In E. J. Lawler, B. Markovsky, C. Ridgeway, & H. A. Walker (Eds.), *Advances in group processes* (Vol. 9, pp. 237–280). Greenwich, CT: JAI.

Morgan, B. B., Glickman, A. S., Woodard, E. A., Blaiwes, A. S., & Salas, E. (1986). *Measurement of team behaviors in a Navy environment* (NTSC Tech. Rep. No. 86–014). Orlando, FL: Naval Training Systems Center.

Murdock, P. E. (1989). Group cohesiveness and productivity: A closer look. *Human Relations, 42,* 771–785.

Murnighan, J. K, & Conlon, D. E. (1991). The dynamics of intense work groups: A study of British string quarters. *Administrative Science Quarterly, 36,* 165–186.

O'Reilly, C. A., & Caldwell, D. (1979). Informational influence as a determinant of perceived task characteristics and job satisfaction. *Journal of Applied Psychology, 64,* 157–165.

Salancik, G. R., & Pfeffer, J. (1978). A social information processing approach to job attitudes and task design. *Administrative Science Quarterly, 23,* 224–253.

Salas, E. (1993, January/February). Team training and performance. *Psychological Science Agenda,* pp. 9–11.

Stasser, G. (1992). Pooling of unshared information during group discussions. In S. Worchel, W. Wood, & J. A. Simpson (Eds.), *Group process and productivity* (pp. 48–67). Newbury Park, CA: Sage.

Stata, R. (1989). Organizational learning: The key to management innovation. *Sloan Management Review, 30,* 63–74.

Staw, B. M., Sandelands, L. E., & Dutton, J. E. (1981). Threat-rigidity effects in organizational behavior: A multi-level analysis. *Administrative Science Quarterly, 26,* 501–524.

Steiner, I. D. (1972). *Group process and productivity.* New York: Academic Press.

Tajfel, H., & Turner, J. C. (1986). The social identity theory of inter-group behavior. In S. Worchel & W. Austin (Eds.), *The social psychology of intergroup relations* (2nd ed., pp. 7–24). Pacific Grove, CA: Brooks-Cole.

Tuckman, B. W. (1965). Developmental sequence in small groups. *Psychological Bulletin, 63,* 384–399.

Webb, S., & Smith, A. (1991, June). IS training survey: Manufacturing training holds up as recession continues. *Industrial Society,* pp. 13–15.

Wegner, D. M. (1986). Transactive memory: A contemporary analysis of the group mind. In G. Mullen & G. Goethals (Eds.), *Theories of group behavior* (pp. 185–208). New York: Springer-Verlag.

Wegner, D. M., Erber, R., & Raymond, P. (1991). Transactive memory in close relationships. *Journal of Personality and Social Psychology, 61,* 923–929.

Wegner, D. M., Giuliano, T., & Hertel, P. (1985). Cognitive interdependence in close relationships. In W. J. Ickes (Ed.), *Compatible and incompatible relationships* (pp. 253–276). New York: Springer-Verlag.

Wexley, K. N., & Latham, G. P. (1981). *Developing and training human resources in organizations.* Glenview, IL: Scott, Foresman.

White, S. E., & Mitchell, T. R. (1979). Job enrichment versus social cues: A comparison and competitive test. *Journal of Applied Psychology, 64,* 1–9.

Wilder, D. A. (1986). Social categorization: Implications for creation and reduction of intergroup bias. In L. Berkowitz (Ed.), *Advances in experimental social psychology* (Vol. 19, pp. 291–355). Orlando, FL: Academic Press.

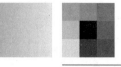

The Common Knowledge Effect: Information Sharing and Group Judgment

Daniel Gigone and Reid Hastie • Department of Psychology, University of Colorado

The hypothesis that the influence of an item of information on a group judgment is directly related to the number of group members who hold that information before group discussion was tested. Three-member groups read short descriptions of students and were asked to make individual and then group consensus judgements about those students' grades in the course. Information held by all members before group discussion had more influence on the group judgments than information held by only 1 member. However, no effect of information distribution was found when controlling for member judgments, suggesting that the impact of the information, and hence the effects of distribution across members, was mediated by its impact on individual-member prediscussion judgments. The group judgments were no more accurate than the average of the member judgments. Group members were not aware of the common knowledge effect's influence of their use of information.

The exchange and sharing of information is an important process in decision-making groups. The ability of groups to consider more information and to consider information from diverse sources is the primary reason that groups are expected to make better decisions than individuals acting alone. Members bring different informational resources to the group, which can be pooled to produce a group decision that is of higher quality than any of the group members could have produced with less complete information. Decision-making committees are often brought together for the express purpose of making a more informed decision through the exchange of initially unshared information. Committee members are often chosen with different backgrounds so that the committee will be able to make decisions based on a wider range of information. However, if groups do not pool information effectively, they will not make better decisions than individual decision makers.

The exchange of information in a group judgment task is essential when the various items of information are not initially available to all group members. In many group judgment situations, as when committee members are chosen from different backgrounds, individual group members are likely to bring different items of information to the group. In such a case, each group member can only base his or her opinion on the information that he or she brings to the task and any information that is exchanged with the group by other group members. If items of information are not exchanged, the group judgment will be based on incomplete information.

Stasser and his colleagues (Stasser, Taylor, & Hanna, 1989; Stasser & Titus, 1985, 1987) have invented a useful method to study the effects of information distributions across group members under controlled laboratory conditions. They gave subjects information about hypothetical candidates for the position of student body president. Some items of information were shared by all of the group members and some were unshared, held by only one of the group members. In some experimental conditions, 66% of the information about each candidate was fully shared, whereas in other conditions, only 33% of the information about each candidate was shared. Groups were then convened and asked to make a consensus decision on which of the candidates was most qualified for the position. The basic paradigm has been repeated with different-sized groups, with different total amounts of information about each of the hypothetical candidates, with different proportions of the information shared and unshared, with structured and unstructured group discussions, and with the overall available information biased toward one of the three candidates or the available information distributed to make the candidates equally attractive. Dependent measures have included the candidate selected, pre- and post discussion recall of informational items, pre- and post discussion individual judgments, and observational measures of the items of information that were exchanged during group discussion.

Stasser's studies showed that subjects generally do not effectively pool unshared information. Groups are more likely to discuss shared information than unshared information. This tendency increased with larger groups, higher overall information load, and a higher percentage of unshared information. Moreover, the tendency to discuss shared information biased the final group judgment in the direction of the initial information distribution. This bias occurred when the available information, if fully exchanged, should have led to a judgment in favor of a different candidate than the one who was initially favored. Only when there was a low overall information load and a high percentage of unshared information was there substantial discussion of the unshared information, and even here there was still a substantial bias in group decisions caused by the initial information distribution pattern.

Stasser explained his results in terms of an information sampling model (Stasser & Titus, 1985).

He claimed that the discussion bias toward shared information can be explained by looking at the probability that any one item of information will be recalled by any one of the group members. The task is disjunctive, because only one group member needs to remember an item in order for it to be discussed by the group. Thus, there is a higher overall probability that a shared item will be recalled by one of the group members than that an unshared item will be recalled by the only group member who possesses it. Stasser was able to use his information sampling model to explain his results concerning group size, information load, and level of information sharing.

However, Stasser's information sampling model fails to tell the whole story about information sharing and group judgment. It assumes that group judgments are the result of a quantitative summation of evidence for and against each candidate, that the group decision process is dominated by "informational influence" or "persuasive arguments" (cf. Burnstein, 1982; Deutsch & Gerard, 1955). His model, because it explains biased judgments in terms of the simple probability of discussion of an item of information, weights all items of information equally in the determination of the group judgment. Moreover, because the model focuses exclusively on the discussion of information, it does not necessarily account for all of the mechanisms that could lead to differences in influence between shared and unshared information. For example, unshared information that contradicts the prevailing opinions might be seen as more surprising and informative than unshared information that is in accordance with the prevailing opinions, and thus it may have a greater impact on the group discussion and its outcome (cf. Hastie, 1984). Also, information that is used to form an individual judgment might be weighted differently than information that is learned later through group discussion.

The present study was therefore designed to look more closely at the relationship between information sharing and the influence of information on group judgments. Specifically, it was designed to test the hypothesis that an item of information will have more influence on the judgment of a group when it is shared than when it is unshared. What we will call the "common knowledge effect" hypothesis can be stated more precisely: "The influence of a particular item of information is directly and positively related to the number of group members who have knowledge of that item before the group discussion and judgment."

Intuition suggests two ways in which shared information could have a relatively large influence on group judgments. First, information held by group members will likely influence their individual judgments. Those judgments, in turn, will influence the group judgment. A piece of information that is held by several group members will affect all of those members' prediscussion judgments and will therefore have a larger influence on the group judgment simply because of its impact on the members' prediscussion judgments. For example, information from a job candidate's job talk will influence the judgments that the audience members form about that candidate. When the hiring committee meets to make a group judgment about that candidate, the committee members probably will express their own judgments, which were influenced by the job talk. Even if the job talk itself is not mentioned, its impact will be conveyed through the members' opinions.

Second, as Stasser has emphasized, shared information can have an undue influence on the group judgment because it is a common reference point for the group members. Shared information might then be more likely to be discussed and evaluated during group discussion. The hiring committee might spend more time discussing members' impressions of the job talk, which all group members have attended, than the candidate's publications, which only a few members have read. If the group discussion focuses on shared information, that information could have inordinate influence on the group judgment. One goal of the present study is to distinguish between these two possible mechanisms that could mediate the hypothesized common knowledge effect.

In the present study, groups made judgments about the grades received by other undergraduate students in an introductory psychology class. These judgments were based on information about each to-be-judged student's academic ability (e.g., high school grade point average and aptitude test percentile score) and motivation (e.g., enjoyment of the course). Obviously, the given information was relevant to the judgments that were to be made. However, there was likely to be disagreement among group members concerning the importance of the various items of information and the relationship of each item to the course grade of a typi-cal psychology student. The grade judgment task was chosen for two reasons. First, undergraduate subjects should be familiar with making this type of a judgment. They undoubtedly have the opportunity to infer from uncertain information what grade they themselves or other students will receive in a course. Second, the grade judgments can be tested for accuracy. Judgments about a stimulus case can be compared with a criterion, the actual grade that the stimulus student received in the course.

The present study used a task that was designed to maximize the probability that unshared items of information would be discussed by the group. Subjects were assigned to three-member groups. Moreover, the total available information about each to-be-judged student consisted of only six items. In the present study, two of the information items were fully shared, two items were unshared, and two items were known by two of the three group members before any discussion. In addition, subjects made a series of 32 judgments, receiving as a group the same six items of information about each to-be-judged student. Thus, each group member should have been aware of the types of information that were available to the group and which of those he or she did not receive. According to Stasser, all of these factors should have led to a high level of discussion of unshared information. The groups in the present study were the same size as Stasser's smallest groups. Even in the lowest load condition, each of Stasser's subjects had to remember 12 items of information about each of three hypothetical candidates, for a total of 36 items. The present study does not correspond exactly to any of Stasser's levels of sharing, although it could be seen as falling somewhere between the 33% and 66% conditions. However, the common knowledge effect hypothesis predicts that shared information should have more influence on the group judgment, even if the unshared information is discussed fully.

Although the present judgment paradigm has some valuable qualities, questions can be raised concerning its external validity. Artificial groups of subjects made a large number of judgments in a relatively short period of time and at low cost to themselves or others. These conditions might have led subjects to use simple heuristics in making their member and group judgments. Moreover, each group member made a written judgment before the group discussion of each case. Thus, a member might be likely to be committed to his or her initial judgment. Such a commitment effect might discourage members from discussing or considering additional information while they are attempting to reach a group consensus. In sum, the results of the present study would not be of particular interest if they were primarily due to the structure of the research paradigm and if that paradigm did not correspond to common real-world group judgment settings.

However, the present paradigm was analogous to a number of authentic group judgment settings. Many committees meet to make several similar judgments or decisions from a relatively small amount of information. For example, a university petition review committee may make a series of quick judgments concerning the merit of various petitions to waive requirements, extend deadlines, and so on; a college admissions committee will consider the strengths and weaknesses of hundreds of applicants; a salary review committee will meet periodically to assess the amount of salary increase deserved by various employees; and a research grant review panel will meet to review 50 proposals. In each of these cases, the group has limited time in which to make a large number of decisions. In addition, members of such groups might implicitly, or even explicitly, commit themselves to individual judgments before group discussion of each case. For example, each member of the admissions committee might make a recommendation based on his or her individual review of an applicant's file. Only if there is disagreement about a particular applicant might group discussion of that case occur. Moreover, in any of the above examples, judgment-relevant information could be differentially distributed among group members. We contend, therefore, that the present research paradigm is relevant and general.

A recent study by Stasser and Stewart (1992) provides some insight into what might be expected from the present judgment task. They found that the bias resulting from unshared information was greater for judgmental tasks, for which groups make judgments based on an assessment of evidence, than for intellective tasks, for which groups believe that there is a demonstrably correct solution to a problem. Groups that do not believe there is enough information to reach a demonstrably correct answer will be motivated in their information search to reach a consensus. The present judgment task clearly falls on the judgmental end of

the task continuum. Although our subjects were informed that there was a "correct" judgment for each case—the actual grade received by that student—they had no way of demonstrating the correctness of their judgments. Thus, according to Stasser and Stewart, the unequal distribution of information would be likely to bias group judgments in our research task. Likewise, differential distribution of information among group members might bias the judgments of real-world groups such as the ones described above. However, Stasser and Stewart again explained the differences between types of tasks in terms of the tendency of group members to be biased in their sampling of unshared information from memory. We argue that judgment bias in the present task cannot be explained by differential pooling rates for shared and unshared cues.

In his review of group accuracy research, Hastie (1986) made a similar distinction between types of group judgment tasks. He argued that groups tended to be more accurate than their average members only when the task involved a demonstrably correct solution. In the present task, then, a group's judgments would not be expected to be more accurate, on average, than the mean of its members' judgments, at least in the fully shared information control condition. However, with differential distribution of information among group members, a group could have the potential to judge more accurately than the average of its members. Valuable information that was withheld from some group members before their member judgments could be pooled during the group discussion. Thus, whereas the members would typically make many of their judgments without the aid of some judgment-relevant information, the group would be potentially fully informed before every judgment. Such groups might be expected to make more accurate judgments than the average individual group member.

Social judgment theory (Brehmer & Joyce, 1988; Hammond, Stewart, Brehmer, & Steinmann, 1986) is a framework for the analysis of the use of information in judgment. An item of information, which is called a *cue*, has some true relationship with the *criterion*, the true state of the judgment target. There is, for example, some true relationship between the high school grade point average of a sample of students and the grades that they tend to receive in introductory psychology courses. The relationship between cues and the criterion can vary in both strength ("ecological validity") and form. For example, a cue could be more or less strongly related to the criterion and that relationship could be either linear or quadratic. Symmetrically, there is some relationship between each cue and the judgment that is made, and these relationships can vary in strength ("cue utilization") and form.

Because of the symmetric relationships between cues and criterion and between cues and judgment, this formulation is known as the "lens model" of judgment (Brunswik, 1956; Hammond, 1966). The strength and form of the relationships between cues and judgments across multiple judgments is known as the judgment policy of the judge. To the extent that this judgment policy matches the true relationships between criterion and cues, the judgments will be accurate, differing from the criterion only because of random error. In making a judgment, then, the individual or group can be described as using a judgment policy to infer the criterion from the available set of cues.

Across a series of judgments, the judgment policy of an individual or group can be determined by running a regression analysis, with the set of cues used in the task as the independent variables and the judgment that is made as the dependent variable (Hammond et al., 1986; Harmon & Rohrbaugh, 1990; Slovic & Lichtenstein, 1971; Stewart, 1988). The presence of reliable interaction or higher-order coefficients would indicate that there were dependencies between cues or that the form of the cue utilization was nonlinear. Within a judgment task, the relative importance or influence of the cues can be compared by standardizing the regression coefficients to account for the scaling and variation of the cue values. Thus, social judgment theory provides a method for comparing the influence of a cue on judgments under different experimental conditions. Although this statistical policy-capture approach has been used extensively to study the influence of information on individual judgments, it has not, to our knowledge, been used before to study group judgment policies. Other researchers have measured changes in the judgment policies of individuals resulting from the resolution of group judgment conflict (cf. Brehmer & Hammond, 1973).

Thus, the group judgment policy provides one useful summary of the group process. Variations in the group's information usage in making a judgment are reflected in the policy weights that correspond to the different cues. A cue that has a strong influence on the judgments made by the group will be heavily weighted in the group judgment policy. The issue of what affects the utilization of information in group judgment can therefore be restated in terms of the group judgment policy. Those factors that affect the cue utilization weights in the group judgment policy do so through their influence on the group's usage of information in making judgments.

Several factors will affect individual judgment policy weights in a multiple cue judgment task. First, the judgment policy will be influenced by the judge's "theories" about the usefulness of each cue. If a person believes that aptitude test scores are the best predictors of college academic performance, that cue will be weighted heavily in the person's judgments about college course grades. Second, judgments will be influenced by cue-response scale commensurability (Slovic, Griffin, & Tversky, 1990; Slovic & MacPhillamy, 1974). A cue that is expressed on the same scale as the required judgment response is likely to receive more weight than a cue that is more difficult to map onto the response scale. Third, cue order, either in presentation or in discussion, probably affects judgment policy weight. A cue that is always presented first or discussed first might anchor a person's judgments, with later cues leading to adjustments in the judgments. Fourth, the salience or dramatic quality of a cue might affect its weight in judgment. A cue that is presented in a novel typeface or that is likely to evoke a vivid image or an emotional reaction, for example, might have more weight than if it were presented in a less distinctive manner. Finally, we expect that the weight of a cue in the group judgment policy will be influenced by its distribution among group members. The possibility of this last "group level" factor having an influence on cue utilization is the focus of the present study.

According to the common knowledge effect hypothesis, the group will use a different judgment policy if a cue is always shared than if it is always unshared. More specifically, the cue utilization ("weight") for a cue will increase as the number of group members who possess the cue before the group discussion increases.

The common knowledge effect hypothesis can be tested by comparing the utilization of each cue in the judgments of group with different levels of sharing for that cue. According to the hypothesis, the standardized simple regression coefficient for a cue will be larger for a group in which all three group members always receive that item of information than for groups in which only one member ever receives the cue. Cue utilization for the condition in which two members receive that item of information should fall somewhere between the other two conditions. We expected that the judgment policy would be an additive linear relationship between the cue set and the judgments, with no interactions or higher order relationships in the model. With relatively simple judgments being made by nonexperts, in a small amount of time, it seems unlikely that the judges would rely on complex judgment strategies. The validity of this hypothesis about the judgment policies can be evaluated empirically by testing the goodness of fit of more complex models.

Method

Overview

College student subjects met in three-member groups to make judgments about the grades received by 32 stimulus students in an introductory psychology course. Each group member first received information about a stimulus student and made an individual judgment about that student. When all three group members had completed their individual judgments, the stimulus case information and the members' judgments were collected. The group members then discussed that stimulus case until they came to a consensus group judgment. That group judgment was collected and the information about the next stimulus case was distributed to the members. The above steps were repeated for each of the 32 stimulus cases (and for four repeated stimulus cases, which were used as a test of judgment reliability).

Subjects

University of Colorado students participated in the study as partial fulfillment of a research experience requirement of introductory psychology courses. Subjects were randomly assigned to three-member groups, composing three experimental conditions and one control condition. A total of 120 subjects participated as members of 40 groups, with 10 groups assigned to each condition. Seventy-seven of the subjects were male and 43 were female, but no effects of subject gender (individually or in the composition of the experimental groups) were observed in any statistical analysis, and so we will ignore this variable in the remainder of the present report.

Materials

The 32 stimulus cases were selected out of a pool of 504 students who had completed one of several introductory psychology courses during the previous year. Information about these students had been collected both from university records and from a voluntary questionnaire that was distributed at the end of the semester.

Six items of information were chosen as cues for the judgment task. These items consisted of high school grade point average, Scholastic Achievement Test of American College Test percentile score (averaged across the mathematics and verbal sections), self-reported percentage of lectures and recitations attended for the course, self-rated enjoyment of the class, self-rated academic anxiety, and self-rated workload in other courses. These cues were chosen to represent both ability and motivational variables and different strengths of relationship with the received course grades (ecological validity).

The 32 judgment cases were chosen to maximize the variability of the sets of cues to make more easily discernible the relationship between each cue and the judgments that are made. Three individual case profiles were created for each target within each condition. The individual profiles consisted of a piece of paper containing labels and values for each of the included cues. The order of the listed cues varied between stimulus cases and between the three profiles for each stimulus case.

Within each condition, the six informational cues were distributed such that the same two cues were always shared by all three group members, two other cues were always shared by two of the group members, and the remaining two cues were always given to only one group member, with the specific group members receiving a particular unshared cue varying across stimulus cases. Thus, each group member always received four items of information about each stimulus case. If the group members pooled their information, all six cues would be available to them. Between conditions, the cues were distributed such that in the first condition, a given cue (e.g., high school grade point average) was always shared by all three group members, in another condition that cue was always shared by two group members, and in the third condition, that cue was always given to a single group member. Thus, between conditions, each cue varied in the level of sharing.

Finally, a "fully shared information" control condition was run, in which all three group members always received all six of the judgment cues. This control condition was not strictly equivalent to the three experimental conditions, as members in the control condition groups received more information before each judgment than did members in the experimental condition groups. However, one goal of the present research was to compare information utilization of groups with that of their constituent members. Only by presenting all six cues to a member before each of the 32 judgments could we obtain unbiased estimates of the relationship between each cue and that member's judgments, controlling for the other five cues.

Table 1 shows the distribution of information in each of the four conditions.

Procedure

The procedures were the same for all conditions, except for the differences in information distribution that were described above. Participants met in groups of three. Preliminary instructions stated that the experiment was designed to study committee decision making. Subjects were told that they would be making judgments about the grades received by actual introductory psychology students like themselves and that they would be bas-

TABLE 1. Distribution of Information by Experimental Condition: Number of Group Members Sharing Each Cue

Cue	Experimental condition			
	1	2	3	Control
ACT or SAT percentile	1	3	2	3
Attendance percentage	2	3	1	3
High school grade point average	3	1	2	3
Enjoyment	2	1	3	3
Other workload	3	2	1	3
Self-rated anxiety	1	2	3	3

Note. ACT = American College Test; SAT = Scholastic Achievement Test.

ing their judgments on information about these students that was collected from university records and from a questionnaire.

The subjects were next asked to fill out the actual questionnaire from which the self-reported cues (enjoyment of the course, course attendance, and academic anxiety) were collected. They were told that they were completing the questionnaire to see for themselves how the information was collected.

Next, the subjects received a sheet describing each of the cues. They were also informed that the judgment cases would include a representative range of received course grades and that, as in a real committee, they might not receive all of the same information as the other group members.

Subjects were next asked to express their subjective judgment policies for the six included cues by assigning relative weights to the cues, summing to 100, such that the weight for each cue represented how important that cue would be in judging what grade a student received in the introductory psychology course.

The group then completed an example judgment. Each group member was given an individual judgment case containing example cue values. For this practice case, each group member received the same five cues. They were informed that they were to make as accurate an individual grade judgment as possible from the information given by circling one of the 12 grades listed on the bottom of the sheet (from F to A, including pluses and minuses, but excluding F−, F+, and A+). After all three group members had completed the example individual judgment and returned the individual judgment sheets to the experimenter, they were informed that they were to discuss the case until they had reached a group consensus about the grade received by that student in the course. They were told that after a consensus had been reached, one of the members, who had been arbitrarily chosen as the recorder, was to record the group judgment by circling one of the grades on a group judgment sheet. They were informed that they would be taped during the group discussion so that a record could be kept of the content of their discussion.

The subjects then completed the individual and group judgment phases for each of the 32 cases. The cases were presented to each group in a different random order. An audio recording was made of the group discussion portion for each case. After the 32 cases had been completed, four of the original cases were repeated as a check of judgment consistency. The subjects were not informed that they had judged these cases before. The groups completed the 36 judgments in a mean time of 54 min. There were no reliable differences between the mean completion times of the groups in the experimental and control conditions.

After all of the 36 individual and group judgments were completed, the subjects completed a short final questionnaire. In this questionnaire, they were asked to report how accurate they thought the group judgments were, to rank the group members in order of accuracy of member judgments, and to rank the group members in order of influence on the group judgments. In addition, subjects repeated the subjective judgment policy weighting measure. After they completed the final questionnaire, subjects were informed of the true purpose of the study and excused.

Results

Overview

Our analysis is presented in an individual to group order. First, we apply regression analysis to capture some of the abstract characteristics of the judgment task and the judgment "policies" followed by members making individual prediscussion judgments. Then we turn to the analysis of the group judgment process and evaluate the extent to which the common knowledge effect hypothesis appears to be manifested in our results. Finally, we attempt to separate the impacts of the members' prediscussion judgments and the discussion contents on the group judgments, again relying on regression analysis to organize our analysis.

Member Judgments

Reliability. For the member judgments, the average correlation between the first and second judgments for the four stimulus cases that were repeated was .57 for members in the experimental groups and .74 for members in the control group, both of which were reliably greater than zero, $F(1, 29) = 33.0, SD = 0.65, p < .0001$, and $F(1, 9) = 32.7, SD = 0.52, p < .001$, respectively.

There was no difference in average member judgment reliability between experimental conditions, $F(2, 27) = 1.28$, *ns*, or between members in

the experimental groups and members in the control groups, $F(1, 37) = 1.83$, *ns*,

Member judgment policies. If group members were utilizing cue information in a linear additive manner, linear regression can be used to ascertain the judgment policies of the individual group members. Regressing a group member's 32 grade judgments on the values of the corresponding stimulus cues provides a model of cue utilization. Such a procedure cannot be performed for the individual subjects in the three experimental conditions, because those subjects were missing information for every judgment; each subject only received four of the six cues for each case. In their judgments, subjects could not utilize information that they did not have and the regression estimates of judgment policy would be confounded with the experimental manipulation.

However, member judgment policies could be obtained for the subjects in the control condition, in which all three group members always received all six of the stimulus cues for every stimulus case. The absolute average standardized regression coefficients for these group members are shown in Figure 1. The analysis shows that the grade judgments of individual subjects were influenced most heavily by the high school grade point average and aptitude test percentile cues, somewhat less by at-

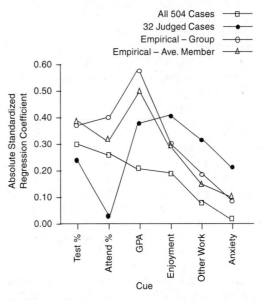

FIGURE 1 ■ Best linear models versus mean group and member empirical judgment policies (control condition groups). (Ave. = average; GPA = grade point average.)

tendance and enjoyment, and very little by other workload and self-rated academic anxiety.

Throughout the analyses, we relied on average results to summarize individual and group judgment policies. In every case, we conducted fine-grained analyses of policies at the appropriate level and observed some variation in the patterns of weights obtained. For example, cluster analyses of the individual judgment policy weights obtained from the control group subjects (who received full six-cue information sets on each judgment trial) revealed three groupings of subjects according to their policies. However, the averaged data provides a fair representation of the typical and predominant patterns of cue utilization in judgment in every case in which we report statistics at that level.

One question of interest is how well the judgment policies of the individual group members matched the optimal linear model weights, summarizing the true relationships between variables. Did the group members use the available information correctly? This question was answered by comparing the individual judgment policies with the best model for the data from which the judgment stimulus cases were chosen. Five hundred four cases in the data set had values for all six of the informational cues that were presented to the subjects. The optimal linear weights were obtained by regressing the actual grades received by the students on the six cues: High school grade point average, aptitude test percentile, attendance, self-rated enjoyment of the course, self-rated academic anxiety, and self-rated other workload. The coefficients in this model represented the ecological validity of the cues—how the cues truly were related to the course grades. The absolute standardized regression coefficients for the 504 cases are also shown in Figure 1. The parameter estimate for other workload was negative, whereas the parameter estimate for anxiety was not reliably different from zero, $F(1, 497) = 0.10$, ns. The model including the six cues as predictors accounted for 29% of the variance in introductory psychology course grades, $F(6, 497) = 33.1$, $p < .0001$.

We also tested for more complex relationships between the cues and the criterion. A test of all of the two-way interactions between pairs of cues revealed reliable positive interactions between the high school grade point average and aptitude test percentile cues, $F(1, 482) = 7.92$, partial $r^2 = .02$, $p < .01$, and between the other workload and the anxiety cues $F(1, 482) = 5.60$, partial $r^2 = .01$, $p <$

.05. In another model testing for the quadratic affect of each cue, we found a positive quadratic effect of high school grade point average, $F(1, 491) = 10.1$, partial $r^2 = .02$, $p < .01$. However, adding the two interactions and the quadratic effect of high school grade point average to the model predicting course grades from the six cues only reduced the error by an additional 4.4%. Therefore, we concluded that a simple linear model adequately describes the true relationships in the data.

The best linear model for the 32 to-be-judged cases is also graphed in Figure 1. The plotted points show the absolute standardized regression coefficients from a model regressing introductory psychology course grade on all six cues. As was noted previously, the 32 cases were chosen to maximize variability in the values of all six cues. The resulting cue-to-grade relationships were somewhat different from the optimal model for all 504 students. The best linear model for the 32 cases accounted for 42% of the variance in course grades, $F(6, 25) = 3.00$, $p < .05$. The coefficients for aptitude percentile, attendance percentage, and other workload were not significantly different from zero. The coefficients for other workload and anxiety were negative. For these 32 cases, the correlation between the predictions from the best linear model for all 504 students and the predictions from the best linear model for the 32 to-be-judged students was $r = .79$, $p < .0001$.

Again, the average individual judgment policies of the control group subjects can be compared with these optimal linear weights. As shown in Figure 1, the subjects relied more on each of the cues than they should have, according to the best linear model. Such an overutilization makes sense, as the judges only had these six cues on which to base their judgment, whereas in the real world there likely are many other variables that covary with introductory psychology grades. Although the overutilization of cues leads to differences between the judged grades and the actual grades, the correlation between judged grades and actual grades would still be high if the two patterns of cue usage are similar.

A comparison of lines in Figure 1 shows that the judgment policies of the individual subjects followed fairly closely the form of the optimal linear weights. The exception to this generalization, the exceptionally high weights for the high school grade point average cue, probably represents a cue-response scale commensurability effect of the type that has been frequently observed in other judgment studies: When a cue is presented on the same scale as the response, it tends to receive a large weight in the judgment policy (Slovic, Griffin, & Tversky, 1990; Slovic & MacPhillamy, 1974). Otherwise, the judgment policies of the individual members in the control groups followed a pattern similar to the best linear model. The average correlation between the 32 judgments of each control group member and the grade for each of the 32 cases that was predicted by the best linear model was .68, which was reliably different from zero, $F(1, 9) = 287.6$, SD = 0.15, $p < .0001$. It appears, therefore, that these subjects were using the available information in a (linear, additive) way that reflects the true relationships between the variables.

Insight. We were also interested in whether the subjects were aware of how they were using the provided information. All of the subjects were asked to give their subjective judgment policies both before and after they made the grade judgments. In each case, the subjects were asked to divide 100 points between the six stimulus cues according to how important they thought each cue should be in the grade judgment. The means for the post judgment subjective judgment policies are shown in Figure 2. A comparison of these mean subjective influence ratings with the average member judgment weights suggests that subjects are unaware of the relatively high influence of the high

school grade point average and aptitude test percentile cues on their judgments.

Accuracy. As a measure of individual judgment accuracy, a correlation was calculated for each subject between his or her individual grade judgments and the actual grades across the 32 stimulus cases. All analyses involving these correlations, and all others in the study using correlations as the dependent variable, were performed after first converting the correlations to Fisher's z scores, to correct for heterogeneity of error variance (Judd & McClelland, 1989). The correlations also were averaged within each group, because the levels of accuracy for the members of a particular group are likely not to be independent from each other.

The average correlations between individual judgments and actual grades for each condition are presented in Table 2. All of the average correlations are reliably greater than zero. The accuracy of the group members' judgments is reliably different among the three experimental conditions, $F(2, 27) = 12.3$, $R^2 = .48$, $p < .001$. This between-conditions difference in member judgment accuracy was expected, because group members in the different conditions received information of different cue validity, on average, because of the manipulation of information sharing. However, it is surprising that the subjects in Condition 2 were the least accurate; those subjects received aptitude percentiles and attendance percentages for every stimulus case, the two cues that should have been the most useful in making judgments. The accuracy of group members in the experimental conditions was not significantly different from the accuracy of group members in the control condition, $F(1, 38) = 2.16$, *ns*. Even though the control group members received more information about each stimulus case (six cues each), they were not more accurate than the experimental group subjects (who received four cues each).

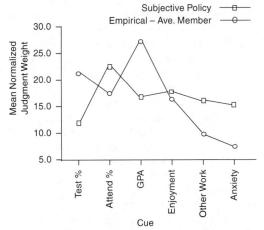

FIGURE 2 ■ Mean postexperiment subjective judgment policy (control condition groups) versus mean member empirical judgment policy (normalized to sum to 100). (Ave. = average; GPA = grade point average.)

TABLE 2. Mean Member Judgment Accuracy by Condition

| Accuracy measure | Experimental condition | | | |
	1	2	3	Control
Correlation: Member judgment vs. actual grade	.41	.23	.32	.38
Correlation: Member judgment vs. grade predicted by best linear model	.59	.60	.56	.68

An alternative measure of accuracy considers the magnitude of the difference between each judgment and the corresponding criterion. Judgments that had patterns of relative differences similar to those of the criterion grades, and therefore a high accuracy correlation, could still be inaccurate in terms of overestimating or underestimating the criterion grades. To explore the absolute accuracy of member judgments, we averaged the absolute differences between each member's judgments and the corresponding criterion grades. This absolute difference measure of accuracy showed the same pattern of differences between conditions, with the groups in Condition 2 being the least accurate and with no mean difference between groups in the experimental conditions and groups in the control conditions.

The social judgment theory analysis suggests another conceptualization of judgment accuracy. According to social judgment theory, an accurate judge would use a judgment policy that is similar to the validity of cues in the environment. Thus, a measure of judge accuracy over multiple judgments would compare the predictions of that judge's judgment policy to the predictions of the best model of cue validity. However, we were not able to estimate the judgment policies of individuals in the experimental conditions. Instead, we computed correlations between the predictions of the best linear model for all 504 cases in the data set and the 32 judgments of each group member. These correlations measure how similar the judgments of each member are to the judgments that he or she would make if the linear relationship of cues to the criteria were known. Table 2 shows the means of these correlations by condition. The mean correlation between best model predictions and member judgments did not differ among experimental conditions or between the experimental conditions and the control condition.

Group Judgments

Reliability. The average correlation between the group judgment for the first and second repetition of the four repeated stimulus cases was .87 for the experimental groups and .84 for the control groups. Both average reliabilities were significantly greater than zero, $F(1, 29) = 65.6$, $SD = 0.79$, $p < .0001$, and $F(1, 9) = 40.0$, $SD = 0.58$, $p < .001$, respectively. There were no differences in average group

reliability between groups in the 3 experimental conditions, $F(2, 27) = 0.66$, *ns*, or between the experimental groups and the control groups, $F(1, 37) = 0.03$, *ns*. For the experimental groups, the group judgments were more reliable, on average, than were the judgments of their members, $F(1, 29) = 17.5$, $SD = 0.68$, $p < .001$; this difference was not significant for the control groups, $F(1, 9) = 2.14$, *ns*.

Group judgment policies (common knowledge effect). At the level of group judgments, regressing the group grade judgments on the six stimulus cue values provides a measure of the influence of each cue on the group judgment. The judgment policies of the full sharing control groups again provide a measure of information usage that is not confounded by differences in information distribution. The mean standardized regression weights for these groups are presented in Figure 1. For these groups, the group judgment policies are very similar to the member judgment policies.

The common knowledge effect hypothesis implies that the experimental groups' judgment policies should differ from condition to condition because of differential distribution of information. Recall our prediction is that the more members who are given a cue, the greater the impact on the group judgment (indexed by the standardized regression weight). To test this hypothesis, a one-way analysis of variance (ANOVA) was performed for each of the six cues. In these analyses, the absolute standardized regression weight for each stimulus cue was used as the dependent measure, with number of group members holding that cue as the between-groups factor. (It should be noted that these six ANOVAs are not independent tests of the hypothesis, as the influence given to any one cue by a group likely affects the influences of the other five cues.)

The relationships between cue distribution and mean regression coefficients for each cue are shown in Figure 3. Significant linear effects of cue "sharedness" on the weight of that cue in the group judgment policy were found for 4 of the 6 stimulus cues. The effect was found for aptitude test percentile, $F(1, 27) = 26.7$, partial $r^2 = .50$, $p < .0001$, attendance percentage, $F(1, 27) = 58.6$, partial $r^2 = .68$, $p < .0001$, high school grade point average, $F(1, 27) = 44.9$, partial $r^2 = .62$, $p < .0001$, and enjoyment, $F(1, 27) = 23.3$, partial $r^2 = .46$, $p < .0001$. For these cues, more sharing led to greater impact.

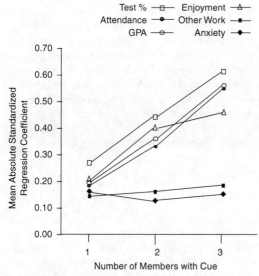

Test % —□— Enjoyment —△—
Attendance —●— Other Work —■—
GPA —○— Anxiety —◆—

FIGURE 3 ■ Effect of cue sharing on group judgment policy weights. (GPA = grade point average.)

TABLE 3. Mean Group Judgment Accuracy by Condition

| Accuracy measure | Experimental condition | | | |
	1	2	3	Control
Correlation: Group judgment vs. actual grade	.50	.29	.41	.43
Correlation: Mean member judgment vs. actual grade	.53	.29	.41	.44
Correlation: Group judgment vs. grade predicted by best linear model	.72	.75	.72	.73
Correlation: Mean member judgment vs. grade predicted by best linear model	.76	.73	.73	.75

If there is a direct linear relationship between level of sharing and influence of a cue, then the coefficient when that cue was shared by two group members should fall near the mean of the other two levels of sharing. Enjoyment was the only cue for which the influence was reliably different when shared by two group members than the average of the other two levels of sharing, $F(1, 27) = 7.81$, partial $r^2 = .22$, $p < .01$. There were no reliable differences between levels of sharing for the influence of other workload or self-rated anxiety cues.

Accuracy. To assess group judgment accuracy, the grade judgments of each group were correlated with the actual stimulus case grades. The average correlations for each condition are reported in Table 3. Again, there were reliable differences in accuracy due to experimental condition, $F(2, 27) = 10.97$, $R^2 = .72$, $p < .001$. The average group accuracy correlations of the experimental conditions and the control condition were not significantly different, $F(1, 38) = 0.39$, *ns*.

We also looked at the average absolute group judgment accuracies, computed as the average absolute difference between a group's judgments and the criterion grades. Again, the pattern of between-groups differences for these scores was similar to that of the judgment–criterion correlations.

Table 3 also shows the mean correlations between the group judgments and the grades predicted by the best linear model. These correlations give an indication of how well the groups were using the case information, in comparison with the true relationships between cues and criterion grades. No significant between-conditions differences were found.

Did the judgments improve as a result of group discussion? To address this question, we compared the group accuracy correlation of each group with the average accuracy correlation of the group's three members. The difference between the accuracy of the group judgments and the accuracy of the individual member judgments was reliable for the experimental conditions, $F(1, 29) = 44.8$, $SD = 0.08$, $p < .0001$, and marginally reliable for the control groups, $F(1, 9) = 4.25$, $SD = 0.09$, $p = .07$. On average, the judgments of the groups were more accurate than the judgments of their constituent members. This difference is easily explained as due to the cancellation of random judgment error through aggregation (cf. Davis, 1969). Simply by statistically pooling their judgments, by averaging them, for example, the three group members would be likely to improve their judgment accuracy.

Of more interest, then, is whether the group judgments were more accurate than the composite judgment obtained by averaging the three member judgments for each case. That is, did the group discussion add any more to judgment accuracy than would have occurred had the members' judgments about each case simply been averaged? The average correlation between the mean of the three member judgments and the actual grades is shown in Table 3. The accuracy of the group judgments was not reliably different from the accuracy of the average of the member judgments for either the groups in the three experimental conditions, $F(1, 29) = 0.90$, ns, or the groups in the control condition, $F(1, 9) = 0.01$, ns. The group judgments were not more accurate than a statistical pooling of the three members' judgments.

To gain a clearer understanding of the relationship between group and member judgment accuracy, we ranked each group's judgment accuracy correlation in relation to the judgment accuracy correlations of its constituent members. A ranking of 1, for example, indicated that the group judged more accurately than any of its members, a ranking of 2 indicated that the group was less accurate than one member, and so on. The mean group versus member accuracy rank was $M = 1.83$ for the experimental groups and $M = 1.90$ for the control groups. In the experimental conditions, 10 of 30 groups were more accurate than any of their members, whereas none was less accurate than all of its members. In the control groups, 4 of 10 groups were more accurate than all of their members and 1 was less accurate than all of its members.

Sniezek and Henry (1989) found that groups with initial judgment disagreement between members made more accurate group judgments than did groups whose members were in agreement. In the present study, groups may have pooled more information, spent more time discussing the case, or paid more attention to unshared information when their initial member judgments were in disagreement. We measured member disagreement about each case by taking the mean of the three absolute differences between pairs of member judgments. We then correlated this measure with the absolute difference between the group judgment and the criterion grade across the 32 cases. These correlations measured the relationship between average member judgment disagreement and group judgment accuracy for each group. Contrary to Sniezek and Henry's findings, the mean disagreement–accuracy correlation was not significantly different from zero for groups in any of the experimental or control conditions. However, the present judgment paradigm differed from the one used by Sniezek and Henry. Their groups made estimates of unfamiliar quantities, the frequency

of deaths from various causes. Therefore, a group member whose judgment was discrepant from the other members may have been more knowledgeable and therefore more accurate. A member who was knowledgeable probably would have little trouble convincing the other group members of his or her opinion. In addition, Sniezek and Henry used the geometric mean as a measure of judgment accuracy, which may have had properties different from our own accuracy measures.

Relationship Between Individual and Group Judgments

Another issue of interest is whether the stimulus cues have any effect on the group judgments, beyond the effect that they have on the individual judgments. Do the groups simply pool the individual member judgments, or do the values of the cues have an additional effect, even when controlling for the individual judgments? This question was addressed by regressing the group judgments on the individual judgments of each of the three group members, along with the set of six stimulus cues. For the experimental conditions, only the coefficient for attendance was reliably greater than zero, $F(1,29) = 8.3$, $SD = 0.12$, $p < .01$. In general, the information that was provided to the groups did not have an effect on the group judgments above and beyond its mediated effect through the group members' judgments.

Even though they are not greater than zero, on average, the direct influences of the cues could be tested to determine whether they show an effect of level of sharing. Again, mean absolute values of the standardized regression coefficients were used as a measure of cue influence. The mean regression weights for each condition are shown in Figure 4. The test of the difference between the unshared (held by one member) and fully shared (held by three members) conditions was not reliable for any of the cues. In this judgment task, information distribution does not appear to have an effect on the group judgment policies. and beyond its effect mediated through the individual judgments.

How, then, are the group members combining their judgments into a group judgment? They might simply be averaging their member judgments. The mean correlation between each group's judgments and the average of its members' judgments was .94 for the groups in the experimental

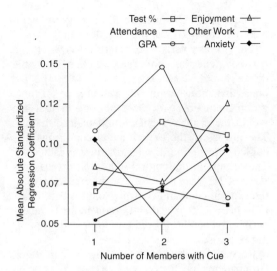

FIGURE 4 ■ Effect of cue sharing on group judgment policy weights, controlling for member judgments. (GPA = grade point average.)

conditions and .96 for the groups in the control conditions, both reliably different from zero. Although the case is strong for an averaging combination rule, some of the groups seemed to be using a different strategy on at least some of the cases. From their group discussion, they seemed to be averaging the closest two members' judgments and ignoring the third member's judgment. The mean correlation between the groups' judgments and the mean of the two closest judgments of their constituent members was .87 for the groups in the experimental conditions and .93 for the groups in the control condition. The difference in fit between the averaging combination rule and the "closest two" combination rule was reliable for both the groups in the experimental conditions and the groups in the control condition, $F(1, 29) = 292.8$, $SD = 0.25$, $p < .0001$, and $F(1, 9) = 12.7$, $SD = 0.23$, $p < .01$, respectively. We also tested a median combination rule. Groups might simply be using the middle member judgment as their group judgment. The mean correlation between the median judgment and the group judgment was $r = .90$ for the groups in the experimental conditions and $r = .93$ for the groups in the control condition. The difference between the fit of the averaging combination rule and the fit of the median combination rule was reliable for the experimental conditions, $F(1, 29) = 14.9$, $SD = 0.18$, $p < .001$, and

marginally reliable for the control condition, $F(1, 9) = 4.67$, $SD = 0.14$, $p = .059$. Thus, the general combination rule for these groups seems to be best described as a simple average of the members' judgments.

We can also examine the present data to determine whether there are any judgment shifts from the initial individual judgments to the group judgment across the 32 cases (Brown, 1986; Myers & Lamm, 1976). There is a slight and consistent tendency for the slope of the regression line to predict the group judgment from the average of the three member judgments to be greater than unity (average slope for the four experimental conditions of 1.05). The interpretation of this small shift is ambiguous as it is both a group polarization shift and a shift toward increased accuracy.

Contents of Group Discussion

The following transcript excerpts provide two examples of typical group discussions, the first by a group in experimental Condition 2 and the second by a group in the control condition.

Example Group Discussion 1 (*Condition* 2).

C plus.

I gave him a D.

I gave him a B minus.

What'd you know that we didn't?

He put down the ultimate lowest for enjoyment of the class.

Oh, really?

So, I'm thinking he must have gotten a bad grade. When he didn't do as well as he'd like, he put down the lowest.

Yeah, he gave a zero, huh?

Yeah.

What'd you . . . Did you have his G.P.A. or anything?

Three point one, and he went to class 82 percent of the time, or something like that.

Yeah, .82 . . . And if you go to class 82 percent of the time . . .

I just. . . . That zero just kind of freaks me out. Why would someone hate a class that much?

He had a five for anxiety.

Five for anxiety? Which is average, right?

Yeah.

So, I don't know. I think he must have gotten a bad grade. I was almost going to give him an F, because he put down a zero.

D plus. Give him a D plus.

I gave him a C or something.

C minus?

How about that?

Yeah.

All right.

Example Group Discussion 2 (control condition).

I gave him a B plus, because his anxiety was pretty high, and his enjoyment was high, but his workload wasn't that bad. And he seemed like a pretty good student.

I gave him a B. It just seemed like he was a good student, and he enjoyed it. His attendance wasn't the best, but I just thought he deserved a B, got a B in the class. So . . .

B plus?

Yeah.

A simple content analysis was performed on the group discussions of 36 of the groups (4 tapes were unusable). Tapes were not coded for 1 group in Condition 1, 1 group in Condition 2, and 2 groups in the control condition. Two coders analyzed the discussions. Each coder listened to half of the discussions within each condition. The coder noted each time that one of the six cues was mentioned by a group member during discussion of each of the 32 cases. As a rough test of the reliability of the coding scheme, both coders coded discussions of 3 of the cases by 8 different groups (2 groups from each condition). During discussion of those 24 cases, one or the other coder noted 92 different cue mentions. The coders were judged to disagree on a coded event any time that one coder marked more mentions of a particular cue than the other did. The coders were in exact agreement on 93.5% (86) of the coded events. Therefore, we are confident that the coding scheme was sufficiently reliable.

Group members almost always pooled their own judgments. On average, 2.93 (of the 3) members' judgments were mentioned during the discussion of each case. The pooling of member judgments did not differ significantly between experimental conditions or between the experimental groups and the control groups.

The pooling rates that are presented below slightly underestimate how much pooling actually occurred during the discussion of a typical case. When the initial judgments of all three group members were in agreement, the members rarely pooled any cues at all. On average, all three group members agreed on 2.71 of the 32 judgments.

The primary variable of interest was whether a particular cue was pooled at least once during the discussion of a case. After a cue had been pooled once, that information was available to all three group members. Any more pooling of that cue would therefore present redundant information. The groups in the experimental conditions discussed a mean of 3.87 cues (of six) for each case. The groups in the control condition discussed a mean of 2.97 cues per case. The difference between the experimental and control groups was reliable, $F(1, 34) = 9.25, p < .005$. Groups in the three experimental conditions did not differ in their pooling rates. $F(2, 25) = 1.23, ns$.

Repeated pooling of a cue might have an effect. Group members might consider a cue that is pooled multiple times during discussion of a single case to be more important than a cue that is only pooled once. Therefore, we also considered the total number of times that each cue was pooled during the discussion of each case. Including repeated pooling of the same cue, groups in the experimental conditions discussed a mean of 5.31 cues for each case. Groups in the control condition discussed a total of 4.05 cues, on average. The difference in total pooling between the experimental groups and the control groups was only marginally significant, $F(1, 34) = 3.27, p = .08$. The total pooling rates of the three experimental conditions did not differ, $F(2, 25) = 0.52, ns$.

In most cases, analyses involving the two variables revealed a similar pattern of results. In the interest of economy, therefore, we only report the analyses involving total pooling rates when they differ qualitatively from those involving the categorical pooling variable. In the between-groups analyses that follow, pooling was averaged across the 32 prejudgment discussions. Thus, the pooling rate for a cue (for the categorical coding) was expressed in terms of the proportion of those 32 discussions during which that cue was mentioned.

First, we looked for a common knowledge effect for information pooling. The mean pooling rates by condition are shown in Figure 5. Cue distribution among members and the discussion of an individual cue were related for five of the six cues. The linear effect of sharing was marginally reliable for the aptitude best percentile cue, $F(1, 25) = 4.11$, partial $r^2 = .14, p = .053$), and reliable for attendance percentage, $F(1, 25) = 14.9$, partial

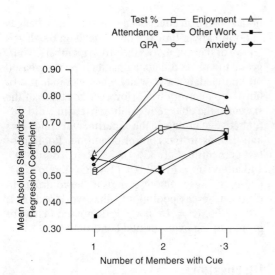

Test % —□— Enjoyment —△—
Attendance —●— Other Work —■—
GPA —○— Anxiety —◆—

FIGURE 5 ■ Effect of cue sharing on rate of cue pooling. (GPA = grade point average.)

$r^2 = .37$, $p < .001$, high school grade point average, $F(1, 25) = 5.97$, partial $r^2 = .19$, $p < .05$, enjoyment, $F(1, 25) = 6.94$, partial $r^2 = .16$, $p < .05$, and other workload cues, $F(1, 25) = 27.8$, partial $r^2 = .53$, $p < .0001$. In addition, the quadratic test comparing the shared-by-two condition with the average of the unshared and fully shared conditions was reliable for attendance percentage, $F(1, 25) = 10.0$, partial, $r^2 = .19$, $p < .001$, and enjoyment, $F(1,25) = 6.05$, partial $r^2 = .19$, $p < .05$, and marginally reliable for other workload, $F(1,25) = 3.10$, partial $r^2 = .11$, $p = .091$. All of the cues besides anxiety were discussed more when they were shared by all three group members than when they were unshared. However, attendance, enjoyment, and other workload were discussed the most when they were shared by two of the three group members. The pattern is only slightly different for the total pools per judgment measure. With that dependent measure, the quadratic effect of cue distribution is not reliable for the other workload cue, $F(1, 25) = 1.08$, ns.

The pooling rates suggest that the effect of cue distribution on cue impact could be due to increased pooling of shared cues. Alternatively, group members might be more likely to pool the cues that have an impact on the group judgments. To explore these possibilities, we tested the effect of each cue's distribution on its impact on the group judgments (mean standardized regression weight),

controlling for the cue's pooling rate. In this test, the linear effect of sharing was reliable for test percentile, $F(1,24) = 13.8$. partial $r^2 = .37$, $p < .005$, attendance percentage, $F(1,24) = 25.9$, partial $r^2 = .52$, $p < .0001$, high school grade point average, $F(1, 24) = 23.3$, partial $r^2 = .49$, $p < .0001$, and enjoyment, $F(1,24) = 10.5$, partial $r^2 = .30$, $p < .005$. The quadratic effect of distribution on cue impact, controlling for pooling, was not significant for any of the cues. Thus, for all 4 cues that originally showed a common knowledge effect (impact of the group judgment), that effect remained when we controlled for between-conditions differences in pooling. However, the quadratic effect of distribution for the enjoyment cue disappeared. Thus, the high impact of enjoyment when it was shared by two group members may have been related to the frequency of pooling of enjoyment in those groups.

Within these same analyses, the test for the effect of pooling on cue impact was also of interest. Each of these tests would show whether the frequency of pooling of a cue was related to the impact of that cue, within levels of sharing. The test was positive and reliable for test percentile. $F(1,24) = 6.68$, partial $r^2 = .22$, $p < .05$, attendance percentage, $F(1,24) = 9.30$, partial $r^2 = .28$, $p < .0001$, and enjoyment, $F(1,24) = 10.5$, partial $r^2 = .27$, $p < .01$, and marginally reliable for high school grade point average, $F(1, 24) = 3.91$, partial $r^2 = .14$, $p = .060$. Within levels of sharing, a cue had more impact on a group's judgments when it was pooled more frequently. For the test percentile, $F(1, 24) = 0.33$, ns, and attendance percentage, $F(1, 24) = 2.37$, ns, cues, however, the effect of mean total pooling was not reliable, suggesting that for those cues, what mattered was whether the cue was pooled during each discussion, not how many times it was pooled.

We also tested for interactions between cue distribution and pooling. These interaction terms test whether the common knowledge effect was weaker (or stronger) for groups that pooled a cue more frequently. None of the interactions was reliable, for either the pooling frequency or the total pooling measures. Thus, the effect of distribution on cue impact does not appear to vary depending on amount of pooling.

We can also ask whether discussion of a cue changes its impact on a group's judgments. If a cue was pooled during discussion, did that information have more of an impact on the subsequent group judgment? Within each group, we estimated regression coefficients for six interaction terms. Each of these terms represented the interaction between the value of a cue and the pooling variable for that cue. Thus, each of these interactions showed whether the impact of a cue depended on whether it was pooled. We then tested whether the means of the six interaction term regression coefficient estimates were significantly different from zero. None of these tests were reliable for either the experimental condition groups or the control condition groups. On average, then, cue impact did not depend on pooling. Only for anxiety did the Cue × Pooling interaction vary significantly between groups in the different experimental conditions, $F(2, 17) = 7.93$, $R^2 = .48$, $p < .005$. Anxiety had the most (negative) impact on group judgments when it was pooled during discussion by groups in the condition in which that cue was fully shared. In general, however, pooling did not influence cue impact, whatever the cue distribution among group members.

We were also interested in changes in pooling rates over trials. Did the group members learn which of the cues were unshared and therefore begin to pool those cues more often, relative to the other cues? Within each group, pooling for each cue was correlated with trial number. Each of these correlations showed whether a cue was pooled more or less often as the group worked through the 32 judgments. These correlations were then averaged across groups. On average, the cues tended to be pooled less often in later trials. For groups in the experimental conditions, the average correlations were significantly less than zero for other workload (mean $r = -.14$), $F(1, 27) = 17.2$, $p < .001$, and anxiety (mean $r = -.11$), $F(1, 27) = 6.62$, $p < .05$, and nearly so for attendance percentage (mean $r = -.06$), $F(1, 26) = 3.96$, $p = .057$. For groups in the control condition, the average correlations were negative and significant for aptitude test percentile (mean $r = -.26$), $F(1, 7) = 5.74$, $p < .05$, attendance percentage (mean $r = -.32$), $F(1, 7) = 10.6$, $p < .05$, and enjoyment (mean $r = -.12$), $F(1, 6) = 10.0$, $p < .05$, and marginally significant for high school grade point average (mean $r = -.13$), $F(1, 7) = 4.05$, $p = .084$. Differences in the degrees of freedom are due to the lack of variation in pooling of some cues by some groups. None of the average correlations were significantly greater than zero.

More important, none of these average correla-

tions showed an effect of cue distribution. Changes in pooling over time did not depend on the distribution of that cue across the group members. Thus, group members did not adjust their pooling based on knowledge about which cues were shared or unshared on every trial. However, for three of the six cues, the change in pooling over time did differ between groups in the experimental conditions and groups in the control condition. Pooling of test percentile, $F(1, 33) = 7.23$, $R^2 = .18$, $p < .05$, and attendance, $F(1, 33) = 11.4$, $R^2 = .26$, $p < .01$, decreased faster among groups in the control condition, whereas pooling of other workload, $F(1, 34) = 7.66$, $R^2 = .18$, $p < .01$, decreased faster for groups in the experimental conditions.

Discussion

The present results demonstrate the hypothesized common knowledge effect. In the context of a group judgment, three-member groups weighed the same information about target students more heavily when it was shared than when it was unshared. Even though groups in all three experimental conditions possessed exactly the same information about the target cases, their use of that information depended on its prediscussion distribution among the individual group members. The predicted effect was highly reliable for four of the six informational cues that were presented for the target cases: aptitude test percentile score, lecture attendance percentage, high school grade point average, and course enjoyment. Each of these four cues had reliably more influence when it was known by all three group members before group discussion than when it was known by only one group member. In addition, the other workload cue showed a slight linear trend, although it did not approach significance.

We want to emphasize the distinctive advantages of our seminal application of social judgment theory's multiple regression analysis framework. We are able to clearly measure, on an interpretable scale, the relative impact of various sources of information (cues) on individual and group judgment. We can analytically separate and compare the strength of mediation through individual-member judgments versus group discussion. And we can represent alternative theories about the group process either in comprehensive sets of equations or in path analysis diagrams. Although we have noted several limitations of the range of applicability of the method, under those conditions where it is appropriate, it performs like a surgeon's scalpel in comparison with the butter knife of conventional approaches to the analysis of the impact of information on group decisions.

Self-rated anxiety was the only informational cue that clearly was not used according to the hypothesis. The influence of the anxiety information did not depend on experimental condition. It could be that anxiety was simply not considered to be useful information in any condition. It did, on average, have the lowest influence of any of the six cues on both member and group judgments. In addition, anxiety was probably a difficult piece of information for groups to use, because it has no clear valence. It is not apparent whether higher self-reported anxiety about academics would be associated with higher or lower course grades or whether that relationship would be curvilinear. In fact, the influence of anxiety over all 32 cases was slightly positive for some groups and negative for others. Uncertainty about the nature of the relationship between anxiety and course grades within the group could have lowered the cue's influence to the point that the experimental manipulation had no effect. Interestingly, self-reported workload in other courses, the only cue with a clear negative valence, was the only other cue that did not clearly follow the expected pattern. Perhaps the common knowledge effect is strongest for information that has a clear, positive valence in the context of the judgments that the group is making.

One issue of interest concerned the linearity of the hypothesized common knowledge effect on those cues whose influence did reflect their distribution across members. That is, does each increase of one in the number of group members sharing a cue lead to an equal increase in the average influence of that cue on the group's judgments? For the course enjoyment cue, the effect of changing the prediscussion information distribution made a larger difference in average influence when moving from the condition in which enjoyment was known by one group member to the condition in which it was known by two than when moving from the condition in which it was known by two group members to the condition in which it was known by all three group members. The comparison was not reliable for any of the other cues. In general, the common knowledge effect is approximately linear, at least for three-member groups.

Further study would be necessary to determine whether something about self-rated enjoyment causes that information to be used differently than the other cues, or whether the nonlinear effect is simply the result of something peculiar in the overall information distribution among the three experimental conditions.

Our regression analyses showed that the stronger influence of fully distributed information cannot easily be explained by differential information pooling. Stasser and his colleagues (Stasser, Taylor, & Hanna, 1989; Stasser & Titus, 1985, 1987) have found that distributed cues are more often mentioned by group members during the group discussion phase of a group judgment task. They have used this information pooling effect to explain their finding that inequitable information distribution can bias the outcome of a group judgment. Direct comparisons with Stasser's results are probably inappropriate because there are many differences between the nature of the task presented to subjects and the experimental procedures in the two research programs. We should note that the present procedure was likely to maximize overall information pooling and therefore to minimize differences in pooling between cues. In each of the 32 grade judgments, individual group members in the experimental conditions only received four of the total of six possible cues, in contrast to Stasser's experiments, in which a larger set of cues had to be remembered by the group members, who were making a single judgment. Moreover, subjects in the present study made a series of 32 judgments, using the same six cues, after having been informed about what kind of information they might expect to see.

The content analysis of the group discussions provided some insight into the relationship between pooling and cue impact. Congruent with Stasser's argument, all of the cues except anxiety were discussed more often when they were fully shared than when they were unshared. Surprisingly, however, 3 of those cues were pooled the most often when they were shared by only two of the three group members. This may indicate that subjects are cognizant of which cues are not fully shared and therefore need to be pooled.

Even though cue distribution and pooling were related, that relationship does not appear to explain the common knowledge effect of distribution on cue impact. When pooling was held constant, the common knowledge effect was still significant for the same 4 cues. Were groups in different conditions to pool one of those cues at the same rate, the impact of that cue on the group judgments would increase monotonically with the level of sharing. Within groups in the same condition, however, the more a cue was pooled, the more impact it had (again, for the aptitude percentile, attendance percentage, high school grade point average, and enjoyment cues). Obviously, the direction of causality in this relationship cannot be specified. It could be, as Stasser suggested, that pooling leads to increased cue impact. On the other hand, a cue that is seen as being more important, and therefore that has more impact, might also be mentioned more frequently during the group discussion. The latter possibility seems more likely. We found no evidence that any cue tended to have more of an impact on the group judgments that followed group discussions during which that cue was mentioned. On average, the within-group interaction terms that tested whether each cue had more of an influence on the group judgment when it was pooled were not significantly different from zero.

In addition, nonsignificant interactions between cue distribution and pooling show that the effect of cue distribution on cue impact did not depend on the level of pooling. Whether groups pooled a particular cue relatively frequently or relatively infrequently, the difference due to differential distribution was the same. Thus, the common knowledge effect was not, for example, produced by those groups that tended not to pool a cue.

In total, the content analysis suggests that, at least in the present research paradigm, differential pooling rates do not mediate differential cue impact. Most of the cues did tend to be pooled more frequently when they were shared and also when they had more impact on the group judgments. However, these effects both occurred when the other was controlled statistically. In addition, the relationship between pooling and impact appeared to occur only, on average, between groups and not judgment to judgment within groups.

Although we are not critical of Stasser's methods (indeed, his research was the inspiration for our own), we highlight one advantage of our application of social judgment theory statistical models (Hammond, Stewart, Brehmer, & Steinmann, 1986). In our study, we are confident that the primary mediator of information distribution effects (e.g., the common knowledge effect) is the differential impact of common and unshared informa-

tion on individual judgments. Stasser's interpretation of behavior in his experimental task in terms of differential impact on the probability that information will be "pooled" in group discussion is most likely correct. Using his group choice task, it might be possible to distinguish between mediation through members' judgments and mediation through evidence pooling. However, we feel that our own paradigm presents a clearer picture of the relative importance of the two influences.

As formulated, the common knowledge effect hypothesis is concerned only with the general effect of information distribution on group judgments. In the present study, however, subjects were first asked to make individual judgments about each target student and then to come to a consensus judgment with the other group members. A simple combination of individual judgments into a group judgment, such as averaging, would result in the common knowledge effect. If group members simply combine their individual judgments into a group judgment, without any further utilization of the information, those cues that have an influence on more of the individual judgments will have more of an influence on the group judgment. On the other hand, the presented information might have an additional effect on group judgments over and above its effect on the individual group members' judgments. That is, the information could have an additional impact on the group judgments, controlling for the impact of the three members' judgments on the group's judgments. Moreover, the additional effect of a particular cue could depend on the number of group members who share that cue before the group discussion. For example, if the pooling of unshared information is affecting the group judgments, then the unshared cues should have more of an effect, when controlling for individual judgments. The groups should adjust their judgments in the direction of previously unshared information, but not in the direction of information that was fully shared. When unshared information is discussed, it provides information that is not already contained in all three member judgments, and therefore that information should have an additional impact on the group judgment. According to the common knowledge effect hypothesis, any such adjustment is not strong enough to overcome the initial bias. On the other hand, the common knowledge effect could be even stronger than originally formulated. The unequal distribution of information could have biased the group judgment even more than would be expected with a linear combination of the member judgments. For example, if a particular cue has an impact on the group discussion every time that it is pooled, and if the cue is pooled more often when it is fully shared than when it is unshared, then that cue would have the greatest additional impact on group judgments in the fully shared condition. Thus, differential pooling rates could augment the initial bias that is due to the impact of information on the individual members' judgments.

In this grade judgment task, none of the cues had more than a slight influence on the group judgments when the members' judgments were partialed out. The average regression weights were not reliably greater than zero for any of the cues, except for the attendance cue. In addition, there were no reliable linear effects of condition on the unmediated influence of the cues. In general, level of prediscussion information sharing does not affect the influence of information on group judgment, controlling for members' judgments. The regression analyses do not provide support for either of the possible effects that were discussed in the previous paragraph. Again, the evidence suggests that information pooling does not play a significant role in the group judgments.

In some ways, the grade judgment task kept the impact of information pooling modest. Because there was no accuracy feedback and no demonstrably correct solution (Stasser & Stewart, 1992), the group members had no way of knowing whether they could improve their accuracy by adjusting their group judgments to reflect pooled information. In addition, the structure of the task encouraged anchoring on the members' judgments. The group members made their individual judgments immediately before they began discussing each to-be-judged case. Moreover, the members made their judgments on the same "commensurate" scale as they used for their group judgment. All of the groups placed considerable weight on the member judgments during discussion. All three group members almost always pooled their member judgments during the discussion of each to-be-judged case. Moreover, as can be seen in the example transcripts, this opinion pooling usually occurred near the beginning of each discussion. Despite task instructions that emphasized the pooling of unshared information and group judgment accuracy, the groups in the present study tended

to emphasize the information provided by the judgments of their constituent members.

Future research might investigate the generality of the common knowledge effect across different judgment tasks. For example, groups might be asked to make judgments for which there are demonstrably correct answers. They might also be provided with feedback concerning the accuracy of each of their judgments. In addition, the task could be modified to reduce the tendency for groups to anchor their judgments on the judgments of their members. Member judgments of all cases could be collected before group discussion of the first case. Alternatively, members and groups could render their judgments on two different, less commensurate response scales. Together or separately, these modifications might increase the influence of information pooling on the group judgments, relative to the impact of the member judgments. However, we emphasize again the similarity of the judgment task used in the present study to some real-world judgments. In a student petition hearing committee, for example, committee members would be likely to render their own implicit or explicit judgments as a case is presented, immediately before group discussion of that case. Moreover, both the members and the committee probably make their judgments on the same or similar response scales. Both members and groups might judge whether the committee should recommend that the petition be accepted or rejected. Although modifications of the judgment task might increase the impact of pooled information on the group judgments, such findings would not invalidate the results of the present study.

One possible explanation for the common knowledge effect is that subjects consciously determine that certain pieces of information are more important, because they are shared for every judgment case. However, even after making a large number of grade judgments, the individual group members are not able to assess accurately how they are using the provided information. In their subjective weightings of the six types of presented information, group members rank the influence of five of the six cues out of order, compared with the actual weights determined by the regression analysis for their group judgments. In addition, they give anxiety and workload in other classes subjective weightings that are a good deal higher than they should be. In reality, these cues, especially anxiety, had little influence on the groups' grade judgments. The subjects had a poor subjective insight into how they actually were using the information to come to a judgment about a case.

The between-conditions differences in judgment accuracy are puzzling on the surface. The groups in Condition 2 were considerably less accurate than groups in any other condition. Yet in these groups, the test percentile and attendance percentage cues were fully shared and thus had a large impact on the group judgments. However, for the 32 to-be-judged cases, attendance percentage was not a particularly good predictor, whereas high school grade point average and enjoyment, both unshared in Condition 2, were good predictors. Those two good predictors had a high impact among groups in Condition 1 (the impact of enjoyment being greatest when shared by two group members), and therefore those groups were the most accurate. Thus, the inability of groups to utilize unshared information did result in reliably different accuracies between the different experimental conditions, even though the results were initially perplexing.

The group judgments were not reliably more accurate than were the averages of the individual judgments in any of the conditions (Hastie, 1986; Hill, 1982). Allowing the group to come to a consensus judgment did not improve judgment accuracy, even though the individual judgments were under informed because of the differential distribution of information. This result was expected for groups in the control condition, in which all group members made fully informed judgments before the group discussion. Groups in Condition 2, at the very least, could have been more accurate had they effectively pooled and weighted the cues that were more predictive of grades in the 32 to-be-judged cases.

What, then, can we conclude about group process with the present group judgment task? Taken together, our results suggest that the groups in the present study tended to use an implicit or explicit averaging combination rule to join their member judgments into a consensus group judgment. They did so even when they discussed judgment-relevant information that had influenced only 1 of the 3 averaged member judgments. That is, the groups did not adjust their judgments to reflect unshared information that was pooled during the group discussion. Our analyses suggest that information discussion in these groups functioned primarily as justification by members for their judgments, rather than as input into the judgment policies of the groups. The primary information that served as input into the groups' judgments was the judgments of their members.

The present study shows the inability of small groups to compensate for the differential distribution of judgment-relevant information among group members. The differential sharing of information affected the judgment policies of the groups. When individual group members pooled their information, the groups failed to take advantage of the cues that were unshared. The group judgments were not any more accurate than the average of the individual judgments, even though the groups were in possession of more information than were any of the individuals. Placing individuals in groups did not result in better judgments than would have been obtained by simply averaging together the judgments of the same individuals.

ACKNOWLEDGMENTS

We thank Charles Judd and David Kenny for their advice concerning data analysis and Garold Stasser, John Rohrbaugh, and Tom Stewart for their suggestions on the research plan. Support for this research was provided by National Science Foundation Grant BNS–8996145.

REFERENCES

Brehmer, B., & Hammond, K. R. (1973). Cognitive sources of interpersonal conflict: Analysis of interactions between linear and nonlinear cognitive systems. *Organizational Behavior and Human Performance, 10*, 290–313.

Brehmer. B., & Joyce, C. R. B. (Eds.). (1988). *Advances in psychology: Vol. 54. Human judgment: The SJT view.* Amsterdam: Elsevier.

Brown, R. (1986). *Social psychology, the second edition.* New York: Free Press.

Brunswik, E. (1956). *Perception and the representative design of psychological experiments.* Berkeley: University of California Press.

Burnstein, E. (1982). Persuasion as argument processing. In H. Brandstatter, J. H. Davis, & G. Stocker-Kreichgauer (Eds.), *Group decision making* (pp. 103–124). San Diego. CA: Academic Press.

Deutsch. M., & Gerard, H. B. (1955). The study of normative and informational social influence on individual judgment. *Journal of Abnormal and Social Psychology, 51*, 629–636.

Hammond, K. R. (Ed.). (1966). *The psychology of Egon Brunswik.* New York: Holt, Rinehart, & Winston.

Hammond, K. R., Stewart, T. R., Brehmer, B., & Steinmann, D. (1986). Social judgment theory. In H. R. Arkes & K. R. Hammond (Eds.), *Judgment and decision making: An interdisciplinary reader* (pp. 56–76). New York: Cambridge University Press.

Harmon, J., & Rohrbaugh, J. (1990). Social judgment analysis and small group decision making: Cognitive feedback effects on individual and collective performance. *Organizational Behavior and Human Decision Processes, 46,* 34–54.

Hastie, R. (1984). Causes and effects of causal attribution. *Journal of Personality and Social Psychology, 46,* 44–56.

Hastie, R. (1986). Experimental evidence on group accuracy. In B. Grofman & G. Owen (Eds.), *Decision research* (Vol. 2, pp. 129–157). Greenwich, CT: JAI Press.

Hill, G. W. (1982). Group versus individual performance: Are N+1 heads better than one? *Psychological Bulletin, 91,* 517–539.

Judd, C. M., & McClelland, G. H. (1989). *Data analysis: A model-comparision approach.* San Diego, CA: Harcourt, Brace, Jovanovich.

Myers, D. G., & Lamm, H. (1976). The group polarization phenomenon. *Psychological Bulletin, 83,* 602–627.

Slovic, P., Griffin, D., & Tversky, A. (1990). Compatibility effects in judgment and choice. In R. M. Hogarth (Ed.), *Insights in decision making* (pp. 5–27). Chicago: University of Chicago Press.

Slovic, P., & Lichtenstein, S. (1971). Comparison of Bayesian and regression approaches to the study of information processing in judgment. *Organizational Behavior and Human Performance, 6,* 649–744.

Slovic, P., & MacPhillamy, D. (1974). Dimensional commensurability and cue utilization in comparative judgment.

Organizational Behavior and Human Performance, 11, 172–194.

Sniezek, J. A., & Henry, R. A. (1989). Accuracy and confidence in group judgment. *Organizational Behavior and Human Decision Processes, 43,* 1–28.

Stasser, G., & Stewart, D. (1992). Discovery of hidden profiles by decision-making groups: Solving a problem versus making a judgment. *Journal of Personality and Social Psychology, 63,* 426–434.

Stasser, G., Taylor, L. A., & Hanna, C. (1989). Information sampling in structured and unstructured discussions of three-and six-person groups. *Journal of Personality and Social Psychology, 57,* 67–78.

Stasser, G., & Titus, W. (1985). Pooling of unshared information in group decision making: Biased information sampling during discussion. *Journal of Personality and Social Psychology, 48,* 1467–1478.

Stasser, G., & Titus, W. (1987). Effects of information load and percentage of shared information on the dissemination of unshared information during group discussion. *Journal of Personality and Social Psychology, 53,* 81–93.

Stewart, T. R. (1988). Judgment analysis: Procedures. In B. Brehmer & C. R. B. Joyce (Eds.), *Human judgment: The social judgment theory view* (pp. 41–74). Amsterdam: North-Holland.

Interpersonal Relationships and Task Performance: An Examination of Mediating Processes in Friendship and Acquaintance Groups

Karen A. Jehn • University of Pennsylvania
Priti Pradhan Shah • University of Minnesota, Twin Cities Campus

This study used multiple methods to examine group processes (information sharing, morale building, planning, critical evaluation, commitment, monitoring, and cooperation) that mediate the effect of relationship level on group performance. The study uses a 2 by 2 experimental design, crossing relationship (friendship vs. acquaintance) as a between-subjects variable and task type (decision making vs. motor) as a within-subject variable. Fifty-three 3-person groups participated in the study, and data from 4 types of meaurement were used to analyze the mediating processes between relationship level and task performance. Friendship groups performed significantly better than acquaintance groups on both decision-making and motor tasks because of a greater degree of group commitment and cooperation. Critical evaluation and task monitoring also significantly increased decision-making performance, whereas positive communication mediated the relationship between friendship and motor task performance.

Friendship is often a consequence of teamwork. Prior relationships, proximity, frequency of communication, and common work goals are factors that facilitate friendship in work groups. Research that investigated friendship at work has provided mixed results regarding the benefits and detriments of friendship on work performance. Despite the belief that friendship is an impediment to productivity because it creates an increased social focus that detracts from the group's work goal (Bramel & Friend, 1987; Homans, 1951), past studies suggest that friendship (often operation- alized as cohesion) in work groups may have such benefits as information sharing, productive conflict, and increased motivation (Berkowitz, 1954; Dailey, 1977; Evans & Dion, 1991; Shah & Jehn, 1993). These contradictory findings regarding relationships and group performance signify a need for a more thorough examination of the processes involved in friendship and acquaintance groups. We argue that one can best conduct this investigation using multiple methods and measurement techniques to examine underlying group processes.

Although group performance studies have examined interpersonal relationship variables (operationalized as group affinity, camaraderie, and cohesion), they have focused primarily on outcomes and have neglected the group process (Evans & Dion, 1991). This focus on outcomes limits the investigation of group processes, although questions about the impact of friendship on group performance are important. Mediating processes are critical to understanding the different behaviors and attitudes in friendship and acquaintance groups that lead to performance differences. Examining underlying group processes should provide a better understanding of performance differences in friendship and acquaintance groups.

In this study, we investigated process differences among friendship and acqaintance groups to determine whether and why friendship among members is beneficial to group performance. First, we integrate group and interpersonal relationship literatures to provide an understanding of the differences between friendship and acquaintance groups. Then, we report on our investigation of communication and behavior in two different task situations (cognitive and motor tasks), considering that group tasks often differ in the skills necessary for high-quality performance (Gladstein, 1984: Jehn, 1995; Van de Ven & Ferry, 1980). Finally, we discuss general behaviors within friendship and acquaintance groups that lead to performance differences and the specific behaviors necessary for superior performance on motor versus cognitive tasks in work groups.

To examine group processes, we proposed a multimethod approach. Whereas most research has focused on a single medium (for exceptions, see Weingart, 1992; Weldon, Jehn, & Pradhan, 1991), a multimethod perspective is critical for understanding and triangulating the dynamics of psychological processes. The use of multiple methods allowed us to more adequately assess the influence of mediating processes and strengthened our understanding of the constructs under study. Constructs are more accurate and reliable when there are multiple operational representations of each (Cook & Campbell, 1979). Thus, we used four measurement methodologies: a postexperimental questionnaire, content-analyzed audiotapes, behavior ratings of videotapes, and objective measures of group behavior and performance.

Friendship and Acquaintance Groups

The interpersonal relationship literature suggests that people distinguish between friendship and acquaintance relationships and that different rules govern people's interactions in the two types of relationships (Clark & Mills, 1993; Clark, Mills, & Powell, 1986; Greenberg, 1983; Pataki, Shapiro, & Clark, 1994). *Friendship groups* are defined as groups with close, interpersonal ties and positive, amiable preexisting relationships among members (Rawlins, 1983, 1989; Wright, 1984). The friendships in these groups are voluntary, mutual, and often communal in that members are concerned about each other's welfare, regardless of benefits gained from the relationship (Clark & Mills, 1979). The friendship are usually not exchange-based (i.e., members are not concerned with reciprocation of benefits).

Acquaintance groups are defined as groups with limited familiarity and contact among members. Members may know each other through casual encounters; however, a strong bond, past history, and depth of mutual knowledge between the parties are lacking. The interaction between acquaintances is not necessarily voluntary or positive, as it is among friends. Although relationships exist on a continuum of intimacy, we followed previous research by focusing on two points (friendship and acquaintance) to assess group process differences (Pataki et al., 1994).

Group Process

Group process is defined as the behavior or interaction patterns among group members (Steiner, 1972; Weldon & Weingart, 1988). Past research on process consultation, team development, and T-group and sensitivity training has assumed that improved interpersonal relationships among group members lead to improved task performance (Guzzo & Shea, 1992). These studies have focused on how interpersonal interactions among group members reduce process loss. *Process loss* is the extent to which group performance is inhibited by misunderstandings, miscommunication, and dislike among group members (Steiner, 1972). Process loss results in wasted group energy and decreased productivity stemming from interpersonal difficulties. Researchers have documented the dysfunctional effects of mistrust, role ambiguity, and communication difficulties on satisfaction in various task groups such as management teams, airline crews, military combat units, mining crews, student groups, and research and development teams (Hackman, 1991). There is little evidence, however, to indicate that improving interpersonal relationships increases work performance (Kaplan, 1979; Sundstrom, de Meuse, & Futrell, 1990; Woodman & Sherwood, 1980).

In addition, past research on cohesiveness and performance has yielded contradictory results (Evans & Dion, 1991; cf. Guzzo & Dickson, 1996; Seashore, 1954). Although friendship and cohesion are two separate constructs, they have numerous commonalities and interdependencies. In particular, both focus on interpersonal affinity among group members. We believe that the interpersonal attraction that is the basis for friendship facilitates cohesion in groups composed of friends. Thus, important insight into friendship groups can be gained by further investigating past research on cohesion. Seashore's work suggests that the relation between cohesion and group performance is contingent on group norms. In highly cohesive groups, norms for high and low performance elicited a high and low level of performance, respectively. Although cohesion and friendship are two separate constructs, both focus on interpersonal affinity among group members. In a recent meta-analysis, Evans and Dion (1991) found a strong positive correlation between cohesion and performance. Because their analysis was conducted only on published studies and were limited to laboratory groups and sports teams, the authors were cautious in their interpretation. Evans and Dion also noted that the analysis of 26 unpublished studies that were based on a larger sample revealed a significant negative correlation. Thus, the direction of the relationship between cohesion and performance is still under debate. We propose that examining the intervening processes between relationship level (i.e., friendship vs. acquaintance) and performance will provide a clearer understanding of the association between the two variables.

Group processes needed for optimal performance also differ depending on the type of task being performed (Jehn, 1995; McGrath, 1984; Steiner, 1972). Processes that are optimal for one task may be detrimental to another. For example, whereas non-task-related conversation can serve as a distraction from the tedium of a repetitive motor task, it may interfere with the cognitive processes required for a complex decision-making task. To investigate the intervening variables between friendship and task performance, we focused in the present study on two different tasks: a cognitive task (decision making) and a repetitive motor task (model building). Cognitive tasks incorporate conceptual skills and problem-solving abilities, whereas repetitive motor tasks (e.g., a manufacturing or assembly-line task) typically emphasize physical skills and speed. The motor task we chose is a maximizing task, according to Steiner (1972), because members were instructed to complete as many models as possible in the time allowed. These two tasks differed fundamentally on the conceptual versus behavioral dimensions cited by McGrath (1984) and were chosen because of the different group processes they require for high-caliber performance (Gladstein, 1984; Gruenfeld & Hollingshead, 1993; McGrath, 1984). We discuss the different group processes necessary for high-caliber performance on these tasks in the next section.

Interpersonal Relationships, Group Process, and Task Performance

We provide empirical support that group processes related to positive interpersonal relations improve group performance. We examined seven processes (information sharing, planning, critical evaluation, morale-building communication, commitment, monitoring, and cooperation) that we predicted would mediate the association between relationship level and task performance of work groups. We believed that we could better understand the complexity of the relation between friendship and performance and the contradictions in past research by examining the interaction patterns in friendship and acquaintance groups. Interactions with friends and interactions with acquaintances are dramatically different, and their differences may affect task performance (Shah & Jehn, 1993).

Information Sharing

A primary difference between friendship and acquaintance groups is the amount and type of communication each generates. Research has shown that individuals share more information with friends than with nonfriends (Newcomb & Brady, 1982: Newcomb, Brady, & Hartup, 1979; Zaccaro & Lowe, 1988). We define information sharing in groups as making statements to other group members about the task. Collective information sharing includes disclosing factual, task-relevant information to other group members (Henry, 1995; Stasser, 1992). Information sharing also encompasses Bales's (1951) notion of task behavior. Active task behavior includes offering opinions, suggestions, and information; passive task behavior includes asking for information, opinions, or suggestions. Talking about the task, expressing feelings and ideas, and freely exchanging task-related thought are examples of information sharing.

Self-disclosure norms common among friends result in candid and copious information exchange (Argyle & Furnham, 1983; Hays, 1985). Network researchers (e.g., Albrecht & Ropp, 1984) have found that social relationships among workers provide the opportunity for more task-related exchanges. More information is shared because of greater contact and trust in friendship relationships (Danowski, 1980; Rawlins, 1983; Roloff, 1987); therefore, we proposed that:

Hypothesis 1a: Friendship groups share more information than acquaintance groups.

Information sharing increases task-focused attention and effort, which in turn increase motor task performance (Weldon et al., 1991). Motor task performance benefits from information shared about unique skills and knowledge about the prescribed way to perform the task. Group performance on cognitive tasks also increases when members share task-relevant information (Stasser & Stewart, 1992). Individuals often bring diverse information and skills to a group. The unique information that each member holds is called unshared information (Larson, Christensen, Abbott, & Franz, 1996; Stasser & Titus, 1985, 1987). Groups who pool this unshared information increase the available informational resources. Small groups who engage in factfinding discussions increase performance by emphasizing important, unique information that members possess (Stasser, 1992). Increasing the sharing of diverse opinions and information about task-related skills and strategies can enhance group performance because valuable information necessary to complete the task becomes salient to all group members (Larson et al., 1996). Therefore, we predicted that:

Hypothesis 1b: Information sharing increases motor task performance.

Hypothesis 1c: Information sharing increases cognitive task performance.[1]

Planning

Planning is a specific type of task-related communication in which group members formulate actions regarding time and function that lead to specific goals (McGrath, 1984). Planning entails specifying task procedures, delegating task responsibility, determining temporal order for task duties, and determining actions necessary to complete the task (Weldon et al., 1991). We investigated explicit in-process planning, that is, verbal planning behavior that takes place while group members work on a task, rather than planning that occurs before the start of a task (Weingart, 1992). When group members discuss whether to perform a certain act, how a certain act should be performed, or who should perform a certain act, they are participating in planning. The open channels of communication present in friendship groups should facilitate planning, assuming that group members are motivated to complete their task. We therefore hypothesized that:

Hypothesis 2a: Friendship groups plan more than acquaintance groups.

Research has shown that planning is positively related to group performance (Dean & Sharfman, 1996; Weldon et al., 1991). Planning influences performance effectiveness in two ways: Group members can share past strategies and implement them, or they can develop or adapt new plans (Hackman & Morris, 1975). High-quality planning reduces coordination problems, which hinder task performance, and increases the likelihood that the group will uncover more efficient and effective plans (Smith, Locke, & Barry, 1990). Coordination, or the integrating of individuals to accomplish a task (Van de Ven, Delbecq, & Koenig, 1976), is necessary for effective collective action. Planning allows group members to work together to best distribute the work, to coordinate the ac-

---

[1] Throughout this section, the "a" hypotheses always refer to the relationship between friendship groups and the mediating process, the "b" hypotheses refer to the relationship between the mediating process and motor task performance, and the "c" hypotheses refer to the relation between the mediating process and cognitive task performance.

tions of individual members, and to open channels for members to share information (Weingart & Weldon, 1991). Research has shown that explicit discussions of strategy improve group productivity (Hackman, Brousseau, & Weiss, 1976) when a task requires coordination (e.g., a motor task) or sharing among members (e.g., a cognitive task). We investigated tasks in which coordination is necessary, that is, tasks in which members are highly interdependent and in which organization leads to improved task performance (Shure, Rogers, Larsen, & Tassone, 1962; Weldon et al., 1991). Therefore, we proposed that:

Hypothesis 2b: Planning increases motor task performance.

Hypothesis 2c: Planning increases cognitive task performance.

Critical Evaluation

Critical evaluation occurs when one or more members finds fault with or judges the quality of other group members. Disagreements or arguments about the way a group member performs her duty, criticism about a member's performance, or disapproval of a member's suggestion are instances of critical evaluation. Critical evaluation includes examining, judging, analyzing, evaluating, and scrutinizing another group member's work.
Studies show that friends manage disagreements differently than nonfriends (Aboud, 1989; Ladd & Emerson, 1984; Nelson & Aboud, 1985). Friends offer more explanations to their partners, make more criticisms, and are more likely to get confirmatory information relative to nonfriends. Gottman and Parkhurst (1980) provided evidence that individuals tolerate disagreements with friends more than with nonfriends. The friends in Gottman and Parkhurst's study tended to disagree and to provide critical feedback in a constructive manner that the receiver perceived as positive and productive. The nonfriends, however, were more likely to be perceived as making assumptions and providing neutral or negative evaluations on the basis of flaws inherent in the person (e.g., flaws in abilities, knowledge, and personality) rather than on circumstances external to the person.
Preexisting personal relationships encourage group members to critically evaluate each other's ideas. Knapp, Ellis, and Williams (1980) have asserted that friends are more likely than nonfriends

to give and receive both positive and negative feedback. Research has shown that criticism and conflict regarding opinions and ideas are more common in close relationships than in acquaintances (Argyle & Furnham, 1983). Roloff (1987) suggested that a supportive environment established by preexisting friendships may foster the questioning and challenging of ideas in a nonthreatening manner. Relational security reduces the fear of retaliation or negative repercussions that result from critical comments. In addition, critical evaluation may be suppressed in acquaintance groups because norms of politeness govern social interaction among strangers (Mikula & Schwinger, 1978). We therefore hypothesized that:

Hypothesis 3a (1): Friendship groups engage in more critical evaluation than acquaintance groups.

Alternatively, research on interpersonal relationships has suggested that people may avoid conflict with friends in order to maintain their relationships. Group members who are friends are often preoccupied with maintaining their relationships and therefore are unwilling to critically evaluate each other's views (Kelley & Thibaut, 1979). Davidson and Duberman (1982) found that participants in dyadic friendship groups experienced fewer arguments than nonfriends. Threats to the relationship often lead to restricted information exchange and processing (Gladstein & Reilly, 1985). Similar values, viewpoints, and experience among members will lead to similar task interpretations, thus reducing the likelihood of disagreements (Lincoln & Miller, 1979; McPherson & Smith-Lovin, 1987). The cohesiveness of friendship groups makes them prone to "groupthink" and consensus building (Janis, 1982). We acknowledge the competing theories regarding the amount of critical evaluation present in friendship groups because of the various norms and psychological processes operating, and we have proposed competing hypotheses. Therefore, in contrast to hypothesis 3a (1), we proposed that:

Hypothesis 3a (2): Acquaintance groups engage in more critical evaluation than friendship groups.

Critical evaluation is an integral component in decision-making tasks, for it enables a group to explore alternatives and make informed decisions. Decision-making performance is improved by analyzing and prioritizing options (Allison, 1971). Critical evaluation can eliminate the negative impact of groupthink (Janis, 1982) by questioning assumptions and increasing the generation of acceptable alternatives (Cosier & Schwenk, 1990). In addition, dissent among members can produce divergent views that enhance decision making (Nemeth, 1986). We therefore hypothesized that:

Hypothesis 3b: Critical evaluation improves cognitive task performance.

Alternatively, critical evaluation can be a hindrance in groups performing routine motor tasks. When procedures are set, the criticism can interfere with efficient processing (Guzzo, 1986). Differences of opinion and criticism can cause stress and irritation, which inhibit performance (Jehn, 1995). According to Gladstein (1984), simple tasks do not require task discussion or evaluation of strategies and may even be harmed by the interference. Thus, we proposed that:

Hypothesis 3c: Critical evaluation decreases motor task performance.

Morale-Building Communication

Communication in work groups involves both task-related communication (e.g., information sharing, planning, and critical evaluation) and non-task-related communication. A frequent form of non-task-related communication is morale-building communication (Weldon et al., 1991). Morale-building communication is defined as communication that encourages group members to perform better by exchanging positive comments about the group's or group member's performance. Offering positive comments, exuding confidence, displaying a positive attitude, providing words of encouragement, and showing enthusiasm are examples of morale-building communication.

Friendship groups often consist of homogeneous individuals with similar interests who are more likely to engage in non-task-related conversation (e.g., gossip) than are individuals in acquaintance groups because of their common interests and experiences (Davidson & Duberman, 1982; Lincoln & Miller, 1979; McPherson & Smith-Lovin, 1987). Positive affect and admiration among friends are likely to result in morale-building communication in task groups (Wright, 1984). Newcomb et al. (1979) found greater positive affective expression and reciprocal praise in friend interactions than in nonfriend interactions. Friends also tend to be more

"ego-supportive" of one another than do nonfriends, which fosters positive, efficacious, encouraging communication among friendship group members (Rawlins, 1989). We therefore proposed that:

Hypothesis 4a: Friendship groups engage in more morale-building communication than acquaintance groups.

An increased level of morale-building communication has both positive and negative consequences, depending on the type of group task. Morale-building communication (e.g., a pep talk) provides a sense of efficacy among group members, arouses their emotions, and thus induces groups to work faster on a repetitive motor task (Bandura, 1982; Bandura, Reese, & Adams, 1982; Thoms, Moore, & Scott, 1996). Morale-building communication also influences performance by increasing group members' effort (Weldon & Weingart, 1988). Thus, we hypothesized that:

Hypothesis 4b: Morale-building communication increases motor task performance.

However, these same morale-building behaviors may interfere with cognitive task performance. Because the quality, rather than the speed, of the decision is the important factor in decision-making task performance, the emotional arousal provided by morale-building communication may not be necessary. In fact, self-efficacy and overconfidence can cause individuals to invest too little in cognitive tasks (Bandura, 1982; Fischhoff, Slovic, & Lichtenstein, 1977). Similarly, non-task-related communication, which creates an amiable working environment in routine tasks, may interfere with the added attentional demands of a decision-making task. In a study of decision-making tasks (Shah & Jehn, 1993), highly emotional exchanges (both positive and negative) detracted from the concentration of group members. Another negative factor that influences performance of cognitive tasks, especially prevalent in friendship groups, is the tendency of group members to socialize rather than focus on the task. The cognitive effort applied to non-task-related discussion involves cognitive resources necessary for effective decision making. Additionally, open communication and self-disclosure can have negative effects, causing interpersonal problems that inhibit productivity (Jehn, 1995; Rawlins, 1983). On the basis of our reasoning, we proposed that:

Hypothesis 4c: Morale-building communication decreases cognitive task performance.

Commitment

Commitment to the work group is defined as the strength of a member's identification and involvement with the group (Mowday, Porter, & Steers, 1982). O'Reilly and Chatman's (1986) analysis of organizational commitment revealed identification as a basis for attachment to an organization, because members desire affiliation with the group. Committed group members feel obligated to the group, identify with the group, are dedicated to the other members, and have emotional ties to the group.

The level of commitment to the group is expected to be higher in friendship groups than in acquaintance groups because members have strong interpersonal ties. Friends focus on the group as an entity and define their identity as part of the group. The emotional attachment present within friendship groups also increases commitment (Brass, 1984). Thus we proposed that:

Hypothesis 5a: Friendship groups have a higher level of commitment than acquaintance groups.

Commitment to the work group causes group members to increase their task effort, regardless of the type of task being performed (Newcomb & Brady, 1982; Whitney, 1994). According to Klein and Mulvey (1995), commitement to and identity with group encourages members to perform well. Identity with the group encourages members to work harder to protect their group and individual identity (Cialdini et al., 1976; Tesser, Millar, & Moore, 1988); this, in turn, enhances performance. Research conducted with groups who performed routine motor tasks demonstrated that high levels of commitment increase group performance (Jehn, 1995; Weldon et al., 1991). Similarly, groups who perform cognitive, nonroutine tasks have higher levels of performance when group members are highly committed to the group (Jehn, 1995; O'Reilly & Caldwell, 1981). Thus, we predicted that:

Hypothesis 5b: Commitment increases motor task performance.

Hypothesis 5c: Commitment increases cognitive task performance.

Task Monitoring

Task monitoring is an administrative step group members take to ensure that the task is completed on time or at all. Task monitoring takes place when members assess their performance progress and the likelihood they will reach their goal (Weldon et al., 1991). For example, for a group with a specific deadline, monitoring behavior includes checking the clock for the time remaining to complete the task and assessing the amount of work remaining.

Attachments within friendship groups as well as group accountability and reputation effects cause members to monitor their behavior to ensure success. Group members who identify with the group and are concerned about reputation effects are more likely to perform the monitoring function (Robinson & Weldon, 1993). Members who are not strongly concerned about the group or identified with the group tend to monitor less. We therefore proposed that:

Hypothesis 6a: Friendship groups engage in more monitoring behavior than acquaitance groups.

Research shows that monitoring behavior in groups is positively related to group performance (Weldon et al., 1991). Task monitoring entails assessing the group's performance on the basis of the time remaining and the group's rate of production. Monitoring enables members to update their level of effort and to identify when different strategies are necessary to increase performance (Robinson & Weldon, 1993). Seeking feedback about the task through monitoring also improves problem solving and strategy development in that members assess current strategies and reevaluate the process (Ashford & Cummings, 1983). Therefore, we proposed that changes made by monitoring would increase group performance on both motor and cognitive tasks:

Hypothesis 6b: Task monitoring increases motor task performance.

Hypothesis 6c: Task monitoring increases cognitive task performance.

Cooperation

Cooperation "aids the performance of another group member or contributes to the ease with which group members coordinate their efforts" (Weldon & Weingart, 1988, p. 22). Cooperation includes members' helping one another with tasks (e.g., handling each other materials) and partaking in mutually beneficial behavior (e.g., trading tasks so that members are more suited to their tasks).

We propose that cooperation is greater in friendship groups than in acquaintance groups because of differences in social exchanges, such as helping behavior and task support. Mutual assistance, or the assumption that individuals can count on one another in times of need, is a characteristic of friendships (Argyle & Furnham, 1983; Davis & Todd, 1982). Whereas norms of equity govern exchange among strangers (Clark & Mills, 1979), equality or need norms are more common among close friends (Austin, 1980; Clark & Reis, 1988). Therefore, friends provide assistance to each other on the basis of needs and desires; strangers or acquaintances do so to reciprocate past benefits or to obtain future reciprocity. Given the open flow of information in close relationships (Roloff, 1987), individuals are more aware of their friends' needs and therefore are better able to provide assistance. Because of obligations, a cooperative orientation, and role expectations inherent in relationships, friends are more likely to pay attention to and fulfill others' needs (Clark, Mills, & Corcoran, 1989; Newcomb et al., 1979). Individuals also feel better after helping a friend (Williamson & Clark, 1992) and are more likely to seek assistance from friends (Harlow & Cantor, 1995; Roloff, Janiszewski, McGrath, Burns, & Manrai, 1988). We therefore proposed that:

Hypothesis 7a: Friendship groups cooperate more than acquaintance groups.

Cooperation among members is a necessary component of superior task performance (Newcomb & Brady, 1982; Whitney, 1994). Group members who help each other on a task can increase their effort and rate of production (Hackman, 1987). Cooperative groups' members share information, pay attention to others, have few communication difficulties, and thus perform better when working on interdependent tasks (Weldon & Weingart, 1988). Therefore we hypothesized that:

Hypothesis 7b: Cooperation increases motor task performance.

Hypothesis 7c: Cooperation increases cognitive task performance.

In sum, we hypothesized that friendship groups would engage in more information sharing, planning, morale-building communication, task monitoring, and cooperation and would have higher levels of commitment than acquaintance groups. We proposed competing hypotheses for the likelihood of critical evaluation in friendship and acquaintance groups on the basis of past research. We hypothesized, in turn, that performance on the motor task would be positively associated with information sharing, planning, morale building, commitment, task monitoring, and cooperation and would be negatively associated with critical evaluation. In contrast, we hypothesized that performance on the cognitive task would be positively associated with information sharing, planning, critical evaluation, commitment, task monitoring, and cooperation and would be negatively associated with morale-building communication. Overall, we suggested that friendship groups would engage in group processes that enhance performance on both motor and cognitive tasks. Thus, our final overall prediction was the following:

Hypothesis 8: Friendship groups perform better on motor and cognitive tasks than acquaintance groups.

Method

Participants

One hundred fifty-nine business students (53 three-person groups) participated in the study. Participants were on average 28.21 years old, worked 40.7 hr a week, and were primarily full-time employees. Thirty-eight percent of the participants were female.

Procedure

The study used a 2 by 2 experimental design, crossing relationship (friendship vs. acquaintance) as a between-subjects variable and task type (cognitive vs. motor) as a within-subjects variable. Each group performed two tasks, cognitive and motor, and completed postexperimental surveys. Task order was counterbalanced. Groups were videotaped during both tasks.

Participants were assigned to groups on the basis of a class survey adminstered 1 week prior to the experimental date, which asked them to identify up to 10 classmates with whom they were friends and had a "close interpersonal relationship." Students who listed each other on this survey were placed in friendship groups. To match our definition of friendship, all 3 members must have had mutually reciprocated ties. This means a participant was placed in a friendship group only if he or she had mutually named both of the other members as close personal friends and was named by the other 2 as a close personal friend. The listing of a friend had to be voluntary and reciprocated by the person named. Those who did not list each other were placed in acquaintance groups (cf. Pataki et al., 1994). The acquaintance groups were therefore composed of 3 members who had not mentioned each other on their lists. There were 78 participants in 26 groups in the friendship condition and 81 participants in 27 groups in the acquaintance condition.

The number of people required to complete the task, task interdependence, and task divisions were controlled across task types. The cognitive task we used was a scorable task that required problem-solving skills (Stasser, Taylor, & Hanna, 1989). Having a scorable task allowed us to compare across groups. Groups were given six completed master of business administration applications and had 30 min to rank the applications on six criteria (academic abilities, interpersonal skills, focus, motivation, career progress, and outside activities) and to make final accept, wait-list, or reject decisions. Groups were asked to match admissions committee decisions for each applicant (i.e., if a group chose "accept" for Applicant 1 and the admissions committee had chosen "accept" for Applicant 1, this equated one match). Groups were not told how many of the six should be accepted, wait-listed, or rejected.

The motor task we used was a model-building task that required routine, repetitive manual labor. Participants were given supplies (Styrofoam balls, glue, Popsicle sticks, aluminum foil, macaroni, string, and Tinker Toys) and were told to build models that matched a given diagram (see Weldon et al., 1991, or Weingart, 1992, for task details). They then built one structure in order to become familiar with the task. The experimenter checked the model to verify that it matched the diagram and gave the member feedback regarding deviations from the diagram. The experimenter then set a timer, which was visible to group members, told them to begin and left the room. Groups had two 10-min sessions and were told their performance would be measured by the number of models completed in each session. To avoid arbitrary goal setting, we told groups that most groups who had performed this task completed eight models per session. Participants were later debriefed. Prior use of this motor task with similar participants indicated that this was a difficult goal (Weldon et al., 1991).

Process Analysis

We used four types of data measurement to analyze the mediating group processes between relationship level and task performance: a postexperimental questionnaire, content-analyzed audiotapes, behavioral ratings of videotapes, and objective measures of individual actions (i.e., number of applications scanned and number of times a member looked at the timer). The perceptual and behavioral measures provided direct and unobtrusive measures of group process. The postexperimental questionnaire provided self-report responses from the participants, the content analysis provided measures of verbal communication, and the behavioral ratings provided measures that focused on noverbal actions, as did the objective measures of ation frequencies taken from the videotapes. We performed triangulation of multiple operationalizations to examine the mediating process that influenced group performance in friendship and acquaintance roups, which provided a rigorous examination of group processes.

Content-analyzed audiotapes. We used a three-step process to analyze the content of group discussions. First, tapes were transcribed by an individual unaware of the hypotheses. To check for accuracy, we randomly selected segments from on third of the audiotapes and compared them with the transcripts. The results indicated that the discussions were accurately transcribed. Second, each transcript was separated into thought units. A thought unit is defined as a "sequence of a few words conveying a single thought" (Weldon et al., 1991, p. 559) and was deemed the appropriate unit for analysis of meaning. Two coders unitized the transcripts; both were blind to condition and one was blind to the hypotheses. Fifteen of the 53 transcripts were unitized by both coders; the others were unitized by one coder. To determine reliability between the coders, we calculated the percentage of disagreement for the 15 transcripts that were unitized by both coders. The results indicated that the coders disagreed on unitizing once for every 100 units. Specific guidelines for unitizing can be found in the Appendix.

Third, raters were trained to classify thought units into eight different categories: information sharing, planning, critical evaluation, morale building, monitoring, commitment, cooperation, and uncodable units (which accounted for fewer than 1% of all thought units, often because of poor tape quality or mumbling). Information sharing units included statements about basic information needed to complete the task (e.g., "There are six applications"; "We can accept as many as we want"; and "We have red, yellow, and green sticks"). Planning units included phrases about how acts should be performed, who should do what, and in what order acts should be performed (e.g., "I'll do the bases and you can do the gluing"; "First let's all read everything though one time"; and "What should I do first?"). Critical evaluation units included statements such as "I think you did that wrong"; "I don't agree with your decision"; and "That model looks awful!" Morale-building units included phrases such as "No problem, we can do it!" and "Okay, we're doing great!" Monitoring was measured by the extent to which group members asked. "How many do we have done now?" or "We have two minutes left." The level of cooperation in each group was determined by the number of times members asked for or offered help or reinforced the common interest of the group (e.g., "Can you hand me that application?" and "We have to work as a team here"). Statements about group commitment included "I really feel like a part of this group" and "I'm certainly committed to us."

Three different raters coded transcripts. All three raters were unaware of condition, and two raters were unaware of the hypotheses. Twenty-one of the 53 transcripts were coded by two of the raters; the others were coded by one rater, once the rate of agreement between all pairs of raters was over 90%. Interrater agreement between the raters was based on the 21 transcripts coded by two of the raters. Kappa, a conservative measure of agreement, was used to determine interrater agreement (Brennan & Prediger, 1981). The average kappa was 96.0%. The category-specific kappas were the following: for information sharing, 88.9%; for planning, 91.1%; for critical evaluation, 99.4%; for morale building, 99.5%; for monitoring, 97.0%; for commitment, 97.8%; for cooperation, 97.3%; and for uncodable units, 97.2%. Kappa was calculated by calculating the number of times that the judges agreed on the category in which to place a unit, dividing by the number of units in the transcript, and adjusting for chance.[2] A complete description of the eight categories, categorization guidelines, and category-specific reliabilities is provided in the Appendix.

Frequencies of behaviors. All acts performed by each member (e.g., wrapping foil around a ball, attaching a green base, moving a box, picking up an application, giving the application to a group member) were recorded from the videotapes by a research assistant who was unaware of the hypotheses. The acts performed by each group member were used to assess the amount of morale-building communication, monitoring, and cooperative acts. Morale-building acts consisted of high-fives, clapping, and backslapping as acts of encouragement among members. Monitoring was measured by the number of times group members looked at or pointed to the timer. The level of cooperation in each group was determined by the number of times members helped one another (e.g., by pointing to information on an application or handing the application to another member in the application task, or by passing materials or assisting in attaching materials to the final structure in the model-building task). These behaviors indicated cooperation among members to complete the task. To check the accuracy of the listings, 15 one-minute segments were viewed by the experimenters. The category-specific kappas for these categories were the following: for morale-building, 100%; for monitoring, 98%; and for cooperation, 98%.

---

[2]Although a sound track was present on the videotapes, we chose to code the verbal behaviors from the audiotapes for two reasons. First, the clarity of the sounds on the audiotape was superior to that on the videotape. Second, our coding scheme used the thought unit as the unit of analysis and was more accurate when we used a hard copy of the transcripts from the audiotapes than when we listened directly to the sound from the videotapes. We realize that by coding only the transcripts, we were unable to capture the nonverbal behaviors associated with the verbal behavior; however, we expected to capture much of the nonverbal behavior in the videotape ratings.

Videotape ratings. The videotapes were also rated by two raters unaware of the hypotheses. The two raters watched each group's videotape four times for both the model-building task and the decision-making task. They rated the actions of each individual and the interaction among group members for each task on information sharing, planning, critical evaluation, morale-building communication, commitment, monitoring, and cooperation. Raters were given definitions of the process variables and were asked about statements such as "This group engaged in a lot of planning" and "This group engaged in a lot of task monitoring." They rated the behaviors on a scale of 1 (*strongly disagree*) to 7 (*strongly agree*). The average interrater agreement was 89.3%, ranging from 85.5% (for planning) to 96% (for cooperation). When raters rated an item farther than 1 point apart, they discussed the item and behavior until they reached agreement. A complete description of the eight categories and items is provided in the Appendix.

Postexperimental questionnaire. Self-reports of information sharing, morale-building communication, planning, critical evaluation, commitment, and cooperation were collected after the model-building task and the decision-making task. For example, commitment was measured by the members' ratings of the following questions: "I was very committed to this work group"; "I would talk up this work group to my friends as a great group"; and "I would be proud to tell others that I am part of this work group." Group members responded to the items on 7-point scales (*strongly disagree* to *strongly agree*). The items that measure each variable in the model are included in Table 1.

Scale development. Scales were developed from the four methods of construct measurement (postexperimental questionnaire, content-analyzed audiotapes, behavioral ratings of the videotapes, and action frequencies) for the seven mediating variables (information sharing, planning, critical evaluation, morale-building communication, commitment, monitoring, and cooperation). We performed a principal-components analysis using an oblique rotation. The reults are provided in Table 1. An oblique rotation was performed to take into account the intercorrelation of the process variables (Kim & Mueller, 1978). A six-component solution was found, on the basis of the scree test and eigenvalues above 1.0.

The first component included four items that measured morale-building communication; the transcript rating of morale building, two items from the video ratings, and one item from the postexperimental questionnaire. Two items were reverse-coded to reflect positive morale building. Also loading on Factor 1 were three items that reflected information sharing: the content-analyzed transcript rating of information sharing, the video rating of open communication, and one item from the postexperimental questionnaire. We labeled this factor Positive Communication and used it to test our hypotheses regarding morale-building communication and information sharing. The Cronbach alpha for Positive Communication was .86.

Cooperation was reflected in the second component by three items of the video raters ("This member was very cooperative"; 'This member engaged in a lot of help-offering behavior"; and "This member put forth a lot of effort"); the number of actions regarding cooperation tallied from the videotapes (e.g., handing, passing, and answering questions); and one item from the postexperimental questionaire ("How cooperative and helpful were your group members?"). The Cronbach alpha for Factor 2, Cooperation, was .79.

The third component included the six items that measured critical evaluation: three items from the postexperimental questionnaire ("How often did people in your work group disagree about opinions regarding the work being done?" "To what extent were there differences of opinion in your work group?" and "How frequently did you have disagreements about the work you did with other people in your work group?"); the critical evaluation component of the content-analyzed audiotapes; and two items from the video rating (e.g., "This group engaged in a lot of critical evaluation" and "This group engaged in a lot of conflicts about ideas"). The Cronbach alpha was .88 for Critical Evaluation, Factor 3.

The fourth component reflected the monitoring behavior of the group members. The behavioral ratings from the videotapes ("This group engaged in a lot of task monitoring") and the content-analyzed audiotape comments regarding monitoring comments (e.g., "How many do we have done?" and "How much time is left?") loaded on this component. The Cronbach alpha for Factor 4, Monitoring, was .98.

TABLE 1. Factor Loadings for Group Process Measures

Measure	Factor 1 (Positive Communication)	Factor 2 (Cooperation)	Factor 3 (Critical Evaluation)	Factor 4 (Monitoring)	Factor 5 (Commitment)	Factor 6 (Planning)
"It is easy to talk openly to all members of this group." (PQ)	**.747**	−.070	.263	−.043	.080	−.081
"This group engaged in very open communication." (VR)	**.738**	−.030	.289	−.075	.071	−.079
Content analysis of information sharing (AT)	**.758**	−.233	.204	−.076	.080	−.027
Content analysis of morale building (AT)	**.566**	.214	.113	−.020	.302	.334
"People were angry about working in this group." (VR)	**−.577**	.367	.147	−.206	.263	.011
"This group engaged in a lot of morale building." (VR)	**.629**	.316	.228	−.028	.279	.038
"I felt a lot of tension in this group." (PQ)	**−.527**	.425	.138	−.084	.275	−.175
"How cooperative and helpful were your group members?" (PQ)	.048	**.815**	.166	.124	.042	.098
Cooperative behavior—handing, passing, answering questions (AF)	.216	**.760**	.039	.198	−.062	.391
"This member engaged in a lot of help-offering behavior." (VR)	.424	**.619**	−.306	−.078	.154	.395
"This member was very cooperative." (VR)	.347	**.600**	−.323	−.093	.096	−.303
"This member put forth a lot of effort." (VR)	.408	**.708**	−.272	−.190	−.060	−.023
"How often did people in your work group disagree about opinions regarding the work being done?" (PQ)	−.293	.406	**.446**	−.256	.009	.079
"To what extent were there differences of opinion in your work group?" (PQ)	−.376	.300	**.501**	−.152	.069	−.059
"How frequently did you have disagreements about the work you did with other people in your work group?" (PQ)	−.367	.359	**.510**	.034	.248	.126
Content analysis of critical evaluation (AT)	−.284	.244	**.537**	.038	.181	.027
"This group engaged in a lot of critical evaluation." (VR)	.067	.329	**.581**	−.136	−.235	.030
"This group engaged in a lot of conflicts about ideas." (VR)	−.108	.403	**−.530**	−.125	.285	.009
"This group engaged in a lot of task monitoring." (VR)	.065	.246	.088	**.759**	−.006	−.074
Content analysis of task monitoring (AT)	.071	.301	.087	**.764**	−.015	−.076
"I was very committed to this group." (PQ)	.230	−.104	.145	.054	**.557**	.188
"I would talk up this work group to my friends as a great group." (PQ)	.282	−.101	.375	−.076	**.619**	.008
"This group was very committed to each other." (VR)	.092	−.005	.451	−.006	**.760**	.098
"This member was very committed to doing well." (VR)	.022	.406	−.296	−.205	**.816**	.097
"This group engaged in a lot of planning." (VR)	.097	.121	.008	−.165	.145	**.536**
"How much disagreement is there about procedures in your work group?" (PQ)	.048	.234	.036	.198	−.067	**.679**
Content analysis of planning (AT)	−.276	−.100	.267	−.152	.069	−.059
Monitoring behavior—check time, check quality. (AF)	.045	−.235	.098	.137	.229	.341

(Continued)

TABLE 1. Continued

Measure	Factor 1 (Positive Communication)	Factor 2 (Cooperation)	Factor 3 (Critical Evaluation)	Factor 4 (Monitoring)	Factor 5 (Commitment)	Factor 6 (Planning)
"I would be proud to tell others that I am part of this work group." (PQ)	.092	.130	−.249	−.205	.230	−.022
Content analysis of commitment (AT)	.155	−.104	.145	.054	.230	.189
"To what extent did you talk about who would do what?" (PQ)	−.068	.064	.140	−.106	.291	.175
"There was a lot of emotional conflict in this group." (PQ)	−.345	.201	.114	−.020	.303	.334
"We engage in very open communication." (PQ)	.201	.115	.104	.098	−.259	−.295
Morale-building behavior—high-fives, clapping (AF)	.116	.098	.244	.249	.298	.023
Content analysis of cooperation (AT)	.001	.218	.166	.124	.042	.098
"How cooperative were you with your group members?" (PQ)	.161	.191	.125	.044	.053	.228
Eigenvalues	7.21	6.14	3.11	1.69	1.54	1.18

Note. N = 159. Boldface is used to indicate significant loading. AF = action frequencies; AT = audio transcripts; PQ = postexperimental questionnaire; VR = video ratings.

The component included two postexperimental questionnaire items that reflected commitment to the group ("I was very committed to this work group" and "I would talk up this work group to my friends as a great group") and the videotape ratings of commitment ("This group was very committed to each other" and "This member was very committed to doing well"). The Cronbach alpha for Factor 5, Commitment, was .82.

Planning was the sixth component and included the behavioral video rating ("This member engaged in a lot of planning") and one item from the postexperimental questionnaire ("How much disagreement is there about procedures in your work group?"). The Cronbach alpha was .71 for Planning, Factor 6. The intercorrelations among the factors ranged from .02 (for Critical Evaluation and Planning) to .36 (for Commitment and Cooperation) with an average of .18.

The principal-components analysis and Cronbach alphas indicate that there is consistency across methods of measurement and that triangulation of multiple methods is an appropriate and robust way to examine the mediating processes between relationship level and group performance.

We averaged the 13 individual-level items to produce composite scores on each variable for each group member. We then averaged these scores across groups to produce group scores of the factors. We performed the eta-squared test for aggre-

gation to detremine whether any two people within the same group were more similar than two people from different groups. The results exceeded .20 for all factors, indicating that it was appropriate to aggregate the factors to the group level (Georgopoulos, 1986, p. 40).

Performance measures. Motor task performance scores were based on the number of models produced. Cognitive task performance was calculated as the degree to which group decisions matched the admissions committee decisions. Comparison with experts' performance is a common way to assess group performance (McGrath, 1984). Cognitive task performance scores were therefore based on the number of times group decisions matched those of the admissions committee.

Results

Manipulation Checks

As shown by t tests, participants in the acquaintance groups were significantly less likely to rate other group members as friends on the postexperimental questionnaire, $M = 3.73$ $(SD = 1.47)$, with $1 = strongly\ disagree$ and $7 = strongly\ agree$, than were participants in friendship groups when responding to the item "The other people in this group are my friends," $M = 5.45$ $(SD = 1.10)$, $t(158) = 11.38, p < .0001$, thus indicating that groups were properly created. The members of friendship groups were also significantly more familiar with one another, $M = 4.62$ ($SD = 1.37$), were more cohesive, $M = 5.74$ ($SD = 1.26$), were more positive regarding interpersonal relations, $M = 4.36$ ($SD = 1.17$), were more amiable, $M = 6.25$ ($SD = 0.84$), had more knowledge about one another's strengths and weaknesses, $M = 3.59$ ($SD = 1.75$), and were more concerned with maintaining their relationships, $M = 5.12$ ($SD = 1.50$) than were members of the acquaintance groups: familiar $M = 2.36$ ($SD = 1.25$), with 1 = *did not know others* and 7 = *knew others very well*, $t(158) = 14.90, p < .0001$; cohesive $M = 4.68$ ($SD = 1.60$), with 1 = *not at all cohesive* and 7 = *very cohesive*, $t(158) = 6.37, p < .0001$; positive $M = 3.75$ ($SD = 1.15$), with 1 = *not at all satisfied* and 7 = *very satisfied*, $t(158) = 3.90, p < .0001$; amiable $M = 5.43$ ($SD = 1.26$), with 1 = *don't like at all* and 7 = *like very much*, $t(158) = 6.53, p < .0001$; knowledge $M = 1.97$ ($SD = 1.31$), with 1 = *not at all familiar with strengths and weaknesses* and 7 = *very familiar with strengths and weaknesses*, $t(158) = 9.02, p < .0001$; contact $M = 4.23$ ($SD = 1.59$), with 1 = *no concern with contact to maintain the relationship* and 7 = *very concerned with contact to maintain the relationship*, $t(158) = 4.98, p < .0001$.

In addition, in the video ratings the friendship groups were viewed as more concerned with the relationship, $M = 3.75$ ($SD = 1.12$), more cohesive, $M = 4.39$ ($SD = 1.28$), and more satisfied, $M = 5.72$ ($SD = 1.32$), than were the acquaintance groups: relationship concern $M = 3.24$ ($SD = 1.02$), $t(52) = 3.48, p < .001$; cohesive $M = 3.87$ ($SD = 1.14$), $t(52) = 3.18, p < .001$; satisfied $M = 5.37$ ($SD = 1.40$), $t(52) = 2.14, p < .03$. Friends also made more cohesive statements, $M = 5.36$ ($SD = 1.51$), such as "We are such a close group" and "Together forever!" than acquaintances, $M = 4.43$ ($SD = 1.72$), $t(52) = 4.97, p < .001$, as rated by the audio transcript raters.

Items regarding task attributes on the postexperimental survey indicated that the tasks differed only on the cognitive and motor dimensions; no significant differences were reported on task interdependence, difficulty, challenge, effort expended, or goal commitment. Significant differences were reported on the extent to which tasks were repetitive: motor task $M = 6.04$ ($SD = 1.31$), decision task $M = 3.34$ ($SD = 1.69$), with 1 = *not at all repetitive*, and 7 = *very repetitive*, $t(307) = 15.51, p < .001$; whether they required cognitive ability: motor task $M = 3.50$ ($SD = 1.23$), decision task $M = 5.98$ ($SD = 1.19$), with 1 = *no cognitive ability required* and 7 = *much cognitive ability required*, $t(307) = 10.52, p < .001$; and whether they required physical labor: motor task $M = 5.60$ ($SD = 1.49$). decision task $M = 1.62$ ($SD = .97$), with 1 = *no physical labor required*, and 7 = *much physical labor required*, $t(307) = 27.57, p < .001$.

Hypotheses Tests

The means by relationship level and task type are shown in Table 2. The number of models produced by a group during the motor task ranged from 1 to 12. The number of correct decisions made by a group (calculated by the degree to which group decisions matched the admissions committee decisions) ranged from 0 to 6. Table 3 provides the intercorrelations for all variables in the model.

Relationship level and group process. The overall multivariate analysis of variance (MANOVA) for relationship was significant, $F(1, 52) = 6.73, p < .001$. Thus, we conducted task by relationship analyses of variance (ANOVAs) to test main effects regarding relationship level and group processes. The performance scores were normalized by task and combined for each group. The main effect of relationship on performance was significant, $F(1, 52) = 10.45, p < .01$, thus supporting Hypothesis 8, that friendship groups perform better than acquaintance groups. Further analysis using t tests indicated that friendship groups produced significantly more models, $M = 9.00$ ($SD = 3.98$), than acquaintance groups, $M = 2.45$ ($SD = 1.28$), $t(52) = 2.43, p < .05$. Friendship groups also matched more admissions committee decisions, $M = 3.10$ ($SD = 1.07$), than acquaintance groups, $M = 2.44$ ($SD = 1.26$), $t(52) = 2.30, p < .05$.

The results of the ANOVAs indicate main effects for relationship on positive communication, commitment, and cooperation. Friendship groups exchanged more positive communication, $M = 4.22$ ($SD = .61$), than acquaintance groups, $M = 3.87$ ($SD = .43$), $F(1, 52) = 6.87, p < .001$, providing some support for the hypotheses that friendship groups share more information (as we predicted in Hypothesis 1a) and exchange more positive morale-building communication (as predicted in Hypothesis 4a). Hypothesis 5a, that friendship groups have a higher level of commitment than acquaintance groups, was supported: Friendship groups were more committed, $M = 5.13$ ($SD =$

TABLE 2. Means and Standard Deviations by Relationship and Task

	Process												
	Positive communication		Planning		Critical evaluation		Commitment		Monitoring		Cooperation		Task performance	
Group	M	SD	M	SD	M	SD	M	SD	M	SD	M	SD	M	SD
	Motor task													
Friendship	4.28	0.61	3.50	1.72	1.56	0.48	5.23	0.88	2.71	1.77	5.06	1.09	9.00	3.98
Acquaintance	3.87	0.39	2.72	1.55	1.78	0.76	4.56	1.03	2.70	1.79	4.76	1.16	2.45	1.28
	Cognitive task													
Friendship	4.16	0.52	3.33	1.64	2.35	0.91	5.03	1.00	2.96	1.81	4.70	1.25	3.10	1.07
Acquaintance	3.87	0.57	2.63	1.36	2.24	0.98	4.19	1.08	2.81	1.74	4.11	1.12	2.44	1.26
	Overall													
Friendship	4.22	0.61	3.42	1.68	1.96	0.91	5.13	1.06	2.84	1.75	4.88	1.18		
Acquaintance	3.87	0.43	2.68	1.45	2.01	0.90	4.37	0.96	2.76	1.76	4.44	1.18		

Note. For friendship group, *n* = 26; for acquaintance group, *n* = 27.

1.06), than acquaintance groups, $M = 4.37$ ($SD = .96$), F (1, 52) = 7.38, $p < .001$. Hypothesis 7a, that friendship groups cooperate more than acquaintance groups, was also supported: Friendship groups were more cooperative, $M = 4.88$ ($SD = 1.18$), than acquaintance groups, $M = 4.44$ ($SD = 1.18$), $F(1,52) = 10.46, p < .01$. There was no main effect for relationship on planning, critical evaluation, or monitoring, contrary to Hypotheses 2a, 3a, and 6a, respectively.

Group processes and task performance. Table 4 illustrates the regression results examining the relation between performance and positive communication, commitment, monitoring, planning, and cooperation, regardless of the task performed. Hypotheses 5b (motor task) and 5c (cognitive task)

were supported: Commitment was positively related to task performance. Task monitoring (Hypotheses 6b and 6c) was also positively related to task performance, as was cooperation (Hypotheses 7b and 7c). Planning (Hypotheses 2b or 2c) and positive communication (Hypotheses 4b and 4c) were not significantly related to task performance.

Group processes mediating relationship and performance. We used the test for mediation described by Baron and Kenny (1986) to test the contribution of the mediating processes between relationship level and task performance. First, the predicted mediators were regressed on relationship level. On the basis of the previous analyses, we excluded planning and monitoring because they were not found to have significant main effects of

TABLE 3. Correlations Between Variables Across Friendship and Age Groups

Variable	1	2	3	4	5	6	7	8	9
1. Critical Evaluation	—								
2. Positive Communication	.22	—							
3. Cooperation	−.89	.15	—						
4. Commitment	−.05	.20	.36	—					
5. Planning	.06	.01	.34	.21	—				
6. Monitoring	.27	.17	.25	.20	.27	—			
7. Relationship	−.03	.39	.17	.36	.09	.06	—		
8. Performance—Motor	−.14	.27	.39	.36	.05	.28	.65	—	
9. Performance—Cognitive	.23	−.14	.38	.32	.22	.26	.46	.46	—

Note. All correlations of greater absolute magnitude than .23 are significant at the $p < .05$ level. Given the multitude of correlations tested (55), there is the possibility of capitalizing on chance. However, only 5%, or approximately 3 of the 55 correlation coefficients, would be significant if chance alone were operating. Our results indicate 26 significant correlation coefficients, thus suggesting the need for further examination.

TABLE 4. Summary of Regression Analysis for Variables Predicting Performance

Variable	B	SE B	β
Positive Communication	0.288	.228	−.127
Planning	0.062	.055	−.190
Commitment	1.340	.134	.432*
Monitoring	1.210	.049	.449*
Cooperation	0.780	.154	.376*

Note. N = 106. R = .55.
*p < .01.

relationship, and we excluded positive communication because it was not significantly related to performance. Commitment and cooperation were significantly related to relationship level (B = .389, p < .001, and B = .184, p < .01, respectively). Second, relationship level was significantly related to the dependent variable, task performance (B = .45, p > .001). Third, the effect of relationship became nonsignificant when the mediator variables were included in the regression analyses on group performance (average B = .09, all ps were ns). Thus, the mediating role of commitment and cooperation on task performance was supported (Baron & Kenny, 1986).

Task type, group process, and performance. To examine the hypotheses that task type moderates the relation between critical evaluation (Hypotheses 3b and 3c) and morale-building communication (Hypotheses 4b and 4c), we conducted regressions separately for each task. We used the positive communication variable to test the hypothesis regarding morale-building communication because it included the items designed to measure morale-building communication. In support of Hypothesis 4b, positive communication was positively related to performance in the motor task (B = .22, p < .001), and in marginal support of Hypothesis 4c, it was negatively related to performance in the cognitive task (B = −.13, p < .07, respectively). In addition, critical evaluation was positively related to performance in the cognitive task but negatively related in the motor task (B = .16, p < .001, and B = −.27, p < .001, respectively). Although friendship did not influence critical evaluation in this study (Hypothesis 3a). Hypotheses 3b and 3c were supported: Critical evaluation was positively related to performance in the cognitive task and negatively related to performance in the motor task.

We included task order as a variable in our de-

sign to control for task experience across tasks. A 2 (task) × 2 (relationship) × 2 (order) ANOVA revealed significant main effects for order on positive communication, $F(1, 52)$ = 5.96, p < .05, and commitment, $F(1, 52)$ = 6.68, p < .05. Groups who performed the cognitive task prior to the motor task had more commitment (M = 4.96) than groups who performed the motor task prior to the cognitive task (M = 4.66). Groups in which the motor task preceded the cognitive task engaged in more positive communication (M = 1.78) than those in which the cognitive task preceded the motor task (M = 1.50).

Discussion

This study provides information about group processes that mediate the effect of relationship level on task performance. The results indicate that several process differences in friendship and acquaintance groups account for the performance superiority of friendship groups on both cognitive and motor tasks. Prior research has suggested that friendship among group members may harm a group's performance, because the group's focus may be on social interaction rather than the task (Bramel & Friend, 1987; Homans, 1951). The results from this study indicate that although friendship groups do communicate more and provide more positive encouragement than acquaintance groups, they also are more committed and more cooperative, which leads to higher performance levels.

Regardless of the type of task the group performed, commitment, cooperation, and task monitoring increased group performance, thus demonstrating why friendship groups performed better than acquaintance groups. There was no significant difference between the amount that friends and acquaintances planned, nor was planning related to performance in either the model-building task or the decision-making task. One explanation is that tacit coordination occurred without discussion (Wittenbaurm, Stasser, & Merry, 1996), which was not captured by our verbal coding scheme. This is unlikely, because our measure of planning included self-report and video rating of nonverbal behaviors; however, the reliability for this scale was one of the lowest (.71). In addition, Argote (1982) found that in organizations, in-process planning improves effectiveness when the task has a high level of uncertainty. In our study we measured only in-process planning, therefore missing any preplanning that might have taken place (Weingart, 1992). In addition, both of the tasks were very structured, with low levels of uncertainty; therefore, it may not be surprising that we did not find significant results for planning and performance.

Similar to Weldon et al. (1991), we found that task monitoring was positively related to task performance. In addition, we expanded Weldon et al.'s model by demonstrating that friendship, cooperation, and commitment increase task performance. Similar to Shah and Jehn (1993), we found that processes in friendship groups are not consistent across tasks. Friendship groups appear to engage in behavior and interaction patterns beneficial to the task they are performing. This suggests a feedback mechanism that may be more common in friendship groups than in acquaintance groups (Guzzo & Dickson, 1996). Poor performance reflects negatively on a group, and it is more difficult to diassociate oneself from a group of friends than from a group of acquaintances (Tesser & Smith, 1980).

Processes not related to performance may be less likely to occur in friendship groups because of associations among members and the strong obligation to be committed to high performance and the maintenance of a good group reputation. For instance, although friendship groups communicated more than acquaintance groups overall, when they worked on the cognitive task, their conversation was more task focused (i.e., they engaged in critical evaluation). Friendship groups also reduced their level of morale building in the cognitive task, where emotional arousal is not necessary for superior performance. Differences in task division in friendship and acquaintance groups also existed. Friendship groups helped each other complete their task components more in the motor task and engaged in more critical evaluation in the cognitive task than did acquaintance groups, who tended to work independently on both tasks. Thus, one implication of this study is the adaptability apparent in friendship groups as compared with acquaintance groups.

A main contribution of this research project is the use of multiple methods to measure the group processes that lead to task performance. Rather than depending solely on one source of data, this project integrated survey responses, coded transcripts, behavioral ratings, and objective measures of individuals' actions to provide a more thorough understanding of the mediating group processes under investigation. The use of multiple methods enabled us to observe the group process constructs from multiple perspectives and strengthened our understanding of the constructs and the relation among them.

Limits of our study suggest interesting directions for future research. Our research focused on a finite task in a limited time frame. The time frame may affect the processes differently depending on the type of task being performed. For instance, if members performing a cognitive task have unlimited time to collect and process information, morale building may produce positive results (as it did in the motor task) rather than negative ones, as our study demonstrated. The motor task in this study focused on manual skill and dexterity, with very little information-processing demands. The time that group members took away from information processing during the cognitive task to engage in morale building might have played a role in decreasing performance. We also found that the counterbalancing of tasks in our design led to a main effect of order. Groups who performed the motor task first had higher levels of positive communication overall than did groups who performed the cognitive task first. Groups who performed the cognitive task first had higher levels of information sharing and commitment. It is interesting that the processes associated with order were based on the variables related to high performance in the first task (e.g., morale building in the motor task). This suggests a learning effect, which we encourage future researchers to investigate.

The results from this study suggest numerous other directions for future inquiry, particularly in the areas of group processes, relationships, and tasks. Although numerous mediating processes have been speculated to influence group performance, our research focused on seven. Future research to identify and investigate other mediating factors, such as conflict, diffusion of responsibility, trust, advice, and workflow patterns, is needed. Our work focused on processes within a group's internal environment. Work by Gladstein (1984) has suggested that both a group's internal and its external environment are important factors in its performance. It would be interesting to investigate whether friendship and acquaintance groups exhibit different external as well as internal group processes. The relationships that exist within a group may result in different interaction patterns with external interfaces. Finally, rather than focus solely on positive relationships within work groups, researchers might also investigate processes in groups where interpersonal dislikes, disputes, and conflicts prevail.

The group process focus of this paper departs from the traditional outcome-focused approaches (for other examinations of group process see Liang, Moreland, & Argote, 1995; Shah & Jehn, 1993; Weingart, 1992; Weldon et al., 1991). Outcome-focused research has provided important information regarding group compostion and performance. However, this line of inquiry provides only a limited understanding of the link between friendship and group performance. Investigating the mediating processes that contribute to superior group performance provides a more comprehensive understanding of the process by which friendship groups outperform acquaintance groups. On a more general level, understanding the processes that mediate group performance is essential to understanding how group dynamics and interaction pattern lead to differing performance levels. Knowledge of the processess necessary for superior performance provides us with the tools necessary to train and manage better performing work teams.

ACKNOWLEDGMENTS

This resarch was supported in part by grants from the Dispute Resolution Research Center at Northwestern University; the University of Minnesota, Twin Cities Campus; and the Reginald H. Jones Center for Management Policy, Strategy, and Organization at the Wharton School of the University of Pennsylvania. We are grateful to Maggie Neale, Keith Weigelt, Craig Fox, and Jeanne Brett for their help and insightful comments on the research project and the experimental design; to Tiffany Galvin, Ha Ngyuen, and Ted Wong for their help in coding the process data; to Mary Eileen Baltes for her editorial skills; and to Sara Yang, Dave Polesky, and Emma Vas for their assistance in data entering and analysis.

REFERENCES

Aboud, F. E. (1989). Disagreement between friends. *International Journal of Behavioral Development, 12*, 495–508.

Albrecht, T. L., & Ropp, V. A. (1984). Communicating about innovation in networks of three U.S. organizations. *Journal of Communication, 34*, 78–91.

Allison, G. T. (1971). *Essence of decision: Explaining the Cuban missile crisis*. Boston: Little, Brown.

Argote, L. (1982). Input uncertainty and organizational coordination in hospital emergency units. *Administrative Science Quarterly, 27*, 420–434.

Argyle, M., & Furnham, A. (1983). Sources of satisfaction and conflict in long-term relationships. *Journal of Marriage and the Family, 45*, 481–493.

Ashford, S. J., & Cummings, L. L. (1983). Feedback as an individual resource: Personal strategies of creating information. *Organizational Behavior and Human Performance, 32*, 370–398.

Austin, W. (1980). Friendship and fairness: Effects of type of relationship and task performance on choice of distribution rules. *Personality and Social Psychology Bulletin, 6*, 402–408.

Bales, R. F. (1951). *Interaction process analysis*. Cambridge, MA: Addison-Wesley.

Bandura, A. (1982). Self-efficacy mechanism in human agency. *American Psychologist, 37*, 122–147.

Bandura, A., Reese, L., & Adams, N. E. (1982). Microanalysis of action and fear arousal as a function of differential levels of perceived self-efficacy. *Journal of Personality and Social Psychology, 43*, 5–21.

Baron, R. M., & Kenny, D. A. (1986). The moderator-mediator variable distinction in social psychological research: Conceptual, strategic, and statistical consideration. *Journal of Personality and Social Psychology, 51*, 1173–1182.

Berkowitz, L. (1954). Group standards, cohesiveness, and productivity. *Human Relations, 7*, 509–519.

Bramel, D., & Friend, R. (1987). The work group and its vicissitudes in social and industrial psychology. *Journal of Applied Behavioral Science, 23*, 233–253.

Brass, D. (1984). Being in the right place: A structural analysis of individual influence in an organization. *Administrative Science Quarterly, 29*, 518–539.

Brennan, R. L., & Prediger, D. J. (1981). Coefficient kappa: Some uses, misuses and alternatives. *Journal of Educational and Psychological Measurement, 41*, 687–699.

Cialdini, R. B., Borden, R. J., Thorne, A., Walker, M. R., Freeman, S., & Sloan, L. R. (1976). Basking in reflected glory: Three (football) field studies. *Journal of Personality and Social Psychology, 34*, 366–375.

Clark, M. S., & Mills, J. R. (1979). Interpersonal attraction in exchange and communal relationships. *Journal of Personality and Social Psychology, 37*, 12–24.

Clark, M. S., & Mills, J. R. (1993). The difference between communal and exchange relationships: What it is and is not. *Personality and Social Psychology Bulletin, 19*, 684–691.

Clark, M. S., Mills, J. R., & Corcoran, D. M. (1989). Keeping track of needs and inputs of friends and strangers. *Personality and Social Psychology Bulletin, 15*, 533–542.

Clark, M. S., Mills, J. R., & Powell, M. (1986). Keeping track of needs in communal and exchange relationships. *Journal of Personality and Social Psychology, 51*, 333–338.

Clark, M. S., & Reis, H. T. (1988). Interpersonal processes in close relationships. *Annual Review of Psychology, 39*, 609–672.

Cook, T., & Campbell, D. (1979). *Quasi-experimentation: Design 7 analysis issues for field settings*. Boston: Houghton Mifflin.

Cosier, R., & Schwenk, C. (1990). Agreement and thinking alike: Ingredients for poor decisions. *Academy of Management Executive, 4*, 81–92.

Dailey, R. C. (1977). The effects of cohesiveness and collaboration on work groups: A theoretical model. *Group and Organization Studies, 2,* 461–469.

Danowski, J. A. (1980). Group attitude uniformity and connectivity of organizational communication networks for production, innovation, and maintenance content. *Human Communication Research, 12,* 251–270.

Davidson, L. R., & Duberman, L. (1982). Friendship: Communication and interactional patterns in same-sex dyads. *Sex Roles, 8,* 809–821.

Davis, K. E., & Todd, M. J. (1982). Friendship and love relationships. *Advances in Descriptive Psychology, 2,* 79–122.

Dean, J. W., & Sharfman, M. P. (1996). Does decision process matter? A study of strategic decision-making effectiveness. *Academy of Management Journal, 39,* 368–396.

Evans, C. R., & Dion, K. L. (1991). Group cohesion and performance: A meta-analysis. *Small Group Research, 22,* 175–186.

Fischhoff, B., Slovic, P., & Lichtenstein, S. (1977). Knowing with certainty: The appropriateness of extreme confidence. *Journal of Experimental Psychology: Human Perception and Performance, 3,* 552–564.

Georgopoulos, B. S. (1986). *Organizational structure, Problem solving and effectiveness.* San Francisco: Jossey-Bass.

Gladstein, D. L. (1984). Groups in context: A model of task group effectiveness. *Administrative Science Quarterly, 29,* 499–517.

Gladstein, D. L., & Reilly, N. P. (1985). Group decision making under threat: The tycoon game. *Academy of Management Journal, 28,* 613–627.

Gottman, M. T., & Parkhurst, J. T. (1980). A developmental theory of friendship and acquaintanceship processes. In W. A. Collins (Ed.). *Minnesota Symposium on Child Psychology* (pp. 197–253). Hillsdale. NJ: Erlbaum.

Greenberg, J. (1983). Equity and equality as clues to the relationship between exchange participants. *European Journal of Social Psychology, 13,* 195–196.

Gruenfeld, D., & Hollingshead, A. B. (1993). Sociocognition in work groups: The evolution of group integrative complexity and its relation to task performance. *Small Group Research, 24,* 383–405.

Guzzo, R. A. (1986). Group decision making and group effectiveness in organizations. In P. S. Goodman (Ed.), *Designing effective work groups* (pp. 34–71). San Francisco: Jossey-Bass.

Guzzo, R. A., & Dickson, M. W. (1996). Teams in organizations: Recent research on performance and effectiveness. *Annual Review of Psychology, 47,* 307–338.

Guzzo, R. A., & Shea, G. P. (1992). Group performance and intergroup relations in organizations. In M. D. Dunnette & L. M. Hough (Eds.), *Handbook of industrial and organizational psychology* (pp. 262–313). Palo Alto, CA: Consulting Psychologists Press.

Hackman, J. R. (1987). The design of work teams. In J. Lorsch (Ed.), *Handbook of organizational behavior* (pp. 315–342). Englewood Cliffs, NJ: Prentice Hall.

Hackman, J. R. (1991). *Groups that work (and those that don't).* San Francisco: Jossey-Bass.

Hackman, J. R., Brousseau, K. R., & Weiss, J. A. (1976). The interaction of task design and group performance strategies in determining group effectiveness. *Organizational Behavior and Human Performance, 16,* 350–365.

Hackman, J. R. & Morris, C. G. (1975). Group tasks, group interaction process, and group performance effectiveness: A review and proposed integration. In L. Berkowitz (Ed.).

Advances in experimental social psychology (pp. 1–56). New York: Academic Press.

Harlow, R. E., & Cantor, N. (1995). To whom do people turn when things go poorly? Task orientation and functional social contacts. *Journal of Personality and Social Psychology, 69,* 329–340.

Hays, R. B. (1985). A longitudinal study of friendship development. *Journal of Personality and Social Psychology, 48,* 909–924.

Henry, R. (1995). Improving group judgment accuracy: Information sharing and determining the best member. *Organizational Behavior and Human Decision Processess, 62,* 190–197.

Homans, G. C. (1951). *The human group.* New Brunswick, NJ: Transaction.

Janis, I. L. (1982). *Groupthink: Psychological studies of policy decisions and fiascos.* Boston: Houghton Mifflin.

Jehn, K. A. (1995). A multimethod examination of the benefits and deteriments of intragroup conflict. *Administrative Science Quarterly, 40,* 256–282.

Kaplan, R. E. (1979). The conspicuous absence of evidence that process consultation enhances task performance. *Journal of Applied Behavioral Science, 15,* 346–360.

Kelley, H. H., & Thibaut, J. W. (1979). *Interpersonal relations.* New York: Wiley.

Kim, J., & Mueller, C. W. (1978). *Introduction to factor analysis.* Beverly Hills, CA: Sage.

Klein, H. J., & Mulvey, P. W. (1995). Two investigations of the relationships among group goals, goal commitment, cohesion, and performance. *Organizational Behavior and Human Decision Processes, 61,* 44–53.

Knapp, M. L., Ellis, D. G., & Williams, B. A. (1980). Perceptions of communication behavior associated with relationship terms. *Communication Monographs, 47,* 262–278.

Ladd, G. W., & Emerson, E. S. (1984). Shared knowledge in children's friendships. *Developmental Psychology, 20,* 932–940.

Larson, J., Christensen, C., Abbott, A., & Franz, T. (1996). Diagnosing groups: Charting the flow of information in medical decision-making teams. *Journal of Personality and Social Psychology, 71,* 315–330.

Liang, D., Moreland, R., & Argote, L. (1995). Group versus individual training and group performance: The mediating role of transactive memory. *Personality and Social Psychology Bulletin, 21,* 384–393.

Lincoln, J. R., & Miller, J. (1979). Work and friendship ties in organizations: A comparative analysis of relational networks. *Administrative Science Quarterly, 24,* 181–199.

McGrath, J. (1984). *Groups: Interaction and performance,* Englewood Cliffs, NJ: Prentice Hall.

McPherson, J. M., & Smith-Lovin, L. (1987). Homophilly in voluntary organizations: Status distance and the composition of face-to-face groups. *American Sociological Review, 52,* 370–379.

Mikula, G., & Schwinger, T. (1978). Intermember relations and reward allocation: Theoretical considerations of affects. In H. Brandstatter, J. H. Davis, & H. Schuler (Eds.), *Dynamics of group decisions,* Beverly Hills, CA: Sage.

Mowday, R. T., Porter, L. W., & Steers, R. (1982). *Organizational linkages: The psychology of commitment, absenteeism, and turnover.* New York: Academic Press.

Nelson, J., & Aboud, F. E. (1985). The resolution of social conflict between friends. *Child Development, 56,* 1009–1017.

Nemeth, C. J. (1986). Differential contributions of majority and minority influence. *Psychological Review, 93,* 1–10.

Newcomb, A. F., & Brady, J. E. (1982). Mutuality in boys' friendship relations. *Child Development, 53,* 392–395.

Newcomb, A. F., Brady, J. E., & Hartup, W. W. (1979). Friendship and incentive conditions as determinants of children's task-oriented social behavior. *Child Development, 50,* 878–881.

O'Reilly, C., & Caldwell, D. (1981). The commitment and job tenure of new employees: Some evidence of postdecisional justification. *Administrative Science Quarterly, 26,* 597–616.

O'Reilly, C., & Chatman, J. (1986). Organizational commitment and psychological attachment: The effects of compliance, identification, and internalization on prosocial behavior. *Academy of Management Journal, 71,* 492–499.

Pataki, S. P., Shapiro, C., & Clark, M. S. (1994). Children's acquisition of appropriate norms for friendships and acquaintances. *Journal of Social and Personal Relationships, 11,* 427–442.

Rawlins, W. K. (1983). Negotiating close friendship: The dialectic of conjunctive freedoms. *Human Communication Research, 9,* 255–266.

Rawlins, W. K. (1989). A dialectical analysis of the tensions, functions, and strategic challenges of communication in young adult friendships. In J. Anderson (Ed.), *Communication yearbook* (Vol. 12, pp. 157–189). Newbury Park, CA: Sage.

Robinson, S., & Weldon, E. (1993). Feedback seeking in groups: A theoretical perspective. *British Journal of Social Psychology, 32,* 71–86.

Roloff, M. E. (1987). Communication and reciprocity within intimate relationships. In M. E. Roloff & G. R. Miller (Eds.), *Interpersonal processes* (pp. 1–46). Newbury Park, CA: Sage.

Roloff, M. E., Janiszewski, C. A., McGrath, M. A., Burns, C. S., & Manrai, L. A. (1988). Acquiring resources from intimates: When obligation substitutes for persuasion. *Human Communication Research, 14,* 364–396.

Seashore, S. E. (1954). *Group cohesiveness in the industrial work group.* Ann Arbor: University of Michigan Press.

Shah, P., & Jehn, K. A. (1993). Do friends perform better than acquaintances? The interaction of friendship, conflict, and task. *Group Decision and Negotiation, 2,* 149–165.

Shure, G., Rogers, M., Larsen, I., & Tassone, J. (1962). Group planning and task effectiveness. *Sociometry, 14,* 263–282.

Smith, K., Locke, E., & Barry, D. (1990). Goal setting, planning, and organizational performance: An experimental simulation. *Organizational Behavior and Human Decision Processes, 46,* 118–134.

Stasser, G. (1992). Information salience and the discovery of hidden profiles by decision-making groups: A "thought experiment." *Organizational Behavior and Human Decision Processes, 52,* 156–181.

Stasser, G., & Stewart, D. (1992). Discovery of hidden profiles by decision-making groups: Solving a problem versus making a judgment. *Journal of Personality and Social Psychology, 63,* 426–434.

Stasser, G., Taylor, L. A., & Hanna, C. (1989). Information sampling in structured and unstructured discussions of three-and six-person groups. *Journal of Personality and Social Psychology, 57,* 67–78.

Stasser, G., & Titus, W. (1985). Pooling of unshared information in group decision making: Biased information sampling during discussion. *Journal of Personality and Social Psychology, 48,* 1467–1478.

Stasser, G., & Titus, W. (1987). Effects of information load and percentage of shared information on the dissemination of unshared information during group discussion. *Journal of Personality and Social Psychology, 53,* 81–93.

Steiner, I. D. (1972). *Group process and productivity.* San Diego, CA: Academic Press.

Sundstrom, E., de Meuse, K. P., & Futrell, D. (1990). Work teams: Applications and effectiveness. *American Psychologist, 45,* 120–133.

Tesser, A., Millar, M., & Moore, J. (1988). Some affective consequences of social comparison and reflection processes: The pain and pleasure of being close. *Journal of Personality and Social Psychology, 54,* 49–61.

Tesser, A., & Smith, J. (1980). Some effects of friendship and task relevance of helping: You don't always help the one you like. *Journal of Experimental Social Psychology, 16,* 582–590.

Thoms, P., Moore, K., & Scott, K. (1996). The relationship between self-efficacy for participating in self-managed work groups and the Big Five personality dimensions. *Journal of Organizational Behavior, 17,* 349–362.

Van de Ven, A., Delbecq, A., & Koenig, R. (1976). Determinants of coordination modes within organizations. *American Sociological Review, 41,* 322–338.

Van de Ven, A., & Ferry, D. (1980). *Measuring and assessing organizations.* New York: Wiley.

Weingart, L. (1992). Impact of group goals, task component complexity, effort, and planning on group performance. *Journal of Applied Psychology, 77,* 682–693.

Weingart, L., & Weldon, E. (1991). Processes that mediate the relationship between a group goal and group member performance. *Human Performance, 4,* 33–54.

Weldon, E., Jehn, K. A., & Pardhan, P. (1991). Processes that mediate the relationship between a group good and improved group performance. *Journal of Personality and Social Psychology, 61,* 555–569.

Weldon, E., & Weingart, L. (1988, August). *A theory of group goals and group performance.* Paper presented at the annual meeting of the Academy of Management, Anaheim. CA.

Whitney, K. (1994). Improving group task performance: The role of group goals and group efficacy. *Human Performance, 7,* 55–78.

Williamson, G. M., & Clark, M. S. (1992). Impact of desired relationship type on affective reactions to choosing and being required to help. *Personality and social Psychology Bulletin, 18,* 10–18.

Wittenbum, G., Stasser, G., & Merry, C. (1996). Tacit coordination in anticipation of small group task completion. *Journal of Experimental SocialPsychology, 32,* 129–152.

Woodman, R. W., & Sherwood, J. J. (1980). The role of team development in organizational effectiveness: A critical review. *Psychological Bulletin, 88,* 166–186.

Wright, P. H. (1984). Self-referent motivation and the intrinsic quality of friendship. *Journal of Social and Personal Relationships, 1,* 115–130.

Zaccaro, S. J, & Lowe, C. A. (1988). Cohesiveness and performance on an additive task: Evidence for multidimensionality. *Journal of Social Psychology, 128,* 547–558.

Appendix

Coding of Transcripts

GUIDELINES FOR UNITIZING

1. The unit of analysis is a "thought unit"; thus, each separate thought should be separated.
2. Acknowledgment of a previous statement is a separate unit (e.g., [Okay], [but I think we should also glue]).
3. Conjunctions separate a thought.
4. Check to see whether the sentence would convey the same content if the preceding or ending phrase were omitted. If not, the two phrases are coded as two units. If so, then code it as one unit. "Wait, they need Popsicle sticks" is coded as two units. However, "Hey, they need Popsicle sticks" would be coded as one unit.
5. Ignore the word *oh*.

GUIDELINES FOR CATEGORIZING STATEMENTS ON AUDIOTAPES

1. Do not draw inferences about the purpose of a statement or intent of the speaker in order to assign a code. Use the rules of content.
2. Categorize a unit as a particular type of statement only when it is clearly an example of that category. If the content is ambiguous, categorize the statement as uncodable.
3. Context can be used to determine the content of a unit. Consider previous statement first. Refer to next statements if previous statement does not help.
4. If the speaker repeats his or her remark at the request of another group member, code the repetition.
5. Use a hierarchy. First, decide whether a statement involves planning, monitoring, critical evaluation, or cooperation. If not, but the unit has to do with building structures or making decisions, then the statement is information sharing.
6. Responses to and acknowledgment of a category are given the same code as that category.

DESCRIPTION OF CONTENT CATEGORIES FOR AUDIO CODING

1. *Information sharing*. Questions and statements about supplies in the motor task and criteria regarding admission standards or application questions in the decision-making task, task-relevant discussions and information, and advice statements that do not constitute planning.
2. *Planning*. Questions and statements about whether a certain act has been or should be performed, how a certain act should be performed, and who is performing, can perform, or should perform a certain act. How the job should be divided.
3. *Critical evaluation*. Disagreements or arguments over the order in which the task should be done or about the way a group member is performing his or her duties in the motor task. Disagreements about the caliber of applicants in the decision–making task.
4. *Morale-building communication*. Positive evaluation of the group's or a group member's ability to perform well.
5. *Commitment*. Statements about the attachment to the group and the desire to be part of the group.
6. *Monitoring*. Questions or statements about the number of models produced or applications completed, the number of each remaining, a goal, and the time passed or remaining in the work session.
7. *Cooperation*. Statements about how members can help one another, offers of assistance, and requests for help.
8. *Uncodable*. Units of which the content is unclear, even when the context is considered, unfinished statements or questions, and indications by the transcriptionist that something was said but was indecipherable.

Rating Actions and Behaviors

VIDEO RATING CATEGORIES

In each of the following categories, quoted phrases are the layperson definitions given to the raters.

INFORMATION SHARING

"Talk a lot, very willing to discuss": This behavior is characterized by lots of talking; free expressions of ideas thoughts, and feelings; and free exchange of thoughts through speech or signals. Information sharing may also entail being able to criticize without being apologetic as well as talking, expanding discussion, and questioning rather than just agreeing or nodding.

PLANNING

"Formulating actions regarding time and function that will lead to specific goals": This behavior involves a strategy worked out before or during a task to accomplish the required goal (e.g., who should do which task, how the task should be performed, and the like).

Examples:
For model building, deciding who should string balls, make bases, make stick sets, and so forth, and deciding how best to accomplish the task (e.g., string balls first and then wrap foil around middle ball or wrap foil around ball first and then string balls accordingly).
For MBA applications, deciding how many applications each member should read, deciding the criteria to use in accepting or rejecting, and deciding whether to read applications individually or as a group.

CRITICAL EVALUATION

"Critically evaluate each other's ideas or works": this behavior is characterized by differences of opinion, disagreement on the decisions made among group members, disagreement on who should do what or how something should be done, and arguments.

Examples:
For model building, conflicts over how to string the balls or in what order to build the model and disagreement over the quality of the work performed or how the task was made.
For MBA applications, disagreement on the qualifications on the applicants and disagreement over whether to accept or reject the application.

MORALE-BUILDING COMMUNICATION

"Encouraging to perform better and positive reactions about the member's or a group's performance": This behavior involves motivating others by offering positive comments, setting an example for others to follow, and displaying leadership; by exuding confidence, cheerfulness, and a positive attitude; and by providing words of encouragement and showing enthusiasm.

COMMITMENT TO GROUP

"Attachment to group": This behavior is marked by wanting to stay and do things with the group; tending to things; making sure everyone gets things done; feeling emotionally tied to the group; feeling dedicated to members and the task at hand; feeling obligated to group members.

Examples:
High levels of commitment are demonstrated when a member expends time and energy to make sure that the group gets along; works well with together members in completing the task; and shows high levels of morale building, critical evaluation, planning, and the like. Average levels of commitment are demonstrated by members working together to get the task done without much of a sense of obligation to remain together.
Low levels of commitment are demonstrated by a lack of dedication, caring about what others think or do, and physical or mental effort expended.

TASK MONITORING

"Assessing the performance and the likelihood that the group will reach its goal."

Examples:
Looking at the timer, counting the number of models, pacing oneself to ensure completion of task or monitoring the performance of others ot ensure that they get done on time, and stopping what one is doing when time is running out to help others complete a whole model.

COOPERATION

"Behavior that aids the performance of another group member or contributes to the ease with which group members coordinate their efforts; mutual assistance; helping": this behavior involves working together toward achieving a common goal and displaying mutually beneficial behavior.

Examples:
Cooperation includes asking for help (e.g., members indicating that they are unsure of how

to do something) and offering help (e.g., for model building, members handing each other material, indicating where things are so other members do not have to search, anticipating others' needs by wrapping a ball or helping with stringing; for the MBA application task, handing each other applications or providing each other with grades or GMAT scores).

CONCERN WITH FRIENDSHIP (MANIPULATION CHECK)

"Close, interpersonal tie; a positive, amiable pre-existing relationship": This behavior is characterized by knowing, liking, or trusting another person; being able to communicate openly and freely; no inhibitions among members; feeling comfortable in the presence of other members; and closer interpersonal relationships. Friendship may include laughing, joking around, and having a good time with each other.

COHESIVENESS (MANIPULATION CHECK)

"Esprit de corps, group spirit, would like to work in this group again, attraction among members, closeness (not necessarily friendship of satisfaction)": This behavior is marked by unity among group members, and ability to get along or to perform as a group, and an ability to get along and perform well even though members may not be friends.

Procedural Justice

Justice is a key issue for understanding organizational behavior. Early conceptions of justice, such as equity theory (Adams, 1965; Walster, Berscheid, & Walster, 1973; Walster, Walster, & Berscheid, 1978), argued that people judge an outcome as fair when the ratio of their own inputs and outputs equals the ratio of the inputs and outputs of comparison others. Equity theory and other related conceptions of justice, such as relative deprivation theory (Crosby, 1976), are theories of *distributive justice* because they focus on the fairness of outcomes that people receive. *Procedural justice* concerns questions about the fairness of the processes and procedures (Thibaut & Walker, 1975; Lind & Tyler, 1988; Tyler & Lind, 1992). Thibaut and Walker's (1975) groundbreaking development of procedural justice led to the development of a new field of theoretical and empirical research that revealed that people's reactions to outcomes are affected by their perceptions of the process. Furthermore, subsequent research has revealed that the distinction between procedural and distributive justice is not merely a conceptual one invented by theorists, but arises naturally in people's cognitions about justice. Initial procedural justice research was conducted primarily to distinguish procedural justice concerns from distributive justice concerns. For example, experiments manipulated procedures while holding outcomes constant and found main effects for procedure (cf. Walker et al., 1974). It is helpful to distinguish the many definitions and theories concerning procedural versus distributive justice.

Self-Interest Model of Procedural Justice

One of the basic ideas in Thibaut and Walker's (1975) explanation of procedural justice effects was that people, finding themselves in conflict and having little success in negotiating a settlement, would have to turn to a third party to resolve the dispute. Accordingly, they would have concerns about controlling the process, as it would affect their outcomes. Thus, Thibaut and Walker's model suggests that people seek control over decisions because they are fundamentally concerned with their own outcomes. It is this concern that leads people to attend to issues of control and, in situations in which they cannot have decision control, to seek process control. According to Lind and Tyler (1988), Thibaut and Walker's conception of procedural justice is based upon self-interest.

Group Value Model

It was anomalous empirical findings that led Lind and Tyler (1988) to develop a different version of procedural justice, embodied in the group-value model. Specifically, some empirical investigations showed noninstrumental effects, such that people are concerned about process, independent of outcome (see the first article in this section by Lind, Kanfer, & Earley, 1990).

The group-value model is based on a group identification model (cf. Tajfel, 1978). Tyler and Lind noted that individuals in groups were more likely to put aside their own self-interest and act in a way that helps all group members than pure self-interest models would predict. The group-value model assumes that group membership is a powerful aspect of social life. Two elements govern much cognition and behavior with respect to groups and organizations: group identity, or the factors that distinguish the group from other social entities, and group procedure, which specifies the authority relations and the formal and informal social processes that regulate much of the group's activity. Procedures operate as norms of decision making that regulate much of a group's process. When procedures are in accord with the fundamental values of the group and the individual, a sense of procedural justice results. The second article in this section provides an empirical examination of specific elements of the group-value model in groups (Tyler, 1989). Lind, Kulik, Ambrose, and De Vera Park (1993) have examined the group-value model in corporations.

Relational Model of Authority

The relational model of authority (Tyler & Lind, 1992) focuses on the conditions under which an authority is perceived to be a legitimate decision maker and is given discretionary power to make decisions for a committee. According to Tyler and Lind, several aspects are legitimacy are important, with three of them central to the theory: feelings of trust in the authority, willingness to accept decisions, and feelings of obligation to follow the rules authorities implement. As a direct test of this model, Tyler and Degoey (1995) examined people's willingness to restrain themselves during a naturally occurring social dilemma situation—the 1991 California water shortage.

Fairness Heuristic Theory

Fairness heuristic theory is based on the group-value model of procedural justice and the relational model of authority (Tyler & Lind, 1992). The theory assumes that because ceding authority to another person provides an opportunity for exploitation and exclusion, people feel uncertain and uncomfortable about their relationship with an authority. Therefore, people ask themselves whether the authority can be trusted not to exploit them or threaten their social identity (cf. Huo, Smith, Tyler, & Lind, 1996; Lind & Tyler, 1988; Tyler & Lind, 1992). The most common approach is to establish a fairness judgment, which then serves as a heuristic that guides the interpretation of subsequent events. Consequently, empirical studies should expect to reveal biases in terms of the presentation of information and timing of information on judgments (cf. van den Bos, Lind, Vermunt, & Wilke, 1997).

Reactions to Injustice

Given that organizational actors are concerned with how their outcomes compare to others, empirical studies have investigated how perceptions of inequity affect behavior. For example, Brockner et al. (1994) focused on how procedural and distributive concerns affect survivors' and victims' reactions in inequity. The third article in this section, by Greenberg (1993), focuses on a highly nonnormative organization behavior, stealing, and its relationship to perceptions of injustice.

REFERENCES

Adams, S. (1965). Inequity in social exchange. In L. Berkowitz (Ed.), *Advances in experimental social psychology* (Vol. 2). New York: Academic Press.

Brockner, J., Konovsky, M., Cooper-Schneider, R., Folger, R., Martin, C., & Bies, R. J. (1994). Interactive effects of procedural justice and outcome negativity on victims and survivors of job loss. *Academy of Management Journal, 37,* 397–409.

Crosby, F. (1976). A model of egoistical relative deprivation. *Psychological Review, 83,* 85–113.

Greenberg, J. (1993). Stealing in the name of justice: Informational and interpersonal moderators of theft reactions to underpayment inequity. *Organizational Behavior and Human Decision Processes, 54,* 81–103.

Huo, Y. J., Smith, H. J., Tyler, T. R., & Lind, E. A. (1996). Superordinate identification, subgroup identification, and justice concerns: Is separatism the problem; is assimilation the answer? *Psychological Science, 7*(1), 40–45.

Lind, E. A., & Tyler, T. R. (1988). *The social psychology of procedural justice.* New York: Plenum.

Lind, E. A., Kanfer, R., and Earley, P. C. (1990). Voice, control, and procedural justice: Instrumental and noninstrumental concerns in fairness judgments. *Journal of Personality and Social Psychology, 59,* 952–959.

Lind, E. A., Kulik, C. T., Ambrose, M., & De Vera Park, M. V. (1993). Individual and corporate dispute resolution: Using procedural fairness as a decision heuristic. *Administrative Science Quarterly, 38,* 224–251.

Tajfel, H., Ed. (1978). *Differentiation between social groups: Studies in the social psychology of intergroup relations.* New York: Academic Press.

Thibaut, J., & Walker, L. (1975). *Procedural justice: A psychological analysis.* Hillsdale, NJ: Lawrence Erlbaum.

Tyler, T. R. (1989). The psychology of procedural justice: A test of the group-value model. *Journal of Personality and Social Psychology, 57,* 830–838.

Tyler, T. R., & Degoey, P. (1995). Collective restraint in social dilemmas: Procedural justice and social identification effects on support for authorities. *Journal of Personality and Social Psychology, 69*(3), 482–497.

Tyler, T. R., & Lind, E. A. (1992). A relational model of authority in groups. *Advances in Experimental Social Psychology, 25,* 115–191.

van den Bos, K., Lind, E. A., Vermunt, R., & Wilke, H. A. M. (1997). How do I judge my outcome when I do not know the outcome of others? The psychology of the fair process effect. *Journal of Personality and Social Psychology, 72*(5), 1034–1046.

Walker, L., LaTour, S., Lind, E. A., & Thibaut, J. (1974). Reactions of participants and observers to modes of adjudication. *Journal of Applied Social Psychology, 4*(4), 295–310.

Walster, E., Berscheid, E., & Walster, G. W. (1973). New directions in equity research. *Journal of Personality and Social Psychology, 25,* 151–176.

Walster, E., Walster, G. W., & Berscheid, E. (1978). *Equity: Theory and research.* Boston: Allyn & Bacon.

Suggested Readings

Brockner, J., Wiesenfeld, B. M., & Martin, C. L. (1995). Decision frames, procedural justice, and survivors' reactions to job layoffs. *Organizational Behavior and Human Decision Processes, 63*(1), 59–68.

Lind, E. A. (1980). Procedure and outcome effects on reactions to adjudicated resolution of conflicts of interest. *Journal of Personality and Social Psychology, 39*(4), 645–653.

Lind, E. A., Kray, L., & Thompson, L. (1998). The social construction of injustice: Fairness judgments in response to own and other's unfair treatment by authorities. *Organizational Behavior and Human Decision Processes, 75*(1), 1–22.

Tyler, T. R., & Degoey, P. (1995). Collective restraint in social dilemmas: Procedural justice and social identification effects on support for authorities. *Journal of Personality and Social Psychology, 69*(3), 482–497.

van den Bos, K., Vermunt, R. & Wilke, H. A. M. (1997). Procedural and distributive justice: What is fair depends more on what comes first than on what comes next. *Journal of Personality and Social Psychology, 72*(1), 95–104.

van den Bos, K., Lind, E. A., Vermunt, R., & Wilke, H. A. M. (1997). How do I judge my outcome when I do not know the outcome of others? The psychology of the fair process effect. *Journal of Personality and Social Psychology, 72*(5), 1034–1046.

Voice, Control, and Procedural Justice: Instrumental and Noninstrumental Concerns in Fairness Judgments

E. Allan Lind • American Bar Foundation, Chicago, Illinois
Ruth Kanfer • University of Minnesota
P. Christopher Earley • University of Minnesota

One hundred seventy-nine undergraduate Ss took part in a study of the effect of instrumental and noninstrumental participation on distributive and procedural fairness judgments. In a goal-setting procedure, Ss were allowed voice before the goal was set, after the goal was set, or not at all. Ss received information relevant to the task, irrelevant information, or no information. Both pre-and postdecision voice led to higher fairness judgments than no voice, with predecision voice leading to higher fairness judgments than postdecision voice. Relevant information also increased perceived fairness. Mediation analyses showed that perceptions of control account for some, but not all, of the voice-based enhancement of procedural justice. The results show that both instrumental and noninstrumental concerns are involved in voice effects.

Since the earliest studies of the psychology of procedural justice (Thibaut & Walker, 1975; Walker, LaTour, Lind, & Thibault, 1974), it has been known that the opportunity to present information relevant to a decision enhances judgments of the fairness of the decision-making procedure. This finding, termed the "process control effect" by Thibaut and Walker (1978) and the "voice effect" by Folger, is probably the best-documented phenomenon in procedural justice research.[1] Numerous studies, conducted in natural settings as well as in the laboratory, have made it clear that the voice effect enhances procedural fairness even when the individual making the fairness judgment has no direct control over the decision itself (e.g.,

Folger, 1977; Kanfer, Sawyer, Earley, & Lind, 1987; LaTour, 1978; Lind, Kurtz, Musante, Walker, & Thibaut, 1980; Lind, Lissak, & Conlon, 1983; Tyler, 1987; Tyler, Rasinski, & Spodick, 1985): Apparently, as long as there is an opportunity to express one's views and opinions before the decision is made, procedural fairness is enhanced.

Given the reliability and strength of the voice effect, it is not surprising that virtually every theory and conceptual analysis of procedural justice processes has attempted to explain the psychological

---

[1]In this article we will use the term *voice* rather than *process control* because voice seems to best capture the essential condition for the effect.

processes that produce the effect. Early theories of procedural justice (Leventhal, 1980; Thibaut & Walker, 1975, 1978) sought to explain procedural justice phenomena with reference to the perceiver's assumptions about the outcomes that various procedures would generate. These theories attributed the voice effect to beliefs about the instrumental consequences of input. The voice effect is explained by presuming that persons given an opportunity to express their views will believe that voice will help them control their outcomes—their arguments might persuade the decision maker to provide a better outcome—and that these expectations lead to higher procedural fairness judgments. In the leading instrumental theories voice is seen as fair because it increases the probability of either a favorable outcome (Leventhal, 1980) or an equitable outcome (Thibaut & Walker, 1978). Instrumental theories of procedural justice and related models are still favored by many procedural justice researchers (e.g., Brett, 1986; Vidmar, in press).

At least two recent theories of procedural justice (Lane, 1988; Lind & Tyler, 1988, pp. 230–240) have sought to explain procedural justice phenomena in terms of the symbolic and informational consequences of procedures, rather than in terms of the procedure's capacity to provide good outcomes. Lind and Tyler proposed a "group-value" model, which argues that the voice effect stems from the implication that those accorded an opportunity to present information are valued, full-fledged members of the group enacting the procedure. People value voice because it suggests that their views are worthy of hearing, according to Lind and Tyler, and procedures that accord people status in this way are viewed favorably, whatever their likely effects on the outcome of the procedure. Lane took a similar position (pp. 179–180) when he described the opportunity to be heard as a "dignity good" that citizens value in government procedures.

There is a middle ground in the debate between instrumental and noninstrumental theories of procedural justice. Notwithstanding their advancement of noninstrumental group-value theory, Lind and Tyler (1988) ultimately concluded that the field will eventually adopt a position intermediate between instrumental theories of procedural justice and theories that explain procedural justice in terms of the symbolic implications of procedures. After reviewing numerous studies, Lind and Tyler

pointed out that the entire range of procedural justice phenomena can be explained only if it is accepted that fairness judgments are driven both by instrumental, informed self-interest concerns and by noninstrumental, group-value concerns (pp. 240–241). They called for new theories that integrate both types of concerns in explaining the psychology of procedural justice.

In the context of these theoretical disagreements about the processes underlying the voice effect, an important empirical question is whether voice effects can be shown to occur in situations where it is clear that the exercise of voice cannot influence the outcome of the procedure. Folger (1986) has pointed out the importance of this question and reviewed the literature relevant to it. He found only three studies that explicitly addressed the question, all reported in an article by Tyler et al. (1985). However, none of the Tyler et al. studies provides a true experimental test of noninstrumental mediation of the voice effect: One study is a correlational study of traffic court defendants' perceptions of control, voice, and fairness; the second is a correlational study of student evaluations of grading procedures; and the third is a hypothetical scenario study in which subjects did not actually experience the procedures and outcomes they rated. The two correlational studies leave unanswered, of course, critical questions concerning the direction of causality. The hypothetical scenario study can only determine whether subjects *believe* that voice would enhance their procedural fairness judgments beyond voice's instrumental value; the study does not prove that such effects actually occur. Previous studies have demonstrated that scenario studies often arrive at conclusions that are at variance to those of true experiments, both in social psychological research in general (e.g., Freedman, 1969) and in procedural justice research in particular (e.g., Lind et al., 1983).

We sought to give the theoretical debate about instrumental and noninstrumental processes in voice effects a stronger empirical basis by testing noninstrumental effects experimentally. Specifically, we tested whether procedural justice judgments were enhanced by an opportunity to voice one's views *after* the decision had been made. If voice effects are attributable solely to the symbolic or status-enhancing consequences of being able to express one's views, as the noninstrumental theories have suggested, then postdecision voice should enhance perceived fairness as much as predecision voice. On the other hand, if voice effects are due solely to the belief that voice will lead to a better decision, as instrumental theories suggest, then postdecision voice will lead to no greater perceived procedural fairness than no voice at all. And if both instrumental and noninstrumental concerns are important in procedural fairness judgments, then postdecision voice should lead to some enhancement of perceived fairness, but not as much as does predecision voice.

It should be noted that it is certainly conceivable that postdecision voice might lead to *lower* procedural justice judgments than does no voice at all. There is evidence that, under some circumstances, people actively reject procedures that appear to offer process control but that do not provide any real input into the decision-making process. Folger and his colleagues (Folger, 1977; Folger, Rosenfield, Grove, & Corkran, 1979; Folger, Rosenfield, & Robinson, 1983) have conducted a number of studies of what is termed the *frustration effect*. These experiments showed that people react quite negatively to ostensibly high voice procedures when repeated unfavorable outcomes or communications from others focus attention on possible biases that might subvert the impact of their voice. Lind and Tyler (1988, pp. 183–184) argued that frustration effects occur only when the procedure is blatantly biased, but absent further empirical evidence it is certainly possible that unbiased postdecision voice will decrease perceived justice.

We studied the effects of voice in the context of a procedure for setting performance goals. During the past decade, theory and research in the goal-setting literature has focused on the influence of participative procedures (procedures that permit an opportunity for input) on goal acceptance and subsequent task performance. A number of studies have examined whether participation in the goal-setting process enhances goal acceptance and task performance (e.g., Erez, Earley, & Hulin, 1985; Latham, Erez, & Locke, 1988; Latham & Saari, 1979; for reviews see, e.g., Kanfer, in press; Latham & Lee, 1986; Locke & Schweiger, 1979; Locke, Shaw, Saari, & Latham, 1981). Some of the explanations for why participation in goal setting may exert beneficial effects resemble explanations of the voice effect on procedural fairness. For example, participation may provide an opportunity to influence the goal that is ultimately established (an instrumental explanation). Alterna-

tively, even when workers' preferences are not implemented, the participative process may convey to the workers that organizational superiors are concerned with the workers' attitudes (a noninstrumental explanation). Another explanation of the effects of participation in goal setting focuses on the information that workers might gain about the task in the process of discussing goals (Locke, Latham, & Erez, 1988). That is, participation might enhance goal acceptance and performance by providing workers with knowledge about how to approach the task, thereby enhancing task-specific self-efficacy expectations.

In this study we tested the effects of voice across three conditions relevant to this last, information-provided explanation of participative goal setting. We manipulated the information provided to the subject by the experimenter. In one condition, the experimenter provided information on strategies that might improve performance on the task. In another condition, the experimenter provided information that was of interest to the subjects but that was unrelated to the task, and in a third condition the experimenter provided no information at all.

If the provision of task-relevant information during discussion serves to increase self-efficacy expectations, then the increased sense of competence associated with heightened self-efficacy expectations might reduce the need to exert influence on the goal assignment. If instrumental theories of procedural justice are correct, we would expect that the provision of task-relevant information would enhance subjects' efficacy expectations, enhance perceptions of goal fairness, and diminish the effects of voice compared with the irrelevant and no-information conditions (cf. Locke & Latham, 1990, pp. 147–148). Thus, instrumental theories of justice predict both a main effect for information and an interaction of information and voice on fairness ratings. In contrast, noninstrumental theories of procedural justice would predict that the provision of interesting information, whether relevant or not, provides individuals with recognition of their involvement and membership in the work group (cf. Bies & Moag, 1986). From the noninstrumental perspective, therefore, both relevant and irrelevant information would be expected to enhance procedural fairness judgments relative to the no-information condition. In contrast to an instrumental explanation, noninstrumental theories of procedural justice would not predict an interaction between the task information provided to the subject and the voice effect.

Method

Subjects

One hundred eighty male undergraduate students participated in the experiment in partial fulfillment of a requirement in an introductory course in psychology.[2] Twenty subjects were randomly assigned to each cell of the experimental design. Data from one subject (in the predecision voice/relevant-information condition) were incomplete and were not used in the analyses reported below.

Experimental Design

The experimental design was a 3 (Procedure: no voice, postdecision voice, and predecision voice) × 3 (Information From Experimenter: no information, irrelevant information, and relevant information) complete factorial design.

Experimental Procedure

The subjects were told that they were participating in a study of performance using a typical student activity: the construction of course schedules. They were told that the experimenter was interested in how students put together their class schedules and that the findings of the study would be reported to the registrar's office for use in deciding how to schedule classes at the university. It was stressed that the experimenter wanted to learn about student's approaches to course scheduling in order to improve the scheduling process.

Each subject was seated in a separate experimental cubicle and given written instructions on how to perform the course scheduling task. The subjects were then told to perform the scheduling task for 5 min as a practice trial. After the practice trial, the experimenter entered the room and collected the schedules the subjects had completed. The subjects then received instructions for the main, goal-setting portion of the experiment.

The subjects were told that they would be given a goal for the number of schedules to be completed during the second, final phase of the experiment. In the *predecision voice* procedure condition, the experimenter first told the subjects that he was tentatively thinking of setting a goal of 12 schedules during the 15-min time frame allotted for the final work period. The experimenter said that he wanted to take the subjects' views into account, however, and he encouraged them to express their opinions concerning the task and the goal. After listening to the subject's views—which invariably included an expressed desire for a lower goal—the experimenter assigned a work goal of 10 schedules in the final work period. (On the basis of pilot testing, it was known that the goal of 10 course schedules in 15 min was a very difficult but attainable goal.) The predecision voice condition thus mirrors the voice procedures used in most previous research, with the additional characteristic that the voice clearly appears to be successful in influencing the goal. In the *postdecision voice* procedure condition, the experimenter told the subjects that he had already decided on a goal of 10 schedules and that this goal would not be changed regardless of what the subject said. The experimenter said he was nonetheless interested in the subjects' views and encouraged the subjects to express their opinions concerning the task and the goal that had been set. As in the predecision voice condition, the subjects in the postdecision voice condition always said that they would prefer a lower goal. After listening to the subjects' views, the experimenter reiterated the work goal of 10 schedules. Thus, any perception of control in the postdecision voice condition would run contrary to both the experimenter's explicit denial of any influence of the subjects' input and his failure to change the goal. In the *no-voice* condition, the experimenter simply announced the work goal of 10 schedules without soliciting comments either before or after the goal was set. The instructions and the communication from the subjects took place through an intercom system, and the experimenter spoke with a calm and reassuring tone.

The experimenter then enacted the information-from-experimenter manipulation, with the rationale of filling time until the second work session

---

[2] Of course, our use of only male subjects precludes us from testing for gender-based differences in procedural justice judgments. Recent research (Lind et al., 1989) tested for gender differences in procedural justice judgments in a naturalistic setting and found none. This is not to say that such differences do not occur, but we know of no study that has shown differences between the procedural justice judgments of men and those of women.

was due to start. In the *relevant-information* condition, he informed the subject of several strategies that would be useful in achieving the goal. For example, the experimenter pointed out that different schedules could be produced by rotating blocks of classes intact while changing only a single class. In the *irrelevant-information* condition, the experimenter addressed the subjects for an equivalent period of time (3 min), providing information on university calendar events. In the *no-information* condition, the experimenter simply asked the subjects to wait a few minutes.

The subjects were then asked to complete a brief questionnaire. After they had completed the questionnaire, they were instructed to begin working on the task. After 15 min the subjects were told to cease working, and the completed schedules were collected. The main questionnaire, which included all of the measures reported below, was administered after the subjects had completed the task but before they were given any feedback about their performance.

Measures

The experimental questionnaire contained two 5-point rating scales on perceptions of justice: Procedural fairness judgments were solicited in a question asking how fair was the way the goal was set, and outcome fairness judgments were solicited in a question asking how fair the assigned goal was. Perceptions of control were assessed with a 5-point scale asking how much control the subject had over the goal. A 5-point scale asking how much information the subject gave to the experimenter about the goal constituted a check on the manipulation of voice (i.e., the opportunity to present information), and a 9-point scale asking how much information the subject had concerning the goal and task constituted a check on the efficacy of the information-from-experimenter manipulation. The subjects were asked to rate, using a 10-point scale, the degree to which they had adopted the goal given them by the experimenter. Ratings of feelings of efficacy with respect to the scheduling task were solicited with a 5-point scale asking how well the subject thought he or she did on the task. The subjects were also asked to rate how much they liked the experimenter, using a 5-point scale. Finally, performance on the task was measured by counting the number of schedules the subject completed during the 15-min work period.

Results

Manipulation Checks

To gauge the subjects' perceptions of the experimental conditions, we conducted a multivariate analysis of variance (MANOVA) on ratings of the opportunity for voice, the subject's control over the goal assignment, the amount of information the subject had about the task and goal, perceptions of efficacy, and how much the subject liked the experimenter. The analysis showed significant main effects for both manipulations: for the voice manipulation, multivariate $F(10, 332) = 11.83$, $p < .001$; for the information-from-experimenter manipulation, multivariate $F(10, 332) = 5.08$, $p < .001$. The voice manipulation produced significant univariate main effects on the ratings of the opportunity for voice, $F(2, 170) = 52.54$, $p < .001$; on the ratings of control over the goal, $F(2, 170) = 34.00$, $p < .001$; and on ratings of perceived efficacy in performing the task, $F(2, 170) = 6.22$, $p < .002$. Neither the multivariate test of the Voice × Information interaction nor any of the univariate tests of the interaction were significant. The subjects' ratings of how much they liked the experimenter were generally in the neutral range of the scale and were not affected by either of the manipulations or by their interaction.

The subjects felt they had given the experimenter more information in the predecision voice condition ($M = 3.96$) than in the postdecision voice condition ($M = 3.27$), and that they had given the experimenter more information in the postdecision condition than in the no-voice condition ($M = 1.87$). Scheffé post hoc pairwise comparisons (Kirk, 1968, pp. 188–189) among the three treatment conditions showed that all three voice conditions differed significantly in the amount of information subjects felt they had given the experimenter (critical $S_{.05} = .51$). The subjects also felt that they had more control over the assigned goal in the predecision voice condition ($M = 3.26$) than in the postdecision voice condition ($M = 2.52$) and more control in the postdecision voice condition than in the no-voice condition ($M = 1.68$). For perceptions of control, the post hoc pairwise comparisons showed that each of the three voice conditions differed from the others (critical $S_{.05} = .47$). For perceptions of efficacy, post hoc Scheffé tests showed that the no-voice condition ($M = 2.73$) differed significantly from the predecision voice condition (M = 3.28), but that the postdecision voice condition (M = 2.98) did not differ significantly from either of the other conditions (critical $S_{.05}$ = .38).

The significant multivariate main effect for the information-from-experimenter manipulation appears to be due to univariate main effects on ratings of the amount of information the subject felt he or she had received about the task and goal, $F(2, 170)$ = 14.14, p < .001, and on ratings of perceived efficacy, $F(2, 170)$ = 7.65, p < .001. Subjects felt that they had received more information in the relevant-information condition (M = 5.45) than in the irrelevant-information condition (M = 3.80) or the no-information condition (M = 3.15). Scheffé post hoc comparisons on ratings of information received showed that the relevant-information condition differed significantly from the two other conditions and that the irrelevant-information and no-information conditions did not differ significantly (critical $S_{.05}$ = 1.23). Post hoc Scheffé tests also showed that the relevant-information condition led to feelings of greater efficacy (M = 3.34) than did either the irrelevant-information condition (M = 2.78) or the no-information condition (M = 2.87); the latter two conditions did not differ from each other (critical $S_{.05}$ = .38).

Procedural and Outcome Fairness Judgments

Table 1 shows the cell means for subjects' ratings of the fairness of the way the goal was assigned—procedural fairness—and their ratings of the fairness of the assigned goal itself—outcome fairness. We tested the effects of the voice manipulation

with a priori contrasts comparing the two voice conditions with the no-voice condition and comparing the postdecision voice condition with the predecision voice condition. (Recall that the prediction from noninstrumental theories of procedural justice is that only the former contrast will be significant, and the prediction from instrumental theories of procedural justice is that only the latter contrast will be significant.) A MANOVA showed significant multivariate and univariate effects for both variables on both contrasts: The voice conditions produced higher ratings of procedural and outcome fairness than did the no-voice condition, multivariate $F(2, 169)$ = 23.15, p < .001; for procedural fairness, $F(1, 170)$ = 42.11, p < .001; for outcome fairness, $F(1, 170)$ = 32.19, p < .001, and the predecision voice condition produced higher ratings of procedural and outcome fairness than did the postdecision voice condition, multivariate $F(2, 169)$ = 6.21, p < .002; for procedural fairness, $F(1, 170)$ = 9.62, p < .002; for outcome fairness, $F(1, 170)$ = 10.56, p < .001.[3] Thus, the fairness ratings provided support for both instrumental and noninstrumental theories of procedural justice.

Both fairness variables also showed a significant effect for the information-from-experimenter manipulation, multivariate $F(4, 338)$ = 3.64, p < .006; for procedural fairness, $F(2, 170)$ = 3.71, p

[3] It is conceivable that the significant contrast of the voice to the no-voice conditions was due solely to the very high fairness ratings of the predecision voice condition. However, Scheffé post hoc comparisons revealed that for both fairness variables, all pairwise comparisons among the voice conditions were significant (critical $S_{.05}$ = .43 for procedural fairness, and critical $S_{.05}$ = .45 for outcome fairness).

TABLE 1. Cell Means: Perceived Fairness

Information from experimenter	Communication to experimenter			
	None	Postdecision	Predecision	M
Perceived procedural fairness				
None	2.15	3.00	3.40	2.85
Irrelevant	2.55	2.95	3.80	3.10
Relevant	2.60	3.50	3.90	3.33
M	2.43	3.15	3.70	
Perceived outcome fairness				
None	2.00	2.80	3.10	2.63
Irrelevant	2.15	2.25	3.10	2.50
Relevant	2.20	3.10	3.74	3.01
M	2.11	2.72	3.31	

Note. Entries are cell means on 5-point scales; higher values indicate perceived fairness.

< .03; for outcome fairness, $F(2, 170) = 4.20, p <$ .02. Scheffé tests of pairwise comparisons among the information-from-experimenter categories showed that relevant information differed significantly from no information in terms of procedural fairness and that relevant information differed from irrelevant information in terms of outcome fairness; all other pairwise comparisons were not significant. Neither fairness variable showed a significant interaction effect, multivariate $F < 1.0$; for procedural fairness, $F < 1.0$; for outcome fairness, $F(2, 170) = 1.20, ns$.

Perceptions of Control and the Voice Effect

The patterns of mean fairness ratings appear to be generally supportive of a mixed model of procedural fairness, showing both instrumental and noninstrumental voice effects. However, the finding that postdecision voice led to greater perceived control than no voice at all makes the pattern of means somewhat more ambiguous than would otherwise have been the case. Subjects in the postdecision voice condition appear to have believed they had some control, even though they were told explicitly that their input could not affect the goal the experimenter assigned and even though the goal remained the same after their input. As we note below, these elevated control ratings may have been due to an illusion of control effect in the postdecision voice condition or they may have been the result of generally enhanced feelings of group involvement.

If the enhanced feelings of control in the postdecision voice condition are the result of an illusion of control, however, one could argue that the fairness findings could be accounted for entirely within an instrumental theory of procedural justice judgments, providing that the theory was based on *subjective* rather than *objective* control. Additional analyses are needed to determine whether perceived control mediated all of the voice effect. We conducted mediational analyses (Baron & Kenny, 1986) to test whether the voice effect could be attributed entirely to perceptions of control. Baron and Kenny (p. 1177) pointed out several criteria that must be met to sustain the assertion that a variable mediates an effect: The mediator must be affected by the independent variable, the dependent variable must be affected by the independent variable, and the relationship between the independent variable and the dependent variable must be attenuated or disappear when variance attributable to the mediator is removed. The first criterion is met for perceptions of control by virtue of the significant voice effect on the control ratings. The second criterion is met by virtue of the voice effects on the fairness ratings.

To test the third Baron and Kenny criterion, we conducted analyses of covariance (ANCOVAS), removing the effects of perceived control prior to testing the contrasts among the three voice conditions. The analyses showed that the contrast between the two voice conditions and the no-voice condition remained significant for ratings of procedural fairness, $F(1, 169) = 4.65, p < .04$, but the variance accounted for by the contrast was markedly reduced (without removing variance mediated by control, $\eta^2 = .19$; after removing variance mediated by control, $\eta^2 = .03$). For the contrast of the voice conditions to the no-voice conditions on ratings of outcome fairness, the ANCOVA showed no significant effect ($F < 1.0$; $\eta^2 = .16$ without control ratings removed, and $\eta^2 = .01$ with control ratings removed). When variance attributable to the control ratings was removed in the ANCOVA, neither fairness variable showed a significant contrast between the postdecision voice and the predecision voice conditions (both $Fs < 1.0$; for procedural fairness, $\eta^2 = .05$ without control ratings removed and $\eta^2 = .004$ with control ratings removed; for outcome fairness, $\eta^2 = .06$ without control ratings removed and $\eta^2 = .004$ with control ratings removed). These analyses suggest that the control ratings can account for some, but not all, of the voice effect on procedural fairness ratings.

Goal Acceptance and Performance

A MANOVA of the number of schedules produced in the test period and of subjects' ratings of the extent to which they accepted the goal they were assigned showed a significant main effect for the voice manipulation, multivariate $F(4, 338) = 9.83$, $p < .001$; for goal acceptance, $F(2, 170) = 7.61, p < .001$; for performance, $F(2, 170) = 19.94, p < .001$. Goal acceptance was higher for both the predecision voice condition ($M = 5.93$) and the postdecision voice condition ($M = 5.67$) than for the no-voice condition ($M = 4.33$; critical $S_{.05} = 1.08$). Similarly, performance was higher in the predecision voice condition ($M = 6.58$) and the postdecision voice condition ($M = 5.85$) than in the no-voice condition ($M = 4.67$; critical $S_{.05} = .76$).

The MANOVA also showed a significant main effect for the information-from-experimenter manipulation, multivariate $F(4, 338) = 21.38$, $p < .001$; for goal acceptance, $F(2, 170) = 5.43$, $p < .005$; for performance, $F(2, 170) = 46.86$, $p < .001$. Relevant information led to greater acceptance of the goal ($M = 6.14$) than either irrelevant information ($M = 4.93$) or no information ($M = 4.85$; critical $S_{.05} = 1.08$), and relevant information also led to better performance ($M = 7.42$) than either irrelevant information ($M = 4.93$) or no information ($M = 4.77$; critical $S_{.05} = .76$).

There was a significant multivariate interaction between the voice manipulation and the information-from-experimenter manipulation, multivariate $F(8, 338) = 2.05$, $p < .001$; for goal acceptance, $F < 1.0$, ns; for performance, $F(4, 170) = 2.31$, $p < .06$. The interaction appears to be due to an especially strong difference in performance between the postdecision voice cell and the no-voice cell within the relevant-information condition.

Discussion

The experiment has a number of important implications for understanding the psychology of procedure. The voice effects on acceptance of the goal and on performance add to a growing body of evidence showing that voice affects a variety of organizational attitudes and behaviors (see, e.g., Earley & Lind, 1987; Greenberg, 1987; Lissak, 1983). By and large, voice appears to promote positive attitudes toward supervisors, tasks, and goals and to lead to better performance. At least one study (Kanfer et al., 1987) has found lower performance when workers are allowed voice, however.

The fairness effects of the information-from-experimenter manipulation show that relevant information, which promotes feelings of efficacy, can also promote the perception that task-related procedures and assignments are fair. As we noted earlier, this finding is congruent with instrumental theories of justice: Relevant information made the subjects feel that they were better at the task, and this may have made the goal seem less extreme and therefore fairer. By rendering the outcome more fair, the relevant information may have made

the procedure that produced the outcome seem fairer. We had hypothesized on the basis of group-value theory that even irrelevant information might make the subjects feel more involved and therefore lead them to view the procedures as fairer. The mean procedural fairness rating in the irrelevant-information condition appears to be somewhat higher than that in the no-information condition, but the difference is not statistically significant. It is not possible to determine whether our hypothesis was incorrect or whether the irrelevant-information manipulation was simply not strong enough to produce the hypothesized effect.

The most important implications of the study have to do with the psychological processes involved in the voice effect. The results of the present experiment show these processes to be more complex than is suggested by any of the current theories of procedural justice. The experiment produced relatively strong evidence that issues of control are an important factor in producing voice effects, but it also showed that not all of the effect of voice was due to control.

Consider first the experimental findings—the mean differences we observed on the procedural and outcome fairness variables. It is clear that, at least within the context and subject population we studied, fairness judgments are enhanced by the opportunity to voice opinions even when there is no chance of influencing the decision. At the same time, it is clear that voice *with* the possibility of influence (and in our experiment with evidence of successful influence) leads to even greater perceived fairness. The postdecision voice condition shows the level of procedural fairness that occurs if only symbolic processes are at work, and the predecision voice condition shows the level of procedural fairness that occurs if both instrumental and symbolic processes are at work. Therefore, the difference between procedural justice ratings for the no-voice condition and those for the postdecisional voice condition provides an indication of the strength of symbolic voice processes, whereas the difference between postdecision voice and predecision voice provides an indication of the strength of instrumental voice processes over and above symbolic processes. The mean values we observed suggest that the symbolic voice effect is at least as strong as the instrumental voice effect: The difference in procedural justice ratings between the no-voice condition and the post-decision voice condition is slightly larger (difference = .72) than the difference between the postdecision voice condition and the predecision voice condition (difference = .55).

The findings with respect to perceived control should also be taken into account. In spite of what seemed to us to be a very strong statement to the subjects about the absence of any possible influence on the decision in the postdecision voice condition and in spite of a clear demonstration of the ineffectiveness of postdecision voice in changing the goal, subjects in this condition reported feeling more control over the outcome than did subjects in the no-voice condition. There are at least two possible explanations for this rather surprising finding. First, the subjects might have felt more control in the postdecision voice condition because the opportunity for voice made them feel more at ease with the experimental setting and its social milieu. The same symbolic factors that were hypothesized to enhance perceived fairness in the postdecision voice condition might also enhance perceived control: To be allowed to express one's views implies that one is a full-fledged member of the experimental group, and this in turn leads to feelings of security and control over the situation (see Lind & Tyler, 1988, pp. 236–237). Alternatively, postdecision voice might have produced an illusion of control (Langer, 1983; Taylor & Brown, 1988).[4] Whichever interpretation is correct, it is interesting to note that similar effects, showing exaggerated perceptions of control in the context of a variety of decision-making procedures, have been seen in other studies (Earley & Lind, 1987; Lind, 1975; Pepitone, 1950).

As we noted earlier, if the high control ratings in the postdecision voice condition are indeed due to an illusion of control—and there is no way of discriminating between the two explanations in the present study—then one could argue that the differences in procedural justice judgments reflect instrumental processes in that they were produced by differences in *subjective* control. Our mediation analyses showed, however, that even under this most favorable interpretation of the data, instrumental models could not account for all of the voice effect. Taken as a whole, then, our study shows that both instrumental and noninstrumental processes are at work. It appears that the early emphasis in procedural justice research on procedure as means to outcomes was in error, but our data make it clear also that it is premature to conclude, as Tyler et al. (1985) did, that "people seem

insensitive to whether their heightened process control is linked to actual control over decisions" (p. 79). It is time for researchers and theorists to become more sophisticated about what drives procedural justice judgments: The answer to the instrumental-noninstrumental debate is that both sides are right, but neither side is entirely right.

The results of the experiment also show that analyses of procedural justice need to be more sophisticated with respect to the psychology of voice. In much of the early research on procedural justice, the major concern was with how procedures that differed in terms of objective power relations might affect fairness judgments (Thibaut & Walker, 1975). It was generally assumed that perceptions of control more or less matched the objective power associated with various procedures. Our data show that voice procedures that are radically different in objective control can produce rather similar perceptions of control and, for that matter, rather similar fairness judgments. In this respect, the present study stresses the subjectivity of justice, a perspective long evident in distributive justice theories (e.g., Adams, 1965; Reis, 1981) but often ignored in procedural justice theory and research. The present study shows, as has other recent research, that what ultimately matters for fairness judgments is not the objective level of outcomes or the objective characteristics of procedures, but instead the subjective evaluations of the variables that underlie fairness judgments (Greenberg & Cohen, 1982; Lind et al., 1989; Paese, Lind, & Kanfer, 1988).

The subjectivity of control and fairness in voice effects also shows a potential for the abuse of voice-based enhancement of procedural fairness judgments. Cohen (1985, 1988) has raised concerns about deceptive uses of the voice effect to promote the appearance of procedural justice. Cohen pointed out that people could be given the appearance of voice—they might be allowed or

---

[4]It is possible, of course, that the subjects simply did not understand the statement or that some other aspect of the experimenter's behavior led them to believe that they could influence the goal they were assigned. The former explanation seems to us unlikely in view of the emphasis placed on the procedure manipulation in running the experiment and in light of the fact that the postdecision voice condition did produce lower control ratings than the predecision voice condition. This explanation is difficult to prove or disprove, but seems to us unlikely in light of the absence of any differences in ratings of the likableness of the experimenter.

even encouraged to express their views to the decision maker—when, in reality, the decision maker has no intention of considering the input. Such "false consciousness" of control could lead the individuals in question to believe that the decision-making procedure was fair even though, by objective criteria, it is patently unfair. Cohen noted that the objective unfairness of such procedures is exacerbated if the decision maker uses the appearance of justice to advance his or her own interests at the expense of those subject to the procedure. If the perception of fairness is enhanced even in the face of the relatively straightforward denial of control involved in our postdecision voice condition, voice-enhanced fairness is all the more likely to occur in situations where a decision maker actively hides the ineffectiveness of input—conditions that may well be more common in the real world than is postdecision voice.

ACKNOWLEDGMENTS

The research reported here was supported in part by grants from the University of Illinois Research Board and the National Science Foundation (SES-85-18597) to E. Allan Lind, and by grants from the University of Minnesota Graduate School and the National Science Foundation (SES-89-10743) to Ruth Kanfer.

We wish to express our appreciation to Ronald Cohen, Tom Tyler, and three anonymous reviewers for their comments on an earlier version of this article.

REFERENCES

Adams, J. S. (1965). Inequity in social exchange. In L. Berkowitz (Ed.), *Advances in experimental social psychology* (Vol. 2, pp. 267–299). San Diego, Academic Press.

Baron, R. M., & Kenny, D. A. (1986). The mediator-moderator variable distinction in social psychological research: Conceptual, strategic, and statistical considerations. *Journal of personality and Social Psychology, 51*, 1173–1182.

Bies, R. J., & Moag, J. S. (1986). Interactional justice: Communications criteria of fairness. In R. Lewicki, M. Bazerman, & B. Sheppard (Eds.), *Research on negotiation in organizations* (Vol. 1, pp. 43–55). Greenwich, CT: JAI Press.

Brett, J. M. (1986). Commentary on procedural justice papers. In R. Lewicki, M. Bazerman, & B. Sheppard (Eds.), *Research on negotiation in organizations* (Vol. 1. pp. 81–90). Greenwich, CT: JAI Press.

Cohen, R. L. (1985). Procedural justice and participation. *Human Relations, 38*, 643–663.

Cohen, R. L. (1998, August). *Fabrications of justice*. Paper presented at the International Conference on Social Justice and Societal Problems, Leiden, The Netherlands.

Earley, P. C., & Lind, E. A. (1987). Procedural justice and participation in task selection: The role of control in mediating justice judgments. *Journal of Personality and Social Psychology, 52*, 1148–1160.

Erez, M., Earley, P. C., & Hulin, C. L. (1985). The impact of participation on goal acceptance and performance: A two step model. *Academy of Management, 28*, 50–66.

Folger, R. (1977). Distributive and procedural justice: Combined impact of "voice" and improvement on experienced inequity. *Journal of Personality and Social Psychology, 35*, 108–119.

Folger, R. (1986). Mediation, arbitration, and the psychology of procedural justice. In R. Lewicki, M. Bazerman, & B. Sheppard (Eds.), *Research on negotiation in organizations* (Vol. 1, pp. 57–79). Greenwich, CT: JAI Press.

Folger, R., Rosenfield, D., Grove, J., & Corkran, L. (1979). Effects of "voice" and peer opinions on responses to inequity. *Journal of Personality and Social Psychology, 37*, 2253–2261.

Folger, R., Rosenfield, D., & Robinson, T. (1983). Relative deprivation and procedural justifications. *Journal of Personality and Social Psychology, 45*, 268–273.

Freedman, J. L. (1969). Role playing: Psychology by consensus. *Journal of Personality and Social Psychology, 13*, 107–114.

Greenberg, J. (1987). Reactions to procedural injustice in payment distributions: Do the ends justify the means? *Journal of Applied Psychology, 72*, 55–61.

Greenberg, J., & Cohen, R. L. (1982). Why justice? Normative and instrumental interpretations. In J. Greenberg & R. Cohen (Eds.), *Equity and justice in social behavior* (pp. 437–466). San Diego, CA: Academic Press.

Kanfer, R. (in press). Motivation theory and industrial/organizational psychology. In M. D. Dunnette (Ed.), *Handbook of industrial and organizational psychology* (vol. 1, 2nd ed.). Palo Alto, CA: Consulting psychologists Press.

Kanfer, R, Sawyer, J., Earley, P. C., & Lind, E. A. (1987). Participation in task evaluation procedures: The effects of influential opinion expression and knowledge of evaluative criteria on attitudes and performance. *Social Justice Research, 1*, 235–249.

Kirk, R. E. (1968). *Experimental design: Procedures for the behavioral sciences*. Belmont, CA: Brooks/Cole.

Lane, R. E. (1988). Procedural goods in a democracy: How one is treated versus what one gets. *Social Justice Research, 2*, 177–192.

Langer, E. J. (1983). *The psychology of control*. Beverly Hills, CA: Sage.

Latham, G. P., Erez, M., & Locke, E. A. (1988). Resolving scientific disputes by the joint design of crucial experiments by antagonists: Application of the Latham-Erez dispute regarding participation in goal setting. *Journal of Applied Psychology, 73*, 753–772.

Latham, G. P., & Lee, T. W. (1986). Goal setting. In E. A. Locke (Ed.), *Generalizing from laboratory to field settings* (pp. 101–118). Lexington, MA: Lexington Books.

Latham, G. P., & Saari, L. M. (1979). The effects of holding goal difficulty constant on assigned and participatively set goals. *Academy of Management Journal, 22*, 163–168.

LaTour, S. (1978). Determinants of participant and observer satisfaction with adversary and inquisitorial modes of adjudication. *Journal of Personality and Social Psychology, 36*, 1531–1545.

Leventhal, G. S. (1980). What should be done with equity theory? New approaches to the study of fairness in social relationships. In K. Gergen, M. Greenberg, & R. Willis

(Eds.), *Social exchange: Advances in theory and research* (pp. 27–55). New York: Plenum Press.

Lind, E. A. (1975). The exercise of information influence in legal advocacy. *Journal of Applied Social Psychology, 5,* 127–143.

Lind, E. A., Kurtz, S., Musante, L., Walker, L., & Thibaut, J. W. (1980). Procedure and outcome effects on reactions to adjudicated resolution of conflicts of interests. *Journal of Personality and Social Psychology, 39,* 643–653.

Lind, E. A., Lissak, R. I., & Conlon, D. E. (1983). Decision control and process control effects on procedural fairness judgments. *Journal of Applied Social Psychology, 13,* 338–350.

Lind, E. A., MacCoun, R. J., Ebener, P. A.,, Felstiner, W. L. F., Hensler, D. R., Resnik, J., & Tyler, T. R. (1989). *The perception of justice: Tort litigants' views of trials court-annexed arbitration, and judicial settlement conferences.* Santa Monica, CA: RAND Corporation.

Lind, E. A., & Tyler, T. R. (1988). *The social psychology of procedural justice.* New York: Plenum Press.

Lissak, R. I. (1983). *Procedural fairness: How employees evaluate procedures.* Unpublished doctoral dissertation, University of Illinois, Champaign.

Locke, E. A., & Latham, G. P. (1990). *A theory of goal setting and task performance.* Englewood Cliffs, NJ: Prentice-Hall.

Locke, E. A., Latham, G. P., & Erez, M. (1988). The determinants of goal commitment. *Academy of Management Review, 13,* 23–39.

Locke, E. A., & Schweiger, D. (1979). Participation in decision-making: One more look. In B. Staw (Ed.), *Research in organizational behavior* (pp. 265–339). Greenwich, CT: JAI Press.

Locke, E. A., Shaw, K. N., Saari, L. M., & Latham, G. P. (1981). Goal setting and task performance: 1969–1980. *Psychological Bulletin, 90,* 125–152.

Paese, P., Lind, E. A., & Kanfer, R. (1988). Procedural fairness and work group responses to performance evaluation systems. *Social Justice Research, 2,* 193–205.

Pepitone, A. (1950). Motivational effects in social perception. *Human Relations, 3,* 57–76.

Reis, H. (1981). Self-presentation and distributive justice. In J. Tedeschi (Ed.), *Impression management theory and social psychological research* (pp. 269–291). New York: Plenum Press.

Taylor, S. E., & Brown, J. D. (1988). Illusion and well-being: A social psychological perspective on mental health. *Psychological Bulletin, 103,* 193–210.

Thibaut, J., & Walker, L. (1975). *Procedural justice: A psychological analysis..* Hillsdale, NJ: Erlbaum.

Thibaut, J., & Walker, L. (1978). A theory of procedure. *California Law Review, 66,* 541–566.

Tyler, T. R. (1987). Conditions leading to value expressive effects in judgments of procedural justice: A test of four models. *Journal of Personality and Social Psychology, 52,* 333–344.

Tyler, T. R., Rasinski, K., & Spodick, N. (1985). The influence of voice on satisfaction with leaders: Exploring the meaning of process control. *Journal of Personality and Social Psychology, 48,* 72–81.

Vidmar, N. (in press). The origins and consequences of procedural fairness, *Law & Social Inquiry.*

Walker, L., LaTour, S., Lind, E. A., & Thibaut, J. (1974). Reactions of participants and observers to modes of adjudication. *Journal of Applied Social Psychology, 4,* 295–310.

The Psychology of Procedural Justice: A Test of the Group-Value Model

Tom R. Tyler • Northwestern University and American Bar Foundation

Research on the psychology of procedural justice has been dominated by Thibaut and Walker's (1975) theory about the psychology of procedural preference. That theory suggests that people are concerned with their direct and indirect control over decisions. Lind and Tyler (1988) proposed a group-value theory that suggests that several noncontrol issues—the neutrality of the decision-making procedure, trust in the 3rd party, and the information the experience communicates about social standing—influence both procedural preferences and judgments of procedural justice. This study examines 3 issues. The first is whether judgments about neutrality, trust, and social standing have an independent impact on judgment of procedural justice. The results suggest that they do. The second is how Thibaut and Walker's control theory developed. The results suggest that control issues are central to the setting studied by Thibaut and Walker—disputes—but are less important in other situations. Finally, the implications of these findings for a group-value theory of procedural justice are examined.

In their 1975 book on procedural justice, Thibaut and Walker suggested that people's reactions to third-party allocation and dispute—resolution decisions are influenced by the fairness of the decision-making procedures, independent of the influence of either the favorability or the fairness of the decisions reached. This procedural justice effect has since been widely replicated in legal, industrial, political, and interpersonal settings (see Lind & Tyler, 1988). It is now a well-established fact that people care about the justice of allocation and decision-making procedures.

In addition to suggesting that people care about procedural justice, Thibaut and Walker (1975) articulated a psychological model to explain procedural preferences. That model suggests that the distribution of control between the participants and the third party is the key procedural characteristic shaping people's views about both fairness and desirability. Thibaut and Walker distinguished between two types of control: process control and decision control. *Process control* refers to participants' control over the presentation of evidence; *decision control* refers to participants' control over the actual decisions made.

Underlying the control model are several important assumptions. The most obvious is that people focus on their direct and indirect control over the decisions made by the third party. It is assumed that people are not concerned with their long-term relationship to the third party or to the institutions they represent. In other words, people are primarily concerned about their relationship to the person or people with whom they have a dispute. Their concerns include an interest in the specific dispute they are engaged in and a concern about maintaining a long-term, productive exchange relationship with other parties to the dispute. As people's concern in dealing with a third party is with the dispute at issue, it is control over aspects of the procedure related to the resolution of the dispute that are central to the control model (Thibaut & Walker, 1975, 1978).

Research subsequent to Thibaut and Walker (1975) has generally followed the control model by focusing its attention on the distribution of control within various types of procedure (see Lind & Tyler, 1988, for a review). That research supports Thibaut and Walker's suggestion that the distribution of control within a procedure influences assessments of its procedural fairness (Lind & Tyler, 1988), so Thibaut and Walker's control theory has been widely confirmed. In their original theory of control, Thibaut and Walker placed their primary emphasis on decision control, viewing process control as an indirect means of exerting decision control. In contrast, subsequent research has suggested that (a) process control is usually more important than decision control, and (b) process control is important even if it is not linked to decision control (Lind, Lissak, & Conlon, 1983; Tyler, 1987; Tyler, Rasinski, & Spodick, 1985). As Thibaut and Walker predicted, people care about control. However, their concerns about control do not correspond to the predictions of Thibaut and Walker's control model.

Group-Value Model

Lind and Tyler (1988) proposed a different conception of the psychology of procedural justice, one that they labeled the *group-value model*. The group-value model suggests that there are important aspects of the psychology of procedural justice that are not represented in Thibaut and Walker's (1975) control model. The group-value model assumes that people are concerned about their long-term social relationship with the authorities or institutions acting as third parties and do not view their relationship with third parties as a one-shot deal. Instead, people care about their relationship with the third party. This leads them to be concerned with three noncontrol issues: the neutrality of the decision-making procedure, trust in

the third party, and evidence about social standing. It is predicted that these three group-value issues will have an effect on reactions to experiences that is independent of the influence of outcome favorability or the distribution of control.

The basic assumption of the group-value model is that people value membership in social groups; that is, group identification is psychologically rewarding. People want to belong to social groups and to establish and maintain the social bonds that exist within groups. Research shows that people establish such connections if given even the most tenuous basis for group identification (Brewer & Kramer, 1986; Kramer & Brewer, 1984; Messick & Brewer, 1983; Tajfel, 1981; Tajfel & Turner, 1979).

One reason that people seek group membership is that groups provide a source of self-validation (Festinger, 1954), giving their members information about the appropriateness of their attitudes and values. Groups also provide emotional support and a sense of belonging. Finally, groups are important sources of material resources. For these reasons, people find evidence that they are accepted members of social groups rewarding and are troubled by evidence that they are being rejected by the groups to which they belong (Cartwright & Zander, 1953; Schachter, 1951).

The groups that people identify with and belong to can be either small groups (such as family, friendship, or work groups) or large organizations. In addition, people identify with and belong to local, state, and national legal and political groups. This study focuses on people's identification with their common membership in a legal-political system, which has formalized rules, institutions, and authorities. Although the legal system is a larger group than a family, friendship, or work group, people nonetheless identify strongly with the legal-political system and feel a striking sense of personal obligation to legal and political authorities (Tyler, in press). This identification continues to occur, although in a weaker form, both within minority groups and among the poor.

Neutrality

In a long-term relationship, people cannot always have what they want. Instead, they must compromise and sometimes defer to others' desires and needs. Hence, a simple focus on outcome favorability in any specific situation is not realistic. People must think about their outcomes over time. Given that people cannot easily focus on short-term outcome favorability, how can they evaluate whether their outcomes from the group are reasonable? Lind and Tyler (1988) suggested that people assume that, over time, all will benefit fairly from the application of fair procedures for decision making. The first implication of a group-value perspective, therefore, is that people will focus on whether the authority has created a neutral arena (i.e., a "level playing field") in which to resolve their problem or conflict, instead of focusing on whether they receive a favorable outcome in any given decision. In any particular situation people will be concerned with having an unbiased decision maker who is honest and who uses appropriate factual information to make decisions.

Trust

In addition to leading to a focus on the neutrality of decision-making procedures, the long-term nature of group membership leads people to focus on the intentions of third parties. Formal authorities, like judges, are given a large element of discretion about the way in which procedures are enacted (Tyler & Bies, in press). Their use of that discretion is shaped by their intentions. Trust involves the belief that the intentions of third parties are benevolent, that they desire to treat people in a fair and reasonable way.

The intentions of authorities are especially important because current interactions allow people to predict the future (Heider, 1958). Because people are in organizations for the long term, their loyalty depends on their predictions about what will happen in the long term. For this reason, people's commitment to the group changes as their attributions about the intentions of the authorities change. If they believe that the authorities are trying to be fair and to deal equitably with them, they develop a long-term commitment to the group.

Standing

Third, people care about their standing in the group. Interpersonal treatment during social interactions gives people information about their sta-

tus within the group. If people are treated rudely, they know that the authority they are dealing with regards them as having low status within the group. Conversely, polite and respectful treatment communicates that the authorities involved regard them as having high status in the group. Similarly, if authorities show respect for individuals' rights as a group member, individuals gain knowledge that those rights will be respected, whereas abuse of one's rights brings their existence into question. When the police harass minorities or treat them rudely, for example, they communicate to members of those groups both their low social standing and the fact that the authorities may not protect them and may, in fact, even hurt them.

Why Did Thibaut and Walker Develop a Control Theory?

This study examines why, if noncontrol variables are an important determinant of reactions to experiences with legal authorities, Thibaut and Walker's (1975) research resulted in a control theory. One hypothesis is that their control theory is appropriate for their research setting—dispute resolution—but does not generalize to other settings.[1] Several recent studies have lent plausibility to this possibility by suggesting that people assess the fairness of procedures in different ways under different circumstances (Barrett-Howard & Tyler, 1986; Lissak & Sheppard, 1983; Sheppard & Lewicki, 1987; Sheppard, Saunders, & Minton, 1988; Tyler, 1988).

Thibaut and Walker's (1975) research is also limited in the type of people they studied. Their work typically used college or law students as subjects (and as third parties). Sears (1986) has pointed out that college-student participants differ in many respects from the general population. In particular, (a) college students tend to be oriented toward cognitive and verbal skills, and may have viewed control over the opportunity to present evidence and arguments as a particularly key feature of pro-

---

[1]Although very important, dispute resolution in formal courtroom trials is not the typical type of experience that people have with legal authorities. The random sampling approach used in this study led to a random sample of people's experiences with legal authorities. In the sample, only 7% of people's experiences involved going to court to resolve a dispute (out of 23% who went to court for any reason).

cedural justice, and (b) questions of group identification and long-term group loyalty were not particularly salient to college students, who are less oriented toward long-term group relationships. In addition, the participants were members of artificially created, short-term groups, and probably felt limited loyalty to those groups. It is also possible, therefore, that Thibaut and Walker's theory of procedure would have differed if they had used a broader sample of the population as subjects.

Group-Value Model

Finding noncontrol effects supports the hypotheses of the group-value model. It does not, however, demonstrate the validity of that model, if other theories can also potentially explain the findings reported. To support the group-value interpretation, it is necessary to show that people care about neutrality, trust, or standing because they care about group status and group membership.

This study includes two types of analysis that more directly test the group-value explanation for the importance of noncontrol issues. The first involves distinguishing between the three different group-value concerns: neutrality, trust, and standing. Of these, standing is the most directly linked to group-value issues. If people prefer information about their status in the group to favorable outcomes, that preference directly supports a group-value interpretation. Trust is also linked to the group-value model when people's trust in the intentions of the authority they have dealt with is being generalized to the group. In other words, if people believe that they will never again deal with the particular judge they have encountered, then that judge is a symbol of the group, and reactions to him or her support a group-value model. If people are involved in a continuing relationship with the third party, then concern about the third party's intentions may reflect either group-value or social exchange concerns. In contrast to standing and trust, neutrality can be explained by both group-value and social exchange models. Hence, evidence that standing and trust matter is especially supportive of a group-value interpretation.

The group-value model also predicts that those people who are committed to the social group will care particularly strongly about group-value issues. In other words, the meaning of procedural justice will be different for such people, who will regard

control issues as less central to definitions of procedural justice. Social exchange theory conversely predicts that more committed group members will care more about control. Hence, exploring the relation between commitment and definitions of procedural justice provides a second way to differentiate the group-value and social exchange models of procedural justice.

Method

Subjects

The data used in this study were obtained through survey interviews with a random sample of the population of Chicago. The interviews were conducted over the telephone during the spring of 1984. The sample of telephone numbers called represented a random sample of existing numbers in the city of Chicago, and 63% of the numbers yielded completed interviews. Some respondents had had several experiences with different legal authorities. Those respondents were asked questions about their most important experience. The use of a random sampling approach leads to a broad range of experiences with legal authorities, including appearances in court (22%), calls to the police for help (47%), and being stopped by the police (31%). The sample included 652 residents of Chicago interviewed following an experience with legal authorities.

Materials

Independent Variables

Outcome favorability. Outcome favorability was assessed in both absolute and relative terms.[2] The absolute quality of the outcome was determined by coding respondent statements indicating the nature of the experience's outcome. In the case of calls to the police, respondents were asked whether the police had solved the problem about which they were called. In situations in which the respondent had been stopped by the police, respondents were asked whether the police had cited them for a violation of the law and whether they had arrested the respondent or taken him or her to a police sta-

---

[2] For the complete wording of all questions and the frequency of all responses, write to Tom Tyler.

tion. With court cases, respondents were asked to indicate whether the outcome of their case was positive or negative. To form an Outcome Favorability scale, the previously outlined judgments of outcome favorability were weighted by the self-reported seriousness of the problem.

Outcome favorability was also assessed relative to four standards of reference. First, respondents were asked to compare their experience with experiences they have had in the past. Second, they were asked to compare their experience with their expectations before the experience, however derived. Third, they were asked to compare their experience with what they thought generally happened to other members of the public. Finally, they were asked to compare their experience with recent experiences of their friends, family, or neighbors.

Control. Process control was assessed by asking respondents how much opportunity they had had to present their problem or their side of the case before decisions were made about how to deal with it. Decision control was assessed by asking respondents how much influence they had over the decisions that were made by the third party. Responses to the two items were correlated ($r = .57$), so the process and decision control items were averaged to form a single control index ($\alpha = .72$).

Neutrality. Neutrality was operationalized as proper behavior, factual decision making, and a lack of bias. Lack of bias in the authorities' behavior was established by asking respondents whether their treatment or the outcome of their interaction was influenced by their race, sex, age, nationality, or some other characteristic of them as a person. In addition, in those cases in which there was a dispute between parties, respondents were asked whether the legal authorities involved had favored one party over another. The three items were highly correlated (mean $r = .54$, $\alpha = .78$).

Neutrality also included propriety or impropriety of behavior. Impropriety was assessed by combining responses to two questions: whether the authorities "did anything that was improper of dishonest" and whether officials had lied. The two items were highly correlated ($r = .44$, $\alpha = .61$).

Finally, neutrality included factual decision making. The factual quality of decision making was assessed in two ways. First, respondents were asked whether the authority involved had "gotten the information they needed to make good decisions about how to handle" the problem. Second,

respondents were asked whether the authorities had tried to "bring the problem into the open so that it could be solved." The two items were highly correlated ($r = .59$, $\alpha = .74$).

To construct the Neutrality scale, subscales were created reflecting each of the three elements of neutrality. Each subscale was created by counting the number of instances of nonneutrality mentioned. The three subscales were found to be positively correlated ($r = .21$), so a Neutrality scale was created by averaging the three subscales ($\alpha = .44$).

Trust. Trust is linked to inferences about the intentions of the authorities. People's impressions about those intentions were assessed by asking respondents to indicate how much effort the authority had made to be fair to them. The assumption that underlies this operationalization of trust is that people use the intentions of the authority dealt with to predict the future behavior of all authorities. In other words, people both (a) predict from the past to the future and (b) generalize from an experience with one or two people to the future behavior of all legal authorities.

To test the reasonableness of the assumptions underlying this operationalization of trust, the degree to which people predict and generalize was tested. Respondents were asked both how typical the authorities they dealt with were of all such authorities, and how much information their experience gave them about how legal authorities would act toward them in the future. These two judgments were combined into a single-scale Generalization scale, and various aspects of experience were used to predict generalization. As predicted, the degree of trust was found to predict the degree of generalization ($\beta = 0.23$, $p < .001$). Generalization was also related to whether the authorities were polite and showed respect for people's rights ($r = .20$, $p < .01$). Outcome favorability did not predict generalization (absolute $r = .11$, *ns*; relative $r = .00$, *ns*). Control did not predict generalization ($r = .10$, *ns*). Finally, neutrality did not predict generalization ($r = .10$, *ns*).

Standing. Information about social standing is conveyed by the quality of the interpersonal treatment a person receives from third parties. Standing was measured in two ways. First, respondents were asked whether the authorities had been polite to them. They were also asked whether the authorities had shown respect for their rights. These two measures were highly correlated ($r =$

.73), so they were averaged to form a Standing scale ($\alpha = .84$).

Although distinct conceptually, the different psychological judgments outlined are not independent of one another. The three operationalizations of the group-value model are intercorrelated (mean $r = .58$), as well as being correlated with the control index (mean $r = .53$) and with outcome favorability (mean $r = .34$). Similarly, control judgments are related to outcome favorability ($r = .32$).

Dependent Variables

Four dependent variables were used in the analysis. The first was the respondents' judgment about the fairness of the procedures used during their experience with the police or courts. Respondents were asked how fair the procedures used by the authorities had been and how fairly they had been treated. These two items were highly correlated ($r = .81$), and were averaged to form a single scale indexing procedural justice ($\alpha = .90$). Respondents were also asked about the fairness of the outcome of their experience. They were asked about the fairness of the outcome and whether they had received what they deserved. These two items were highly correlated ($r = .78$), so a single scale of outcome fairness was formed by averaging ($\alpha = .88$). The correlation between the Procedural Fairness and Outcome Fairness scales was .74.

Respondents also indicated their affect toward the authorities they had dealt with by indicating whether they felt angry, frustrated, or pleased with the authorities. These three items were highly correlated (mean $r = .56$), so an Affect scale was created by averaging responses ($\alpha = 79$).

Finally, respondents were asked to evaluate the overall fairness of the authorities, that is, to generalize from their own experience with particular police officers or judges to views about whether those authorities generally treat citizens fairly. Respondents first indicated how fairly the police or courts treat people and handle their problems. They also indicated how often the police (courts) treat people fairly. Finally, they indicated how fairly they thought that they would be treated by the police (courts) if they were to deal with them in the future. These items were highly correlated (mean $r = .49$ for the police items; mean $r = .46$ for the court items), so they were averaged to form a single scale ($\alpha = .74$ for the police; $\alpha = .72$ for the courts). All respondents were given a score for the scale reflecting their views about the fairness of the authorities they had dealt with (the police or the courts).

Control Variables

Thirteen variables were measured for use as control variables. Six are demographic variables: education, income, self-described political liberalism-conservatism, age, sex, and race. Five are characteristics of the experience: the authority dealt with, whether a dispute was involved, whether the interaction was voluntary, and the self-reported importance of the outcome and of the quality of treatment by the authorities. Finally, two general questions were included that index beliefs about whether the authorities generally treat citizens equally.

People's commitment to the social group was also used as a control variable in the analysis. That commitment was measured in two ways. First, support for legal authorities was assessed. Eight items were used to establish affective attachment to those authorities, including "I feel proud of the [police/courts]" and "I respect the [police/courts]." Those items were correlated (mean $r = .40$, $\alpha = .84$), so they were averaged to form a single index of support. Perceived obligation to obey legal authorities was also assessed using a six-item scale, consisting of items such as "I always try to follow the law, even if I think that it is wrong." Those items were also positively correlated (mean $r = .18$). so they were averaged to form an obligation scale ($\alpha = .57$).

Results

Do Neutrality, Trust, and Standing Matter?

The first question is whether neutrality, trust, and standing explain variance in people's reactions to their experiences with legal authorities that cannot be explained by judgments about control or the favorability of outcomes. If these noncontrol issues are important, they should explain significant amounts of independent variance when variations in control and outcome favorability are controlled for. One way to test for such an idependent influence is through a multiple regression equation with independent variable indexes reflecting outcome favorability, control, neutrality, trust, and social standing.

Table 1 shows the extent to which each of the independent variables under consideration can explain variance in the dependent variables when considered (a) alone or (b) in addition to whatever variance has already been explained by all of the other variables in an equation. The results strongly suggest that neutrality, trust, and standing are a key input into people's reactions to their experiences with third parties. They consistently explain a significant amount of independent variance. In fact, they always explain more variance in the dependent variables than do control issues, irrespective of whether they are considered alone or in addition to other variables.

In the case of procedural justice judgments, for example, neutrality, trust, and standing explain 65% of the variance in procedural justice judgments if considered alone ($p < .001$), and 22% of variance in procedural justice judgments that cannot be explained by outcome favorability or control judgments ($p < .001$). Control issues, in contrast, explain 39% of the variance in procedural justice judgments when considered alone ($p < .001$), and only 1% of unique variance ($p < .001$), Similarly, outcome favorability explains 21% of the variance in procedural justice judgments when considered alone ($p < .001$), and 1% of unique variance ($p < .001$), Neutrality, trust, and standing similarly dominate judgments of distributive justice, affect toward third parties, and beliefs about the justice of legal authorities.

A second type of regression analysis uses beta weights to explore the magnitude of the influence of the independent variables. This analysis allows the independent influence of each of the three noncontrol variables—neutrality, trust, and standing—to be examined. The beta weight shown in Table 2 suggest that issues of trust and of standing within the group are especially important in shaping both people's judgments about whether they have received procedural justice and their reactions to their experience. Both of these judgments are more important than either control judgments or outcome favorability. Neutrality is most important when the issue of concern is outcome fairness. If people are deciding whether the outcome of their experience is fair, they place weight on the neutrality of the decision-making procedure. Such concerns are more important than control issues. Outcome justice judgments are also linked to the favorability of the outcome.

Controlling for Potentially Confounding Third Variables

Because the data used in this study are correlational, it is always possible that the results reported represent a spurious joint association of the variables examined to some unassessed third variable. Such a possibility can never be definitively refuted, as all such possible third variables can never be identified and included in the equation. The possibility of a spurious result can be minimized, however, by including plausible third variables in the equation as controls. In addition to presenting the regression analysis already outlined, Table 2 presents a similar analysis that includes control variables reflecting individual and situational differences.

The results of the regression analysis with added

TABLE 1. The Ability of Each Variable to Explain Variance

Independent variable	Procedural justice Alone (%)	Unique (%)	Distributive justice Alone (%)	Unique (%)	Affect toward authorities Alone (%)	Unique (%)	Beliefs about the justice of the authorities Alone (%)	Unique (%)
Absolute and relative outcome favorability	21	1	34	16	16	2	12	3
Control	39	1	23	0	26	1	12	0
Group-value variables	65	22	50	20	49	19	23	8
Total	68		66		52		26	

Note. $n = 652$. The percentages reported in the Alone variance columns represent the amount of variance explained by the factor(s) when entered into an equation alone. The percentages reported in the Unique variance columns represent the amount of variance explained by each psychological factor above what can be explained by all of the other factors. All nonzero entries are $p < .001$.

TABLE 2. The Influence of Differing Psychological Characteristics

Independent varible	Procedural justice	Distributive justice	Affect toward authorities	Beliefs about the justice of the authorities
	Without third variable controls			
Outcome favorability				
Absolute	.16***	.19***	.15***	.20***
Relative	.07**	.31***	−.01	.05
Control	.17***	.03	.11**	.05
Group-value issues				
Neutrality	.15***	.27***	.10*	.01
Trust	.30***	.27***	.25***	.23***
Group standing	.29***	.17***	.31***	.18***
Total	68%	66%	52%	26%
	With third variable controls			
Outcome favorability				
Absolute	.15***	.13***	.16***	.13**
Relative	.06*	.37***	.00	.01
Control	.19***	.10**	.11**	.09
Group-value issues				
Neutrality	.13***	.24***	.10*	−.02
Trust	.31***	.33***	.24***	.18***
Group standing	.28***	.20***	.28***	.12**
Total	69%	70%	52%	47%

Note. All entries are standardized regression coefficients for an equation in which all terms were entered simultaneously.
* $p < .05.$ ** $p < .01.$ *** $p < .001.$

control variables suggest that introducing third-variable controls has essentially no influence on the conclusions previously outlined regarding the importance of neutrality, trust, and standing. All of the regression analyses that include control variables continue to support the suggestion that noncontrol issues have an independent influence on procedural justice judgments and reactions to experience.[3]

Why Did Thibaut and Walker Develop a Control Theory?

To test the possibility that the choice of setting or of participants influenced the psychological model of procedural justice developed, an analysis was conducted to examine the criteria used by different types of people, and by people in different situations, to define the fairness of procedures. Respondents were divided into subgroups along two dimensions: personal differences and situational differences. Each variable was used in a regression analysis of the type already outlined in the discussion of differences in levels of group commitment. As before, interaction terms were added to a regression of outcome, control, and group-value criteria on judgments of procedural justice. In the cases in which a significant interaction effect was found, separate regression analyses were conducted for each of the two subgroups defined by the situational variable being considered. A comparison of the beta weights within these two regression equations shows the relative importance of the various aspects of procedural justice within each subgroup.

[3] A second possible confounding influence is the effect of prior views about authority in general on interpretations of particular experiences. Because control judgments are more experience specific, and group-value judgments are more global, group-value judgments may be more influenced by prior attitudes. To test this possibility, panel data collected on 291 respondents were analyzed. Those respondents were interviewed both before and after their experiences (see Tyler, in press, for a fuller description of this sample). A replication of the analysis shown in Tables 1 and 2 was conducted, with additional variables added to reflect attitudes toward authority before the experience. With these additional variables in the equation, significant group-value effects continued to be found with all four dependent variables. The additional controls had essentially no influence on judgments of procedural justice, distributive justice, or affect. They diminished, but did not eliminate, the effect of group-value judgments on generalizations to views about the fairness of the authorities. Hence, potential confounds with prior attitudes are not an explanation for group-value effects.

To test the possibility that different types of people do not define procedural justice in the same way, the six demographic variables (race, sex, income, education, age, and liberalism) were used as variables for subgroup analyses. The subgroup analyses yielded no significant differences in the importance of control in the definition of a fair procedure. Of the 18 interactions created by the three group-value variables, only one was statistically significant.[4]

It is also possible that the importance of control or of the group-value issues in defining procedural justice varies depending on the nature of the situation in which people are dealing with legal authorities. Seven situational dimensions were used to explore this possibility: the authority dealt with (police or courts), whether a dispute was involved, whether the experience was voluntary, whether the outcome was favorable, the importance to the respondent of receiving a favorable outcome, and the importance to the respondent of receiving fair treatment from the authorities. Two additional scales were used that measured people's general views about whether the legal authorities treat all citizens equally. The first scale asks respondents whether all citizens are treated equally, and the second asks whether the particular group to which the respondent belongs is treated worse than others.[5]

Unlike the findings in the case of demographic differences, subgroup analysis using situational differences revealed several variations in the role of control in defining the meaning of procedural justice. In two of the seven cases—that is, in the case of variations in whether a dispute was involved and whether the outcome was favorable—significant variations in the importance of control were found. Control was a significantly more important determinant of procedural justice judgments in dispute settings and when outcomes were unfavorable. These findings suggest that Thibaut and Walker's (1975) focus on control is due to their focus on disputes, not to their use of college students as participants.

Do More Committed People Care More About Group-Value Issues?

The previously outlined results suggest that people generally care about neutrality, trust, and standing. If these concerns reflect the concerns identi-

fied by group-value theory, those people who are more committed to the social group should care particularly strongly about them. To test this suggestion, two variables tapping group loyalty were used for subgroup analysis. The first is support for legal authorities, an affective measure of positive feeling toward the police and courts. The second is the perceived obligation to obey those authorities.[6] Respondents were divided into subgroups by dividing the sample at the median.

Regression analysis was used to explore subgroup differences in the role of group-value issues in defining procedural justice. In the regression analyses performed, as in those shown in Table 2, an equation was run that included all psychological factors as independent variables. In addition, an interaction term was included for the interaction of the subgroup variable—loyalty to the group—with each psychological factor. Finally, a term was included to reflect the main effect of the subgroup variable itself. All respondents were included in the analysis.

The results of the subgroup analysis—shown in Table 3—support the hypothesis that those more committed to a group care more about group-value issues. For both variables, group-value issues are more important among those with greater commitment to legal authorities. In the case of support, those high in support defined procedural justice significantly more strongly in terms of the neutrality of the decision-making procedure, and those low in support defined procedural justice signifi-

---

[4]Minority group members were found to place significantly greater weight on evidence about their social standing than did White group members.

[5]As previously noted, it is important to remember that evaluations of the legal authorities were influenced by the respondents' experiences; that is, those who thought that they were fairly treated evaluated the legal authorities more positively. Interestingly, views about whether the authorities treat citizens equally were found to be unrelated to anything involving past experience (mean $r = .05$, ns). Although this issue suggests an important caution in interpreting the findings reported here, this analysis is concerned with the meaning of procedural justice. It seems less likely that people change their views about what constitutes procedural justice as a result of their experience.

[6]Using support and obligation as variables in this analysis requires one caution. Because the experiences being discussed occurred before the interview, whereas attitudes were assessed at the time of the interview, the experiences may have influenced attitudes. In fact, they did (see Tyler, in press). In this case, however, that problem is less important because the issue is the meaning of procedural justice.

TABLE 3. Group Commitment Influences on the Meaning of Procedural Justice

	Support			Obligation		
Independent variable	High	Low	Difference	High	Low	Difference
Absolute outcome favorability	.03	.26***	*	.14***	.20***	–
Relative outcome favorability	.00	.19***	–	.10**	.09	–
Control	.15**	.17*	–	.21***	.20***	–
Neutrality	.20***	.10*	*	.12**	.16**	–
Trust	.35***	.27***	–	.38***	.22***	*
Standing	.30***	.35***	–	.26***	.32***	–
Total(R^2)	61%	71%		68%	68%	

Note. The entries in each column are beta weights from an equation in which all six psychological factors are entered simultaneously. An asterisk in the difference column indicates that the interaction term was statistically significant at $p < .05$ or greater in an equation including main effects and interactions.
* $p < .05$. ** $p < .01$. *** $p < .001$.

cantly more strongly in terms of the favorability of their outcome. In the case of obligation, those high in commitment to legal authorities defined procedural justice significantly more strongly in terms of their trust in the authorities. Although these findings support the theory, it is also important to recognize that the level of support is weak. There are six opportunities for group-value variables to interact with commitment, and only two of those interactions are significant. It is important not to overstate the strength of this finding: It is significant, but weak. Neither of the two measures of commitment resulted in a significant control interaction, although those low in support were found to care more about the favorability of the outcomes they obtained.

Discussion

Thibaut and Walker's (1975) initial theory of procedural justice emphasized the role of control judgments in shaping people's assessments about the fairness of procedures. The results of this study support their suggestion that control issues do matter. The findings suggest strongly, however, that a broader perspective on the psychology of procedural justice explains a great deal about the psychology of procedural justice that cannot be understood using control theories. When issues of neutrality, trust, and standing are examined, they explain more about people's reactions to their experiences than do variations in perceived control or outcome favorability.

The importance of judgments about neutrality, trust, and standing suggests that people care about

more than the issue or problem that initially brings them to a third party. People care about their relationship to the third party. They react to evidence about how that person makes decisions, to information about their intentions, and to the interpersonal context of their interaction with each other.

These findings help to explain two anomalous findings in the control literature. Those findings are that, although Thibaut and Walker (1975) focused on decision control, studies typically find that (a) having process control is more important to people's feelings of being fairly treated than is having decision control, and (b) people value process control even when it is not linked to decision control (Lind et al., 1983; Tyler, 1987; Tyler et al., 1985). These findings are understandable if the importance of people's connection to authorities is recognized. Those with problems value the opportunity to present their problems to authorities. By allowing people to bring problems to them, authorities reaffirm people's social standing and their right to call on the organization for help. Tyler (1987) supported this interpretation by finding that the opportunity to address authorities is only valuable if people believe that what they say has been considered by the authorities when a decision is being made. People's standing in the group is not validated by being ignored, and being ignored would not suggest that an organization is responsive to appeals for help.

Hence, the results suggest the need to broaden the theoretical framework within which procedural justice is understood beyond the control theory articulated by Thibaut and Walker (1975). One theoretical framework that suggests a broader framework is that proposed by Leventhal (1980).

Leventhal (1980) suggested six criteria that might influence judgments about the justice of a procedure. Four of those criteria are aspects of third-party neutrality: consistency, bias suppression, accuracy, and correctability. A fifth criterion is *ethicality*, by which Leventhal meant compatibility with prevailing moral and ethical standards. That criterion is similar to the issue of standing in the group, although Leventhal did not explicitly link the use of ethical standards to the question of standing in the group. Finally, like Thibaut and Walker, Leventhal suggested that control is important. In his framework, control is referred to as *representation*. Hence, many of the findings of this study are anticipated in Leventhal's discussion of procedural justice. Leventhal, however, did not frame his discussion of these issues in terms of people's long-term connection to social groups, as does group-value theory.

An interesting question raised by these findings is why neutrality, trust, and standing were not more important in Thibaut and Walker's (1975) original theory of the psychology of procedural justice. The results of the subgroup analysis suggest why control emerged as the key issue in their work. Within the context of disputes, control is the major issue defining the justice of procedures. On the other hand, disputes represent only one context within which people deal with legal authorities. In other contexts noncontrol concerns are more important.

Thibaut and Walker's (1975) control theory of procedural justice is based on the social exchange model of Thibaut and Kelley (1959). That model stresses people's instrumental concerns in their interaction with others. The group-value model, in contrast, emphasizes the importance that people place on membership in social groups. Both models suggest that people care about long-term group membership, but the models link that concern to different issues. Social exchange theories link such concerns to an interest in rewards from the group, and group-value theories link it to information about group status.

The findings of this study support a group-value interpretation of procedural justice concerns. They do so in several ways. First, issues of standing and trust are more important than the issue of neutrality. Because standing and, to a lesser degree, trust more directly reflect group-value concerns than does neutrality, their importance to those studied supports a group-value interpretation of the find-

ings reported here. This finding provides very strong support for the group-value model of procedural justice effects, as those indicators that are most strongly linked to group-value theory are the most important, and those most strongly linked to social exchange theory are the least important.[7]

The group-value interpretation of noncontrol effects is also supported by the finding that those who are more committed to the group care more about group-value issues. Although consistent with the predictions of group-value theory, this finding is weaker than the first finding. Only two of six possible interactions are significant. In contrast, however, there is no support for the social exchange theory prediction that more committed group members, who should be more invested in securing group outcomes, care more about their degree of control over outcomes.

The value that people place on group membership has two implications. First, people have a long-term commitment to the group and to its authorities, rules, and institutions. Instead of focusing on a single outcome, people look for evidence suggesting whether, over time, they will benefit fairly from group membership. Second, people value favorable social standing in the group. Hence, information about such standing, which is linked to the interpersonal aspects of interaction with authorities, is important and shapes people's interpretations of their experiences.

The group-value model argues for a broader conception of the meaning of procedural justice than is presented in the control model. It suggests that people in organizations focus on their long-term association with a group and with its authorities and institutions. People expect an organization to use neutral decision-making procedures enacted by trustworthy authorities so that, over time, all group members will benefit fairly from being members of the group. They also expect the group and its authorities to treat them in ways that affirm their self-esteem by indicating that they are valued members of the group who deserve treatment with respect, dignity, and politeness (Barber, 1983; Bies & Shapiro, 1987; Lane, 1988).

Another group-value issue is standing in the

---

[7]The absolute importance of standing and trust should be distinguished from their importance relative to issues of neutrality. One potential explanation for the relative weakness of the Neutrality scale is that it is the least reliably measured of the three constructs.

group, which is reflected in the quality of the interpersonal treatment people experience when dealing with authorities. Lane (1988) noted that one of the most important aspects of procedural justice to citizens dealing with political authorities is that the procedures used support their sense of self-respect. Similarly, Tyler and Folger (1980) examined citizen–police contacts and found that a key issue to citizens in such contacts was a "recognition of citizen rights" (p. 292). Similarly, Bies and Shapiro (1987) examined job applicants' reactions to job interviews in a corporate recruiting setting and found that candidates reacted to the politeness of their treatment, as well as to the neutrality issues of decision-maker bias, consistency, and honesty.

The linkage of procedural justice to issues of group identification also suggests the possibility that there will be limits to the areas in which procedural-justice issues arise, with those limits being defined by the contours of people's group identifications. This suggestion corresponds to the argument in the distributive justice literature that concerns about distributive justice will occur within cooperative communities (Deutsch, 1985; Opotow, 1987). The findings of Tyler (in press) support this suggestion. Tyler found that people who are more committed to the institutions represented by authorities pay more attention to issues of procedural justice when they evaluate those authorities.

It is also possible that the range of procedural justice is limited by the expectation of future interaction. If people recognize that they will not be in a relationship with the other person in the future, they may feel less concerned with maintaining a social bond with that person, and may focus less heavily on issues of procedural justice. Although this idea has not been directly tested, several studies have suggested that people pay less attention to issues of procedural justice when they regard the maintenance of group harmony as a less important issue (Barrett-Howard & Tyler, 1986; Tyler & Griffin, 1989).

ACKNOWLEDGMENTS

This article is based on a paper presented at the 96th annual meeting of the American Psychological Association, Atlanta, Georgia, on August 15, 1988. I thank Faye Crosby, Robert Folger, and Allan Lind for comments on that talk. I also thank Harry Reis and five anonymous reviewers for very helpful comments on a draft of this article. The data used in this paper were collected through use of funds provided by the Law and Social Science Program of the National Science Foundation (SES-8310199).

REFERENCES

Barber, B. (1983). *The logic and limits of trust*. New Brunswick, NJ: Rutgers University Press.

Barrett-Howard, E., & Tyler, T. R. (1986). Procedural justice as a criterion in allocation decisions. *Journal of Personality and Social Psychology, 50*, 296–304.

Bies, R. J., & Shapiro, D. L. (1987). Processual fairness judgments: The influence of causal accounts. *Social Justice Research, 1*, 199–218.

Brewer, M. B., & Kramer, R. (1986). Choice behavior in social dilemmas: Effects of social identity, group size, and decision framing. *Journal of Personality and Social Psychology, 50*, 543–549.

Cartwright, D., & Zander, A. (1953). *Group dynamics*. New York: Harper & Row.

Deutsch, M. (1985). *Distributive justice*. New Haven, CT: Yale University Press.

Festinger, L. (1954). A theory of social comparison processes. *Human Relations, 7*, 117–140.

Heider, F. (1958). *The psychology of interpersonal relations*. New York: Wiley.

Kramer, R. D., & Brewer, M. B. (1984). Effects of group identity on resource use in a simulated commons dilemma. *Journal of Personality and Social Psychology, 46*, 1044–1057.

Lane, R. E. (1988). Procedural goods in a democracy: How one is treated versus what one gets. *Social Justice Research, 2*, 177–192.

Leventhal, G. S. (1980). What should be done with equity theory? New approaches to the study of fairness in social relationships. In K. Gergen, M. Greenberg, & R. Willis (Eds.), *Social exchange* (pp. 27–55). New York: Plenum Press.

Lind, E. A., Lissak, R. E., & Conlon, A. E. (1983). Decision control and process control effects on procedural fairness judgments. *Journal of Applied Social Psychology, 4*, 338–350.

Lind, E. A., & Tyler, T. R. (1988). *The social psychology of procedural justice*. New York: Plenum Press.

Lissak, R. I., & Sheppard, B. H. (1983). Beyond fairness: The criterion problem in research on dispute resolution. *Basic and Applied Social Psychology, 13*, 45–65.

Messick, D. M., & Brewer, M. B. (1983). Solving social dilemmas. In L. Wheeler & P. Shaver (Eds.), *Review of personality and social psychology* (Vol. 4, pp. 11–44). Beverly Hills, CA: Sage.

Opotow, S. V. (1987, August). *Modifying the scope of justice: An experimental examination*. Paper presented at the 95th annual convention of the American Psychological Association, New York.

Schachter, S. (1951). Deviation, rejection, and communication. *Journal of Abnormal and Social Psychology, 46,*. 190–207.

Sears, D. O. (1986). College sophomores in the laboratory: Influences of a narrow data base on social psychology's view of human nature. *Journal of Personality and Social Psychology, 51*, 515–530.

Sheppard, B. H., & Lewicki, R. J. (1987). Toward general principles of managerial fairness. *Social Justice Research, 1*, 161–176.

Sheppard, B. H., Saunders, D., & Minton, J. (1988). Procedural justice from the third-party perspective. *Journal of Personality and Social Psychology, 54,* 629–637.

Tajfel, H. (1981). Social stereotypes and social groups. In J. C. Turner & H. Giles (Eds.), *Intergroup behavior.* Chicago: University of Chicago Press.

Tajfel, H., & Turner, J. (1979). An integrative theory of intergroup conflict. In W. G. Austin & S. Worchel (Eds.), *The social psychology of intergroup relations.* Monterey, CA: Brooks/Cole.

Thibaut, J., & Kelley, H. H. (1959). *The social psychology of groups.* New York: Wiley.

Thibaut, J., & Walker, L. (1975). *Procedural justice: A psychological analysis.* Hillsdale, NJ: Erlbaum.

Thibaut, J., & Walker, L. (1978). A theory of procedure. *California Law Review, 66,* 541–566.

Tyler, T. R. (1987). Conditions leading to value-expressive effects in judgments of procedural justice: A test of four models. *Journal of Personality and Social Psychology, 52,* 333–344.

Tyler, T. R. (1988). What is procedural justice?: Criteria used by citizens to assess the fairness of legal procedures. *Law and Society Review, 22,* 301–355.

Tyler, T. R. (in press). *Why people obey the law: Procedural justice. legitimacy and compliance.* New Haven, CT: Yale University Press.

Tyler, T. R., & Bies, R. (in press). Interpersonal aspects of procedural justice. In J. S. Carroll (Ed.), *Advances in applied social psychology: Business settings.*

Tyler, T. R., & Folger, R. (1980). Distributional and procedural aspects of satisfaction with citizen—police encounters. *Basic and Applied Social Psychology, 1,* 281–292.

Tyler, T. R., & Griffin, E. (1989, August). *Managing the allocation of scarce resources: Using procedures to justify outcomes.* Paper presented at the Academy of Management, Washington, DC.

Tyler, T. R., Rasinski, K., & Spodick, N. (1985). The influence of voice on satisfaction with leaders: Exploring the meaning of process control. *Journal of Personality and Social Psychology, 48,* 72–81.

Stealing in the Name of Justice: Informational and Interpersonal Moderators of Theft Reactions to Underpayment Inequity

Jerald Greenberg • The Ohio State University

In a laboratory study, 102 undergraduate students performed a clerical task for which they were either equitably paid or underpaid. The payment was explained using either high or low valid information in either a high or low interpersonally sensitive manner. Subjects then took their own pay and were led to believe the experimenter would not be able to determine exactly how much they actually took. It was found that equitably paid subjects took precisely the amounts they were allowed to take, whereas underpaid subjects took more than they were permitted (i.e., they stole). The degree of stealing was moderated by the validity of the information given (high valid information reduced stealing more than low valid information) and the degree of interpersonal sensitivity shown (high sensitivity reduced stealing more than low sensitivity). These effects combined additively, such that theft was greatest in the low valid information/low sensitivity condition and least in the high valid information/high sensitivity condition (in which the mean amount taken was not significantly higher than the permitted amount). The practical and theoretical implications of these findings are discussed.

How do people respond to being inequitably underpaid? Most of our current knowledge regarding this question is derived from Adams's (1965) theory of inequity which postulates that individuals who are underpaid are likely to respond by lowering their inputs (i.e., their work contributions) or by attempting to raise their outcomes (i.e., job-related rewards, such as pay). A considerable amount of research has supported equity theory's claim that underpayment inequity leads to lowered job performance (e.g., Lord & Hohenfeld, 1979; Pritchard, Dunnette, & Jorgenson, 1972). Also in support of equity theory, underpaid workers paid on a piece rate basis have been found to produce more goods of lower quality—a means of raising their outcomes without also raising their inputs (for a review, see Pritchard, 1969). Such reactions effectively redress states of underpayment inequity by restoring an equitable balance between one's outcome/input ratio and that of a comparison standard (Greenberg, 1982).

Theft as a Reaction to Inequity

Another form of reaction to underpayment inequity that has been recognized by social scientists is disruptive, deviant behavior, such as vandalism and theft (Hollinger & Clark, 1983). For example, anthropological accounts of pilferage among employees have been based on workers' expressed beliefs that theft is "a morally justified addition to wages . . . an entitlement due from exploiting employers" (Mars, 1974, p. 224). According to equity theory, acts of employee theft may be an effective means of increasing one's outcomes in order to reduce feelings of underpayment inequity. In fact, a recent study by Greenberg (1990a) has shown that in manufacturing plants in which a temporary 15% pay cut was introduced, the workers felt highly underpaid and employee theft rates were as much as 250% higher than occurred under normal pay conditions. Given the very costly impact of employee theft on companies—from $5 billion to $10 billion annually according to estimates by the American Management Association (1977)—the need to understand the conditions affecting underpayment-induced employee theft is paramount.

Some insight into the processes underlying inequity-induced theft is suggested by recent research and theory demonstrating that perceptions of fair treatment and outcomes depend not only on the level of one's outcomes, but also on the explanations given for those outcomes (for reviews, see Bies, 1987; Folger & Bies, 1989; Greenberg, 1990b; Greenberg, Bies, & Eskew, 1991; Tyler & Bies, 1990). In general, research in this area has found that negative outcomes perceived as being unfair when they were not adequately explained were perceived as being fairer when they were accompanied by thorough and informative explanations (e.g., Bies & Shapiro, 1988; Bies, Shapiro, & Cummings, 1988; Greenberg, 1991). Relevant to the issue of employee theft, Greenberg (1990a) found that the theft rate in a plant of underpaid workers was considerably lower when the basis for their underpayment was thoroughly and sensitively explained to them ($M = 5.7\%$) than when limited information was given in an insensitive manner ($M = 8.9\%$) (the base rate of theft was 3.7%).

Although such findings clearly illustrate the mitigating impact of explanations on costly reactions to inequity, they suffer from several limitations. For one, because the investigation was conducted in a field setting, it lacked the degree of random assignment to conditions, and high degree of experimental control needed to unambiguously establish causality. Another limitation of the

Greenberg (1990a) study that dictates the need for a follow-up laboratory study is the compound nature of the explanation variable. That is, the explanation given for the pay cut was administered in a manner that intentionally combined two potentially distinct contributors—the quality of the information given, and the interpersonal sensitivity demonstrated in the interaction. By basing his explanation manipulation on past research showing that people tend to associate these variables (Bies *et al.*, 1988), Greenberg's (1990a) field findings are limited by a built-in naturalistic confounding in need of disentangling in laboratory research. In other words, understanding how explanations act to reduce inequity-induced theft requires that a clear experimental distinction be made with respect to *what* is said, and *how* the message is communicated.

Informational and Interpersonal Moderators of Inequity Reactions

If one carefully examines the many variables that have been found to influence perceptions of fairness, it becomes clear that both interpersonal and informational factors are implicated—specifically, the *validity of the information* provided as the basis for decision-making (i.e., information that is verifiably correct and thus worthy of use in decision-making) and the *interpersonal sensitivity* shown regarding the personal affects of the decision (i.e., displays of empathy and concern for the individual). Indeed, these factors are closely related to several rules of procedural fairness identified by Leventhal (1980). To illustrate the prevalence of both informational and interpersonal elements of justice perceptions I will consider some of the variables identified in recent literature reviews highlighting the importance of explanations on perceptions of fairness (e.g., Folger & Bies, 1989; Greenberg *et al.*, 1991; Tyler & Bies, 1990).

A good example of the confusion within this literature may be seen in evidence showing that perceptions of fairness are enhanced when attention is paid to employees' viewpoints. In support of this idea, survey evidence by Reutter (1977) suggests that the perceived fairness of employee suggestion systems is related to the degree to which all suggestions are carefully considered and decisions about them are communicated in a tactful manner (for a review, see Folger & Greenberg, 1985, pp. 168–171). Clearly, both the nature of the information considered (careful evaluation of the suggestion) and the communicator's interpersonal concern (providing a tactful review of the suggestion) are involved in assessments of the system's fairness.

The same can be said about recent research on the adequacy of accounts given for decisions. In this connection, Bies and Shapiro (1987, 1988) found that when a boss provided an explanation why it was necessary to refuse an employee's request, employees felt less disapproval toward the bosses and perceived greater fairness of the decision making process than when no explanations were given. Thus, claims of mitigating circumstances (e.g., financial constraints) may enhance the acceptance of negative outcomes (e.g., rejection of budget proposals). Further research by the same investigators (Bies et al., 1988) has revealed that explanations for rejection may only enhance perceptions of fairness when the reasoning in support of the explanation was judged to be adequate and when it was communicated sincerely (Bies et al., 1988). Thus, both the appropriateness of the information used and the interpersonal sensitivity shown are involved in perceptions of fairness.

A final example of this phenomenon may be seen in Bies' (1986) findings that honest messages were perceived as fairer than dishonest ones. Even here, both interpersonal and informational factors appear to be involved. To wit, a truthful message not only imparts more valid information, but it also reflects the communicator's willingness to treat recipients in a moral and ethical manner. In conclusion, the enhanced fairness found to result from explanations and other procedural variables may well be due to the interpersonal and informational elements underlying those procedures.

Hypotheses

As this review of the literature suggests, it appears that reactions to potentially unfair situations are mitigated in part by the *validity of the information* provided and in part by the *interpersonal sensitivity* shown. That is to say, considerations of fairness appear to involve both the use of valid decision-making criteria (e.g., careful consideration of relevant facts, reliance on accurate information) as well as sensitive interpersonal treatment

(e.g., tactful communication of outcomes, expressions of sincerity). The explicit role of these variables on reactions to an underpayment inequity is considered in the present investigation.

Operationally, the present study confronted some subjects with a situation in which underpayment was manipulated by telling them that they were supposed to be paid $3 instead of the $5 they originally were promised (the underpaid group). No change in the promised pay rate was manipulated in the equitably paid, control group. Participants were then allowed to take their own pay in a situation in which it appeared that the actual amount of money they took could not be detected. Because they were encouraged to take the amount of pay they expected (and which was established as the going rate), equitably paid subjects were expected to refrain from stealing—that is, taking more than the $5 promised them. Specifically, it was hypothesized as follows:

Hypothesis 1. Equitably paid subjects will not take significantly more than the amount promised them ($5).

Moreover, because the situation confronted by equitably paid subjects already discouraged stealing, there was no reason to believe that the amount of money they took would be differentially influenced by either the validity of the information presented to them or the interpersonal sensitivity of their treatment. While such procedural and interpersonal factors may mitigate reactions to unfair outcomes (Bies & Shapiro, 1987, 1988), they may have little incremental impact on reactions to already fair outcomes (Greenberg, 1987). Thus, it was hypothesized as follows:

Hypothesis 2a. The amount of pay taken by equitably paid subjects will not differ significantly as a function of information validity.

Hypothesis 2b. The amount of pay taken by equitably paid subjects will not differ significantly as a function of interpersonal sensitivity.

By contrast, it was expected that subjects asked to take less than the initially promised amount (underpaid group) would redress the inequity by taking more than they were supposed to (i.e., they would steal additional money to reduce the inequity). Thus, it was hypothesized as follows:

Hypothesis 3. Subjects whose pay rate is unfairly reduced (underpaid group) will take more money than the $3 they were permitted to take. (Thus, in general, underpaid subjects will be expected to steal.)

Further complicating this effect is the tendency for inequities to be mitigated by the use of valid information and sensitive interpersonal treatment (Bies *et al.*, 1988; Greenberg, 1990a). Applying these variables to the present experiment, it was expected that the tendency for underpaid subjects to take more than $3 would be reduced by the imparting of thorough and accurate information about the reduced pay in an interpersonally sensitive manner. Thus, it was hypothesized as follows:

Hypothesis 4a. Underpaid subjects will take significantly less pay (i.e., they will steal less) when they are given high valid information about how their pay rate is determined than when they are given low valid information.

Hypothesis 4b. Underpaid subjects will take significantly less pay (i.e., they will steal less) when they are treated with high interpersonal sensitivity than when treated with low interpersonal sensitivity.

Because there is no evidence to suggest that information validity and interpersonal sensitivity qualify each other in any way, no significant interactions were expected between these two variables. However, given evidence suggesting that each factor alone influences perceptions of fairness (Bies *et al.*, 1988), their effects were expected to be additive. As such, the combined impact of both variables was expected to be greater than their individual effects. Consistent with this reasoning, it was hypothesized as follows:

Hypothesis 5a. Underpaid subjects given high valid information about how their pay was determined who are also treated in a high interpersonally sensitive manner will take lower pay (i.e., steal less) than underpaid subjects in the other conditions. (In other words, their mean theft rate will be lowest.)

Hypothesis 5b. Underpaid subjects given low valid information about how their pay was determined who are also treated in a low interpersonally sensitive manner will take higher pay (i.e., steal more) than underpaid subjects in the other conditions. (In other words, their mean theft rate will be highest.)

Method

Subjects and Design

The final pool of participants in the study consisted of 102 undergraduate students at a midwestern university who volunteered to participate in a study allegedly concerned with "consumers' use of sales catalogs," requiring them to look-up and record the prices of items appearing in catalogs. As part of the recruitment procedure they were promised $5 for a session described as lasting approximately 1 h. (Pilot testing revealed that people from the same population from which the subjects were drawn believed this constituted fair compensation.) There were 58 males and 44 females; their mean age was 20.5 years. Ten additional subjects were scheduled to participate, but did not complete the experiment either because they failed to agree to participate in the study after the task was described to them ($n = 2$) or because they were unable to stay for the allotted time ($n = 8$).

A $2 \times 2 \times 2$ complete factorial design was used in which the independent variables were *payment* (equitably paid or underpaid), *interpersonal sensitivity* (high or low), and *information validity* (high or low). Approximately equal numbers of subjects (ranging from 11 to 14) were assigned to each cell of the design. The unequal cell counts resulted from the 10 dropouts noted above. In no case was a subject's responses excluded from the study after any data were collected.

Procedure

Participants were scheduled individually to appear at a room on a university campus. Upon arrival they were told that they would be participating in a study designed to measure how quickly and accurately people could find items in a department store catalog. The task described to participants required them to go through a list of items appearing on a printed sheet, find their prices in a department store catalog, and record those prices in blank spaces provided on the sheet. The rationale was given that the experimenter was interested in seeing how the design of catalogs affected people's ability to use them. They were reminded that they would be paid $5 at the end of the 1-h session for performing the task and completing some questionnaire items. This task was used because of its high degree of acceptance among participants demonstrated in earlier studies, and because it has been found that participants have no preconceived ideas regarding what constitutes equitable payment for this task, thereby making it a suitable platform for launching inequity manipulations (e.g., Greenberg, 1983, 1987).

After the task was described and subjects consented to participate, they were taken to a nearby room and seated at a desk equipped with the materials needed to perform the task: item pricing sheets, a department store catalog, and pencils. After allowing 45 min for participants to perform the task, the experimenter entered their work rooms and asked them to stop working. At this point, the various experimental manipulations were carried out.

Payment. The payment manipulation was affected either by telling the subjects that they would be paid the $5 promised for participating (equitable payment) or that they would be paid a lower amount, $3 (underpayment). Because additional information about the payment manipulation was incorporated into the other manipulations, further description of the manner in which this factor was manipulated follows below.

Informational validity. The informational validity variable manipulated the amount and quality of information used as the basis for determining payment. Specifically, the high valid information conditions were consistently characterized by: (a) the use of directly acquired information (b) from an expert source, (c) that is publicly revealed, and (d) doublechecked with an independent source. By contrast, the low valid manipulations relied on: (a) the use of hearsay information, (b) from a person of undisclosed expertise, (c) that is kept private, and (d) not independently verified. These elements of the informational validity variable follow from research in the field of attitude change in which similar factors have been found to contribute to the acceptance of messages as valid sources of information contributing to the changing of attitudes (McGuire, 1985).[1] Moreover, pilot research has independently verified that each of these elements contributes to assessments of informational validity.[2]

To enhance realism, statements regarding the payment and information about its determination were incorporated with each other.[3] Thus, *underpaid–high valid information* subjects were instructed that they would be paid less than the promised amount and were given a considerable amount of information in support of that decision. Specifically, they were told:

> While you were working, I found out from my supervisor that our research sponsor is really only paying $3 instead of the $5 you were promised. As you can see from this document [experimenter shows participant fake budget figures], this is the

---

[1] Although the term "informational validity" is used as the name of the variable that appears to capture the essence of the complex manipulation used, it is prudent to caution that the phrase fails to reflect all possible shadings of interpretation suggested by the verbal phrases used as the basis of the operationalization. For example, as one reviewer has noted, it is possible that the manipulation may have caused differences in the perceived characteristics of the person presenting the information as well as differences in the quality of the information itself. However, such possibilities are an inevitable consequence of *any* complex manipulations based on differing verbal content. The major implication of this point is that care should be exercised in interpreting the manipulation solely on the basis of the label used to define it.

[2] A pilot study was conducted requiring subjects (drawn from the same population as the main study) to judge the perceived validity of information gained through the use of (a) directly acquired vs. hearsay information, (b) statements by experts vs. statements by persons of undisclosed expertise, (c) data that are willingly shared vs. data that are not shared, and (d) data that are double-checked with an independent source vs data that are not double-checked with an independent

source. It was found that the perceived level of informational validity was significantly higher for the first element of each pair, thereby empirically justifying the use of each of these subcriteria as the basis for deriving the manipulation.

[3] Although manipulations of the information communicated and the interpersonal sensitivity used to communicate it were made independently, one reviewer has noted the possibility that subjects might draw inferences about the communicator's sensitivity on the basis of the information itself. As such, readers are cautioned that there may be an inherent potential confounding between the variables at the phenomenological level. It also should be noted that differences in the phrasing of manipulations were required in order to incorporate both manipulations together in a logical way. For this reason, it is prudent to advise that some combinations of conditions are potentially confounded by the inclusion of slightly different types of information. However, the risk of doing so was judged to be less serious than combining potentially "purer" combinations of manipulations that appeared unnatural. Indeed, the results of manipulation check data (disclosed later) provide no support for the possibility that the manipulations had any effects other than those intended.

amount that was planned in the original budget proposal. To make sure, I also called the project's budget officer and was reassured of this figure. Because of a typographical error, some participants did get $5, but this was a mistake. Starting now, you can get only $3.

In the *equitable–high valid information* condition subjects were instructed that they would be paid exactly the stated amount and were given a considerable amount of information in support of that decision. Specifically, they were told:

While you were working, I verified with my supervisor that our research sponsor is paying the $5 you were promised. As you can see from this document [experimenter shows participant fake budget figures], this is the amount that was planned in the original budget proposal. To make sure, I also called the project's budget officer and was reassured of this figure. Everyone who participates is getting paid $5.

In the low information conditions, participants received much less assurance regarding the appropriateness of the stated pay rates. Specifically, in the *underpayment–low valid information* condition, participants were told:

While you were working, I heard from someone in the hall that our research sponsor is really only supposed to be paying $3, instead of the $5 you were promised. As a result, that's what I'll be paying you.

In the *equitable–low valid information* condition, participants were told: "As I told you, our research sponsor is paying $5 for this study, so that's what I'll be paying you."

Interpersonal sensitivity. Following the administration of the payment information, additional comments were made that helped create the interpersonal sensitivity manipulation (abbreviated as sensitivity). These remarks varied in terms of the degree of caring and sensitivity shown the participant with respect to their pay rate. Specifically, the high sensitivity conditions were characterized by: (a) repeated expressions of remorse (or satisfaction) and (b) attempts to dissociate from (or associate with) the outcome. Low sensitivity conditions were characterized by: (a) expressions of disinterest with the participants' outcomes and (b) claims of greater concern with one's own personal outcomes. Such operational guidelines are in keeping with suggestions from the literature describing interpersonally sensitive behavior in social

contexts (Hornstein, 1976). They are also justified by the results of pilot tests (analogous to those described for the informational validity variable in footnote 2) showing that subjects perceive these dimensions to be differentially suggestive of interpersonal sensitivity.

As in the case of the information validity variable, these remarks were tailored slightly to the payment condition.

In the *high sensitivity–underpayment* condition, the experimenter expressed considerable regret about the underpayment. Specifically, he said:

You really got a bad deal and I feel very sorry for you. I know it's only a $2 difference, but I feel awful for misleading you. Please recognize that it's not my fault, and that I would pay you more if I could. You seem like such a nice person, I really hate to have to do this to you. I don't want to upset you. It's probably not much consolation, but I feel very badly about this myself.

In the *high sensitivity–equitable payment* condition, the experimenter expressed considerable satisfaction about the participant's fair payment. Specifically, he said:

You really got a fair deal, and I feel good for you. I'm glad you were able to get paid $5 for this job; you deserve it. You seem like such a nice person, I'm really glad that this all worked out all right for you.

By contrast to the highly sensitive treatment accorded participants in these conditions, much less sensitivity was shown in the low interpersonal sensitivity conditions. Specifically, in both the *low sensitivity–underpayment* condition, and the *low sensitivity–equitable payment* condition, participants were told, "That's the way it is; I don't make the rules around here. I really don't care how much you get paid. I don't care too much about how much others get; I'm more concerned about how much I get paid myself."

Payment procedure/theft measure. After the final interpersonal sensitivity remarks were made, the experimenter announced that he would have to go down the hall to begin another experimental session. At this point, he reached into his hip pocket and removed a handful of money, some one-dollar bills, as well as some quarters, nickels, dimes, and pennies, and placed it on a nearby desk. The experimenter's seemingly disorganized state helped create the impression that he was unaware of the exact amount of money he put on the table.

Reinforcing this image, he said, "I have to go down the hall now to begin another session, so [reaching into his pocket] I'll just have to leave you some money to pay yourself with. I don't know how much is here, but it look's like there's more than enough for you. Just take the $5 ($3) you are supposed to be paid and leave the rest on the table." This procedure made it possible for participants to take as much money as they wanted without believing that the experimenter would be able to tell how much was actually taken. In actuality, there was a total of $10.42 available: 7 one-dollar bills, 6 quarters, 11 dimes, 12 nickels, and 22 pennies, making it possible for the experimenter to determine exactly how much subjects took.

As he was leaving, the experimenter handed the participants a questionnaire in a large manila envelope and asked them to complete it and return it to the envelope before putting it into a large stack of other envelopes on a table in the corner of the room. This procedure was used to lead subjects to believe that their responses could not be identified (although, of course, they could, because of coding marks surreptitiously placed on the envelope). It was necessary to promote the belief of anonymity in order to minimize the threat of a social desirability bias that could have been activated had subjects believed that the experimenter could identify their responses. A similar procedure was used successfully in earlier research (e.g., Greenberg, 1983, 1987).

Questionnaire measures. In support of the cover story, participants were asked to complete several questionnaire items focusing on their reactions to the task at hand. Among these were 16 items that were relevant to the present study. These tapped: justice perceptions (9 items), manipulation checks (4 items), and supplementary measures (3 items). Unless otherwise noted, the questions were completed using a scale ranging from 1, labeled "not at all," to 7, labeled "extremely."

The nine *justice perception* items were written in a manner that made them both sensitive to the concerns of the present study and consistent with various conceptual perspectives regarding the forms of justice assessed—distributive (Deutsch, 1985; Leventhal, 1976), procedural (Greenberg, 1986a; Lind & Tyler, 1988), and interactional (Bies & Moag, 1986). Thus, although the measures were ad hoc, they were carefully connected to established conceptual bases (see Greenberg, 1990c).

Three items measured perceptions of *distribu-* *tive justice*: (a) "How fair is the amount of pay you were given to perform this task?" (b) "To what extent was the amount of the payment you received appropriate for the task performed?" and (c) "To what extent was your pay in keeping with prevailing pay standards?" Coefficient α was .93.

Three items measured perceptions of *procedural justice*: (a) "How fair was the method used to determine your pay?" (b) "To what extent were proper rules and procedures used to determine your pay?" and (c) "How consistent and unbiased was the method used for establishing your pay?" Coefficient α was .84.

Three items measured perceptions of *interactional justice*: (a) "To what extent was the experimenter concerned about your fair treatment during the study?" (b) "How fair was the experimenter in considering your needs and well-being?" and (c) "To what degree did the experimenter give fair consideration to your personal feelings?" Coefficient α was .88.

Four items were included as *manipulation checks*. To assess the validity of the payment manipulation subjects were asked, "How much money did the experimenter say you should be paid for this study?" A scale ranging from $1 to $7 in one-dollar increments was used to record the responses. A follow-up question asked, "Is this __ less than, __ equal to, or __ more than (check one) the amount you expected when you first showed up?" To assess the validity of the information validity manipulation subjects were asked, "How much information were you given about the rate of pay you were supposed to receive?"[4] Finally, to assess the validity of the interpersonal sensitivity manipulation subjects were asked, "How much personal concern did the experimenter show for you?"

Three *supplementary measures* were included to gain insight into subjects' feelings about their self-payment behavior. The first question asked, "To what extent do you believe you were acting honestly or dishonestly in taking the pay you did?" The response scale ranged from 1, "very dishonestly," to 7, "very honestly," with the midpoint labeled, "neither honestly nor dishonestly."

---

[4]Because low valid information may be readily discounted, it follows that differences in the sheer amount of information received would be perceived if the informational validity variable were successful. In hindsight, however, a more direct measure tapping the overall perceived validity of the information (or its subcomponents; see footnote 1) would have been more appropriate.

A second question asked, "How justified or unjustified were you in taking the amount of pay that you did?" The response scale ranged from 1, "completely unjustified," to 7, "completely justified." A third question asked, "How fair or unfair was it for you to take the amount of pay you took?" The response scale ranged from 1, "completely unfair," to 7, "completely fair," Because the responses to these two questions were highly correlated ($r = .91$), they were combined to form a single "perceived justification" measure.

Debriefing. Upon leaving their work rooms, the participants were intercepted by the experimenter, who then dehoaxed them and debriefed them about the true purpose of the experiment. The discussion continued until such time as the participants appeared to fully understand and accept the nature of the study and the need to use deception (Greenberg & Folger, 1988). During the course of the debriefing, no participants expressed any suspicions about the true purpose of the study. The pay of all subjects who took less than the $5 promised was supplemented so that their actual final pay totaled $5. Effectively, then, no subjects were really underpaid.

Results

Manipulation Checks

All manipulation check questionnaires (except the check-list item) were based on $2 \times 2 \times 2$ factorial univariate analyses of variance (ANOVAs). For the payment manipulation check, the only significant source of variance was a significant payment effect, $F(1, 94) = 126.88$, $p < .0001$, revealing that underpaid subjects reported that they were supposed to be paid less than the equitably paid subjects ($Ms = 3.06$ vs. 5.00, respectively). Moreover, these means did not differ significantly from the

$3 and $5 manipulated values, in both cases, $t < 1.00$, ns. The follow-up question revealed that: (a) all subjects in the underpaid group acknowledged that the amount they were told to take was less than they expected, and (b) all subjects in the equitably paid group acknowledged that the amount they were told to take was equal to what they expected. Together, these data reveal that the payment manipulation was unequivocally successful in differentiating payment conditions as desired.

For the informational validity item, the only significant source of variance was the significant main effect of the informational validity manipulation, $F(1, 94) = 96.80$, $p < .0001$. This effect reflected the tendency for more information to be perceived as given in the high information condition than in the low information condition ($Ms = 5.41$ vs. 3.02, respectively). Thus, the informational validity manipulation was successful in creating conditions in which different amounts of information were recognized as being imparted.

For the sensitivity item, the only significant source of variance was the significant main effect of the sensitivity manipulation, $F(1, 94) = 186.46$, $p < .0001$. This effect reflected the tendency for greater sensitivity to be recognized as given in the high sensitivity condition than in the low sensitivity condition ($Ms = 5.70$ vs. 2.66, respectively). Thus, the sensitivity manipulation was successful in creating conditions in which different amounts of sensitivity were recognized as being used in communicating with subjects.

Tests of Hypotheses

Because the hypotheses were based on the amount of money taken as a function of payment, validity, and sensitivity, a $2 \times 2 \times 2$ factorial ANOVA was performed on these data. A summary of this analy-

TABLE 1. Summary of Analysis of Variance for Amount of Pay Taken

Source	df	MS	F	p	w^2
Payment (A)	1	33.35	114.68	.0001	.39
Interpersonal sensitivity (B)	1	2.51	8.14	.0053	.10
Informational validity (C)	1	1.64	5.33	.0232	.08
A × B	1	2.63	8.52	.0044	.11
A × C	1	1.43	4.64	.0338	.04
B × C	1	0.06	0.18	.6688	.00
A × B × C	1	0.13	0.44	.5105	.00
Residual	94	0.31			

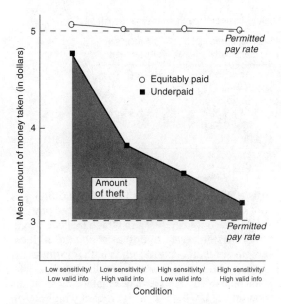

FIGURE 1 ■ Mean amount of pay taken as a function of experimental conditions.

sis appears in Table 1, and a summary of all the various cell means appears in Fig.1.

Hypothesis 1. Hypothesis 1 claimed that equitably paid workers would not take more than the $5 promised them. Inspection of the means constituting the almost flat line for the equitable condition at the $5 level across the top of Fig. 1 visually confirms the hypothesis. More formally, a simple effects test revealed that the four means were not significantly different from each other, $F < 1.00$, ns, nor were any of them significantly different than $5, t$ values < 1.00. Thus, Hypothesis 1 was supported.

Hypothesis 2. Hypothesis 2a claimed that informational validity would not influence the amount of money taken by equitably paid subjects. A subset of the means in the significant payment × informational validity interaction (identified in

Table 1) bears on this interaction. These means are shown in Table 2. As hypothesized, Table 2 shows that equitably paid subjects took relatively equal amounts of payment regardless of whether they received high valid information or low valid information.

Hypothesis 2b claims that sensitivity will not influence the amount of money taken by equitably paid subjects. A subset of the means in the significant payment × sensitivity interaction (identified in Table 1) bears on this interaction. These means are shown in Table 3. As hypothesized, Table 3 shows that equitably paid subjects took relatively equal amounts of payment regardless of whether they were treated with high or low interpersonal sensitivity.

Hypothesis 3. Hypothesis 3 claimed that underpaid subjects would take significantly more than the $3 they were asked to pay themselves. The overall amount of pay taken by underpaid workers was $3.84, an amount significantly higher than $3, $t(51) = 7.49$, $p < .001$, thus confirming hypothesis 3. Cell-by-cell comparisons of the means in the underpaid condition (see lower line on Fig. 1) to $3 revealed that significantly higher pay was taken by subjects in the low sensitivity–low information condition, $t(13) = 6.78$, $p < .005$, the low sensitivity–high information condition, $t(11) = 3.55$, $p < .005$, and the high sensitivity–low information condition, $t(13) = 3.14$, $p < .005$, but not in the high sensitivity–high information condition, $t(11) = 1.41$, ns. Thus, only when sensitivity and information were both high did subjects refrain from stealing.

Hypothesis 4. Hypothesis 4a claimed that the use of high valid information would reduce the amount of money taken by underpaid subjects. A subset of the means in the significant payment × informational validity interaction (identified in Table 1) bears on this interaction. These means are shown in Table 2. As hypothesized, Table 2

TABLE 2. Mean Amount of Pay Taken as a Function of Payment and Informational Validity

Payment	Low valid information	High valid information	Comparison (two-tailed)
Equitable payment	$M = 5.02$ $SD = 0.07$ $n = 23$	$M = 5.00$ $SD = 0.17$ $n = 27$	$t(48) = 0.62$, ns
Underpayment	$M = 4.07$ $SD = 0.89$ $n = 28$	$M = 3.58$ $SD = 0.74$ $n = 24$	$t(50) = 2.19$, $p < .05$

TABLE 3. Mean Amount of Pay Taken as a Function of Payment and Interpersonal Sensitivity

Payment	Low interpersonal sensitivity	High interpersonal sensitivity	Comparison (two-tailed)
Equitable payment	$M = 5.00$ $SD = 0.17$ $n = 25$	$M = 5.00$ $SD = 0.10$ $n = 25$	$t(48) = 0.10$, ns
Underpayment	$M = 4.17$ $SD = 0.85$ $n = 26$	$M = 3.52$ $SD = 0.73$ $n = 26$	$t(50) = 2.99$, $p < .01$

shows that underpaid subjects took significantly less pay when they were given high valid information than when they were given low valid information.

Hypothesis 4b claimed that sensitivity would reduce the amount of money taken by underpaid subjects. A subset of the means in the significant payment × sensitivity interaction (identified in Table 1) bears on this interaction. These means are shown in Table 3. As hypothesized, Table 3 shows that underpaid subjects took significantly less pay when they were treated with high sensitivity than when they were treated with low sensitivity.

Hypothesis 5. As Table 1 reveals, the interaction between informational validity and interpersonal sensitivity was not significant. However, the individual effects of these variables were significant. A simple effects test determined that the underpaid subjects differed in their theft rate across all levels of information and sensitivity, $F(3,94) = 64.20$, $p < .0001$. Visually inspecting the means associated with this simple main effect, the line shown at the bottom of Fig. 1 reveals that for underpaid subjects, the effects of sensitivity and validity were additive. That is, each contributed some to the overall tendency to reduce theft. When both were high, theft was least; when both were low, theft was greatest. Specifically, for underpaid subjects, the overall pattern of significant differences in theft rates (using Newman–Keuls tests with α = .05) was as follows: low sensitivity, low validity > low sensitivity, high validity = high sensitivity, low validity > high sensitivity, high validity.

Consistent with hypothesis 5a, the lowest amount of theft occurred when both informational validity and interpersonal sensitivity were high. Newman–Keuls tests revealed that the mean in this condition ($M = 3.32$) was significantly lower than the mean for any of the other three conditions. Moreover, as noted in conjunction with hypoth-

esis 3, the mean pay taken in this condition was not significantly higher than the required pay rate of $3 (the only condition in which this occurred).

Consistent with hypothesis 5b, the highest amount of theft occurred when both informational validity and interpersonal sensitivity were low. Newman–Keuls tests revealed that the mean in this condition ($M = 4.45$) was significantly higher than the mean of any of the other three conditions.

Justice Perception Measures

Responses to all justice perception items were analyzed using 2 × 2 × 2 factorial univariate ANOVAs. These analyses were justified in view of the high degree of statistical independence between the measures (mean $r = .04$). Interestingly, it was found that for each of the three measures, the only significant source of variance found was for the variable most closely associated with that measure.

Specifically, for the distributive justice measure, a significant main effect was found for payment, $F(1,94) = 485.59$, $p < .0001$, reflecting the greater perceived fairness of pay provided in the equitable condition than in the underpaid condition (Ms = 5.91 vs. 2.22, respectively). For the procedural justice measure, a significant main effect was found for informational validity, $F(1,94) = 444.17$, $p < .0001$, such that procedures were recognized as being procedurally fairer when high valid information about pay determination was provided than when low valid information was provided (Ms = 5.53 vs. 2.64, respectively). Finally, for the interactional justice variable, a main effect was found for sensitivity, $F(1,94) = 254.85$, $p < .0001$, reflecting the tendency for subjects to recognize the greater degree of interactional justice shown by an individual demonstrating high degrees of interpersonal sensitivity than by one demonstrating low degrees of interpersonal sensitivity ($Ms = 5.46$ vs. 2.71, respectively).

Supplementary Questionnaire Measures

The questionnaire tapping subjects' self-perceived honesty–dishonesty of their pay-taking behavior revealed a significant main effect for the payment variable, $F(1,94) = 6.92, p < .01$. Subjects reported being more honest ($M = 5.11$) in the equitably paid condition than in the overpaid condition ($M = 3.31$). Because these means were on opposite sides of the scale midpoint, it appears that subjects distinguished between the honesty and the dishonesty of their actions (as opposed to simply a difference between degrees of either pole alone).

Finally, no significant sources of variance were found for the perceived justification measure. This was the result of the tendency for subjects to report that their pay-taking behavior was uniformly fair and justified (overall $M = 6.01$).

Discussion

The present findings support equity theory's (Adams, 1965) claim that people who are inequitably underrewarded will respond by increasing their outcomes. In the present study, they did so by taking rewards in excess of the amount they were permitted—that is, by stealing. Such deviant behavior is consistent with Kemper's (1966) notion of "reciprocal deviance," according to which theft may result when employees believe that their employers defaulted on their role obligations to them, thereby encouraging further deviant acts. That is precisely what appears to have happened in this study. Not surprisingly, it was found that underpaid subjects perceived their stealing as being honest, but also completely fair and justifiable. Indeed, earlier research has also found that unfairly paid workers believe that acts of stealing are morally justified as sources of outcome to which they are entitled (Mars, 1973, 1974). Although earlier field studies of employee theft behavior (e.g., Greenberg, 1990a; Hollinger & Clark, 1983) provide aggregate data suggesting that theft is associated with feelings of underpayment, the present laboratory findings clearly demonstrate that stealing is a direct causal effect of the use of an underpayment procedure.

Interestingly, the incidence of theft behavior was reduced independently by each of two variables—the validity of the information provided about the underpayment and the interpersonal sensitivity shown the underpaid victim. Previous research has shown that these factors make people more willing to accept undesirable outcomes and the individuals responsible for them (Bies & Shapiro, 1987, 1988; Bies et al., 1988); The present findings extend this line of research by demonstrating that valid information and high sensitivity also moderate reactions to unfair outcomes. Thus, each of these factors lessened the degree to which redressing inequity was attempted. High levels of both factors led to no significant attempts to redress underpayment inequity, whereas low levels of both factors led to extreme attempts to redress the inequity. As such, it may be said that informational validity and interpersonal sensitivity work individually and together to facilitate acceptance of inequities, thereby moderating efforts at redressing them.

Implications

Several aspects of these findings are noteworthy. First, by disentangling the informational and interpersonal contributions of explanations that are frequently intercorrelated in naturalistic settings (Bies et al., 1988), it is now possible to understand more precisely what it is about explanations that makes them so effective as mechanisms facilitating the acceptance of fairness judgments (Bies, 1987; Greenberg, 1990b). Such information can raise questions about existing research. For example, in several studies, Tyler (1984, 1988, 1990) has found that people are more likely to accept authority figures' judgments as fair when they believe those authorities considered their own viewpoints. Why? Both informational validity and interpersonal sensitivity may be involved. Hearing another's viewpoint may improve the validity of the information used, and/or it may demonstrate concern for that individual's feelings. Thus, it is unclear to what degree each underlying variable is responsible for the demonstrated effects. By revealing the separate and combined effects of these elements, the present study paves the road for future researchers to more precisely examine this issue.

Beyond the obvious scientific benefits of explaining why an effect occurs, these findings may also have practical significance. Specifically, learning what factors encourage acceptance of undesirable outcomes may be useful for designing techniques for facilitating judgment acceptance (e.g., impression management techniques; Greenberg, 1990b). In fact, simply knowing that explaining underpayment situations in a highly informative and interpersonally sensitive manner may reduce employee theft is itself a valuable piece of information that can be used for combating this extremely disruptive form of inequity reduction.

Another interesting aspect of the present findings is that the different degrees of inequity redress shown were not linked to concomitant beliefs in distributive fairness. Indeed, equity theory claims that the differential effects at reducing an underpayment would be associated with differential perceptions about the strength of the inequity (Greenberg, 1984). That is, greater perceived inequities would be associated with greater attempts to redress them. In the present study, this occurred only at the extremes—that is, distributive justice was seen as being violated in the underpayment condition (where the stealing occurred) but not in the equitable payment condition (where no stealing occurred). However, it was *not* found that perceptions of distributive justice were associated with the differential attempts of redress inequities caused by the information and sensitivity variables. Redress behavior continued although no less distributive justice was perceived. Instead, when a lack of information raised redress efforts, procedural justice was perceived as being violated, and when low interpersonal sensitivity raised redress efforts, interactional justice was perceived as being violated. As such, it appears that differential willingness to redress underpayment is motivated by perceptions of procedural justice and interactional justice, as well as by distributive justice (as traditionally established).

An important implication of these findings is that it extends equity theory's (Adams, 1965) claims regarding the mediational effects of inequity perceptions on inequity redress behavior (see Greenberg, 1984). Apparently, attempts to redress inequity may be motivated by the belief not only that the outcomes are distributively unfair, but also that the procedures used and the interpersonal treatment received were unfair. Such a theoretical extension is an intriguing possibility in need of investigation in future research. For now, however,

showing that people discriminate between informational and interpersonal aspects of justice perceptions argues against the recent trend toward incorporating the two together as different aspects of procedural justice (Folger & Bies, 1989; Tyler & Bies, 1990). At least until the interpersonal aspects of justice are better understood, attempts to fold interactional justice into procedural justice may be seen as a premature move toward parsimony (Greenberg, 1990c).

Limitations and Qualifications

It should be noted that various aspects of the present laboratory study may have encouraged theft behavior. Specifically, it may be claimed that subjects in the present study were provided ample opportunities to steal (excess money was left in front of them) and that the experimenter implicitly condoned stealing by providing this opportunity. It is in fact true that opportunities for theft to occur were necessary for the experiment to be conducted, and that sanctions against stealing were not implemented. Both factors have been shown to influence employee theft (Astor, 1972; Horning, 1970). Moreover, the circumstances encouraging theft as a behavioral act were strong. Specifically, participants had only a limited, transient relationship with their victims, the effects of the theft were assumed to be focused on an impersonal source, and participants did not expect to be subject to retaliation. Given that such factors have been shown to encourage inequitable acts under certain conditions (Greenberg, 1978, 1986b), it is easy to appreciate how the present study facilitated the possibility of theft as a reaction to underpayment inequity.

Although the present study may have paved the way for theft reactions to occur, this is only a limitation insofar as one would be interested in comparing different possible reactions to inequity. However, it is important to keep in mind that one common purpose of a laboratory study (including the present one) is to see what people *would do* in certain circumstances (Greenberg & Folger, 1988). Previous field research has already established that people *actually do* steal in response to feelings of underpayment (Greenberg, 1990a; Hollinger & Clark, 1983). The value of the present study comes not from attempts to generalize what might happen in the field, but understanding what processes might be operating in that context. It is precisely because the field is an impossible place to gain control of the many variables that make theft more or less likely to occur that the need to isolate variables of interest in the laboratory is warranted. Indeed, it was the need to isolate variables of interest that often covary in naturalistic settings that stimulated the present study.

This justification for the use of the laboratory is not to imply that the present study is without limitations. The most important limitation is based on the idea that the relative strength of the interpersonal sensitivity and informational validity variables was a function of the script used to manipulate levels of these variables. Although the experimental scripts used gave both factors prominence in the present study (demonstrating that they *can* be involved), it would be misleading to conclude that informational validity and interpersonal sensitivity are always relatively equal determinants of reactions to unfairness. In fact, it is an interesting possibility that in certain contexts, only one factor or the other may be an involved, or both factors may be involved interactively. For example, if an individual's interpersonal sensitivity can be attributed to strong normative pressures ("he had to behave that way"), people may be unwilling to use that factor as an element in judging the fairness of that person's behavior (Jones & Davis, 1965). Thus, although the present study demonstrates that interpersonal sensitivity and information integrity may moderate reactions to inequity, it should not be implied that these factors would always operate as demonstrated here.

Although the present research represents an advance over previous studies in which informational and interpersonal variables have been confounded (e.g., Bies & Shapiro, 1987; Greenberg, 1990a), it underscores the need for further refinement of these variables. As noted earlier, the manipulations of interpersonal sensitivity and informational validity were, of necessity, complex and composed of many different elements. As a result, it is not possible to identify the relative contributions of the individual elements from which the manipulations were composed. For this reason, readers should exercise caution in generalizing beyond the present results. Moreover, follow-up research should be directed at refining these variables if their unique effects are to be ultimately identified. This caution is raised in recognition of the possibility that identifying a complex set of variables with a single condition name might fail to reflect the unique impact of its component parts. Given the possibility that specific elements of the manipulations used may be differentially involved in producing the present results, future research is needed to more precisely pinpoint the most potent elements of the informational and interpersonal variables studied.

Finally, it should be noted that the present study was designed so that subjects would express their feelings of underpayment by stealing. However, as equity theory (Adams, 1965) notes, it is also possible for underpaid workers to react in other ways, such as by cognitively reevaluating their outcomes (Greenberg, 1989), or by lowering their work contributions (Pritchard *et al.*, 1972)—options that were not viable in the present context. It is important to note that moral and ethical constraints against stealing may make it a relatively less preferable form of expression (Shull, Delbecq, & Cummings, 1970)—but apparently, a relatively common reaction to inequity in certain circumstances (Greenberg, 1990a). As such, it would appear to be worthwhile for future researchers to consider the conditions under which responses to underpayment inequity may take the form of theft as opposed to other, more socially acceptable, options. Indeed, the more general questions of when various reactions to inequity will occur, and how they are interrelated, remain one of the most serious limitations of equity theory (Greenberg, 1989, 1990c).

ACKNOWLEDGMENTS

The author gratefully acknowledges the contributions of the following colleagues to an earlier version of this article: Robert Bies, Joel Brockner, Robert Folger, Deborah Shapiro, and Tom Tyler.

REFERENCES

Adams, J. S. (1965). Inequity in social exchange. In L. Berkowitz (Ed.), *Advances in experimental social psychology* (Vol. 2, pp. 267–299). New York: Academic Press.

American Management Association. (1977, March). *Summary overview of the "state of the art" regarding information gathering techniques and level of knowledge in three areas concerning crimes against business: Draft report*. Washington, DC: National Institute of Law Enforcement and Criminal Justice, Law Enforcement Assistance Administration.

Astor, S. D. (1972). Who's doing the stealing? *Management Review, 61,* 34–35.

Bies, R. J. (1986, August). *Identifying principles of interactional justice: The case of corporate recruiting.* Paper presented at the meeting of the Academy of Management, Chicago, IL.

Bies, R. J. (1987). The predicament of injustice: The management of moral outrage. In L. L. Cummings & B. M. Staw (Ed.), *Research in organizational behavior* (Vol. 9, pp. 289–319). Greenwich, CT: JAI Press.

Bies, R. J., & Moag, J. S. (1986). Interactional justice: Communication criteria of fairness. In R. J. Lewicki, B. H. Sheppard, & B. H. Bazerman (Ed.), *Research on negotiation in organizations* (Vol. 1, pp. 43–55). Greenwich, CT: JAI Press.

Bies, R. J., & Shapiro, D. L. (1987). Interactional fairness judgments: The influence of causal accounts. *Social Justice Research, 1,* 199–218.

Bies, R. J., & Shapiro, D. L. (1988). Voice and justification: Their influence on procedural fairness judgments. *Academy of Management Journal, 31,* 676–685.

Bies, R. J., Shapiro, D. L., & Cummings, L. L. (1988). Causal accounts and managing organizational conflict: Is it enough to say it's not my fault? *Communication Research, 15,* 381–399.

Deutsch, M. (1985). *Distributive justice.* New Haven, CT: Yale Univ. Press.

Folger, R. (1977). Distributive and procedural justice: Combined impact of "voice" and improvement on experienced inequity. *Journal of Personality and Social Psychology, 35,* 108–119.

Folger, R., & Bies, R. J. (1989). Managerial responsibilities and procedural justice. *Employee Responsibilities and Rights Journal, 2,* 79–90.

Folger, R., & Greenberg, J. (1985). Procedural justice: An interpretive analysis of personnel systems. In K. M. Rowland & G. R. Ferris (Eds.), *Research in personnel and human resources management* (Vol. 3, pp. 141–183). Greenwich, CT: JAI Press.

Greenberg, J. (1978). Effects of reward value and retaliative power on allocation decisions: Justice, generosity, or greed? *Journal of Personality and Social Psychology, 36,* 367–379.

Greenberg, J. (1982). Approaching equity and avoiding inequity in groups and organizations. In J. Greenberg & R. L. Cohen (Ed.), *Equity and justice in social behavior* (pp. 389–435). New York: Academic Press.

Greenberg, J. (1983). Self-image versus impression management in adherence to distributive justice standards: The influence of self-awareness and self-consciousness. *Journal of Personality and Social Psychology, 44,* 5–19.

Greenberg, J. (1984). On the apocryphal nature of inequity distress. In R. Folger (Ed.), *The sense of injustice* (pp. 167–188). New York: Plenum.

Greenberg, J. (1986a). Differential intolerance for inequity from organizational and individual agents. *Journal of Applied Social Psychology, 16,* 191–196.

Greenberg, J. (1986b). Determinants of perceived fairness of performance evaluations. *Journal of Applied Psychology, 71,* 340–342.

Greenberg, J. (1987). Reactions to procedural injustice in payment distributions: Do the means justify the ends? *Journal of Applied Psychology, 72,* 55–61.

Greenberg, J. (1989). Cognitive re-evaluation of outcomes in response to underpayment inequity. *Academy of Management Journal, 32,* 174–184.

Greenberg, J. (1990a). Employee theft as a reaction to underpayment inequity: The hidden costs of pay cuts. *Journal of Applied Psychology, 75,* 561–568.

Greenberg, J. (1990b). Looking fair vs. being fair: Managing impressions of organizational justice. In B. M. Staw & L. L. Cummings (Ed.), *Research in organizational behavior* (Vol. 12, pp. 111–157). Greenwich. CT: JAI Press.

Greenberg, J. (1990c). Organizational justice: Yesterday, today, and tomorrow. *Journal of Management, 16,* 401–434.

Greenberg, J. (1991). Using social accounts to manage impressions of performance appraisal fairness. *Employee Responsibilities and Rights Journal, 4,* 51–60.

Greenberg, J., Bies, R. J., & Eskew, D. E. (1991). Establishing fairness in the eye of the beholder: Managing impressions of organizational justice. In R. Giacalone & P. Rosenfeld (Eds.), *Applied impression management: How image making affects managerial decisions* (pp. 111–132). Newbury Park, CA: Sage.

Greenberg, J., & Folger, R. (1988). *Controversial issues in social research methods..* New York: Springer-Verlag.

Hollinger, R. D., & Clark, J. P. (1983). *Theft by employees.* Lexington, MA: Lexington Books.

Hornstein, H. A. (1976). *Cruelty & kindness.* Englewood Cliffs, NJ: Prentice–Hall.

Horning, D. (1970). Blue collar theft: Conceptions of property, attitudes toward pilfering, and work group norms in a modern industrial plant. In E. O. Smigel & H. L. Ross (Eds.), *Crimes against bureaucracy* (pp. 46–64). New York: Van Nostrand Reinhold.

Jones, E. E., & Davis, K. E. (1965). From acts to dispositions: The attribution process in person perception. In L. Berkowitz (Ed.), *Advances in experimental social psychology* (Vol. 2, pp. 45–68). New York: Academic Press.

Kemper, T. D. (1966). Representative roles and the legitimization of deviance. *Social Problems, 13,* 288–298.

Leventhal, G. S. (1976). The distribution of rewards and resources in groups and organizations. In L. Berkowitz & E. Walster (Ed.), *Advances in experimental social psychology* (Vol. 9, pp. 91–131). New York: Academic Press.

Leventhal, G. S. (1980). What should be done with equity theory? In K. J. Gergen, M. S. Greenberg, & R. H. Willis (Ed.), *Social exchange: Advances in theory and research* (pp. 27–55). Plenum: New York.

Lind, E. A., & Tyler, T. (1988). *The social psychology of procedural justice.* New York: Plenum.

Lord, R. G., & Hohenfeld, J. A. (1979). A longitudinal field assessment of equity effects on the performance of major league baseball players. *Journal of Applied Psychology, 64,* 19–26.

Mars, G. (1973). Chance, punters, and the fiddle: Institutionalized pilferage in a hotel dining room. In M. Warner (Ed.), *The sociology of the workplace* (pp. 200–210). New York: Halsted Press.

Mars, G. (1974). Dock pilferage: A case study in occupational theft. In P. Rock & M. McIntosh (Eds.), *Deviance and control* (pp. 209–228). London: Tavistock Institute.

McGuire, W. J. (1985). Attitudes and attitude change. In G. Lindzey & E. Aronson (Eds.), *Handbook of social psychology* (3rd ed., Vol. 2, pp. 233–346). New York: Random House.

Pritchard, R. A. (1969). Equity theory: A review and critique. *Organizational Behavior and Human Performance, 4,* 75–94

Pritchard, R. D., Dunnette, M. D., & Jorgenson, D. O.(1972). Effects of perceptions of equity and inequity on worker performance and satisfaction. *Journal of Applied Psychology, 56,* 75–94.

Reutter, V. G. (1977). Suggestion systems: Utilization, evaluation, and implementation. *California Management Review, 19,* 78–89.

Shull, F. A., Delbecq, A. L., & Cummings, L. L. (1970). *Organizational decision making.* New York: McGraw–Hill.

Tyler, T. R.(1984). The role of perceived injustice in defendants' evaluation of their courtroom experience. *Law and Society Review, 18,* 51–74.

Tyler, T. R.(1988). What is procedural justice? *Law and Society Review, 22,* 301–335.

Tyler, T. R. (1990).*Why people follow the law: Procedural justice, legitimacy, and compliance.* New Haven, CT: Yale Univ. Press.

Tyler, T. R., & Bies, R. J. (1990). Beyond formal procedures: The interpersonal context of procedural justice. In J. Carroll (Ed.), *Applied social psychology and organizational settings* (pp. 77–98). Hillsdale, NJ: Erlbaum.

Relationships and Trust

Fundamentals of Relationships: Interdependence

Virtually all organizational interaction unfolds in the context of dyadic or group interaction. The interdependence among organizational actors is an essential component of organizational life. As Lewin (1948) notes, "The essence of a group is interdependence. . . . A change in the state of any subpart changes the state of any other subpart. . . . Every move of one member will, relatively speaking, deeply affect the other member" (pp. 84–88). Interdependence theory is a comprehensive analytic framework for understanding interpersonal processes (Kelley, 1979; Kelley & Thibaut, 1969, 1978; Thibaut & Kelley, 1959). One's interdependence orientation has proven to be one of the more useful theoretical analyses for understanding key processes in relationships.

Relationships and Emotion

It is difficult to study relationships without studying emotion. One of the key challenges of organizational life is regulating the emotion aroused by the actions—or absence of expected actions—of others. Nearly all models of social competence propose, and many empirical studies have demonstrated, that optimal regulation involves neither overcontrol (i.e., inhibition of emotion) nor undercontrol (i.e., lack of impulse control). In the first article in this section, Tesser, Millar, and Moore's self-evaluation maintenance (SEM) model (1988) is derived from social comparison

305

theory (Festinger, 1954). The basis of the SEM model is that people are concerned with how they compare to others. The self-evaluation maintenance model proposes that there are two affective responses to successful accomplishment by a close other: (1) reflection, in which the self "basks in the reflected glory" of the other's performance; and (2) comparison, which engenders jealousy. Tesser et al. propose that whether a person takes joy or resentment from the good fortune of another organizational member is a function of how relevant the task is for the self (the higher the relevance, the more likely a threat perception) and the closeness of the relationship to the other. Thus, Tesser et al. propose that a reflection process occurs when another organizational actor outperforms the self on a task that is low in relevance to the self and when that person is interpersonally close to us. Tesser et al. use a number of dependent measures, such as pleasantness of facial expressions, to test their theory across three experiments.

Trust in Relationships

The second article in this section examines interpersonal trust in organizations and, in particular, the factors that influence the development of trusting relationships and the impact of trust on behavior and performance. McAllister's (1995) paper is an excellent example of a field study of 194 managers who reported on cross-functional relationships with peers. Although McAllister's study does not allow causal conclusions, the paper's main value is its theorizing about the distinction between cognitive and affective trust. The results indicate that cognition-based trust is higher than affect-based trust, which supports the theory that cognition-based trust is necessary for affect-based trust to develop.

Social Networks

The social networks point of view is that the nature and impact of interpersonal relationships depends not on psychological factors such as attraction, but rather on features such as power, influence, resources, and communication channels (Hall & Wellman, 1985). Moreover, dyads do not exist in isolation; rather, they are embedded in large multiple-person networks. This idea is reflected in the variables that social network analyses study, such as network size, density (i.e., the extent to which members of a person's network associate directly with each other), homogeneity (i.e., the similarity of network members), frequency of contact, multiplexity (i.e., the number of different resources exchanged by two network members).

In the third article in this section, Krackhardt (1990) essentially argues that knowledge is power. In particular, Krackhardt argues that an accurate perception of one's own informal networks in the organization can be a form of power, independent of the actual structure of the network. Krackhardt presents a field study of this hypothesis in a small entrepreneurial firm. The critical measure was the accuracy of "perceived" networks and "actual" networks. Organizational members who had more accurate networks were rated as more powerful by others in the organization. Of course, this study, as well as all correlational research, suffers from causal ambiguity. However, Krackhardt is careful to note the limitations of the study.

REFERENCES

Festinger, L. (1954). *A theory of cognitive dissonance.* Evanston, IL: Row, Peterson.

Hall, A., & Wellman, B. (1985). Social networks and social support. In S. Cohen and S. L. Syme (Eds.), *Social support and health* (pp. 23–41). New York: Academic Press.

Kelley, H. H. (1979). *Personal relationships.* Hillsdale, NJ: Lawrence Erlbaum.

Kelley, H. H., & Thibaut, J. (1969). Group problem solving. In G. Lindzey and E. Aronson (Eds.), *Handbook of social psychology* (pp. 1–101). Reading, MA: Addison-Wesley.

Kelley, H. H., & Thibaut, J. (1978). *Interpersonal relations: A theory of interdependence.* New York: Wiley.

Krackhardt, D. (1990). Assessing the political landscape: Structure, cognition, and power in organizations. *Administrative Science Quarterly, 35,* 342–369.

Lewin, K. (1948). *Resolving social conflicts: Selected papers on group dynamics.* Gertrude W. Lewin (Ed.). New York: Harper & Row.

McAllister, D. (1995). Affect and cognition-based trust as foundations for interpersonal cooperation in organizations. *Academy of Management Journal, 38*(1), 24–59.

Tesser, A., Millar, M., & Moore, J. (1988). Some affective consequences of social comparison and reflection processes: The pain and pleasure of being close. *Journal of Personality and Social Psychology, 54,* 49–61.

Thibaut, J., & Kelley, H. H. (1959). *The social psychology of groups.* New York: Wiley.

Suggested Readings

Kramer, R. M. (1999). Trust and distrust in organizations: Emerging perspectives, enduring questions. *Annual Review of Psychology, 50,* 569–598.

MacCrimmon, K. R., & Messick, D. M. (1978). A framework for social motives. *Behavioral Science, 21,* 86–100.

McClintock, C. G., & Liebrand, W. B. G. (1988). The role of interdependence structure, individual value orientation, and another's strategy in social decision making: A transformational analysis. *Journal of Personality and Social Psychology, 55,* 396–409.

Rousseau, D. M., Sitkin, S. B., Burt, R. S., & Camerer, C. (1998). Not so different after all: A cross-discipline view of trust. *Academy of Management Review, 23*(3), 393–404.

Sitkin, S. B. (1995). *On the positive effect of legalization on trust: Research on negotiation in organizations* (Vol. 5, pp. 185–217). Greenwich, CT: JAI Press.

Some Affective Consequences of Social Comparison and Reflection Processes: The Pain and Pleasure of Being Close

Abraham Tesser, Murray Millar, and Janet Moore
• Institute for Behavioral Research, University of Georgia

A self-evaluation maintenance (SEM) model of social behavior was described. According to the comparison process, when another outperforms the self on a task high in relevance to the self, the closer the other the greater the threat to self-evaluation. According to the reflection process, when another outperforms the self on a task low in relevance to the self, the closer the other the greater the promise of augmentation to self-evaluation. Affect was assumed to reflect threats and promises to self-evaluation. In three studies, subjects were given feedback about own performance and the performance of a close (friend) and distant (stranger) other on tasks that were either low in self-relevance (Study 2) or that varied in self-relevance (Studies 1 and 3). In Study 1 ($N = 31$), subjects' performance on simple and complex tasks after each feedback trial served as a measure of arousal. Being outperformed by a close other resulted in greater arousal than being outperformed by a distant other. In Study 2 ($N = 30$), evaluative ratings of words unrelated to task performance served as an indirect measure of affect. Results indicated that when relevance is low, more positive affect is associated with a friend's outperforming the self than either a friend's performing at a level equal to the self or being outperformed by a stranger. In Study 3 ($N = 31$), subjects received feedback while their facial expressions were monitored. Pleasantness of expression was an interactive function of relevance of task, relative performance, and closeness of comparison other. The results of all three studies were interpreted as being generally consistent with the SEM model.

After a decade of research on cold cognition, social psychology is beginning to enjoy the warm embrace of affect and emotion (Abelson, 1983; Clark, Milberg, & Ross, 1983; Fiske, 1982; Roseman, 1984; Zajonc, 1980). The research described here also deals with emotion. It emphasizes the role of social circumstances in producing affect.

Affect and emotion have played an important mediating role in several theories of social phenomena, such as aggression (e.g., Geen & Quanty, 1977; Zillman, 1978), helping behavior (e.g., Batson, Duncan, Ackerman, Buckley, & Birch, 1981; Cialdini & Kenrick, 1976; Isen & Levin, 1972; Piliavin, Dovidio, Gaertner, & Clark, 1982), and close relationships (Berscheid, 1983; Gottman

& Levenson, 1984). Our studies examine the role of affect in social comparison and reflection processes.

The notion of social comparison (Festinger, 1954; Goethals, 1984; Suls & Miller, 1977), an important perspective in social psychology, has been with us for a long time. The concept of basking in reflected glory, although less influential, was introduced some 10 years ago (Cialdini et al., 1976). Our studies are based on a self-evaluation maintenance (SEM) model that integrates these two ideas into a system in which affect may play a crucial role.

Self-Evaluation Maintenance (SEM) Model

The SEM model assumes that persons behave in a manner that will maintain or increase self-evaluation and that one's relationships with others have a substantial impact on self-evaluation. The SEM model is composed of two dynamic processes. Both the *reflection process* and the *comparison process* have as component variables the closeness of another and the quality of that other's performance. These two variables interact in affecting self-evaluation but do so in opposite ways in each of the processes.

Self-evaluation may be raised to the extent that a close (in a unit-relation sense; Heider, 1958) other performs very well on some activity; that is, one can bask in the reflected glory of the close other's good performance. For example, one can point out (to oneself and others) one's close relationship with one's friend the rock star and thereby increase one's own self-evaluation. The better the other's performance and the closer the psychological relationship, the more one can gain in self-evaluation through the reflection process.

The outstanding performance of a close other can, however, cause one's own performance to pale by comparison and decrease self-evaluation. Being close to another invites comparison, and the other's good performance could result in one's own performance looking bad, thereby adversely affecting self-evaluation. Again, the better the other's performance and the closer the psychological relationship, the greater the loss in self-evaluation through the comparison process.

It should be apparent from the description that the reflection and comparison processes depend on the same two variables but have opposite effects on self-evaluation: When closeness and performance are high, there is a potential gain in self-evaluation through the reflection process but there is a potential loss through the comparison process. According to the SEM model, the relevance of another's performance to one's self-definition determines the relative importance of the reflection and comparison processes. Following social comparison theory, another's performance is relevant to an individual's self-definition to the extent that the performance is on a dimension that is important to the individual's self-definition and to the extent that the other's performance is not so much better or worse than the individual's own performance that comparisons are rendered difficult. If the other's performance is highly relevant, the comparison process will be relatively important and one will suffer by comparison with a close other's better performance. If the other's performance is minimally relevant, the reflection process will be relatively important and one can enhance self-evaluation by basking in the reflected glory of a close other's better performance. (A more elaborated treatment of the model's constructs and dynamics can be found in Tesser, 1986, and Tesser & Campbell, 1983.)

On the Mediating Process

Direct empirical tests of the model have focused only on behavior: changes in closeness (e.g., Pleban & Tesser, 1981), attempts to change another's performance (e.g., Tesser & Smith, 1980), and changes in relevance (e.g., Tesser & Campbell, 1980). There has been no attempt to measure self-evaluation. We viewed self-evaluation as

a hypothetical construct, a theoretical fiction which is used to organize and make comprehensible the relationships among the variables that have empirical indicants, i.e., relevance, performance, closeness, Similarly, self-evaluation maintenance is viewed as a hypothetical process much like "dissonance reduction" is viewed as a hypothetical process in dissonance theory. Neither dissonance reduction nor self-evaluation maintenance is directly measured or observed, but both models are testable because they make specific predictions concerning the observable antecedents and observable consequences of the hypothesized process. (Tesser & Campbell, 1983, pp. 8–9)

Although the SEM model has been useful in accounting for the relevant behaviors (see Tesser, 1986, for a review), there have been no tests directed at its mediating processes. If self-evaluation processes are real, how might they be detected? We believe that the operation of these processes is often relatively fast and, even more important, outside of conscious awareness (see Tesser's, 1986, section on awareness). Therefore, self-reports may have limited utility. However, if these processes are real, they should also manifest themselves in more unobtrusive measures of change in affect and arousal. Threats to self-evaluation should result in negative affect, whereas enhancements to self-evaluation should lead to positive affect.

The SEM Model and Affect

There is some previous research using self-reported affect that is consistent with the SEM assumption. In studying social-comparison jealousy, Salovey and Rodin (1984) gave participants feedback that they performed well or poorly on a dimension that was relevant or irrelevant to their self-definition. They also provided information that another participant had performed well on either the relevant or irrelevant dimension. From the perspective of the SEM model, the condition that poses the greatest threat to self-evaluation is the one in which the participant performs poorly on a relevant dimension and the other performs well on this dimension. Salovey and Rodin found that participants in this condition reported more anxiety, more depression, and less positivity of mood than did participants in any of the seven other conditions.

When one person helps another, the person receiving help is implicitly demonstrating inferior performance. When the help takes place on a dimension relevant to the recipient's self-definition, comparison processes should come into play, and the closer the relationship of the helper, the greater the threat to self-evaluation. Nadler, Fisher, and Ben-Itzhak (1983) had participants try to solve a mystery. The task was described as tapping important skills (high relevance) or luck (low relevance). The participant's solution was wrong and he was given a clue from either a friend (close other) or a stranger (distant other). Some participants went through this experience once and some went through it twice. Participants then rated their affect on a series of scales. From the perspective of the model, the most threatening condition is the one in which help was received twice from a friend on the relevant task. This condition was indeed associated with the most negative affect, and none of the other conditions appeared to differ from one another.

Although these two studies suggest that conditions presumed to result in threat to self-evaluation are associated with negative affect, more research is needed. For example, do conditions presumed to maximize self-evaluation (i.e., the outstanding performance of a close other on a low-relevance dimension) produce positive affect? Furthermore, the studies depended on self-reports of affect. The studies to be described examine both threatening and enhancing conditions and unobtrusive behavioral outcroppings of arousal and facial expressions to index affect.

Study 1: SEM and Arousal

The SEM model is a motivational model. Theoretically, persons strive to maintain a positive self-evaluation. Therefore, threats to self-evaluation or promises of gain in self-evaluation ought to be arousing. A number of models of emotion suggest that both positive and negative emotion are arousing (e.g., Clark et al., 1983; Russell's, 1980, circumplex model; the jukebox models of Mandler, 1975, and Schacter, 1964). The SEM model is quite specific about the conditions that threaten a loss and those that promise a gain in self-evaluation. High-relevance activities activate the comparison process and create the potential for threat (by the better performance of a close other). Low-relevance activities activate the reflection process and create the promise of a gain (also by the better performance of a close other).

Arousal has known effects on task performance. It tends to facilitate or speed up the performance of simple (low response competition) tasks and to interfere with or slow down the performance of complex (high response competition) tasks (e.g., Spence, 1956; Zajonc, 1965). We consider here two tasks. The *primary task* is either high or low in personal relevance and is the task with which the individual is concerned. The *secondary task* is incidental to the primary task but varies in complexity. It is included in order to detect changes in arousal.

According to the SEM model, when a primary performance dimension is high in relevance, the comparison process is activated and threat increases with the relative performance of another, particularly a close other. If arousal results from this threat, performance on a simple secondary task should be facilitated, and performance on a complex secondary task should be degraded with the other's, particularly a close other's better performance. When a primary performance dimension is low in relevance, the promise of gain to self-evaluation should increase with the other's relative performance, particularly a close other. If arousal is associated with the promise of gain in self-evaluation, we should expect to find that simple secondary tasks are facilitated and complex secondary tasks are degraded with the other's, particularly a close other's, better performance.

In statistical terms, these predictions lead to the expectation of a three-factor interaction on performance: Closeness × Other's Performance × Task Complexity. If the comparison process or the reflection process are differentially effective in producing arousal, the relevance variable should also enter into the interaction, that is, Relevance × Closeness × Performance × Complexity. However, we have no specific hypotheses about the relative strengths of the comparison and reflection processes.

Research (e.g., Spence, Farber, & McFann, 1956) concerning arousal and task performance has benefited from the inclusion of the Taylor (1953) Manifest Anxiety Scale, a scale that has been construed as a measure of general drive (arousal). It is included because it is expected to facilitate performance on the simple task and interfere with performance on the complex task. Research on sociopathy has shown that persons who score low on the Socialization scale of the California Psychological Inventory (Gough, 1964) show less arousal (electrodermal response) to noxious stimuli (e.g., Hare, 1978). Furthermore, Waid and Orne (1982) have shown that these subjects also perform less well on a nonstressful, high-response-conflict task. Because persons who score low on the Socialization scale show fewer arousal effects, this scale was included with the expectation that the predictions from the model would be better supported among more socialized individuals. Finally, we also included a measure of self-esteem (Rosenberg, 1965), although we had no directional predictions concerning this measure.

(See Tesser & Campbell, 1982a and 1983, for a discussion of individual differences in self-esteem and self-evaluation maintenance processes.)

Method

Overview

Subjects reported to the experiment location with a friend. After measuring the relevance of social sensitivity and creativity to their self-definition, we separated the two and seated each before a microcomputer. The computer administered a series of items purporting to measure creativity and social sensitivity. After the subject responded to each item, she was given feedback that she had done either better or worse than either her friend or a stranger. Following the feedback, subjects completed a simple or complex motor task (typing a single digit five times or five different digits as fast as they could). Item type (social sensitivity vs. creativity), relative performance, comparison other (friend vs. stranger), and complexity of task were systematically manipulated such that each subject was exposed once to all 16 possible combinations.

Subjects

Seventeen pairs of female friends ($N = 34$) were recruited from an introductory psychology pool. They signed up for a study on "social sensitivity, creativity, and social judgment" and received course credit for their participation.

Procedure

Subjects participated in one friendship pair at a time. When they arrived for their session, they were told that the study concerned the relationships among social sensitivity, creativity, and social judgment. They were also given an overview of the tasks that they would be asked to complete. Each subject then filled out a questionnaire intended to measure the relevance of creativity and social sensitivity to their self-definition. There were two 7-point items to measure each: To what extent do you consider yourself a creative (socially sensitive) person? How important is it for you to be a creative (socially sensitive) person?

Subjects were then taken to separate rooms and seated before a microcomputer. They were told that they would be given a series of items that accurately measured social sensitivity and creativity. They were also told that they would be receiving feedback following their response to each item concerning their performance and the performance of their friend or a stranger (someone who had previously participated in the study). They were told to pay attention to the feedback. After the item feedback, subjects were told they would have to type a number into the computer as quickly as they could in order to "keep participants [i.e., themselves] alert during the feedback period." Subjects were then given examples to familiarize them with this aspect of the procedure.

Design. Each subject was confronted with 16 trials conforming to a completely balanced 2 (item type: creativity vs. social sensitivity) × 2 (performance feedback: self better than other vs. other better than self) × 2 (closeness; friend vs. stranger) × 2 (task complexity: simple vs. complex). The order of trials was randomized for each subject. The social sensitivity items provided subjects with an interpersonal problem and a solution to which they could respond yes or no. For example, "An older brother dominates his younger sister. Whenever the sister tries to show her independence, the older brother becomes aggressive. Should the younger sister be encouraged to limit her contacts with her older brother?" The creativity items asked subjects to indicate whether one word had something to do with three other words. For example, subjects were asked to indicate whether the word *red* was related to the three words *happy, selfish,* and *heart.* Following the subjects' response to each item, they learned that their answer was either better or worse than that of the other (friend or stranger), that is, self was correct and other incorrect or vice versa.

Measuring arousal. After the feedback had been visible for 10 s, it disappeared from the screen and the subject was prompted to type in five numerical digits as quickly as possible. The simple task (low response competition) consisted of a single, randomly selected digit repeated 5 times. The complex task (high response competition) consisted of five randomly selected (with replacement) digits. The dependent variable, recorded by the computer, was the speed with which these numbers were entered.

Postexperimental questionnaires. On completion of the computer task, subjects returned to the first room and completed several additional questionnaires. One asked them to indicate how well they, their friend, and the stranger did on the social sensitivity and creativity items. These items were framed in terms of percentage correct (free response) and "compared to the average subject" (7-point scale anchored with *bad/good*). Subjects also filled out Rosenberg's (1965) Self-Esteem Scale, the Socialization scale of the California Personality Inventory (Gough, 1964), and Taylor's (1953) Manifest Anxiety Scale. Finally, subjects were completely debriefed and all their questions answered.

Results

Recall our expectations. The threat of comparison results from the better performance of another, particularly a close other, on a relevant dimension. The promise of reflection also results from the good performance of another, particularly a close other, but on an irrelevant dimension. Both the threat of comparison and the promise of reflection should result in arousal. Because closeness and performance interact to produce comparison (when relevance is high) and reflection (when relevance is low), closeness and performance should interact in producing arousal. Arousal, in turn, should facilitate performance on the simple task and interfere with performance on the complex task. Because these effects go in opposite directions, the overall prediction is for a three-factor interaction: Performance × Closeness × Complexity.

Our index of secondary task performance was the amount of time taken to complete the task. The analysis of variance (ANOVA) of this index included four within-subjects factors: 2 (relevance) × 2 (performance) × 2 (closeness) × 2 (complexity). Relevance was defined as a within-subjects factor (i.e., idiographically) by separately summing the responses to the two items included to measure the relevance of social sensitivity and the two items included to measure the relevance of creativity. For each subject, the topic that had the larger sum was classified as high in relevance and the one with the smaller sum was classified as low in relevance. (Three subjects were dropped because there was no difference in the relevance of the two areas.)

Several effects emerged. First, there was a huge task-complexity effect, $F(1, 30) = 378.78, p < .001$. Although this effect is not surprising, it serves to validate the complexity manipulation: The simple task ($M = 2.3$ s) took substantially less time than the complex task ($M = 3.8$ s). The next two effects, a performance main effect, $F(1, 30) = 6.44$, $p < .02$, and a Complexity × Performance interaction, $F(1, 30) = 4.65$, $p < .05$, should be interpreted in terms of the final, more interesting effect. As predicted, the Performance × Closeness × Complexity interaction was also significant, $F(1, 30) = 4.52$, $p < .05$. As seen in Figure 1, the interaction is of the appropriate form.

Because arousal is inferred from the differential effects on simple and complex tasks, the three-factor interaction is decomposed in terms of the simple interactions with task complexity, that is, the Closeness × Complexity interactions and the Performance × Complexity interactions.[1] Where other outperforms self, as closeness increases (from stranger to friend), there is a slowing down on the complex task and a speeding up on the simple task, $t(60) = 2.60$, $p < .01$.[2] This effect is slightly reversed ($t < 1$) when the self outperforms the other. Similarly, if we look only at the close other, the friend, as performance increases (from self better to other better), there is a slowing down on the complex task and a speeding up on the simple task, $t(60) = 3.02$, $p < .01$. This effect is slightly reversed ($t < 1$) when the other is distant, the stranger.

The relevance of a topic to one's self-definition determines the relative importance of the comparison and reflection processes. Because we assumed that comparison and reflection processes would have similar effects on arousal, we did not expect relevance necessarily to moderate the predicted interaction. In fact, it did not ($F < 1$). To make this lack of effect meaningful, however, it is important to show that relevance was adequately varied.

First, as noted, each of the subjects included in the analysis rated one of the topics as more relevant than the other: On a scale varying from 2 to 14 with 8 as the midpoint, the mean rating of the low-relevance activity was 8.87 and the mean rating of the high-relevance activity was 11.52.[3] Second and more important, relevance must have been adequately varied because it had a significant impact on other variables. Subjects were asked on the postexperimental questionnaire to rate performance and indicate the percentage correct for themselves, their friend, and the stranger on the computer tasks. Recall that subjects received feedback that they and the others did better than one another an equal number of times, and that was true for both the high-and low-relevance topics. These responses were analyzed in a 2 (relevance) × 3 (person: self vs. friend vs. stranger) within-subjects ANOVA. Focusing on the rating of performance, there was an effect of person, $F(2, 54) = 8.27$, $p < .001$: Friends ($M = 2.95$) were rated as

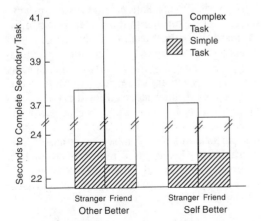

FIGURE 1 ■ Study 1: Time taken (in seconds) to complete simple and complex secondary tasks as a combined function of performance feedback (self better vs. other better) and closeness of other (friend vs. stranger). (This figure originally appeared in Tesser, in press, and is reproduced here by permission.)

[1]It is worth noting that although both simple and complex tasks show the expected pattern of means, as seen in Figure 1, most of the variance in differences between tasks comes from the complex task. Indeed, a separate analysis of the simple task yields no significant effects. Perhaps there is a floor effect at work with this task.

[2]Because the direction of these simple interaction effects was predicted, one-tailed t tests were used for assessing their significance. These t tests are simply the square root of the F test for the appropriate simple effect. (The relation between t and F with 1 degree of freedom is $F = t^2$.) There are 60 degrees of freedom because the appropriate error term in this repeated-measures analysis is the pooled error terms from the three-factor interaction (with 30 df) and the relevant two-factor interaction (with 30 df), in this case, Closeness × Complexity (Winer, 1962).

[3]Both means are on the high side of the scale midpoint, yet we are arguing that one is high and the other low in relevance. Perhaps our argument is wrong. On the other hand, it seems very difficult to interpret these scale values in absolute terms. Clearly, it is socially desirable to say that these dimensions are important. The scales have no fixed origin. Also, there are no norms on a representative set of dimensions for comparison. Perhaps, then, the numbers should be interpreted in relative terms.

performing better than self ($M = 3.52$) or stranger ($M = 3.54$). Furthermore, there was a significant main effect of relevance, $F(1, 27) = 10.93$, $p < .01$. Because the interaction approached significance, $F(2, 27) = 3.65$, $p = .08$, and is meaningful, we probed the simple effects. It was only for self that high-relevance performance ($M = 3.18$) was significantly better than low-relevance performance ($M = 3.86$), $F(1, 81) = 5.29$, $p < .05$. The corresponding comparisons for friend ($Ms = 2.93$ vs. 2.96) and stranger ($Ms = 3.50$ vs. 3.57) did not approach significance. The outcomes for the percentage-correct measure were similar. The person effect was only marginally significant, $F(2, 54) = 2.56$, $p < .10$, but there was a significant overall relevance effect, $F(1, 27) = 6.73$, $p < .02$. Because the interaction did not approach significance, we did not follow up with formal statistical tests. However, it is worth noting that the effect of relevance for self ($Ms = 63\%$ vs. 57%) was larger than that for friend ($Ms = 66\%$ vs. 63%) or stranger ($Ms = 61\%$ vs. 60%). In sum, the relevance variable had effects on perceptions of performance, and these effects were most pronounced for the self, as might be expected.

Subjects responded to a number of personality measures including self-esteem, the Socialization scale of the California Psychological Inventory, and the Taylor Manifest Anxiety Scale. Each was split at the median and, in turn, added as a between-subjects factor to the basic ANOVA of the response times. The predicted interaction (Performance × Closeness × Complexity) was snot moderated by any of these variables. For some subjects, social sensitivity was more relevant than creativity ($n = 24$), whereas the reverse was true for the remaining subjects ($n = 7$). This classification was also added as a between-subjects factor to the basic ANOVA. Again, there was no moderating effect.

Discussion

When a close other does better than the self, performance on a complex task worsens but performance on a simple task is facilitated. From these data we conclude that arousal results when a close other performs better than the self. Furthermore, the relevance of the performance domain does not appear to moderate this effect. In short, the superior performance of close others affects our emotion more than does the superior performance of

distant others. Indeed, there is some evidence that the mere anticipation of a close other's performance can be arousing. For example, Brenner (1973) found that when individuals in a group take turns reading words, they have a difficult time remembering the words read just before their own turn. More interesting from our perspective, they also have a difficult time remembering the words read just before a friend's turn.

We interpret the arousal results to indicate that both the loss in self-evaluation associated with the social comparison process and the gain in self-evaluation associated with the social reflection process manifest themselves in arousal. Although we have some evidence that the relevance manipulation was successful, we have no directional evidence of the operation of these two processes. That is, arousal can index both positive and negative effect, and we argue that it is doing that in this study. Another interpretation, one that could be derived from a social comparison perspective,[4] is simply that being outperformed by another, particularly a close other, produces negative affect (and arousal) regardless of the level of relevance. What seems to be needed now to make the case for the reflection process is a demonstration that being outperformed by another can sometimes reduce negativity. Specifically, according to the SEM model, reduced negativity (or increased positivity) should be associated with being outperformed by a close other on a low-relevance dimension. Study 2 was run in an attempt to provide such evidence. Before turning to that study, however, we address briefly the question of self-reports.

Subjects' self-reports, in addition to providing evidence concerning the validity of the relevance variable, showed an interesting pattern of distortion. Although they received feedback that each of the actors (self, friend, stranger) had performed equally well, subjects indicated that their friend had performed better than self or stranger. Such charitable but distorted self-reports have also been observed by Tesser and Campbell (1982b). We take these reports to mean that persons often like to

---

[4]The label *social comparison perspective is* used to refer to a broad view on social behavior rather than any single statement of social comparison theory (e.g., Festinger, 1954). Although this alternative explanation has the flavor of social comparison theory, we know of no particular version that makes this specific prediction, nor are we aware of any studies of arousal per se conducted in the social comparison tradition.

say nice things about those who are close to them. Perhaps this is simply a generalization from the kind of interaction that may go on inside a close relationship in attempts to maintain that relationship (see Brickman & Bulman, 1977).

Study 2: Positive Affect and the Reflection Process

The results of Study 1 are quite consistent with the SEM model, but they are consistent with other theoretical positions as well, most notably a social comparison perspective. When relevance is high, the predictions of the social comparison perspective and the SEM model are the same: Being outperformed by another, particularly a close other, will produce negative affect (and arousal). The predictions diverge for affect (but not necessarily arousal) in the low-relevance case. The social comparison perspective continues to predict negative affect (and arousal) with the better performance of a close other. The SEM model, on the other hand, posits a reflection process. A close other's better performance when relevance is low provides the opportunity for basking in the reflection of the other's good performance and hence should be associated with relatively more positive affect (and arousal).

What is needed, then, for interpretive clarity is a set of low-relevance conditions that vary with respect to relative performance and closeness and a directional measure of affect, that is, one that is sensitive to differences in positivity and negativity. Under such low-relevance conditions both the social comparison perspective and the SEM model predict a Performance × Closeness interaction, but the form of those interactions differ: Stating it in terms of positivity of affect, the social comparison perspective predicts the least positivity when the close other outperforms the self; the SEM model predicts the most positivity when the close other outperforms the self.

This study provides a site for examining the relative merit of these opposing predictions. Subjects received feedback that a close (friend) or distant (stranger) other performed about the same or better than the self on a low-relevance test. After receiving feedback, subjects made evaluative ratings of unfamiliar words. Because we believe that affective changes are often fast and not subject to conscious awareness, we wanted a non-self-report

measure of affect. Positivity and negativity of the ratings of words unrelated to the performance dimension, an indirect index of affect (e.g., Clark & Isen, 1982; Isen & Shalker, 1977), was therefore used as our primary measure. Subjects also responded to a self-report measure of affect on the postexperimental questionnaire.

The only individual difference measure used in the study was a measure of self-esteem (Rosenberg, 1965). No specific predictions were made about the influence of this variable.

Method

Subjects

Thirty-four female undergraduates comprising 17 friendship pairs were recruited for a study ostensibly on the relation between personality and the perception of others. Four subjects were dropped because of experimenter errors in procedure, leaving a total of 30 participants in the study.

Procedure

Subjects were scheduled in groups of 4 (two friendship pairs).[5] When they arrived, they were asked to fill out the self-esteem scale and a questionnaire designed to measure their interests. The interest measure actually measured the relevance of a number of dimensions (e.g., movies, science, television, health and fitness, photography) to the subject's self-definition. For each dimension, subjects were asked on a 7-point scale anchored with *strongly agree* and *strongly disagree* how interested they were (e.g., "I enjoy movies a great deal and go to the movies whenever I can") and how knowledgeable they were (e.g., "I know more about movies than most people").

After completing these measures, each subject was given an opportunity to say a little about herself so that the others might form a first impression. While the subjects were engaged in this activity, the experimenter determined each subject's least relevant dimension from the interest inventory. Subjects' ratings on the question concerning their

---

[5]If only one friendship pair arrived for the study, those subjects assigned to feedback about a distant other were told that they were receiving feedback on the performance of the last participant who had answered questions on that particular topic.

contact with the particular topic and the question concerning their knowledge about the topic were summed to form one score. Subjects also were asked to rank order the six interest areas according to knowledge about the topic. This rank ordering was used to determine the subjects' least relevant dimension when there was a tie between summed scores. The mean rating of the selected dimension was 12.78 on a scale that varied from 2 (high relevance) to 14 (low relevance). The topic that subjects rated lowest in terms of interest and knowledge was the topic about which they were subsequently quizzed.

Subjects then were given the following cover story:

> In the next phase of the study you will be interacting with a computer that will produce questions about an area to be randomly selected from among those on the interest inventory. The computers are interconnected so that some of you will be getting feedback about how another is responding to the same questions. Although you will know who the feedback concerns, you will not know who, if anyone, is getting feedback on your performance. Finally, some of you may not get feedback on anyone.

In order to forestall questions, subjects were told that after the computer phase they would be given another exercise in which they would learn a little more about one another before giving their final impressions of each other. Subjects then were taken to separate booths and seated before a microcomputer.

Manipulating the Independent Variables

Each subject was confronted with 30 questions from an area that she had marked as least relevant to her self-definition. After each block of five items, subjects were told how many of the preceding items they had answered correctly and how many of these same items their friend (close condition) or one of the new acquaintances (distant condition) had answered correctly. In the *equal* performance condition, subjects learned, with some variability over trials to bolster credibility, that they had correctly answered approximately the same number of items (15) that the other had answered correctly (16). In the *other-better* condition, the subject learned that the other (23 correct) had outperformed her (7 correct).

Measuring Affect

While subjects remained in the booths, the experimenter returned and told each subject that it would take a few more minutes to get the materials ready for the next phase of the study. Further more, each subject was told that while she was waiting she might wish to help out a graduate student by doing some ratings. Subjects were shown a stack of cards with an unfamiliar word printed on each card (e.g., *Catarhh, Obol, Perdol*) and paper containing places to write and rate each word on a 7-point semantic differential scale (*pleasant-unpleasant*). They were shown how to use the scale to rate the pleasantness of the words.[6] The experimenter then left. The average rating given on the pleasantness scale served as an indirect measure of subjects' affect (Clark & Isen, 1982; Isen & Shalker, 1977).

When the experimenter returned, approximately 7 min later, a final questionnaire designed to check on the performance manipulation and to assess self-reported affect was administered. Finally, all 4 subjects were brought back together, probed for suspicion regarding the hypotheses, and thoroughly debriefed.

Results

Performance Manipulation

When subjects had been outperformed by the other, they rated their performance as significantly poorer ($M = 6.01$) than when they performed equal to the other ($M = 4.00$), $F(1, 25) = 13.05, p < .001$. When subjects were outperformed by the other, they rated the other's performance as significantly better ($M = 2.73$) than when they had performed equally ($M = 4.00$), $F(1, 25) = 6.55, p < .02$. When asked to rate who had done better on a scale with endpoints *I did much better* and *She did much better*, subjects who had been outperformed were more inclined to rate toward the other-did-better end of the scale ($M = 6.31$) than when they performed

---

[6]Subjects were told that the number they completed, or even whether they worked at all, was completely up to them. Originally we had hoped to use helping as an indirect index of positive affect/mood (e.g., Isen & Levin, 1972). Because almost all subjects rated some of the words, this was not possible. The 5 (of 20) subjects who rated no words came from each of the four conditions, so differential selection does not seem to be an important problem.

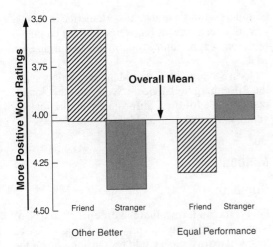

FIGURE 2 ■ Study 2: Effects of closeness (friend vs. stranger) and relative performance (other better vs. equal) on pleasantness ratings of words unrelated to task performance.

equally (M = 3.94), $F(1, 25)$ = 51.43, p < .0001. Neither the closeness nor the Closeness × Performance effects were significant in any of these analyses. Performance appears to have been successfully manipulated.

Affect

Our major measure of affect was the mean evaluative rating of the first five words subsequent to the feedback. (Two subjects used in this analysis rated fewer than five words.) These data were analyzed in terms of a 2 (performance) × 2 (closeness) ANOVA. The means associated with these conditions are illustrated in Figure 2.

Both the social comparison perspective and the SEM model predict a Closeness × Performance interaction. This component is significant, $F(1, 21)$ = 6.44, p < .02. The theoretical perspectives differ, however, with respect to the expected pattern of the interaction: The SEM model anticipates the most positivity and the social comparison perspective the least positivity in the close-other-better cell. As seen in Figure 2, the pattern of means is consistent with the SEM prediction. Analyses of simple effects revealed that the close-other-better cell (M = 3.57) was more positive than the close-other-equal cell (M = 4.29), $F(1, 21)$ = 5.06, p < .05, and more positive than the distant-other-bet-

ter cell (M = 4.38), $F(1, 21)$ = 5.94, p < .05. Neither of the remaining simple effects was significant (F < 1).

A self-report affect measure was taken on the postexperimental questionnaire. Subjects responded to four 7-point semantic differential scales (*pleasant–unpleasant, proud–not proud, dissatisfied–satisfied,* and *angry–not angry*) to indicate their feelings while working on the interest test. These ratings were summed and subjected to an ANOVA similar to the one just reported. None of the effects were significant.

Both of the analyses reported here were also run with a median split on the self-esteem scale as an additional factor. In no case did self-esteem significantly affect the outcomes.

Discussion

This study dealt with the effects of closeness and performance on affect when a performance dimension is low in personal relevance. Different theoretical viewpoints can be seen as making differing predictions concerning these effects. A simple social comparison perspective might predict that being outperformed by another, particularly a close other, should result in negative affect (even when relevance is low), whereas the SEM model assumes that the reflection process becomes important when relevance is low and the better performance of a close other has the potential for joy. The pattern of results was consistent with the latter expectation. A close other's better performance was associated with the most positive affect, even though that performance was associated with the self's poorer performance in both relative and absolute terms (see Tesser & Campbell, 1980).

The measure of affect that showed the predicted effects was indirect and immediate. A more direct, self-report measure given approximately 7 min after the feedback revealed no systematic effects. Obviously, there are a number of potential explanations for this discrepancy. Perhaps the effects are rather short-lived and would have shown themselves on an immediate self-report, or perhaps the effect is so subtle that it doesn't register in conscious awareness.

Study 2 was undertaken to help clarify the results of Study 1. In Study 1 closeness and performance interacted to produce arousal, and relevance had no impact. We argued, however, that the arousal was indexing negative affect in the case of high relevance and positive affect in the case of low relevance. Study 2 showed the pattern of affect predicted to be associated with low relevance. However, Study 2 focused only on low-relevance conditions, and the operations used in Studies 1 and 2 differed somewhat, making comparisons difficult. What is needed now is a study in which both high and low relevance conditions are present and in which it is possible to track differences in positivity and negativity in affect.

Study 3: SEM and Facial Expression

Study 3 was designed to provide more evidence for the comparison and reflection processes by examining the positivity and negativity of affect in all the conditions relevant to the SEM model. The primary measure of affect used in this study was the pleasantness of facial expressions. Facial indexes of affect have been found useful in a variety of contexts (e.g., Barden, Garber, Duncan, & Masters, 1981; Ekman & Oster, 1979; Zuckerman, Klorman, Larrance, & Spiegel, 1981).

The SEM model assumes that threats to self-evaluation are unpleasant and increases in self-evaluation are pleasant. Further more, the theory is explicit in specifying the conditions that promise to reduce or augment self-evaluation. When the task is high in relevance, the comparison process is important and a close other's better performance should lead to more negative affect than should a distant other's better performance. On the other hand, when relevance is low, the reflection process is important, and a close other's better performance should lead to more positive affect than should a distant other's better performance. In sum, all three factors (relative performance, relevance, and closeness) should interact in producing affective responses.

Study 3 uses a paradigm similar to that used in Study 1: Subjects take a test high in relevance to their self-definition and a test low in relevance. A friend (close other) and a stranger (distant other) are purported to respond to the same test items. For each item, subjects are given feedback containing three elements of information: type of item (high or low relevance), relative performance (self better vs. other better), and the closeness of the comparison other (friend vs. stranger). These variables define eight trials that represent a complete replication of a factorial design composed of the

complete crossing of the three elements. Subjects' affective response, as registered in their facial expression, was monitored continuously during each trial.

As in Study 1, the Taylor Manifest Anxiety scale, the Rosenberg Self-Esteem Scale, and the Socialization scale, of the California Psychological Inventory were administered.

Method

Subjects

Forty-six undergraduate women (23 pairs of friends) taking introductory psychology classes received extra course credit for participation. One participant was dropped from further consideration because of failure to follow experimental instructions.

Procedure

Each friendship pair was informed by a male experimenter that the purpose of the study was to measure esthetic judgment and logical thinking ability. The experimenter gave a short definition of each ability and explained that participants would be required to complete two computer tasks designed to measure these abilities. Before completing the tasks, the participants were asked to fill out a four-item questionnaire. The questionnaire was designed to assess the relevance of each domain to the participant's self-definition. They rated on 7-point scales the extent to which they thought of themselves as having good esthetic judgment (logical thinking ability) and how important it was for them to have good esthetic judgment (logical thinking ability).

Each friend was then escorted to a separate room and seated at a microcomputer. The experimenter explained that the microcomputer would require them to perform eight games: four logical thinking games and four esthetic judgment games. After they finished playing each game, the computer would automatically score their performance and provide feedback. In addition, the computer would tell them how well their friend, who was working on the terminal in the next room, performed on the same game. However, if their friend had not completed or was not assigned a similar game, they would receive information on the performance of a subject who had participated earlier in the study. The experimenter then left the room and the microcomputer gave participants directions on how to play the games as well as an opportunity to practice both the logical thinking and esthetic judgment games. After the practice games, four logical thinking and four esthetic judgment trials were presented with preassigned feedback randomly ordered.

Participants were given a questionnaire designed to assess their perceptions of their performance, their friend's performance, and the stranger's performance on the esthetic judgment and logical thinking games. A further questionnaire asked participants to report how they felt in each of the eight feedback conditions; they rated on 7-point scales the extent to which they felt good or bad when they received the eight types of feedback. Participants then completed the Rosenberg Self-Esteem Scale (Rosenberg, 1965), the Socialization scale of the California Psychological Inventory, and the Taylor Manifest Anxiety Scale. Finally, participants were questioned concerning the experimental hypotheses, debriefed, and released.

Computer Tasks

An interception task that ostensibly measured logical thinking and a pattern creation task that ostensibly measured esthetic judgment were used. The logical thinking task required participants to intercept a target airplane in a 12 × 11 matrix. Each time participants moved one unit, the target airplane moved one unit. The target airplane's movements were random except when participants were to receive poor performance feedback. On these trials the computer moved the target so that it was impossible to hit. Participants were informed that the computer evaluated their logical ability not only by whether they intercepted the target but also by examining the pattern or strategy they used to intercept the target.

The esthetic judgment game required participants to take an existing pattern and make it more esthetically pleasing by changing the symbols used to make the pattern and the amount of space between symbols. With each pattern, participants were given four chances to make it look pleasing. After each attempt, the modified pattern was presented to the participant. Participants were informed that the computer would evaluate their esthetic judgment not only on the basis of the final

pattern they created but on the basis of the means in which they attempted to make the pattern esthetically pleasing.

Feedback

At the end of each trial, the computer presented information ostensibly reporting on the participants' performance and the performance of either their friend or an earlier participant. Each participant received feedback representing each level of the three variables (friend vs. stranger, logical thinking vs. esthetic judgment; self-better vs. other better), creating eight feedback conditions. Self-better feedback was created by giving the participant a score between 70th and 90th percentile and the comparison person a score between 20th and 50th percentile; other-better feedback was created by reversing these scores. The order in which the feedback conditions were presented was counterbalanced across subjects. After the feedback had been presented, subjects could terminate the feedback and initiate the next trial by pressing a designated key on the computer. The time spent examining the feedback was recorded by the computer.

Dependent Measure

Cameras behind a one-way mirror in the experimental rooms recorded the participants' facial responses during the game-playing behavior and feedback. The computer illuminated a light recorded on the videotape to signal when the participant was receiving feedback. Two raters later viewed the tapes and, when the light signal was on, rated the pleasantness of participants' facial responses to the feedback by using a 7-point scale anchored by *unpleasant* (7) and *pleasant* (1). Raters were blind to feedback conditions.

Results

Reliability of Facial Ratings

Two persons independently rated the pleasantness of each subject's face in each condition; these ratings were summed to yield a pleasantness score. (Because of difficulty with the video equipment, data for 2 subjects were deleted, leaving 43 subjects.) Reliability of ratings was assessed for each subject by computing a coefficient alpha over the

TABLE 20.1. Pleasantness of Facial Expressions as a Function of Relative Performance, Personal Relevance, and Closeness of Other

Other (closeness)	Self-better performance		Other-better performance		M
	High relevance	Low relevance	High relevance	Low relevance	
Friend	7.10	7.77	7.97	7.39	7.56
Stranger	8.71	7.74	8.03	8.55	8.26
M	7.90	7.76	8.00	7.97	7.91

Note. Numbers have a potential range of 2 (most pleasant) to 14 (most unpleasant).

eight conditions in which each subject was observed. Reliability was satisfactory. Only 5 subjects had alphas under .60; the mean alpha was .81 and the median alpha .93.

Analysis of Facial Ratings

Relevance was defined as in Study 1: The two relevance items for each topic were summed (2 = maximal relevance; 14 = minimal relevance), and the topic that had the larger sum was classified as high relevance ($M = 4.48$) and the topic that had the smaller sum was classified as low relevance ($M = 6.45$; see Footnote 3). For 17 subjects logical ability was more relevant; for 14 subjects esthetic judgement was more relevant. Twelve subjects were dropped because there was no difference in the relevance of the two areas.

Pleasantness ratings were analyzed in a 2 (relevance) × 2 (closeness) × 2 (performance) repeated-measures ANOVA. The means associated with this analysis are presented in Table 1. The SEM model predicts both a two-way interaction (Relevance × Performance) and a three-way interaction (Relevance × Closeness × Performance). The two-factor interaction was not significant ($F < 1$), but the three-factor interaction was significant, $F(1, 30) = 4.72, p < .04$. The only other effect even to approach significance was that due to closeness, $F(1, 30) = 3.18, p = .08$. Facial expressions were more pleasant in connection with feedback to a friend than a stranger.

As one might guess, knowing that the predicted Relevance × Performance interaction did not emerge, the pattern of means producing the three-factor interaction does not, in absolute terms, completely conform to predictions. On the other hand, the pattern does conform to theoretical expectations in relative terms (see Tesser, in press, for a discussion of the importance of relative predic-

tion or interactions in testing SEM predictions).

We assume that SEM functioning is not the only thing that determines behavior in general or pleasantness of facial expression in this particular instance. For example, the SEM model makes some absolute predictions about the difference in pleasantness between friend and stranger. It predicts that being outperformed by a friend should be more threatening (more unpleasant) than being outperformed by a stranger on a relevant task. As seen in Table 1, this was not the case. However, independent of SEM functioning, as noted, more pleasant expressions tend to be associated with feedback about a friend than with feedback about a stranger. This effect is not anticipated by the SEM model but it is not particularly surprising. Because it is present, we must look at this closeness effect relative to the closeness effect in other conditions. (The closeness effect is defined as the difference in pleasantness to friend vs. stranger, with positive numbers meaning more pleasantness to friend.)

Fortunately, the SEM model is unambiguous in telling us where to look for relative differences. When the self outperforms the other, there should be no threat due to comparison even if the performance dimension is self-relevant. Thus, the closeness effect under other-better, high-relevance conditions should be less positive than under self-better, high-relevance conditions. Figure 3 illustrates these closeness effects as deviations from the overall difference in pleasantness to the friend and stranger. As can be seen, the difference in these effects is in the predicted direction and is significant, $t(60) = 1.74, p < .04$ (see Footnote 2).

When relevance is low the reflection process is important. So, in absolute terms, there should be more pleasantness associated with a friend than with a stranger when the other performs better. Although this absolute difference is in the appropriate direction, it could be due to the general dif-

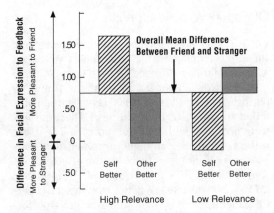

FIGURE 3 ■ Study 2: Difference in pleasantness of facial expression to close (friend) and distant (stranger) other as a combined function of performance feedback (self better vs. other better) and relevance of task to subjects' self-definition.

ference in facial pleasantness alluded to earlier. So, again, we pursue our strategy of relative comparisons. On a low-relevance dimension, if the self outperforms the other then one cannot bask in the other's good performance. Thus, the closeness effect under other-better, low-relevance conditions should be more positive than the closeness effect under self-better, low-relevance conditions. As shown in Figure 3, this difference is in the predicted direction although not significant, $t(60) = 1.30$, $p < .10$.

The comparison of closeness effects between other-better, high-relevance conditions and self-better, high-relevance conditions is actually the simple Closeness × Performance interaction at high relevance. The comparison of closeness effects between other better, low relevance and self better, low relevance is actually the simple Closeness × Performance interaction at low relevance. These simple interactions go in opposite directions as predicted. Thus, an overall test of the entire set of relative predictions is the Closeness × Performance × Relevance interaction. As reported earlier, this source of variation was clearly significant.

Still focusing on Figure 3, another set of comparisons is possible. Earlier we compared closeness effects as a function of performance while holding relevance constant. The model also has something to say about the effects of relevance while holding performance constant. It suggests that the other-better, high-relevance condition should be associated with a smaller closeness ef-

fect than should the other-better, low-relevance condition. That is, in the former condition closeness should increase the loss due to comparison, and in the latter it should increase the gain due to reflection. The relative sizes of the effect are in the expected direction but do not approach significance, $t(60) = 1.14$. When the dimension is high in relevance, there is a potential threat of comparison. If self outperforms other, then threat is avoided. When the dimension is low in relevance, there is a potential gain due to reflection. When self outperforms other, that promise is unfulfilled. Thus, the closeness effect associated with the former condition (threat avoidance) should be more positive than that associated with the latter condition (loss of potential gain). It is, $t(60) = 1.71$, $p < .05$. These predictions, like those made earlier, are also confirmed as a set by the presence of the significant Closeness × Performance × Relevance interaction.[7]

---

[7]Subjects were also asked to indicate on the postexperimental questionnaire how they felt on a 7-point scale (*bad* = 1, *good* = 7) under each of the eight conditions defined by the experiment (e.g., "How did you feel when you were told: That you had performed worse than your friend on the esthetic judgement game"). These ratings were analyzed with the same analysis used for the facial affect ratings. If subjects' self-ratings of moods reflected the mood exhibited in their faces, we would expect a Relevance × Performance × Closeness interaction. This source of variation was not significant ($F < 1$). There were, however, some other effects. The commonsensical expectation that people will feel better when they perform better rather than worse than the other emerged ($Ms = 5.62$ vs. 2.73), $F(1, 32) = 92.72, p < .0001$. Performance and relevance interacted in affecting these self-reports, $F(1, 32) = 6.60$, $p < .02$. When the other performed better, there was more positive self-reported affect when the task was low in relevance ($M = 2.89$) than when the task was high in relevance ($M = 2.56$) $F(1, 64) = 6.73, p < .02$. When the self performed better, there was more positive affect when the task was high in relevance ($M = 5.74$) than when the task was low in relevance ($M = 5.50$), $F(1, 64) = 3.70, p < .06$. Closeness and relevance also interacted, $F(1, 32) = 4.99, p < .04$. When the other was a friend, subjects felt better when the feedback was on a low-relevance task ($M = 4.23$) than when it was on a high-relevance task ($M = 4.08$), $F(1, 64) = 4.17, p < .04$. When the other was a stranger, task relevance made no difference ($F < 1$). It is difficult to know precisely how to interpret these self-reports. They were taken later and are retrospective accounts. The affective changes may have been short-lived, or memory may have been a problem. The subjects were asked about eight different situations and may simply have been confused. It is also possible that the affective changes were too subtle even to register consciously. Perhaps such limitations caused subjects to rely on implicit theories to generate their ratings. Because of these problems and ambiguities, we will have no more to say about these ratings.

Individual Differences

For some subjects, logical ability was more relevant than esthetic judgment. For the remaining subjects the reverse was true. When this between-subjects factor was added to the analysis, the predicted three-factor interaction remained significant, $F(1, 29) = 4.35$, $p < .05$, and was not moderated by which task was most relevant ($F < 1$).

Subjects also responded to three personality measures. Each was split at the median and added in turn as a factor to the basic ANOVA. As in Study 1, scores on the California Psychological Inventory did not change the results. However, self-esteem and manifest anxiety did moderate the results. When self-esteem was added to the analysis, the predicted Relevance × Closeness × Performance interaction remained significant, $F(1, 29) = 6.02$, $p < .03$, but was moderated by self-esteem, $F(1, 29) = 3.87$, $p < .06$. An analysis of simple effects revealed that the three-factor interaction was significant among subjects with low self-esteem, $F (1, 29) = 9.77$, $p < .01$, but not among subjects with high self-esteem ($F < 1$). Similarly, when manifest anxiety was added to the analysis, the overall Relevance × Closeness × Performance interaction remained significant, $F(1, 29) = 6.57$, $p < .02$, but was moderated by anxiety, $F(1, 29) = 3.89$, $p < .06$. The Relevance × Closeness × Performance interaction was significant among high-anxiety subjects, $F(1, 29) = 8.85$, $p < .01$, but not among low-anxiety subjects ($F < 1$). Not surprisingly, self-esteem and anxiety were highly correlated in this sample ($r = -.73$). In sum, the affective responses predicted by the SEM model seem to be more closely associated with persons low in self-esteem and high in anxiety.

Time to Inspect Feedback

The computer kept track of how long subjects inspected the feedback (time elapsed from the onset of the feedback until the subject asked for the next trial). Inspection times were analyzed in the same repeated-measures ANOVA used for the facial affect. Only one effect emerged as significant. Subjects spent more time with the feedback when their performance was superior ($M = 8.73$ s) than when it was inferior ($M = 7.59$ s), $F(1, 32) = 4.63$, $p < .04$.

Questionnaire Responses

The feedback was designed so that subjects were superior and inferior to their friend and the stranger an equal number of times on each task. Subjects rated their own, their friend's, and the stranger's performance on the two tasks. (Four participants failed to complete these ratings.) These ratings were analyzed with a 2 (relevance) × 3 (person: self vs. friend vs. stranger) repeated-measures ANOVA. As in Study 1, there was an effect of person, $F(2, 56) = 5.73$, $p < .01$. Friend's performance ($M = 4.79$) was rated as better than the self's performance ($M = 4.31$) and the stranger's performance ($M = 4.29$). Also as in Study 1, there was an overall relevance effect, $F(1, 29) = 5.08$, $p < .05$.

Again, however, the relevance effect was significant only for the self ($M = 4.59$ vs. 4.03), $F(1, 84) = 10.33$, $p < .01$, and not for the friend ($M = 4.79$ vs. 4.79) or the stranger ($M = 4.34$ vs. 4.24).

Discussion

The facial-expression results from Study 3 are surprising in two respects: the effects that did not emerge and the effects that did emerge. From a commonsense perspective we might have expected to find overall more pleasant affect associated with self's better performance than with other's better performance. More subtly, we might even have expected an interaction with relevance such that the performance difference in pleasantness would be more pronounced when the task was high in self-relevance than when it was low in self-relevance. (Such an effect would also be anticipated by the SEM model.) These intuitively expected effects did not emerge in the facial expressions. If these were the only results, it would be parsimonious to conclude that the rated facial expressions were simply too insensitive to register what may be small differences in affect. However, these were not the only results. Indeed, the facial expressions are capable of registering effects. The facial expressions showed, at least in relative terms, a significant pattern of differences that were consistent with some of the SEM predictions.

Why the predicted Performance × Relevance effect did not emerge on the facial measure is puzzling. It is particularly puzzling in that the more complex three-factor interaction did emerge. However, the three-factor interaction does provide some support for the affect hypotheses derived from the SEM model. The model consists of a system of three interacting variables that are summarized in terms of two processes, a comparison process and a reflection process. So the predictions are complex. When the task is high in relevance and another does better, there is greater potential pain from comparison with a close other than with a distant other. When the task is low in relevance and another does better, there is greater potential gain in self-evaluation via the reflection from a close other than from a distant other. Thus, given a high-relevance task, there should be a reduction in facial pleasantness to the friend (relative to the stranger) as performance changes from self better to other better. Given a low-relevance task, there should be an increase in facial pleasantness to the friend (relative to the stranger) as performance changes from self better to other better. It is precisely this set of relative differences in affect that combined to produce the obtained three-factor interaction. Thus, although there were important predictions that failed to receive support in these data, there were some predictions that were supported.

There is another interpretation of which the reader should be aware. Our theoretical focus has been on the conditions in which the other outperforms the self. The self-better conditions serve as points of comparison. In interpreting the data we have relied on differences between these two sets of means. Variability in these differences is driven by variability in both the other-better and self-better conditions. If there were nothing else going on in the situation we would expect more action in the other-better conditions, but on the contrary, there appears to be more variability in the self-better conditions. Thus, it is possible that the pattern we have interpreted as support for the SEM model is attributable not to the relative impact of comparison and reflection processes but rather they may be ultimately due to non-predicted effects of relevance and closeness on affect under the self-better conditions.

In Study 1 and 2, individual differences did not have any effects. In this study, the three-factor interaction was marginally more pronounced for in-dividuals low rather than high in self-esteem and also more pronounced for those high rather than low in manifest anxiety. Because these two variables are so highly correlated, we do not discuss them separately but rather focus only on the self-esteem aspect of their commonality. We had no prior prediction regarding self-esteem: On the one hand one might expect people with high self-esteem to engage in SEM processes more than those with low self-esteem. Their high self-esteem could be the result of engaging in such processes. On the other hand, a threat to self-evaluation or the promise of a gain in self-evaluation might be more consequential for persons low in self-esteem. Thus, persons low in self-esteem might engage in SEM processes more. Self-esteem has often been measured in this research program, and frequently its effects are minimal. However, on balance, as was the case in this study, persons low in self-esteem tend to engage in SEM processes more than do persons high in self-esteem. (See Tesser & Campbell, 1982a and 1983, for a review and discussion.) Brockner (1983) has also noted that persons low in self-esteem show greater responsiveness (plasticity) to social psychological variables than do persons high in self-esteem. Perhaps in this case the potential changes in self-evaluation have more impact for those with low rather than high self-esteem, and that impact shows itself in facial expressions. [8]

Questionnaire responses regarding performance in this study were similar to those in Study 1. Personal relevance affected judgments of own performance but not judgments of other's performance. Friend's performance was rated as better than own or stranger's performance. Both of these effects represent distortions of the feedback. The relevance effect seems understandable. Subjects may simply wish to see themselves as performing better on the dimension that is more relevant to their self-definition, and the wish is the sire of the perception. Or subjects may generally perform better on tasks more relevant to the self than on tasks less relevant to the self, and the ratings may

---

[8]Because the personality instruments were given after the experimental manipulations, one might argue that the manipulations affected the personality responses rather than vice versa. This does not seem likely to us because all the manipulations were within-subjects, and hence all the subjects were exposed to identical conditions.

simply be a generalization of that state of affairs. Why friends are rated as performing best is puzzling. Perhaps this represents an attempt at a modest self-presentation; perhaps it represents a generalization of attempts to maintain smooth interactions (Brickman & Bulman, 1977); or perhaps it represents a feminine tendency to avoid competition (e.g., Bond & Vinacke, 1961; Gilligan, 1982).

General Discussion

We have suggested that much social behavior can be understood as the result of two antagonistic processes: A comparison process and a reflection process. We have also suggested that the motive underlying these processes is the maintenance of a positive self-evaluation. Finally, we argued that threats and promises to self-evaluation should result in changes of affect. Thus, tracking affect could help evaluate the tenability of the model. This was the goal of our research.

The results of the three studies are encouraging. When another outperforms the self compared with when the self outperforms the other, the closer the other, the greater the threat if the task is high in relevance (comparison process) and the greater the promise if the task is low in relevance (reflection process). Study 1 showed that conditions presumed to lead to increased threat or increased promise seemed to be associated with greater arousal (speeded-up performance of simple tasks and slowed-down performance of complex tasks).

Interpreting the low-relevance results of Study 1 was difficult. The SEM model suggests that the better performance of a close other produces arousal because of the positivity of reflection. A social comparison perspective suggests that the better performance of a close other generates threat (negative affect and arousal) even on low-relevance tasks. In Study 2, closeness and relative performance on a low-relevance task were manipulated. Results favored the SEM model. An indirect measure of affect revealed the most positivity and least negativity when the self was outperformed by a close other on a low-relevance task.

In Study 3 we used a different measure of directional changes in affect and pleasantness of facial expression, and we explored these changes in both high-and low-relevance circumstances. When the task was high in relevance, pleasantness of affect associated with the close other (relative to the distant other) decreased as performance changed from self better to other better. On the other hand, when the task was low in relevance, pleasantness of affect associated with the close other (relative to the distant other) increased an performance changed from self better to other better. These results offer partial support for the SEM model and suggest that the closeness of others increases the pain of comparison and the pleasure of reflection.

ACKNOWLEGMENTS

We are grateful for support provided by National Institute of Mental Health Grant 1RO1MH41487–01. We gratefully acknowledge the helpful comments of Jennifer Campbell, Norbert Kerr, Peter Salovey, Thomas Wills, and three anonymous reviewers. A preliminary report of Studies 1 and 3 is presented in Tesser (in press).

REFERENCES

Abelson, R. P. (1983). Whatever became of consistency theory? *Personality and Social Psychology Bulletin, 9,* 37–54.

Barden, R. C., Garber, J., Duncan, S. W., & Masters, J. C. (1981). Cumulative effects of induced affective states in children: Accentuation, inoculation, and remediation. *Journal of Personality and Social Psychology, 40.* 750–760.

Batson, C. D., Duncan, B. D., Ackerman, P., Buckley, T., & Birch, K. (1981). Is empathic emotion a source of altruistic motivation? *Journal of Personality and Social Psychology, 40,* 290–302.

Berscheid, E. (1983). Emotion. In H. H. Kelley, E. Berscheid, A. Christensen, J. H. Harvey, T. L. Huston, G. Levinger, E. McClintock, L. A. Peplau, & D. R. Peterson (Eds.), *Close relationships* (pp. 110–168). New York: Freeman.

Bond, J. R., & Vinacke, W. E. (1961). Coalitions in mixed-sex triads. *Sociometry, 24,* 61–75.

Brenner, M. (1973). The next-in-line effect. *Journal of Verbal Learning and Verbal Behavior, 12,* 320–323.

Brickman, P., & Bulman, R. J. (1977). Pleasure and pain in social comparison. In J. Suls & R. L. Miller (Eds.), *Social comparison processes: Theoretical and empirical perceptions* (pp. 149–186). Washington, DC: Hemisphere.

Brockner, J. (1983). Low self-esteem and behavioral plasticity: Some implications. In L. Wheeler & P. Shaver (Eds.), *Review of personality and social psychology* (Vol. 4, pp. 237–271). Beverly Hills, CA: Sage.

Cialdini, R. B., Borden, R. J., Thorne, A., Walker, M. R., Freeman, S., & Sloan, L. R. (1976). Basking in reflected glory: Three (football) field studies. *Journal of Personality and Social Psychology, 34,* 366–375.

Cialdini, B., & Kenrick, D. T. (1976). Altruism as hedonism: A social development perspective on the relationship of negative mood state and helping. *Journal of Personality and Social Psychology, 34,* 907–914.

Clark, M. S., & Isen, A. M. (1982). Toward understanding the relationship between feeling states and social behavior. In A. Hastorf & A. M. Isen (Eds.), *Cognitive social psychology* (pp. 73–108). New York: Elsevier North-Holland.

Clark, M. S., Milberg, S., & Ross, J. (1983). Arousal cues arousal-related material in memory: Implications for understanding effects of mood on memory. *Journal of Verbal Learning and Verbal Behavior, 22,* 633–649.

Ekman, P., & Oster, H. (1979). Facial expressions of emotions. *Annual Review of Psychology, 30,* 527–554.

Festinger, L. (1954). A theory of social comparison processes. *Human Relations, 7.* 117–140.

Fiske, S. T. (1982). Schema triggered affect: Applications to social perception. In M. S. Clark & S. T. Fiske (Eds.), *Affect and cognition: The 17th Annual Carnegie Symposium on Cognition* (pp. 55–78). Hillsdale, NJ: Erlbaum.

Geen, R. G., & Quanty, M. B. (1977). The catharsis of aggression: An evaluation of a hypothesis. In L. Berkowitz (Eds), *Advances in experimental social psychology* (Vol. 10, pp. 2–23). New York: Academic Press.

Gilligan, C. (1982). *In a different voice.* Cambridge: Harvard University Press.

Goethals, G. R. (1984, August). *Social comparison theory: Psychology from the lost and found.* Paper presented at the annual convention of the American Psychological Association, Toronto.

Gottman, J. M., & Levenson, R. W. (1984). Why marriages fail: Affective and physiological patterns in marital interaction. In J. C. Masters & K. Yarkin-Levin (Eds.), *Boundary areas in social and developmental psychology* (pp. 67–106). New York: Academic Press.

Gough, H. G. (1964). *Manual for the California Psychological Inventory.* Palo Alto, CA: Consulting Psychologists Press.

Hare, R. D. (1978). Electrodermal and cardiovascular correlates of psychopathy. In R. E. Hare & D. Schalling (Eds.), *Psychopathic behavior: Approaches to research* (pp. 126–139). London: Wiley.

Heider, F. (1958). The psychology of interpersonal relations. New York: Wiley.

Isen, A. M., & Levin, P. F. (1972). The effect of feeling good on helping: Cookies and kindness. *Journal of Personality and Social Psychology, 21,* 384–388.

Isen, A. M., & Shalker, T. E. (1977). *Do you "accentuate the positive, eliminate the negative" when you are in a good mood?* Unpublished manuscript, University of Maryland, Baltimore County, Catonsville.

Mandler, G. (1975). *Mind and emotion.* New York: Wiley.

Nadler, A., Fisher, J. D., & Ben-Itzhak, S. (1983). With a little help from a friend: Effect of single or multiple act aid as a function of domain and task characteristic. *Journal of Personality and Social Psychology, 44,* 310–321.

Piliavin, J. A., Dovidio, J. F., Gaertner, S. L., & Clark, R. D. (1982). Responsive bystanders: The Process of intervention. In V. J. Derlega & J. Grzelak (Eds.), *Cooperation and helping behavior* (pp. 281–304). New York: Academic Press.

Pleban, R., & Tesser, A. (1981). The effects of relevance and quality of another's performance on interpersonal closeness. *Social Psychology Quarterly, 44,* 278–285.

Rosenberg, M. (1965). *Society and the adolescent self-image.* Princeton, NJ: Princeton University Press.

Roseman, I. (1984). Cognitive determinants of emotion: A

structural theory. In P. Shaver (Ed.), *Review of Personality and Social Psychology* (Vol. 5, pp. 11–36). Beverly Hills, CA: Sage.

Russell, J. A. (1980). A circumplex model of affect. *Journal of Personality and Social Psychology. 39,* 1161–1178.

Salovey, P., & Rodin, J. (1984). Some antecedents and consequences of social-comparison jealousy. *Journal of Personality and Social Psychology, 47,* 780–792.

Schacter, S. (1964). The interaction of cognitive and physiological determinants of emotional state. In L. Berkowitz (Ed.), *Advances in experimental social psychology* (Vol. 1, pp. 49–79). New York: Academic Press.

Spence, K. W. (1956). *Behavior theory and conditioning.* New Haven, CT: Yale University Press.

Spence, K. W., Farber, I. E., & McFann, H. H. (1956). The relation of anxiety (drive) level to performance in competitional and noncompetitional paired-associates learning. *Journal of Experimental Psychology, 52,* 296–305.

Suls, J. M., & Miller, R. L. (Eds.). (1977). *Social comparison processes: Theoretical and empirical perspectives.* Washington, DC: Hemisphere.

Taylor, J. A. (1953). A personality scale of manifest anxiety. *Journal of Abnormal and Social Psychology, 48,* 285–290.

Tesser, A. (1986). Some effects of self-evaluation maintenance on cognition and action. In R. M. Sorrentino & E. T. Higgins (Eds.), *The handbook of motivation and cognition: Foundations of social behavior* (pp. 435–464). New York: Guilford Press.

Tesser, A. (in press). Toward a self-evaluation maintenance model of social behavior. In L. Berkowitz (Ed.), *Advances in experimental social psychology* (Vol. 20). New York: Academic Press.

Tesser, A., & Campbell, J. (1980). Self-definition: The impact of the relative performance and similarity of others. *Social Psychology Quarterly, 43,* 341–347.

Tesser, A., & Campbell, J. (1982a, August). *Self-evaluation maintenance processes and individual differences in self-esteem.* Paper presented at the annual convention of the American Psychological Association, Washington, DC.

Tesser, A., & Campbell, J. (1982b). Self-evaluation maintenance and the perception of friends and strangers. *Journal of Personality, 50,* 261–279.

Tesser, A., & Campbell, J. (1983). Self-definition and self-evaluation maintenance. In J. Suls & A. Greenwald (Eds.), *Social psychological perspectives on the self* (Vol. 2, pp. 1–31).

Tesser, A., & Smith, J. (1980). Some effects of friendship and task relevance on helping: You don't always help the one you like. *Journal of Experimental Social Psychology, 16,* 583–590.

Waid, W. W., & Orne, M. T. (1982). Reduced electrodermal response to conflict, failure to inhibit dominant behaviors, and delinquency proneness. *Journal of Personality and Social Psychology, 43,* 769–774.

Winer, B. J. (1962). *Statistical principles in experimental design.* New York: McGraw-Hill.

Zajonc, R. B. (1965). Social facilitation, *Science, 149,* 269–274.

Zajonc, R. B. (1980). Feeling and thinking: Preferences need no inferences. *American Psychologists, 35,* 151–176.

Zillman, D. (1978). Attribution and misattribution of excitatory reactions. In J. H. Harvey, W. Ickes, & R. E. Kidd (Eds.), *New directions in attribution research* (Vol. 2, pp. 335–368). New York: Wiley.

Zuckerman, M., Klorman, R., Larrance, D. T., & Spiegel, N. H. (1981). Facial, autonomic, and subjective components of emotion: The facial feedback hypothesis vs. the externalizer-internalizer distinction. *Journal of Personality and Social Psychology, 41,* 929–944.

Affect- and Cognition-Based Trust as Foundations for Interpersonal Cooperation in Organizations

Daniel J. McAllister • Georgetown University

This study addressed the nature and functioning of relationships of interpersonal trust among managers and professionals in organizations, the factors influencing trust's development, and the implications of trust for behavior and performance. Theoretical foundations were drawn from the sociological literature on trust and the social-psychological literature on trust in close relationships. An initial test of the proposed theoretical framework was conducted in a field setting with 194 managers and professionals.

Trust . . . tends to be somewhat like a combination of the weather and motherhood; it is widely talked about, and it is widely assumed to be good for organizations. When it comes to specifying just what it means in an organizational context, however, vagueness creeps in.

—Porter, Lawler, & Hackman, 1975: 497

Recent developments in the organizational sciences reflect the importance of interpersonal trust relationships for sustaining individual and organizational effectiveness. Researchers have recognized trust's influence on coordination and control at both institutional (Shapiro, 1987, 1990; Zucker, 1986) and interpersonal levels of organization (Granovetter, 1985; Pennings & Woiceshyn, 1987). Because economic action is embedded within networks of social relationships (Bradach & Eccles, 1989; Fichman & Levinthal, 1991; Granovetter, 1985; Larson, 1992), researchers have argued that efficiency within complex systems of coordinated action is only possible when interdependent actors work together effectively. Trust between such actors is seen as a determining factor (Pennings & Woiceshyn, 1987; Seabright, Leventhal, & Fichman, 1992).

For managers and professionals in organizations, developing and maintaining trust relationships is especially important. As boundary spanners, managers work through critical horizontal ties to external constituencies on which their departments or organizations depend (Mintzberg, 1973; Sayles, 1979). Given the complexity and uncertainty inherent in managerial work and the amount of mutual accommodation it involves, effective horizontal working relationships within organizations are also critical (Gabarro, 1990; Sayles, 1979). As Thompson (1967) observed, under conditions of uncertainty and complexity, requiring mutual adjustment, sustained effective coordinated action is only possible where there is mutual confidence or trust.

Although trust's importance has been acknowledged, the matter of how it develops and functions has received little systematic theoretical attention The present work develops and tests a theoretical model based on the sociological literature on trust (Barber, 1983; Lewis & Wiegert, 1985; Luhman,

327

1979; Shapiro, 1990; Zucker, 1986) and social-psychological work on trust close relationships (Johnson-George & Swap, 1982; Rempel, Holmes, & Zanna, 1985). The present research was designed to contribute to understanding of the nature and functioning of interpersonal trust relationships by (1) distinguishing between two principal forms of interpersonal trust—cognition-based trust, grounded in individual beliefs about peer reliability and dependability, and affect-based trust, grounded in reciprocated interpersonal care and concern—(2) identifying factors influencing the development of each form of trust, and (3) examining the implications of each trust form for coordination-relevant behavior, including monitoring to control peers, defensive behavior, monitoring to assist peers, and interpersonal citizenship behavior.

Theoretical Foundations

Interpersonal trust is a pervasive phenomenon in organizational life. Trust enables people to take risks: "where there is trust there is the feeling that others will not take advantage of me" (Porter et al., 1975: 497). Trust is based on the expectation that one will find what is expected rather than what is feared (Deutsch, 1973). Thus, competence and responsibility as central to understandings of trust (Barber, 1983; Cook & Wall, 1980; Shapiro 1990). At times an individual's trust in others is centered more on how they make decisions that affect him or her than on how they behave: "Do they consider my interests and welfare?" Finally, trust encompasses not only people's beliefs about others, but also their willingness to use that knowledge as the basis for action (Luhmann, 1979). Combining these ideas yield a definition of interpersonal trust as the extent to which a person is confident in, and willing to act on the basis of, the words, actions, and decisions of another.

Principal Forms of Interpersonal Trust: Affect- and Cognition-Based Trust

Interpersonal trust has cognitive and affective foundations (Lewis & Wiegert, 1985). Trust is cognition-based in that "we choose whom we will trust in which respects and under what circumstances, and we base the choice on what we take to be 'good reasons,' constituting evidence of trustworthiness" (Lewis & Wiegert, 1985: 970). The amount of

knowledge necessary for trust is somewhere between total knowledge and total ignorance (Simmel, 1964). Given total knowledge, there is no need to trust, and given total ignorance, there is no basis upon which to rationally trust. Available knowledge and "good reasons" serve as foundations for trust decisions, the platform from which people make leaps of faith, like those involved in trusting (Luhmann, 1979; Simmel, 1964).

Past measures of trust in organizational settings suggest that competence and responsibility are central elements (Butler, 1991; Cook & Wall, 1980). Reliability and dependability have also been included in measures of interpersonal trust in close relations (Johnson-George & Swap, 1982; Rempel et al., 1985). Reliability and dependability expectations must usually be met for trust relationships to exist and develop (Zucker, 1986) and evidence to the contrary provides a rational basis for withholding trust (Luhmann, 1979; Shapiro, 1987, 1990).

Affective foundations for trust also exist, consisting of the emotional bonds between individuals (Lewis & Wiegert, 1985). People make emotional investments in trust relationships, express genuine care and concern for the welfare of partners, believe in the intrinsic virtue of such relationships, and believe that these sentiments are reciprocated (Pennings & Woiceshyn, 1987; Rempel et al., 1985). Ultimately, the emotional ties linking individuals can provide the basis for trust.

Empirical evidence from the social-psychological literature on trust in close relationships supports this distinction between the two forms of trust. Johnson-George and Swap (1982) identified, distinguished between, and reliably measured two dimensions of trust they labeled "reliableness" and "emotional trust." Similarly, Rempel and colleagues (1985) distinguished between "dependability" and "faith" (emotional security) as unique forms of trust. Organizations abound with relationships based on dependability and faith (Pennings & Woiceshyn, 1987) in which moderate expressions of interpersonal care and concern are not uncommon (Granovetter, 1985; Griesinger, 1990; Pennings & Woiceshyn, 1987). Drawing on this theoretical distinction between forms of interpersonal trust, I hypothesized that

Hypothesis 1: Relationships of interpersonal trust among managers in organizations are characterized by two dimensions—cognition-based trust and affect-based trust.

Figure 1 outlines the theoretical framework developed in the following discussion. The sequence of relationships is from peer attributes and behavior, through focal manager assessments of peer trustworthiness, to focal manager behavioral responses, and ultimately to focal manager and peer performance alike.

Factors Influencing Managerial Trust Relationships

Antecedents of cognition-based trust. In organizations, the extent to which a manager will be willing to vest cognition-based trust in peers may depend on the success of past interaction, the extent of social similarity, and organizational context considerations (Zucker, 1986). First, because working relationships are typically personal and extend over time, it is possible for people to consider the track record of peers, or how they have carried out role-related duties in the past, when assessing trustworthiness (Cook & Wall, 1980; Granovetter, 1985). Evidence that a peer's behavior is consistent with norms of reciprocity and fairness and that the peer follows through on commitments is vital (Lindskold, 1978; Stack, 1988). In working relationships involving high interdependence, peer performance can have a determining impact on personal productivity, and evidence that peers carry out role responsibilities reliably will enhance a manager's assessments of a peer's trustworthiness. Accordingly,

> Hypothesis 2a: The level of a manager's cognition-based trust in a peer will be positively associated with the extent of that peer's reliable role performance.

Second, social similarity between individuals can influence trust development. Groups of individuals with similar fundamental characteristics, such as ethnic background, may have an advantage over diverse groups in their ability to create and maintain trusting working relationships. Light (1984) documented the tendency of ethnic minority entrepreneurs to conduct business through co-ethnic rather than interethnic social circles. More fundamentally, self-categorization theorists have observed that individuals tend to group themselves with others on the basis of objective attributes such as race, age, and gender (Turner, 1987) and that such internal classifications influence beliefs and attitudes. Individuals are more likely to perceive outgroup members as dishonest, untrustworthy,

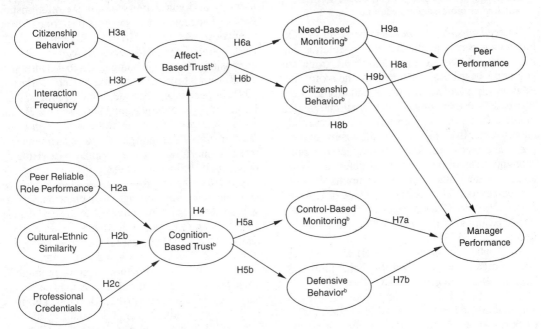

a Direction of relationship is from peer to manager.
b Direction of relationship is from manager to peer.

FIGURE 1 ■ Theoretical model outlining the role of trust in interpersonal relationships in organizations.

and uncooperative than they are to so perceive in-group members (Brewer, 1979). Notwithstanding the potential beliefs of diversity for organizations, which include enhanced creativity, access to a broader set of environmental resources, and more, the possibility that cultural similarity facilitates the creation and maintenance of trust in organizations merits recognition. Accordingly,

> Hypothesis 2b: The level of a manager's cognition-based trust in a peer will be greater when the two are culturally or ethnically similar.

Third, formal organizations, through formal role specifications, specify boundaries for trust relationships (Baier, 1985; Fox, 1974) and professional credentials serve as clear signals of role preparedness. Educational institutions, professional associations, and credentialing agencies manufacture trust by providing guarantees to would-be trusters through certification that individuals meet standards for acceptability in a larger professional community (Zucker, 1986). Professional standing can be maintained over time through continued membership and participation in relevant professional associations. Thus,

> Hypothesis 2c: The level of a manager's cognition-based trust in a peer will be greater for peers with higher professional credentials.

Antecedents of affect-based trust. Although external factors making the behavior of relationship partners predictable provide foundations for cognition-based trust, insights into the motives of relationship partners provide foundations for affect-based trust. Findings from attribution research indicate that behavior recognized as personally chosen rather than role-prescribed, serving to meet legitimate needs, and demonstrating interpersonal care and concern rather than enlightened self-interest may be critical for the development of affect-based trust (Clark & Mills, 1979; Clark, Mills, & Powell, 1986; Clark & Waddell, 1985; Holmes, 1978; Holmes & Rempel, 1989; Kelly, 1979; Rempel et al., 1985).

Such behavior corresponds well with descriptions of organizational citizenship behavior (OCB; Organ, 1988; Smith, Organ, & Near, 1983). Organ defined OCB as behavior intended to provide help and assistance that is outside an individual's work role, not directly rewarded, and conductive to effective organizational functioning. Smith, Organ, and Near defined altruism, a specific form

of OCB, as behavior "directly and intentionally aimed at helping a specific person in face-to-face situations" (1983: 657). Altruistic behavior may provide an attributional basis for affect-based trust. Being extra-role, it can be viewed as being personally chosen, and not being directly rewarded, it cannot easily be attributed to enlightened self-interest (MacKenzie, Podsakoff, & Fetter, 1991). Accordingly,

> Hypothesis 3a: The level of a manager's affect-based trust in a peer will be positively associated with the level of that peer's citizenship behavior directed toward the manager.

Because affect-based trust is grounded in an individual's attributions concerning the motives for others' behavior, it should be limited to contexts of frequent interaction, where there are sufficient social data to allow the making of confident attributions (Lewis & Wiegert, 1985). Thus,

> Hypothesis 3b: The level of a manager's affect-based trust in a peer will be positively associated with the frequency of interaction between the manager and the peer.

The relationship between cognition- and affect-based trust. Although much of the research on affectivity in organizations and on the relationship between affect and cognition has focused on unanchored mood states (Brief & George, 1992; Burke, Brief, George, Roberson, & Webster, 1989), increasing attention is being given to the interpersonal foundations of affectivity (Isen & Baron, 1991; Longenecker, Jaccoud, Sims, & Gioia, 1992; Park, Sims, & Motowidlo, 1986; Tsui & Barry, 1986). Research on affect and cognition in close relationships has highlighted the development of interpersonal affect upon a cognitive base (Holmes & Rempel, 1989; Rempel et al., 1985). Cognition-based trust, or reliableness, is seen as "more superficial and less special" than emotional trustworthiness (Johnson-George & Swap, 1982: 1316). Faith (Rempel et al., 1985: 98) is characterized by a greater investment of time and emotion than are dependability and reliability.

For working relationships among managers, some level of cognition-based trust may be necessary for affect-based trust to develop; people's base-line expectations for peer reliability and dependability must be met before they will invest further in relationships. Where baseline expectations are not yet established, individuals may be inclined to attribute extra-role conduct to ingratiation and impression management rather than to care and concern. Once an individual has established a track record for reliability and dependability, and thus some level of cognition-based trust exists, confident attributions concerning the motivations for that person's citizenship behavior may follow. Accordingly,

> Hypothesis 4: A manager expressing high levels of cognition-based trust in a peer will also report high affect-based trust in that peer.

Two comments qualify this developmental perspective on the relationship between affect- and cognition-based trust. First, given the distinctive antecedents and consequences posited, affect-based trust should be viewed as a distinct form of interpersonal trust rather than as a higher level of trust. Second, as affect-based trust matures, the potential for the decoupling of trust forms and for reverse causation (affect-based trust influencing cognition-based trust) increases. Zajonc observed that "once formed, an evaluation is not easily revoked . . . Affect often persists after a complete invalidation of its original cognitive basis" (1980: 157). Holmes and Rempel (1989) observed that as affect-based trust develops, key attributions, such as "This colleague genuinely cares about me," become incorporated into a stable and global picture of a partner's motives. In time, ascribed motives are taken as permanent and left unquestioned, even in the face of disconfirming evidence. Transgressions are discounted in advance or explained away. Thus, once a high level of affect-based trust has developed, a foundation of cognition-based trust may no longer be needed.

Consequences of Managerial Beliefs About Peer Trustworthiness

Control-based monitoring and defensive behavior. Where one person, interdependent with another, cannot count on that individual to be dependable and reliable, he or she can take steps to manage the uncertainty inherent in the situation. Monitoring to control the untrustworthy individual is one likely response (Bradach & Eccles, 1989; Pennings & Woiceshyn, 1987; Williamson, 1974). As Ouchi observed, "People must either be able to trust each other or to closely monitor each other if they are to engage in cooperative enterprises" (1979: 846).

Besides assuring some minimal level of peer performance, managers must perform their own duties with little disturbance, buffer themselves from the influence of others, and protect their personal interests (Ashforth & Lee, 1990). Individuals behave defensively, for example, when they make requests for assistance well ahead of the time they are needed, draw upon multiple and redundant sources when making requests for the assistance, expend extra resources working around and avoiding others, and use official and formal (rather than informal) means to document requests (Ashforth & Lee, 1990). Two hypotheses follow:

> Hypothesis 5a: A manager expressing a high level of cognition-based trust in a peer will engage in little control-based monitoring of that peer.

> Hypothesis 5b: A manager expressing a high level of cognition-based trust in a peer will direct little defensive behavior toward that peer.

Within this theoretical framework, control-based monitoring and defensive behavior are behavioral consequences of cognition-based trust alone. In practical terms, for affect-based trust to develop, some level of cognition-based trust must already exist, and it can be expected that where cognition-based trust is present, levels of monitoring and defensive behavior will be low. Likely consequences of affect-based trust are outlined below.

Need-based monitoring and interpersonal citizenship behavior. Relationships characterized by affect-based trust resemble so-called communal relationships (Clark, Mills, & Corcoran, 1989; Clark, Mills, & Powell, 1986). Research findings show that individuals in communal relationships are more inclined to keep track of associates' needs than are individuals in exchange relationships. What drives need-based monitoring is not the desire to generate future obligations or to reciprocate benefits received, but rather an understanding of the communal nature of the relationship: "In a communal relationship, the idea that a benefit is given in response to a benefit that was received is compromising, because it calls into question the assumption that each member responds to the needs of the other" (Clark & Mills, 1979; 13). In communal relationships, partners appear less inclined to keep track of personal inputs on joint tasks (Clark, 1984) and to feel exploited by unrequited helping (Clark & Waddell, 1985). They take on their partners' problems as their own, develop a tacit awareness of partners' needs, and learn how to respond appropriately (Holmes & Rempel, 1989). Similarly, in affect-based-trust relationships, sensitivity to the personal and work-related needs of associates should be high. Accordingly,

> Hypothesis 6a: A manager expressing a high level of affect-based trust in a peer will engage in a great amount of need-based monitoring of that peer.

Individuals expressing high affect-based trust in peers may also direct a great amount of interpersonal citizenship behavior toward them. Increased assistance may follow naturally either from an increased awareness of peer needs (the product of need-based monitoring) or from a desire to assist peers in meeting their personal objectives and to express felt care and concern tangibly. Although Organ and Konovsky asserted that "characteristic OCB has a deliberate, controlled character, somewhat akin to conscious decision making rather than expressive emotional behavior" (1989: 162), I argue that when a great amount of citizenship behavior is directed toward a focal individual, the behavior has expressive, noncalculated qualities. Accordingly,

> Hypothesis 6b: A manager expressing a high level of affect-based trust in a peer will direct a great amount of interpersonal citizenship behavior toward that peer.

It is important to note that no direct relationship between a peer's interpersonal citizenship behavior and a manager's citizenship behavior is posited. Observation of a direct relationship would demonstrate the influence of reciprocity and exchange norms (Holmes, 1978; Holmes & Rempel, 1989). Within the proposed framework, peer conduct (citizenship directed toward a focal manager) influences the focal manager's affect-based-trust perceptions through its expressive qualities. Those perceptions in turn influence the manager's citizenship behavior toward the peer. The latter's citizenship behavior becomes an expressive act rather than an obligation-discharging and equilibrium-restoring act of reciprocation.

Performance Implications of Cognition- and Affect-Based Trust

Apart from a general assumption of the efficacy of trust relations as a lubricant to the social system, facilitating coordinated action (Arrow, 1974; Ouchi, 1979; Williamson, 1974), existing research contains little on how trust effects performance outcomes. The behavioral consequences of trust may provide one line of explanation. Managerial and professional work involves mutual adjustment and accommodation within a multiple constituency context (Sayles, 1979; Tsui, 1984). Trusting peers should receive enhanced performance assessments to the extent that the behavioral consequences of trust further organizational ends. If trust helps to further organizational ends, it should be associated with supervisor assessments of the performance of trusting and trusted individuals.

Performance implications of defensive behavior and control-based monitoring. In general, monitoring and defensive behavior represent nonproductive uses of finite managerial resources. Allocating work energies to pursuits like monitoring (Alchian & Demset, 1972; Baker, Jensen, & Murphy, 1988) and defensive behavior (Ashforth & Lee, 1990; Kahn, Wolfe, Quinn, & Snoek, 1964) involves a trade-off: Managers engaging in excessive monitoring and defensive behavior will have fewer resources remaining with which to accomplish fundamental work objectives. Accordingly,

> Hypothesis 7a: The level of a manager's control-based monitoring of peer will be negatively associated with supervisor assessments of the manager's performance.

> Hypothesis 7b: The level of a manager's defensive behavior toward a peer will be negatively associated with supervisor assessments of the manager's performance.

Performance implications of need-based monitoring and citizenship behavior. Organizations depend on the discretionary contributions of their members to maintain efficiency and coordination; one has only to witness the disruption that occurs when employees limit their contributions exclusively to what is specified in their job descriptions to realize that this is the case (Katz, 1964). Organizations must also depend on employees to use their skills and energies wisely so that contributions are maximized—organizations need employees who work not only harder but smarter. An essential ingredient in working smarter is undoubtedly paying attention and looking for opportunities to make constructive contributions.

Thus, need-based monitoring and citizenship behavior by focal managers may enhance assessments of their contributions, especially assessments provided by supervisors and others whose interests are aligned with those of the organization. Two hypotheses follow:

Hypothesis 8a: The level of a manager's need-based monitoring of a peer will be positively associated with supervisor assessments of the manager's performance.

Hypothesis 8b: The level of a manager's interpersonal citizenship behavior directed toward a peer will be positively associated with supervisor assessments of the manager's performance.

Performance enhancement is likely to be a principal motivator for need-based monitoring. Need-based monitoring arises when individuals feel responsible for the needs of others and wish to respond to those needs (Clark et al., 1989). Pearce and Gregerson argued that "felt responsibility is a psychological state that may play an important role in numerous aspects of job performance and deserves further research attention" (1991: 843). Indeed, need-based monitoring and assistance behavior that addresses work-related needs should enhance peer performance. Two hypotheses complete the theoretical framework:

Hypothesis 9a: The level of a manager's need-based monitoring of a peer will be positively associated with supervisor assessments of the peer's performance.

Hypothesis 9b: The level of a manager's interpersonal citizenship behavior directed toward a peer will be positively associated with supervisor assessments of the peer's performance.

Methods

Respondents

A sample of 194 managers and professionals, including men and women from various industries, reported on cross-functional dyadic relationships with peers at work. Individuals enrolled in, and alumni of, the executive master's of business administration (EMBA) program of a major university in Southern California were requested to participate and to nominate peers from work to participate with them. In examining relations among middle and upper-level managers, I focused on relations of lateral interdependence (Sayles, 1979), where the impact of trust's presence or absence was expected to be pronounced (Thompson, 1967).

Each EMBA affiliate agreeing to participate nominated-two peers, so triads were formed. Triad members separately completed surveys describing various aspects of their working relationships with one another. Respondents provided two forms of data: (1) information concerning one triad member from the perspective of a focal manager, and (2) information concerning the second triad member from the perspective of a peer. Data collected from respondents were combined to form manager-peer dyad records. Of the 197 individuals initially contacted, 80 agreed to participate, a 41 percent acceptance rate. Given the level of commitment involved (questionnaire response, as well as nominating peers), this response rate is well within accepted limits. The nominated peers were not associated with the EMBA program, and the response rate at the second stage of the study was 81 percent (194 of 240 EMBA students, alumni, and nominated peers). From the data collected, I constructed 175 complete manager-peer dyad records, which formed the basis for the present research. The initial contacts also identified one person, in most cases a superior, familiar with the performance of all triad members to provide performance information; the superior's response rate was 86 percent.

The respondents were, for the better part, mature (an average age of 38 years), well-educated (57 percent with some graduate training, 28 percent with undergraduate degrees) individuals with considerable organizational experience (an average professional tenure of 11.7 years). The profile of respondents by age and gender corresponds well with that of the population of EMBA students and alumni (average age 37 years, 74.8 percent men). Although further information on the population from which respondents the drawn was not available, it appeared likely that they were representative of the population.

Procedures

Initial contacts agreeing to participate in this study were directed to think of peers (not supervisors or subordinates), from functional areas different from their own, with whom they had significant work-related interaction. After a contact identified three to five people with whom he or she worked the best" and three to five with whom he or she "worked less well," the individual selected one person from each list to participate in the study with him or her. The working relationships examined were task-oriented, not limited to close friendships, and varied along the critical dimensions of trust. By stipulating that the people chosen should interact with one another at work, I ensured the existence of three separate dyads in each organization.[1] I used a randomization procedure to assign individuals to focal manager–peer dyads and to allocate reporting roles within dyads. The statistical independence of observations was maintained by having no respondents provide information from the perspective of one role (focal manager or peer) for more than one dyad.[2]

Measures

Except for the performance data provided by superiors, dyad members provided all data for this study. Given the dyad-specific nature of the information involved, I considered these sources most authoritative. Focal managers reported on peer trustworthiness and behavioral responses to peers (control-based monitoring, defensive behavior, need-based monitoring, and citizenship behavior). Peers provided exogenous data (interaction frequency, citizenship behavior, reliable role performance, educational attainment, and ethnic background).

Affect- and cognition-based trust. A new measure to assess affect- and cognition-based trust levels was developed for use in this study. The measure consists of 11 items, 6 assessing levels of cognition-based trust, and 5 assessing affect-based trust; respondents indicated, on a scale ranging from 1 (strongly disagree) to 7 (strongly agree), their agreement with various statements about a specific peer at work.

Drawing on a review of the literature and on available measures of interpersonal trust (Cook & Wall, 1980; Johnson-George & Swap, 1982; Rempel et al., 1985; Rotter, 1971), I created an initial pool of 48 items. Eleven organizational behavior scholars, provided with definitions of affect- and cognition-based trust, classified these items as tapping cognition-based trust, affect-based trust, both forms of trust, or neither form of trust. Based on an analysis of expert evaluations, I created a subset of 20 unambiguous items, 10 items for each form of trust. I used results of an exploratory factor analysis of pretest data from a group of employed M.B.A. and undergraduate business students to further reduce the measure to the 11

strongest-loading items. Table 1 gives the wording and confirmatory analysis results for this trust measure and for the behavioral response measures, which are discussed in the next section. Reliability estimates (Cronbach's alphas) for the cognition- and affect-based trust measures are .91 and .89, respectively.

Behavioral response measures. The questionnaire contained 25 items designed to measure behavioral responses associated with trusting or distrusting peers. Respondents reported the extent to which they agreed that certain actions described their behavior toward a specific peer on a seven-point scale (1, strongly disagree, to 7, strongly agree). Fourteen items measuring control-based monitoring, defensive behavior, and need-based monitoring were original to the present study, developed from a review of the literature and pretested on the group described above. Eleven items assessed citizenship behavior, 6 of which were drawn from Williams and Anderson's (1991) measure and rephrased to address assistance to specific individuals rather than organization members in general and 5 of which were developed to more fully tap the domain of the construct.

Initial exploratory factor analyses were conducted on parallel data that were collected but not

---

[1] The procedure used here is similer to that used by Tsui (1984). Manipulation checks revealed that it was effective in controlling self-selection tendencies and building variation along the critical trust dimensions. Nominating individuals expressed greater affect- and cognition-based trust in peers selected from the people with whom they worked best than in those with whom they worked less well (pairwise *t*-tests, *p* < .001). Also, nominated peers from the first list expressed greater affect-and cognition-based trust in the nominating individuals than did peers from the second list (pairwise *t*-tests, *p* < .05).

[2] By random assignment, triad members were assigned roles as respondents (1, 2, or 3). The three focal manager → peer dyads addressed were as follows: 1 × 2, 2 × 3, and 3 → 1. Thus, respondent 1 provided information from the perspective of a focal manager for his or her relationship with respondent 2 and information from the perspective of a peer for his or her relationship with respondent 3. Although I collected complete data for all relationships within each triad, dyad-specific data collected for use in hypothesis testing were collected first. By collecting respondent 1's assessment of his or her trust in respondent 2 before collecting information on his or her trust in respondent 3, the relevant assessment received was absolute rather than comparative. This method allowed efficient use of respondents (data concerning three dyads were collected from each set of three respondents) and maintained independence of observations. Further, parallel data collected but not used in hypothesis testing could be used for preliminary analyses of new measures developed in the study.

TABLE 1. Results of Confirmatory Factor Analysis for Behavioral Response and Interpersonal Trust Measures[a]

Items	Lambdas
Affect-based trust	
We have a sharing relationship. We can both freely share our ideas, feelings, and hopes.	.89
I can talk freely to this individual about difficulties I am having at work and know that (s)he will want to listen.	.82
We would both feel a sense of loss if one of us was transferred and we could no longer work together.	.81
If I shared my problems with this person, I know (s)he would respond constructively and caringly.	.79
I would have to say that we have both made considerable emotional investments in our working relationship.	.66
Cognition-based trust	
This person approaches his/her job with professionalism and dedication.	.90
Given this person's track record, I see no reason to doubt his/her competence and preparation for the job.	.86
I can rely on this person not to make my job more difficult by careless work.	.81
Most people, even those who aren't close friends of this individual, trust and respect him/her as a coworker.	.77
Other work associates of mine who must interact with this individual consider him/her to be trustworthy.	.73
If people knew more about this individual and his/her background, they would be more concerned and monitor his/her performance more closely.[b]	.69
Need-based monitoring	
Even when others think everything is fine, I know when (s)he is having difficulties.	.76
This person doesn't have to tell me in order for me to know how things are going for him/her at work.	.72
Affiliative citizenship behavior	
I take time to listen to this person's problems and worries.	.79
I have taken a personal interest in this individual.	.78
I frequently do extra things I know I won't be rewarded for, but which make my cooperative efforts with this person more productive.	.72
I pass on new information that might be useful to this person.	.65
I willingly help this individual, even at some cost to personal productivity.	.62
When making decisions at work that affect this individual, I try to take his/her needs and feelings into account.	.40
I try not to make things more difficult for this person by my careless actions.	.17
Assistance-oriented citizenship behavior	
I help this person with difficult assignments, even when assistance is not directly requested.	.90
I assist this person with heavy work loads, even though it is not part of my job.	.84
I help this person when (s)he has been absent.	.71
Monitoring and defensive behavior	
I find that this person is not the sort of coworker I need to monitor closely.[b]	.85
The quality of the work I receive from this individual is only maintained by my diligent monitoring.	.81
I have sometimes found it necessary to work around this individual in order to get things done the way that I would like them to be done.	.73
I keep close track of my interactions with this individual, taking note of instances where (s)he does not keep up her/his end of the bergain.	.72
I have found it necessary to make inquiries before responding to this person's requests for assistance. This ensures that my interests are protected.	.62
Rather than just depending on this individual to come through when I need assistance, I try to have a backup plan ready.	.56

[a]The lambdas are reported from the completely standardized solution. Chi-square with 362 degrees of freedom is 681.64 (p < .001). Comparative fit index is .90. Calculated from null of 3,646.90 with 406 degrees of freedom.
[b]Item was reverse-coded.

used to test hypotheses in the present research (see footnote 1). I extracted four factors with acceptable psychometric properties (eigenvalue greater than 1.0, $\alpha > .60$) and retained them for confirmatory analysis with the present respondents: control-based monitoring and defensive behavior items together (factor 1), citizenship behavior with strong affiliative content (factor 2), citizenship behavior involving congenial assistance (factor 3), and need-based monitoring (factor 4).

To assess the adequacy of the derived trust and behavioral response measures for use with the present research sample and to test the discriminant validity of trust and behavioral response measures, I conducted a confirmatory factor analysis using LISREL 7 (Jöreskog and Sörbom, 1989). I computed the comparative fit index (CFI), a fit measure that prevents the underestimation of fit likely to occur in small samples, to assess the fit of the factor structure to the data (Bentler, 1990) and examined correlations among factors to assess the discriminant validity of measures. Table 1 reports results.

Overall, the model fit the data well (CFI = .90). All factor loadings (lambdas) on specified factors were significant ($t > 1.96$). Reliability estimates (α) for affiliative citizenship behavior, assistance-oriented citizenship behavior, need-based monitoring, and monitoring and defensive behavior measures were .79, .85, .69, and .87, respectively. However, several correlations among latent constructs were considerable, with off-diagonal elements in the phi-matrix exceeding .60.

Because I obtained trust and behavioral response measures from a single source, it was important to demonstrate substantive differences between these measures. Within the LISREL framework, discriminant validity can be assessed in part by constraining a single phi coefficient (ϕ_{ij}) to 1.0, refitting the model, and testing the resulting change in the chi-square measure of model fit (Anderson & Gerbing, 1988; Bagozzi & Yi, 1988). I conducted this analysis for each of four correlations exceeding .60. With one exception, constraining ϕ_{ij} to 1.0 resulted in a significant worsening in model fit, indicating a real difference in the measures. The relationship between cognition-based trust and monitoring and defensive behavior measures was found to be −.85, and the constrained-coefficient model did not yield a change in model fit ($\Delta\chi^2 = .71$, $df = 1$, n.s.). Because monitoring and defensive behavior could not be empirically distinguished from negative cognition-based trust, I decided to retain the cognition-based trust measure and exclude the monitoring and defensive behavior measure from further use in this study.

Exogenous variables. Reliable role performance was measured with four items drawn from Williams and Anderson's (1991) measure of organization-directed citizenship behavior and in-role behavior. Respondents assessed, on a seven-point scale ranging from 1, "almost never," to 7, "al-most always," the extent to which each behavior described was characteristic of their behavior on the job. Frequency of interaction was measured with four items adapted from an instrument developed by Wilson (1988). Respondents described the frequency of various forms of their work-related interaction with a focal manager on a seven-point scale ranging from 1 (once or twice in the last six months) to 7 (many times daily). Citizenship behavior, afflictive and assistance-based, was measured with items identical to those used for focal manager citizenship behavior.

Table 2 reports confirmatory factor analysis results for the exogenous scales and item wordings. The four-factor solution provides an adequate fit for the data (CFI = .90, $t > 1.96$, all loadings). Reliability estimates for interaction frequency, peer affiliative citizenship behavior, peer assistance-oriented citizenship behavior, and peer reliable role performance are .91, .81, .82, .77, respectively.

Demographic data, including education level, age, gender, and ethnicity, were collected to develop a basic demographic profile of the respondents. Further, I used these data to derive measures of cultural-ethnic and gender similarity, and professional status. A binary variable for cultural-ethnic similarity was created, with focal manager—peer dyads whose members reported similar ethnic backgrounds (e.g., white-white, Hispanic-Hispanic) coded 1 and those whose members reported different ethnic backgrounds coded 0. I created a similar binary measure for similarity in gender and one for the assessment of professional standing (attended a university at the master's or doctoral level = 1, at most an undergraduate degree = 0). this breakdown was appropriate because only 16 percent of the respondents did not already possess some sort of four-year university degree.

Performance. Tsui's three-item measure of reputational effectiveness (Tsui, 1984) and one additional item were used to measure focal manager and peer performance. Supervisors were asked to consider the total job, including job-specified duties, additional activities not formally required, and the dependability of focal managers and peers, and to assess their satisfaction with various aspects of each target individual's job performance on a seven-point scale ranging from 1 (not at all) to 7 (entirely). Performance measures were found to be reliable ($\alpha = .92$). Table 3 reports confirmatory factor analysis results and item wordings.

TABLE 2. Results of Confirmatory Factor Analysis for Exogenous Measures[a]

Items	Lambdas
Interaction frequency	
How frequently does this individual initiate work-related interaction with you?	.95
How frequently do you initiate work-related interaction with this person?	.94
How frequently do you interact with this person at work?	.90
How frequently do you interact with this person informally or socially at work?	.66
Peer affiliative citizenship behavior	
I take time to listen to this person's problems and worries.	.82
I willingly help this individual, even at some cost to personal productivity.	.70
I have taken a personal interest in this individual.	.69
I pass on new information that might be useful to this person.	.65
I frequently do extra things I know I won't be rewarded for, but which make my cooperative efforts with this person more productive.	.61
When making decisions at work that affect this individual, I try to take his/her needs and feelings into account.	.54
I try not to make things more difficult for this person by my careless actions.	.34
Peer assistance-oriented citizenship behavior	
I help this person when (s)he has been absent.	.82
I help this person with difficult assignments, even when assistance is not directly requested.	.78
I assist this person with heavy work loads, even though it is not part of my job.	.74
Peer reliable role performance	
This person adequately completes assigned duties.	.76
This person performs all tasks that are expected of him/her.	.71
This person fulfills responsibilities specified in job description.	.64
This person meets formal performance requirements of the job.	.60

[a] The lambdas are reported from the completely standardized solution. Chi-square with 129 degrees of freedom is 256.01 ($p < .001$). Comparative fit index is .90. Calculated from null of 1,688.53 with 153 degrees of freedom.

Analyses

Using LISREL 7 (Anderson & Gerbing, 1988; Jöreskog & Sörbom, 1989), I took a two-stage approach to structural equation model fitting and assessment, assessing measurement properties of the model prior to considering structural relation-ships between constructs. Within the structural equation modeling framework used, multiple observed indicators (the individual scale items) were used to measure latent constructs. In testing the theoretical framework, I fitted 11 nested models, each incorporating different assumptions about model parameters, to the data.

TABLE 3. Results of Confirmatory Factor Analysis for Performance Measures[a]

Items	Lambdas
Assessor rating of focal manager's performance	
Overall, to what extent do you feel that this person is performing his/her total job the way you would like it to be performed?	.96
To what extent has this person met all of your expectations in his/her roles and responsibilities?	.93
To what extent are you satisfied with the total contribution made by this person?	.82
If you had your way, to what extent would you change the manner in which this person is doing his/her job?	.71
Assessor rating of peer performance	
Overall, to what extent do you feel that this person is performing his/her total job the way you would like it to be performed?	.95
To what extent has this person met all of your expectations in his/her roles and responsibilities?	.94
To what extent are you satisfied with the total contribution made by this person?	.82
If you had your way, to what extent would you change the manner in which this person is doing his/her job?	.72

[a] The lambdas are reported from the completely standardized solution. Chi-square with 19 degrees of freedom is 99.57 ($p < .001$). Comparative fit index is .93. Calculated from null of $45.73 with 28 degrees of freedom.

The first two models were used to assess measurement properties. An initial null model specifying no relations among observable variables represented the poorest-fitting model and provided a baseline for computation of the normed comparative fit index. A measurement model with the paths between observable variables and associated latent constructs freed and latent constructs allowed to correlate freely was fitted to the data. As during measure development, I assessed the discriminant validity of constructs by constraining correlations among constructs to zero and examining the change in chi-square.

To test hypotheses concerning the structural relationships among variables, I took a nested-models approach (Anderson & Gerbing, 1988). I arrayed nine nested structural models between the measurement model—the best-fitting model, with structural relationships among latent constructs assumed to be perfectly estimated—and the null model and compared them using chi-square difference tests. First, the theoretical model, with all

paths not specifically hypothesized to exist fixed to zero, was specified. Figure 2 presents the structural relationships in this model from which four variables—defensive behavior, control-based monitoring, social similarity, and professional status—are omitted. The combined measure of monitoring and defensive behavior was found to be insufficiently distinct from cognition-based trust to warrant inclusion, and the categorical measures of social similarity (gender and ethnic background) and professional status were not suitable for inclusion within the LISREL model.[3]

In addition, three constrained-parameter and five

---

[3]LISREL parameter estimates are distorted when categorical variables are included in the analysis as interval scale measures. PRELIS provides for the computation of "polychoric" correlation coefficients between categorical variables and "polyserial" correlation coefficients between categorical and continuous variables as substitutes for Pearson product-moment correlations, but this procedure requires a sample of more than 20 subjects and considerable computational power (Jöreskog & Sörbom, 1988, 1989).

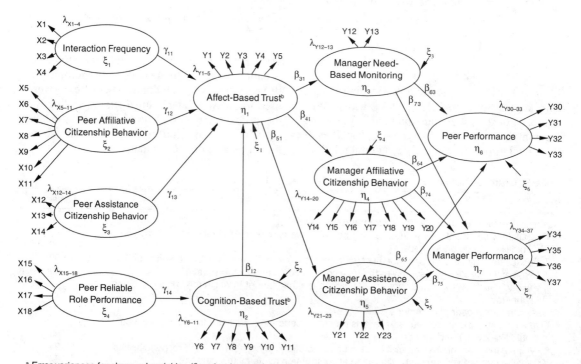

[a] Error variances for observed variables (δ and ε elements) and correlations among latent exogenous variables (Φ_{ij} elements) have been omitted for the sake of clarity.
[b] Direction of relationship is from manager to peer.

FIGURE 2 ■ Structural parameters included in the theoretical model[a]

relaxed-parameter models were fitted to the data. For the constrained models, I fixed the sets of relationships hypothesized to exist to zero and assessed chi-square difference tests between these models and the theoretical model. These tests indicated whether these models included paths that should have been omitted. The three constrained-parameter models can be specified as follows: in model C1, paths from exogenous variables to affect- and cognition-based trust are fixed to zero ($\gamma_{11} = \gamma_{12} = \gamma_{13} = \gamma_{24} = 0$); in model C2, paths from cognition- and affect-based trust to behavioral response measures are fixed to zero ($\beta_{31} = \beta_{41} = \beta_{51} = 0$); and in model C3, paths from behavioral response to performance measures are fixed to zero ($\beta_{63} = \beta_{64} = \beta_{65} = \beta_{73} = \beta_{74} = \beta_{75} = 0$). Examining the impact of sets of constrained paths in addition to examining the significance of individual paths is important where the constructs involved are significantly correlated (Niehoff & Moorman, 1993). A significant difference in fit between structural models would provide support for fundamental relationships hypothesized in the model.

For the relaxed-parameter models, I freed sets of structural paths fixed to zero in the theoretical model and conducted chi-square difference tests. These tests indicate the potential importance of relationships not yet specified. The five relaxed-parameter models examined can be specified as follows: in model R1, additional paths from exogenous variables to affect- and cognition-based trust are freed ($\gamma_{21}, \gamma_{22}, \gamma_{23}, \gamma_{14}$); in model R2, additional paths from cognition- and affect-based trust to behavioral response variables are freed ($\beta_{32}, \beta_{42}, \beta_{52}$); in model R3, paths from exogenous variables to behavioral response variables are freed ($\gamma_{31}, \gamma_{32}, \gamma_{33}, \gamma_{34}, \gamma_{41}, \gamma_{42}, \gamma_{43}, \gamma_{44}, \gamma_{51}, \gamma_{52}, \gamma_{53}, \gamma_{54}$); in model R4, paths from trust to performance are freed ($\beta_{61}, \beta_{62}, \beta_{71}, \beta_{72}$); and in model R5, paths from exogenous variables to performance are freed ($\gamma_{61}, \gamma_{62}, \gamma_{63}, \gamma_{64}, \gamma_{71}, \gamma_{72}, \gamma_{73}, \gamma_{74}$).

Given my focus on theory testing, I made no attempt to develop a best-fitting model by adding paths based on modification indexes, deleting nonsignificant variables and paths, allowing observable variables to load on more than one latent factor, allowing correlated measurement errors, and so forth. It should also be noted that reversals in causal ordering and reciprocal causation, especially as they concern the relationship between cognition and affect-based trust, were not examined.[4] Nevertheless, within the nested-models framework, considering constrained-parameter models allowed for detection of potential errors of commission (specifying unnecessary relationships) and considering relaxed-parameter models allowed for identification of potential errors of omission (excluding relationships that might have theoretical and practical significance). A specific advantage of the nested-models approach to theory testing is its potential for exploring relationships, not yet included in a model, that may have theoretical relevance (Anderson & Gerbing, 1988).

In addition to structural equation modeling, ordinary-least-squares (OLS) regression analysis was used to examine Hypotheses 2b (the relationship between cultural-ethnic similarity and cognition-based trust) and 2c (the relationship between a peer's professional status and a manager's cognition-based trust). I regressed cognition-based trust on all causally prior (exogenous) variables. For this analysis, I computed scales as the average of their indicator items. Multiple regression analysis is well established as an acceptable method for path computation in path analysis (Pedhazur, 1982).

Result

Assessment of the Measurement Model

Table 4 presents correlations among all study variables. Table 5 reports results from the nested-models analysis, including structural path coefficients and model fit statistics.

The measurement model represents a confirmatory factor analysis of all scales used in the study. The normed comparative fit assessments for the confirmatory factor analyses of portions of the model (see Tables 1, 2, and 3) all met or exceeded .90, a generally accepted standard for acceptability, but the comparative fit index for the measurement model was .87. This finding mirrors Niehoff and Moorman's (1993) observation that as the number of latent variables included in a model increases, a researcher's ability to fit models, even those with strong theoretical support, decreases.

---

[4]For two reciprocally related parameters to be overidentified, it is necessary for each to have an instrument, an exogenous variable affecting one but not the corresponding variable (Kenny, 1979; Schaubroeck, 1990). In the case of the relationship between affect- and cognition-based trust, I found no significant instrument for cognition-based trust and accordingly, could not examine reciprocal causation.

TABLE 4. Correlations and Descriptive Statistics[a]

Variables	Means	s.d.	1	2	3	4	5	6	7	8	9	10	11	12	13	14
Focal manager attitudes and behavior																
1. Cognition-based trust	5.43	1.29	(.91)													
2. Affect-based trust	4.71	1.47	.63***	(.89)												
3. Need-based monitoring	4.44	1.33	.01	.31***	(.69)											
4. Manager citizenship behavior, affiliative	5.23	0.98	.43***	.71**	.43***	(.79)										
5. Manager citizenship behavior, assistance	4.03	1.57	.19**	.48***	.48***	.67***	(.85)									
Peer attributes and behavior																
6. Reliable role performance	6.22	0.60	.06	-.07	-.05	.02	.07	(.77)								
7. Professional status	1.43	1.24	.09	.08	-.18**	.05	-.03	.05								
8. Peer citizenship behavior, affiliative	5.19	1.06	.13*	.39***	.23***	.32***	.27***	-.05	.07	(.81)						
9. Peer citizenship behavior, assistance	3.63	1.61	.09	.22**	.23***	.23***	.33***	-.03	.00	.52***	(.82)					
Relationship considerations																
10. Ethnic similarity	0.73	0.44	-.05	-.02	-.09	.00	-.01	-.08	.08	-.04	-.07					
11. Gender similarity	0.69	0.47	.03	.13*	.08	.15*	.16*	-.05	-.15*	.16*	.07	.03				
12. Interaction frequency	4.67	1.64	.19**	.39***	.34***	.35***	.41***	-.06	-.02	.49***	.40***	.04	.14*	(.91)		
Effectiveness measures																
13. Peer performance	5.06	1.27	.40***	.18**	-.08	.12	.03	.14*	.06	.13*	.10	-.13	-.09	.11	(.92)	
14. Focal manager performance	5.07	1.26	.15*	.26***	.02	.23**	.00	.05	.01	.16*	.08	-.05	-.08	.03	.22	(.92)

[a] Cronbach's alphas appear on the diagonal for multiple-item measures.
* $p < .05$
** $p < .01$
*** $p < .001$

Given the fact that this analysis included 11 distinct latent constructs, the achieved model fit is reasonable.

Four correlations among latent measures exceeded .60: the relationships between peer affiliative and assistance-oriented citizenship behavior, focal manager affiliative and assistance-oriented citizenship behavior, focal-manager-reported affect- and cognition-based trust, and focal manager affect-based trust and affiliative citizenship behavior. In part, these excessive coefficients reflect the fact that measures were obtained from a single source. As in initial scale development, I assessed discriminant validity by constraining phi coefficients (ϕ_{ij}) for pairs of constructs to 1.0 and conducting chi-square difference tests. For each pair of constructs, constraining the correlation to 1.0 made model fit significantly worse. This finding that these measures are better understood as distinct than joined, although not ruling out the presence of common method variance, supports the argument that method covariation alone cannot adequately account for the relationships observed (Podsakoff & Organ, 1986).

Assessment of the Structural Model

Results from the nested-models analysis (Table 5) indicate that the theoretical model provides only a limited explanation for the structural relationships among the variables. The measurement model's comparative fit index of .87 approximates the fit that would be achieved (given the present data) with the structural portion of the LISREL model perfectly fitted. Accordingly, the theoretical

TABLE 5. Structural Parameter Estimates for Nested-Models Analysis[a]

Path Coefficient	Measurement Model	Theoretical Model	Constrained Models			Relaxed Models					Null Model
			1	2	3	1	2	3	4	5	
β_{12}		.63***	.68***	.68***	.63***	.60***	.72***	.64***	.63***	.63***	
β_{31}		.36***	.36***		.37***	.38***	.92***	.25*	.36***	.37***	
β_{41}		.86***	.86***		.85***	.87***	1.20***	.81***	.85***	.86***	
β_{51}		.56***	.57***		.56***	.57***	1.07***	.48***	.56***	.56***	
β_{63}		−.20*	−.19*	−.15		−.20*	−.31***	−.20*	−.12	−.20*	
β_{64}		.31**	.31	.25**		.32***	.38**	.33***	.10	.23*	
β_{65}		−.12	−.12**	−.11		−.12	−.13	−.12	.00	−.15	
β_{73}		−.14	−.14	−.15		−.14	−.11	−.13	−.17	−.10	
β_{74}		.52***	.53***	.45***		.54***	.56***	.53***	.47*	.49***	
β_{75}		−.27**	−.27**	−.22**		−.27**	−.33**	−.29**	−.26**	−.25**	
γ_{11}		.22**		.19*	.22**	.20**	.21***	.20**	.22**	.22**	
γ_{12}		.24*		.26**	.24*	.22*	.17	.23*	.24*	.24*	
γ_{13}		−.02		−.06	−.02	−.02	.04	−.03	−.02	−.02	
γ_{24}		.07		.07	.07	.10	.06	.07	.08	.09	
γ_{14}						−.03					
γ_{21}						.15					
γ_{22}						.13					
γ_{23}						−.04					
β_{32}							−.75***				
β_{42}							−.44***				
β_{52}							−.67***				
γ_{31}								.23*			
γ_{32}								−.14			
γ_{33}								.27			
γ_{34}								−.11			
γ_{41}								.06			
γ_{42}								.07			
γ_{43}								.17			
γ_{44}								.07			
γ_{51}								.21*			
γ_{52}								−.28*			
γ_{53}								.37***			
γ_{54}								.05			
β_{61}									−.20		
β_{62}									.50***		
β_{71}									.13		
β_{72}									−.11		
γ_{61}										.06	
γ_{62}										.16	
γ_{63}										.01	
γ_{64}										.23**	
γ_{71}										−.15	
γ_{72}										.17	
γ_{73}										−.05	
γ_{74}										.14	
χ^2	1,843	2,032	2,068	2,230	2,061	2,025	1,973	1,999	2,010	2,015	7,089
df	1,072	1,107	1,111	1,111	1,113	1,103	1,104	1,095	1,103	1,099	1,176
CFI	.87	.84	.84	.81	.84	.84	.85	.85	.85	.85	.00
$\Delta\chi^2$			36***	198***	29***	7	59***	33***	22***	17	5.057***	
Δdf			4	4	6	4	3	12	4	8	69	

[a]Standardized path coefficients are reported. They represent relationships between variables within the theoretical model presented in Figure 2. Chi-square difference tests were computed on the basis of the deviation from the theoretical model.
*p < .05
**p < .01
***p < .001

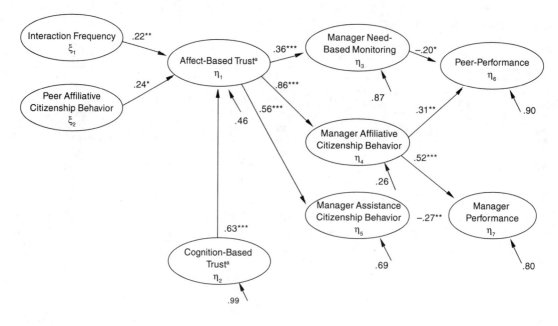

^aDirection of relationship is from manager to peer.
* p < .05
**p < .01
***p < .001

FIGURE 3 ■ Derived path coefficients based on a structural equation analysis of the theoretical model.

model's index of .84 may appear reasonable. Yet a chi-square difference test comparing the two models indicates that the measurement model provides a significantly better fit to the data than does the theoretical model ($\Delta\chi^2 = 189$, $\Delta df = 58$, $p < .001$).

Figure 3 presents significant standardized path coefficients for the theoretical model. Also included are error terms (ξs) for the structural equations. In standardized form, error coefficients represent the proportion of variance in each equation not accounted for in the structural model. Quite clearly, portions of the model fit the data better than others—for instance, 54 percent of the variance in affect-based trust was accounted for in the theoretical model, but only 10 percent of the variance in peer performance was explained. The theoretical framework may best be viewed as addressing antecedents and consequences of affect-based trust and not as comprehensively explaining the antecedents of performance.

Results from the nested-models analysis clarify the nature of the theoretical model's misspecification. In general, results of chi-square difference tests between that model and the constrained

models indicate that fundamental relationships do exist between peer attributes and a focal manager's trust in peers, between the manager's trust in peers and his or her behavioral responses, and between those responses and performance outcomes. For each of the three constrained models, fit was significantly worse than the fit of the theoretical model. Thus, the paths that were included in the model should have been included. On the other hand, model fit assessments were significantly improved with the freeing of additional paths; those from focal manager trust beliefs (affect- and cognition-based) to behavioral responses, from antecedents to behavioral responses, and from trust to performance. Thus, considering additional relationships among study variables might enrich the model.

The Distinction Between Cognition- and Affect-Based Trust

Strong support was found for the distinction between cognition-based and affect-based trust predicted in Hypothesis 1. First, exploratory findings with parallel data and confirmatory analysis results with the present sample (Table 1) indicate that the two-factor representation of affect- and cognition-based trust fits the data well. The two factors were shown to be reliable. Second, the pattern of relationships between the forms of trust and the other variables included in the study differ considerably. In the theoretical model, peer affiliative citizenship behavior was found to be positively associated with focal manager affect-based trust in peers but unrelated to cognition-based trust. Combining insights derived from the theoretical model with observations from the relaxed model in which additionl paths between focal manager trust in peers and behavioral responses are freed suggests that although a focal manager's affect-based trust in peers is positively associated with need-based monitoring of peers and assistance-oriented citizenship behavior, cognition-based trust may be negatively associated with these variables. Thus, affect-based trust and cognition-based trust represent distinct forms of interpersonal trust.

Interpersonal Hypotheses: Relating Peer Attributes and Behavior to Trust Perceptions

In general, peer attributes and behavior were found to be related to focal manager assessments of peer trustworthiness (Table 5). Model fit assessments were appreciably worse with paths from hypothesized antecedents to trust constrained to zero; the change in chi-square between the theoretical model and the first constrained model was 36, $p < .001$. Further analysis indicated, as is apparent in Figure 3, that relationships between peer attributes and affect-based trust in particular explain this finding.

It was hypothesized that a manager's cognition-based trust in peers would be greater under three conditions: when peers exhibited high levels of reliable role performance (Hypothesis 2a), when the parties had cultural-ethnic similarity (Hypothesis 2b), and when peers had strong professional credentials (Hypothesis 2c). Hypothesis 2a was examined in the structural equation assessment of the theoretical model (Figure 3). The path from reliable role performance to focal manager cognition-based trust was not significant. Hypotheses 2b and 2c were examined in the supplementary

OLS regression analysis and were also not supported. Regression analysis results, in which level of cognition-based trust was regressed on all causally prior variables, were not significant ($F = 1.60$, n.s.). Thus, findings do not support Hypotheses 2a, 2b, and 2c.

Hypotheses 3a and 3b, however, were strongly supported. I hypothesized that focal managers would express strong affect-based trust in peers engaging in interpersonal citizenship behavior (Hypothesis 3a) and in those with whom the managers interacted frequently (Hypothesis 3b). Significant, positive paths from interaction frequency and peer affiliative citizenship behavior to affect-based trust ($\gamma_{11} = .22$, $p < .01$; $\gamma_{12} = .24$, $p < .05$) supported predictions. Assistance-based citizenship behavior, however, was not found to be associated with affect-based trust.

Intrapersonal Hypotheses: Relationships Among Trust Perceptions and Behavioral Responses

Hypotheses 4, 5, and 6, addressing relationships among focal manager beliefs about peer trustworthiness and focal manager behavior, were generally supported. First, the hypothesis that cognition-based trust would be a positive predictor of affect-based (Hypothesis 4) was strongly supported ($\beta_{12} = .63$, $p < .001$). Second, results of the nested-models analysis demonstrated that managers' assessments of peer trustworthiness were associated with the managers' behavior toward their peers. Fit assessments were appreciably worse with paths associating focal manager trust perceptions with focal manager behavioral responses (β_{31}, β_{41}, and β_{51}) constrained to zero ($\Delta\chi_2 = 198$, $p < .001$). As Hypotheses 5a and 5b, concerning the behavioral consequences of cognition-based trust, were not tested, this finding is best understood as substantiating relationships from affect-based trust to its behavioral consequences only.

Results supported the hypotheses predicting that the affect-based trust local managers expressed in peers would be positively associated with the managers' need-based monitoring of peers (Hypothesis 6a) and interpersonal citizenship behavior toward them (Hypothesis 6b). Paths from focal manager affect-based trust in peers to need-based monitoring, affiliative citizenship behavior, and assistance-oriented citizenship behavior were, as shown in Figure 3, all significant ($\beta_{31} = .36$, $p <$ 001; $\beta_{41} = .86$, $p < .001$; $\beta_{51} = .56$, $< .001$).

Performance Implications Hypotheses

In general, the behavioral consequences of trust were found to be related to supervisor assessments of performance. As the results of the nested-models comparison of the theoretical model with the third constrained model indicate (Table 5), model fit assessments were appreciably worse with paths from behavioral response latent constructs to performance measures (β_{63}, β_{64}, β_{65}, β_{73}, β_{74}, and β_{75}) constrained to zero ($\Delta\chi^2 = 29$, $p < .001$). Hypotheses 7, 8, and 9 address specific relationships among behavioral response and performance variables. Again, as Hypotheses 7a and 7b were not tested in this analysis, findings are best understood as substantiating the relationship between the behavioral consequences of the affect-based trust and performance outcome measures.

Results also only partially supported Hypotheses 8a and 8b. Focal manager need-based monitoring of peers was not positively associated with supervisor assessments of focal manager performance as hypothesized (Hypothesis 8a). Nevertheless, consistent with Hypothesis 8b, the path from focal manager affiliative citizenship behavior directed toward peers to supervisor assessments of focal manager performance was significant ($\beta_{74} = 52$, $p < .001$). An interesting, nonhypothesized finding was a significant negative path from assistance-based citizenship behavior to focal manager performance ($\beta_{75} = -.27$, $p < .01$). It may be that people see expressive acts of interpersonal help and assistance serving more of a maintenance than a task function as aiding performance but see other practical acts of help and assistance as detracting from performance. This anomalous finding suggests that organizations may particularly value the expressive qualities of interpersonal citizenship behavior. It may also be that expressive conduct is more salient to supervisors than task-oriented assistance.

Hypotheses addressing the relationship between focal manager behavior and peer performance (Hypothesis 9a and Hypothesis 9b) were not supported. Nested-models analysis results do not show focal manager need-based monitoring of peers to be positively associated with peer performance. Indeed, for the theoretical model, focal manager need-based monitoring of peers was found to be

negatively associated with peer performance ($\beta_{63} = -.20$, $p < .05$). This finding may reflect managers' tendency to look for opportunities to assist peers in real need of assistance (signified by their having low performance assessments). That is, the true causal ordering may be the reverse of that depicted in Figure 2.

Consistent with Hypothesis 9b, a significant positive relationship between focal manager affiliative citizenship behavior and peer performance was observed in the theoretical model ($\beta_{64} = .31$, $p < .01$). Yet when I examined this relationship at the same time as possible direct relationships between trust and performance outcomes, in the fourth relaxed model, this path was nonsignificant.

In summary, results did not support the hypotheses concerning the antecedents of cognition-based trust (2a through 2c). They did support hypotheses concerning the antecedents of affect-based trust (3a, 3b, and 4). The hypotheses concerning the behavioral consequences and performance implications of cognition-based trust were not tested. The hypotheses concerning the behavioral consequences of affect-based trust (6a and 6b) were supported. Partial support emerged for two of four hypotheses concerning the performance implications of affect-based trust.

Discussion

The Nature of Interpersonal Trust

The findings of this research indicate that the beliefs of managers about the trustworthiness of peers can be measured along two dimensions, the extent of affect-based trust and the extent of cognition-based trust. In general, levels of cognition-based trust were higher than levels of affect-based trust, a finding consistent with the understanding that some level of cognition-based trust is necessary for affect-based trust to develop. Further, results indicate that, although cognition- and affect-based trust may be causally connected, each form of trust functions in a unique manner and has a distinct pattern of association to antecedent and consequent variables.

More theoretical work is needed to address the factors that can influence the development of cognition-based trust; such information should enrich understanding of cognition-based trust itself.

Theory-based predictors of cognition-based trust—a peer's reliable role performance, professional credentials, and social-ethnic similarity—were not found to be associated with cognition-based trust. One factor not addressed in the study was the local reputation of a peer as dependable and reliable. Supervisor assessments of peer performance were found to be strongly associated with a focal manager's cognition-based beliefs about peer trustworthiness ($r = .40, p < .001$). Quite likely, what others think about the dependability of a peer will influence personal evaluations of that peer. Future research will need to address reputational effects.

Observed differences in the pattern of relationships between forms of trust and predictor and consequence variables underscore the importance of considering not only the level but also the form of trust. In past research on citizenship behavior in organizations, authors have argued that trust and citizenship behavior are positively associated (Organ, 1990; Podsakoff et al., 1990). The present research indicates that there may be negative relationships between a focal manager's cognition-based trust in a peer and his or her affiliative- and assistance-oriented citizenship behavior toward the peer ($\beta_{42} = -.44, p < .001; \beta_{52} = -.67, p < .001$).[5]

Interpersonal Trust and Coordination

Focal managers expressing high affect-based trust in peers were shown to be more inclined to look for opportunities to meet peers' work-related needs and to engage in productive intervention. In the complex, uncertain situations involving reciprocal interdependence, typical in managerial and professional work, traditional mechanisms of coordination (rules, plans, routines, and such) are usually inadequate as contingencies cannot always be properly planned for (Katz, 1964; Thompson, 1967). Under these conditions, coordination is a continuous process in which all the actors involved adjust their actions to one another (Follett, 1937) and self-initiated mechanisms of coordination are critical. Need-based monitoring and citizenship-behavior represent self-initiated steps that can promote coordination under turbulent conditions.

Findings did not generally support the hypotheses addressing the performance implications of behavioral responses to trust. One notable exception was the positive relationship found between focal manager affiliative citizenship behavior and

supervisor assessments of focal manager performance. Interestingly enough, focal manager assistance-based citizenship behavior was negatively associated with supervisor assessments of focal manager performance. As defined here, affiliative citizenship behavior differed from assistance-oriented citizenship behavior in that it involved personal assistance, was affect-laden and expressive, and served more of a maintenance than a task function. The logic behind managers' placing greater value on affiliative citizenship behavior than on more practical acts of interpersonal help and assistance merits systematic attention in future research.

The Social Fabric of Managerial Working Relationships

The current findings demonstrate the importance of affect-based trust relationships and the expressive qualities of interpersonal behavior. These findings extend current thinking on the nature of personal relationships among managers and professionals in organizations. Management scholars have recognized for some time that a considerable amount of managerial work is accomplished through interpersonal interaction and that the nature of the interpersonal relationships between managers and peers can determine their ability to get work accomplished (Gabarro, 1990; Mintzberg, 1973; Sayles, 1979). Less acknowledged, however, has been the affective element of these interpersonal relationships. The understanding has been that "because working relationships generally exist to accomplish tasks while social relationships [do] not, task achievement, task instrumentality and task-specific competence are especially important in work relationships, while affect and self-disclosure are less important" (Gabarro, 1990: 79). Given this view of affective factors as being somehow less important, their role in ongoing working relationships has remained unaddressed. In contrast, the focus here was on the inherent social nature of managerial work and on enhancing understanding of working relationships in organizations by recognizing their commonalities with other types of social relationships.

---

[5]This finding may not be all that surprising. An individual who sees a peer as dependable and reliable, competent and capable, may have little reason to offer assistance, as little assistance appears to be needed.

The expressive qualities of behavior in organizations should receive more systematic treatment in future research. Findings from the present theoretical model show that peer affiliative citizenship behavior in particular, rather than citizenship behavior in general, is associated with managers' affect-based trust in peers and that peer affiliative citizenship behavior is associated with managers' affiliative citizenship behavior only indirectly, through affect-based trust. Exploratory findings from a relaxed-parameter model with paths from antecedents of trust to managers' behavioral responses freed show peer assistance-based citizenship behavior to be positively associated with managers' assistance-oriented citizenship behavior ($\gamma_{53} = .37$, $p < .001$) but not with affect-based trust. It appears that managers distinguish between instrumental assistance from peers, which generates debts, and assistance from peers that is primarily demonstrative or expressive. As Kahn (1993) observed, exchanges of resources, time, information, counseling, and services can all serve more than instrumental purposes and, with appropriate affective content, can function as essential mechanisms of social support. In a study of interpersonal dyadic relationships within network-form organizations, Larson quoted an executive as stating, "The [extra] effort to help is as important as the help itself. The relationship has to be attended to" (1992, 89).

It appears that it is not unusual for managers, even those from different areas of functional specialization and different organizational units, to develop relationships of care and concern for one another and for such sentiments to constitute an important basis for trust. Indeed, over 60 percent of the focal managers in this study, discussing their beliefs about their trust in peers, believed that, to some extent, they could talk freely with a specific peer and know that he or she would want to listen and respond constructively and caringly. Approximately 50 percent of the respondents believed that both they and the specific peers had made significant emotional investments in the working relationships and that both would feel a sense of loss of one or the other were transferred and they could no longer work together.

These findings support Seabright and colleagues' contention that "it is hard to imagine the development of highly specific relationship capital that does not engender some element of social ties" (1992, 155). Granovetter's general observation that "continuing economic relations often become overlaid with social content that carries strong expectations of trust and abstention from opportunism" (1985, 490) can be given added specificity—the sentiments of care and concern that connect individuals provide a principal foundation for this trust. Despite the prevalence of relationships of affect-based trust, very little theory or data exist to either guide understanding of the implications of such trust relationships for the individuals involved and their organizations or to distinguish these relationships from those based solely on cognition-based trust. The present research is an initial step toward articulating a theoretical framework for future research on how relationships of affect-based trust between managers in organizations influence their behavior and performance.

Study Limitations

The present findings should be interpreted in light of the study's limitations. First, because almost 75 percent of the study's participants were highly educated men, the findings are best interpreted as evidence concerning working relationships between such individuals. Further research is needed to establish the generalizability of these findings to other sorts of working relationships. Second, given the cross-sectional design, causality cannot be established from this study alone. My focus was on examining whether the pattern of relationships among variables was consistent with a specific causal understanding (Bobko, 1990). The present findings are an initial step on the road to causality determination. Supplemental longitudinal field studies and controlled laboratory experiments will both prove useful in future research. Finally, the disciplined confirmatory assessment of the theoretical framework through the nested-models analysis indicates that there remains considerable room for improvement in the fit of the theoretical model. Insights from the relaxed-parameter analyses, including possible negative paths from cognition-based trust in peers to need-based monitoring, affiliative citizenship behavior, and assistance-oriented citizenship behavior indicate ways in which the model can be enriched, but these insights must be understood as exploratory. Further theoretical and empirical work is needed to demonstrate that these findings are not unique to this sample and study.

Conclusion

This article assesses a theoretical framework for studying interpersonal trust in organizations, the factors influencing the development of trust relationships, and the mechanisms by which trust influences behavior in interdependent relationships and ultimately, the efficiency with which coordinated action is maintained. Empirical findings from an initial test of the framework support the fundamental distinction made between two principal forms of trust and the argument that each form should be understood. Further, the results of the research point to the importance of understanding the affective qualities of working relationships and the expressive qualities of various forms of interpersonal conduct.

Over fifteen years ago Burns (1977) expressed concern over existing conceptions of the role of the informal social relationships in organizations. Burns noted that Roethlisberger and Dickson saw the informal organization "as a receptacle for observations about the behavior, relationships, the sentiments and beliefs . . . taken to be irrelevant to the formal organization or incompatible with it," and that Barnard saw it as "an essential adjunct to formal organization." For Burns the theoretical and practical relevance of the informal organization went much further. He argued that "essential organizational processes involving actual operations and work are grounded in the person-to-person relationships formed by people at work, and as such constitute the necessary counterpart and complement to the control systems maintained by the management structure" (1977: 308).

In the present research, informal relations have been examined with the understanding that they are central to the real work of organizations. Findings establish the affective foundations upon which trust between managers is built as an essential counterpart to other foundations for interpersonal trust and highlight affect-based trust's role in facilitating effective coordinated action in organizations.

ACKNOWLEDGMENTS

I am grateful to Jone Pearce, Anne Tsui, and Lyman Porter for their guidance and advice in this research, conducted as part of my doctoral dissertation at the University of California, Irvine. Special words of appreciation are due to Susan Ashford and two anonymous reviewers for their insightful comments and constructive feedback on several earlier drafts of this article.

REFERENCES

Alchian, A. A., & Demsetz, H. 1972. Production, information costs, and economic organization. *American Economic Review, 62,* 777–795.

Anderson, J. C., & Gerbing, D. W. 1988. Structural equation modeling in practice: A review and recommended two-step approach. *Psychological Bulletin, 193,* 411–423.

Arrow, K. 1974. *The limits of organization.* New York: Norton.

Ashforth, B. E., & Lee, R. T. 1990. Defensive behavior in organizations: A preliminary model. *Human Relations, 43,* 621–648.

Bagozzi, R. P., & Yi, Y. 1988. On the evaluation of structural equation models. *Journal of the Academy of Marketing Science, 16,* 74–94.

Baier, A. 1985. Trust and antitrust, *Ethics, 96,* 231–260.

Baker, G. P., Jensen, M. C., & Murphy, K. J. 1986. Compensation and incentives: Practice vs. theory. *Journal of Finance, 43,* 593–616.

Barber, B. 1983. *The logic and limits of trust.* New Brunswick, NJ: Rutgers University Press.

Bentler, P. M. 1990. Comparative fit indexes in structural models. *Psychological Bulletin, 107,* 238–246.

Bobko, P. 1990. Multivariate correlational analysis. In M. D. Dunnette & L. M. Hough (Eds.), *Handbook of industrial and organizational psychology* (2d ed., Vol. 1: 636–686). Palo Alto, CA: Consulting Psychologists Press.

Bradach, J. L., & Eccles, R. G. 1989. Price, authority, and trust: From ideal types to plural forms. *Annual Review of Sociology, 15,* 97–118.

Brewer, M. B. 1979. In-group bias in the minimal intergroup situation: A cognitive-motivational analysis. *Psychological Bulletin, 86,* 307–324.

Brief, A. P., & George, J. M. 1992. Feeling good—doing good: A conceptual analysis of the mood at work-organizational spontaneity relationship. *Psychological Bulletin, 112,* 310–329.

Burke, M. J., Brief, A. P., George, J. M., Roberson, L., & Webster, J. 1989. Measuring affect at work: Confirmatory analyses of competing mood structures with conceptual linkages to cortical regulatory systems. *Journal of Personality and Social Psychology, 57,* 1091–1102.

Burns, T. 1977. *The BBC: Public institution and private world.* New York: Holmes & Meier Publishers.

Buller, J. K. 1991. Towards understanding and measuring conditions of trust: Evolution of a conditions of trust inventory. *Journal of Management, 17,* 643–663.

Clark, M. S. 1984. Record keeping in two types of relationships. *Journal of Personality and Social Psychology, 47,* 549–557.

Clark, M. S., & Mills, J. 1979. Interpersonal attraction in exchange and communal relationships. *Journal of Personality and Social Psychology, 37*(1), 12–24.

Clark, M. S., Mills, J., & Corcoran, D. M. 1989. Keeping track of needs and inputs of friends and strangers. *Personality and Social Psychology Bulletin, 15,* 533–542.

Clark, M. S., Mills, J., & Powell, M. C. 1986. Keeping track of needs in communal and exchange relationships. *Journal of Personality and Social Psychology, 51,* 333–338.

Clark, M. S., & Waddell, B. 1985. Perceptions of exploitation in communal and exchange relationships. *Journal of Social and Personal Relationships, 2,* 403–418.

Cook, J., & Wall, T. 1980. New work attitude measures of

trust, organizational commitment and personal need non-fulfillment. *Journal of Occupational Psychology, 53,* 39–52.

Deutsch, M. 1973. *The resolution of conflict: constructive and destructive processes.* New Haven: Yale University Press.

Fichman, M., & Levinthal, D. A. 1991. Honeymoons and the liability of adolescence: A new perspective on duration dependence in social and organizational relationships. *Academy of Management Review, 16,* 442–468.

Follett, M. P. 1937. The process of control. In L. Gulick & L. Urwick (Eds.), *Papers on the science of administration* (pp. 161–169). New York: Institute of Public Administration.

Fox, A. 1974. *Beyond contract: Work, power and trust relations.* London: Faber & Faber.

Gabarro, J. 1990. The development of working relationships, In J. Galagher, R. E. Kraut, & C. Egido (Eds.), *Intellectual teamwork: Social and technological foundations of cooperative work* (pp. 79–110). Hillsdale, NJ: Erlbaum.

Granovetter, M. S. 1985. Economic action and social structure: The problem of embeddedness. *American Journal of Sociology, 91,* 481–510.

Griesinger, D. W. 1990. The human side of economic organization. *Academy of Management Review, 15,* 478–490.

Holmes, J. G. 1978. The exchange process in close relationships: Microbehaviors and macro motives. In M. J. Lerner & S. C. Lerner (Eds.), *The justice motive in social behavior: Adapting to times of scarcity and change* (pp. 261–284). New York: Plenum.

Holmes, J. G., & Rempel, J. K. 1989. Trust in close relationships. In C. Hendrick (Ed.), *Close relationships* (pp. 187–220). Newbury Park: Sage.

Isen, A. M., & Baron, R. A. 1991. Positive affect as a factor in organizational behavior. In L. Cummings & B. M. Staw (Eds.), *Research in organizational behavior* (Vol, 13, pp. 1–53). Greenwich, CT: JAI Press.

Johnson-George, C. E., & Swap, W. C. 1982. Measurement of specific interpersonal trust: Construction and validation of a scale to assess trust in a specific other. *Journal of Personality and Social Psychology, 43,* 1306–1317.

Jöreskog, K. G., & Sörbom, D. 1988. *PRELIS.* Mooresville, IN: Scientific Software.

Jöreskog, K. G., & Sörbom, D. 1989. *LISREL 7.* Mooresville, IN: Scientific Software.

Kahn, R. L., Wolfe, D. M., Quinn, R. P., & Snoek, J. D. 1964. *Organizational stress: Studies in role conflict and ambiguity.* New York: Wiley.

Kahn, W. A. 1993. Caring for the caregivers: Patterns of organizational caring. *Administrative Science Quarterly, 38,* 539–563.

Katz, D. 1964. The motivational basis of organizational behavior. *Behavioral Science, 9,* 131–146.

Kelly. H. H. 1979. *Personal relationships: Their structures and process.* Hillsdale, NJ: Erlbaum.

Kenny, D. A. 1979. *Correlation and causality.* New York: Wiley.

Larson, A. 1992. Network dyads in entrepreneurial settings: A study of the governance of exchange relationships. *Administrative Science Quarterly, 37,* 76–104.

Lewis, J. D., & Weigert, A. 1985. Trust as a social reality. *Social Forces, 63,* 967–985.

Light, I. 1984. Immigrant and ethnic enterprise in North America. *Ethnic and Racial Studies, 7,* 195–216.

Lindskold, S. 1978. Trust development, the GRIT proposal, and the effects of conciliatory acts on conflict and cooperation. *Psychological Bulletin, 85,* 772–793.

Longenecker, C. O., Jaccoud, A. J., Sims, H. P., Jr., & Gloia, D. A. 1992. Quantitative and qualitative investigations of affect in executive judgment. *Applied Psychology: An International Review, 41,* 21–41.

Luhmann, N. 1979. *Trust and power.* Chichester: Wiley.

MacKenzie, S. B., Podsakoff, P. M., & Fetter, R. 1991. Organizational citizenship behavior and objective productivity as determinants of managerial evaluations of salespersons performance. *Organizational Behavior and Human Decision Processes, 50,* 123–150.

Mintzberg, H. 1973. *The nature of managerial work.* New York: Harper & Row.

Niehoff, B. P., & Moorman, R. H. 1993. Justice as a mediator of the relationship between methods of monitoring and organizational citizenship behavior. *Academy of Management Journal, 36,* 527–556.

Organ, D. W. 1988, *Organizational citizenship behavior: The good soldier syndrome.* Lexington, MA: Lexington Books.

Organ, D. W. 1990. The motivational basis of organizational citizenship behavior. In B. M. Staw & L. L. Cummings (Eds.), *Research in organizational behavior* (vol. 12, pp. 43–72). Greenwich, CT: JAI Press.

Organ, D. W., & Konovsky, M. 1989. Cognitive versus affective determinants of organizational citizenship behavior. *Journal of Applied Psychology, 74,* 157–164.

Ouchi, W. G. 1979. A conceptual framework for the design of organizational control mechanisms. *Management Science, 25,* 833–848.

Park, O. S., Sims, H. P., Jr., & Motowidlo, S. J. 1986. Affect in organizations: How feelings and emotions influence managerial judgment. In H. P. Sims, Jr., & D. A. Gioia (Eds.), *The thinking organization* (pp. 215–237). San Francisco: Jossey-Bass.

Pearce, J. L., & Gregerson, H. B. 1991. Task interdependence and extrarole behavior: A test of the mediating effects of felt responsibility. *Journal of Applied Psychology, 76,* 838–844.

Pedhazur, E. J. 1982. *Multiple regression in behavioral research: Explanation and prediction* (2nd ed.). New York: Holt, Rinehart, & Winston.

Pennings, J. M., & Woiceshyn, J. 1987. A typology of organizational control and its metaphors. In S. B. Bacharach & S. M. Mitchell (Eds.), *Research in the sociology of organizations* (Vol. 5, pp. 75–104). Greenwich, CT: JAI Press.

Podsakoff, P. M., MacKenzie, S. B., Moorman, R. H., & Fetter, R. 1990. Transformational leader behaviors and their effects on followers' trust in leader, satisfaction, and organizational citizenship behaviors. *Leadership Quarterly, 1,* 107–142.

Podsakoff, P. M., & Organ, D. W. 1986. Self-reports in organizational research: Problems and prospects. *Journal of Management, 12,* 531–544.

Porter, L. W., Lawler, E. E., & Hackman. J. R. 1975. *Behavior in organizations.* New York: McGraw-Hill.

Rempel, J. K., Holmes, J. G., & Zanna, M. D. 1985. Trust in close relationships. *Journal of Personality and Social Psychology, 49,* 95–112.

Rotter, J. B. 1971. Generalized expectancies for interpersonal trust. *American Psychologist, 35,* 1–7.

Sayles, L. R. 1979. *Leadership: What effective managers really do . . . and how they do it.* New York: McGraw-Hill.

Schaubroeck, J. 1990. Investigating reciprocal causation in organizational behavior research. *Journal of Organizational Behavior, 11,* 17–28.

Seabright, M. A., Leventhal, D. A., & Fichman, M. 1992. Role of individual attachments in the dissolution of interorganizational relationships. *Academy of Management Journal, 35,* 122–160.

Shapiro, S. P. 1987. The social control of impersonal trust. *American Journal of Sociology, 93,* 623–658.

Shapiro, S. P. 1990. Collaring the crime, not the criminal: Reconsidering the concept of white-collar crime. *American Sociological Review, 55,* 346–365.

Simmel, G, 1964. *The sociology of Georg Simmel* (K. H. Wolff, trans.). New York: Free Press.

Smith, C. A., Organ. D. W., & Near, J. P. 1983. Organizational citizenship behavior: Its nature and antecedents. *Journal of Applied Psychology, 68,* 653–666.

Stack, L. C. 1988. Trust. In H. London & J. E. Exner, Jr. (Eds.), *Dimensionality of personality* (pp. 561–579). New York: Wiley.

Thompson, J. D. 1967. *Organizations in action.* New York: McGraw-Hill.

Tsui, A. S. 1984. A role-set analysis of managerial reputation. *Organizational Behavior and Human Performance, 34,* 64–96.

Tsui, A. S., & Barry, B. 1988. Interpersonal affect and rating errors. *Academy of Management Journal, 29,* 586–599.

Turner, J. C. 1987. *Rediscovering the social group: A self-categorization theory.* Oxford: Blackwell.

Williams, L. J., & Anderson, S. E. 1991. Job satisfaction and organizational commitment as predictors of organizational citizenship and in-role behaviors. *Journal of Management, 17,* 601–617.

Williamson, O. E. 1974. *Markets and hierarchies.* New York: Free Press.

Wilson, D. O. 1988. *Effects of task uncertainty upon link multiplexity for high and low performance project teams.* Unpublished doctoral dissertation, University of California, Irvine.

Zajonc, R. B. 1980. Feelings and thinking: Preferences need no inferences. *American Psychologist, 35,* 151–175.

Zucker, L. G. 1986. The production of trust: Institutional sources of economic structure, 1840–1920. In B. M. Staw & L. L. Cummings (Eds.), *Research in organizational behavior* (Vol. 8, pp. 55–111). Greenwich, CT: JAI Press.

Assessing the Political Landscape: Structure, Cognition, and Power in Organizations

David Krackhardt • Cornell University

This paper argues that an accurate cognition of informal networks can itself be a base of power, above and beyond power attributable to informal and formal structural positions. To explore this claim, a small entrepreneurial firm was studied. Perceptions of the friendship and advice networks were compared to "actual" networks. Those who had more accurate cognitions of the advice network were rated as more powerful by others in the organization, although accuracy of the friendship network was not related to reputational power.

The Bush team apparently failed to understand that Sen. Tower, though he had served in the Senate for 24 years, didn't leave behind a reservoir of good feeling. "I don't think they understood how despised John Tower was by his peers while he was there." says Democratic consultant Mark Siegel. [From an article analyzing why Bush failed to win confirmation of John Tower as secretary of defense, *Wall Street Journal,* March 10, 1989]

In his seminal book on power, Pfeffer (1981) included a chapter on how to assess who has power in organizations. He argued that this is an important question not only for researchers but also for political actors in organizations. That is, it is not enough to have power; one should also know the political lay of the land—how much and what kinds of power others have. Pfeffer quoted Pettigrew (1973: 240) at the beginning of this chapter: "An accurate perception of the power distribution in the social arena in which he lives is . . . a necessary prerequisite for the man seeking powerful support for his demands."

But how does one assess the political landscape in an organization? One way of addressing this question is to identify the key political actors in the organization, a task about which Pfeffer had much to say. But simply identifying the most powerful actors may not give sufficient information to anticipate the overall dynamics of resistance and support for political acts. Additional questions about these actors come to mind: Are these powerful actors organized such that they tend to act in unison? Do they represent different political constituencies? Precisely whom does each have influence over? Beyond knowing who is powerful, it is useful to know how the powerful and powerless are organized or structured. As Bailey (1969: 108) noted: "The man who correctly understands how a particular structure works can prevent it from working or make it work differently with much less effort than a man who does not know these things."

One way to approach the answers to these deeper questions about the political landscape is to study access to and the control of information flow in the organization (Pettigrew, 1973). As far back as 1965, Hubbell derived both a measure of the power of individual actors and an identification of powerful coalitions, using the actors' networks of ties. Laumann and Pappi (1976) documented how power accrued to those in central network positions in a community of elites. Brass (1984) discovered that centrality in work-related communication networks was a robust predictor of power in a printing company. As Pfeffer (1981: 130) stated: "Clearly the power that comes from information control . . . derives largely from one's position in both the formal and informal communication networks."

More to the point, the study reported in this paper suggests that power accrues not only to those who occupy central network positions in organizations but also to those who have an accurate perception of the network in which they are embedded. An individual who has an astute knowledge of where the network links are can have a substantial advantage. First, this information provides a good assessment of who is powerful in the organization, since the central actors in the network can be easily ascertained. Knowing who the central—and powerful—actors are in the organization is essential political knowledge. Second, this information can be used to identify where the coalitions are in an organization. Knowing where the coalitions are, how large they are, and where their support comes from gives one an edge in anticipating resistance and in mobilizing support for action or change. Third, an accurate assessment of the network can also reveal the weaknesses in political groups by exposing holes, gaps, and locations of lack of support for any particular coalition. Thus understanding the network provides a source of power independent of centrality in the network.

The central point in this paper is precisely that: Cognitive accuracy of the informal network is, in and of itself, a base of power. Both the concepts of power and cognitive accuracy are further developed below. In addition, I will argue that these two concepts are embedded in a structural context that must be taken into account in any empirical exploration.

Power

There has been much disagreement as to the precise meaning of power. Some writers have referred to it as the ability to get things done despite the will and resistance of others, the ability to "win"

political fights, or a capacity to outmaneuver the opposition (Bierstadt, 1950; Emerson, 1962). Others (e.g., McClelland, 1975; Kanter, 1979; Roberts, 1986) have stressed the positive sum nature of power, suggesting it is the raw ability to mobilize resources to accomplish some end (without specific reference to organized opposition). Still others refer to power as the ability to control premises of actions, such that power becomes almost unobservable (Bachrach and Baratz, 1962; Lukes, 1974; Mizruchi, 1983). Salancik and Pfeffer (1977) preferred to ignore these distinctions, noting that, while academics may quibble over the definition of power, those actually experiencing the effects of power in the real world seem to exhibit a consensus as to who has it.

Without fully resolving this debate, it is reasonable to assume that the answer to the question of who has power depends in part on an answer to the question, Power to do what? If the influence being sought is within the routine operation of the organization, then people who are "experts," people in "authority," and, generally, people who know how things work around the organization are likely to be seen as powerful. If, however, the influence entails a radical departure from prior operations, then the uncertainty that emerges is likely to arouse emotional responses to influence attempts. Affect-laden issues such as trust, respect, or liking may become important in evaluating who has the ability to mobilize support for the radical change (Krackhardt and Stern, 1988). In such cases, the powerful person may be someone who has referent power (French and Raven, 1968) or charisma (House, 1977; Bradley, 1987; Fiedler and House, 1988) in the organization rather than someone who simply has authority or expertise.

Following the advice of Pfeffer (1981), I have included multiple kinds of power in this study. The assumption is that some actors are powerful because they are acknowledged as adept at getting things done in the organization, despite some resistance (e.g., Brass, 1984) and that some actors are influential because of an ascribed individual trait that reflects intangible qualities of trust and personal charm. These two different assessments of power are offered as ones that actors will readily recognize as influence bases in organizations: the ability to get things done in spite of resistance and the ability to influence people through personal appeal and magnetism (which is termed charisma).

Cognitive Social Structure and Accuracy

Cognitive accuracy, the major independent variable in this study of power, requires the development and measure of two subsidiary concepts. First, one must identify a standard or "actual" network against which accuracy can be measured.[1] Second, one must assess each individual's cognitive representation of this standard. Accuracy, then, is simply how well the individual's cognitive map approximates the standard.

Both the "actual" and cognitive maps of the network can be derived from what has been called cognitive social structures (Krackhardt, 1987). Networks on any given relation have been traditionally represented by a square matrix, R_{ij}, where i is the sender of a relation and j is the receiver of the relation. Krackhardt argued that such relations might be fruitfully represented by three dimensions $R_{i,j,k}$ where k is the perceiver of the relation from i to j. There are several implications of this framework for looking at networks. For one, relationships are often based on people's perceptions and interpretations and not necessarily on observable, behavioral fact. For example, if two people act cordially toward each other, but underneath that cordiality they despise each other, it does not make sense to call them friends even though they may be observed to act like friends. Another implication of this three-dimensional framework is that the perceptions of the relationship from i to j can vary substantially. Person i may have a different view of the i-to-j relationship than person j has; both of these views may differ from that of a third bystander, person k. Krackhardt (1987: 119–125) found that such perceptions do vary considerably.

The current study was motivated by the question: How closely does each person's perception of the network approximate the "actual" network and how does this relate to power? To address this question, two types of aggregations were employed: The set of N individual perceived maps of the whole network, called "slices" of $R_{i,j,k}$; and the "actual" network, as defined by the two people actually involved in the relationship, referred to as the locally aggregated structure, or LAS (Krackhardt, 1987).

Just as power itself is a multidimensional concept, network relationships may be assessed on several dimensions. But the specific question is, what network relations are critical for the assessment of power? For example, a network composed

of incidental communication links, such as perfunctory "Hello's," may not be as rich in power information as a network composed of critical advice relationships. The study reported here was based on the cognitive social structures for two different types of networks that have been shown to be useful in understanding the dynamics of informal organizations (e.g., Lincoln and Miller, 1979; Burt, 1982: 25; Brass, 1984; Krackhardt and Porter, 1985, 1986). First, the advice network (who goes to whom for work-related advice) represents the instrumental, workflow-based network in the organization. The second network assessed was the friendship network, or what Lincoln and Miller (1979: 186) called the "primary network." This latter network is not necessarily linked to the routine work done in the organization, but it does capture important affective and social bonds that can affect trust, especially in times of change (Krackhardt and Stern, 1988).

Structural Influences

In pursuing issues of power, one cannot ignore critical contextual and structural factors that also operate to give certain actors privilege and power in an organization. Brass (1984) found that centrality in the informal network itself predicts power. But centrality also has important theoretical links to cognition (see Krackhardt, 1987, for a comparison of different types of centrality). A series of studies has found that central involvement in a social system increases one's ability to "see" the social system accurately (Freeman and Romney, 1987; Freeman, Romney, and Freeman, 1987). Freeman, Freeman, and Michaelson (1988) noted that "social intelligence," the ability to discern social groups and boundaries, evolves over time as participants gain experience in the social group. Freeman and Romney (1987) demonstrated that people's ability to recall social structure accurately was a function of whether they were members of the core group or were peripheral, transitory members. These results, combined with Brass's (1984)

---

[1] I use the term "actual" in quotes here and throughout this paper to quality its familiar meaning. The relationships referred to here may include behavioral components, but these behaviors in and of themselves do not define the relationships. Thus, "actual" networks are not defined by behaviors, per se, between actors, and therefore are not directly observable. Rather, the existence of an actual relationship is defined consensually by the two actors engaged in the relationship.

findings, suggest that centrality in the informal structure can lead to both cognitive accuracy and power.

Another structural power base that cannot be ignored is the formal position a person has in the organization. Clearly, those with more authority will have more power, on the average, than those with less authority. In addition, those higher in the organizational chart are responsible for a larger part of the organization. A first-line supervisor is responsible for the activities of his or her immediate subordinates. A manager of several supervisors is responsible for these supervisors and ultimately for the activities of all their subordinates. People's positions require them to pay attention to the way in which those under them work together and relate to each other. Thus, those higher up in the organization will have, by virtue of their position, a better opportunity to observe and take note of a larger part of the informal network. Consequently, they are likely to have a more accurate picture of the informal network. This should be particularly true in a small, entrepreneurial firm, where the owners/managers are known to be heavily involved in the details and day-to-day workings of the entire organization.

Those higher in the formal organization are forced to relate to a wider base of people. A first-line supervisor must coordinate the activities of a limited number of people, all of whom are likely to interact informally with each other and be doing similar work. A top-level manager must coordinate the activities of supervisors and managers from different functions and sectors of the organization. This responsibility gives higher-level managers more central positions in the formal organization, in that they will find themselves dealing with more issues that surface between departments or groups. This formal role is likely, in turn, to lead to opportunities to be in the middle of the informal network, acting as a bridge between groups of employees. Therefore, it is expected that formal hierachical level will also contribute to network centrality.

There are thus both structural and cognitive power bases in an organization. While it is proposed here that cognitive accuracy is a power base in and of itself, one must take into account the fact that this cognitive power base is influenced by formal and informal structural factors. Since these structural factors are sources of power in their own right, these sources are explicitly included as

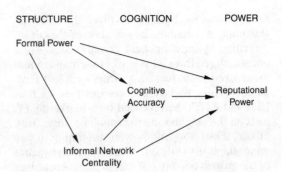

Figure 1 ■ Model relating structure, cognition, and power.

part of the cognitive model of power presented here.

Figure 1 displays this model, which relates structure, cognition, and power. Formal structure is shown as an exogenous variable leading directly to informal structure, cognitive accuracy, and power. Informal structure, in turn, contributes to cognitive accuracy and power. Finally, in accordance with the central theme of this paper, cognitive accuracy is predicted to contribute to power over and above the power already explained by the structural factors. This last link represents the main proposition of this paper:

Proposition: Controlling for formal and informal bases of power, cognitive accuracy of the informal network will be correlated with individual power in the organization.

To test the model in Figure 1 and the proposition posed above, a network study was conducted of a small hi-tech firm. Questionnaire and interview data were collected from which the cognitive social structures and "actual" networks were determined, and each employee provided assessments of how powerful and charismatic every employee was in the organization. From these data, the central proposition and model were tested directly.

Method

The Site

A small, entrepreneurial firm, called here Silicon Systems, was selected for study. The firm was located in an area known for its many small, start-up firms as well as some more established ones.

Silicon Systems' business involved the sales, installation, and maintenance of state-of-the-art information systems in client organizations. Their clients ranged from local banks to schools to medium-sized manufacturing firms to R&D labs. Until recently, their largest competitors, such as IBM and AT&T, had focused their marketing efforts on the neighboring metropolitan areas. But, of late, these competitors were beginning to pay more attention to Silicon Systems' market because of the growth potential of that market. According to the top managers of Silicon Systems, the small firm's competitive edge rested in its ability to respond more efficiently to idiosyncratic customer demands.

Silicon Systems was wholly owned by the three top managers, each of whom owned an equal share. All employees worked in the single-floored building owned by the company. They saw each other regularly, although the installers spent many days at sites rather than in the office. Thus, employees were familiar with each other to varying degrees, and each had an opinion about every other employee, with the occasional exception of new hires.

The firm had grown from three people to 36 people in fifteen years. Much of this growth occurred in the five years previous to the study. Most of these years had been profitable and the owners anticipated no downward trend in their business.

Reputational Measure of Power

A reputational measure of power was developed following the work of Brass (1984). In his study of nonsupervisory personnel, he obtained ratings from each person's supervisor and nominations of "who is influential" from the nonsupervisors. Such estimates have bias problems, since ratings are not based on comparable sources. One supervisor may provide higher overall ratings than another, even though the latter has more powerful subordinates. And, as Brass noted, nominations of colleagues who are "influential" have potential availability-bias problems stemming from the fact that respondents are likely to list only people who are currently salient in their minds. Moreover, it provides a dichotomous value that hides people's views of the degree of power they ascribe to their colleagues. The limitations of these measures were unavoidable because of the size of Brass's sample ($N = 160$). Despite these limitations, however,

Brass demonstrated reasonable internal consistency using different sources and different methods, and his reputational measures correlated well with his nonreputational measure of power, future promotion.

Because Silicon Systems was so small, the question of reputational power could be addressed more directly by asking each employee to rate all the employees (including him- or herself) on the two dimensions of power: the ability to get things done despite resistance and the ability to influence through personal magnetism (charisma). This procedure avoided the problem of availability bias, incomparable sources, and dichotomization. Moreover, with this multiple-source method, the internal reliability of the two power scores can be estimated. The directions for this part of the questionnaire operationally defined the two measures for the respondent:

> There are many ways in which people influence each other in the workplace. We are interested in two of these: charisma and power. For purposes of this questionnaire, we will define charisma as the influence derived from personal magnetism. A person who is charismatic tends to generate loyalty and enthusiasm in others. Power, on the other hand, is the ability to get things done that the power-holder wants done, in spite of whatever resistance he or she may encounter. People who are powerful can get most of what they want.

Each person rated each other person on a 7-point Likert scale on both charisma and the ability to get things done (potency). Two anchors were provided for each scale: "Not at all charismatic" to "Highly charismatic" for charisma, and "Not at all powerful" to "Highly powerful" for potency.

Formal Position

While power derived from formal position may be ambiguous in some larger organizations, this organizational base of power was quite clear in Silicon Systems. There were three distinct levels of formal authority. At the top level were the three owner-managers. Even though they took on different responsibilities and had different titles, they were equal partners and made all major company decisions jointly. The next level consisted of five managers, each of whom had supervisory responsibility over certain operational features in the organization. The remaining 28 employees had no formal supervisory title or authority. Formal position, then, was scored as follows: each of the three owners was given a formal position score of 3; the five managers were given a formal position score of 2; the remaining 28 employees were given a formal position score of 1.

Cognitive Accuracy

The cognitive social structure is a three-dimensional array of linkages, $R_{i,j,k}$, among a set of N actors, where i is the sender of the relation, j is the receiver of the relation, and k is the perceiver of the relation. Using Krackhardt's (1987) methodology, a questionnaire was designed to assess the cognitive social structure of two relations in the organization, friendship and advice. The directions for the "advice" section of the questionnaire were as follows:

> In this section, you will find a set of similar questions with a list of people after each question. The question is: "Who would this person go to for help or advice at work?" That is, if this person had a question or ran into a problem at work, who would they likely go to to ask, for advice or help? Please answer the question by placing a check next to the names of all the people the person is likely to go to. . . . Some people may go to several people for help or advice. Some may only go to one person. Some may not go to anyone, in which case do not check anyone's name under that question.

These directions were followed by 36 questions (e.g., "Who would Cindy Stalwart go to for help or advice at work?"), each asking the same question about a different employee. Each of these 36 questions was followed by a list of 35 names, any of which the respondent could check off in response to the question.

Similarly, another section of the questionnaire asked about friendship. The directions for this section paralleled those in the previous section and are reproduced here in part:

This time the question is: "Who would this person consider to be a personal friend?" Please place a check next to all the names of those people who that person would consider to be a friend of theirs.

Again, the question was repeated 36 times, once for each employee's name (e.g., "Who would Cindy Stalwart consider to be a personal friend?"), and each question was followed by a list of 35 names, any number of which the respondent could check off.

Two different aggregations of these cognitive social structures provided the basis for the two independent variables, "actual" network and "perceived" network. Each is specifically defined below.

Actual network. While recent work in the area of recall of network relations has cast doubt on an informant's ability to relate accurately to whom they actually talk on any given day (see Bernard et al., 1984, for a review), Freeman, Romney, and Freeman (1987) have shown that people are remarkably good at recounting enduring patterns of relations that they have with others. Thus, while people may not remember whom they talked to today or this week, they can accurately tell you whom they are in the habit of relating to over an extended period of time. Consistent with these results, Brass (1984) found that the workflow network in his study closely corresponded to the network reported by respondents. Since it is these enduring relational patterns that are of interest—as evidenced by the wording in the questions—the locally aggregated structure, or LAS (Krackhardt, 1987), was used as a proxy for the "actual" network. The LAS is an aggregation defined by the local participants in the network. It mimics the typical form in which network data are collected. Technically, the definition is as follows for the "actual" advice and friendship networks:

$$R_{i,j}^* = \begin{cases} 1 \text{ if } R_{i,j,i} = 1 \text{ and } R_{i,j,i} = 1 \\ 0 \text{ otherwise.} \end{cases}$$

Both i and j must agree that i goes to j for help and advice before the j $i \to j$ link is recorded as existing in the "actual" advice network.[2] Similarly, both i and j must agree that i considers j a friend before the $i \to j$ link is recorded as existing in the "actual" friendship network. Since the relationship is defined as existing when both parties agree that it exists, this measure of the "actual" network is direct and has obvious face validity.

Cognitive accuracy. Each participant's cognition of the network was taken simply from the set

---

[2]Since three of the 36 employees chose not to fill out the questionnaire, the following decision rules were used to deal with missing values if either $R_{i,j,i}$ or $R_{i,j,j}$ but not both, were missing, then $R_{i,j}$ was equal to the nonmissing value. If both were missing, then a voting scheme was used to determine the presence of a tie: $R_{i,j} = 1$ if $\frac{1}{n} \sum_{k=1}^{n} R_{i,j,k} \geq .5$ for all nonmissing k; else, $R_{i,j} = 0$.

of responses he or she selected on the network questionnaire. These responses are technically defined for person k as:[3]

$$R_{k_{i,j}} = \begin{cases} 1 \text{ if } R_{i,j,k} = 1 \text{ and } k \neq i \text{ and } k \neq j: \\ 0 \text{ if } R_{i,j,k} = 0 \text{ and } k \neq i \text{ and } k \neq j \end{cases}$$

There are several measures that can be used to assess the degree to which a person's perceived links correspond to the actual links. In a general form, the following 2×2 table portrays all the relevant information:

One could use simple percentages here to assess accuracy, such as percentage of links correctly identified $[d/(d + b)]$.

But such simple percentages do not take into account other types of accuracy. For example, one could just as easily argue that the percentage of nonlinks correctly identified as nonlinks $[a/(a + c)]$ is an important component of accuracy, or perhaps the percentage of identified links that are correct $[d/(d + c)]$ or the percentage of identified nonlinks that are correct $[a/(a + b)]$.

There exists a family of measures of correspondence for such 2×2 tables, measures that account for the information contained in all four of the above percentages. Fifteen such measures were reviewed and analyzed for desirable properties by Gower and Legendre (1986). Of these measures, one (called S_{14} in their article) stood out by exhibiting high resolution (appropriate sensitivity to small changes in correspondence) and low nonlinearity (low distortion at extreme values). This correspondence measure is defined as follows[4]:

$$S_{14} = \frac{ad - bc}{\sqrt{(a+c)(b+d)(a+b)(c+d)}}$$

Using simple arithmetic, this formula can be rewritten to show how this statistic combines the four percentages referred to earlier:

$$S_{14} = \sqrt{\left(\frac{a}{a+c} - \frac{b}{b+d}\right)\left(\frac{a}{a+b} - \frac{c}{c+d}\right)}$$

Given its statistically superior properties and appropriateness in this case, the S_{14} statistic was used to measure the degree of correspondence between an individual's map of the network and the "actual" network. Henceforth, I refer to this mea-

sure as the accuracy score for individual k, since it is how accurate the individual is in recounting the "actual" network that is of theoretical interest here. ADVACCUR and FRNACCUR are the variable names given to the accuracy scores for each respondent's cognitive map of the advice and friendship network, respectively.

Centrality

The graph-theoretic concept of centrality has a long and distinguished history in the area of network analysis (Bavelas, 1948; Stephenson and Zelen, 1989). The three most common measures of centrality—degree, closeness, and betweenness —are compared and reviewed by Freeman (1979).[5]

Of the three indices, betweenness is the one most closely, aligned with the idea of power; as Freeman (1979) put it, the individual who is in between other actors has more control over information flow from one sector of the network to another. That person becomes a gatekeeper of information flow. Moreover, betweenness is an indication of the nonredundancy of the source of information. To the extent that a person is connected to different parts of the network, and therefore has access to different, nonredundant sources of information, that person will have a wider variety of information at his or her disposal.

All three of these measures can be illustrated

---

[3]This aggregation contains only perceptions of ties (and nonties) between dyads in which ego (k) is not involved. The local ties (defined as those where $k = i$ or $k = j$) are excluded from this set of perceived ties because to include them would confound the measures of cognitive accuracy and the actual network, which is based on local ties only. In fact, this exclusion does not alter the subsequent results substantially. Only a small fraction of observations (2/36, or less than 6 percent) is eliminated. The correlations between accuracy scores that include local ties and scores that exclude local ties are .96 and .95 for advice and friendship, respectively. Nonetheless, to avoid even the small degree of confounding that does occur, these local ties were excluded in the analysis reported here.

[4]This statistic has also been called the point correlation coefficient and is equal to the value obtained by computing a simple Pearson correlation coefficient between the original elements in $R^*_{i,j}$ and Rk_{ij}.

[5]Another class of measures in network analysis, most strongly associated with Hubbell (1965), Bonacich (1987), and Salancik (1986), also carries the name "centrality." But the measures developed by these authors are aimed more at the concept of asymmetric status hierarchy, or "being at the top," than they are at the idea of "being at the center," which is the idea behind the graph theoretic measures used here.

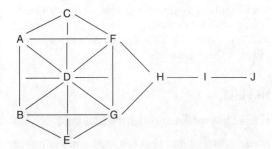

FIGURE 22.2 ■ Network exhibiting a kite structure.

by the position of actors in the hypothetical network in Figure 2. I call this network a "kite structure," and it represents the smallest network I have found in which the centrality based on each of the three measures reveals different actors as the most central in the network. Degree centrality is defined as the number of links connected to the person. For example, D has the most links, with a degree centrality of 6. Closeness centrality is defined as the inverse of the average path distance between the actor and all others in the network. Persons F and G have the highest closeness centralities in the network.

Betweenness is somewhat more complicated in its definition Using Freeman's (1979) notation, betweenness centrality is defined as follows:

$$C_B(k) = 2 \sum_{i}^{n} \sum_{j}^{n} \left[\frac{g_{ij}(k)}{g_{ij}} \right]$$

for all unordered triples $i,j,k (i < j$, and $i \neq j \neq k$ where n is the number of nodes in the network, g_{ij} is the number of geodesics (shortest paths) between nodes i and j in the network, and $g_{ij}(k)$ is the number of geodesics from i to j that include k. If one thinks of a network as a roadmap, and one starts at point i and travels to point j, the question is does one travel through point k to get there? To the extent that k lies on the shortest paths between each pair (i,j), then k would be said to have high betweenness centrality. In Figure 2. H has the highest betweenness centrality. H, in essence, can block or control communication from one end of the network to the other. H also has access to parts of the network that are not connected to each other, allowing richer, more differentiated information to reach H, D, F, and G are "better connected" (have more connections) than H, but their connections

are connected to each other, so that the information contained within these various parts tends to be redundant.

Centrality is expected to lead to power because it provides an exclusive control of information flow. In comparing the three centrality measures, Freeman (1979: 221) argued that a "person in such a position [such that he or she has a high betweenness score] can influence the group by withholding or distorting information in transmission." As such, betweenness captures the essence of what I mean theoretically by the concept of centrality. Moreover, since betweenness suggests access to differentiated quarters in the network, it is reasonable to argue that a person with the best betweenness position in the network stands to have a broader, more accurate overall picture of the network. Consequently, I used Freeman's betweenness index to measure centrality in this study.

Asymmetric relations. Freeman's review of graph-theoretic measures of centrality is based on symmetric graphs: the relationships represented in the network are assumed to be reciprocated. For example, if person A communicates with person B, then it is assumed that person B communicates with person A. Relations in this study, however, were not inherently symmetrical. Simply because A goes to B for advice does not mean that B goes to A for advice. It is even possible that friendships might be nonsymmetrical. One can imagine a situation in which A considers B a personal friend but B does not consider A a personal friend.

There are two ways to treat these asymmetries. On the one hand, one could assume that information only travels in the one direction specified by the asymmetric relation. For example, if A goes to B for advice, then one could assume that relevant information flow is from B to A and not vice versa. On the other hand, it may be more reasonable to assume that information flows in both directions as the result of an exchange, independent of who initiates the exchange. That is, just because A defers to B (by going to B for advice) does not mean that no information is passed from A to B in the exchange. In fact, by the very act of asking for advice. A is providing B with information about what A is doing or what is going on around A. For this reason, I assumed, in this study, that the presence of a relationship from A to B indicates an opportunity for an exchange of information in both directions, from A to B and from B to A. To operationalize this assumption, the measurement of centrality of an actor in the network was based on a symmetrized form of $R*$ defined as follows:

$$R^*_{s_{i,j}} = \begin{cases} 1 \text{ if } R^*_{ij} = 1 \text{ or } R^*_{j,i} = 1; \\ 0 \text{ otherwise.} \end{cases}$$

Advice centrality and friendship centrality are the variable names representing the betweenness centrality of each actor in the "actual" advice and friendship network, respectively.

Table 1 contains the raw data for the analysis performed in this study. The two parts of the power variable are given separately. Data are not included for persons 13, 24, and 35 because they did not fill out the network questionnaire and were therefore excluded from the analysis. The ID number

is the number I assigned to the respondent for identification. The raw data on the cognitive social structure choices for the advice network are provided in the Appendix.

Results

Reliability of Dependent Variables

It was assumed that people's reputation of power in the organization was an attribute of the individual whose reputation was being assessed. That is, since the firm was small, it was assumed everyone had a reasonably consistent and reliable view of how much power any other person might have. To the extent that everyone reaches a consensus on the reputational power of any individual, then

TABLE 1. Power, Positional, and Accuracy Scores

ID	Potency	Charisma	Formal position	Advice centrality	Friend centrality	Advice accuracy	Friend accuracy
1	2.193	3.000	1	0.82	0.00	0.481	0.386
2	2.843	5.281	1	0.14	64.85	0.332	0.344
3	2.750	3.625	1	0.00	10.66	0.373	0.390
4	3.612	4.838	1	0.00	31.04	0.425	0.331
5	6.187	3.843	2	119.77	0.00	0.485	0.292
6	5.625	4.875	2	37.18	53.43	0.459	0.334
7	3.531	4.468	1	1.15	0.70	0.422	0.310
8	2.354	2.258	1	0.40	0.00	0.371	0.155
9	2.871	4.906	1	0.00	1.59	0.441	0.398
10	3.437	4.656	1	9.48	0.00	0.332	0.199
11	2.531	3.968	1	0.00	16.72	0.429	0.383
12	1.718	2.218	1	14.54	5.61	0.211	0.329
14	2.580	3.516	1	0.00	14.90	0.313	0.187
15	2.766	3.566	1	2.79	1.42	0.429	0.301
16	6.225	5.290	3	19.38	41.72	0.419	0.323
17	5.322	4.906	2	34.22	0.00	0.514	0.340
18	4.483	4.468	1	4.75	1.66	0.435	0.332
19	6.875	4.875	3	97.61	62.30	0.410	0.349
20	3.687	4.593	1	4.96	39.57	0.378	0.362
21	3.586	4.482	1	8.16	54.15	0.413	0.355
22	3.093	4.218	1	2.23	0.00	0.352	0.275
23	1.687	2.500	1	0.14	0.00	0.416	0.352
25	2.645	3.354	1	33.02	0.00	0.390	0.177
26	3.031	5.000	1	0.43	4.13	0.474	0.414
27	5.031	4.187	2	19.14	1.36	0.397	0.336
28	2.812	4.281	1	0.00	0.00	0.499	0.291
29	5.062	5.625	1	31.31	96.39	0.384	0.361
30	4.125	4.281	2	32.65	8.19	0.430	0.441
31	3.200	3.892	1	0.00	0.00	0.422	0.380
32	1.741	2.225	1	0.00	0.00	0.378	0.325
33	2.906	4.625	1	1.63	39.35	0.301	0.381
34	2.937	4.187	1	0.00	11.63	0.469	0.406
36	6.069	4.800	3	0.66	0.00	0.417	0.220

the faith one can have in these reputational assessments increases.

To assess this assumption of consensus, or reliability. Cronbach's α was calculated for each of the two reputational measures, charisma and potency. Cronbach's α is an overall measure of agreement on a variable of interest, in this case, reputational power. The formula for Cronbach's α is provided by Carmines and Zeller (1979: 44):

$$\alpha = \frac{N\rho}{1 + \rho(N-1)}$$

where N is the number of scores an individual received (or 33, one from each respondent who filled out the questionnaire), and ρ is the average interrater correlation, or agreement, between all distinct pairs of the 33 respondents. An individual correlation between two raters was determined by correlating their ratings of the 36 people in the firm on their reputational power. The score is high to the extent that everyone agrees (i.e., there is small variance) on each person's power score relative to the distribution of scores received by individual people.

Both charisma and potency had high reliability coefficients (Cronbach's α = .96 and .99, respectively), demonstrating that there was very high consensus in the organization on who was influential on each of these dimensions. The correlation between the two power indicators was .63, indicating considerable overlap between the two measures. For this reason, the two measures were combined into a single dependent variable, overall power, using the factor scores from the first component of a principal components analysis (PCA) of the two variables.[6]

The means, standard deviations and intercorrelations among all the variables used in this study are presented in Table 2.[7]

To test more completely the model in Figure 1, a set of hierarchical regressions was performed on the dependent variable, overall power. The results are presented in Table 3 as reduced form equations (Cohen and Cohen, 1983: 361–366).[8] Formal position explains 43 percent of the variance in overall power. The two informal structure sources of power, centrality in the advice and friendship networks, add another 17 percent of explained variance (significant at the .007 level). Note, however, that advice centrality is not significant in the equation; only centrality in the

friendship network is significantly related to power when controlling for formal position ($\rho < .01$). It appears, then, that any advantage a person has by being central in the routine advice network is attributable to his or her formal position of power in the organization.[9]

In equation 3 of Table 3, cognitive accuracy on the advice and friendship networks explains an additional 8.2 percent variance ($\rho < .047$). Again, however, only one of the two added variables is significant: accuracy on the advice network. Understanding the friendship network is not significantly related to one's power reputation over and above being in the center of the networks and having a position of formal authority.

---

[6]The factor scores of a simple, two-variable PCA are a linear function of the sum of the z-scores of each variable: that is, each variable contributes equally to the variance in the factor scores. Whenever one performs a PCA on two variables, the first eigenvalue will always = $1 + r$ (1.628, in the present case), and the variance explained by this factor will be $1 + r/2$ (here, .814).

[7]As a supplemental overall test of the proposition, a full canonical analysis was performed on all seven variables. Potency and charisma were the dependent variables; cognitive accuracy in both the advice and friendship network were the independent variables; and the controlling variables, centrality in each of the informal networks and formal position, were partialled out of the canonical analysis. While this analysis produced two canonical factors, only the first of them was significant ($r < .05$). The canonical correlation was equal to .455, over three times its standard error (.147).

[8]Statistical tests in this paper are based on the usual OLS estimates of second moments. Such tests assume that observations are independent of one another. Recent literature questions this assumption in social science phenomena (Doreian, 1980; Dow, Burton, and White, 1982; Doreian, Teuter, and Wang, 1984). This problem has been found to be particularly severe in network research when the unit of analysis is the dyad (Krackhardt, 1988). Here, however, this network autocorrelation problem is attenuated by the fact that the dyadic data are aggregated to the individual-actor level of analysis before statistical tests are performed, and this Krackhardt-type problem is therefore not encountered.

[9]At the recommendation of one reviewer, these analyses were replicated using closeness centrality in place of betweenness centrality. The argument for closeness centrality is that it may be a better predictor of cognitive accuracy, since it represents that average path distance an actor is away from everyone else on the average. Using closeness, the results paralleled those found in Table 3, except that closeness was a weaker predictor than betweenness had been. In fact, closeness in the advice network was negatively, albeit in significantly, correlated with advice accuracy ($r = -.17$). Substituting closeness for betweenness in equation 2 of Table 3 results in an R^2 of .520 (vs. .597 when betweenness is used). While the strength of the predictions was reduced, each of the coefficients that were significant in Table 3 remained significant when closeness was used in place of betweenness.

TABLE 22.2. Means, Standard Deviations, and Correlations among Variables (N = 33)

Variable	Mean	S.D.
Power	0	1.00
Advice accuracy	.406	.0624
Friend accuracy	.326	.0704
Advice centrality	14.443	27.3039
Friend centrality	17.014	25.1941
Formal position	1.333	.6454

Correlation structure					
Variable	Power	1	2	3	4
1. Advice accuracy	.340*				
2. Friend accuracy	.146	.282*			
3. Advice centrality	.453**	.210	.031		
4. Friend centrality	.506**	.172	.236	.222	
5. Formal position	.656***	.240	.041	.566***	.161

*$p < .05$: **$p < .01$; ***$p < .001$.

However, an understanding of the advice network is significantly related to one's power reputation.

These results reveal an interesting juxtaposition of effects. Clearly, formal authority is correlated with reputed power, as expected, but the two networks relate in different ways to one's power base. Centrality in the friendship network—not the advice network—is a key factor in reputed power; but it is cognitive accuracy of the advice network—and not the friendship network—that adds a sig-

nificant amount of explained variance to one's power reputation.

A closer inspection of the simple relationships among the variables in Table 2 provides a partial explanation for these findings. Advice centrality and friendship centrality are both strong simple predictors of power (.45 and .51, respectively). But, while advice centrality is correlated with formal authority (.57), friendship centrality is not significantly related (.16). Most of the variance in power explained by advice centrality is already explained

TABLE 22.3. Hierarchical Regression Analysis of Reduced-Form Equations with Reputational Power as Dependent Variable*

Independent variables	(1)	Equation (2)	(3)
Formal position	1.017***	.879***	.782***
	(.210)	(.222)	(.210)
Advice centrality		.0015	−.0004
		(.005)	(.005)
Friend centrality		.161**	.0195***
		(.0048)	(.0049)
			5.091**
Advice accuracy			(2.02)
Friend accuracy			−.559
			(1.74)
R^2	.431	.597	.678
Hierarchical test of model			
ΔR^2		.166	.082
F		5.966	3.425
d.f		2,29	2,27
p		.007	.047

*$p < .05$; **$p < .01$; ***$p < .001$.
* Standard errors are in parentheses.

by formal authority: those central in the advice network are also those with higher authority. Since friendship centrality is not related to formal authority, however, it provides a unique contribution to power in the second step of the hierarchical regression. Knowledge of the advice network does not significantly covary with formal authority and therefore also provides a unique contribution to power in the third step of the regression.

Discussion

The network analysis conducted on Silicon Systems confirms the major proposition of this study, that an accurate picture of the informal network significantly correlates with power. But, the overall model presented in Figure 1, relating structural factors to cognition and power, received only qualified support (see Table 2). As predicted, formal position is significantly related to power and advice centrality. Contrary to the model's predictions, formal position does not significantly correlate with cognitive accuracy. Also, contrary to prior research (Freeman and Romney, 1987), centrality was not directly related to cognitive accuracy. Since these simple correlations were not confirmed in Table 2, more elaborate tests of the path coefficients for Figure 1 were not necessary, beyond the overall tests provided for by the hierarchical regressions reported in Table 3.

The question remains why the other relationships in Figure 1, which form the theoretical building blocks for the basic proposition of this paper, were not confirmed. One possible explanation for the lack of support for parts of the causal model may rest in the size of the firm. Because the firm is small, people all know each other and are relatively better informed on each other's relationships than they might be in a large organization. Thus, being in the center of the network or at the top of the formal hierarchy does not provide as strong an informational edge over others' vantage points. Perhaps in a larger organization, where many people are not even aware of each other's existence, these structural advantages may prove more predictive of cognitive accuracy. Future research on this topic could shed light on whether these results are generalizable to—or perhaps even enhanced in—larger firms.

Since the structural links to cognitive accuracy were not confirmed, the test of the major proposi-

tion of this study could have been reduced to a simple correlation between cognitive accuracy and reputational power without controlling for formal or informal positional power. It was necessary, nonetheless, to present the analysis in full, controlling for these theoretically important sources of power. The amount of variance in power explained by cognitive accuracy in the advice network alone was 11.6 percent ($= .341^2$); the direct contribution of the two accuracy indicators in equation 3 in the hierarchical analysis was 8.2 percent. This difference indicates that, as predicted by the theory, there is some, albeit small, spurious correlation due to structural effects. In the conservative approach taken here, the hierarchical test of the main proposition removes this spuriousness.

The study showed that reputational power of the members of the firm was significantly related to cognitive accuracy of the advice network, not the friendship network. Perhaps this is an indication of the extent to which power surrounded those who were capable of handling relatively routine operational problems. In answering questions about influence and power, employees were responding according to their experiences in their day-to-day lives in the organization. As mentioned above, those people in the "advice" network, the experts, are likely to derive power from such routine situations. Had the organization faced a nonroutine situation such as a crisis, however, it is possible that an understanding of the friendship network could have been more predictive of power in dealing with the crisis. Dealing with crises does not require routine information but, rather, it requires trust (Krackhardt and Stern, 1988). It is reasonable to speculate that understanding the friendship network, which better represents the trust relations in the organization, could prove more critical than understanding the advice network in such a nonroutine situation. Of course, this is only speculation, since the data reported here do not involve anything but routine operations.

Caveats and Limitations

The theory presented at the beginning of the paper argued that knowledge of the network is in its own right a base of power above and beyond the power accrued through other formal and informal bases. This causal claim leads directly to the prediction of association. However, as is always the case in field studies such as this, one cannot infer the causal link from the data. There are three possible reasons for an association between two variables, A and B: A leads to B, B leads to A, or there is a third variable (or set of variables) that leads to both A and B, in which case we say that the relationship is spurious. It is worth speculating about each of these possible reasons for the underlying association.

In the current study, the theoretical claim underlying the observed association is that network knowledge leads to reputational power. But is it possible that one's reputation as a powerful person leads to a better understanding of the social network? Perhaps, for instance, as one becomes reputed to have more power, one is fed differentially more social information. However, if this were the case, then it is likely that this differential focus of information would in turn lead to the actor becoming central in the network, and partialling out network centrality would remove the association between reputational power and network knowledge.

A more serious concern is whether the observed relationship is spurious. Despite some statistical attempts to control for clear sources of spuriousness, there are potentially an infinite number of variables that are unaccounted for. For example, suppose that power reputation is an attribution based on the fact that certain people are closer to the action in the organization. suppose that being closer to the action also gives people certain advantages in knowing the social network. Then one could argue that the observed relationship between reputational power and network knowledge is spurious. In part, one could also argue that being "closer to the action" is already controlled for by controlling for centrality in the network; but then again, it may not control for all of it. I have controlled for what I argued to be the most reasonable sources of spuriousness. But, clearly, one cannot conclude that all sources of spuriousness have been eliminated. One reason for including the raw data in this paper was to invite scholars to explore alternative models that might explain the reported relationships.

Power. Another important issue surrounds the use of the term "power" in this study. The literature on power in organizations is extensive, and on a theoretical level, this study sheds light on only a small part of that literature. The emphasis here is on the power induced through information flows in the informal network. Dependencies and power

in an organization can emanate from many sources, not simply how information is passed from one person to the next. For example, I have no indication of the important workflow interdependencies (cf. Brass, 1984). Nor am I able to locate the critical resources or who has control over them (cf. Pfeffer and Salancik, 1978). Nor do I have information on who is performing the important functions in the organization and the exclusivity with which they perform them (see Dubin, 1957: 62, for the first explicit treatment of this two-component definition of power). My use of the term "power" in this study is relatively specialized and may not generalize to other conceptualizations or other contexts. Whether understanding the social network has any bearing on whether an individual has control over critical resources is an interesting question that must be left to future research.

Secondly, there is a methodological limitation to this study, one discussed in full by Pfeffer (1981: 54–57). Using reputation to measure the relative power of an individual has potential biases. The measure assumes that the raters know who is powerful and that they are willing to tell the researcher honestly what they know. Despite these possible problems, Pfeffer (1981: 56–57) noted that when raters seem to agree on their power attributions, "this consensus and consistency in power ratings provides some evidence for at least a shared social definition of the distribution of power." Given the high reliability scores of the components of the reputational measure in this study, I share Pfeffer's conclusion that at least I have demonstrated that there is consensus in the power attributions.

Conclusion

This paper demonstrates that knowledge of the relevant network is itself associated with reputational power, independent of other structural bases of power. In particular, further work exploring the importance of the structure of different kinds of relations in organizations may prove fruitful in understanding the dynamics of organizational behavior.

As Mintzberg (1983: 1) put it, "Power is a major factor, one that cannot be ignored by anyone interested in understanding how organizations work and end up doing what they do." The contribution in this paper is to focus on how political actors themselves gain power by following in the footsteps of organizational scientists in understanding and identifying the power bases in the political arenas in which they operate. A meta-power emerges here: the power of power. If power is the ability to influence a target, then meta-power is an indirect power derived from knowing and using the power others have to influence the target. Given all the attention paid to structural and resource bases of power, it is surprising that so few have investigated the power due to such political knowledge.

REFERENCES

Bachrach, P., and M.S. Baratz. 1962 "The two faces of power." American Political Science Review, 56: 947–952.

Bailey, F.G. 1969 Strategems and Spoils: A Social Anthropology of Politics. Oxford: Blackwell.

Bavelas, Alexander. 1948 "A mathematical model for group structure." Human Organization, 7: 16–30.

Bernard, H. Russell, Peter Killworth, David Kronenfeld, and Lee Sailer. 1984 "The problem of informant accuracy: The validity of retrospective data." Annual Review of Anthropology, 13: 495–517.

Bierstadt, Robert. 1950 "An analysis of social power." American Sociological Review, 15: 730–738.

Bonacich, Philip. 1987 "Power and centrality: A family of measures." American Journal of Sociology, 92: 1170–1182.

Bradley, Raymond T. 1987 Charisma and Social Structure: A Study of Love and Power. Wholeness and Transformation New York: Paragon.

Brass, Daniel J. 1984 "Being in the right place: A structural analysis of individual influence in an organization." Administrative Science Quarterly, 29: 518–539.

Burt, Ronald S. 1982 Toward a Structural Theory of Action. New York: Academic Press.

Carmines, Edward G., and Richard A. Zeller. 1979 Reliability and Validity Assessment. Beverly Hills, CA: Sage.

Cohen, Jacob, and Patricia Cohen. 1983 Applied Multiple Regression/Correlation Analysis for the Behavioral Sciences. Hillsdale, NJ: Erlbaum.

Doreian, Patrick. 1980 "Linear models with spatially distributed data: Spatial disturbances or spatial effects?" Sociological Methods and Research, 9: 29–60.

Doreian, Patrick, Klaus Teuter, and Chi-Hsein Wang. 1984 "Network autocorrelation models: Some Monte Carlo results." Sociological Methods and Research, 13: 155–200.

Dow, Malcolm M., Michael L. Burton, and Douglas R. White. 1982 "Network autocorrelation: A simulation study of a foundational problem in regression and survey research." Social Networks, 4: 169–200.

Dubin, Robert. 1957 "Power and union management relations." Administrative Science Quarterly, 2: 60–81.

Emerson, Richard M. 1962 "Power-dependence relations." American Sociological Review, 27: 31–41.

Fiedler, Fred, and Robert J. House. 1988 "Leadership theory and research: A report of progress." In Cary L. Cooper and Ivan T. Robertson (eds.), International Review of Industrial and Organizational Psychology: 73–92. New York: Wiley.

Freeman, Linton C. 1979 "Centrality in social networks: Conceptual clarification." Social Networks, 1: 215–239.

Freeman, Linton C., Sue C. Freeman, and Alaina G. Michaelson. 1988 "On human social intelligence." Journal of Social and Biological Structures, 11: 415–425.

Freeman, Linton C., and A. Kimball Romney. 1987 "Words, deeds and social structure." Human Organization, 46: 330–334.

Freeman, Linton C., A. Kimball Romney, and Sue C. Freeman. 1987 "Cognitive structure and informant accuracy." American Anthropologist, 89: 310–325.

French, John R.P., and Bertram Raven. 1968 "The bases of social power" In Dorwin Cartwright and Alvin Zander (eds.), Group Dynamics, 3d ed.: 259–269. New York: Harper & Row.

Gower, J.C., and Pierre Legendre. 1986 "Metric and Euclidean properties of dissimilarity coefficients." Journal of Classification, 3: 5–48.

House, Robert J. 1977 "A 1976 theory of charismatic leadership." In J.G. Hunt and L.L. Larson (eds.), Leadership: The Cutting Edge (189–207) Carbondale, IL: Southern Illinois University Press.

Hubbell, Charles H. 1965 "An input-output approach to clique identification." Sociometry, 28: 377–399.

Kanter, Rosabeth Moss. 1979 "Power failure in management circuits." Harvard Business Review, July/August: 65–75.

Krackhardt, David. 1987 "Cognitive social structures." Social Networks, 9: 109–134.
1988 "Predicting with networks: Nonparametric multiple regression analysis of dyadic data." Social Networks, 10: 359–381.

Krackhardt, David, and Lyman W. Porter. 1985 "When friends leave: A structural analysis of the relationship between turnover and stayers' attitudes." Administrative Science Quarterly, 30: 242–261.
1986 "The snowball effect: Turnover embedded in communication networks." Journal of Applied Psychology. 71: 50–55.

Krackhardt, David, and Robert N. Stern 1988. "Informal networks and organizational crises: An experimental simulation." Social Psychology Quarterly, 51: 123–140.

Kruskal, Joseph B., and Myron Wish. 1978 Multidimensional Scaling. Beverly. Hills, CA: Sage.

Laumann, Edward O., and Franz U. Pappi. 1976 Networks of Collective Action: A Perspective on Community Influence Systems. New York: Academic Press.

Lincoln, James R., and Jon Miller. 1979 "Work and friendship ties in organizations: A comparative analysis of relational networks." Administrative Science Quarterly, 25: 181–199.

Lukes, S. 1974 Power: A Radical View. London: MacMillan.

McCelland, David C. 1975 Power: The Inner Experience. New York: Irvington.

Mintzberg, Henry. 1983 Power in and around organizations. Englewood Cliffs; NJ: Prentice-Hall.

Mizruchi, Mark S. 1983 "Who controls whom? An examination of the relation between management and boards of directors in large American corporations." Academy of Management Review, 8: 426–435.

Pettigrew, Andrew M. 1973 The Politics of Organizational Decision-Making. London: Tavistock.

Pfeffer, Jeffrey. 1981 Power in Organizations. Boston: Pitman.

Pfeffer, Jeffrey, and Gerald Salancik. 1978 The External Control of Organizations. New York: Harper & Row.

Roberts, Nancy. 1986 "Organizational power styles: Collective and competitive power under varying organizational conditions." Journal of Applied Behavioral Science. 22: 443–458.

Salancik, Gerald R. 1986 "An index of subgroup influence in dependency networks." Administrative Science Quarterly, 31: 194–211.

Salancik, Gerald R., and Jeffrey Pfeffer. 1977 "Who gets power and how they hold onto it: A strategic-contingency model of power." Organizational Dynamics, 5: 3–21.

Stephenson, Karen, and Marvin Zelen. 1989 "Rethinking centrality: Methods and examples." Social Networks, 11: 1–37.

APPENDIX: Cognitive Social Structure of Advice Network

Below are the raw cognitive social structure (CSS) scores for the advice network for all 33 respondents who completed the questionnaire. The number to the left of the equal sign is the ID number of the respondent. The 36×36 matrix represents that respondent's slice of the CSS. The diagonals of each slice are undefined and are so indicated with an x.

$$
1 =
\begin{pmatrix}
x0010100000000000110000100100000000000 \\
0x00100000000000000000000000010000000 \\
00x011000000000010000000100000000 \\
000x00000000000110100000100000000 \\
0000x0000000000001000000000100000000 \\
00001x000000000001000000010000000000 \\
000101x000000000011000000010100000000 \\
0000100x00000000000000000010000000 \\
00000000x1000000100000000000001000000 \\
000000000x000001010000000010000000 \\
0000100000x00000010000000010000000 \\
00000100000x001011000000010000000 \\
00001000000x0000000000000010000000 \\
0000100000000x000000000000010000000 \\
00001000000000x0000000000010000000 \\
000000000000000x00100000000000000001 \\
0000000000000000x0100000000000000 \\
0001000000000010x1010000010000000000 \\
000000000000001000x0000000000000001 \\
0000100000000000000x0000001000000000 \\
0000100000000000010x00000100000000 \\
0000000001000000100000x000000010000000 \\
000010000000000000000x0001000000000 \\
0001010000000000110100x001000000000 \\
00001000000001001000000x00000000000 \\
0000100000000000001000000x0000000010 \\
00000000000001001001000000000x0000000 \\
000000000000010010010000000x00000000 \\
00001000000000000001000000000x0000000 \\
0000000000000011100000000000x000000 \\
000000000000000100100000000000x00000 \\
00001000000000000000000000000100x0000 \\
00001000000000000001000000001000x000 \\
00001000000000000001000000010000x00 \\
0000000000000001001000000000000x1 \\
0000000000000001001000000000000x
\end{pmatrix}
$$

$$
2 =
\begin{pmatrix}
x0010000000000000010000010010000000000 \\
0x0110000000000000000000000010000000 \\
00x011000000000100100000000000000 \\
100x0000000000010010000001000000000 \\
0000x1000000000010010000001000000000 \\
00100x000000000100100000000000000 \\
000110x000000000011000000010000000000 \\
0000100x00000000010000000000000000 \\
00000000x10000010100000000010000000 \\
000000001x0000010100000000001000000 \\
0000100000x00000010000000010000000 \\
10100100000x00000100000000000000000 \\
000010000000x00100100000000010000000 \\
01001010000x000000000000010000000 \\
0000101000000x000000000000000000000 \\
00001000000000x0010000000000100001 \\
000010001100000x0100000000001000000 \\
10010000000000010x100001001000000000 \\
000000000000000000x000000000000000000 \\
0000110000000011000x0000001000000011 \\
00001000000000000010x0000000000000 \\
00001000110000000100x00000010000100 \\
000000000000000000000x0000000000000 \\
0100101000100110001000x000010001000 \\
00001000100100100100000x01100010000 \\
00001100000000010010000000x0000000010 \\
100110000000010110000100x000000000010 \\
00110000000010110001000x000000000 \\
0000010000010010010000001000x00100001 \\
000010000000000000100000000x0000000 \\
00001000110000010100000000001000x000 \\
00001000001001001000000000000x00000 \\
0100101100100110001001000001100x1000 \\
00001000000000100100000000001000x000 \\
00001000010000000001000000010000x00 \\
0000110000000001001000000000000x0 \\
00001000000000100100000000000000x
\end{pmatrix}
$$

$$
3 = \left(\begin{array}{l}
x0000100000000000100000001000000000\\
0x001000000000000010000000010000000\\
00x011000000000000000001000000000\\
000x000000000000011000001000000000\\
0000x1000000000001010000000000000\\
00001x0000000000010000000000000000\\
000100x0000000000110000000000000000\\
0000100x00000000000100000000000000\\
00000000x100000100000000000100000\\
000000001x000001000000000000100000\\
0000100000x00000010000000010000000\\
00100100000x00000000000010000000000\\
00001000000x001001000000000000000\\
0000101100000x0000010100000010001000\\
00001000000000x0000010100000010000100\\
0000010000000000x001000000000100001\\
00000100000000000x01010000001000000\\
00000000000000000x100000001000000000\\
0000000000000000000x0000000000000000\\
000011000000000001x00000000010001000\\
000000000000000001010x000000000000\\
000000000100000010100x000000001000000\\
010000110010011000100x00000010010000\\
00011000000000001100000x001001000000\\
0000110000010010010000x00000100000\\
0000010000000000000000x0000000010\\
00000000000000000010000x000000000\\
000001000001001000000000100x00000000\\
0000100000000000001000000000x0000000\\
000000000000000101010000000x000000\\
00000000000000100100000000000x00001\\
01000001000011000100100000100x0000\\
00000000000000000001010000001000x100\\
000000000000000000010000011000x00\\
000001000000000010010000000000000x1\\
0000000000000000100100000000000000x
\end{array}\right)
$$

$$
4 = \left(\begin{array}{l}
x000010000000000000000000000000000\\
0x00100000000000000000000000000000\\
00x001000000000000000000000000000\\
000x00000000000000000001000000000\\
0000x0000000000001000000000000000\\
00000x0000000000010000000000000000\\
0000010x0000000000000000000000000\\
000100x000000000000000000000000000\\
00000000x0000000000000001000000\\
000000000x000010000000000000000\\
0000100x0000000000000000000000\\
00000100000x000000000000000000\\
00000000000x001000000000000000\\
0000100000000x00000000000000000\\
00001000000000x0000000000000000\\
0000000000000000x00000010000000\\
000010000000000000x0000000000000\\
00001000000000000000x0000000000\\
0000000000000000000x000001000000\\
000000000000000010000x0000000000\\
00001000000000000000x00000000000\\
00001000000000000000000x0000000000\\
0000000000010000000000x0000000000\\
00001000000000000000000x000000000\\
00000000000010000000000x000000000\\
0000010000000000000000000x00000000\\
0000100000000000000000000x000000\\
000000000000010000000000000x00000\\
00001000000000000000000000x0000\\
000010000000000000000000000x0000\\
0000000010000000000000000000300x00\\
00000000000000000010000000000000x0\\
000000000000000010010000000000000x
\end{array}\right)
$$

$$
5 = \left(\begin{array}{l}
x00001000000000000000000000000000000\\
0x00100000000000100000000000000000\\
00x001000000000000000000000000000\\
000x00000000000000000001000000000\\
0000x0000000000010000000000000000\\
00001x00000000010000000000000001\\
000010x0000000000000000000000000\\
0000100x000000000000000000000000\\
00000000x00000010000000000010000000\\
000000000x0000010000000000000000\\
0000100000x000000000000010000000\\
00000100000x000000000000000000000\\
00001000000x001000000000000000000\\
0000101000000x00000000000000000000\\
000001000000000x0000000000000010000000\\
000010000000000x101000000000000001\\
00001000000001x010000000000000001\\
0000000000000000x100000010000000000\\
000010000000001110x0000000000000001\\
0000010000000000000x00000010000000\\
00001000000000000010x00000000000000\\
0000100010000000000000x0000010000000\\
000010000000000000000x00000100000000\\
00001000000010010010000x00000000000\\
00000100000000000000000x0000000000\\
000000000000000001000000x000000000\\
00000000000010010000000010x00000000\\
00001000000000000000000x001000000000\\
0000100000010010010000x0000000000\\
000000010000000000000000x0000000\\
0000000000000000010000000x000000\\
000000000000000010010000000000x00000\\
00001000000000000000000000000100x1000\\
000010000000000000000000000001000x000\\
00001000100000000000000000000x00\\
0000000000000000010010000000000000x1\\
00000000000000000100100000000000000x
\end{array}\right)
$$

$$
6 = \left(\begin{array}{l}
x00001000000000001100000001000000010\\
0x001000001000000000000000000000000\\
00x00100000000001000000000000000000\\
000x100000000001100000010000000000\\
0000x00000000001000000000000000000\\
00001x000000000101000000000000000\\
000010x000000000000000000000000000\\
0010110x0000000000000000000000000\\
00000000x000000000010000000110000000\\
010000000x000001000000000000000000\\
0000100000x00000000000000000010000000\\
00100100000x0000000000000000000000010\\
000010000000x001011000000100000000\\
0000100000000x00000000000000000000\\
00001000000000x00000000000000000000\\
000000000000000x001000000000000001\\
00001000000000000x01000000000000000\\
00010000000000000x10000000000000000\\
000010000000000100x0000000000000001\\
000010000000000001x0000000010000000\\
000010000000000010x0000000000000000\\
00001000000000001000x00000000000000\\
0000100000000000000x0000000000000000\\
00001100000000000010000x001000000000\\
00000100000100100100000x00000000000\\
000001000001000000010000x0000000010\\
100001000000000011000000x000000000\\
000000000001001000000000100x00000000\\
000010001000000001000000000x0000000\\
0000000000000000010000000x000010\\
00000100000000100100000000000x00000\\
00001000000000000000000000000x000\\
00001000000000000000000000000x000\\
00001000000000000000000000000x00\\
000001000000001011000000000000x0\\
0000000000000000100100000000000000x
\end{array}\right)
$$

$$
7 = \begin{pmatrix}
x00001000000000000000000001000000000\\
0x011000000000000000000000000000000000\\
00x0010000000000000000000000000000000000\\
000x000000000000010000000010000000000\\
0000x000000000010010000000000000000001\\
00000x0000000001001000000100000000001\\
000110x00000000010000000000000000000\\
000100x000000000000000000000000000000\\
00000000x000000100000000000011000000\\
000000000x0000000100000000000000000000\\
0000100000x000000010000000000000000000\\
00000100x0000000000000000000000000000\\
000000000000x00100100000000000000000\\
0000101000000x000010000000000000000000\\
00001000000x00000100000x001000000000\\
000000000000000x00100000000000000001\\
0000100000000000x01010000001000000\\
00000000000000000x1010000100000000\\
000000000000000001000x000000000000001\\
0000100000000000000x00100000100000000\\
00000000000000000110x000001000000\\
000000000000001001000000x0000000000\\
000100000000000000000x000000000000\\
000010000000000010000x0010000000000\\
0000000000000000100000000x00000000\\
000000000000000000000000000x000000010\\
0000000000000001101001000000x00000000\\
00000000000010010000000000x00000000\\
00011000000000000000000000000x0000000\\
0000000000000000101000000000x000000\\
00000000000000010010000000000x00000\\
000010000000000000000000000000x0000\\
00001000000000000000000000001000x000\\
000010001000000010000000000000000x00\\
000000000000000010000000000000000x0\\
000000000000000100100000000000000x\\
\end{pmatrix}
$$

$$
8 = \begin{pmatrix}
x00001000000000000000000001000000000\\
0x00100000000000000000000000000000000\\
00x0010000000000000000000000000000000\\
000x0000000000001000000010000000000\\
0000x001000000010000000000000000000\\
00100x0000000000010000000000000000\\
000010x00000000000000000000000000\\
0010110x010000011000100000000000000\\
00000000x1000001000000000011000000\\
000000010x000000100000000000000000\\
0000100000x000000000000000000000000\\
00000000000x000000000000000000000\\
000010010000x0010000000000000000000\\
00001000000x0000000000000000000000\\
00000100000000x000000000000000000\\
00000000000000x000000000000000000\\
0000000000000000x010000000000000000\\
00000000000000000x0000000010000000\\
0000000000000000x00000000000000000\\
00000000000000000x0000000000000000\\
00001000000000010x00001000000000\\
0000000010000010000x0000000000000\\
0000100000000000000x0000000000000\\
00010000000000000x001000000000000\\
00010010000000000000x000000000000\\
0000010000000000000000x0000000000\\
0000000000000000000000x00000000\\
00000000000000000000000x00000000\\
00010000000000000000000x0000000\\
00000000010000010000000000x000000\\
000000000000001000000000000x0000000\\
0000100000000000000000000000x0000\\
0000100000000000000000000000x000\\
00010000000000000000000000000x00\\
00000000000100000000000000000x0\\
00000000000000010010000000000000x\\
\end{pmatrix}
$$

$$
9 = \begin{pmatrix}
x00101000000000001000000001000000000\\
0x001000100000000000000000010000000\\
00x001000000000000000000000000000000\\
000x000000000000010000001000000000\\
0000x1000000000010100000000000000000\\
00001x000000000001010000000000000000\\
000110x0000000000000000000000000000\\
0000100x000000000000000000000000000\\
00000000x0000001000000000000001000000\\
000010001x00000100000000000001000000\\
0000100000x0000001000000010000000\\
00100100000x000000000000010000000\\
00000000000x00110000000000000010000000\\
0000100000000x00000000000001000000\\
00001000000000x0000000000000100000\\
00010000000000x000000001000000000\\
00001000000000000x01000000000000001\\
100100000000000x0000000001000000000\\
00000000000000100x000000000000001\\
00001000000000000x0001000010000000\\
00001000000000001010x00000000000000\\
00000000010000010000x0000000000000\\
00001000000000000000x0000000000000\\
0000100000000000000000x001000000000\\
000000000001001000000x0000000000000\\
00001100010000000000000x0000000010\\
00001000000001010100000x000000000\\
0000000000001001000000001100x00000000\\
000010000000000000010000000x0000000\\
0000100000000001010000000x000000\\
000000001000001100000000001z00000\\
000010000000000000000100000100x0000\\
00001000000000000001010000000x000\\
0000100001000001000010000000000x00\\
0000010000000000010000000000000x1\\
00000000000000010010000000000000x\\
\end{pmatrix}
$$

$$
10 = \begin{pmatrix}
x01111000100000011000010010000000000\\
0x011110000000010000000010100000000\\
00x001000110000000000000000110000000\\
010x000001000000110010000010000000000\\
0000x10000000001001000000100000000\\
00001x0000000000010000000000000010\\
100110x10000000010010000010100000000\\
0001100x0000000010010000010000000000\\
00001000x1000001000000000001000000\\
000011000x00000010001000001000000000\\
0100001100x00000001000000010000000\\
01000100000x00000000000010000000010\\
00001000100x0010000000000000000000\\
0100001100000x0000100000000010001000\\
0100001100000x000010000000010001000\\
000000000000x0010000000000000000\\
0000100000000010x010000000000000000\\
0001100000000000x100000010000000000\\
00000000000000000100x000000000000\\
00001001000000000x00000000100000000\\
00000000000000000010x0000000000000000\\
0010000010000001100x000100000000000\\
01001011001001100001000x00000100010000\\
0001000001000000110000x001000000000\\
00001000000000100000000x00000000000\\
00001001000010000000000x0000000010\\
00100000000000000110000000x00000000\\
00000000000010010000000100x001000000\\
00011000010000001000010010x0000000\\
0000100000000010100000000x000000\\
000000000000000010100000000x00000\\
01001011001001100001000000100x1000\\
00001000000000000010000000010000x000\\
00001000010000010000100000000000x00\\
00000000000000010010000000000x1\\
10000000000000010010000000000000x\\
\end{pmatrix}
$$

$$
11 = \begin{pmatrix}
x0000100000000000000000001000000010 \\
0x0010000000000001000000001000000000 \\
00x001000000000000000000000000000000 \\
000x0000000000001000000001000000000 \\
0000x000000000000100000001000000000 \\
00000x0000000001001000000000000000 \\
000010x0000000000010000001010000000 \\
0000100x000000000001000010000000000 \\
00001000x10000001000000000001000000 \\
000010010x100000010000000001000000 \\
000000001x000000100000000001000000 \\
0000000000x00000000000000000000000 \\
00100100000x0000000000001000000010 \\
000010000000x001001000000010000000 \\
0000101000100x0000010000000010000000 \\
00001000000000x000010000000010000000 \\
00001000000000000x0101000000000000000 \\
00011000000000000x1000000010000000 \\
000011000000000100x00000000000000000 \\
0000100000000000000x00000010110000000 \\
0000100000000000000010x0000000000000 \\
0000100001000000100000x00000000000000 \\
00001010000000000000100x0000010000000 \\
0000100000000000000000x001000000000 \\
00000000000100100000000x00000000000 \\
00100100000000000000000x0000000010 \\
00011000000000000110000x000000000 \\
000000000000100100000000x00000000 \\
00001000000000000000100000x0000000 \\
0000100011000000100010000100x000000 \\
0000010000000010000000000000x000000 \\
000010000010000100000000000100x1000 \\
0000000100010000000100000000100x10 \\
00001000010000010000100000001000x00 \\
00000000000000010010000000000000x0 \\
0000000000000001001000000000000000x
\end{pmatrix}
$$

$$
12 = \begin{pmatrix}
x0111111000100001100001001000000010 \\
0x101111000001100011011001001001111110 \\
11x111111001111100111011011111100111110 \\
101x010011010000111010010110010000010 \\
0110x111001101100011011100110100011110 \\
10101x000001000101000001011100000010 \\
111111x100110110011100110110100011110 \\
1011110x0001000001101000011000000010 \\
10010100x100000011100000001001000010 \\
100101001x00000011100001011001000010 \\
0110111100x0011000110110010010011110 \\
10111100000x10000110001111100000010 \\
101001000001x001001000000110100100011 \\
0110111100100x100011011001001001111110 \\
01101111001001x0001101100100100111110 \\
000011000000100x0010010000000100100011 \\
1000010011000000x010000100100000010 \\
10110100110100001x10000101100100000010 \\
100011001100000110x0000010110011001100011 \\
0110111100011000110001x011101000010011110 \\
000011001100000001010x00000100001000010 \\
0110111000100111000110x100100010011110 \\
01101110001000111011011101x0010110011110 \\
101111001101000011101001x011001000010 \\
0000010000011001001001000001x10100100011 \\
11101111000111111001101101x0010111111 \\
101101001101000011101001011x001000010 \\
000001000001100100100001010x00100011 \\
0110111000100110001101100100x0011110 \\
100101011100000011100001001001x000010 \\
0000010000001001010010000001101000x00011 \\
01101110001001100011011001001001x1110 \\
0110111000100110001101100100100011x110 \\
011011100111001101110100100010011x110 \\
00000100000001001010000001000000000x1 \\
000001000000100100100000000000010001x
\end{pmatrix}
$$

$$
14 = \begin{pmatrix}
x0000000000000001000000001000000000 \\
0x001000000000000000000000000000000 \\
00x00000000000000000000000000000000 \\
000x000000000000000000000000000000 \\
0000x000000000000010000000000000000 \\
00000x000000000001000000000000000000 \\
000010x000000000000000000000000000 \\
0000100x000000000000000000000000000 \\
00000000x100000000000000000000000000 \\
000010000x00000000000000000000000000 \\
0000100000x0000000000000000000000000 \\
00000000000x0000000000000000000000 \\
000000000000x0010000000000000000000 \\
0000100000000x0000000000000000000000 \\
0000100000000x00000000000000000000 \\
0000000000000000x001000000000000000000 \\
00000000000000000x00000000000000000000 \\
0000000000000000000x10100000000000000 \\
000000000000000000100x00000000000000 \\
0000100000000000000x0000000000000000 \\
0000000000000000000000x000000000000 \\
000010000000000000000x0000000000000 \\
00000000000000000000000x000000000000 \\
000000000000000000000000x00000000000 \\
00001000000000000000000000x000000000 \\
0000000000000000000000000x0000000000 \\
0000100000000000000000000000x0000000 \\
000000000000000000000000000x00000000 \\
00010000000000000000000000000x0000000 \\
00000000100000000000000000000x000000 \\
0000000000000001000000000000000x0000 \\
00001000000000000000000000000000x00 \\
0000100000000000000000000000000x00 \\
00000000000000001000000000000000x0 \\
0000000000000001001000000000000000x
\end{pmatrix}
$$

$$
15 = \begin{pmatrix}
x000010000000000000000000001000000000 \\
0x00100000000000000000000000010000000 \\
00x011000000000000000000000000000000 \\
000x00000000000001001000001000000000 \\
0000x000000000101010000001000000000 \\
00101x000000000001000000001000000000 \\
001110x0000000010010000001010000000 \\
0000000x00000000000000000000000000 \\
00000000x100000010000000000001000000 \\
100010001x0000001000010000101100000 \\
0000100000x0001000010010000000000 \\
10000100000x00000000000000000000010 \\
000011100000x0110101100000101010000 \\
0000101000000x1000010000000000000 \\
00001010000000x000001001000010000000 \\
000010000001000x00100000010001000001 \\
00001000000000000x0101000010010000000 \\
0001100000000000x1010000010000000000 \\
00001000000001000x0000000010000000001 \\
00001000000000000x0001001010000000 \\
00001000000000001100x000000100000000 \\
00101100000001000100x01001010000000 \\
0100101000000010000110x1000010000000 \\
101111000000000001001000x001000000010 \\
00001100000100100100000x01100100000 \\
10000100000000000000000x0000000010 \\
00101100000000000101000000x000000000 \\
00000100000010010000000000x00100000 \\
01101100000000100111010000000x000000 \\
0000100000000010100000000000x000000 \\
00000000000000010010000000000x00001 \\
0100101000000010001100000000100x0000 \\
00101010000000100000000000000x000 \\
0010100001000000000010000000000x00 \\
00000100000000000010000010000000x0 \\
000000000000000010010000000000000x
\end{pmatrix}
$$

$$
16 = \begin{pmatrix}
x0010100000000001110000100110 0100000 \\
0x0010000000000000000000000000000000 \\
00x00100000000000000000000000000000 \\
100x01000000000011100001001000000010 \\
0000x10000000011010100000000000001 \\
00001x0000000011010000000000000011 \\
000010x00000000000000000000000000 \\
0001100x0000000000000000000000000 \\
00000100x0000001010000000001000000 \\
000000000x00000101000000001000000 \\
0000100000x00000000000000000000000 \\
00000100000x0000000000000000000000 \\
000011000000x0011010000010100100001 \\
0000100000000x000000000000000000 \\
0000100000000x0000000000000000000 \\
000011000000100x1010000010110110011 \\
00001000010000000x01000000000001000001 \\
1001000000000000x100001001000000000 \\
00001100000000100x010000001000000011 \\
00001000000000000x00000000000000000 \\
00001000000000011010x000000000000000 \\
00001000000000000000x000000000000000 \\
00001000000000000000x0000000000000 \\
1001100000000000011110000x001000000000 \\
00001100000100110100000x00000100001 \\
00000100000000000000000x0000000000 \\
10000000000000000101010000x001000000 \\
0000000000001001001000001000x00000001 \\
00001000000000000001000000000x0000000 \\
00001000000001101000000000x000001 \\
000011000100100110101000100000x00001 \\
00001000000000000000000000000x0000 \\
00001000000000000000000000000x000 \\
0001000000000000000000000000000x00 \\
0000000000000100100000000000000x1 \\
00000100000000110100000000000000x
\end{pmatrix}
$$

$$
17 = \begin{pmatrix}
x00101000000000010000000001000000000 \\
0x0000000000000000010000000010000000 \\
10x00100000000000000000000000000000 \\
000x0000000000011000000001000000000 \\
0000x0000000001010000000001000000 \\
00001x0000000010000000000001000000 \\
000010x0000000000000000000000000 \\
0001100x0000000000000000000000000 \\
00000000x100000000000000000001000000 \\
000000000x00000010000000000001000000 \\
0000100000x00000001000000010000000 \\
00001000000x00000000000010000000000 \\
000010000100x0011000000010100000000 \\
00001000000000x0000010000000010000000 \\
00001000000000x000010000000010000000 \\
00001000000000x10100000000001000000 \\
00001000000000x0101000001000000 \\
000000000000000x100000001000000000 \\
00001000000000110x01000000001000001 \\
00001000000000000x0000000001000000 \\
000010000000001010x000000010000000 \\
00000000010000001000x00000000000000 \\
00001000000000000100x0000010000000 \\
00001000000001010000x001001000000 \\
00001100010000110000000x00000000000 \\
00000100000000000000000x0000000000 \\
00000000000000010000000x000000000 \\
00001000000010010000000000x00000000 \\
00001000000000001000000000x0000000 \\
000010000000001010000000000x000000 \\
00000000000000110100000000000x000000 \\
00001000000000001100000000000x0000 \\
00001000000000001000000001000x000 \\
0000000001000001000010000000000x00 \\
00000000000000001101000000000000x1 \\
00000100000000011010000000000000x
\end{pmatrix}
$$

$$
18 = \begin{pmatrix}
x00001000000000000000000001000000000 \\
0x0110000000000010000000001010000000 \\
00x0010000000000000000000000000000 \\
000x00000000000010010010010000000000 \\
0000x0000000000010100000000000000 \\
00000x000000000010000000000000000 \\
000110x00000000010000000010000000 \\
0000100x000000000000000000010000000 \\
00000000x10000001000000000001000000 \\
000000001x0000010000000000001000000 \\
0001001000x00000000000000010000000 \\
10000100000x0000000000000010000000 \\
000000000000x0010000000000000000000 \\
0000101000000x000000000000010000000 \\
00001000000000x00000000000010000000 \\
00000000000001100x0010000010010010001 \\
0000000001000000x0001000000001000000 \\
0001000000000000x101000001000000000 \\
00001000000001100x0000000000000000001 \\
00001000000000000x0000001000000010000 \\
00000000000000000100x000001000000000 \\
0001000010000000000x000000000000000 \\
00001000000000000000x0000010000000 \\
00001000000000000100x001000000000 \\
00000000000010010000000x00000100000 \\
00001000000000000000000x000000000 \\
0001000000000000100100100x000000000 \\
00000000000010010000000100x00000000 \\
00001000000000000000000000x0000000 \\
00000000100000100000000000000x000000 \\
00000000000001000000000000000x00000 \\
000010000000000000000000000100x0000 \\
00001000000000000000000001000x000 \\
00001000100000000000000000000x00 \\
000000000000000010000000000000000x1 \\
00000000000000001001000000000000001x
\end{pmatrix}
$$

$$
19 = \begin{pmatrix}
x00001000000000001100000001000000000 \\
0x00100000000001011000000001000000000 \\
00x01100000000000100000000000000000 \\
000x100000000000111010010010010000000 \\
0000x1000000000110101000001001000000 \\
00001x000000001001000000001000000010 \\
00110x00000000100000000010010000000 \\
0000100x0000000100000001000000000 \\
00000000x1000001010000000001000000000 \\
000011000x0000011101000001001000000 \\
0000101000x0000000000000000010001000 \\
0000010000x00000000000001000000010 \\
000011000000x0011110100000101 1000000 \\
0000101000000x00000000000000010001000 \\
00001000000000x0000000001010000000 \\
00001100000100x01101000001010000001 \\
00001100010000011x1101000001001000001 \\
00000100000000001x100001001001000000 \\
00001000100000111x0100100001000001 \\
000011100100000000111x1000001011000000 \\
00001100000000011110x000001001000000 \\
00001100000000011101x01001011000000 \\
000010000000000000101100x0000001000000 \\
000111100000001110100x001011000000 \\
00001100000000110100000x01001000001 \\
000011000000000001000000x0000000010 \\
001111100000000001110100100x001000000 \\
00001100000010010010000000110x00000000 \\
000111100000000011110010010x1000000 \\
00001110000000001110100100100x000010 \\
000110000001000100000000000000x00000 \\
000010000000000000001000000000100x1000 \\
00001000000000010010000100101100x000 \\
00001000010000010000100000011001x00 \\
0000100000000010010000010000000000x1 \\
000011000000000010010000000000000001x
\end{pmatrix}
$$

$$20 = \begin{pmatrix}
x000000000000000001001000001000000000 \\
0x001000000000000001000000000010000000 \\
00x001000000000000000000000000000000000 \\
000x000000000000001000000001000000000 \\
0000x000000000001001100000000010000000 \\
00000x000000001001000000000000000000 \\
000010x000000000111000001000000000 \\
0000100x000000000000000000000000000 \\
00000000x1000001001000000010000000 \\
000000001x000001000000000001000000 \\
0000100000x000000001000000010000000 \\
00000100000x000000000000010000000000 \\
000000000000x0010011000000010000001 \\
0000100000000x00001000000010000000 \\
00001000000000x00001000000010000000 \\
00000000000000x001000000000000000000 \\
0000000010000001x010000000000100000 \\
0001000000000000x000001001000000000 \\
00001000000000100x1000000010000000 \\
0001000000000001001x000000010000000 \\
000010000000000000011x000000010000000 \\
00000000100000001001 0x00000011000000 \\
00010000000000000000100x00000010000000 \\
10010000000000000010000x001000000000 \\
0000100000010010010000x0001000000 \\
000001000000000000000000x0000000010 \\
1001000000000000000100100x000000000 \\
000010000001001001000100x10000000 \\
0000100000000001001100000000x0000000 \\
00000000110000010010000000 1x000000 \\
0000000000000001001000000000x00000 \\
0001000000000000000100000000100x0000 \\
00001000000000000001000000001000x000 \\
00001001000000010010000000011000x00 \\
0000000000000001000000000000000x0 \\
000010000000000110110000001010000000x
\end{pmatrix}$$

$$21 = \begin{pmatrix}
x0001100000000000001010000010 0 uu00000000 \\
0x001000000000000001000000000010000000 \\
00x011000000000000101000001000000000 \\
000x110000000000011010000010000000000 \\
0000x100000000000101000000000000000 \\
00000x000000000000101000000000000000 \\
000010x000000000001000000000010000000 \\
0000100x000000000101000000000000000 \\
00000000x000000100010000000100 0000 \\
00001000x0000001010000000001000000 \\
0000100000x00000000000000000010000000 \\
0000100000x0000000000000010000000 \\
000011000000x001001000000000000000 \\
0000100000000x00000000000000010000000 \\
0001000000000x000010100000000010000000 \\
00000000000000x0100000000000000001 \\
0000000000000000x010000000000000000 \\
000001000000000x1010000010000000000 \\
00011000000000x010100000000000000 \\
0001100000000000x1100000000000000 \\
00001100000000000010x00000010000000 \\
000010000000000010111x00000011000000 \\
000010000000000000000x0000000010 \\
000111000000000001111 00x001000000000 \\
00001100000000100001000x01000000000 \\
000001000000000000000000x0000000010 \\
00000000000000000010100000x000000000 \\
0000000000001001000000000100x00000 \\
00001100000000001010000000x1000000 \\
000011000000000101010000000x1000000 \\
00000100000000100100000000000x00000 \\
000000000000000000000010000001 00x0000 \\
0000100000000001000000000001000x000 \\
00001100000000101001000000010000x00 \\
000001000000000010000001000000000x0 \\
00000000000000001000000000000000000x
\end{pmatrix}$$

$$22 = \begin{pmatrix}
x001010000000000011000010010 00000000 \\
0x01101000000000010000000010100 00000 \\
00x011000000000000100000000000000000 \\
000x1000000000000100000000010000000 \\
0001x0000000000001110001001010000000 \\
00100x00000000001001000000000000000 \\
000110x000000000100000010010000000 \\
0001100x000000001000000010000000 \\
00000000x10000010000000000011000000 \\
001011000x0000011000101001000000100 \\
0001100000x0000010000010000010001000 \\
10100100000x0000000000010000000000 \\
000010000000x0010110000001010000000 \\
0001100000x100100000100100000001000 \\
000110100000000x001000001001010000000 \\
001011000000100x001000000000000000 \\
001011000100000x010010000000100100 \\
10001000000000000x100001001000000000 \\
00101100000000110x0000000000000000 \\
001110000000000011x0001001010000000 \\
0001100000000001110x0010010000000000 \\
001011001000001110x0100100100000100 \\
01011010001001101101 01x1001010001100 \\
100110000000000011000 10x000010000000 \\
00001000000010010110100x0001000000 \\
00011100010000001000000x0000000010 \\
0000100100000 000011000000x000000000 \\
000010000000100110100000000x01000000 \\
001110001000000001000010010x0000000 \\
00011000000001101000000000x000000 \\
00000100000000100100000000000x00000 \\
01101010001001101001010000010100x1100 \\
011111010000000000110100000001000x000 \\
00111100010000011000101001010000x00 \\
100C01000000000000000000000000000x0 \\
00101100000000001101000000011000010001x
\end{pmatrix}$$

$$23 = \begin{pmatrix}
x00100000000000001000001001000000000 \\
0x01100000000000000000000000010000000 \\
00x00100000000000010000000010000000 \\
000x0000000000001100000001000000000 \\
0000x000000000001001010000000000001 \\
00001x000000000001000000001000000000 \\
000110x0000000011010000001000000000 \\
0000100x000000000001000000000000000 \\
00000000x10000001000000000001000000 \\
000000001x000001000000000001000000 \\
000000000x0000000000000000000000000 \\
00001100000x00000000000000000000010 \\
0000000000x0010000000000000000001 \\
000000100000x0000000100000010000000 \\
00001000000x00000100100010000000 \\
000010000001001x0110100000010001001 \\
000001000000000x01010000011000000 \\
001100000000000x1010000001000000 \\
0000110000000001010x010000010000000 \\
0000101010000000111x1001001010000000 \\
00110001000000000111 0x0000010001000000 \\
000010000100000011100x0001011000000 \\
000111101000000111101 0x1001011000001 \\
0001100000000011101 00x001011000000 \\
001001000001000101100000x01100000001 \\
0000000000000000010000 00x0000000010 \\
000000000000000010100000x000000001 \\
000000000000100100000000x00000001 \\
000011000000000111010010010x1000000 \\
000010000000010101000000000x000000 \\
00000000000000100000000000000x00001 \\
000000100000010000001011000100x0000 \\
0000001000000000010000000001000x0000 \\
0000100000000010101101000011000x00 \\
000000000000000000100000100000000x0 \\
000001000000000110100000000100010001x
\end{pmatrix}$$

$$25 = \begin{pmatrix}
x011010001001001011000011110000000010 \\
0x1011000001001001100001101100000010 \\
10x011000000000010000001000000000010 \\
101x1100000000011100001001000000010 \\
0000x111100010011011100011111110000011 \\
10101x0000110011010100011100010011 \\
001010x110001000111100001101110000010 \\
1010110x0000100110101000011110000010 \\
00001100x100100010101000011011000010 \\
100011001x0010010100100101001000110 \\
0010100000x00000011000001001000000 10 \\
10101100000x10011010000001111001000110 \\
1010111111101x001111110011111111100011 \\
00101000000000x00001100000100100000010 \\
00101000000000x0001100000001000000010 \\
100011001001100x111010001111101100011 \\
0000110010010001x0101000011000000011 \\
10101100000000001x101001001000000010 \\
1011111000000100111x010011110111100011 \\
0010110000001001101x1000110011000010 \\
00001100000000011010x000011001000010 \\
00101000110000010100x00010001000110 \\
00101000000000000001100x00100100000010 \\
10010100000000001110100x011000000010 \\
1010111111101100111111000x1110110011 \\
100011000001100100100000 1x0100100011 \\
1000010000000011101001000x001000000 \\
0010110000110010010000000110x01100011 \\
001011001000000110110000100x0000010 \\
000010001100000101010001000x000010 \\
1000010000000100110100000110001x00011 \\
001010000000000011000000000100x0010 \\
0010100000000000011000000001000x010 \\
0000100010000010101001000000x10 \\
0000000100010010010000011000000 00x1 \\
0000010000011001101000000100000 10001x
\end{pmatrix}$$

$$26 = \begin{pmatrix}
x000010000000000001000000010000000000 \\
0x0010000000000000001000000010000000 \\
00x0010000000000000000000000000000000 \\
000x10000000000011010000001000000000 \\
0000x1000000000010010000000000000001 \\
00001x00000000001001000000000000000 \\
000010x000000000010000000000000000 \\
0000100x000000001000000000000000000 \\
00000000x1000000100000000000001000000 \\
000010000x00000010000000000000000000 \\
0000101000x000000010000000010000000 \\
00000100000x0000000100000010000000 \\
000011000000x0010110000000000001000000 \\
0000101000000x000001000000010000000 \\
00001000000000x00000000000010000000 \\
00000000000000000x001000000000000001 \\
00001000000000001x0100000000000000001 \\
000000000000000000x1010000001000000000 \\
000000000000000100x00000000000000001 \\
00001000000000001x000000000000000000 \\
0000010000000010010x000000000000000 \\
0000000001000000010000x00000000000000 \\
0000010000000000100x000000010000000 \\
00010000010000001110000x001001000000 \\
000011000000000100100000x000000000000 \\
000001000000000001000000x0000000000 \\
0000010000000000010100000x001000000 \\
00001100000001001000000000100x00000000 \\
00001100000000001000000000x0000000000 \\
00001000000000000101000000000x000000 \\
0000000000000010010000000000x00001 \\
0000010100000000001100000000100x0000 \\
000011100000000000011000000001000x000 \\
0000000001000000100000100000000000x00 \\
0000000000000000100100000000000000x1 \\
0000000000000001001000000000000000x
\end{pmatrix}$$

$$27 = \begin{pmatrix}
x00101000000000001000000001000000000 \\
0x000000000000000000000000000000000 \\
00x001000000000000000000000000000000 \\
000x000000000011000000010001000000 \\
0000x0000000000010000000000000000 \\
00000x000000000001000000000000000 \\
000110x0000000010000000010000000000 \\
0000100x0000000000000000000000000 \\
00000000x0000001000000000001001000000 \\
000000000x000001100000000100100000 \\
000000000x000000000000000000000000 \\
00001000000x000000000000000000000000 \\
000000000000x001110000000100100000 \\
000000000000x0000000000000000000000 \\
00000000000000x0000000000000000000 \\
0000000000000x0110000001001000000 \\
000000000000000x110000001001000000 \\
00000000000000001x100000001001000000 \\
00001000000000011x0000001001000000 \\
00001000000000001x0000000100000000 \\
0000000000000000000x0000001001000000 \\
0000000001000000100000x00001001000000 \\
000000000000000000x0000000000000000 \\
0000000000000001110000x001001000000 \\
000000000000100111000000x01001000000 \\
0000100000000000000x0000000000000 \\
0000000000000001100000000x001000000 \\
0000000000010010000000000x00000000 \\
000010000000000011000000010x1000000 \\
00001000000000001110000x001001000000 \\
00000000000000000000000000000x0000 \\
00000000000000000000000000000x000 \\
0000000000000000000000000000x00 \\
0000000000000001001000000000000x1 \\
0000000000000001001000000000000x
\end{pmatrix}$$

$$28 = \begin{pmatrix}
x001110000000000011000000010000000000 \\
0x001000000000000010000000010000000 \\
00x001000000000000000000000000000000 \\
000x000000000001000000010000000000 \\
0000x000000000010010000000000000000 \\
00001x0000000000100000000000000000 \\
000010x0000000010000000000000000000 \\
0001100x00000000100000001000000000 \\
00000000x1000000100000000000001000000 \\
000010001x00000100000000000001000000 \\
0000100000x00000010000000010000000 \\
10100100000x000000000000010000001000 \\
000111010000x0010110000101100000000 \\
0000100000000x0000000000000000000000 \\
0001000000000x000000000000000000000 \\
000010000000000x00100000000000000001 \\
000100011000001x0100000000001000001 \\
00011000000000000x100000001000000000 \\
00001100000000000x0000000001000000001 \\
0001000000000000001x0000001010000000 \\
0000100000000010010x000000000000000 \\
0001000110000001000x000000001000000 \\
000010000000000000100x0000001000000000 \\
00001000000000000010000x001000000000 \\
00001101010000011010100 0x01111000000 \\
000001000000000000000000x0000000010 \\
00011000000000011000000x000000000 \\
00011000000100100100000101x00000000 \\
0000100000000000001000000000x0000000 \\
000100011000000100000000000x000000 \\
000000000001001000000000100100x00000 \\
0000100000000000000000000000100x0000 \\
00001000000000000000000000000x000 \\
00010001000000100000000000000000x00 \\
0000100000000000000000000000000x1 \\
0000000000000001101000000000000001x
\end{pmatrix}$$

$$
29 = \begin{pmatrix}
x00001000000000000000000001000000000 \\
0x0011000000000000000000000010000010 \\
00x001000000000000000000000000000010 \\
000x00000000000000000000001000000010 \\
0000x10000000001001000000000000000 \\
00000x00000000011010000000010000011 \\
000011x0000000001000000000001000010 \\
0001110x100000000100000000001001000010 \\
00000100x0000001000000000001000010 \\
000011000x00000010000000000011000010 \\
0000110000x0000000100000101000010 \\
00000100000x0000000000000001000000 \\
000011101000x001101000010010110000011 \\
0000110000000x00000000000010000010 \\
00001100000000x010000010010000010 \\
00001100000100x0100000001000000001 \\
0000110011000001x01001000000110000111 \\
00001010000000000x0000000001000000010 \\
00001100000000110x000000010010000011 \\
000011000000000000x0000000010000000 \\
00000000000000000000x0000000010000000 \\
0000110001000000010000x0000000000000 \\
00001100000000000000000x00001000010 \\
000011000000100100000000x001001000010 \\
0000100000000001001000000x0000000011 \\
00000100000000010010000x000000000011 \\
00011100110010011110000000x001000000 \\
00011100110010011110000000010x1000011 \\
00001100110000001010000000101x100010 \\
00001100000001001001000000000x00011 \\
00001100000000001001000000000100x0010 \\
000011000000000100100000000001000x010 \\
0000100011000001000010000001000x00 \\
00000100000001001000000000000000x1 \\
00001000000000000100000001001000000x
\end{pmatrix}
$$

$$
30 = \begin{pmatrix}
x0010100000000001000000001000000000 \\
0x0010000100000000000000000010000000 \\
00x001000000000000000000000000000000 \\
000x10000100000001100000001001000000 \\
0000x0000000000010101000001001000000 \\
00001x00000000001010000000001000010 \\
000110x0000000000110001001001000000 \\
0000100x00000000100000001001000000 \\
00000000x100000010000000000001000000 \\
000000001x0000001000000000001000000 \\
0000101000x0000000000000010000000 \\
10000100000x000000000000010000000 \\
0000000000000x001001000000000001000000 \\
0000100000000x000001000000010000000 \\
00001000000000x000000000000010000000 \\
000001000000000x101000000001000011 \\
00001000010000000x010000001001000001 \\
00010000000000000x10000001001000000 \\
00001100000000110x0000001001000011 \\
000110010000000010x00000001011000000 \\
000000000000000001010x00001001000000 \\
00000000010000001000x00000000000000 \\
000001000000000000000x0000010000000 \\
00011000000000001000000x001001000000 \\
00000100010010010010000x00001100000 \\
00000100000000000000000x0000000010 \\
001100000000000001110000000x001000000 \\
00001100000010000000001000x00100000 \\
000010000000000001000000000x0000000 \\
00001000000000001110000000100x000000 \\
00000100000100100000000000001x00000 \\
00001000000000000000000000000100x0000 \\
00001000000000000000000000001000x000 \\
00000000010000000000000000000x0000000010 \\
00000000000000010010000010000000x1 \\
00000000000000010010000000000000000x
\end{pmatrix}
$$

$$
31 = \begin{pmatrix}
x00000000000000000000000001000000000 \\
0x00100000000000000000000000000000000 \\
00x001000000000000000000000000000000 \\
000x00000000000001000000010000000000 \\
0000x0000000000001000000000000000000 \\
00000x000000000001000000000000000000 \\
000010x0000000000000000000000000000 \\
0000100x000000000000000000000000000 \\
00000000x00000010000000000000000000 \\
000000000x0000001000000000000000000 \\
0000100000x000000000000000000000000 \\
00000100000x0000000000000000000000 \\
000000000000x0010000000000000000000 \\
0000100000000x00000000000000000000 \\
0000100000000x00000000000000000000 \\
00000000000000x0010000000000000001 \\
000000000000000x0100000000000000000 \\
0000000000000000x10000001000000000 \\
0000000000000000100x00000000000000001 \\
00001000000000000x0000000000000000 \\
000000000000000000010x000000000000000 \\
00001000000000000000x000000000000000 \\
000000000000000000010x0000000000000 \\
0000100000000000000000x00000000000 \\
00000000000000000010000x0000000000 \\
000000000000000100000000x000000000 \\
000010000000000000000000x000000000 \\
00000000000000000100000000x00000000 \\
00001000000000000000000000x0000000 \\
00000000000000001001000000000x00000 \\
000010000000000000000000000x0000 \\
00001000000000000000000000000x000 \\
000010000000000000000000000000x00 \\
0000000000000000010000000000000x1 \\
000000000000000100100000000000000x
\end{pmatrix}
$$

$$
32 = \begin{pmatrix}
x00000000100000001000001001000000000 \\
0x0010101000000000000000000010000000 \\
10x001000000000000000000000000000000 \\
100x100001000000100000001000000000 \\
0000x00001001001011000001000000001 \\
00001x000000000010000001000000000 \\
010010x0000000000001000000001011000000 \\
0000100x010000000110100001000000000 \\
00000000x1000001000000000011000000 \\
000000000x00100110001001001111000000 \\
0000100000x001000001010000010001000 \\
10000100000x0000000000000000010 \\
00001100010x00100100001011000000 \\
0100101000100x1000010011000010001100 \\
01001000000000x00001001000010001000 \\
000011000001100x101000001000100000 \\
000010001100000x1000101001101100000 \\
000010000100100x1000000001011000000 \\
00001010010010010x0000001111100000 \\
00001000000000001x0000001010000000 \\
00001001010010011101x000001010000000 \\
00001001100100111100x01001001000100 \\
010010000000101010000x001010000000 \\
000011000001000111100x001010000000 \\
00001000000010010011000x01000000001 \\
0000100000000000000100x0000000010 \\
00000000000000011110000000x000000001 \\
000000000000100110100000001x01100000 \\
000010000001001011000000x0000000 \\
00001000100100111100000000x0000000 \\
000010000001001111000001001000x00000 \\
00001000000011010000000000100x0000 \\
010010100010010100110101000010000x000 \\
010010001100100111101000001111000x00 \\
00001100000000011000000000000000x0 \\
000000000000000100100000000000000x
\end{pmatrix}
$$

$$
33 = \begin{pmatrix}
x0010100000000000110000000010000000000 \\
0x0010000000000000101000000001000000000 \\
00x011000000000000010000000000010000000 \\
000x1000000000000011000010010000000000 \\
0000x1001001000101110000010110001000 \\
00000x00000000000000000000000000000000 \\
000110x1000000000010010000010000000000 \\
0000100x00000000000100000000000000000 \\
00001000x1000000100000000000010000000 \\
000000000x0000000000100000000000000100 \\
0000101000x0000000010000000010001000 \\
10100100000x000000000000010000000010 \\
00000000000x0000000000000000000000000 \\
0000100001100x000000000100000100000 \\
00001000000000x00101100000010001000 \\
000000000000000x00000000000000000000 \\
000000001000000x000010000000001000100 \\
10010000000000000x101001001000000000 \\
000000000000000000x000000000000000000 \\
00001000100000000001x0001000011000000 \\
000000000000000000000x00000000000000 \\
00000000110000000000000x000000001000100 \\
01001010001000100011100x0000010001000 \\
100100000000000000110000x001000000000 \\
0000100000000100100000000x00100000000 \\
00001100000000000000000000x0000100010 \\
10011000000000000010010000x0000000000 \\
0000000000000010010000000100x00000000 \\
00110100010010000000000000x1001000 \\
00001000110000001000000000000x000000 \\
0000010000000010000000000000000x00000 \\
000010100010010000100000000100x1000 \\
00001110000010000100000001001000x010 \\
0000000001000001000010000000001000x00 \\
00001100000000000100000100000000x0 \\
0000000000000000010010000000000000x
\end{pmatrix}
$$

$$
34 = \begin{pmatrix}
x000100000000000001000000001000000000 \\
0x0010000000000000010000000000010000000 \\
00x001000000000000010000000000000000000 \\
000x0000000000000001010010010000000000 \\
0000x00000000000110101000000010000000 \\
00100x0000000000010000000000000000000 \\
000010x0000000000010000000000000000000 \\
0000100x00000000001000000000000000000 \\
00000000x1000001010000000001000000 \\
000010000x00000101000000000000000000 \\
0000100000x000000100000000010000000 \\
00000100000x00000010000010000000000 \\
000000000000x001001000000000000000000 \\
0000100000000x000010000000010000000 \\
0000100000000x0001000000000x00000000 \\
0000000000000000x001010000000000001 \\
00000000000000000x01010000000010000000 \\
00000000000000000x100000001000000000 \\
00001000000000110x000000001000000001 \\
000010000000000001x0000000000000000 \\
000011000000000011010x000000000000000 \\
00000001000001010x00x0000000000000000 \\
000010000000000001000x0000000000000 \\
00001000000000000010100x001000000000 \\
000010000000100110000000x00000000000 \\
0000100000000000001000000x0000000010 \\
0000000000000000010100100x000000000 \\
0000000000000100100100000000x00000000 \\
00001000000000000010100000000x0000000 \\
00000000000000001010000000000x000000 \\
0000000000000001001000000000000x00011 \\
00001000000000001000000000100x0000 \\
00001000000000001000000000001000x000 \\
000000001000000101000000000000000x00 \\
000000000000000010010000000000000x1 \\
000000000000000010010000000000000000x
\end{pmatrix}
$$

$$
36 = \begin{pmatrix}
x00100000000000001100000001000000000 \\
0x001010000000000000000000000010000000 \\
00x0010000000000000000000000010000000 \\
000x000000000000010010000001000000000 \\
0000x010000000011011100000010010000000 \\
00001x00000000011010000000000000000011 \\
000010x0000010000111000000010000000 \\
0000100x000000001101000001000000000 \\
0000100x1000001101000000000011000000 \\
00001000x10000011010000000000011000000 \\
000000000x00000101000000000001000000 \\
0000101000x000000001000000010000000 \\
00000100000x1000000000000010000000010 \\
000010000000x0011010000010000010 \\
0000101000000x00001000000000010000000 \\
0000101000000x0000100000000010000000 \\
000011000000100x10100000000000001 \\
0000110001000001x01000000000001000001 \\
0000000000000000x1000000001000000000 \\
000011000000000110x0000000001000001 \\
0000101000000001001x0000000010000000 \\
00001000000000001010x000000000000000 \\
0000100000000000010101x00000000000000 \\
0000101000000000000100x0000010000000 \\
00000000000000000110000x001000000000 \\
0000110000010010010000x10000100001 \\
0000010000000010000000000x0000000011 \\
00001000000000000010100000x000000000 \\
00000000000000100000000100x00000001 \\
0000101000000000000100000000x0000000 \\
000010000000000110100000000x000000 \\
000000000000000100100000000000x00001 \\
000010010000000000010000000100x0000 \\
00001010000000000010000000010000x000 \\
00001010000000000010000000010000x00 \\
0000000000000000100100000000000000x1 \\
000011000000000011010000000000000001x
\end{pmatrix}
$$

Values, Norms, and Politics

This section collects articles that speak to how organizational actors structure organizational systems, rules, and norms and how those systems in turn affect the organizational actor. Thus, the papers in this section do not represent a well-worn theme in micro OB, but rather represent landmark papers in terms of the ideas and concepts they have provided independently.

The first paper in the section, by Kerr (1975), represents a departure from most of the papers in this book in that it draws upon a case study and examples as its empirical base. Kerr cogently, and in many cases, humorously, argues that organizational leaders often erect reward systems that run counter to their own self-interest, in terms of benefiting the firm. Kerr bases his argument on behavioral theories of reward and punishment and makes the simple argument that rewards increase the occurrence of particular behaviors while punishments decrease them. Kerr provides compelling examples from war, medicine, and universities that point to a disturbing dissociation between the behaviors that these organizations hope to reward and what they actually reward in practice.

Tetlock's research on accountability exerted a tremendous impact in bridging esoteric studies of paper-and-pencil decision making with real organizational scenarios. Tetlock's argument is simple to the point of obvious: He argues that organizational actors who are accountable for their decisions will make more deliberate and thoughtful decisions compared to those decision makers who are not accountable. The beauty of Tetlock's accountability theory is the empirical demonstration of accountability and his creation of a new and apt metaphor for the organizational actor: that of a naïve politician. In the second article, Tetlock (2000) undertakes a field experiment of managers' evaluations of a variety of organizational problems. Tetlock finds that political ideology and cognitive style are consistent predictors of the value spins that managers place on decisions at the micro, meso, and macro levels of analysis.

The third article, by Miller (1999), on the "norm of self-interest," appears at first glance to be yet another attempt to dismantle the powerful rationality assumption that hovers over behavioral science. However, upon closer inspection, Miller's argument is more subtle: He takes it for granted that people have motivations that are not always self-interested, but that the norm of self-interest has become so pervasive that it acts as a form of pluralistic ignorance. Thus, people explain their own behavior as self-interested in a post-hoc fashion, but in fact, the actual cause of their behavior is not self-interested. Miller suggests that certain conditions may augment the self-interest fallacy.

REFERENCES

Kerr, S. (1975). On the folly of rewarding A, while hoping for B. *Academy of Management Journal, 18*(4), 769–775.

Miller, D. T. (1999). The norm of self-interest. *American Psychologist, 54* (12), 1053–1060.

Tetlock, P. E. (2000). Cognitive biases and organizational correctives: Do both disease and cure depend on the politics of the beholder? *Administrative Science Quarterly, 45,* 293–326.

Suggested Readings

Eisenberger, R., Rhoades, L., & Cameron, J. (1999). Does pay for performance increase or decrease perceived self-determination and instrinsic motivation? *Journal of Personality and Social Psychology, 77*(5), 1026–1040.

Tetlock, P. E., & Kim, J. I. (1987). Accountability and judgment processes in a personality prediction task. *Journal of Personality and Social Psychology, 52*(4), 700–709.

Tetlock, P. E., Peterson, R. S., & Lerner, J. S. (1996). Revising the value pluralism model: Incorporating social content and context postulates. In C. Seligman, J. M. Olson, & M. P. Zanna (Eds.), *The psychology of values: The Ontario Symposium* (Vol. 8, pp. 25–49). Mahwah, NJ: Lawrence Erlbaum Associates.

Tetlock, P. E., Kristel, O., Elson, B., Green, M., & Lerner, J. (2000). The psychology of the unthinkable: Taboo tradeoffs, forbidden base rates and heretical counterfactuals. *Journal of Personality and Social Psychology, 78*(5), 853–870.

Zucker, L. G. (1977). The role of institutionalization in cultural persistence. *American Sociological Review, 42,* 726–743.

On the Folly of Rewarding A, While Hoping for B

Steven Kerr • Ohio State University

Illustrations are presented from society in general, and from organizations in particular, of reward systems that "pay off" for one behavior even though the rewarder hopes dearly for another. Portions of the reward systems of a manufacturing company and an insurance firm are examined and the consequences discussed.

Whether dealing with monkeys, rats, or human beings, it is hardly controversial to state that most organisms seek information concerning what activities are rewarded, and then seek to do (or at least pretend to do) those things, often to the virtual exclusion of activities not rewarded. The extent to which this occurs of course will depend on the perceived attractiveness of the rewards offered, but neither operant nor expectancy theorists would quarrel with the essence of this notion.

Nevertheless, numerous examples exist of reward systems that are fouled up in that behaviors which are rewarded are those which the rewarder is trying to *discourage,* while the behavior he desires is not being rewarded at all.

In an effort to understand and explain this phenomenon, this paper presents examples from society, from organizations in general, and from profit making firms in particular. Data from a manufacturing company and information from an insurance firm are examined to demonstrate the consequences of such reward systems for the organizations involved, and possible reasons why such reward systems continue to exist are considered.

Societal Examples

Politics

Official goals are "purposely vague and general and do not indicate . . . the host of decisions that must be made among alternative ways of achieving official goals and the priority of multiple goals . . ." (8, p. 66). They usually may be relied on to offend absolutely no one, and in this sense can be considered high acceptance, low quality goals. An example might be "build better schools." Operative goals are higher in quality but lower in acceptance, since they specify where the money will come from, what alternative goals will be ignored, etc.

The American citizenry supposedly wants its candidates for public office to set forth operative goals, making their proposed programs "perfectly clear," specifying sources and uses of funds, etc. However, since operative goals are lower in acceptance, and since aspirants to public office need acceptance (from at least 50.1 percent of the people), most politicians prefer to speak only of official goals, at least until after the election. They of course would agree to speak at the operative level if "punished" for not doing so. The electorate could do this by refusing to support candidates who do not speak at the operative level.

Instead, however, the American voter typically punishes (withholds support from) candidates who frankly discuss where the money will come from, rewards politicians who speak only of official goals, but hopes that candidates (despite the reward system) will discuss the issues operatively. It is academic whether it was moral for Nixon, for example, to refuse to discuss his 1968 "secret plan" to end the Vietnam war, his 1972 operative goals concerning the lifting of price controls, the reshuffling of his cabinet, etc. The point is that the reward system made such refusal rational.

It seems worth mentioning that no manuscript can adequately define what is "moral" and what is not. However, examination of costs and benefits, combined with knowledge of what motivates a particular individual, often will suffice to determine what for him is "rational."[1] If the reward system is so designed that it is irrational to be moral, this does not necessarily mean that immortality will result. But is this not asking for trouble?

War

If some oversimplification may be permitted, let it be assumed that the primary goal of the organization (Pentagon, Luftwaffe, or whatever) is to win. Let it be assumed further that the primary goal of most individuals on the front lines is to get home alive. Then there appears to be an important conflict in goals—personally rational behavior by those at the bottom will endanger goal attainment by those at the top.

But not necessarily! It depends on how the reward system is set up. The Vietnam war was indeed a study of disobedience and rebellion, with terms such as "fragging" (killing one's own commanding officer) and "search and evade" becoming part of the military vocabulary. The difference in subordinates' acceptance of authority between World War II and Vietnam is reported to be considerable, and veterans of the Second World War often have been quoted as being outraged at the mutinous actions of many American soldiers in Vietnam.

Consider, however, some critical differences in the reward system in use during the two conflicts. What did the GI in World War II want? To go home.

And when did he get to go home? When the war was won! If he disobeyed the orders to clean out the trenches and take the hills, the war would not be won and he would not go home. Furthermore, what were his chances of attaining his goal (getting home alive) if he obeyed the orders compared to his chances if he did not? What is being suggested is that the rational soldier in World War II, *whether patriotic or not,* probably found it expedient to obey.

Consider the reward system in use in Vietnam. What did the man at the bottom want? To go home. And when did he get to go home? When his tour of duty was over! This was the case *whether or not* the war was won. Furthermore, concerning the relative chance of getting home alive by obeying orders compared to the chance if they were disobeyed, it is worth noting that a mutineer in Vietnam was far more likely to be assigned rest and rehabilitation (on the assumption that fatigue was the cause) than he was to suffer any negative consequence.

In his description of the "zone of indifference," Barnard stated that "a person can and will accept a communication as authoritative only when . . . at the time of his decision, he believes it to be compatible with his personal interests as a whole" (1, p. 165). In light of the reward system used in Vietnam, would it not have been personally irrational for some orders to have been obeyed? Was not the military implementing a system which *rewarded* disobedience, while *hoping* that soldiers (despite the reward system) would obey orders?

Medicine

Theoretically, a physician can make either of two types of error, and intuitively one seems as bad as the other. A doctor can pronounce a patient sick when he is actually well, thus causing him needless anxiety and expense, curtailment of enjoyable foods and activities, and even physical danger by subjecting him to needless medication and surgery. Alternately, a doctor can label a sick person well, and thus avoid treating what may be a serious, even fatal ailment. It might be natural to conclude that physicians seek to minimize both types of error.

---

[1]In Simon's (10, pp. 76–77) terms, a decision is "subjectively rational" if it maximizes an individual's valued outcomes so far as his knowledge permits. A decision is "personally rational" if it is oriented toward the individual's goals.

Such a conclusion would be wrong.[2] It is estimated that numerous Americans are presently afflicted with iatrogenic (physican *caused*) illnesses (9). This occurs when the doctor is approached by someone complaining of a few stray symptoms. The doctor classifies and organizes these symptoms, gives them a name, and obligingly tells the patient what further symptoms may be expected. This information often acts as a self-fulfilling prophecy, with the result that from that day on the patient for all practical purposes is sick.

Why does this happen? Why are physicians so reluctant to sustain a type 2 error (pronouncing a sick person well) that they will tolerate many type 1 errors? Again, a look at the reward system is needed. The punishments for a type 2 error are real: guilt, embarrassment, and the threat of lawsuit and scandal. On the other hand, a type 1 error (labeling a well person sick) "is sometimes seen as sound clinical practice, indicating a healthy conservative approach to medicine" (9, p. 69). Type 1 errors also are likely to generate increased income and a stream of steady customers who, being well in a limited physiological sense, will not embarrass the doctor by dying abruptly.

Fellow physicians and the general public therefore are really *rewarding* type 1 errors and at the same time *hoping* fervently that doctors will try not to make them.

General Organizational Examples

Rehabilitation Centers and Orphanages

In terms of the prime beneficiary classification (2, p. 42) organizations such as these are supposed to exist for the "public-in-contact," that is, clients. The orphanage therefore theoretically is interested in placing as many children as possible in good homes. However, often orphanages surround themselves with so many rules concerning adoption that it is nearly impossible to pry a child out of the place. Orphanages may deny adoption unless the applicants are a married couple, both of the same religion as the child, without history of emotional or vocational instability, with a specified minimum income and a private room for the child, etc.

If the primary goal is to place children in good homes, then the rules ought to constitute means toward that goal. Goal displacement results when these "means become ends-in-themselves that dis-

place the original goals" (2, p. 229).

To some extent these rules are required by law. But the influence of the reward system on the orphanage's management should not be ignored. Consider, for example, that the:

1. Number of children enrolled often is the most important determinant of the size of the allocated budget.
2. Number of children under the director's care also will affect the size of his staff.
3. Total organizational size will determine largely the director's prestige at the annual conventions, in the community, etc.

Therefore, to the extent that staff size, total budget, and personal prestige are valued by the orphanage's executive personnel, it becomes rational for them to make it difficult for children to be adopted. After all, who wants to be the director of the smallest orphanage in the state?

If the reward system errs in the opposite direction, paying off only for placements, extensive goal displacement again is likely to result. A common example of vocational rehabilitation in many states, for example, consists of placing someone in a job for which he has little interest and few qualifications, for two months or so, and then "rehabilitating" him again in another position. Such behavior is quite consistent with the prevailing reward system, which pays off for the number of individuals placed in any position for 60 days or more. Rehabilitation counselors also confess to competing with one another to place relatively skilled clients, sometimes ignoring persons with few skills who would be harder to place. Extensively disabled clients find that counselors often prefer to work with those whose disabilities are less severe.[3]

Universities

Society *hopes* that teachers will not neglect their teaching responsibilities but *rewards* them almost entirely for research and publications. This is most true at the large and prestigious universities. Cliches such as "good research and good teaching go

---

[2]In one study (4) of 14,867 films for signs of tuberculosis, 1,216 positive readings turned out to be clinically negative; only 24 negative readings proved clinically active, a ratio of 50 to 1.

[3]Personal interviews conducted during 1972–1973.

together" notwithstanding, professors often find that they must choose between teaching and research oriented activities when allocating their time. Rewards for good teaching usually are limited to outstanding teacher awards, which are given to only a small percentage of good teachers and which usually bestow little money and fleeting prestige. Punishments for poor teaching also are rare.

Rewards for research and publications, on the other hand, and punishments for failure to accomplish these, are commonly administered by universities at which teachers are employed. Furthermore, publication oriented resumés usually will be well received at other universities, whereas teaching credentials, harder to document and quantify, are much less transferable. Consequently it is rational for university teachers to concentrate on research, even if to the detriment of teaching and at the expense of their students.

By the same token, it is rational for students to act based upon the goal displacement which has occurred within universities concerning what they are rewarded for. If it is assumed that a primary goal of a university is to transfer knowledge from teacher to student, then grades become identifiable as a means toward that goal, serving as motivational, control, and feedback devices to expedite the knowledge transfer. Instead, however, the grades themselves have become much more important for entrance to graduate school, successful employment, tuition refunds, parental respect, etc., than the knowledge or lack of knowledge they are supposed to signify.

It therefore should come as no surprise that information has surfaced in recent years concerning fraternity files for examinations, term paper writing services, organized cheating at the service academies, and the like. Such activities constitute a personally rational response to a reward system which pays off for grades rather than knowledge.

Business Related Examples

Ecology

Assume that the president of XYZ Corporation is confronted with the following alternatives:

1. Spend $11 million for antipollution equipment to keep from poisoning fish in the river adjacent to the plant; or

2. Do nothing, in violation of the law, and assume a one in ten chance of being caught, with a resultant $1 million fine plus the necessity of buying the equipment.

Under this not unrealistic set of choices it requires no linear program to determine that XYZ Corporation can maximize its probabilities by flouting the law. Add the fact that XYZ's president is probably being rewarded (by creditors, stockholders, and other salient parts of his task environment) according to criteria totally unrelated to the number of fish poisoned, and his probable course of action becomes clear.

Evaluation of Training

It is axiomatic that those who care about a firm's well-being should insist that the organization get fair value for its expenditures. Yet it is commonly known that firms seldom bother to evaluate a new GRID, MBO, job enrichment program, or whatever, to see if the company is getting its money's worth. Why? Certainly it is not because people have not pointed out that this situation exists; numerous practitioner oriented articles are written each year to just this point.

The individuals (whether in personnel, manpower planning, or wherever) who normally would be responsible for conducting such evaluations are the same ones often charged with introducing the change effort in the first place. Having convinced top management to spend the money, they usually are quite animated afterwards in collecting arigorous vignettes and anecdotes about how successful the program was. The last thing many desire is a formal, systematic, and revealing evaluation. Although members of top management may actually *hope* for such systematic evaluation, their reward systems continue to *reward* ignorance in this area. And if the personnel department abdicates its responsibility, who is to step into the breach? The change agent himself? Hardly! He is likely to be too busy collecting anecdotal "evidence" of his own, for use with his next client.

Miscellaneous

Many additional examples could be cited of systems which in fact are rewarding behaviors other than those supposedly desired by the rewarder. A few of these are described briefly below.

Most coaches disdain to discuss individual accomplishments, preferring to speak of teamwork, proper attitude, and a one-for-all spirit. Usually, however, rewards are distributed according to individual performance. The college basketball player who feeds his teammates instead of shooting will not compile impressive scoring statistics and is less likely to be drafted by the pros. The ballplayer who hits to right field to advance the runners will win neither the batting nor home run titles, and will be offered smaller raises. It therefore is rational for players to think of themselves first, and the team second.

In business organizations where rewards are dispensed for unit performance or for individual goals achieved, without regard for overall effectiveness, similar attitudes often are observed. Under most Management by Objectives (MBO) systems, goals in areas where quantification is difficult often go unspecified. The organization therefore often is in a position where it *hopes* for employee effort in the areas of team building, interpersonal relations, creativity, etc., but it formally *rewards* none of these. In cases where promotions and raises are formally tied to MBO, the system itself contains a paradox in that it "asks employees to set challenging, risky goals, only to face smaller paychecks and possibly damaged careers if these goals are not accomplished" (5, p. 40).

It is *hoped* that administrators will pay attention to long run costs and opportunities and will institute programs which will bear fruit later on. However, many organizational reward systems pay off for short run sales and earnings only. Under such circumstances it is personally rational for officials to sacrifice long term growth and profit (by selling off equipment and property, or by stifling research and development) for short term advantages. This probably is most pertinent in the public sector, with the result that many public officials are unwilling to implement programs which will not show benefits by election time.

As a final, clear-cut example of a fouled-up reward system, consider the cost-plus contract or its next of kin, the allocation of next year's budget as a direct function of this year's expenditures. It probably is conceivable that those who award such budgets and contracts really hope for economy and prudence in spending. It is obvious, however, that adopting the proverb "to him who spends shall more be given," rewards not economy, but spending itself.

Two Companies' Experiences

A Manufacturing Organization

A midwest manufacturer of industrial goods had been troubled for some time by aspects of its organizational climate it believed dysfunctional. For research purposes, interviews were conducted with many employees and a questionnaire was administered on a companywide basis, including plants and offices in several American and Canadian locations. The company strongly encouraged employee participation in the survey, and made available time and space during the workday for completion of the instrument. All employees in attendance during the day of the survey completed the questionnaire. All instruments were collected directly by the researcher, who personally administered each session. Since no one employed by the firm handled the questionnaires, and since respondent names were not asked for, it seems likely that the pledge of anonymity given was believed.

A modified version of the Expect Approval scale (7) was included as part of the questionnaire. The instrument asked respondents to indicate the degree of approval or disapproval they could expect if they performed each of the described actions. A seven point Likert scale was used, with one indicating that the action would probably bring strong disapproval and seven signifying likely strong approval.

Although normative data for this scale from studies of other organizations are unavailable, it is possible to examine fruitfully the data obtained from this survey in several ways. First, it may be worth noting that the questionnaire data corresponded closely to information gathered through interviews. Furthermore, as can be seen from the results summarized in Table 1, sizable differences between various work units, and between employees at different job levels within the same work unit, were obtained. This suggests that response bias effects (social desirability in particular loomed as a potential concern) are not likely to be severe.

Most importantly, comparisons between scores obtained on the Expect Approval scale and a statement of problems which were the reason for the survey revealed that the same behaviors which managers in each division thought dysfunctional were those which lower level employees claimed were rewarded. As compared to job levels 1 to 8 in Division B (see Table 1), those in Division A claimed a much higher acceptance by management of "conforming" activities. Between 31 and 37 percent of Division A employees at levels 1–8 stated that going along with the majority, agreeing with the boss, and staying on everyone's good side brought approval; only once (level 5–8 responses to one of the three items) did a majority suggest that such actions would generate disapproval.

Furthermore, responses from Division A workers at levels 1–4 indicate that behaviors geared toward risk avoidance were as likely to be rewarded as to be punished. Only at job levels 9 and above was it apparent that the reward system was positively reinforcing behaviors desired by top management. Overall, the same "tendencies toward conservatism and apple-polishing at the lower levels" which divisional management had complained about during the interviews were those claimed by subordinates to be the most rational course of action in light of the existing reward system. Management apparently was not getting the behaviors

TABLE 1. Summary of Two Divisions' Data Relevant to Conforming and Risk-Avoidance Behaviors (Extent to Which Subjects Expect Approval)

Dimension	Item	Division and Sample	Total Responses	Percentage of Workers Responding		
				1, 2, or 3 Disapproval	4	5, 6, or 7 Approval
Risk Avoidance	Making a risky	A, levels 1–4 (lowest)	127	61	25	14
	decision based on	A, levels 5–8	172	46	31	23
	the best information	A, levels 9 and above	17	41	30	30
	available at the time,	B, levels 1–4 (lowest)	31	58	26	16
	but which turns out	B, levels 5–8	19	42	42	16
	wrong.	B, levels 9 and above	10	50	20	30
	Setting extremely high	A, levels 1–4	122	47	28	25
	and challenging	A, levels 5–8	168	33	26	41
	standards and goals,	A, levels 9+	17	24	6	70
	and then narrowly	B, levels 1–4	31	48	23	29
	failing to make them.	B, levels 5–8	18	17	33	50
		B, levels 9+	10	30	0	70
	Setting goals which	A, levels 1–4	124	35	30	35
	are extremely easy to	A, levels 5–8	171	47	27	26
	make and then	A, levels 9+	17	70	24	6
	making them.	B, levels 1–4	31	58	26	16
		B, levels 5–8	19	63	16	21
		B, levels 9+	10	80	0	20
Conformity	Being a "yes man"	A, levels 1–4	126	46	17	37
	and always agreeing	A, levels 5–8	180	54	14	31
	with the boss.	A, levels 9+	17	88	12	0
		B, levels 1–4	32	53	28	19
		B, levels 5–8	19	68	21	11
		B, levels 9+	10	80	10	10
	Always going along	A, levels 1–4	125	40	25	35
	with the majority.	A, levels 5–8	173	47	21	32
		A, levels 9+	17	70	12	18
		B, levels 1–4	31	61	23	16
		B, levels 5–8	19	68	11	21
		B, levels 9+	10	80	10	10
	Being careful to stay	A, levels 1–4	124	45	18	37
	on the good side of	A, levels 5–8	173	45	22	33
	everyone, so that	A, levels 9+	17	64	6	30
	everyone agrees	B, levels 1–4	31	54	23	23
	that you are a great	B, levels 5–8	19	73	11	16
	guy.	B, levels 9+	10	80	10	10

it was *hoping* for, but it certainly was getting the behaviors it was perceived by subordinates to be *rewarding*.

An Insurance Firm

The Group Health Claims Division of a large eastern insurance company provides another rich illustration of a reward system which reinforces behaviors not desired by top management.

Attempting to measure and reward accuracy in paying surgical claims, the firm systematically keeps track of the number of returned checks and letters of complaint received from policyholders. However, underpayments are likely to provoke cries of outrage from the insured, while overpayments often are accepted in courteous silence. Since it often is impossible to tell from the physician's statement which of two surgical procedures, with different allowable benefits, was performed, and since writing for clarifications will interfere with other standards used by the firm concerning "percentage of claims paid within two days of receipt," the new hire in more than one claims section is soon acquainted with the informal norm: "When in doubt, pay it out!"

The situation would be even worse were it not for the fact that other features of the firm's reward system tend to neutralize those described. For example, annual "merit" increases are given to all employees, in one of the following three amounts:

1. If the worker is "outstanding" (a select category, into which no more than two employees per section may be placed): 5 percent;
2. If the worker is "above average" (normally all workers not "outstanding" are so rated): 4 percent;
3. If the worker commits gross acts of negligence and irresponsibility for which he might be discharged in many other companies: 3 percent.

Now, since (a) the difference between the 5 percent theoretically attainable through hard work and the 4 percent attainable merely by living until the review date is small and (b) since insurance firms seldom dispense much of a salary increase in cash (rather, the worker's insurance benefits increase, causing him to be further overinsured), many employees are rather indifferent to the possibility of obtaining the extra one percent reward and therefore tend to ignore the norm concerning indiscriminant payments.

However, most employees are not indifferent to the rule which states that, should absences or latenesses total three or more in any six-month period, the entire 4 or 5 percent due at the next "merit" review must be forfeited. In this sense the firm may be described as *hoping* for performance, while *rewarding* attendance. What it gets, of course, is attendance. (If the absence-lateness rule appears to the reader to be stringent, it really is not. The company counts "times" rather than "days" absent, and a ten-day absence therefore counts the same as one lasting two days. A worker in danger of accumulating a third absence within six months merely has to remain ill (away from work) during his second absence until his first absence is more than six months old. The limiting factor is that at some point his salary ceases, and his sickness benefits take over. This usually is sufficient to get the younger workers to return, but for those with 20 or more years' service, the company provides sickness benefits of 90 percent of normal salary, tax-free! Therefore . . .)

Causes

Extremely diverse instances of systems which reward behavior A although the rewarder apparently hopes for behavior B have been given. These are useful to illustrate the breadth and magnitude of the phenomenon, but the diversity increases the difficulty of determining commonalities and establishing causes. However, four general factors may be pertinent to an explanation of why fouled up reward systems seem to be so prevalent.

Fascination with an "Objective" Criterion

It has been mentioned elsewhere that:

> Most "objective" measures of productivity are objective only in that their subjective elements are a) determined in advance, rather than coming into play at the time of the formal evaluation, and b) well concealed on the rating instrument itself. Thus industrial firms seeking to devise objective rating systems first decide, in an arbitrary manner, what dimensions are to be rated, . . . usually including some items having little to do with organizational effectiveness while excluding others that do. Only then does Personnel Division churn out official-looking documents on which all dimensions chosen to be rated are assigned point values, categories, or whatever (6, p. 92).

Nonetheless, many individuals seek to establish simple, quantifiable standards against which to measure and reward performance. Such efforts may be successful in highly predictable areas within an organization, but are likely to cause goal displacement when applied anywhere else. Over-concern with attendance and lateness in the insurance firm and with number of people placed in the vocational rehabilitation division may have been largely responsible for the problems described in those organizations.

Overemphasis on Highly Visible Behaviors

Difficulties often stem from the fact that some parts of the task are highly visible while other parts are not. For example, publications are easier to demonstrate than teaching, and scoring baskets and hitting home runs are more readily observable than feeding teammates and advancing base runners. Similarly, the adverse consequences of pronouncing a sick person well are more visible than those sustained by labeling a well person sick. Team-building and creativity are other examples of behaviors which may not be rewarded simply because they are hard to observe.

Hypocrisy

In some of the instances described the rewarder may have been getting the desired behavior, notwithstanding claims that the behavior was not desired. This may be true, for example, of management's attitude toward apple-polishing in the manufacturing firm (a behavior which subordinates felt was rewarded, despite management's avowed dislike of the practice). This also may explain politicians' unwillingness to revise the penalties for disobedience of ecology laws, and the failure of top management to devise reward systems which would cause systematic evaluation of training and development programs.

Emphasis on Morality or Equity Rather than Efficiency

Sometimes consideration of other factors prevents the estalishment of a system which rewards behaviors desired by the rewarder. The felt obliga-

tion of many Americans to vote for one candidate or another, for example, may impair their ability to withhold support from politicians who reruse to discuss the issues. Similarly, the concern for spreading the risks and costs of wartime military service may outweigh the advantage to be obtained by commiting personnel to combat until the war is over.

It should be noted that only with respect to the first two causes are reward systems really paying off for other than desired behaviors. In the case of the third and fourth causes the systems *is* rewarding behaviors desired by the rewarder, and the systems are fouled up only from the standpoints of those who believe the rewarder's public statements (cause 3), or those who seek to maximize efficiency rather than other outcomes (cause 4).

Conclusions

Modern organization theory requires a recognition that the members of organizations and society possess divergent goals and motives. It therefore is unlikely that managers and their subordinates will seek the same outcomes. Three possible remedies for this potential problem are suggested.

Selection

It is theoretically possible for organizations to employ only those individuals whose goals and motives are wholly consonant with those of management. In such cases the same behaviors judged by subordinates to be rational would be perceived by management as desirable. State-of-the-art reviews of selection techniques, however, provide scant grounds for hope that such an approach would be successful (for example, see 12).

Training

Another theoretical alternative is for the organization to admit those employees whose goals are not consonant with those of management and then, through training, socialization, or whatever, alter employee goals to make them consonant. However, research on the effectiveness of such training programs, though limited, provides further grounds for pessimism (for example, see 3).

Altering the Reward System

What would have been the result if:

1. Nixon had been assured by his advisors that the could not win re-election except by discussing the issues in detail?
2. Physicians' conduct was subjected to regular examination by review boards for type 1 errors (calling healthy people ill) and to penalties (fines, censure, etc.) for errors of either type?
3. The President of XYZ Corporation had to choose between (a) spending $11 million dollars for antipollution equipment, and (b) incurring a fifty-fifty chance of going to jail for five years?

Managers who complain that their workers are not motivated might do well to consider the possibility that they have installed reward systems which are paying off for behaviors other than those they are seeking. This, in part, is what happened in Vietnam, and this is what regularly frustrates societal efforts to bring about honest politicians, civic-minded managers, etc. This certainly is what happened in both the manufacturing and the insurance companies.

A first step for such managers might be to find out what behaviors currently are being rewarded. Perhaps an instrument similar to that used in the manufacturing firm could be useful for this purpose. Chances are excellent that these managers will be surprised by what they find—that their firms are not rewarding what they assume they are. In fact, such undesirable behavior by organizational members as they have observed may be explained largely by the reward systems in use.

This is not to say that all organizational behavior is determined by formal rewards and punishments. Certainly it is true that in the absence of formal reinforcement some soldiers will be patriotic, some presidents will be ecology minded, and some orphanage directors will care about children. The point, however, is that in such cases the rewarder is not *causing* the behaviors desired but is only a fortunate bystander. For an organization to *act* upon its members, the formal reward system should positively reinforce desired behaviors, not constitute an obstacle to be overcome.

It might be wise to underscore the obvious fact that there is nothing really new in what has been said. In both theory and practice these matters have been mentioned before. Thus in many states Good Samaritan laws have been installed to protect doctors who stop to assist a stricken motorist. In states without such laws it is commonplace for doctors to refuse to stop, for fear of involvement in a subsequent lawsuit. In college basketball additional penalties have been instituted against players who foul their opponents deliberately. It has long been argued by Milton Friedman and others that penalties should be altered so as to make it irrational to disobey the ecology laws, and so on.

By altering the reward system the organization escapes the necessity of selecting only desirable people or of trying to alter undesirable ones. In Skinnerian terms (as described in 11, p. 704), "As for responsibility and goodness—as commonly defined—no one . . . would want or need them. They refer to a man's behaving well despite the absence of positive reinforcement that is obviously sufficient to explain it. Where such reinforcement exists, 'No one needs goodness.'"

REFERENCES

1. Barnard, Chester I. *The Functions of the Executive* (Cambridge, Mass.: Harvard University Press, 1964).
2. Blau, Peter M., and W. Richard Scott. *Formal Organizations* (San Francisco: Chandler, 1962).
3. Fiedler, Fred E. "Predicting the Effects of Leadership Training and Experience from the Contingency Model," *Journal of Applied Psychology*, Vol. 56 (1972), 114–119.
4. Garland, L. H. "Studies of the Accuracy of Diagnostic Procedures," *American Journal Roentgenological, Radium Therapy Nuclear Medicine*, Vol. 82 (1959), 25-38.
5. Kerr, Steven. "Some Modifications in MBO as an OD strategy." *Academy of Management Proceedings,* 1973, pp. 39–42.
6. Kerr, Steven. "What Price Objectivity?" *American Sociologist*, Vol. 8 (1973), 92–93.
7. Litwin, G. H., and R. A. Stringer, Jr. *Motivation and Organizational Climate* (Boston: Harvard University Press, 1968).
8. Perrow, Charles. "The Analysis of Goals in Complex Organizations," in A. Etzioni (Ed.), *Readings on Modern Organizations* (Englewood Cliffs, N. J.: Prentice-Hall, 1969).
9. Scheff, Thomas J. "Decision Rules, Types of Error, and Their Consequences in Medical Diagnosis," in F. Massarik and P. Ratoosh (Eds.), *Mathematical Explorations in Behavioral Science* (Homewood, Ill.: Irwin, 1965).
10. Simon, Herbert A. *Administrative Behavior* (New York: Free Press, 1957).
11. Swanson, G. E. "Review Symposium: Beyond Freedom and Dignity," *American Journal of Sociology*, Vol. 78 (1972), 702–705.
12. Webster, E. *Decision Making in the Employment Interview* (Montreal: Industrial Relations Center, McGill University, 1964).

Cognitive Biases and Organizational Correctives: Do Both Disease and Cure Depend on the Politics of the Beholder?

P. E. Tetlock • The Ohio State University

The study reported here assessed the impact of managers' philosophies of human nature on their reactions to influential academic claims and counter-claims of when human judgment is likely to stray from rational-actor standards and of how organizations can correct these biases. Managers evaluated scenarios that depicted decision-making processes at micro, meso, and macro levels of analysis: alleged cognitive biases of individuals, strategies of structuring and coping with accountability relationships between supervisors and employees, and strategies that corporate entities use to cope with accountability demands from the broader society. Political ideology and cognitive style emerged as consistent predictors of the value spins that managers placed on decisions at all three levels of analysis. Specifically, conservative managers with strong preferences for cognitive closure were most likely (a) to defend simple heuristic-driven errors such as overattribution and overconfidence and to warn of the mirror image mistakes of failing to hold people accountable and of diluting sound policies with irrelevant side-objectives; (b) to be skeptical of complex strategies of structuring or coping with accountability and to praise those who lay down clear rules and take decisive stands; (c) to prefer simple philosophies of corporate governance (the shareholder over stakeholder model) and to endorse organizational norms such as hierarchical filtering that reduce cognitive overload on top management by short-circuiting unnecessary argumentation. Intuitive theories of good judgment apparently cut across levels of analysis and are deeply grounded in personal epistemologies and political ideologies.

Experimental research on judgment and choice casts us, human beings, in a less-than-flattering light (Goldstein and Hogarth, 1996; Gilovich, Griffin, and Kahneman, 2000). We fall prey, it has been claimed, to a wide assortment of errors and biases. We are too quick to draw conclusions about others, too slow to change our minds, excessively confident in our predictions, and prone to give too much weight to irrelevant cues (such as sunk costs) and too little weight to relevant ones (such as opportunity costs). Although this grim portrait has been qualified by the recent proliferation of dual-process models of judgment and choice that in the spirit of Simon (1955), bestow on people some limited capacity to decide how to decide (see Chaiken and Trope, 1999, for a collection of current cognitive-manager models), the dominant emphasis in the last quarter century of experimental work has clearly been on judgmental shortcomings. The question remains, though, how organizational theorists should react to this burgeoning evidence of deviations from rationality at the individual level of analysis. March and Olsen (1989, 1995) have constructed a useful inventory of key conceptual stumbling blocks likely to trip up confident reductionists who propose one-size-fits-all normative frameworks for assessing rationality across levels of analysis. The relevant standards for gauging quality of decision making hinge on the relative importance that observers from varying organizational and political perspectives place on (1) making judgments and decisions in accord with utilitanan or rule-based models of human thought, (2) clarifying or obfuscating the underlying organization is committed to sacrosanct societal values such as equal opportunity, environmental protection, or balancing work and family (Meyer, 1983).

Taken in its entirety, this Marchian inventory warns us that the normative standards that are useful in defining good judgment in the laboratory can be deeply misleading in organizational settings that are characterized by sharp contests for power and status, intense accountability pressures from conflicting constituencies, prickly principal-agent relationships, and enormous uncertainty about what should be done next. We should not be astonished, therefore, when work-a-day managers have the temerity to second-guess the normative pronouncements of high-profile experimental researchers. We should also not be astonished to discover systematic rifts in the opinions that managers themselves hold about what counts as a cognitive bias and about the types of organizational reforms that are likely to correct these biases, either by changing how employees think or by altering their thresholds for expressing particular thoughts.

Some theorists will treat disagreements over cognitive biases and organizational correctives as presumptive evidence that one camp must be right and the other wrong. Right and wrong take on clear-cut meanings within the intuitive-scientist framework, preoccupied as it is with maximizing epistemic goals, or within the intuitive-economist framework, preoccupied as it is with maximizing utilitarian goals in competitive markets that ruthlessly punish suboptimal practices. When the task

is well-defined, there are rigorous mathematical baselines—derived from Bayes' theorem and decision theory—for gauging exactly how mistaken people are.

By contrast, right and wrong rapidly devolve into tendentious categorizations within a multifunctional theory of judgment and choice that incorporates less-well-defined goals and task constraints, such as projecting desired social identities to key constituencies, proclaiming fealty to sacred values, and defending the normative order. From a multifunctional perspective, disagreements over cognitive biases and organizational correctives count as presumptive evidence that the disputants subscribe to distinctive ideological worldviews that rest on diverging assumptions about human nature and the social order, about how to understand social reality and navigate oneself through it, and about the goals that give purpose to one's life and define one's relationship to various social structures. Confronted by disagreements over what is rational and how to fix alleged departures from rationality, the appropriate response is to trace these disagreements to their philosophical and ideological roots.

The current article proceeds from the premise that managers' opinions about cognitive biases and organizational correctives are rooted in competing epistemological and ideological worldviews, although most managers take pride in thinking of themselves as pragmatic problem solvers and resist characterizations of their views as either philosophical or ideological. Following research precedents in the literature on cognitive styles (Kruglanski and Webster, 1996; Tetlock, 1998), the study reported here assessed personal epistemologies along a cognitive-style continuum that gauged strength of preference for conceptual simplicity and explanatory closure. At one end of the continuum are distaste for ambiguity and protracted debate and endorsements of the views that the social world is fundamentally simple, as are the most effective strategies of coping with it. At the other end are a high comfort level for dissonance and uncertainty and endorsements of the views that the social world is enormously complex and pluralistic and the most effective coping strategies for dealing with it require multifaceted perspective taking and trade-offs.

Following research precedents in the literature on political ideology in mass and elite samples

(Lipsett and Raab, 1978; McClosky and Brill, 1983; Tetlock, 1984; Sniderman and Tetlock, 1986), ideological worldviews were assessed with a battery of items that tap views of human nature as well as endorsements of individualistic, egalitarian, environmentalist, and traditional conservative values. Consistent with past work on public attitudes, especially on elites (Kinder, 1998), it was impossible to forge a psychometrically defensible one-dimensional measure of ideology. A two-dimensional model did, however, fit the patterns of covariation among beliefs. The model includes (1) an authoritarianism factor, anchored at one end by authoritarian conservatism, characterized by an unapologetic defense of hierarchies and suspicions about the trustworthiness of the model employee, and at the anti-authoritarian egalitarian end by a distaste for hierarchy and a more benign view of humanity; and (2) a libertarianism factor, anchored at one end by libertarian conservatism, which is characterized by an enthusiastic embrace of market solutions, deep skepticism of government, and a view of humanity as resourceful, rational, and self-reliant, and, at the anti-libertarian egalitarian end, by a distaste for the cut-throat competition of capitalism, a fear of externalities, and a view of humanity as fragile and in need of protection by a caring state.

The guiding idea was that cognitive style and ideological worldview would jointly predict managerial reactions to a broad assortment of scenarios pitched at micro, meso, and macro levels of analysis. Predictions focused on (a) the soundness of strategies and styles of individual decision making; (b) the soundness of strategies of structuring and coping with accountability relationships; and (c) the soundness of competing political schemes for organizing accountability systems at the corporate or societal level.

Micro-Level: Cognitive Biases

One possible predictor of what counts as a cognitive bias in social perception is baseline assumptions about the trustworthiness of other people. How prone are others to take advantage of the inevitable incompleteness of even the most formal contracts (not to mention informal understandings based on the proverbial handshake)? How wise is it to pressure others to live up to their ends of social bargains by indicating that one has a low

threshold for drawing inferences about character even when extenuating circumstances exist? Other things being equal, the more pessimistic one's view of human nature, the more egoistic, calculating, and self-serving one should suppose others to be and the more likely one should be to approve of quickly drawing strong conclusions about the characters of employees who violate moral or performance norms of the organization. Drawing on past surveys of public opinion (McClosky and Brill, 1983; Sniderman and Tetlock, 1986), the following hypotheses are advanced:

H1: Authoritarian conservatives should subscribe to a more jaundiced view of humanity than do those on the ideological left.

H2: Authoritarian conservatives should rise to the normative defense of the fundamental attribution error by insisting both that the alleged error is not all that erroneous (people are often untrustworthy) and that it is often prudent (it is better, on average, to indict the occasional innocent soul than it is to fail to punish the sinful masses of defectors).

A second set of hypotheses highlight managers' opinions of the rationality and resilience of fellow human beings. The more doubts one harbors about the intellectual maturity of one's fellow human beings, about their tolerance for ambiguity and dissonance, the more prone one will be to adopt a hardball, authoritarian model of the ideal leader that springs right out of Machiavelli's advice to Renaissance princes. Drawing again on research on public opinion (Sniderman and Tetlock, 1986), as well as on cognitive style (Kruglanski and Webster, 1996), the following hypotheses are advanced:

H3: Authoritarian conservatives, especially those with strong preferences for cognitive closure, should most doubt the intellectual, emotional, and political maturity of subordinates.

H4: Authoritarian conservatives, especially those with strong preferences for cognitive closure, should display a pronounced affinity for leaders with simple, decisive styles of self-presentation that conceal private doubts and cloak imminent trade-offs under artful rhetoric.

At this juncture, skeptics might suspect that the apparent normative divergence between the laboratory classifications of effects as errors and biases and managers' assessments merely rests on a misunderstanding over levels of analysis. Conservative respondents may still see overconfidence, escalating commitment to sunk costs, and trade-off denial as private cognitive vices; they just also see them as public or political necessities. The disagreement revolves around what leaders need to do to sustain useful social illusions. To test whether authoritarian conservatives with strong preferences for closure subscribe to different theories of good judgment or of rhetorical manipulation, or perhaps both, we need to compare their reactions to private decision-making procedures as well as to public posturing. Here, though, there are reasons for predicting ideological effects in both private and public contexts. Drawing on survey research (Sniderman and Tetlock, 1986), archival content-analysis studies of political decision making (Tetlock, 1984), and laboratory studies of cognitive style (Kruglanski and Webster, 1996), it is hypothesized:

H5: Authoritarian conservatives should most strongly defend managers who (a) are confident in their private assessments of challenges (even if they are systematically overconfident); (b) believe that failure to stay the course with fundamentally good ideas is a more common error-than trying to recoup sunk costs by pouring resources into red-ink hemorrhaging projects; and (c) believe that exaggerating the complexity of problems is a more common error than overreliance on simple, intuitive rules of thumb.

A third dimension along which organizational theorists, and quite possibly managers, vary is their assumptions about the goals of judgment and choice (Tetlock, 1985; Tetlock and Boettger, 1989). Some subscribe to a monistic conception in which it is a bad idea to dilute core business objectives—efficiency and profit maximization—with ancillary goals that create unnecessary or distracting trade-offs (Jensen and Meckling, 1976); others subscribe to more pluralistic conceptions that place numerous moral and political constraints on the pursuit of efficiency (Etzioni, 1996). These observations lead to the following hypotheses:

H6: Anti-libertarian egalitarians should most object to factoring into policy deliberations statistical base rates that, however probative, work to the disadvantage of traditionally disadvantaged groups (e.g., setting insurance premiums in ways that reflect covariation between actuarial risk and racial ethnic classification).

H7: Libertarian conservatives should take least umbrage at taboo trade-offs such as those that affix dollar values to human life.

Meso-Level: Strategies for Accountability Systems

Opinions about what constitutes a cognitive bias or moral defect, and how pervasive those biases or defects are among the work force, should be closely coupled to opinions about how to design accountability systems that prevent these all-too-human shortcomings from impeding or tainting organizational functions. This argument leads to the tight-accountability-leash hypothesis:

H8: Authoritarian conservatives and those with strong preferences for cognitive closure should approve of bosses who give their subordinates well-defined job missions and monitor subordinates closely, whereas anti-authoritarian egalitarians should see good rationales for creating some degree of normative ambiguity and of encouraging imaginative thought experiments that undercut traditional ways of doing things.

A closely related argument is that these ideological and cognitive-stylistic preferences for order and discipline should seep into evaluations of how employees respond to accountability pressures from higher-ups:

H9: Authoritarian conservatives and those with strong preferences for cognitive closure should be more favorable to employees who have confident and decisive personas and who offer unequivocal recommendations, whereas anti-authoritarian egalitarians and those with weak closure preferences should favor employees with more self-critical and reflective personas who acknowledge uncertainty and enumerate complex trade-offs.

One recurring controversy in designing accountability systems concerns the relative emphasis to place on process accountability, which holds employees responsible for observing the correct decision-making procedures, and outcome accountability, which holds employees responsible for bottom-line performance indicators and permits considerable improvisation in pursuit of these objectives (cf. Chubb and Moe, 1990, on the accountability norms and relative bureaucratic overhead of private and public schools). Here the expectation is that egalitarians should favor process over outcome accountability but that authoritarian and libertarian conservatives should hold the opposite preference (Wilson, 1989):

H10: Anti-libertarian egalitarians fear the unfairness of holding people accountable for outcomes that are only partly under their control and, hence, are more willing to forgive those who fail but who followed the right procedures.

H11: Libertarian conservatives fear the perverse incentives created by shifting from a problemsolving focus on maximizing external outcomes to a ritualistic focus on observing prescribed routines. They tend to identify process accountability with the most notorious inefficiencies of public sector organizations. Authoritarian conservatives should share this concern but also worry about making performance appraisal unnecessarily cumbersome and opening the door to endless justifications and excuses for non-performance.

Yet another set of hypotheses predicts ideological variation in managerial reactions to accountability dilemmas that implicate classic problems of distributive and procedural justice. A recurring theme in the literature on distributive justice is the tension between efficiency, which requires directing resources to those who will use them most productively, and equality, which requires subsidizing the less productive (Messick, 1993). These ideological cleavages in the broader society should manifest themselves in managerial ideology:

H12: Anti-libertarian and anti-authoritarian egalitarians should resist concentrating budget cuts on the least productive, whereas libertarian and authoritarian conservatives should have no such compunctions.

With respect to procedural justice, there is the classic tension between the desire of authorities to enforce rules and the countervailing concern that everyone should feel that they had a fair say. The guiding hypotheses are:

H13: Anti-authoritarian and anti-libertarian egalitarians should be more sympathetic to employees who resisted decisions from above that ignored their point of view, sympathy that should extend not just to employees exercising the voice option (protest) and exit option (resignation) but even to employees engaging in conduct of dubious morality (loophole exploitation).

H14: Authoritarian conservatives should be more sympathetic to employees who defer to commands from above (conservatives are not embarrassed about talking about "subordinates") and more inclined to regard protestors as whiners and malcontents, quitters as disloyal, and loophole exploiters as cheaters.

H15: Libertarian conservatives should also back upper management but less out of affinity for hierarchy and more out of deference to the core precepts of market pricing, formal contracts, and property rights. Their reactions to loophole exploiters should be harsh, but their reactions to protestors should be muted (they are less upset by insubordination), and their reactions to those who exit may even be positive (resourceful, self-reliant people don't passively accept ill-treatment, they find a better deal in the labor market).

Macro-Level: Attitudes Toward Corporate Governance

How should accountability relationships within the organization as a whole, and between the organization and the broader society, be structured? Working from the assumption that people who like simplicity in their immediate working environment prefer simplicity in the wider social universe one hypothesis is that:

H16: Authoritarian conservatives and those with strong preferences for cognitive closure should be skeptical of multiple-advocacy systems that require soliciting and integrating inputs from a wide range of perspectives prior to reaching decisions and enthusiastic about hierarchical, top-down, decision systems that place a lot of authority in a few hands and permit rapid implementation of new initiatives.

This split between egalitarians and conservatives may be rooted in distinct cognitive and moral sources: those on the right should be both more dubious of the added utility of soliciting diverse inputs as a means to the end of better decisions (subordinates may actually detract from the quality of debate) and less committed to the egalitarian goal of giving voice, and the attendant sense that one has been heard, to the hoi polloi as a moral end in itself. Building on the same psycho-logic:

H17: Authoritarian conservatives who most value hierarchy and parsimony (seek rapid closure) will display stronger support for the shareholder model of corporate governance, a stringently monistic accountability regime that calls on management (the agents) to work single-mindedly toward the goal of greater financial returns to shareholders (the principals), and greater skepticism toward the stakeholder model, a more open-ended pluralistic accountability regime that calls on management to balance the contradictory demands of a cacophony of clamorous constituencies.

This preference for the shareholder model need not be rooted entirely in cognitive-stylistic affinity for accountability systems that make it easier to determine whether management is doing a good job. Libertarian as well as authoritarian conservatives should be especially sympathetic to the interests of the capitalized principals (who possess the moral trump card of rightful ownership and whose interests should be advanced as an end in itself), as well as more supportive of a single-minded focus on efficiency (Jensen and Meckling, 1976). Critical though they indisputably are to the long-term profitability of the enterprise, stakeholders "have not put their money where their mouths are" and occupy a distinctly secondary place in both the moral and pragmatic schemes of things. This argument leads to the following hypotheses:

H18: Libertarian and authoritarian conservatives will endorse the shareholder over the stakeholder model of corporate governance on the practical grounds that the shareholder model works better and on the moral grounds that property rights should trump other claims.

H19: Anti-libertarian and anti-authoritarian egalitarians will invoke mirror-image arguments to justify the stakeholder model: (a) given the pluralistic and interdependent character of modern business environments, it does not make practical sense to exclude key voices from the policy setting process; (b) economic underdogs and the traditionally disadvantaged have a moral right to be heard and won't be unless granted places on boards of directors (Etzioni, 1996).

In testing the above hypotheses, this study examined the patterns of consistency in managerial judgments of the soundness of decision-making practices and accountability procedures at micro, meso, and macro levels of analysis. The study focuses on the main and interactive effects of two key predictors of these patterns, ideological worldview and the cognitive-style construct of preference for simplicity and explanatory closure, but it also assessed a host of potential control variables, including private and public sector employment, gender, income, age, and education. Finally, although the current study is largely an exercise in hypothetico-deductive social science, there is an exploratory inductive dimension to the research design. In-depth interviews with ideological subsets of managers probed their justifications for their judgments at the different levels of analysis.

Method

Questionnaires were distributed to approximately 650 middle-managers in three public sector organizations (employing, on average, 5,000 persons) and three private-sector organizations (employing, on average, 4,500 persons). Of the managers in the target population, 39 percent ultimately responded to all or most of the questionnaire, yielding a sample of 259 managers who averaged 43.2 years of age, had 5.1 years of higher education, and had 8.2 years of experience in coordinating and supervising staffs that ranged in size from 4 to 210. The sex ratio was seven males to every three females. Data collection occurred in 1996 and 1997. The private-sector organizations included an insurance company and two high-technology firms; the public-sector organizations were civilian agencies of the federal government that specialized in national security or intelligence analysis and a state-level educational bureaucracy. Both individual respondents and organizational representatives were assured of the absolute confidentiality of all responses. The questionnaires were analytically partitioned into three components: ideological worldview, cognitive style, and preferred managerial styles, which measured reactions to micro, meso, and macro scenarios.

Ideological worldview. These items relied on 7-point semantic-differential-style scales to assess ideological self-identification, using a question adapted from the National Election Studies ("Overall, do you consider yourself to be a liberal or conservative?"), as well as views of the trustworthiness of other people ("Most people are looking for ways of getting away with something," and "When you treat employees with fairness and consideration, you can count on them to do the right thing even when no one is looking."), the resourcefulness and rationality of others ("People lower down in organizations generally understand a lot more than they are given credit for." "Even the strongest among us fall on hard times and need help from the community," and "A useful maxim in dealing with employees is KISS—keep it simple, stupid."), the willingness to defend explicit hierarchies ("I am not at all embarrassed to talk about 'subordinates' or 'people working under me in the chain of command,'" "It is not a perfect relationship but generally the higher in an organization you look, the more talented and hardworking the people tend to be," and "It sounds old-fashioned but obedience is an important virtue."). the willingness to defend the single-minded pursuit of profit-maximization ("It is a bad idea to mix business goals with concerns for social justice," and "Human progress owes a lot to innovators who had the courage of their convictions"), the relative importance of "avoiding being taken advantage of" versus "failing to reach mutually beneficial relationships with others," the necessity of strong leadership ("Most people are without direction in the absence of strong leadership."), enthusiasm for free markets (they "stimulate growth and prosperity"), wariness of markets ("We need government to protect us from the income inequality that results from unregulated free markets" or "to protect us from the damage to the natural environment that results from unregulated markets"), and attitudes toward government ("Overall, in our society today, government creates a lot more problems than it solves.").

Cognitive style. These cognitive style items were mostly adapted from Kruglanski and Webster's (1996) need-for-closure scale. They assessed tolerance for ambiguity ("I dislike questions that can be answered in many different ways," and "It is annoying to listen to someone who cannot seem to make up his or her mind.") and strength of personal preference for simple comprehensive explanations of phenomena, for working on problems with clear-cut solutions, and for working in homogeneous as opposed to heterogeneous social units ("The world is fundamentally a far simpler place than it initially seems to be"; "Even after I have made up my mind about something. I am always eager to consider a different opinion"; "I usually make important decisions quickly and confidently"; "When considering most conflict situations, I can usually see how both sides can be right"; "I prefer interacting with people whose opinions are very different from my own"; "It is better to accomplish one objective really well than it is to try to accomplish two or more objectives and do only a so-so job").

Micro Scenarios: Cognitive Biases

Fundamental attribution error. A pair of scenarios assessed approval of managers who varied in their receptiveness to employees' accounts for failure to achieve organizational goals. Half of the respondents were randomly assigned to the experimental condition in which they first read a scenario describing a prime managerial candidate for the fundamental attribution error—a manager with a low threshold for drawing strong conclusions about the character of his employees from performance data alone:

> J. M. adopts a "no-excuses" approach to evaluating the people who report to him. He feels that most people are just far too inventive at concocting stories for failing to achieve organizational goals. He therefore holds people strictly accountable for objective performance indicators, taking into account only relatively extreme extenuating circumstances.

After rating the manager, these respondents then read a scenario that described an empathic manager who seemed a prime candidate for the flipside inferential bias, hyper-receptivity to any and all situational explanations that people might advance for their conduct:

> L. V. thinks it a bad idea to base evaluations of the people reporting to him on so-called objective performance indicators. He needs to hear the employees' perspectives on why they failed or succeeded in achieving key organizational goals and always bases his evaluation primarily on the accounts that employees provide of what is actually going on in both the business and their personal lives.

The other half of the respondents read the scenarios in the opposite order. Dependent variables included eight descriptive phrases to which managers responded on 1-9 unipolar scales, ranging from "not at all characteristic" to "extremely characteristic." The traits were selected to capture the negative and positive value spins that could plausibly be attached to both managerial stances toward employees. The most negative value spin on the fundamental attribution error is that it reveals a "harsh" and "punitive" style of management; the most positive value spin is that it reveals "uncompromisingly high standards" and "a commitment to a no-nonsense, no-excuses working style" (alpha = .81). The most negative value spin on the flipside of the fundamental attribution error—hypersensitivity to situational accounts—is that such managers are "gullible" and "tolerant of low or inconsistent standards" (alpha = .84).

An additional single-item measure of attitude toward the fundamental attribution error was "Managers always run the risk in evaluating employees of two possible mistakes: (a) failing to hold them responsible for outcomes that they could and should have controlled; (b) holding them responsible for outcomes that they could not reasonably be expected to control." Participants then rated (on a 1–9 scale), the relative frequency and seriousness of these two errors in work settings today (with 9 representing the view that b is "by far the more common serious error").

Overconfidence. A second pair of counterbalanced scenarios explored evaluations of managers who viewed either over-or underconfidence as the more serious vice:

> It is always possible to make one of two basic mistakes in decision-making: to be underconfident (to doubt that one has useful information in hand when one really does) or to be overconfident (to think one has useful information in hand when one really does not). But L. B./N. R. is convinced that underconfidence/overconfidence is much the more serious threat to high-quality decision-making and that [priority should be given to encouraging critical analysis of core assumptions, even if that slows decision making down] [priority should be given to advancing compelling arguments and mobilizing enthusiasm for what looks like the best option, even if it means acting too quickly].

Dependent variables captured positive value spins on over-confidence (decisive, possesses a can-do attitude), as well as negative value spins (rigid/closed-minded, arrogant) (alpha = .76) and positive value spins on underconfidence (flexible/open-minded, possesses capacity for self-criticism), as well as negative value spins (indecisive, wishy-washy) (alpha = .78). In addition, a single-item measure of attitude toward over-and underconfidence explicitly distinguished between private thought and public self-presentation. Respondents rated their degree of preference (on a 9-point scale) for two styles of leadership: "M. V. believes that however many doubts about a decision he may harbor privately, he needs to project confidence that he has the right answer to employees" versus " A. V. believes that if he has private doubts about a decision, it is a good idea to share those concerns with employees."

For *staying the course versus abandoning sunk costs,* participants rated the relative frequency of one of two mistakes that managers nowadays can make: they "are more likely to make the mistake of prematurely abandoning a good idea that runs into trouble" or "to make the flipside mistake of persevering too long with a bad idea and spending good money after bad." *Simple heuristics versus complex choice strategies* was assessed by the following item: "Which mistake do you think managers nowadays are more likely to make: to rely too heavily on simple, intuitive rules of thumb grounded in practical experience or to exaggerate the complexity of the issues at stake and to spend far too much time and energy seeking expert advice and developing complex decision-making procedures?" A single-item measure of *taboo trade-offs* explored reactions to a cost-benefit analysis that placed a dollar value on human life:

> S. J. is an auto-industry executive who received a confidential cost-benefit analysis which indicated that the expected cost of correcting a potential safety defect is $900 million whereas the expected benefits (reduced legal liability from fewer injuries and deaths) is just $300 million, a 3:1 ratio in favor of taking no action. How do you think he should respond?: Should he go along with the recommendation and not undertake the repairs or reject the report's recommendation and order the potential safety defect corrected?

A single-item measure of morally suspect base rates explored the profit-maximization rooted in egalitarian/fairness concerns:

> G. B. is an executive who discovered that, although the actuarial risk factors used to compute homeowners' insurance premiums are statistically and financially well designed to maximize profits and are not open to legal challenge, the net result of using these risk factors is that poor people, who come disproportionately from minority groups, wind up paying higher percentage premiums. How do you think he should respond? Should he keep the current profit-maximizing policies in place or alter the current profit-maximizing policy and reduce the burden on the poor communities, notwithstanding the adverse effect on the corporate bottom line?

Meso Scenarios: Coping with Accountability

Preemptive self-criticism versus defensive bolstering was assessed with a pair of scenarios that posed the following problem:

Senior management has asked K. M. for his views on which projects in his division should be put on the "fast track." The "favorites" of senior management are at this point impossible to guess. He responds by [offering a complex and balanced appraisal of the pros and cons of each project, anticipating the key criticisms that can be leveled at each, and specifying the trade-offs that management confronts] [singling out the projects he considers most promising and making as powerful and compelling a case as he can for those options.]

Dependent variables included the same trait scales used in assessing reactions to over- and underconfidence, given that experimental evidence has shown that self-critical thought attenuates and bolstering amplifies overconfidence (Tetlock and Kim, 1987).

Open-ended versus directive accountability was assessed with the following pair of scenarios:

D. F. runs a policy planning group that consists of professionals with varying expertise. [He sees it as his job to guide the group by giving his opinion first and by laying out a clear discussion agenda that keeps meetings brief. He finds that this procedure helps to set definite boundaries on what it is and is not useful to consider.] [He sees it as his job to encourage the group members to think as creatively as possible and, to this end, he rarely reveals his opinion before everyone has had a say. Although meetings may be long, he believes that the process often reveals important new perspectives.]

Bipolar rating scales included positive and negative spins on open-ended accountability (open- versus closed-minded) and on directive accountability (well organized/poorly organized).

Process versus outcome accountability was assessed on the following pair of scenarios:

M. R. runs the purchasing department for his organization. [His philosophy is that employees are paid to implement carefully designed procedures for making deals with outside providers of goods and services. As long as employees follow the specified procedures for selecting high-quality products at competitive bids, employees know they won't get into trouble—even if the resulting price paid is too high.] [His philosophy is that employees are paid to get the best possible prices for high-quality products. The purchasing procedure guidelines are just that—guidelines, not fixed rules. Employees who pay too high a price or who buy defective merchandise jeopardize their careers. Following procedures is no defense.]

Positive value-spin descriptions of the process-accountability manager included fair and systematic; negative spins included rule-bound and bureaucratic (alpha = .75). Positive value spin descriptions of the outcome-accountability manager included resourceful and effective; negative value spins included excessively demanding and unfair (alpha = .83).

A pair of scenarios assessed managers' reactions to the necessity to concentrate or diffuse the pain of cuts:

B. G. just learned that the department received a 10% cut in its annual operating budget. He responds [by trying to distribute the burden of the cuts fairly and equally across all employees who work for him] [by trying to maximize the efficiency of his organization—laying off those employees who contribute the least to productivity and streamlining operations by introducing new technology that reduces the need for future hiring].

Dependent variables captured positive and negative value spins that liberals and conservatives might place on the egalitarian versus efficiency responses to austerity. The positive value spin on concentrating the cuts on the least productive was that this policy "promotes profitability and efficiency" and "sends the right message to employees who take their jobs for granted"; the negative value spin was that this policy "violates the trust the workers have placed in the organization" (the implicit social contract) and "erodes the loyalty toward the organization and breeds cynicism and distrust." Alpha for the 4-item scale was .79. The positive value spin on diffusing the cuts is that sharing burdens equally was "morally right in itself" and also "promotes solidarity at the workplace"; the negative value spin was that this policy is merely "a cowardly dodge to avoid controversy" and "is short-sighted and likely to destroy the organization in the long term." Alpha for this 4-item scale was .76.

Scenarios assessing voice, exit, exploitation, and loyalty probed reactions to resistance to accountability that take the form of protest (exercising the voice option) looking for another job (exercising the exit option) and strategic exploitation of loopholes in the accountability guidelines:

P. T. learns that the work unit he manages will be expected in the coming year to achieve an increase in productivity he considers unreasonably and unfairly large. His unit was not consulted at all during the process of setting the new productivity standard. The firm is doing well and in no danger of insolvency. P. T. [protests by providing a detailed set of reasons why he considers the new standards to be both unreasonable and unfair to his work unit] [resigns to take another job] [looks for loopholes in the new accountability guidelines that allow him to "play games with numbers" in ways that artificially inflate the perceived productivity of his unit] [keeps his objections to himself and does the best he can do to achieve the new performance standards].

Dependent variables captured positive and negative value spins on voice (alpha = .75), exit (alpha = .82), subversion (alpha = .77), and compliance (alpha = .80): voice (whiny, ineffective/honest, principled), exit (disloyal, opportunistic/self-reliant, autonomous), subversion (cheater, fraud/reasonable response to unreasonable demands, resourceful), and compliance (easily bullied, submissive/can-do attitude, loyal worker).

Macro Scenarios: Accountability Regimes

A pair of scenarios assessed preferences for multiple advocacy versus hierarchical filtering as styles of organizational decision making:

Top management in this organization have worked together a long time and know each other well [They think it most important to make decisions efficiently, minimizing unnecessary discussion and getting to the key points quickly. Accordingly, they have streamlined the decision process, requiring top managers to justify important decisions to the group but rarely requiring them to go outside the group to solicit critical suggestions.] [They think it most important to subject important decisions to thorough, critical analysis from a variety of viewpoints inside and outside the organization, even if it is time consuming. Accordingly, top managers can never be sure of the types of objections that might be raised to their proposals in decision-making meetings.]

Dependent variables included positive value spins on hierarchical filtering ("permits decisive action in rapidly changing situations," "preserves clear lines of authority") and on multiple advocacy ("compels decision makers to confront unpleasant facts," "prevents the error of acting impulsively") and negative spins on hierarchical filtering ("encourages an overconfident and clique-

ish attitude at the top," "promotes a rigid, authoritarian structure") and on multiple advocacy ("creates a serious risk of waffling and paralysis," "promotes anarchy—everyone wants a say on everything"). Alpha for hierarchical-filtering scales was .79 and, for multiple advocacy, .86.

This pair of scenarios probed implicit philosophies of corporate governance with respect to shareholder versus stakeholder:

Corporation x is founded on the philosophy that it exists [for one overriding purpose—to maximize return to shareholders—and that, if every corporation were faithful to this mission, the net long-term result would be a vibrant economy that produces the greatest prosperity for the greatest number] [to achieve a variety of sometimes conflicting goals, including providing competitive returns to shareholders, ensuring all employees of good livelihoods and respectful treatment, maintaining good relations with customers, suppliers, and local communities, and pursuing sound social and environmental policies. In this view, if every corporation were faithful to these multiple missions, the net long-term result would be a fundamentally more decent and just society.]

Dependent variables included positive value spins on the two models of governance (shareholder: "keeps the faith with investors," "maximizes efficiency and long-term viability of the organization"; stakeholder: "keeps faith with the society as a whole," "promotes social justice") and negative value spins (shareholder: "short-sighted profit maximizing," "dehumanizes everyone but the investors"; stakeholder: "creates a blank check for lazy, inept, or corrupt managers," "prevents managers from making tough decisions critical for long-term survival"). Alpha for the shareholder scale was .84 and, for the stakeholder scale, .81.

Exploratory interviews. Priority was placed on intensively examining respondents with unusually coherent and well defined ideological world views. Accordingly, libertarian conservatives who were interviewed had high scores on the factor by that name (preference for market-based solutions and distaste for government intervention, coupled with faith in people as rational and resilient) and low to moderate scores on the authoritarianism factor (an aversion to hierarchy). Egalitarians had low scores on both the libertarianism and authoritarianism factors. Authoritarian conservatives had high scores on the factor by that name and middle-range scores on the libertarianism factor (their scores on this factor should be inflated by their support for market solutions but should be deflated by their skepticism about the rationality of their fellow citizens). Finally, moderates or centrists scored in the middle range of both factors and were interviewed for comparison purposes. Interviews were conducted with 26 managers who represented four distinct political points of view: eight authoritarian conservatives, seven egalitarians, five libertarian conservatives, and six moderates or centrists. These interviews explored the explanations that managers offered for their reactions to each scenario from the structured questionnaire.

Results

Independent-variable scales. Maximum-likelihood factor analysis indicated that the preference for-simplicity and explanatory closure (PSEC) scale was reasonably unidimensional. The scale as a whole possessed adequate internal reliability (alpha = .77). By contrast, the same factor-analytic procedure indicated that the best representation of the underlying correlational structure of the measures of ideological worldview was two-dimensional. Table 1 presents the variable loadings that emerged from the two-factor oblimin rotated matrix. The first factor captured authoritarian conservatism. High-loading items included doubts about the trustworthiness of others, skepti-

cism that even employees who have been treated fairly well will reciprocate by "doing the right thing when no one else is looking," placing a greater priority on avoiding exploitation (being taken for a sucker) than on failing to achieve mutually beneficial agreements, the belief that obedience is an important and underrated virtue, the belief that people are rudderless without strong leadership, and wariness of government intervention in the economy. Low scores captured anti-authoritarian egalitarianism: a distaste for obedience and hierarchies, a relatively benign view of people as decent and fair, and a willingness to give those lower down in the pecking order the benefit of the doubt.

The second factor captured libertarian conservatism, highlighting items that tapped into faith in free markets, wariness of government intervention in the economy, and a view of people as rational, resourceful, and self-reliant. Low scores captured anti-libertarian egalitarianism: support for a safety-net state that redistributes income and carefully watches for negative externalities of free-market behavior, doubts about how meritocratic society really is, doubts about great-man theories of social progress, and a view of individual human beings as fragile and in need of considerable social support. Interestingly, high scorers on both factors tended to label themselves as conservative and Republican, and low-scorers tended to label themselves as Democrats and liberal, in the con-

TABLE 1. Variable Loadings in Rotated Factor Matrix from Maximum-Likelihood Analysis

Variable	Authoritarian conservatism	Libertarian conservatism
Self-identification as conservative	.22	.19
Untrustworthiness of other people	.38	.04
Can count on employees doing right thing when no one is looking	−.35	.00
Underlings understand a lot	−.22	.02
Even the strong need help	.14	.27
"Keep it simple, stupid"	.41	.08
Embarrassed by talk of "subordinates"	−.27	−.10
System is meritocratic	.30	.26
Obedience is an underrated virtue	.29	.00
Don't mix business goals with social justice	.25	.41
Society owes much to courageous innovators	.16	.49
Avoiding exploitation less important than joint gain	-.37	.02
People are rudderless without leaders	.43	−.05
Free markets promote prosperity	.21	.46
Need government to check impact of free markets on inequality	−.20	−.35
Need government to check impact of free markets on the environment	−.11	−.09
Government creates more problems than it solves	.24	.38

ventional late-twentieth century sense of that term. Alphas for the resulting scales were .84 and .78, respectively.

Although scores on the two factors are moderately positively correlated ($r = .22$), it is a mistake to attribute much significance to that relationship, hinging as it does on the proportion of items pertaining to skepticism of government and support for markets (inflating the correlation) versus the proportion of items tapping views of human nature and support for authority and hierarchy (depressing the correlation). The low positive correlation between authoritarian conservatism and preference for cognitive closure ($r = .21$) is less easily dismissed, replicating as it does a longstanding body of work on the links between cognitive style and ideology (Lipsett and Raab, 1978; Tetlock, 1984). It is worth stressing, though, that confirmatory factor analysis applied to all indi-

vidual-difference predictors supports that factorial distinctness of authoritarian conservatism and preference for cognitive closure.

Multiple regressions. Table 2 summarizes a series of multiple regressions that used the two-factor measure of ideological worldview and the measure of cognitive style as predictors of what counts as both cognitive bias and organizational corrective. Control variables included private-public sector employment, seniority, income, education, and gender. Table 3 presents the mean evaluative reactions of respondents who scored in the top and bottom tertiles of the measures of ideological worldview and need for closure (the most consistent predictors) to each of the scenarios and their variants.

As the regression coefficients in Table 2 and the means in Table 3 reveal, ideology in its two-factor form proved a robust predictor of reactions across

TABLE 2. Coefficients of Multiple Regression Predictors of Evaluations of Micro, Meso, and Macro Scenarios

Scenarios	R^2	Key Predictors (Standardized Betas)		
		Authoritarian conservatism	Libertarian conservatism	Need closure
Cognitive biases				
Overattribution	.26	.38**	.10	.30*
Underattribution	.24	−.36**	−.07	−.24**
Overconfidence (private thought)	.22	.25**	.23*	.27**
Underconfidence (private thought)	.20	−.29**	−.22*	−.23**
Overconfidence (public self-presentation)	.19	.23*	.22*	.03
Sunk-cost justification serious problem	.18	−.29*	.01	−.25
Complex heuristics trump simple	.25	−.35*	−.02	−.32*
Use morally suspect base rate	.17	.25*	.27*	.02
Make taboo trade-off	.12	.08	.31*	−.01
Coping with accountability				
Preemptive self-criticism	.23	−.33**	.02	−.34**
Defensive bolstering	.22	.26**	.01	.23*
Directive accountability	.15	.22*	.03	.19*
Open-ended accountability	.14	−.23*	.00	−.19*
Process accountability	.11	.03	−.25*	.13
Outcome accountability	.13	.14	.28*	.09
Diffuse cuts/minimize protest	.24	−.28**	−.32**	−.07
Concentrate cuts/maximize efficiency	.23	.24*	.33**	−.10
Protest (voice)	.19	−.26**	−.18	−.14
Exit	.18	.02	.38**	.02
Loophole exploitation	.29	−.34**	−.33**	.00
Loyalty	.17	.26*	.18*	.02
Designing accountability systems				
Shareholder	.31	.31**	.39**	.10
Stakeholder	.27	-.29**	−.35**	−.08
Hierarchical filtering	.18	.30**	−.04	.26*
Multiple advocacy	.17	−.20*	.01	−.28*

* $p < .01$; ** $p < .05$.

levels of analysis. With respect to putative cognitive biases, support emerged for H1 and H2. Authoritarian conservatives were more favorable to the no-excuses manager (who committed the fundamental attribution error of insensitivity to situational explanations) and less favorable to the empathic manager (who committed the flipside error of hypersensitivity to excuses that deflect responsibility for non-performance). There was also an unusually powerful association between certain single-item questions and reactions to the diverging attributional styles of managers. Respondents were especially positive toward the no-excuses manager and skeptical about the effectiveness of the sensitive manager to the degree that (a) they suspected "most people are continually looking for what they can get away with"; (b) they placed high importance on "preventing others from taking advantage of them"; and (c) they felt that managers erred far more often in the direction of letting employees off the hook for outcomes they could control than in wrongly blaming employees for

outcomes they could control (all r's > .30). Indeed, the conservatism factor ceased to predict reactions to these scenarios after controlling for these three items [partial $r(240) = 0.09$]. Suspiciousness of human nature, which loads highly on the authoritarianism but not on the libertarianism factor, may thus be driving this effect.

Consistent with past psychological work on cognitive style, managers with strong preferences for cognitive closure, regardless of ideology, were more likely to defend the fundamental attribution error. This result suggests that the psychological appeal of the alleged error is also rooted in aversion to the ambiguity that inevitably arises in weighing justifications and excuses for failure. Summary social justice simplifies life.

Authoritarian and libertarian conservatives had similar reactions to the over-/underconfidence scenarios. Consistent with H3, H4, and H5, both camps reacted favorably toward the manager who felt that overconfidence was, all other things being equal, a less serious error than underconfidence

TABLE 3. Mean Evaluations of Scenarios*

Scenarios	Bottom and Top Tertiles		
	Low/high conservatism	Low/high libertarianism	Low/high need closure
Overattribution	3.10 vs. 5.12	3.86 vs. 4.03	3.52 vs. 5.03
Underattribution	5.21 vs. 3.99	4.39 vs. 4.32	4.83 vs. 3.86
Overconfidence (private thought)	4.02 vs. 5.22	4.35 vs. 4.91	4.21 vs. 5.03
Underconfidence (private thought)	5.08 vs. 3.80	4.28 vs. 3.74	4.71 vs. 3.72
Overconfidence (public posturing)	3.86 vs. 6.02	4.12 vs. 5.73	4.41 vs. 5.55
Sunk-cost justification serious problem	6.02 vs. 3.52	5.05 vs. 5.37	6.15 vs. 3.71
Complex heuristics trump simple	6.33 vs. 3.66	5.14 vs. 5.01	5.99 vs. 3.18
Use morally suspect base rate	3.22 vs. 5.21	3.15 vs. 5.35	3.66 vs. 4.08
Make taboo trade-off	4.46 vs. 4.71	3.85 vs. 5.53	4.03 vs. 4.25
Preemptive self-criticism	5.39 vs. 4.21	4.78 vs. 4.98	5.54 vs. 4.22
Defensive bolstering	5.05 vs. 5.47	4.70 vs. 4.91	4.04 vs. 5.54
Directive accountability	4.72 vs. 6.05	5.15 vs. 5.25	4.42 vs. 5.89
Open-ended accountability	5.42 vs. 4.59	5.08 vs. 5.03	5.61 vs. 4.48
Process accountability	5.23 vs. 5.33	5.26 vs. 3.88	5.14 vs. 5.41
Outcome accountability	4.84 vs. 5.45	4.32 vs. 5.75	5.08 vs. 5.24
Diffuse cuts/minimize protest	4.85 vs. 2.80	5.04 vs. 2.71	3.76 vs. 4.03
Concentrate cuts/maximize efficiency	3.29 vs. 5.35	3.07 vs. 5.65	4.08 vs. 4.25
Protest (voice)	4.62 vs. 3.13	4.14 vs. 3.65	4.33 vs. 4.20
Exit	4.13 vs. 4.25	3.49 vs. 5.45	4.12 vs. 4.17
Loophole exploitation	3.76 vs. 2.83	3.80 vs. 2.70	3.53 vs. 3.55
Loyalty	4.93 vs. 5.38	4.62 vs. 5.17	4.31 vs. 4.86
Shareholder	3.37 vs. 5.21	3.16 vs. 5.37	4.20 vs. 4.31
Stakeholder	5.52 vs. 3.06	5.23 vs. 3.26	4.40 vs. 4.10
Hierarchical filtering	3.37 vs. 4.89	3.90 vs. 3.83	3.41 vs. 4.26
Multiple advocacy	5.45 vs. 4.21	4.73 vs. 4.59	4.99 vs. 4.32

*Higher scores indicate a more positive evaluation of the manager, coping strategy, or accountability regime.

in both private decision making and public self-presentations to employees. Again, though, a more fine-grained analysis revealed especially powerful associations between certain items and reactions to the over- versus underconfident managers. Partial correlation analysis revealed that authoritarian conservatism ceased to predict reaction to the scenarios after controlling for endorsement of the maxim that, in dealing with employees, it is important to "keep it simple, stupid." Libertarian conservatism ceased to predict reactions after controlling for endorsement of the claim that human progress owed a lot to innovators with the courage of their convictions. Thus, although the two camps on the right agreed, they did not have the same reasons for taking this common stand. Support could be rooted in fear and distrust or in hope and techno-optimism.

Also consistent with H4 and H5, authoritarian conservatives were the most favorably disposed toward managers who thought that abandoning good ideas that had run into temporary trouble was a more common mistake than persevering with bad ideas (and vainly trying to save face and recoup sunk costs) and that excessive "complexification" was a more common mistake than excessive simplification in decision making. Libertarian conservatism predicted neither sentiment.

The cognitive-style predictions received more mixed support. As Kruglanski and Webster (1996) predicted, the stronger are managers' preferences for closure, the more support they offered for overconfidence, for staying the course, and for simplifying decision processes. But cognitive style did not predict support for overconfidence in public self-presentation, and none of the expected conservatism-by-cognitive-style interactions materialized.

Consistent with H6, authoritarian conservatives and libertarian conservatives were largely on the same ideological wave-length in their reactions to the morally suspect base rate. Unlike the anti-authoritarian and anti-libertarian egalitarians, these two groups refrained from condemning a business practice that, in pursuit of profit, harmed traditionally disadvantaged groups. This stance was rooted, according to partial-correlation analysis, in the degree to which respondents thought it a bad idea to mix business goals with concerns for social justice. There was also some support for H7: libertarian conservatives, not now joined by authoritarian conservatives, were virtually alone in

refraining from condemning the executive who committed the taboo trade-off of affixing an explicit dollar value to human life.

Managers' reactions to strategies of structuring accountability were consistent with H8: authoritarian conservatives and those with strong closure preferences stood out as most critical of open-ended accountability (in which the boss keeps subordinates guessing about where he stands) and most supportive of directive accountability, in which the boss squarely assumes the mantle of responsibility for setting priorities. Partial correlation analysis suggested that this effect was partly rooted in the belief that people are rudder-less without strong leadership.

With respect to strategies of coping with accountability, consistent with H9, both authoritarian conservatism and the preference for cognitive closure scale predicted the attribution of more positive traits to decision makers who coped with accountability by taking clear simple stands from which they could not be easily swayed. Authoritarian conservatism and preference for closure were also negatively associated with the attribution of more positive traits to decision makers who coped with accountability by engaging in pre-emptive self-criticism and by weighing legitimate competing perspectives against each other. The expected conservatism-by-cognitive-style interactions did not emerge.

There was only partial support for H10 and H11. As expected, libertarian conservatives were the stoutest defenders of outcome accountability and most critical of process accountability, which they disparaged as "just more bureaucracy" and "rules for the sake of rules." Unexpectedly, however, they were not joined by authoritarian conservatives who seemed quite ambivalent about the relative emphasis that should be placed on process and outcome accountability.

In the results for the more overtly political strategies of coping with accountability, support emerged for H12, that authoritarian and libertarian conservatives would be more likely than their egalitarian counterparts to (a) condemn the manager who, in their view, avoided the tough decisions by spreading budget cuts equally rather than targeting the cuts at the least productive and then restructuring to compensate for shifts in the division of labor; and (b) applaud the manager who "bit the bullet" and "allocated scarce resources more rationally."

The ideological agreement broke down somewhat, however, in reactions to the voice, exit, exploitation, and loyalty scenarios. Relative to the low scores on the two factors, authoritarian and libertarian conservatives were both more likely to deplore the subversive, loophole-exploiting response to rising accountability demands and, to a lesser extent, more likely to applaud the loyalty response (all in accord with H13 and H14). But, in accord with H15, libertarian conservatives had a much more positive reaction to the exit response (competent individuals exercising choices in self-correcting labor markets) than did the authoritarian conservatives, who saw the same conduct as rather opportunistic. Authoritarian conservatives also had a more negative reaction to protest than did the libertarians, but not a more negative reaction to cheaters, contrary to H15, a null result probably attributable to a floor effect on the rating scales for cheaters.

Finally, sharp ideological cleavages emerged in managers' evaluations of macro scenarios that explored the tensions between the hierarchical-filtering and multiple-advocacy models of internal corporate governance and the tensions between the shareholder-stakeholder models of external corporate governance. Consistent with H16, authoritarian but not libertarian conservatives judged top management more favorably when it relied on hierarchical filtering to simplify the decision process (screening out weak or irrelevant arguments), whereas anti-authoritarian egalitarians reserved the most praise for top managers who embraced a multiple-advocacy style of decision making that gave priority to considering inputs from a wide range of interest groups within the organization. Consistent with H17 and H18, authoritarian and libertarian conservatives alike judged top management more favorably when it favored a monistic accountability regime centered around shareholders, whereas low scorers on these two factor-analytic scales moved in the opposite direction, attributing the most positive traits to top managers who endorsed the pluralistic regime of accountability to stakeholders. Inconsistent with H17, the preference-for-closure scale failed to predict preferences for accountability regimes at this most macro level. The stands that middle-level managers took on the shareholder-stakeholder debate reflected abstract political sympathies (property rights of well-capitalized principals versus human rights of economic underdogs) more than personal cognitive style. Whether this result would hold up for top management—whose working lives are more tightly linked to the mode of corporate governance—is an open question.

General observations. Overall, the measures of ideology, and to a lesser extent cognitive style, were the statistically dominant predictors. Moreover, the cognitive style results roughly paralleled those for authoritarian conservatism, with high scorers on the need-for-closure scale resembling authoritarian conservatives in their preference for simple decision-making styles across levels of analysis, but most noticeably at the micro and meso levels. The expected interactive effects of conservatism and cognitive style never emerged.

Among the control variables entered into the regressions, private-sector employment and gender had significant zero-order correlations with decision-style preferences. With only a few exceptions, however, the effects of these alternative predictors disappeared in the multiple regressions. The exceptions included a tendency for women to prefer an openness to situational explanations for performance shortfalls and for public-sector managers to prefer to avoid controversy by spreading the pain of budget cuts equally across constituencies. There was also some tendency for ideology effects to be larger (and justifications for policy preferences to be longer) the more years managers had spent in institutions of higher learning.

Supplementary Analyses of Qualitative Data

The interviews had three guiding objectives. The first was to assess the explanations that managers offered for preferring one or another style of making decisions or of structuring accountability. Could these free-flowing, stream-of-consciousness justifications be mapped onto the conceptual framework advanced earlier, which traces diverging conceptions of good judgment to more fundamental divergences in ideological worldview and in cognitive style? Does a qualitative analysis of the accounts that managers advance for their questionnaire responses point us in the same explanatory direction as do the multiple regression analyses reported earlier? The second objective was to assess the degree to which respondents possessed an intuitive awareness of the types of arguments that might be advanced for alternative answers to the questionnaire and the degree to which they accepted or disparaged these alternative outlooks. The third was to assess managers' willingness, in principle, to change their minds if it turned out that some of the factual arguments underpinning alternative answers were correct.

Fundamental attribution error. When queried, managers quite readily acknowledged the role of fundamental assumptions about human nature in shaping their openness to subordinates' accounts for failing to satisfy performance expectations. As the regression results led us to expect, the less trustworthy and committed they thought employees were ("to do the right thing when no one is looking"), the greater their reluctance to accept accounts. Managers with strong opinions on the perils of overattribution or underattribution virtually always had an accompanying horror story. Those who deplored overattribution usually had, ready at hand, there-but-for-the-grace-of-God-go-I parables in which decent, hardworking folks are temporarily overwhelmed by forces outside of their control—bad marriages, disease, depression, problem children—but eventually overcome these forces and become esteemed members of the organization, an outcome that would have been impossible if their bosses had not been caring and empathic ("open doors, open ears, open minds"). Sometimes, the managers recalled that they themselves were once in the role of the floundering subordinate. By contrast, those most concerned with the perils of underattribution came armed with stories that cut in the opposite direction: parables of free-riders exploiting gullible managers, in which shady characters concoct one cockamamie excuse or justification after another for non-performance and, in the process, harm coworkers, the managers in charge, and the organization as a whole. One manager waxed Shakespearian, "To be kind I must be cruel." One does no one any favors by pretending that poor performance is not poor or does not impose burdens on others who wind up suffering financial penalties or taking on extra work. A few of these tough managers even had stories about receiving thank-you notes from people they had fired. These reformed slackers and ne'er do wells eventually came to appreciate the wake-up call (cf. Rodgers, Taylor, and Foreman, 1992).

Styles of decision making and of structuring accountability. Managers justified their preferences for certain styles of decision making, in part,

by invoking competing views of human nature. Some managers, especially authoritarian conservatives, subscribed to an implicit theory of leadership that stressed the importance of always projecting can-do confidence to others and not acknowledging errors as long as those errors can be "spun" into sound decisions: "If you don't believe in yourself, don't expect others to believe in you" (one defense of overconfidence at the level of private thought), and "Hamlets don't inspire confidence—you need to show a little bluster to get the troops moving" (a defense at the level of public self-presentation). Others, especially anti-authoritarian egalitarians, subscribed to the view that one gains the long-term respect of others by honestly admitting one's shortcomings and displaying a willingness to heed constructive criticism and make timely mid-course corrections.

But rationales for decision-making styles were also rooted in competing views of the challenges confronting the organization. Some managers, especially authoritarian conservatives, explicitly declared that, in many choice situations, one quickly reaches the point of diminishing marginal returns for further information search and analysis, whereas other managers, especially egalitarians, were equally explicit about the need to be wary of "premature closure." Popular refrains among those most skeptical of the value of protracted cognitive assessments of problems included "Time is money," "Real managers make decisions, they don't talk about them," "On-the-one-hand-and-on-the-other presentations get tiresome very quickly," and, most crudely, "S–t or get off the pot." Those more sympathetic to protracted cognitive assessments were equipped with fewer snappy aphorisms, but the gist of their comments was plain enough: "Learn to live with uncertainty," and "As soon as you stop hearing that little voice in the back of your mind saying 'you might be wrong,' you are definitely in trouble." These cleavages in managers' intuitive theories of decision making thus mirror themes in the now vast literature on contingency theories of social cognition and decision making (Chaiken and Trope, 1999) and the ongoing controversy over when simple heuristics generate as accurate assessments and as utility-enhancing decisions as do more complex and effort-demanding methods of making up one's mind (Gigerenzer and Todd, 1999).

Libertarian conservatives, with their dislike of rule-bound systems that constrain individual initiative, were harshest in their evaluations of the process-accountability manager ("He personifies what was wrong with the old approach to running businesses," and "That's how you get $1000 toilet seats.") and most favorable to the outcome-accountability manager ("who pays the people working for him the highest compliment: they are smart and they should use their smarts."). Authoritarian conservatives and egalitarian liberals had more mixed reactions, winding up on approximately the same locations on the rating scales but for somewhat different reasons. Moralistic conservatives rated both managers quite favorably. They resonated to the structure that the process-accountability manager gave employees and to the no-nonsense, results orientation of the outcome-accountability manager. Egalitarians were also quite favorable to both managers. They resonated to the procedural fairness of the process regime and to the autonomy to stray from guidelines in the outcome regime, although the latter reaction was qualified by concern that the outcome accountability regime might unfairly assume more potential employee control over outcomes than is humanly possible.

Authoritarian conservatives offered the most positive evaluations of the executive who ran meetings quickly and directed discussion down avenues he deemed productive ("Isn't this what leaders are supposed to do?") and the least positive evaluations of the executive who adopted a low profile in group discussions in order to stimulate creativity ("I understand the rationale but it looks like dilly-dallying and passing the buck to me."). Libertarian conservatives and egalitarians had one of their rare moments of convergence: they both made more positive character attributions to the manager who encouraged creativity among subordinates ("a reasonable strategy for encouraging open expression of unpopular opinions") and less positive attributions to the manager who played a more proactive role in steering the conversation ("He seems to want an echo chamber for his own views.").

Moral boundaries on the thinkable. Libertarian conservatives were least appalled by the life-money trade-off, often taking the position that no product is perfectly safe and that the market will punish manufacturers who sell particularly unsafe products. As one libertarian commented, "If people really wanted perfectly safe cars, they'd drive in tanks and accept 10-mile-per-hour speed limits.

The hypocrisy . . . is overwhelming." Nonetheless, even this libertarian reluctantly endorsed recall, because "the public-relations hit could easily exceed the legal tab." The only other libertarian who thought the company should recall the cars with the potential defect did so not on the grounds that it was immoral to monetize life, a taboo trade-off (Tetlock, Peterson, and Lerner, 1996; Fiske and Tetlock, 1997) but, rather, on the grounds that the company may not have been fully honest with its customers about the risks to their safety and thus prevented the customers from making money-life trade-offs of their own. By contrast, egalitarians were quite vehement in denouncing resistance to a vehicle recall, and their irritation focused on the taboo character of the trade-off ("Decent human beings just aren't supposed to dollarize human life," and "Who would want to do business with a company that doesn't care about your safety? It's just one more step and we start saying the lives of the poor are worth a lot less than those of the rich."). Authoritarian conservatives fell between libertarian conservatives and egalitarians. They shared the libertarian view that nothing is perfectly safe (and therefore that taboo trade-offs are an inevitable part of life) but shared the egalitarians' repugnance for the explicitness with which the cost-benefit analysis translated lives into money. Unlike the egalitarians, though, who invoked a secular morality to express their repugnance, authoritarian conservatives tended to use the religious language of "sin" and even "evil." One authoritarian conservative nicely captured the ambivalence of this faction toward taboo trade-offs: "I am not an idiot. I know that businesses and their customers can't put 100% emphasis on safety. But we shouldn't be so upfront about putting a dollar value on human life. Call it hypocrisy if you want. I think it is degrading. Society must treat some things as sacred."

Egalitarians were also most upset about the executive who kept in place a premium policy that boosted profits but hurt racial minorities and the poor, whereas libertarian and authoritarian conservatives were least bothered. Indeed, libertarians were unapologetic backers of the executive who retained the profit-maximizing scheme ("He was honoring his responsibilities to his firm and to the shareholders, not pandering to pressure groups. If he wants to give to charity, let him spend his own money, not other people's.").

Shareholder-stakeholder controversy. Managers

for this study were drawn largely from the middle ranks of large organizations and had little experience making decisions that required answering directly either to shareholder or stakeholder representatives. Here, we thus entered a realm remote from the cognitive and interpersonal challenges that participants faced in their everyday lives—answering pressing questions such as "Is this person trustworthy or competent?" and "Should I decide now or give it more thought?" The tension between the two models of corporate governance struck many as a tad contrived. In the words of one skeptical centrist, "I don't get it. How can you please shareholders if everyone—from the customers to the politicians—is furious with you? And how can you keep stakeholders happy if you don't have any money to spread around?" That said, though, the interviews also revealed why ideology still predicted preferences for models of corporate accountability. Authoritarian and libertarian conservatives gravitated toward the shareholder model largely for the ideologically correct reason, the primacy of property rights: shareholders are owners of the corporation and managers are their agents.

Authoritarian conservatives also occasionally added a procedural reason, an almost visceral distaste for messy accountability arrangements that blur lines of authority ("Where's the boss in this system and how will we ever know if he's doing a good job?") and that make it difficult to hold anyone accountable for anything ("Where does the buck stop in a setup like that?"). Egalitarians also arrived at the "right" answer (the stakeholder model) for largely the right political reasons: the need to protect the weak and control negative externalities ("There need to be some checks and balances on corporations." "How else can the little people be heard?" and "What's wrong with a bit more democracy in the workplace?").

Acknowledging the legitimacy of other perspectives. Although many respondents were aware of arguments against the positions they preferred, awareness should not be confused with tolerance, less still, willingness to change one's mind. In the controversy over corporate governance, conservatives, both authoritarian and libertarian, understood stakeholder concerns and the necessity of taking them into account as a means to the end of profit maximization. But they feared that egalitarian efforts to promote the stakeholder vision rested on a fundamental misunderstanding both of human

nature and of capitalism that would impair long-term growth by enmeshing corporate executives in ever more elaborate webs of communitarian regulations ("You can't do anything until the local politicians, labor unions, environmentalists, minority-rights activists, and other assorted opportunists have all had their palms crossed with silver.") and by creating an inexhaustible source of excuses for poorly performing managers to put off long-suffering shareholders. As one freshly minted M.B.A. pontificated, "The stakeholder model aggravates the principal-agent problem at the heart of corporate capitalism—it gives agents too much wiggle room to evade their responsibility to promote the principal's interest." Those on the egalitarian left often understood the value of "incentivizing" management to make the hard choices that are necessary to promote growth but felt that the concentration of power and wealth had just become too lop-sided: "People who like the shareholder model are just out for number one and they really don't give a damn what happens to anybody else," and, more philosophically, "Society created corporations and it has the right to define the rules that they operate under."

At the micro end of the continuum of questions posed, there is also considerable awareness of the reasons for taking a position on the other side. In terms of the fundamental attribution error, authoritarian conservatives sometimes conceded that they might be too hard on employees (in this case, too slow to acknowledge legitimate excuses) but insisted that although many might think them hard-hearted, they had no difficulty living with themselves: "Somebody has to draw a line somewhere," and "It is only human nature to keep testing the limits." Egalitarians sometimes acknowledged that they might be "suckers" but thought the balance the were striking was best for themselves ("I can look myself in the mirror.") and for the organization ("People who feel respected will respect the company.").

In the language of decision theory, most managers, when challenged, acknowledged that there was no dominant (trade-off-free) option. But this acknowledgment was rarely spontaneous and tended to be grudging and perfunctory. In the language of cognitive-consistency theory, managers seem to have rather thoroughly rationalized their preferred styles of thinking, evaluating, and acting. Perceptions of facts and endorsements of values were in close alignment, if a characteristic managerial stance emerged from the interviews, it appears to have been belief-system overkill, in which participants insisted that their preferred working style minimizes the more common type of error (factual claim) and the more serious type of error (largely a moral or value judgment). Authoritarian conservatives put priority on minimizing what, for convenience, might be called Type II errors, such as failing to hold employees accountable for outcomes potentially under their control, exaggerating the complexity of fundamentally simple problems, pursuing additional information beyond the point of diminishing marginal returns, abandoning sound policies that run into temporary trouble, and resisting misguided efforts to make the decision process more democratic, pluralistic, and, in their view, chaotic. This policy posture was justified by maintaining that these Type II errors were both more likely and more serious than the logically complementary errors that tend to preoccupy anti-authoritarian and anti-libertarian egalitarians and that do so for roughly mirror-image reasons.

Discussion

Opinions about cognitive biases and organizational correctives hinge on the ideological worldview and cognitive style of the beholder. Most fundamentally, managers of varying political persuasions subscribe to markedly different assumptions about human nature that, in turn, shape their underlying philosophies of governance.[1] Authoritarian conservatives believe that "most people" look for and exploit loopholes in accountability systems, whereas anti-authoritarian egalitarians believe that most people will refrain from exploiting loopholes as long as they feel fairly treated. These competing views lead, among other things, to different assessments of the fundamental attribution error. Authoritarian conservatives deem it prudent managerial practice to communicate to subordinates a low tolerance for justifications and excuses that invoke situational causes for conduct that falls short of organizational expectations. People will be more motivated to behave properly if they believe that improper behavior will almost automatically tarnish their reputations—a social variant of the legal doctrine of strict liability. From an authoritarian-conservative perspective, failing to hold people responsible for outcomes that they could

have controlled is arguably a more serious error than holding people responsible for outcomes that they could not control. By contrast, the anti-authoritarian egalitarians see the fundamental attribution error as punitive, not prudent. They disagree with conservatives about both the frequency with which subordinates will invent specious justifications and fictitious excuses for substandard performance and the relative importance of avoiding Type I errors (condemning the innocent) versus Type II errors (acquitting the guilty), deploring the former error to a greater degree.

Authoritarian conservatives and those with a strong preference for cognitive closure were also more likely to concur with the sentiment that the world is often far simpler than it initially appears to be. They viewed simplicity as evidence of insight, not simple-mindedness, whereas low scorers on these scales viewed complexity as evidence of thoughtfulness, not confusion. Authoritarian conservatives also believed that lack of will power and of commitment to principles are common human failings, whereas anti-authoritarian egalitarians believed that an unwillingness to entertain self-critical thoughts and to reexamine basic assumptions are common human failings. Extending previous work in political psychology on the connections between political ideology and cognitive style, these competing views of the world translated quite directly into different evaluations of a host of putative biases, including the relative perils of over- and underconfidence, of staying the course versus escalating commitment to sunk costs, of simple versus complex choice heuristics, of preemptive self-criticism versus defensive bolstering as strategies of coping with accountability, and of directive versus open-ended strategies of structuring accountability. These two groups' markedly different evaluations of overconfidence and of staying the course are emblematic. Authoritarian conservatives believe that the can-do determination and optimism of the overconfident decision maker more than offsets the risk of persevering with a wrong assessment of the situation (cf. Staw and

---

[1]From Aristotle to the *Federalist Papers,* there are numerous precedents for assigning a foundational role to assumptions about human nature in philosophies of governance. It is perhaps surprising, therefore, that the topic has received as little attention as it has in contemporary behavioral and social science (for exceptions to this generalization, see Lane, 1973; Wrightsman, 1974).

Ross, 1980). Anti-authoritarian egalitarians believe that the capacity of self-critical thinkers to realize quickly that they are on the wrong path more than offsets the risk of prematurely abandoning a good policy that has run into temporary difficulties. And, at the level of self-presentation, they think it a bad idea for managers to wear a worry-free mask and stress the benefits of keeping coworkers (they dislike the term "subordinates") reasonably fully informed.

Ideologically grounded disagreements over human nature and the causal structure of the social world parallel in key respects disagreements over how to manage people, at both a micro and macro level. Authoritarian conservatives and their high-preference-for-cognitive-closure allies approve of managers who communicate their policy preferences clearly to subordinates and approve of subordinates who respond equally decisively, whereas low scorers on these scales see advantages in encouraging open, balanced debate and cultivating an atmosphere of normative ambiguity that keeps coworkers guessing, at least for a while. Those on the political left—and this now includes both anti-authoritarian and anti-libertarian egalitarians—also offer more muted negative evaluations of the manager who responds in a borderline-dishonest, loophole-exploiting manner to an accountability regime perceived as unjust. Some egalitarian managers see such behavior as an understandable human bid to "empower onself" when confronted by insensitive or arrogant authorities, with even occasional quasi-Marxist warnings about alienating and dehumanizing those lower in the packing order.

At the most macro level, both authoritarian and libertarian conservatives favored the monistic regime of accountability solely to shareholders ("It is hard enough to do one thing well, less still half a dozen."), whereas the anti-authoritarian and anti-libertarian egalitarians embraced the value of accountability to a host of constituencies whose interests would often have to be combined in different ways in different situations ("Corporations can't be allowed just to focus on making money," and "There is more to running a society than just efficiency.").

Looking back on the full range of correlations between ideology and managerial policy preferences, it becomes clear that the more macro the issue domain, the more likely authoritarian and libertarian conservatives were to agree. As one might expect from the variable loadings in the rotated factor matrix, high scorers on both dimensions defended property rights and free markets (unless national security/sovereignty issues were implicated, in which case support from authoritarian conservatives quickly fades) and opposed what they frequently saw as misguided government efforts to help the less competitive and to dampen fictitious externalities. By contrast, the more micro the issue, the more likely authoritarian and libertarian conservatives were to be temperamentally and stylistically at odds with each other, agreeing strongly with each other only on the adaptive value of overconfidence and on the appropriateness of using morally suspect base rates. Libertarians tended to be more cognitively flexible (or, if one prefers, unprincipled), less preoccupied with precedent, status, and hierarchy (or, if one prefers, less loyal to existing organizational structures), and more prone to have an upbeat assessment of their fellow humans (or, if one prefers, an unrealistic or naive assessment). In certain respects, libertarian conservatives resembled anti-authoritarian egalitarians, especially in their lack of enthusiasm for deference and obedience to established ways, but breaking abruptly with this outlook when questions tapped into broader attitudes toward social equality, markets, and government. And, in certain respects, authoritarian conservatives resembled the anti-libertarian egalitarians, especially in their doubts about the self-sufficiency of the isolated individual, but breaking sharply with this camp on the more macro questions of societal and economic organization. In brief, this data set allows us to observe in a managerial microcosm the cross-cutting tensions documented by survey researchers in society at large between authoritarian conservatism/secular liberalism and economic individualism/egalitarianism (Kinder, 1998). If nothing else, the current results demonstrate that organizational behaviorists err if they suppose that these deep differences in worldviews do not insinuate themselves into a wide array of managerial preferences and practices. There is no "Chinese wall" between attitudes toward work and toward politics.[2]

---

[2]The current approach to assessing managerial ideology draws on political psychological research on cognitive style and ideological worldviews. There are intriguing parallels, though, with sociological and cultural-anthropological work on rational and normative ideologies of control in managerial discourse (cf. Fiske, 1991; Barley and Kunda, 1992).

Taken as a whole, the pattern of findings suggests the usefulness of revisiting a much maligned but still standing distinction in philosophy and social science, that between facts and values. One unresolved issue concerns the degree to which ideological disagreements over cognitive biases and organizational correctives are rooted either in competing views of the facts (How likely is this or that inferential error?) or in competing values (How important is it to avoid this or that inferential error?). Disagreements rooted in competing appraisals of a common reality should, in principle, be resolvable via recourse to evidence. From this standpoint, if we could persuade conservatives that they have exaggerated the degree to which people are inherently untrustworthy and prone to exploit empathic managers, conservatives should become less tolerant of the fundamental attribution error. Or if we could persuade low-need-for-closure respondents that simple heuristics perform as well as more complex decision rules developed through grueling hours of group discussion (cf. Gigerenzer and Todd, 1999), these respondents might be quicker to realize when they have reached the point of diminishing returns for further deliberation.

By contrast, disagreements rooted in values should be profoundly resistant to change. Authoritarian conservatives may so detest being suckers that they are willing to endure a high rate of falsely rejecting employees' accounts. Libertarian conservatives might oppose the (confiscatory) stakeholder model even when confronted by evidence that concessions in this direction have no adverse effects on profitability to shareholders. Expropriation is expropriation, no matter how prettified. And some egalitarians might well endorse the stakeholder model, even if shown compelling evidence

that it reduces profits. Academics who rely on evidence-based appeals to change minds when the disagreements are rooted in values may be wasting everyone's time.

Placed in the broadest perspective, the current findings remind us that decision theorists are not the only people with strong opinions on the nature of good judgment and rationality. Decision theorists characteristically adopt an explicitly prescriptive stance to their subjects of study: there are right answers that can be derived from well-defined axiomatic systems of logic such as Bayes theorem or expected utility theory or game theory. To paraphrase John Milton in "Paradise Lost," their task is to explain the ways of God to man, not the ways of man to God, where God translates for early twenty-first-century audiences as the eternal truths of mathematical models of choice.

The intuitive theories of good judgment that many managers possess are not anchored in mathematical axioms and do not have a rigorous hypothetico-deductive structure. Rather, these intuitive theories are a conceptual mish-mash: loose amalgams of hunches that rest on speculative assumptions about human nature (How prone are people to exploit loopholes in rules and accountability regimes?), the efficacy of simple rules of thumb, and ultimately, the nature of the good society (How should we structure accountability ground rules so as to strike reasonable balances among such diverse values as efficiency, autonomy, equality, and fairness?). Insofar as this mish-mash coheres, and it often does not, psychological theory suggests that it does so in response to a combination of intrapsychic-consistency pressures to justify one's working style to oneself—Am I doing the right thing?—and self-presentational pressures to justify one's working style to others (cf. Schlenker, 1985).

Strictly speaking, there is no direct contradiction between logic and psycho-logic, between the formal prescriptivism of decision theory and the informal ideological hunches of decision makers who cope with messy human and organizational realities from day to day. Indeed, there is a rough complementarity. Formal prescriptive theories make minimal assumptions about the external world but extensive assumptions about how decision makers should integrate cues once they have been assigned likelihood or utility values, whereas intuitive theories make extensive assumptions about the world but are notoriously vague on the

---

Libertarian conservatives fall toward the rational extreme with their almost exclusive emphasis on market-pricing and calculated self-interest as the bases of working relationships inside and outside the organization. Authoritarian conservatives and anti-libertarian and anti-authoritarian egalitarians, each in their own fashion, put more emphasis on the normative bases of working relationships, with authoritarian conservatives stressing what Fiske (1991) called authority ranking (the organization as legitimate command hierarchy with superiors and subordinates), anti-libertarian egalitarians stressing communal sharing (the organization as extended family with obligations to care for needy members), and anti-authoritarian egalitarians stressing equality matching (the organization as a network of colleagues bound together in reciprocity networks).

precise rules for combining elementary beliefs and preferences into final judgments. But there is also a palpable tension. Micro-economic reductionists might be tempted to argue that disagreements grounded in ideology and cognitive style are merely atavistic vestiges of a more primitive social order, soon to be swept away by the intensification of competitive market forces that have ever-closer-to-zero tolerance for obfuscation, fuzzy thinking, and self-serving posturing. What counts is what works, and it is only a matter of time before we are all converted into Bayesian belief updaters converging on common truths about human nature, the social world, and how best to go about understanding both. This is a crude but popular variant of the end-of-ideology and end-of-history theses (Friedman, 1999; Fukuyama, 1992). Other scholars, of a more pluralistic bent, might stubbornly insist, with Immanuel Kant and Isaiah Berlin, that from the crooked timber of humanity, no straight thing can be built, and that it will prove impossible to banish ideological posturing and human imperfections from business (Berlin, 1990). Even in perfectly competitive markets pulsating signals at the speed of light, there will be numerous niches of ever changing shape and size where each ideological worldview can survive, even thrive. In this view, if one is willing to concede that human nature is at least as bafflingly complex as that conceptual prototype of economic efficiency, the stock market, where bullish and bearish observers seem fated to co-exist indefinitely in dialectical interdependence, why should one resist the notion that an equally broad spectrum of managerial opinion on human nature will prove sustainable in the face of even ferocious market competition?

ACKNOWLEDGMENTS

I appreciate the support of National Science Foundation grant #SBR 9505680 and the Institute of Personality and Social Research at the University of California, Berkeley, and the Mershon Center of The Ohio State University. I also thank the research participants and their employers for donating valuable time in completing a series of questionnaires that were admittedly a tad tedious. I hope that they feel the resulting contribution to knowledge justifies the cost. Finally, I thank Sara Bassett, Rachel Szteiter, Megan Berkowitz, Meaghan Quinn, Jeannette Poruban, Charles McGuire, Dan Newman, Orie Kristel, Mark Polifroni, and Beth Elson for research assistance, and Rod Kramer and Linda Johanson for valuable comments on the manuscript.

REFERENCES

Barley, S. R., and G. Kunda 1992 "Design and devotion: Surges of rational and normative ideologies of control in managerial discourse." Administrative Science Quarterly, 37: 363–399.

Berlin, I. 1990 The Crooked Timber of Humanity. New York: Knopf.

Chaiken, S., and Y. Trope 1999 Dual Process Models of Social Cognition. New York: Guilford.

Chubb, J. E., and T. Moe 1990 Politics, Markets, and America's Schools. Washington, DC: Brookings Institution.

Etzioni, A. 1996 Macro Socio-economics: From Theory to Activism. Armonk. NY: M. E. Sharpe.

Fiske, A. P. 1991 Structures of Social Life: The Four Elementary Forms of Human Relations. New York: Free Press.

Fiske, S., and S. Taylor 1991 Social Cognition. New York: McGraw-Hill.

Fiske, S., and P. E. Tetlock 1997 "Taboo trade-offs: Reactions to transactions that transgress spheres of justice." Political Psychology, 18: 255–297.

Friedman, T. 1999 The Lexus and the Olive Tree. New York: Farrar, Strauss, & Giroux.

Fukuyama, F. 1992 The End of History and the Last Man. New York: Free Press.

George, A. L. 1980 Presidential Decision Making in Foreign Policy: The Effective Use of Information and Advice. Boulder, CO: Westview.

Gigerenzer, G., and P. M. Todd 1999 Simple Heuristics That Make Us Smart. New York: Oxford University Press.

Gilovich, T., D. Griffin, and D. Kahneman (eds.) 2000 Inferences, Heuristics and Biases: New Directions in Judgment under Uncertainty. New York: Cambridge University Press.

Goldstein, W., and R. Hogarth 1996 Research on Judgement and Decision Making: Currents, Connections, and Controversies. New York: Cambridge University Press.

Hirschman, A. 1970 Exit, Voice, and Loyalty: Responses to Decline in Firms, Organizations, and States. Cambridge, MA: Harvard University Press.

Janis, I. L., and L. Mann 1977 Decision Making: A Psychological Analysis of Conflict, Choice, and Commitment. New York: Free Press.

Jensen, M., and W. Meckling 1976 "Theory of the firm: Managerial behavior, agency costs, and ownership structure." Journal of Financial Economics, 3: 305–360.

Kagel, J. H., and A. E. Roth (eds.) 1995 The Handbook of Experimental Economics. Princeton, NJ: Princeton University Press.

Kinder, D. 1998 "Opinion and action in the realm of politics." In D. Gilbert et al. (eds.), Handbook of Social Psychology, 2: 778–867. New York: McGraw Hill.

Koehler, J. 1996 "The base rate fallacy reconsidered: Descriptive, normative and methodological challenges." Behavioral and Brain Sciences, 19: 1–53.

Kruglanski, A. W., and D. M. Webster 1996 "Motivated closing of the mind: 'Seizing' and 'freezing'." Psychological Review, 103: 263–268.

Lane, R. 1973 "Patterns of political belief." In J. Knutson (ed.), Handbook of Political Psychology: 83–116. San Francisco: Jossey-Bass.

Lipsett, S., and E. Raab 1978 The Politics of Unreason. Standford, CA: Stanford University Press.

March, J. M., and J. P. Olsen 1989 Rediscovering Institutions. New York: Free Press.

1995 Democratic Governance. New York: Free Press.

McClosky, H., and A. Brill 1983 Dimensions of Tolerance. New York: Russell Sage Foundation.

Messick, D. M. 1993 "Equality as a decision heuristic." In B. Mellers and J. Baron (eds.). Psychological Perspectives on Justice: 11–31. New York: Cambridge University Press.

Meyer, J. W. 1983 "Conclusion: Institutionalization and the rationality of formal organizational structure." In J. W. Meyer and W. R. Scott (eds.), Organizational Environments: Ritual and Rationality: 266–299. Beverly Hills, CA: Sage.

Rodgers, T. J., W. Taylor, and R. Foreman 1992 No Excuses Management. New York: Doubleday.

Schlenker, B. R. (ed.) 1985 The Self and Social Life. New York: McGraw-Hill.

Simon, H. 1955 "A behavioral model of rational choice." Quarterly Journal of Economics, 69: 99–118.

Simonson, I. 1989 "Choice based on reasons: The case of attraction and compromise effects." Journal of Consumer Research, 16: 158–174.

Sniderman, P., and P. E. Tetlock 1986 "Interrelationship of political ideology and public opinion." In M. Herman (ed.), Handbook of Political Psychology: 62–96. San Francisco: Jossey-Bass.

Staw, B. M., and J. Ross 1980 "Commitment in an experimenting society: A study of the attribution of leadership from administrative scenarios." Journal of Applied Psychology, 65: 249–260.

Tetlock, P. E. 1984 "Cognitive style and political belief systems in the British House of Commons." Journal of Personality and Social Psychology: Personality Processes and Individual Differences, 46: 365–375.

1985 "Accountability: The neglected social context of judgment and choice." In B. M. Staw and L. L. Cummings (eds.), Research in Organizational Behavior, 7: 297–332. Greenwich, CT: JAI Press.

1992 "The impact of accountability on judgment and choice: Toward a social contingency model." Advances in Experimental Social Psychology, 25: 331–376.

1998 "Close-call counterfactuals and belief system defenses: 'I was not almost wrong but I was almost right.'" Journal of Personality and Social Psychology, 75: 230–242.

1999 "Accountability theory: Mixing properties of human agents with properties of social systems." In J. Levine, L. Thompson, and D. Messick (eds.), Shared Cognition in Organizations: The Management of Knowledge: 117–137. Hillsdale, NJ: Eribaum.

Tetlock, P. E., and Boettger 1989 "Accountability: A social magnifier of the dilution effect." Journal of Personality and Social Psychology, 57: 388–398.

Tetlock, P. E., and J. Kim 1987 "Accountability and judgement in a personality prediction task." Journal of Personality and Social Psychology: Attitudes and Social Cognition, 52: 700–709.

Tetlock, P. E., O. Kristel, B. Elson, M. Green, and J. Lerner 2000 "The psychology of the unthinkable: Taboo trade-offs, forbidden base rates, and heretical counterfactuals." Journal of Personality and Social Psychology (in press).

Tetlock, P. E., R. Peterson, and J. Lerner 1996 "Revising the value pluralism model: Incorporating social content and context postulates." In C. Seligman, J. Olson, and M. Zanna (eds.), Ontario Symposium on Social and Personality Psychology: Values: 25–51. Hillsdale, NJ: Erlbaum.

Tyler, T. R. 1990 Why People Obey the Law. New Haven, CT: Yale University Press.

Wilson, J. Q. 1989 Bureaucracy: What Government Agencies Do and Why They Do It. New York: Basic Books.

Wrightsman, L. S. 1974 Assumptions about Human Nature: A Social-psychological Analysis. Monterey, CA: Brooks/Cole.

The Norm of Self-Interest

Dale T. Miller • Princeton University

The self-interest motive is singularly powerful according to many of the most influential theories of human behavior and the layperson alike. In the present article the author examines the role the assumption of self-interest plays in its own confirmation. It is proposed that a norm exists in Western cultures that specifies self-interest both is and ought to be a powerful determinant of behavior. This norm influences people's actions and opinions as well as the accounts they give for their actions and opinions. In particular, it leads people to act and speak as though they care more about their material self-interest than they do. Consequences of misinterpreting the "fact" of self-interest are discussed.

With the publication of *Leviathan,* Thomas Hobbes (1651/1950) enthroned self-interest as the cardinal human motive, a status it enjoys to this day (Schwartz, 1986). The sovereignty of the self-interest motive has not gone unchallenged, of course. Critics have charged that the power accorded self-interest, especially by neoclassical economics, promotes a misleading and impoverished view of the human agent that is as dangerous as it is demeaning. A more adequate view of human agent, dissenters contend, acknowledges the power of many additional, sometimes dominating, motives, such as public spiritedness (Etzioni, 1988; Mansbridge, 1994), empathy (Batson, 1991; Kohn, 1990), commitment (Sen, 1977), and justice (Lerner, 1980; Tyler, Boeckmann, Smith, & Huo, 1997).

That the explanatory power of the self-interest assumption has been the major focus of the self-interest debate is understandable, but it has also proven limiting. In particular, it has forestalled consideration of the theory's causal power—a serious omission, as the assumption of self-interest is not simply an abstract theoretical concept but a collectively shared cultural ideology (Kohn, 1990; Lerner, 1982; Miller & Ratner, 1996; Sampson, 1983; Wallach & Wallach, 1983). Demonstrating that the theory of self-interest has causal power—specifically, that it plays a role in its own confirmation—is the main objective of this article.

Scientific theories, by generating self-knowledge and self-images, are always at risk of becoming self-fulfilling (Berger & Luckmann, 1966; Gergen, 1973, 1982; Schwartz, 1997; Wallach & Wallach, 1983). Nowhere would this risk seem greater than in the case of the self-interest assumption, for the image of humans as being predominantly self-interested is central not only to neoclassical economics but to many other influential theories of human behavior, including evolutionary biology, behaviorism, and psychoanalytic theory (Etzioni, 1988; Kohn, 1990; Schwartz, 1986; Wallach & Wallach, 1983). Indeed, the self-fulfilling properties of the self-interest assumption have frequently been commented on (Kagan, 1989; Kohn, 1990; Lerner, 1982; Schwartz, 1997).

How exactly does the assumption that humans are self-interested become a self-fulfilling prophecy? Previous analyses of the self-fulfilling impact of the self-interest assumption have focused on the role that the theory plays in the structuring and configuring of social institutions (Etzioni, 1988; Kohn, 1990; Lerner, 1982; Schwartz, 1997). According to these arguments, the image of humans as being self-interested leads to the creation of the kinds of social institutions (e.g., workplaces, schools, governments) that transform the image into reality. The present analysis accepts the premise that a positive feedback loop exists between theory and social structure and that this loop contributes importantly to theory confirmation (Schwartz, 1997). I seek to go further, however, and show that scientific theory also impinges on individual consciousness and interpersonal behavior. More specifically, I attempt to show that the theory of self-interest has spawned a norm of self-interest, the consequence of which is that people often act and speak in accordance with their perceived self-interest solely because they believe to do otherwise is to violate a powerful descriptive and prescriptive expectation.

Defining the Norm of Self-Interest

The norm of self-interest prescribes that people pursue their self-interest, but, more than this, it prescribes that they pursue their self-interest narrowly defined. To satisfy the strictures of the self-interest norm, people's actions must conform to, at least crudely, the strictures of neoclassical economic theory. Acting so as to maximize positive emotions (e.g., pride) or minimize negative emotions (e.g., guilt) while meeting many definitions of self-interested behaviors (see Mansbridge, 1990b) does not meet the standards of most rational choice models nor, as we shall see, those of the self-interest norm. The latter requires that the interests motivating people be material ones (e.g., economic profit).

Consider the act of donating to charity as an example. It is often claimed that acts of this type, even anonymous ones, are self-interested because they serve various psychological interests of the self, such as self-esteem enhancement or guilt reduction (Frank, 1988; Mansbridge, 1990b). Such motivational constructions, however, do not satisfy the logic of most rational choice models (e.g.,

Mueller, 1979; Olson, 1965), because the fact that actors "feel good" after contributing to a public good (e.g., a new museum) is of no material consequence to them. Indeed, according to many rational choice models, the only truly rational action taken with respect to public goods is to partake of them without contributing to them—after all, public goods exist whether one contributes to them or not.[1] The norm of self-interest does not go so far as to mandate that people eschew charitable donation in favor of free riding, but it has, as we shall see, led the layperson to feel increasingly uncomfortable donating to charity in the absence of a tangible quid pro quo.

The Layperson as Self-Interest Theorist

If a scientific theory is to exert power over people's behavior, its validity must be widely acknowledged. This precondition certainly seems to be met in the case of the self-interest assumption, for the belief in the power of self-interest, far from being confined to theoreticians closeted in ivory towers, is held, in some form or another, by people in all segments of society: politicians, policy analysts, educators, captains of industry, athletic coaches, and, most importantly, the layperson. That the average person is a self-interest theorist, and one in the neoclassical mode at that is well-documented in general surveys (Kohn, 1990; Wuthnow, 1991) as well as in more systematic studies (Miller & Ratner, 1996, 1998). For example, the layperson believes that people's attitudes and behaviors are highly influenced by monetary incentives as well as by other personal stakes (Miller & Ratner, 1996, 1998). Thus, people who would benefit materially from the implementation of a social policy are expected to have more favorable attitudes toward that policy than are people who would not. Similarly, those offered financial compensation for undertaking a socially beneficial act (e.g., giving blood) are expected to be more willing to undertake it than are those who are not. The most impressive evidence that individuals are self-interest theorists is the finding that the predictive power they accord self-interest is largely unaffected by

---

[1]Defining self-interest psychologically also seems personally unpersuasive to rational choice practitioners—at least, research shows that economists donate significantly less to charities than do members of other professions (Frank, Gilovich, & Regan, 1993).

the explanatory power it has for their own behavior. Even when people's own attitudes toward a social policy are incongruent with their acknowledged level of vested interest in it (either too positive or too negative), they still think that the attitudes of others will be congruent with their self-interest (Miller & Ratner. 1998).

The finding that laypersons believe fervently in the power of self-interest to shape attitudes and behaviors will strike few as surprising, certainly not those social scientists who adhere to the central assumptions of rational choice theory (see Green & Shapiro, 1994). However, it should give pause to anyone familiar with the large body of research showing consistently weak links between self-interest and social attitudes (see Sears & Funk, 1990, 1991). The small actual effects of self-interest stand in sharp relief to the substantial assumed effects of self-interest and as such pose a puzzle: How is it that people come to embrace the theory of self-interest when everyday life provides so little evidence of it? To answer this question, a closer examination of self-interest rhetoric is in order.

The Origins of the Layperson's Belief in the Self-Interest Motive

Knowledge pertaining to the relative power of different motives is acquired through the same means as are other forms of social knowledge: instruction and experience. Consider first how instruction might foster the belief in the potency of self-interest. Every culture, through its scientific theories, provides its members with answers to fundamental questions about the nature of the human condition (Fiske, Kitayama, Markus, & Nisbett, 1998; Shweder, 1991). As Schwartz (1997) described this process, "science creates concepts, ways of understanding the world and our place in it, that have enormous effect on how we think and act" (p. 21). Few questions about the nature of the human condition are as important as that of the source of human action, and most cultures forge collective representations that specify both what does motivate people (descriptive theories) and what should motivate people (prescriptive theories). The dissemination of these collective representations takes both direct and indirect routes.

Direct instruction. Repeated instruction (whether at the parent's knee or in the classroom) on the power of self-interest is unlikely to be lost on its audience. Unfortunately, there has been very little research on the extent or effect of socialization of this type. What evidence there is, however, suggests that self-interest motivation can indeed be taught. For example, Frank et al. (1993) demonstrated that efforts to evangelize on behalf of the self-interest motive can produce converts even among those who could be assumed to already have strong theories of human motivation (i.e., college students).

The specific question addressed by Frank et al. (1993) was this: Does exposing college students to the precepts and findings of rational choice theory influence the power they perceive self-interest has, or at least should have, over their own lives and that of the average other? The researchers examined this question by assessing students' responses at both the beginning and end of the semester to two ethical dilemmas ("Would you return a lost envelope with $100 in it?" and "Would you report a billing error that benefited you?"). Students were members of one of two different microeconomics classes or of a class unrelated to economics (astronomy). Of the economics classes, one was taught by an instructor who specialized in game theory (a field in which self-interest is axiomatic), the other, by an instructor who specialized in economic development in Maoist China. The results supported the hypothesis that studying economics can foster self-interest. Over the course of the semester, the responses of students in the game theorist's class increased in self-interest more than did those of students in the other economist's class; these latter students' responses, in turn, increased more in self-interest than did those of students in the control (astronomy) professor's class. Similar changes emerged on measures assessing students' expectations of the actions of the average person.

The most significant finding of Frank et al. (1993) for the present analysis is that the experience of taking a course in microeconomics actually altered students' conceptions of the appropriateness of acting in a self-interested manner, not merely their definition of self-interest. Instruction in economics, it would appear, does not make cynics out of students by persuading them that the motivation behind people's actions, whatever it appears to be, is inevitably self-interest. Frank et al.'s (1993) participants did not emerge from Economics 101 believing that it actually is in one's self-interest to report a favorable billing error because, for example, it preempts guilt or fosters a reputation for honesty. Rather, they emerged apparently believing that not reporting a favorable billing error, in addition to being self-interested, is also the rational and appropriate action to take, however guilty one feels doing so.

Indirect instruction. One need not take a course in microeconomics to learn about the descriptive and prescriptive power of self-interest, of course. The putative power of self-interest can be communicated much more subtly. For example, myriad daily appeals to the self-interest motive reinforce the belief that this motive should be powerful. More than merely pointing out the instrumental value of a particular activity (e.g., "ethics pay"), these appeals communicate an important message about the virtue of instrumental value: It is good to pursue what pays. Thus, appeals to self-interest, although explicitly pointing to the means by which the goal of self-interest can be achieved, implicitly point to the wisdom and appropriateness of pursuing self-interest (Frey, 1997; Kohn, 1990).

This last point suggests a novel perspective on the finding that people's sensitivity to their self-interest increases after it has been made salient to them (Green & Cowden, 1992; Sears & Lau, 1983). Pointing out to people where their material self-interest lies may make it salient to them, but it also makes the norm of self-interest salient to them, and it may be due as much to the latter as to the former that this intervention leads them to act more in accordance with self-interest. As an illustration, consider then-candidate Ronald Reagan's famous refrain in the 1980 U.S. presidential campaign: "Ask yourself, are you better off today than you were four years ago?" This refrain reflected a message as well as a question. In addition to asking voters to reflect on the link between their self-interest and their electoral choice, it instructed them on what should motivate their choice of political candidate—self-interest. In effect, by telling voters that a vote for him would be good for their pocketbook, Reagan was telling them that it was normative to vote on the basis of their pocketbook. It is interesting to note that the correlation between self-interest (defined by personal financial situation) and candidate preference in the 1980 U.S. presidential election was only .08 (Sears & Funk, 1991). However, it rose to a more substantial .36 by 1984 (Lau, Sears, & Jessor, 1990), tempting one to speculate that the tenor of the self-interest-celebrating rhetoric of Reagan's first term contributed to the social construction of voting behavior (and perhaps to many other aspects of social life) as being something that self-interest does and should dominate. People, it would appear, can be taught to act "naturally."

Why Does Personal Experience Not Invalidate Self-Interest Indoctrination?

Self-interest rhetoric may be ubiquitous in contemporary society, but social science research suggests that this will not be the message of everyday social experience. For example, research suggests that everyday experience should reveal self-interest to be related only weakly, if at all, to people's attitudes toward social policies (Sears & Funk, 1990, 1991) and to their satisfaction with the outcomes provided by social institutions (Tyler, 1990). However, this assumes that social actors are as comfortable revealing divergences between their self-interest and their attitudes as they are revealing convergences, which as we shall see, is not the case. The fact is that people's everyday actions and words exaggerate the actual power self-interest has over them, thereby providing the layperson with spurious "evidence" of the power of self-interest. In this way, everyday experience not only fails to contradict societal rhetoric but actually reinforces it.

The Norm of Self-Interest and Behavior

Social norms can be defined as shared perceptions of appropriate behavior that possess the power to induce people to act publicly in ways that deviate from their private inclinations (Miller & Prentice, 1996). The norm of self-interest is a case in point: It induces people to act publicly in ways that maximize their material interests, whether or not they are so inclined privately. This norm, like most other norms, reflects both a descriptive belief (people are self-interested) and a prescriptive belief (people ought to be self-interested). Either of these beliefs is sufficient to induce the layperson to act more in line with self-interest than he or she might personally be inclined to do.

The power of the norm of self-interest does not end with its influence on people's behavior. By influencing behavior and rhetoric it also influences lay theories as well as more formal theories of human behavior. The reason for this is simply that the layperson (along with the professional observer) frequently interprets evidence of the strength of the norm of self-interest to be evidence of the strength of the motive of self-interest. The consequence of this misinterpretation is a strengthening of the norm itself. How precisely the norm of self-interest contributes to a false impression of the inevitability and naturalness of the self-interest motive is the topic to which we now turn.

Descriptive Power

The expectation that others will act in a particular way frequently leads people to act similarly (see Darley & Fazio, 1980; Miller & Turnbull, 1986; Snyder & Stukas, 1998). There are at least two reasons why the expectation of self-interested behavior from others could lead people to act (contrary to their private preferences) in a self-interested manner themselves and thereby unwittingly provide further evidence of the power of self-interest. One reason people pursue self-interest when they anticipate self-interested behavior from others is the fear that to do otherwise would lead to their exploitation. This dynamic is nicely captured in experimental games where the more individuals expect those with whom they are interacting to pursue a self-interested strategy the more inclined they are to pursue a self-interested strategy themselves (Bouas & Komorita, 1996; Kelley & Stahelski, 1970; Messé & Sivacek, 1979). The experience of experimental games or any similarly structured social relationship thus reinforces people's belief that individuals are "out for themselves" and leaves them even more convinced that pursuing a competitive orientation is the rational and appropriate thing to do (Kelley & Stahelski, 1970; Miller & Holmes, 1975).

A second reason people pursue self-interest when they anticipate self-interested behavior from others is the fear that to do otherwise would be a waste of time and effort. This assumption is common in situations where actors must decide whether to undertake action on behalf of a cause they support but in which they, like most potential actors, have no personal stake. Individuals in this circumstance tend to assume that their supportive position is not shared by others and hence that any action of theirs is likely to be solitary and ineffectual (Miller & Ratner, 1998). As Coontz (1992) described this dynamic, "The major barrier to social involvement is not people's commitment to a purely individualistic way of life but their feeling of helplessness, the fear that they are the only people who feel this way" (p. 284).

Prescriptive Power

The descriptive component of the norm of self-interest primarily affects behavior by influencing an actor's calculation of the material consequences of deviating from a self-interested course of action. In contrast, the prescriptive component of the norm of self-interest primarily affects behavior by influencing the actor's calculation of the social consequences of deviating from a self-interested course of action. The fear that deviating from one's material self-interest will provoke dismay, suspicion, or derogation can be as powerful a deterrent as the fear that it will prove futile or render one vulnerable to economic exploitation.

For an example of how the prescriptive component of a self-interest norm can affect behavior, consider once again the experimental game context. A reliable finding in this context is that decisions made by groups tend to be more self-interested than those reached by individuals (Schopler & Insko, 1992). The traditional explanation for this finding points to the feelings of anonymity and diffusion of responsibility experienced by individuals in groups. Ratner (1999), however, has speculated that enhanced self-interest in groups may actually reflect the prescriptive component of the self-interest norm, reasoning that even if people themselves are comfortable pursuing a non-self-interested course in such a situation, their belief that their teammates are not leads them to embrace a competitive team strategy. Supporting her speculation. Ratner (1999) found participants in an experimental game believed that their teammates were less comfortable with a cooperative strategy than they themselves were, and this belief led the individuals to play more competitively when their outcomes and those of their teammates were interdependent.

People's wish to avoid the disapprobation of peers and observers is not the only reason they conform to the norm of self-interest. Even when deviation would neither affect nor be known by anyone else, actors might still override their private preferences and conform to the dictates of narrowly defined self-interest simply because they have internalized the belief that it is appropriate and rational to do so (Tyler, Huo, & Lind, 1999). Thus, although research consistently demonstrates that even positive material outcomes (e.g., high grades) can leave people upset if they are produced by procedures that people consider unfair, most people are reluctant to express their dissatisfaction in these circumstances, because they have internalized the belief that one ought not to be upset when the bottom line favors the self (Greenberg, 1987). Of course, by concealing from public view their dissatisfaction with unfairly produced positive outcomes, people only provide further evidence of the (social) fact that people are self-interested.

The Norm of Self-Interest and Accounts for Behavior

The norm of self-interest influences more than the actions people take and the attitudes they express. It also influences the accounts people provide for their actions and opinions (Mills, 1963). The easiest way to avoid the negative reactions behavioral and attitudinal deviations from material self-interest provoke is simply to refrain from taking such actions or expressing such attitudes. However, it is also possible to normalize seemingly deviant actions or opinions by providing accounts for them that emphasize their basis in self-interest (Miller & Ratner, 1996). The prominence of self-interest-speak in behavioral accounts can be seen in the different reasons people provide for their voting preferences at different temporal points. Sears and his colleagues have found that the relation between self-interest and voting behavior is much higher in exit polls than in either preelection or postelection surveys (Sears & Lau, 1983). Whether people distort their votes in the direction of their self-interest or vice versa, it appears clear that people who have recently cast a vote are motivated to tell a story that closely links their vote with their self-interest (see also Stein, 1990).

People also provide self-interested accounts when asked to explain their attitudes. An interesting example of this is provided by a study in which researchers examined the impact vested interest had on Whites' attitudes toward school busing as a means of achieving racial integration (Green & Cowden, 1992; Sears & Funk, 1990). When asked to explain their position, most opponents of busing focused on narrowly defined self-interest arguments: concern for their children's safety, diminished property values, inconvenience

to kids, and so forth (Sears & Funk, 1990). However, the data also indicated that whether or not respondents were parents or property owners had virtually no affect on the likelihood of their expressing an antibusing position. It would appear, then, that although people were comfortable acknowledging to an interviewer that they were opposed to busing, they were not comfortable offering an account for that opposition that did not focus on material self-interest.

People's motivation to make their actions appear self-interested is not limited to the political sphere. They seem motivated to cast even highly pro-social acts in terms of self-interest (Lerner, 1982). For example, on the basis of extensive interviews and surveys, Wuthnow (1991) claimed that although people actually engage in many acts of genuine compassion, they are loathe to acknowledge that these acts may have been motivated by genuine compassion or kindness. Instead, people offer pragmatic or instrumental reasons for them, saying things such as "It gave me something to do" or "It got me out of the house." Indeed, the people Wuthnow interviewed seemed to go out of their way to stress that they were not a "bleeding heart," "goody two-shoes," or "do-gooder."

On the basis of Wuthnow's findings, it would appear that accounts for actions that emphasize self-interest, rather than diminishing the actions, actually may normalize or license them. Self-interest provides a sufficient account for what might otherwise seem inexplicable, Interestingly, the claim that people—at least Americans—often conceal their more noble sentiments under the guise of self-interest is not new. Over 150 years ago, the French social philosopher Alexis de Tocqueville observed that "Americans . . . enjoy explaining almost every act of their lives on the principle of self-interest . . . I think that in this they often do themselves less than justice, for sometimes in the United States, as elsewhere, one sees people carried away by the . . . spontaneous impulses natural to man. But the Americans are hardly prepared to admit that they do give way to emotions of this sort" (1835/1969, p. 546).

Why Does Self-Interest Predict Behavior Better Than Attitudes?

Self-interest, as we have seen, does not fare well at predicting people's attitudes toward social policies. It fares much better, however, at predicting social action. Consider a study by Regan and Fazio (1977). This study found no relation between undergraduates' attitudes regarding the circumstances of a campus housing shortage at their university and whether the students were personally inconvenienced by the shortage: All students expressed considerable hostility. This study did find, however, a strong relationship between vested interest and behavior: Undergraduates' willingness to take direct steps to alleviate the problem was highly dependent on whether they were personally inconvenienced by the current policy. A second study that demonstrates the greater impact of self-interest on behavior than on attitudes was reported by Sivacek and Crano (1982). This study found that college students who were affected most by a proposal to increase the legal drinking age in their state (those who would be prohibited from drinking for two or more years) were no more opposed to the proposal than were students who were affected least by it (those who were close to or already at the proposed new drinking age). The former were more willing to make phone calls to oppose the increase, however. A third relevant study (Green & Cowden, 1992), previously described, found that Whites who owned property or who had school-age children were no more opposed to a school busing policy than were Whites who had no material stake in the policy. The former, however, were much more likely to join antibusing organizations.

How are we to interpret the significantly stronger relation between material self-interest and social action than between material self-interest and social attitudes? One possibility focuses on the different thresholds that must be reached to express an attitude versus to take an action. Although one might not require a vested interest in a cause to express an attitude supporting it, one might require a level of motivation only having a stake in the issue can provide to convert a supportive attitude into a supportive action. As Green and Cowden (1992) have argued, the prospect of behavioral involvement (unlike the request for an opinion) forces people to consider cost and hence prompts self-interest reflection. In their words, the potential political actor must first ask him- or herself "Is it worth it?"

That survey research underestimates the "political wallop" of self-interest is certainly one reason why there might be a stronger link between self-interest and behavior than between self-interest and attitudes, but there is another possibility suggested by the self-interest-as-norm analysis. Namely, to the extent that acting without a vested interest is perceived by actors and observers to be norm violating, individuals who support a cause in which they have no stake will be hesitant to take action on behalf of that cause, not because they lack an incentive but because they lack a justification. By this account, the question the political actor needs to answer is not "Is it worth it?" but "Is it appropriate?"

Self-Interest as Standing

The existence of a norm of self-interest means that people who lack a stake in a cause will feel uncomfortable taking action on its behalf. However willing they might be to invest time and money on a cause's behalf, people will be inhibited from doing so if they feel it is not their place to act. The judicial concept of legal standing provides an instructive metaphor for this process. According to the United States Supreme Court (*Sierra Club v. Morton,* 1972), not everyone is entitled to bring forward a case for legal review. To qualify as having legal standing for judicial review, a person must show that he or she has suffered or will suffer some injury, economic or otherwise. So, for example, moral outrage at the injurious behavior of another without demonstrable personal injury would not be sufficient grounds for bringing legal action. Because of this definition of legal standing, it will always be possible to point to the basis in self-interest of any judicial action. Obviously, however, this fact would not be grounds for concluding that the human impulse to right wrongs is invariably confined to wrongs that affect the actor personally. The strength of the relationship between self-interest and legal action says much about the normative position of the court but possibly little about the motivating power of self-interest. A similar claim could be made about the strength of the relationship between self-interest and social action: It says much about the normative position of the court of public opinion but possibly little about the motivating power of self-interest. The court of public opinion declares that a person must have psychological standing (vested interest) to undertake action on behalf of a cause or person. A supportive attitude without a vested interest is insufficient to provoke action. Thus, self-interest, whether in the legal or social domain, may play as big a role in legitimating and justifying behavior as it does in motivating it.

Providing the Nonvested With Standing

To the extent that it is their perceived lack of psychological standing that inhibits nonvested individuals from acting on behalf of causes they support, framing the call to action so as to provide these individuals with standing (although not with vested interest) should increase their willingness to act. Individuals on whom standing has been conferred, even if they do not have vested interest, should feel free to act. A recent study by Ratner and Miller (1999) supports this reasoning. Specifically, Ratner and Miller found that nonvested actors who supported a particular cause were much more likely to take action on its behalf when the organization supporting the cause possessed a name that legitimated the involvement of nonvested as well as vested actors. Indeed, when provided with standing by means of the organization's inclusive title, nonvested actors (who were as supportive of the cause as vested actors) participated at a rate comparable to the vested actors. In summary, at least one reason why nonvested individuals are inhibited from converting their supportive attitudes into supportive actions is that they feel it is "not their place" to act.

Do Incentives Increase Charitable Donations by Increasing Motivation or Justification?

If people attribute their pro-social acts to self-interest so as not to appear motivated by compassion, it stands to reason that they would also welcome those opportunities that provided them with self-interested accounts for acting compassionately. This logic may, knowingly or unknowingly, underlie the practice of offering potential charity donors some product (e.g., light bulbs, return address labels, magazine subscriptions) in exchange for their donations. The commonness of this practice suggests the net profit elicited by product-for-donation exchanges exceeds that elicited by strict charity appeals alone. If so, one explanation for

the success of the strategy might be that the offer of an exchange creates a fiction that permits people to act on their impulse to help without committing themselves to unwanted psychological burdens, such as a public or private image as a "do-gooder" or an enduring, open-ended relationship with the victim group (Lerner, 1980; Lerner, Miller, & Holmes, 1976; Miller, 1977). In effect, the exchange fiction provides a psychological cover for individuals who wish to express their compassion and concerns with justice without having to reveal, or even recognize, their motives.

In a test of the exchange fiction hypothesis, J.G. Holmes, Miller, and Lerner (1999) had a group of experimenters approach students on a university campus with one of a variety of charity appeals. The design was complicated, so only the most relevant conditions are discussed here. The key manipulations were the seriousness of the victims' need (high vs. low) and the presence or absence of an exchange (a candle). The pattern of donation rates supported the prediction. When the victims' need was high (and so presumably was the sympathy they elicited), the offer of an exchange increased people's donation rate threefold; when the victims' need was low (and so presumably was the sympathy they elicited), the offer of an exchange had no significant effect.

The J.G. Holmes et al. (1999) study reveals the need for caution when interpreting the link between material incentives and charitable donations. Interpreting this link to suggest that people are disinclined to give if they are not compensated for doing so may be an accurate empirical description (people do give more when they are offered an incentive), but it is not necessarily an accurate psychological interpretation. Incentives, as we have seen, serve not so much to motivate charitable giving as to disinhibit such giving by providing a justification for it. The justificatory role of incentives comes into play when people care about a cause and want to help but are inhibited from doing so, as it appears was the case for the individuals in the high-need condition of the J.G. Holmes et al. study.

In summary, incentives may be a necessary and sufficient factor in charity campaigns, but their role may be more legitimating than motivating. When people receive a quid pro quo (e.g., a tax deduction) for their assistance, they do not have to feel like a do-gooder. They can construe their action as something to feel good about but not as something that is inconsistent with collective representations of what constitutes acceptable forms of motivation. From the perspective of the present analysis, it is the mere existence of an incentive (e.g., a tax deduction), not its size, that is critical in eliciting greater donation rates. To the extent that an incentive provides the excuse for giving, all that is important is that one be offered.

Conclusion

To inquire about the role played by self-interest in human affairs is to inquire about the essence of human nature, which is why this question has sustained debate among social and political theorists for centuries (see Hirschman, 1977; S. Holmes, 1990; Sen, 1977; Smith, 1776/1963). With the rising prominence of rational choice models of behavior in recent decades, the intensity of the self-interest debate has only increased (e.g., Downs, 1957; Mueller, 1979; Olson, 1965). The sweeping claims of these models have provoked a torrent of conceptual and empirical critiques (see Elster, 1986; Mansbridge, 1990a). Rational choice theorists have stood their ground, however, typically either dismissing the cases presented as isolated instances and therefore mere exceptions to the general rule or reinterpreting them so as to render them consistent with the rational (self-interested) position (see Green & Shapiro, 1994).

The significance of the evidence adduced by critics of rational choice theory is an interesting and important question, but it is not the question addressed here. This article addresses the significance of the evidence adduced by the proponents of rational choice theory. The question, in effect, is What are we to make of evidence suggesting that material self-interest is a powerful force in people's lives? The thesis of the article is that this evidence is inherently ambiguous because the ideology of self-interest, widely celebrated in individualistic cultures, functions as a powerful self-fulfilling force. The assumption of self-interest contributes to its own confirmation in at least two ways. First, individualistic cultures structure their social institutions to reflect their belief that people are naturally disposed to pursue their self-interest, which results in these institutions fostering the very behavior their structure pre-supposes occurs

naturally (Lerner, 1982; Schwartz, 1997). Second, as argued here, individualistic cultures spawn social norms that induce people to follow their material self-interest rather than their principles or passions, whether the latter be noble or ignoble. Stated more boldly, people act and sound as though they are strongly motivated by their material self-interest because scientific theories and collective representations derived from those theories convince them that it is natural and normal to do so. As Kagan (1989) observed, "People treat self-interest as a natural law and because they believe they should not violate a natural law, they try to obey it" (p. 283).

Evidence that material self-interest is powerful, therefore, may speak more to the power of social norms than to the power of innate proclivities. Interpreting the presence of self-interested behavior to suggest that self-interest is inevitable and universal rather than historically and culturally contingent only serves to strengthen the layperson's belief that pursuing self-interest is normatively appropriate, rational, and enlightened. The result of this is a positive feedback loop: The more powerful the norm of self-interest, the more evidence there is for the theory of self-interest, which, in turn, increases the power of the self-interest norm (Schwartz, 1997). None of this is to say that self-interest, even narrowly defined, is an insubstantial force in human affairs. But, however strong the disposition to pursue material self-interest may be, it is likely not as strong as the prevalence of self-interested behavior in everyday life suggests. Homo economicus, it should not be forgotten, inhabits a social world.

ACKNOWLEDGMENTS

Kenneth J. Gergen served as action editor for this article.

The preparation of this article was supported by National Institute of Mental Health Grant M1144069. The article benefited greatly from extensive discussions and research collaborations with Melvin Lerner and Rebecca Ratner.

REFERENCES

Batson, C. D. (1991). *The altruism question: Toward a social psychological answer.* Hillsdale, NJ: Erlhaum.

Berger, P. L., & Luckmann, T. (1966). *The social construction of reality.* New York: Doubleday.

Bonas, K. S., & Komorita, S. S. (1996). Group discussion and cooperation in social dilemmas. *Personality and Social Psychology Bulletin, 22,* 1144–1150.

Coontz, S. (1992). *The way we never were.* New York: Basic Books.

Darley, J. M., & Fazio, R. H. (1980). Expectancy confirmation processes arising in the social interaction sequence. *American Psychologist, 35,* 867–881.

Downs, A. (1957). *An economic theory of democracy.* New York: Harper & Row.

Elster, J. (Ed.), (1986). *Rational choice.* New York: New York University Press.

Etzioni, A. (1988). *The moral dimension: Toward a new economics.* New York: Free Press.

Fiske, A. P., Kitayama, S., Markus, H. R., & Nisbett, R. E. (1998). The cultural matrix of social psychology. In D. T. Gilbert, S. T. Fiske, & G. Lindzey (Eds.), *Handbook of social psychology* (4th ed., Vol. 2, pp. 915–981). New York: Oxford University Press.

Frank, R.H. (1988). *Passions within reason: The strategic role of the emotions.* New York: Norton.

Frank, R. H., Gilovich, T., & Regan, D. T. (1993). Does studying economics inhibit cooperation? *Journal of Economic Perspectives, 7,* 159–171.

Frey, B. S. (1997). *Not just for the money: An economic theory of personal motivation.* Brookfield, VT: Elgar.

Gergen, K. J.(1973). Social psychology as history. *Journal of Personality and Social Psychology, 26,* 309–320.

Gergen, K .J. (1982). *Toward transformation in social knowledge.* New York: Springer-Verlag.

Green, D. P., & Cowden, J. A. (1992). Who protests: Self-interest and White opposition to busing. *Journal of Politics, 54,* 471–496.

Green, D. P., & Shapiro, I. (1994). *Pathologies of rational choice theory.* New Haven, CT: Yale University Press.

Greenberg, J. (1987). Reactions to procedural injustice in payment distributions: Do the means justify the ends? *Journal of Applied Psychology, 72,* 55–61.

Hirschman, A. O. (1977). *The passions and interests: Political arguments for capitalism before its triumphs.* Princeton, NJ: Princeton University Press.

Hobbes, T. (1950). *Leviathan.* New York: Dulton. (Original work published 1651)

Holmes, J. G., Miller, D. T., & Lerner, M. J. (1999). *Symbolic threat in helping situations: The "exchange fiction."* Unpublished manuscript. University of Waterloo. Waterloo, Ontario, Canada.

Holmes, S. (1990). The secret history of self-interest. In J. J. Mansbridge (Ed.), *Beyond self-interest* (pp. 267–286). Chicago: University of Chicago Press.

Kagan, J. (1989). *Unstable ideas: Temperament, cognition, and self-* Cambridge, MA: Harvard University Press.

Kelley, H. H., & Stahelski, A. J. (1970). Social interaction basis of cooperators' and competitors' beliefs about others. *Journal of Personality and Social Psychology, 16,* 190–197.

Kohn, A. (1990). *The brighter side of human nature.* New York: Basic Books.

Lau, R. R., Sears, D. O., & Jessor, T. (1990). Fact or artifact revisited: Survey instrument effects and pocketbook politics. *Political Behavior, 12,* 217–242.

Lerner, M. J. (1980). *The belief in a just world,* New York: Plenum.

Lerner, M. J. (1982). The justice motive in human relations and the economic model of man: A radical analysis of facts and fictions. In V. J. Derelega & J. Gizelak (Eds.), *Cooperation and helping behavior: Theories and research* (pp.

249–278). New York: Academic Press.

Lerner, M. J., Miller, D. T., & Holmes, J. G. (1976). Deserving and the emergence of forms of justice. In L. Berkowitz & E. Walster (Eds.), *Advances in experimental social psychology* (Vol. 9, pp. 133–162). New York: Academic Press.

Mansbridge, J. J. (Ed.), (1990a). *Beyond self-interest.* Chicago: University of Chicago Press.

Mansbridge, J. J. (1990b). The rise and fall of self-interest in the explanation of political life. In J. J. Mansbridge (Ed.), *Beyond self-interest* (pp. 3–24). Chicago: University of Chicago Press.

Mansbridge, J. J. (1994). Public spirit in political systems. In H. J. Aron, T. E. Mann, & T. Taylor (Eds.), *Values and public policy* (pp. 146–172). Washington, DC: Brookings Institution.

Messé, L. A., & Sivacek, J. M. (1979). Predictions of others' responses in a mixed-motive game: Self-justification or false consensus? *Journal of Personality and Social Psychology, 37,* 602–607.

Miller, D. T. (1977). Personal deserving verus justice for others: An exploration of the justice motive. *Journal of Experimental Social Psychology, 13,* 1–13.

Miller, D. T., & Holmes, J. G. (1975). The role of situational restrictiveness on self-fulfilling prophecies: A theoretical and empirical extension of Kelley and Stahelski's triangle hypothesis. *Journal of Personality and Social Psychology, 31,* 661–673.

Miller, D. T., & Prentice, D. A. (1996). The construction of social norms and standards. In E. T. Higgins & A. W. Kruglanski (Eds.), *Social psychology: Handbook of basic principles* (pp. 799–829). New York: Guilford Press.

Miller, D. T., & Ratner, R. K. (1996). The power of the myth of self-interest. In L. Montada & M. J. Lerner (Eds.), *Current societal issues about justice* (pp. 25–48). New York: Plenum.

Miller, D. T., & Ratner, R. K. (1998). The disparity between the actual and assumed power of self-interest. *Journal of Personality and Social Psychology, 74,* 53–62.

Miller, D. T., & Turnbull, W. (1986). Expectancies and interpersonal processes. In M. R. Rosenzweig & L. W. Porter (Eds.), *Annual review of psychology* (Vol. 37, pp. 233–256). Palo Alto, CA: Annual Reviews.

Mills, C. W. (1963). Situation actions and vocabularies of motive. In I. L. Horowitz (Ed.), *Power, politics, and people: The collected essays of C. Wright Mills* (pp. 439–449). New York: Oxford University Press.

Mueller, D. C. (1979). *Public choice.* Cambridge, England: Cambridge University Press.

Olson, M. (1965). *The logic of collective action.* Cambridge, MA: Harvard University Press.

Ratner, R. K. (1999). *Overestimating others' concern with self-interest: Consequences for group decision making.* Unpublished doctoral dissertation, Princeton University, Princeton, New Jersey.

Ratner, R. K., & Miller, D. T. (1999). *The norm of self-interest and its effects an social action.* Unpublished manuscript, Princeton University. Princeton, New Jersey.

Regan, D. T., & Fazio, R. (1977). On the consistency between attitudes and behavior; Look to the method of attitude formation. *Journal of Experimental Social Psychology, 13,* 28–45.

Sampson, E. E. (1983). *Justice and the critique of pure psychology.* New York: Plenum.

Schopler, J., & Insko, C. A. (1992). The discontinuity effect in interpersonal and intergroup relations: Generality and mediation. In W. Stroebe & M. Hewstone (Eds.), *European review of social psychology* (Vol. 3, pp. 121–151). Chichester, England: Wiley.

Schwartz, B. (1986). *The battle for human nature.* New York: Norton.

Schwartz, B. (1997). Psychology, idea technology, and ideology. *Psychological Science, 8, 21–27.*

Sears, D. O., & Funk, C. L. (1990). Self-interest in Americans' political opinions. In J. J. Mansbridge (Ed.), *Beyond self-interest* (pp. 147–170). Chicago: University of Chicago Press.

Sears, D. O., & Funk, C. L. (1991). The role of self-interest in social and political attitudes. In M. P. Zanna (Ed.), *Advances in experimental social psychology* (Vol. 24, pp. 2–91). New York: Academic Press.

Sears, D. O., & Lau, R. R. (1983). Indicating apparently self-interested political preferences. *American Journal of Political Science, 27,* 223–252.

Sen, A. K. (1997). Rational fools: A critique of the behavioral foundations of economic theory. *Philosophy and Public Affairs, 6,* 317–344.

Shweder, R. A. (1991). *Thinking through cultures: Expeditions in cultural psychology.* Cambridge, MA: Harvard University Press.

Sierra Club v. Morton, 405 U.S. 727 (1972).

Sivacek, J., & Crano, W. D. (1982). Vested interest as a moderator of attitude–behavior consistency. *Journal of Personality and Social Psychology, 43,* 210–221.

Smith, A. (1963). *An inquiry into the nature and couses of the wealth of nations.* Homewood, IL: Irwin. (Original work published 1776)

Snyder, M., & Stukas, A. A. (1998). Interpersonal processes: The interplay of cognitive, motivational, and behavioral activities in social interaction. *Annual Review of Psychology, 50,* 273–303.

Stein, R. M. (1990). Economic voting for governor and U.S. senator: The electoral consequences of federalism. *Journal of Politics, 52,* 29–53.

Tocqueville, A. de (1969). *Democracy in America* (J. P. Mayer, Ed., & G. Lawrence, Trans.), Garden City, NY: Anchor Press. (Original work published 1835)

Tyler, T. R. (1990). Justice, self-interest, and the legitimacy of legal and political authority. In J. J. Mansbridge (Ed.), *Beyond self-interest* (pp. 171–179). Chicago: University of Chicago Press.

Tyler, T. R., Boeckmann, R. J., Smith, H. J., & Huo, Y. J. (1997). *Social justice in a diverse society.* Boulder, CO: Westview Press.

Tyler, T. R., Huo, Y. J., & Lind, A. E. (1999). Two psychologies of conflict resolution: Differing antecedents of pre-experience choices and post-experience evaluations. *Group Processes and Intergroup Relations, 2,* 99–118.

Wallach, M. A., & Wallach, L. (1983). *Psychology's sanction for selfishness: The error of egoism in theory and therapy.* San Francisco: Freeman.

Wuthnow, R. (1991). *Acts of compassion.* Princeton, NJ: Princeton University Press.

Appendix: How to Read a Journal Article in Social Psychology

Christian H. Jordan and Mark P. Zanna • University of Waterloo

When approaching a journal article for the first time, and often on subsequent occasions, most people try to digest it as they would any piece of prose. They start at the beginning and read word for word, until eventually they arrive at the end, perhaps a little bewildered, but with a vague sense of relief. This is not an altogether terrible strategy; journal articles do have a logical structure that lends itself to this sort of reading. There are, however, more efficient approaches–approaches that enable you, a student of social psychology, to cut through peripheral details, avoid sophisticated statistics with which you may not be familiar, and focus on the central ideas in an article. Arming yourself with a little foreknowledge of what is contained in journal articles, as well as some practical advice on how to read them, should help you read journal articles more effectively. If this sounds tempting, read on.

Journal articles offer a window into the inner workings of social psychology. They document how social psychologists formulate hypotheses, design empirical studies, analyze the observations they collect, and interpret their results. Journal articles also serve an invaluable archival function: They contain the full store of common and cumulative knowledge of social psychology. Having documentation of past research allows researchers to build on past findings and advance our understanding of social behavior, without pursuing avenues of investigation that have already been explored. Perhaps most importantly, a research study is never complete until its results have been shared with others, colleagues and students alike. Journal articles are a primary means of communicating research findings. As such, they can be genuinely exciting and interesting to read.

That last claim may have caught you off guard. For beginning readers, journal articles may seem anything but interesting and exciting. They may, on the contrary, appear daunting and esoteric, laden with jargon and obscured by menacing statistics. Recognizing this fact, we hope to arm you, through this paper, with the basic information you will need to read journal articles with a greater sense of comfort and perspective.

Social psychologists study many fascinating topics, ranging from prejudice and discrimination, to culture, persuasion, liking and love, conformity and obedience, aggression, and the self. In our daily lives, these are issues we often struggle to understand. Social psychologists present systematic observations of, as well as a wealth of ideas about, such issues in journal articles. It would be a shame if the fascination and intrigue these topics have were lost in their translation into journal publications. We don't think they are, and by the end of this paper, hopefully you won't either.

Journal articles come in a variety of forms, including research reports, review articles, and theoretical articles. Put briefly, a *research report* is a formal presentation of an original research study, or series of studies. A *review article* is an evaluative survey of previously published work, usually organized by a guiding theory or point of view. The author of a review article summarizes previous investigations of a circumscribed problem, comments on what progress has been made toward its resolution, and suggests areas of the problem that require further study. A *theoretical article* also evaluates past research, but focuses on the development of theories used to explain empirical findings. Here, the author may present a new theory to explain a set of findings, or may compare and contrast a set of competing theories, suggesting why one theory might be the superior one.

This paper focuses primarily on how to read research reports, for several reasons. First, the bulk of published literature in social psychology consists of research reports. Second, the summaries presented in review articles, and the ideas set forth in theoretical articles, are built on findings presented in research reports. To get a deep understanding of how research is done in social psychology, fluency in reading original research reports is essential. Moreover, theoretical articles frequently report new studies that pit one theory against another, or test a novel prediction derived from a new theory. In order to appraise the validity of such theoretical contentions, a grounded understanding of basic findings is invaluable. Finally, most research reports are written in a standard format that is likely unfamiliar to new readers. The format of review and theoretical articles is less standardized, and more like that of textbooks and other scholarly writings, with which most readers are familiar. This is not to suggest that such articles are easier to read and comprehend than research reports; they can be quite challenging indeed. It is simply the case that, because more rules apply to the writing of research reports, more guidelines can be offered on how to read them.

The Anatomy of Research Reports

Most research reports in social psychology, and in psychology in general, are written in a standard format prescribed by the American Psychological Association (1994). This is a great boon to both readers and writers. It allows writers to present their ideas and findings in a clear, systematic manner. Consequently, as a reader, once you understand this format, you will not be on completely foreign ground when you approach a new research report— regardless of its specific content. You will know where in the paper particular information is found, making it easier to locate. No matter what your reasons for reading a research report, a firm understanding of the format in which they are written will ease your task. We discuss the format of research reports next, with some practical suggestions on how to read them. Later, we discuss how this format reflects the process of scientific investigation, illustrating how research reports have a coherent narrative structure.

TITLE AND ABSTRACT

Though you can't judge a book by its cover, you can learn a lot about a research report simply by reading its title. The title presents a concise statement of the theoretical issues investigated, and/or the variables that were studied. For example, the following title was taken almost at random from a prestigious journal in social psychology: "Sad and guilty? Affective influences on the explanation of conflict in close relationships" (Forgas, 1994, p. 56). Just by reading the title, it can be inferred that the study investigated how emotional states change the way people explain conflict in close relationships. It also suggests that when feeling sad, people accept more personal blame for such conflicts (i.e., feel more guilty).

The abstract is also an invaluable source of information. It is a brief synopsis of the study, and packs a lot of information into 150 words or less. The abstract contains information about the problem that was investigated, how it was investigated, the major findings of the study, and hints at the theoretical and practical implications of the findings. Thus, the abstract is a useful summary of the research that provides the gist of the investigation. Reading this outline first can be very helpful, because it tells you where the report is going, and gives you a useful framework for organizing information contained in the article.

The title and abstract of a research report are like a movie preview. A movie preview highlights the important aspects of a movie's plot, and provides just enough information for one to decide whether to watch the whole movie. Just so with titles and abstracts; they highlight the key features of a research report to allow you to decide if you want to read the whole paper. And just as with movie previews, they do not give the whole story. Reading just the title and abstract is never enough to fully understand a research report.

INTRODUCTION

A research report has four main sections: introduction, method, results, and discussion. Though it is not explicitly labeled, the introduction begins the main body of a research report. Here, the researchers set the stage for the study. They present the problem under investigation, and state why it was important to study. By providing a brief review of past research and theory relevant to the central issue of investigation, the researchers place the study in an historical context and suggest how the study advances knowledge of the problem. Beginning with broad theoretical and practical considerations, the researchers delineate the rationale that led them to the specific set of hypotheses tested in the study. They also describe how they decided on their research strategy (e.g., why they chose an experiment or a correlational study).

The introduction generally begins with a broad consideration of the problem investigated. Here, the researchers want to illustrate that the problem they studied is a real problem about which people should care. If the researchers are studying prejudice, they may cite statistics that suggest discrimination is prevalent, or describe specific cases of discrimination. Such information helps illustrate why the research is both practically and theoretically meaningful, and why you should bother reading about it. Such discussions are often quite interesting and useful. They can help you decide for yourself if the research has merit. But they may not be essential for understanding the study at hand. Read the introduction carefully, but choose judiciously what to focus on and remember. To understand a study, what you really need to understand is what the researchers' hypotheses were, and how they were derived from theory, informal observation, or intuition. Other background information may be intriguing, but may not be critical to understand what the researchers did and why they did it.

While reading the introduction, try answering these questions: What problem was studied, and why? How does this study relate to, and go beyond, past investigations of the problem? How did the researchers derive their hypotheses? What questions do the researchers hope to answer with this study?

METHOD

In the method section, the researchers translate their hypotheses into a set of specific, testable questions. Here, the researchers introduce the main characters of the study—the subjects or participants—describing their characteristics (gender, age, etc.) and how many of them were involved. Then, they describe the materials (or apparatus), such as any questionnaires or special equipment, used in the study. Finally, they describe chronologically the procedures of the study; that is, how the study was conducted. Often, an overview of the research design will begin the method section. This overview provides a broad outline of the design, alerting you to what you should attend.

The method is presented in great detail so that other researchers can recreate the study to confirm (or question) its results. This degree of detail is normally not necessary to understand a study, so don't get bogged down trying to memorize the particulars of the procedures. Focus on how the independent variables were manipulated (or measured) and how the dependent variables were measured.

Measuring variables adequately is not always an easy matter. Many of the variables psychologists are interested in cannot be directly observed, so they must be inferred from participants' behavior. Happiness, for example, cannot be directly observed. Thus, researchers interested in how being happy influences people's judgments must infer happiness (or its absence) from their behavior—perhaps by asking people how happy they are, and judging their degree of happiness from their responses; perhaps by studying people's facial expressions for signs of happiness, such as smiling. Think about the measures researchers use while reading the method section. Do they adequately reflect or capture the concepts they are meant to measure? If a measure seems odd, consider carefully how the researchers justify its use.

Oftentimes in social psychology, getting there is half the fun. In other words, how a result is obtained can be just as interesting as the result itself. Social psychologists often strive to have participants behave in a natural, spontaneous manner, while controlling enough of their environment to pinpoint the causes of their behavior. Sometimes, the major contribution of a research report is its presentation of a novel method of investigation. When this is the case, the method will be discussed in some detail in the introduction.

Participants in social psychology studies are intelligent and inquisitive people who are responsive to what happens around them. Because of this, they are not always initially told the true purpose of a study. If they were told, they might not act naturally. Thus, researchers frequently need to be creative, presenting a credible rationale for complying with procedures, without revealing the study's purpose. This rationale is known as a *cover story,* and is often an elaborate scenario. While reading the method section, try putting yourself in the shoes of a participant in the study, and ask yourself if the instructions given to participants seem sensible, realistic, and engaging. Imagining what it was like to be in the study will also help you remember the study's procedure, and aid you in interpreting the study's results.

While reading the method section, try answering these questions: How were the hypotheses translated into testable questions? How were the variables of interest manipulated and/or measured? Did the measures used adequately reflect the variables of interest? For example, is self-reported income an adequate measure of social class? Why or why not?

RESULTS

The results section describes how the observations collected were analyzed to determine whether the original hypotheses were supported. Here, the data (observations of behavior) are described, and statistical tests are presented. Because of this, the results section is often intimidating to readers who have little or no training in statistics. Wading through complex and unfamiliar statistical analyses is understandably confusing and frustrating. As a result, many students are tempted to skip over reading this section. We advise you not to do so. Empirical findings are the foundation of any science and results sections are where such findings are presented.

Take heart. Even the most prestigious researchers were once in your shoes and sympathize with you. Though space in psychology journals is limited, researchers try to strike a balance between the need to be clear and the need to be brief in describing their results. In an influential paper on how to write good research reports, Bem (1987) offered this advice to researchers:

> No matter how technical or abstruse your article is in its particulars, intelligent nonpsychologists with no expertise in statistics or experimental design should be able to comprehend the broad outlines of what you did and why. They should understand in general terms what was learned. (p. 74)

Generally speaking, social psychologists try to practice this advice.

Most statistical analyses presented in research reports test specific hypotheses. Often, each analysis presented is preceded by a reminder of the hypothesis it is meant to test. After an analysis is presented, researchers usually provide a narrative description of the result in plain English. When the hypothesis tested by a statistical analysis is not explicitly stated, you can usually determine the hypothesis that was tested by reading this narrative description of the result, and referring back to the introduction to locate an hypothesis that corresponds to that result. After even the most complex statistical analysis, there will be a written description of what the result means conceptually. Turn your attention to these descriptions. Focus on the conceptual meaning of research findings, not on the mechanics of how they were obtained (unless you're comfortable with statistics).

Aside from statistical tests and narrative descriptions of results, results sections also frequently contain tables and graphs. These are efficient summaries of data. Even if you are not familiar with statistics, look closely at tables and graphs, and pay attention to the means or correlations presented in them. Researchers always include written descriptions of the pertinent aspects of tables and graphs. While reading these descriptions, check the tables and graphs to make sure what the researchers say accurately reflects their data. If they say there was a difference between two groups on a particular dependent measure, look at the means in the table that correspond to those two groups, and see if the means do differ as described. Occasionally, results seem to become stronger in their narrative description than an examination of the data would warrant.

Statistics *can* be misused. When they are, results are difficult to interpret. Having said this, a lack of statistical knowledge should not make you overly cautious while reading results sections. Though not a perfect antidote, journal articles undergo extensive review by professional researchers before publication. Thus, most misapplications of statistics are caught and corrected before an article is published. So, if you are unfamiliar with statistics, you can be reasonably confident that findings are accurately reported.

While reading the results section, try answering these questions: Did the researchers provide evidence that any independent variable manipulations were effective? For example, if testing for behavioral differences between happy and sad participants, did the researchers demonstrate that one group was in fact happier than the other? What were the major findings of the study? Were the researchers' original hypotheses supported by their observations? If not, look in the discussion section for how the researchers explain the findings that were obtained.

DISCUSSION

The discussion section frequently opens with a summary of what the study found, and an evaluation of whether the findings supported the original hypotheses. Here, the researchers evaluate the theoretical and practical implications of their results. This can be particularly interesting when the results did not work out exactly as the researchers anticipated. When such is the case, consider the researchers' explanations carefully, and see if they seem plausible to you. Often, researchers will also report any aspects of their study that limit their interpretation of its results, and suggest further research that could overcome these limitations to provide a better understanding of the problem under investigation.

Some readers find it useful to read the first few paragraphs of the discussion section before reading any other part of a research report. Like the abstract, these few paragraphs usually contain all of the main ideas of a research report: What the hypotheses were, the major findings and whether they supported the original hypotheses, and how the findings relate to past research and theory. Having this information before reading a research report can guide your reading, allowing you to focus on the specific details you need to complete your understanding of a study. The description of the results, for example, will alert you to the major variables that were studied. If they are unfamiliar to you, you can pay special attention to how they are defined in the introduction, and how they are operationalized in the method section.

After you have finished reading an article, it can also be helpful to reread the first few paragraphs of the discussion and the abstract. As noted, these two passages present highly distilled summaries of the major ideas in a research report. Just as they can help guide your reading of a report, they can also help you consolidate your understanding of a report once you have finished reading it. They provide a check on whether you have understood the main points of a report, and offer a succinct digest of the research in the authors' own words.

While reading the discussion section, try answering these questions: What conclusions can be drawn from the study? What new information does the study provide about the problem under investigation? Does the study help resolve the problem? What are the practical and theoretical implications of the study's findings? Did the results contradict past research findings? If so, how do the researchers explain this discrepancy?

Some Notes on Reports of Multiple Studies

Up to this point, we have implicitly assumed that a research report describes just one study. It is also quite common, however, for a research report to describe a series of studies of the same problem in a single article. When such is the case, each study reported will have the same basic structure (introduction, method, results, and discussion sections) that we have outlined, with the notable exception that sometimes the results and discussion section for each study are combined. Combined "results and discussion" sections contain the same information that separate results and discussion sections normally contain. Sometimes, the authors present all their results first, and only then discuss the implications of these results, just as they would in separate results and discussion sections. Other times, however, the authors alternate between describing results and discussing their implications, as each result is presented. In either case, you should be on the lookout for the same information, as outlined above in our consideration of separate results and discussion sections.

Reports including multiple studies also differ from single study reports in that they include more general introduction and discussion sections. The general introduction, which begins the main body of a research report, is similar in essence to the introduction of a single study report. In both cases, the researchers describe the problem investigated and its practical and theoretical significance. They also demonstrate how they derived their hypotheses, and explain how their research relates to past investigations of the problem. In contrast, the separate introductions to each individual study in reports of multiple studies are usually quite brief, and focus more specifically on the logic and rationale of each particular study presented. Such introductions generally describe the methods used in the particular study, outlining how they answer questions that have not been adequately addressed by past research, including studies reported earlier in the same article.

General discussion sections parallel discussions of single studies, except on a somewhat grander scale. They present all of the information contained in discussions of single studies, but consider the implications of all the studies presented together. A general discussion section brings the main ideas of a research program into bold relief. It typically begins with a concise summary of a research program's main findings, their relation to the original hypotheses, and their practical and theoretical implications. Thus, the summaries that begin general discussion sections are counterparts of the summaries that begin discussion sections of single study reports. Each presents a digest of the research presented in an article that can serve as both an organizing framework (when read first), and as a check on how well you have understood the main points of an article (when read last).

Research Reporting as Story Telling

A research report tells the story of how a researcher or group of researchers investigated a specific problem. Thus, a research report has a linear, narrative structure with a beginning, middle, and end. In his paper on writing research reports, Bem noted that a research report:

> . . . is shaped like an hourglass. It begins with broad general statements, progressively narrows down to the specifics of [the] study, and then broadens out again to more general considerations. (1987, p. 175)

This format roughly mirrors the process of scientific investigation, wherein researchers do the following: (1) start with a broad idea from which they formulate a narrower set of hypotheses, informed by past empirical findings (introduction); (2) design a specific set of concrete operations to test these hypotheses (method); (3) analyze the observations collected in this way, and decide if they support the original hypotheses (results); and (4) explore the broader theoretical and practical implications of the findings, and consider how they contribute to an understanding of the problem under investigation (discussion). Though these stages are somewhat arbitrary distinctions—research actually proceeds in a number of different ways—they help elucidate the inner logic of research reports.

While reading a research report, keep this linear structure in mind. Though it is difficult to remember a series of seemingly disjointed facts, when these facts are joined together in a logical, narrative structure, they become easier to comprehend and recall. Thus, always remember that a research report tells a story. It will help you to organize the information you read, and remember it later.

Describing research reports as stories is not just a convenient metaphor. Research reports *are* stories. Stories can be said to consist of two components: A telling of what happened, and an explanation of why it happened. It is tempting to view science as an endeavor that simply catalogues facts, but nothing is further from the truth. The goal of science, social psychology included, is to *explain* facts, to explain *why* what happened happened. Social psychology is built on the dynamic interplay of discovery and justification, the dialogue between systematic observation of relations and their theoretical explanation. Though research reports do present novel facts based on systematic observation, these facts are presented in the service of ideas. Facts in isolation are trivia. Facts tied together by an explanatory theory are science. Therein lies the story. To really understand what researchers have to say, you need consider how their explanations relate to their findings.

The Rest of the Story

> There is really no such thing as research. There is only search, more search, keep on searching. (Bowering, 1988, p. 95)

Once you have read through a research report, and understand the researchers' findings and their explanations of them, the story does not end there. There is more than one interpretation for any set of findings. Different researchers often explain the same set of facts in different ways.

Let's take a moment to dispel a nasty rumor. The rumor is this: Researchers present their studies in a dispassionate manner, intending only to inform readers of their findings and their interpretation of those findings. In truth, researchers aim not only to inform readers, but also to *persuade* them (Sternberg, 1995). Researchers want to convince you their ideas are right. There is never only one explanation for a set of findings. Certainly, some explanations are better than others; some fit the available data better, are more parsimonious, or require fewer questionable assumptions. The point here is that researchers are very passionate about their ideas, and want you to believe them. It's up to you to decide if you want to buy their ideas or not.

Let's compare social psychologists to salesclerks. Both social psychologists and salesclerks want to sell you something; either their ideas, or their wares. You need to decide if you want to buy what they're selling or not—and there are potentially negative consequences for either decision. If you let a sales clerk dazzle you with a sales pitch, without thinking about it carefully, you might end up buying a substandard product that you don't really need. After having done this a few times, people tend to become cynical, steeling themselves against any and all sales pitches. This too is dangerous. If you are overly critical of sales pitches, you could end up foregoing genuinely useful products. Thus, by analogy, when you are too critical in your reading of research reports, you might dismiss, out of hand, some genuinely useful ideas—ideas that can help shed light on why people behave the way they do.

This discussion raises the important question of how critical one should be while reading a research report. In part, this will depend on why one is reading the report. If you are reading it simply to learn what the researchers have to say about a particular issue, for example, then there is usually no need to be overly critical. If you want to use the research as a basis for planning a new study, then you should be more critical. As you develop an understanding of psychological theory and research methods, you will also develop an ability to criticize research on many different levels. And *any* piece of research can be criticized at some level. As Jacob Cohen put it, "A successful piece of research doesn't conclusively settle an issue, it just makes some theoretical proposition to some degree more likely" (1990, p. 1311). Thus, as a consumer of research reports, you have to strike a delicate balance between being overly critical and overly accepting.

While reading a research report, at least initially, try to suspend your disbelief. Try to understand the researchers' story; that is, try to understand the facts—the findings and how they were obtained—and the suggested explanation of those facts—the researchers' interpretation of the findings and what they mean. Take the research to task only after you feel you understand what the authors are trying to say.

Research reports serve not only an important archival function, documenting research and its findings, but also an invaluable stimulus function. They can excite other researchers to join the investigation of a particular issue, or to apply new methods or theory to a different, perhaps novel, issue. It is this stimulus function that Elliot Aronson, an eminent social psychologist, referred to when he admitted that, in publishing a study, he hopes his colleagues will "look at it, be stimulated by it, be provoked by it, annoyed by it, and then go ahead and do it better. . . . That's the exciting thing about science; it progresses by people taking off on one another's work" (1995, p. 5). Science is indeed a cumulative enterprise, and each new study builds on what has (or, sometimes, has not) gone before it. In this way, research articles keep social psychology vibrant.

A study can inspire new research in a number of different ways, such as: (1) it can lead one to conduct a better test of the hypotheses, trying to rule out alternative explanations of the findings; (2) it can lead one to explore the limits of the findings, to see how widely applicable they are, perhaps exploring situations to which they do not apply; (3) it can lead one to test the implications of the findings, furthering scientific investigation of the phenomenon; (4) it can inspire one to apply the findings, or a novel methodology, to a different area of investigation; and (5) it can provoke one to test the findings in the context of a specific real world problem, to see if they can shed light on it. All of these are excellent extensions of the original research, and there are, undoubtedly, other ways that research findings can spur new investigations.

The problem with being too critical, too soon, while reading research reports is that the only further research one may be willing to attempt is research of the first type: Redoing a study better. Sometimes this is desirable, particularly in the early stages of investigating a particular issue, when the findings are novel and perhaps unexpected. But redoing a reasonably compelling study, without extending it in any way, does little to advance our understanding of human behavior. Although the new study might be "better," it will not be "perfect," so *it* would have to be run again, and again, likely never reaching a stage where it is beyond criticism. At some point, researchers have to decide that the evidence is compelling enough to warrant investigation of the last four types. It is these types of studies that most advance our knowledge of social behavior. As you read more research reports, you will become more comfortable deciding when a study is "good enough" to move beyond it. This is a somewhat subjective judgment, and should be made carefully.

When social psychologists write up a research report for publication, it is because they believe they have something new and exciting to communicate about social behavior. Most research reports that are submitted for publication are rejected. Thus, the reports that are eventually published are deemed pertinent not only by the researchers who wrote them, but also by the reviewers and editors of the journals in which they are published. These people, at least, believe the research reports they write and publish have something important and interesting to say. Sometimes, you'll disagree; not all journal articles are created equal, after all. But we recommend that you, at least initially, give these well-meaning social psychologists the benefit of the doubt. Look for what they're excited about. Try to understand the authors' story, and see where it leads you.

ACKNOWLEDGMENTS

Preparation of this paper was facilitated by a Natural Sciences and Engineering Research Council of Canada doctoral fellowship to Christian H. Jordan. Thanks to Roy Baumeister, Arie Kruglanski, Ziva Kunda, John Levine, Geoff MacDonald, Richard Moreland, Ian Newby-Clark, Steve Spencer, and Adam Zanna for their insightful comments on, and appraisals of, various drafts of this paper. Thanks also to Arie Kruglanski and four anonymous editors of volumes in the series, *Key Readings in Social Psychology* for their helpful critiques of an initial outline of this paper. Correspondence concerning this article should be addressed to Christian H. Jordan, Department of Psychology, University of Waterloo, Waterloo, Ontario, Canada N2L 3G1. Electronic mail can be sent to chjordan@watarts.uwaterloo.ca

REFERENCES

American Psychological Association (1994). *Publication manual* (4th ed.). Washington, D.C.

Aronson, E. (1995). Research in social psychology as a leap of faith. In E. Aronson (Ed.), *Readings about the social animal* (7th ed., pp. 3–9). New York: W. H. Freeman and Company.

Bem, D. J. (1987). Writing the empirical journal article. In M. P. Zanna & J. M. Darley (Eds.), *The compleat academic: A practical guide for the beginning social scientist* (pp. 171–201). New York: Random House.

Bowering, G. (1988). *Errata*. Red Deer, Alta.: Red Deer College Press.

Cohen, J. (1990). Things I have learned (so far). *American Psychologist*, *45*, 1304–1312.

Forgas, J. P. (1994). Sad and guilty? Affective influences on the explanation of conflict in close relationships. *Journal of Personality and Social Psychology*, *66*, 56–68.

Sternberg, R. J. (1995). *The psychologist's companion: A guide to scientific writing for students and researchers* (3rd ed.). Cambridge: Cambridge University Press.

Author Index

Abbott, A., 241
Abelson, R., 47, 51, 60, 308
Aboud, F., 242
Ackerman, P., 308
Adams, J., 105, 273, 289, 299, 300, 301
Adams, N., 243
Adams, S., 261
Adelman, L., 85, 86
Adler, S., 17
Agha, G., 130
Albrecht, T., 241
Alchian, A., 332
Aldrich, H., 13
Alexander, S., 80
Allison, G., 242
Allport, F., 1
Amabile, T., 19
Ambrose, M., 262
American Assembly of Collegiate Schools of Business
    (AACSB), 38
American Management Association, 290
American Psychological Association, 420
Ames, R., 175, 176
Andersen, J., 3
Anderson, J., 336, 337, 338, 339
Anderson, L., 189
Anderson, S., 336
Andrews, D., 205
Argote, L., 164, 170, 186, 204–215, 255
Argyle, M., 241, 242, 245
Arkes, H., 19
Arnold, J., 75
Aronson, E., 51, 59, 60, 426
Arrow, K., 332
Ashford, S., 244
Ashforth, B., 331, 332
Astor, S., 300
Austin, W., 107, 245
Axelrod, R., 141

Bachrach, P., 351
Bagozzi, R., 336
Baier, A., 330
Bailey, F., 350
Baker, G., 332
Baldwin, T., 164, 204

Bales, R., 189, 241
Ball, T., 43, 44
Bandura, A., 3, 15, 16, 243
Banerji, R., 164
Baraz, M., 351
Barber, B., 286, 327, 328
Barden, R., 318
Bar-Hillel, M., 66
Barker, J., 25
Barley, S., 403
Barnard, C., 376
Baron, J., 38
Baron, R., 142, 143, 144, 153, 159, 210, 252, 253, 271, 330
Barrett-Howard, E., 278, 287
Barry, B., 157, 330
Barry, D., 241
Bar-Tal, D., 150
Bassok, M., 163
Bateman, T., 64
Batson, C., 13, 142, 143, 308, 407
Bavelas, A., 356
Bazerman, M., 18, 49, 74, 75, 105–124, 126, 129–140, 131, 157, 165, 166
Beach, L., 48
Beck, H., 193
Becker, G., 98, 101, 102
Bell, D., 3, 121
Bell, H., 205
Bem, D., 59, 423, 425
Ben-Itzhak, S., 310
Bentler, P., 336
Ben Yoav, O., 130, 138
Berger, P., 407
Berkowitz, L., 238
Berlin, I., 405
Bernard, H., 355
Berry, P., 191
Berscheid, E., 105, 261, 308
Beyer, J., 36, 37
Bierstadt, R., 351
Bies, R., 267, 278, 286, 287, 290, 291, 292, 295, 299, 300, 301
Birch, K., 308
Birnbaum, M., 80
Bishop, R., 102
Bjork, R., 205, 212, 214
Blaiwes, A., 205

Blau, P., 11
Block, C., 191
Blumer, C., 19
Bobko, P., 346
Boeckmann, R., 407
Boettger, R., 68, 387
Boles, T., 145, 148
Bonacich, P., 176, 356
Bond, C., 189
Bond, J., 324
Bond, M., 145
Borgatta, E., 189
Borgida, E., 87
Bouas, K., 411
Bouchard, T., 188, 191
Bower, D., 14
Bower, G., 3
Bowering, G., 425
Bowman, E., 83
Boyce, R., 95
Bradach, J., 327, 331
Bradley, R., 351
Brady, J., 241, 244, 245
Bramel, D., 253
Bramel, K., 238
Bransford, J., 164
Brass, D., 244, 351, 352, 354, 362
Brehm, J., 51, 52
Brehmer, B., 219, 220, 234
Brem, S., 170
Brennan, R., 247
Brenner, M., 314
Brett, J., 150, 266
Brewer, M., 127, 174–184, 277, 330
Brickman, P., 315, 324
Brief, A., 330
Briggs, G., 205
Brill, A., 386
Brockner, J., 18, 263, 323
Bromiley, P., 75
Brookshire, D., 92, 97, 98, 101
Brousseau, K., 242
Brown, A., 165
Brown, B., 129, 139, 157
Brown, J., 18, 73, 75, 205, 273
Brown, R., 229
Brunswik, E., 220
Bruun, S., 194
Buckley, T., 308
Bulman, R., 315, 324
Burke, M., 205, 330
Burns, C., 245
Burns, T., 347
Burnstein, E., 217
Burrell, G., 38, 39
Burt, R., 352
Burton, M., 359
Butler, D., 141, 143
Butler, J., 328

Calder, B., 51, 53, 59
Caldwell, D., 9, 14, 17, 207, 244

Camacho, L., 188, 198
Campbell, D., 13, 27, 178, 239
Campbell, J., 38, 309, 310, 311, 314, 317, 323
Campbell, W., 74
Cantor, N., 245
Capen, E., 74
Carlsmith, J., 51, 52, 59
Carmines, E., 359
Carroll, G., 42
Cartwright, D., 277
Casey, J., 189
Cass, J., 80
Catrambone, R., 164, 165
Chaiken, S., 10, 384, 399
Chamberlain, J., 175
Chase, W., 81
Chatman, J., 17, 244
Chisholm, D., 75
Christensen, C., 241
Chubb, J., 387
Cialdini, B., 308, 309
Cialdini, R., 244
Clapp, R., 74
Clark, J., 289, 299, 300
Clark, K., 205
Clark, M., 107, 239, 245, 308, 310, 315, 316, 330, 331, 333
Clark, R., 308
Claudy, J., 82
Clegg, S., 39
Cohen, A., 51, 52
Cohen, D., 103
Cohen, J., 359, 426
Cohen, P., 359
Cohen, R., 273
Cole, S., 33, 41, 42
Coleman, J., 176
Collaros, P., 189
Collins, B., 51, 53
Conlon, A., 277
Conlon, D., 213, 265
Connolly, T., 34, 38, 41
Conrath, D., 106, 109
Cook, J., 328, 329, 334
Cook, T., 27, 239
Coontz, S., 411
Cooper, A., 73
Cooper, J., 51, 52, 160
Corcoran, D., 245, 331
Corkran, L., 267
Corrigan, B., 82, 83, 84, 85, 86
Cosier, R., 243
Coursey, D., 92, 97, 98, 101
Cowden, J., 410, 412, 413
Crandall, R., 87
Crano, W., 413
Crosby, F., 105, 261
Crowne, D., 60
Cummings, L., 244, 290, 301
Curely, S., 68

Daft, R., 38
Dailey, R., 238

Danowski, J., 241
d'Arge, R., 92
Darley, J., 142, 143, 190, 411
Darlington, R., 79
Davidson, L., 242, 243
Davies, D., 213
Davies, G., 212
Davis, D., 75
Davis, K., 245, 301
Davis-Blake, A., 42
Dawes, R., 49, 72, 79–90, 106, 175, 176
Day, R., 205
Dean, J., 241
Deci, E., 59, 106, 109
Degoey, P., 262
deGroot, A., 81
DeGroot, M., 98
DeHarpport, T., 165
Delbecq, A., 241, 301
de Meuse, K., 240
Demset, H., 332
Deutsch, M., 217, 287, 295, 328
De Vera Park, M., 262
Dickson, M., 240, 254
Diehl, M., 188, 189, 190, 191, 194, 198, 200, 201
Dion, K., 207, 238, 239, 240
Doeringer, P., 43
Donahue, E., 150
Donaldson, G., 74
Donaldson, L., 39
Donaldson, S., 190
Doreian, P., 359
Dorris, W., 143
Douglas, A., 142, 144
Dovidio, J., 308
Dow, M., 359
Downs, A., 415
Drews, J., 143
Dröge, C., 13, 16, 17
Druckman, D., 205, 214
Duberman, L., 242, 243
Dubin, R., 22, 26, 362
Duguid, P., 205
Duhaime, I., 74
Dun and Bradstreet, 73
Dunbar, K., 170
Duncan, B., 308
Duncan, S., 318
Dunnette, M., 289
Dutton, J., 13, 214
Dyer, J., 205
Dzindolet, M., 188–204
Dzindolet, T., 185

Earley, P., 265–275
Eccles, R., 327, 331
Echols, C., 165
Edney, J., 175
Edwards, D., 80
Edwards, W., 47, 85
Einhorn, H., 18, 68, 81, 82, 87
Ekman, P., 318

Ellis, D., 242
Elster, J., 415
Emerson, E., 242
Emerson, R., 351
Epple, D., 164
Erber, R., 206
Erez, M., 267
Ernst, G., 164
Eskew, D., 290
Etzioni, A., 387, 389, 407, 408
Evans, C., 207, 238, 239, 240
Ewert, A., 213

Falkenhainer, B., 165
Farber, I., 311
Fazio, R., 411, 413
Ferguson, R., 170
Ferry, D., 239
Festing, L., 27
Festinger, L., 51, 59, 60, 105, 193, 277, 306, 309
Fetter, R., 330
Fichman, M., 327
Fiedler, F., 351
Fischhoff, B., 18, 243
Fishburn, P., 64, 121
Fisher, J., 310
Fiske, A., 403, 409
Fiske, S., 9, 143, 308, 400
Flatt, S., 14
Folger, R., 265, 266, 267, 287, 290, 291, 295, 300
Follett, M., 129, 345
Forbus, K., 163, 164, 165, 170
Ford, J., 164, 204
Forgas, J., 420
Fouraker, L., 105, 122
Fox, A., 330
Fox, J., 176
Frank, R., 408, 409
Franks, J., 164
Franz, T., 241
Freedman, J., 51, 52, 266
Freeman, A., 91
Freeman, J., 17, 27
Freeman, L., 352, 355, 357, 361
Freeman, S., 352, 355
Freese, L., 22
French, R., 351
Freud, S., 3
Frey, B., 176, 410
Friedman, R., 157
Friedman, T., 405
Friend, R., 238, 253
Frieze, I., 60
Fukuyama, F., 405
Funder, D., 143
Funk, C., 9, 409, 410, 412
Furnham, A., 241, 242, 245
Futrell, D., 240

Gabarro, J., 327, 345
Gaertner, S., 308

Galbraith, C., 205
Garber, J., 318
Gardiner, P., 85
Garvey, W., 37
Geen, R., 189, 308
Gentner, D., 126, 163–173
Gentry, G., 143
George, C., 205
George, J., 330
Georgenson, D., 204
Georgopoulos, B., 250
Gerard, H., 217
Gerbing, D., 336, 337, 338, 339
Gergen, K., 407
Gettys, C., 189
Geva, N., 150
Gick, M., 163, 164, 165
Gigerenzer, G., 73, 399, 404
Gigone, D., 186, 216–237
Gillespie, J., 165, 166
Gilligan, C., 324
Gilovich, T., 384, 408
Gioia, D., 330
Giuliano, T., 206, 214
Gladstein, D., 239, 240, 242, 243, 254
Glaser, B., 25
Glickman, A., 205
Goethals, G., 190, 309
Goffman, E., 60, 159
Goldberg, L., 81, 82, 83, 86, 87, 145
Goldberg, S., 150
Goldstein, I., 204, 205
Goldstein, W., 384
Goldstone, R., 165
Goodman, P., 214
Gordon, G., 34, 35, 36, 39, 43
Gottman, J., 308–309
Gottman, M., 242
Gough, H., 311, 312
Gower, J., 356
Graham, W., 189, 198
Granovetter, M., 8, 327, 328, 329, 346
Green, B., 85
Green, D., 409, 410, 412, 413, 415
Greenberg, J., 239, 263, 272, 273, 289–303, 412
Greenhalgh, L., 133
Gregerson, H., 333
Griesinger, D., 106, 328
Griffin, D., 72, 73, 220, 225, 384
Griffin, E., 287
Grove, J., 267
Gruenfeld, D., 240
Gupta, V., 28
Guth, W., 105
Guyer, M., 176
Guzzo, R., 204, 205, 239, 240, 243, 254

Hackman, J., 240, 241, 242, 245
Haggard, E., 192
Hall, A., 306
Hall, J., 214
Hamburger, H., 176

Hammond, K., 82, 85, 86, 219, 220, 234
Hanna, C., 216, 233, 246
Hannan, M., 17, 27, 38
Harari, O., 189
Hare, R., 311
Hargadon, A., 170
Hargens, L., 37
Harkins, S., 189, 190, 193, 194
Harlow, R., 245
Harmon, J., 220
Harris, R., 191
Harrison, J., 74
Hartup, W., 241
Hastie, R., 159, 186, 216–237
Hayes, J., 164
Hayes, R., 205
Hays, R., 241
Hazewinkel, A., 213
Heberlein, T., 102
Heider, F., 106, 142, 149, 278, 309
Heiner, R., 102
Henry, R., 228, 241
Herrigel, E., 27
Hertel, P., 214
Heywood, J., 213
Hill, G., 210, 236
Hirschman, A., 415
Hobbes, T., 407
Hoffman, P., 82
Hogarth, R., 18, 68, 82, 87, 384
Hohenfeld, J., 289
Hollinger, R., 289, 299, 300
Hollingshead, A., 240
Holmes, J., 328, 330, 331, 332, 411, 414
Holmes, S., 415
Holt, R., 81
Holyoak, K., 163, 164, 165
Homans, G., 105, 238, 253
Homans, R., 25, 26
Horning, D., 300
Horwitz, M., 178
House, R., 26, 351
Hovis, J., 92
Howard, J., 80
Hoyt, M., 51, 53
Hrebec, D., 165
Hubbell, C., 350, 356
Hulin, C., 38, 267
Hull, C., 3
Huo, Y., 263, 407, 411
Hyams, N., 198

Ichheiser, G., 142
Inkster, J., 59
Insko, C., 51, 53, 411
Isen, A., 308, 315, 330

Jaccoud, A., 330
Jackson, J., 193
Jackson, S., 213
Jacobs, R., 13

Janis, I., 74, 242, 243
Janiszewski, C., 245
Jehn, A., 187, 238–260
Jenicke, L., 86
Jensen, M., 332, 387, 389
Jervis, R., 150
Jessor, T., 410
Jette, R., 204
John, O., 145, 147, 150, 157
Johnson, C., 188
Johnson-George, C., 328, 330, 334
Jones, E., 51, 52, 143, 159, 301
Jones, R., 52
Jordan, C., 419–428
Jöreskog, K., 336, 337
Jorgenson, D., 289
Joyce, C., 219
Judd, C., 225

Kagan, J., 407, 415
Kagel, J., 74
Kahan, J., 176
Kahn, R., 24, 332
Kahn, W., 346
Kahneman, D., 19, 48, 49, 50, 63–78, 87, 91–104, 106, 107,
    110, 119, 121, 130, 131, 175, 182, 384
Kane, M., 165
Kanekar, S., 201
Kanfer, R., 265–275
Kanter, R., 13, 19, 24, 351
Kaplan, A., 22, 24, 26, 27
Kaplan, R., 240
Katz, D., 24, 332, 345
Katzell, R., 204
Keane, M., 164
Keeney, R., 65
Keller, R., 207
Kelley, H., 9, 59, 106, 141, 143, 150, 159–160, 242, 286,
    305, 411
Kelley, J., 197
Kelly, H., 330
Kelly, L., 88
Kemper, T., 299
Kennedy, P., 165
Kenny, D., 153, 210, 252, 253, 271
Kenrick, D., 308
Kerr, N., 194
Kerr, S., 373, 375–383
Kets de Vries, M., 13, 16, 17
Kim, J., 248, 392
Kinder, D., 386, 403
Kirk, R., 269
Kitayama, S., 409
Klein, H., 244
Klorman, R., 318
Knapp, M., 242
Knetsch, J., 49, 65, 91–104
Knez, M., 101
Knez, P., 92, 97
Knox, R., 59
Kochenberger, G., 64
Koenig, R., 241

Koh, K., 165
Kohen, E., 82, 84, 87
Kohlberg, L., 17
Kohn, A., 407, 408, 410
Komorita, S., 176, 411
Konovsky, M., 332
Konrad, A., 35, 36
Kotovsky, L., 165
Krackhardt, D., 306, 350–372
Kramer, R., 127, 165, 174–184, 277
Krantz, D., 81
Krishnan, R., 170
Kruglanski, A., 385, 386, 387, 390, 397
Kuhn, T., 27, 33, 41, 43
Kukla, A., 60
Kulik, C., 262
Kunda, G., 403
Kurtz, S., 265
Kuypers, B., 213

Labor letter, 204
LaCoursiere, R., 213
Ladd, G., 242
Lakatos, L., 41
Lamm, H., 18, 229
Landau, M., 75
Landers, R., 163, 165
Lane, R., 266, 286, 287
Langer, E., 18, 273
Langton, L., 36
Lapworth, C., 176
Larkey, P., 74
LaRocco, J., 26
Larrance, D., 318
Larrick, R., 126, 141–162
Larsen, I., 242
Larson, A., 327, 346
Larson, J., 241
Latane, B., 190
Latham, G., 205, 267
LaTour, S., 265
Lau, R., 410, 412
Laughhunn, D., 64
Laughlin, P., 205
Laumann, E., 351
Law, K., 164, 165
Lawler, E., 74
Lax, D., 165
Leblebici, H., 36
Lee, R., 331, 332
Lee, T., 267
Lee, W., 53
Legendre, P., 356
Leong, A., 36
Lerner, J., 400
Lerner, M., 407, 408, 412, 414, 415
Levenson, R., 309
Leventhal, D., 327
Leventhal, G., 266, 285–286, 290, 295
Levi, A., 47
Levin, D., 74
Levin, P., 308

Levine, J., 205, 213, 214
Levinthal, D., 327
Lewicki, R., 107, 129, 147, 150, 278
Lewin, K., 305
Lewis, J., 327, 328, 330
Liang, D., 186, 204–215, 255
Libby, R., 83, 87
Lichtenstein, S., 73, 82, 220, 243
Liebrand, W., 176
Light, I., 329
Lin, N., 37
Lincoln, J., 242, 243, 352
Lind, A., 411
Lind, E., 261, 262, 263, 265–275, 276, 277, 278, 285, 295
Linder, E., 51, 52
Lindsey, D., 36
Lindskold, S., 329
Lipsett, S., 386, 395
Lissak, R., 265, 272, 277, 278
Litterer, J., 107, 147, 150
Livingston, J., 106
Locke, E., 131, 241, 267
Lodahl, J., 34, 35, 36, 39, 43
Lodahl, T., 37
Loewenstein, G., 49, 105–124, 159
Loewenstein, J., 125
Loewenstein, T., 126, 163–173
Longenecker, C., 330
Loomes, G., 121
Lopes, L., 48, 66
Lord, R., 289
Lorsch, J., 74
Louche, C., 213
Lovallo, D., 49, 63–78
Lowe, C., 241
Lowe, E., 74
Luckmann, T., 407
Luhman, N., 327, 328
Lukes, S., 351
Lurie, S., 106
Lynch, J., 72

MacCrimmon, K., 64, 68, 73, 106, 109
MacKenzie, S., 330
MacPhillamy, D., 220, 225
Maginn, B., 191
Magliozzi, T., 126, 129–140
Magnier, J., 213
Mandler, G., 310
Mannix, E., 127
Manrai, L., 245
Mansbridge, J., 407, 408, 415
March, J., 23, 24, 25, 43, 63, 74, 76, 385
Markman, A., 165, 166, 170
Markus, H., 16, 409
Marlow, D., 60
Marquardt, D., 79
Mars, G., 290, 299
Marschak, J., 98
Marsden, R., 39, 44
Marwell, G., 40, 105, 175, 176
Masters, J., 318
McAllister, D., 306, 327–349

McArthur, L., 142, 143, 159
McClelland, C., 176
McClelland, D., 351
McClelland, G., 225
McClosky, H., 386
McCrae, R., 145, 157
McFann, H., 311
McGrath, J., 205, 240, 241, 250
McGrath, M., 245
McGuire, W., 60, 293
McKelvey, B., 17
McKersie, R., 129, 130
McPherson, J., 242, 243
Mechanic, D., 14
Meckling, W., 387, 389
Medin, D., 165
Medina, J., 164, 166
Meehl, P., 79, 80, 81
Meeker, R., 176
Mehle, T., 189
Meindl, J., 74
Mendelsohn, G., 143
Merrow, E., 74
Merry, C., 253
Merton, R., 22, 26, 27, 159
Messé, L., 411
Messick, D., 49, 106, 109, 113, 121, 174, 176, 178, 181, 183, 277, 388
Meyer, J., 16, 385
Meyer, M., 28
Michaelson, A., 352
Mikula, G., 242
Milberg, S., 308
Miles, R., 17
Milgram, S., 142
Milgrom, P., 40
Millar, M., 244, 305, 308–326
Miller, D., 13, 16, 17, 374, 407–417
Miller, J., 16, 242, 243, 352
Miller, R., 309
Milliken, F., 75
Mills, C., 412
Mills, J., 107, 239, 245, 330, 331
Miner, J., 38
Minton, J., 278
Mintzberg, H., 25, 327, 345, 362
Mischel, W., 157
Mitchell, T., 207
Mizruchi, M., 351
Moag, J., 267, 295
Moe, T., 387
Moore, J., 244, 305, 308–326
Moore, K., 243
Moore, W., 35, 37, 38
Moorman, R., 339
Moreland, R., 170, 186, 204–215, 255
Morgan, B., 205
Morgan, G., 38, 39
Morris, C., 241
Morris, M., 126, 141–162
Motowidlo, S., 330
Mowday, R., 244
Mueller, C., 248
Mueller, D., 408, 415

Mueller, S., 13
Mullen, B., 188, 189
Mulvey, P., 244
Murdock, P., 207
Murnighan, J., 213
Murphy, K., 332
Musante, L., 265
Myers, D., 18, 229

Nadler, A., 310
Natham, G., 131
Naylor, J., 205
Neale, M., 28, 75, 126, 129–140, 144, 157, 165
Near, J., 330
Nelson, C., 37
Nelson, J., 242
Nemeth, C., 18, 190, 243
Neslin, S., 133
Neuberg, S., 143
Newcomb, A., 241, 243, 244, 245
Newcomb, T., 60
Niehoff, B., 339
Nisbett, R., 30, 87, 142, 143, 159, 409
Northcraft, G., 28
Novick, L., 164, 170

Ofir, C., 72
Olsen, J., 43, 385
Olson, M., 176, 408, 415
Opotow, S., 287
Orbell, J., 106
O'Reilly, C., 9, 14, 17, 207, 244
Organ, D., 330, 332, 340, 345
Orne, M., 311
Orvis, B., 141, 143
Osborn, A., 188
Oster, H., 318
Ouchi, W., 331, 332

Paese, P., 273
Pallak, M., 51
Panman, R., 201
Pappi, F., 351
Park, O., 330
Parkhurst, J., 242
Pataki, S., 239, 246
Paulus, P., 185, 188–204
Pavlov, I., 3
Pearce, J., 333
Pedhazur, E., 339
Pennings, J., 17, 327, 328, 331
Pepitone, A., 273
Perfetto, G., 164
Perrow, C., 24, 27
Peterson, R., 400
Pettigrew, A., 350
Petty, R., 194
Pfeffer, J., 8, 9, 12, 14, 16, 23, 26, 33–46, 47, 207, 350, 351, 362
Pietromonaco, P., 143
Piliavin, J., 308

Piore, M., 43
Pleban, R., 309
Pliske, R., 189
Plott, C., 92, 130
Plous, S., 49
Podsakoff, P., 330, 340, 345
Polanyi, M., 41
Poletes, G., 188, 193
Pondy, L., 34, 143
Porter, L., 244, 328, 352
Powell, M., 239, 330, 331
Pradhan, P., 239
Prediger, D., 247
Prentice, D., 410
Price, D., 34
Pritchard, R., 289, 301
Pruitt, D., 105, 122, 129, 130, 131, 132, 138, 139, 143

Quanty, M., 308
Quinn, R., 332

Raab, E., 386, 395
Rabbie, J., 178
Radlow, R., 150
Raiffa, A., 65
Raiffa, H., 3, 122, 139, 144
Rasinski, K., 265, 277
Ratner, R., 407, 408, 409, 411, 412, 414
Rattermann, M., 163, 164, 165, 170
Raven, B., 351
Rawlins, W., 239, 241, 243
Raymond, P., 206
Redelmeier, D., 66
Reed, H., 87
Reed, L., 60
Reed, M., 39
Reed, S., 164
Reese, L., 243
Reeves, L., 163, 164, 165
Regan, D., 408, 413
Reilly, N., 242
Reis, H., 245, 273
Rempel, J., 328, 330, 331, 332, 334
Remus, W., 86
Rest, S., 60
Reutter, V., 290
Rhode, J., 74
Richardson-Klavehn, A., 212
Roberson, L., 330
Roberts, J., 40
Roberts, N., 351
Robins, R., 143, 145, 159
Robinson, S., 244
Robinson, T., 267
Rodin, J., 310
Rogers, M., 242
Rohrbaugh, J., 220
Roll, L., 75
Roloff, M., 241, 242, 245
Romanelli, E., 18
Romney, A., 355
Romney, K., 352, 361

Ropp, V., 241
Roseman, I., 308
Rosenbaum, M., 201
Rosenbaum, R., 60
Rosenberg, M., 60, 311, 312, 315, 318, 319
Rosenfield, D., 267
Rosenthal, R., 159
Ross, B., 163, 164, 165
Ross, J., 18, 19, 25, 64, 308, 403
Ross, L., 9, 30, 142, 143, 159
Ross, M., 51, 53, 122
Rotter, J., 334
Rowan, B., 16
Rowe, R., 92
Rubin, D., 159
Rubin, J., 18, 105, 122, 129, 139, 157
Ruscher, J., 143
Russell, J., 310

Saari, L., 267
Sabel, C., 43
Safer, M., 142
Salancik, G., 16, 34, 35, 36, 37, 44, 74, 207, 351, 356, 362
Salancik, J., 59
Salancik, R., 26
Salas, E., 188, 205
Salovey, P., 310
Sampson, E., 407
Samuelson, P., 66
Samuelson, W., 65, 74
Sandelands, L., 13, 214
Saunders, D., 278
Sawyer, J., 81, 265
Sayles, L., 327, 332, 333, 345
Schachter, S., 277
Schacter, S., 310
Schein, E., 13
Schelling, T., 141
Schlenker, B., 16, 404
Schmidt, F., 82
Schmitt, D., 105
Schmittberger, R., 105
Schneider, B., 14, 18
Schopler, J., 411
Schulze, W., 92
Schumacher, R., 164
Schwartz, B., 407, 408, 409, 415
Schwarze, B., 105
Schweiger, D., 267
Schwenk, C., 74, 243
Schwinger, T., 242
Scott, K., 243
Scott, R., 11, 106
Scott, W., 16
Seabright, M., 327, 346
Sears, D., 9, 278, 409, 410, 412
Seashore, S., 240
Sebenius, J., 165
Seigel, S., 105, 122
Seligman, M., 75
Sen, A., 415
Sentis, K., 49, 106, 113, 121

Seta, C., 190
Seta, J., 190, 193
Shah, P., 187, 238–260
Shah, S., 214
Shalker, T., 315
Shapira, Z., 63, 74, 76
Shapiro, C., 239
Shapiro, D., 286, 287, 290, 291, 299, 301
Shapiro, I., 409, 415
Shapiro, S., 327, 328
Sharfman, M., 241
Shaw, K., 267
Shaw, R., 74
Shea, G., 239
Sheppard, B., 278
Sherman, S., 51
Sherwood, J., 240
Sherwood, R., 164
Shoda, Y., 157
Shull, F., 301
Shure, G., 176, 242
Shweder, R., 409
Sicoly, F., 122
Sierra Club v. Morton, 413
Simmel, G., 328
Simon, H., 8, 24, 25, 48, 81, 164, 376, 384
Sims, H., 330
Sinden, J., 97
Sivacek, J., 411, 413
Skinner, B., 3
Slovic, P., 81, 82, 220, 225, 243
Smith, A., 204, 415
Smith, C., 330
Smith, E., 149
Smith, H., 263, 407
Smith, J., 254, 309
Smith, K., 241
Smith, R., 74
Smith, V., 92, 101
Smith-Lovin, L., 242, 243
Snee, R., 79
Sniderman, P., 386, 387
Sniezek, J., 228
Snipper, R., 36
Snoek, J., 332
Snow, C., 17
Snow, W., 17
Snyder, M., 159, 411
Sogin, S., 51
Sörbom, D., 336, 337
Spence, K., 310, 311
Spiegel, N., 318
Spodick, N., 265, 277
Spranca, M., 143
Stack, L., 329
Stahelski, A., 150, 159–160, 411
Starbuck, W., 38, 41, 75
Stasser, G., 170, 206, 216, 217, 218, 219, 233, 234, 235, 241, 246, 253
Stata, R., 205
Staw, B., 7, 11–21, 22–32, 34, 48, 51–62, 64, 214, 402
Steers, R., 244
Stein, R., 412

Steiner, I., 186, 213, 239, 240
Steinmann, D., 219, 234
Stephenson, K., 356
Stern, R., 351, 352, 361
Sternberg, R., 426
Stevens, S., 67
Stewart, D., 170, 219, 235, 241
Stewart, T., 219, 220, 234
Stigler, G., 101, 102
Stoner, J., 186
Strauss, A., 25, 141
Strehl, K., 36
Stroebe, W., 176, 188, 189, 190, 191, 194, 198, 200, 201
Stukas, A., 411
Su, K., 126
Su, S., 141–162
Sugden, R., 121
Suls, J., 309
Sundstrom, E., 240
Sutton, R., 22–32, 170
Swalm, R., 64, 65, 68, 70
Swann, W., 142, 143, 159
Swap, W., 328, 330, 334
Sweeney, J., 205

Tajfel, H., 127, 176, 207, 262, 277
Tannenbaum, P., 60
Tassone, J., 242
Taylor, D., 191
Taylor, J., 311, 312, 314, 318, 319
Taylor, L., 216, 233, 246
Taylor, S., 9, 18, 73, 75, 273
Tegar, A., 19
Tesser, A., 244, 254, 305, 306, 308–326
Tetlock, P., 10, 68, 373–374, 384–406
Tetrick, L., 26
Teuter, K., 359
Thaler, R., 49, 65, 91–104, 131
Thibaut, J., 107, 141, 242, 261, 262, 265, 266, 273, 276, 277, 278, 279, 284, 285, 286, 305
Thissen, D., 85
Thomas, K., 143
Thompson, J., 11, 16, 24, 34, 327, 333, 345
Thompson, L., 49, 105–124, 125, 126, 142, 144–145, 157, 163–173
Thoms, P., 243
Thomson, D., 212
Thornton, B., 80
Tiger, L., 73
Titus, L., 189
Titus, W., 216, 217, 233, 241
Todd, M., 245
Todd, P., 399, 404
Torgerson, W., 84
Toulouse, J., 17
Trope, Y., 384, 399
Tsui, A., 330, 332, 334, 336
Tuckman, B., 213
Tuden, A., 34
Turnbull, W., 411
Turner, J., 176, 207, 277, 329
Turner, K., 149

Tushman, M., 18
Tversky, A., 3, 19, 64, 65, 66, 67, 71, 73, 76, 87, 92, 99, 102, 106, 107, 110, 119, 121, 130, 131, 175, 182, 220, 225
Tversky, H., 72, 73
Tyler, T., 261, 262, 263, 265, 266, 267, 273, 276–288, 290, 295, 299, 300, 407, 410, 411

Uchitelle, L., 43
Ury, W., 150

Valley, K., 165
van den Bos, K., 263
Van de Ven, A., 239, 241
Van Leeuwen, M., 189
Van Maanen, J., 27, 30
Van Zante, A., 51
Vermunt, R., 263
Vidmar, N., 266
Vinacke, W., 324
Viscusi, K., 68
Vroom, V., 59
Vye, N., 164

Waddell, B., 330, 331
Wagner, W., 14
Waid, W., 311
Wainer, H., 85
Walker, L., 261, 262, 265, 266, 273, 276, 277, 278, 279, 284, 285, 286
Wall, T., 328, 329, 334
Wallace, H., 82
Wallach, L, 407
Wallach, M., 407
Walster, E., 59, 105, 106, 110, 261
Walster, G., 105, 261
Walton, R., 129, 130
Wang, C., 359
Wang, W., 205
Watson, J., 3
Webb, S., 204
Webster, D., 385, 386, 387, 390, 397
Webster, J., 38, 41, 330
Wegner, D., 205, 212, 214
Wehrung, D., 64, 68, 73
Weick, K., 22, 23, 24, 25, 26, 27, 28, 30, 51, 59, 60
Weidner, M., 150
Weigert, A., 327, 328, 330
Weiner, B., 60
Weingart, L., 239, 241, 242, 243, 245, 246, 254, 255
Weisberg, R., 163, 164, 165
Weiss, H., 17
Weiss, J., 242
Weldon, E., 239, 241, 242, 243, 244, 245, 246, 254, 255
Wellman, B, 306
Wexley, K., 205
Whetten, D., 26
White, D., 359
White, R., 60
White, S., 144, 207
Whitley, R., 34, 37, 41

Whitney, K., 244, 245
Wiggins, N., 82, 84, 87
Wildavsky, A., 76
Wilder, D., 207
Wilke, H., 263
Wilks, S., 85
Williams, A., 92
Williams, B., 242
Williams, K., 190
Williams, L., 336
Williams, M., 214
Williamson, G., 245
Williamson, O., 331, 332
Willig, R., 91
Wills, A., 127
Wilson, D., 336
Wilson, J., 388
Wittenbaurm, G., 253
Woiceshyn, J., 327, 328, 331
Wolfe, D., 332
Wolff, P., 170
Woodard, E., 205
Woodward, J., 16
Word, C., 160

Wright, P., 239, 243
Wurf, E., 16
Wuthnow, R., 408, 412

Yi, Y., 336
Yik, M., 145
Yntema, D., 84
Yoels, W., 36

Zaccaro, S., 241
Zajonc, R., 189, 308, 310, xvii
Zammuto, R., 34, 38, 41
Zander, A., 277
Zanna, M., 160, 328, 419–428
Zeckhauser, R., 65
Zeithaml, C., 64
Zelen, M., 356
Zeller, R., 359
Zillman, D., 308
Ziman, J., 41
Zucker, L., 13, 327, 328, 329, 330
Zuckerman, M., 318

Subject Index

Academy of Management, 12
Academy of Management Journal, 28
Academy of Management Review, 22, 43
Acquaintance groups, 239–257
Administrative Science Quarterly, 22, 28, 29, 30
Affect-based trust, 306, 327–349
American Journal of Sociology, 38
American Psychological Association, 12
American Sociological Association, 12
American Sociological Review, 11, 38
Analytic versus synthetic approach, defined, 2
Application, defined, 2

Ball, George, 52
Bargaining and personality traits, 141–162
"Best alternative to a negotiated agreement" (BATNA), 126
Bootstrapping models of decision making, 82–83
"Bounded rationalist" model, 48
Brainstorming and creativity in groups, 185–186, 188–203
Budgets, reward systems in, 379
Business organizations, reward systems in, 379
"Butt of faulty normative models," 48

Clinical Versus Statistical Prediction: A Theoretical Analysis and a Review of the Evidence (Meehl), 79
Clinton, Bill, 42
Coase theorem in decision making, 99–101, 102–103
Cognition-based trust, 306, 327–349
Cognitive biases and organizational correctives, 384–406
  cognitive biases in, 390–391
  coping with accountability in, 391–394
  fundamental attribution error in, 390–391, 399
"Cognitive miser," 9
Cognitive theories, defined, 3
Common information effect in groups and teams, 186, 216–237
Consensus, in paradigm development, 41–43
Cost-plus contracts, reward systems in, 379
Criterion, 219–221
Cue, 219–221

Decision control, 276
Decision making
  under certainty, 48
  Coase theorem in, 99–101, 102–103
  decision-making theories defined, 4
  domains of, 48–49
  endowment effect in, 91–104
  interpersonal model of, 49–50
  with "isolation error," 49, 63–78
  linear models in, 79–90
  metaphors in, 47–48
  multi-attribute utility theory (MAUT) in, 48
  negotiation as, 125–128, 126
  random linear models in, 84
  in a riskless choice, 48
  under risky choice, 48, 51–62
  social utility in disputes, 105–124
  study of self-justification in investment decisions, 52–62
  under uncertainty, 48
  using bootstrapping, 82–83
Descriptive theories
  cognitive theories, 3
  decision-making theories, 4
  defined, 3
  learning theories, 3
  motivational theories, 3
  role theories, 4
  social exchange theories, 4
Distributive aspects in negotiation, 125
Distributive justice, 261

Ecology, reward systems with, 378
Econometrica, 42
Economic actor, 8
Emotion, in relationships and trust, 305–306, 308–326
Endowment effect
  in decision making, 91–104
  defined, 49
Equity theory, 261
"Error-prone intuitive scientist," 48
Evaluation of training, reward systems in, 378
Experimentation as a research methodology
  defined, 2

Fairness heuristic theory of procedural justice, 263
Fidelity in training programs, 205
Folk wisdom, 2
Friedman, Milton, 383

Friendship groups, 239–257
"Frustration effect," 267
"Fundamental attribution error," 9, 142–144

Group composition, 187, 238–260
Group process, 239
Groups and teams
common information effect in, 186, 216–237
creativity and brainstorming in, 185–186, 188–203
criterion in, 219–221
cue in, 219–221
decision making in, 186
group composition in, 187, 238–260
"group polarization" in, 186
"lens model" of judgment in, 220
production blocking in, 186
role of friendship and acquaintance in, 238–260
social loafing in, 186
transactive memory systems in, 186, 204–215
Group value model of procedural justice, 262, 265–275, 276–288

Improper linear model of decision making, 80–81
Insurance firm, reward system in, 381
Integrative aspects in negotiation, 125
Interpersonal level of analysis, defined, 2
Interpersonal trust in organizations in, 306, 327–349
"Isolation errors," 49, 63–78

Journal articles, reading of, 419–428
Journal of Applied Psychology, 28

Learning theories, defined, 3
"Lens model" of judgment, 220
Leviathan (Hobbes), 407
Linear models of decision making, 79–90
Logic of Collective Action, The (Olson), 176

Macro-organizational behavior, defined, 1
Manufacturing organization, reward system in, 379–381
Medicine, reward systems in, 376–377
Micro-organizational behavior
characteristics of, 1–2
defined, 1
overview of, 1–4
theories in, 2–4
Moral model, 9
"Motivated tactician," 10
Motivational theories, defined, 3
Multi-attribute utility theory (MAUT), 48

Negotiation
accuracy in social perception in, 159
analogical training in, 163–173
bargaining and personality traits in, 141–162
"best alternative to a negotiated agreement" (BATNA) in, 126

components in, 125
as decision making, 126
distributive aspects in, 125
dynamics of self-confirming beliefs in, 159–160
fundamental attribution error in, 142–144
"inert knowledge problem" in, 126, 163–173
integrative aspects in, 125
metaphors for, 125–127
as problem solving, 126, 163–173
social dilemma in, 127, 174–184
as social perception, 126, 141–162
social psychological processes in, 159
New York Times, 42
Nixon, Richard M., 376, 383
Normative theories, defined, 3

Organizational action, models for explanation of, 11–21
Organizational citizenship behavior (OCB), 330
Organization Science, 28
Organizations (March and Simon), 25
Orphanages, reward systems in, 377

Paradigm development, level of, 33–46
Personnel Psychology, 28
Politics, reward systems in, 375–376
"Preconscious actor," 10
Procedural justice
decision control in, 276
defined, 261
fairness heuristic theory of, 263
group value model of, 262, 265–275, 276–288, 277
process control in, 276
reactions/perceptions of, 263, 289–303
relational model of authority in, 262
self-interest model of, 262
"Process control effect," 264
Process loss, 239–240
Proper linear model of decision making, 79–80, 81–82

Qualitative ethnographic research, 2

Random linear models in decision making, 84
Reaction/perception of procedural justice, 263, 289–303
Reagan, Ronald, 410
Rehabilitation centers, reward systems in, 377
Reich, Robert, 42
Relational model of authority, 262
Relationships and trust
affect-based trust in, 306, 327–349
cognition-based trust in, 306, 327–349
interdependence theory in, 305
interpersonal trust in organizations in, 306, 327–349
role of emotion in, 305–306, 308–326
self-evaluation maintenance (SEM) model in, 305–306, 308–326
social networks in, 306, 350–372
Relative deprivation theory, 261
Research in Organizational Behavior (ROB), 22, 27
Retrospective rational model, 8

Reward systems, results/consequences of, 373–383
Riskless choice, 48
Risky choice, decision making under, 48, 51–62
Role theories, defined, 4

"Satisfice," 48
Self-evaluation maintenance (SEM) model, 305–306, 308–326
Self-interest, norm of, 407–417
"Slave to motivational forces," 48
Social dilemma
   choice behavior in, 174–184
   commons dilemma in, 174–175
   public good problem in, 174–175
Social exchange theories, defined, 4
Social model of behavior, 8, 9
Social networks in organizations, 306, 350–372
Social utility functions in decision making, 105–124
Sports, reward systems in, 379
Spreading activation, 3
Synthetic approach, defined, 2

Theory, descriptions and balance of, 22–32
Tower, John, 350
Transactive memory
   group cohesion in, 210
   memory differentiation in, 209–210
   social identity in, 210
   task coordination in, 210
   task credibility in, 210
   task motivation in, 210

Uncertainty, 48
Universities, reward systems in, 377–378

"Vietnam Dollar" phenomenon, 60
Vietnam War, 376
"Voice effect," 264

War, reward systems in, 376

Zen in the Art of Archery (Herrigel), 27